北京大學圖書館特藏文獻叢刊

北京大學圖書館藏
鄒新明 編著

胡適未刊來往書信 上

北京大學出版社
PEKING UNIVERSITY PRESS

圖書在版編目（CIP）數據

北京大學圖書館藏胡適未刊來往書信：全二册 / 鄒新明編著. — 北京：北京大學出版社，2024.1
（北京大學圖書館特藏文獻叢刊）

ISBN 978-7-301-34132-2

Ⅰ.①北… Ⅱ.①鄒… Ⅲ.①胡適（1891—1962）–書信集 Ⅳ.①K825.4

中國國家版本館CIP數據核字(2023)第120768號

書　　　名	北京大學圖書館藏胡適未刊來往書信 BEIJING DAXUE TUSHUGUAN CANG HU SHI WEIKAN LAIWANG SHUXIN
著作責任者	鄒新明　編著
責 任 編 輯	吳冰妮
標 準 書 號	ISBN 978-7-301-34132-2
出 版 發 行	北京大學出版社
地　　　址	北京市海淀區成府路205號　100871
網　　　址	http://www.pup.cn　新浪微博:@北京大學出版社
電 子 郵 箱	編輯部 dj@pup.cn　總編室 zpup@pup.cn
電　　　話	郵購部 010-62752015　發行部 010-62750672 編輯部 010-62756694
印 刷 者	涿州市星河印刷有限公司
經 銷 者	新華書店
	720毫米×1020毫米　16開本　76印張　223千字 2024年1月第1版　2024年1月第1次印刷
定　　　價	380.00元（全二册）

未經許可，不得以任何方式複製或抄襲本書之部分或全部內容。
版權所有，侵權必究
舉報電話：010-62752024　電子郵箱：fd@pup.cn
圖書如有印裝質量問題，請與出版部聯繫，電話：010-62756370

北京大學圖書館特藏文獻叢刊
編輯委員會

主　　編　陳建龍
執行主編　鄒新明
編　　委　鄭清文　別立謙　張麗静　常雯嵐　吳冕　欒偉平　饒益波
編纂者　　陳建龍　鄭清文　別立謙　鄒新明　張麗静　常雯嵐　吳冕
　　　　　欒偉平　饒益波　徐清白　孫雅馨　程援探

北京大學圖書館藏胡適未刊來往書信

編　　著　鄒新明

本書爲國家社會科學基金重大項目"胡適年譜新編"

（項目號：18ZDA198）

階段性成果

"北京大學圖書館特藏文獻叢刊"序

　　北京大學圖書館創建於1898年，初名京師大學堂藏書樓，是中國近現代第一座國立綜合性大學圖書館，專供學人"研究學問，增長智慧"，1912年改爲現名。

　　北京大學圖書館事業得到黨和國家領導人的親切關懷、學校的高度重視和社會各界的熱心支持，歷代圖書館員心繫國家、愛崗敬業、革故鼎新、追求卓越，爲學校整體發展、行業共同進步、國家文化繁榮做出了重要貢獻，在大學圖書館現代化進程中發揮了示範引領作用。

　　125年來，北京大學圖書館已經積累形成了包括古文獻、特藏文獻和普通文獻在內的近千萬册（件）紙質文獻，其中特藏文獻近百萬册（件），蘊含着獨特的歷史底蘊和文化魅力。北京大學圖書館特藏文獻不僅規模宏大，而且種類繁多、內容獨特，大致可歸爲以下四大類：

　　一是晚清民國文獻：晚清民國時期出版的中文圖書（不包括綫裝）、中文報刊、外文報紙（僅包括國內出版）。

　　二是北京大學有關特藏：北大人的著作、北大學位論文、北大名人贈書及手稿，北大校史和館史檔案資料等非書文獻，以及革命文獻。

　　三是西文特藏：西文善本、次善本，西文東方學，中德學會、中法大學舊藏，中法中心藏書，縮微大型特藏，歐盟文獻等。

　　四是其他特藏：非北大名人的贈書、藏書、手稿，零散珍貴特藏等。

　　不難發現，北京大學圖書館特藏文獻不僅是北京大學乃至中國近現代學術文化史的濃縮再現，也是北京大學在馬克思主義的中國早期傳播和中國共產黨建立過程中的傑出貢獻的歷史見證；既是本館百餘年特藏文獻容納百川的厚重積澱，也是近代以來中西文化交流的歷史記錄。

北京大學圖書館向來十分重視特藏的採集和受贈、揭示和組織、整理和研究、保護和利用等工作，2005年設立特藏部，現已改名爲特藏資源服務中心（以下簡稱特藏中心），組建了由十幾名專業館員構成的隊伍。特藏中心在做好基礎工作的同時，積極開展特藏文獻的發掘與整理，已有不少成果問世，如《北京大學圖書館藏西文漢學珍本提要》《烟雨樓臺：北京大學圖書館藏西籍中的清代建築圖像》《胡適藏書目錄》等。這些圖書對於揭示北京大學圖書館特藏資源，推動相關研究，起到了積極作用。

北京大學圖書館特藏文獻的整理研究和出版工作還大有可爲。有鑒於此，北京大學圖書館與北京大學出版社於2017年底簽署了"北京大學圖書館特藏文獻叢刊合作出版協議"，旨在推動北京大學圖書館特藏文獻的整理研究和出版工作，彰顯北京大學薪火相傳的學術傳統，揭示北京大學圖書館博大精深的人文底蘊。"北京大學圖書館特藏文獻叢刊"第一輯出版四種：

《北京大學圖書館藏學術名家手稿》

《北京大學圖書館藏革命文獻圖録》

《北京大學圖書館藏老北大燕大畢業年刊》

《北京大學圖書館藏胡適未刊來往書信》

"北京大學圖書館特藏文獻叢刊"的出版，離不開北京大學出版社的積極合作和鼎力支持，離不開典籍與文化事業部馬辛民主任和武芳、吴遠琴、王應、吴冰妮、沈瑩瑩等編輯的辛勤勞動，在此表示衷心感謝。

"北京大學圖書館特藏文獻叢刊"的出版任重道遠，我們將進一步加強與北京大學衆多院系和有關方面的交流合作，加大文獻整理研究和出版力度，努力將"特藏文獻叢刊"打造成在大學圖書館界和出版界都具有一定知名度的品牌，爲繁榮學術和發展文化做出積極貢獻。

今年10月28日，北京大學圖書館將迎來125周年館慶，"特藏文獻叢刊"的出版無疑也是一種很好的紀念！

北京大學圖書館館長　陳建龍
2023年9月26日

前　言

胡適是中國近現代學術思想史上的著名人物，不僅在史學、哲學、文學等領域有頗多開創性建樹，而且在當時的知識界和思想界有着廣泛而深刻的影響。

胡適非常注重個人檔案資料的保存，加之聲名顯赫，交遊廣泛，僅與胡適有關的書信就數量驚人，無出其右，至今仍不斷有新的發現。

胡適書信的整理出版，最重要的當屬耿雲志先生主編，1994年由黃山書社出版的《胡適遺稿及秘藏書信》。全書共42卷，其中第18—第42卷共25卷爲胡適來往書信，包括胡適手寫信稿和抄件600封左右。900餘人寫給胡適的書信5400餘封，以影印的形式出版，爲胡適研究提供了大量的第一手珍貴史料。

影印出版之外，整理本胡適書信集主要有：

中國社會科學院近代史研究所中華民國史組編《胡適來往書信選》上中下三册，收録胡適1915—1948年來往書信近1400封，最初由中華書局於1979年出版。

耿雲志、歐陽哲生編《胡適書信集》上中下三册，收録胡適本人1907—1962年所寫書信1644封，北京大學出版社1996年出版。

耿雲志、歐陽哲生編《胡適全集》第23—第36卷書信部分，收録胡適1907—1962年所寫書信、函電、明信片2300餘封，安徽教育出版社2003年出版。

潘光哲主編《胡適全集·胡適中文書信集》，在前述整理本的基礎上進行了新的補充，爲目前收録胡適中文書信最全的書信集，臺北胡適紀念館2018年出版。

此外，還有胡適與楊聯陞、雷震、王重民等個人往來書信集的整理出版。

1948年12月，胡適倉促飛離北平，留下102箱藏書和手稿、書信、日記等個人珍貴檔案資料。胡適曾於1957年在紐約立下遺囑，將此102箱藏書和檔案資料贈送北京大學。但由於歷史原因，胡適留在大陸的這批珍貴文獻，主要一分爲二，胡適藏書現由北京大學圖書館收藏，胡適的手稿、書信、日記等珍貴個人檔案現由中國歷史研究院圖書檔案館收藏。上述《胡適遺稿及秘藏書信》即來自後者。

北京大學圖書館藏胡適來往書信，主要發現自胡適的藏書之中。胡適藏書的整理開始於2000年。當年夏季，北京大學對原燕京大學建築群樓頂進行維修加固，存放在這些樓頂的圖書館藏書必須全部搬遷，於是在紅三樓樓頂塵封了近四十年的胡適普通藏書得以搬遷至新館。筆者有幸在當年暑假受時任館長戴龍基教授之託，對胡適藏書做初步整理，並於其中發現了一個文件袋，內裝胡適一批來往中英文書信，主要集中於胡適1938—1942年任駐美大使期間。後來，連同新發現的胡適迄今爲止最早的日記——澄衷學堂日記，結集爲《北京大學圖書館藏胡適未刊書信日記》，由清華大學出版社於2003年影印出版。

北大圖書館胡適藏書的全面系統整理，開始於2005年北大圖書館特藏部成立之後，筆者有幸加入這個新成立的團隊，得以有機會繼續胡適藏書的整理工作。同年夏，臺灣東海大學陳以愛教授來北大圖書館查閱胡適藏書時，轉達了臺北胡適紀念館與北大圖書館合作整理胡適藏書的意向。經多方溝通聯繫，2009年4月，北大圖書館與胡適紀念館正式簽署"胡適藏書目錄整理合作協議"。2010年初，北大館胡適藏書基本整理完畢。我們在系統整理胡適藏書的過程中，對每本書都進行了仔細翻閱，除了記錄書上的題記、批注、印章等信息外，也驚喜地發現了一些夾在書中的書信。我們將這些書信取出單獨保存，並注明出處。當我們整理完胡適藏書後，發現這批書信竟然也有了相當的數量，這就是本書所收胡適書信的主要來源之一。

這部分夾於胡適藏書中的書信，包括中文書信110餘封，英文書信50封，其中不乏著名學者、人物的書信。如曾任北京大學圖書館主任五年、中國共產黨早期創始人之一的李大釗的一封書信，雖然僅寥寥數語，卻是北大圖書館迄今爲止收藏的唯一一封李大釗先生的手跡，非常珍貴。而蔡元培校長給胡適的書信，也屬於北大圖書館館藏中之吉光片羽。其他如吳虞、劉半農、陶孟和、劉文典、高夢旦、王季同、朱經農、胡先驌、顧頡剛、顧孟餘、王世傑、張君勱、沈從文、林語堂、陳榮捷、胡厚宣、魏建功、羅常培、朱士嘉、袁同禮、王靜如、黎錦熙、章廷謙、范振聲、蕭乾、馮沅君等，都是當時知名的學術文化界人物。

本書收錄胡適書信的另外一部分，是胡適駐美大使卸任之後，美國政要、教育、文化界名士給胡適以書信形式寫的留言，共計130封，144頁，涉及的人物有美國總統羅斯福，當時的美國國務卿、陸海軍總司令、司法部長、商務部長，科羅拉多、內華達、伊利諾伊、賓夕法尼亞、紐約、明尼蘇達等州州長，紐約市長，麻省理工學院、耶魯大學、加州大學等校校長，著名作家賽珍珠等。這部分書信，所用信箋整齊劃一，裝在特製的函套內，除了英文書信，還有整理出來的書信目錄打印件，以及一頁說明，用胡適倡導的白話文寫成："這個信劄集，是胡校長適之先生送給北大圖書館的。卅八年一月四日記。"胡適1948年12月已離開北平，故此記錄或爲補記。

這套信劄集很多年一直在北大圖書館北大文庫的著名學者展陳櫃的胡適專櫃中展示，最初筆者對這些書信的來歷頗爲茫然，因爲是同樣的信箋，還曾以爲是找不同人抄錄的。直到後來閱讀《胡適日記全集》，才找到答案。

胡適在1943年1月19日的日記中記："下午去Mrs. James E. Hughes家吃茶，他把他們（Miss Pearl Buck's）收集的美國朝野名人對我去任的信劄一'函'交給我，內有總統、內閣以及各邦總督、中央最高法院全體的信。——雖可寶貴，但他們未得我同意，擅自發函徵求此項書信，實甚使我不安。"值得一提的是，筆者後來在臺北胡適紀念館"胡適檔案檢索系統"中發現，胡適早在1942年11月28日曾爲此事對賽珍珠表示感謝。信中感謝賽珍珠在當月17日爲自己舉辦的宴會，並說自己爲賽珍珠和Mrs. Hughes克服很大的困難爲自己準備的美國朋友的"感謝信"（testimonial letters）這一驚喜的禮物所深深感動，將把此信劄集作爲對自己短暫的外交和從政生涯的獎勵紀念而珍藏。從信中我們可以知道，胡適在當天的宴會上瀏覽了已經收集的部分書信，並在信中希望賽珍珠和Mrs. Hughes將已經收集到的信劄交給自己，不要再麻煩繼續收集了。從胡適日記看，此項收集工作仍然繼續，直到1943年1月。

這些書信可以説是胡適任駐美大使的最好紀念，雖然信中難免溢美之詞，但是其中對胡適任駐美大使期間爲中國抗戰爭取美國援助，以及對於中美文化交流的貢獻的評價，還是頗值得參考的。此外，這些書信中關於與胡適交往的回憶，也頗可補胡適這一時期的日記記録簡略之不足。胡適將此書信集贈與北大圖書館，筆者猜想，可能是由於他認爲這些書信不屬於個人的私密，而是與中國抗戰大局，與中美抗戰期間的政府和民間交往有關，可以爲後來者留一些史料和參考。胡適不能未卜先知，但是他將此書信集贈給北大圖書館，而不是留在個人書信檔案之中，因此避免了這些書信被調撥的命運，而得以保存在北大圖書館，其結局令人頗爲感慨。

　　與胡適令人驚歎的書信量相比，本書收録的只是很小的部分。雖然如此，筆者還是希望本書能夠爲胡適檔案資料的不斷完善作一點小小的貢獻，並爲胡適研究提供新的原始文獻。

　　本書信集從開始整理到現在即將付梓，已經經歷了至少五載光陰。我一直認爲，能夠整理北京大學圖書館的胡適藏書，並由此對相關文獻及背景知識略知一二，是我在北大圖書館工作最大的幸運所在，所以筆者一直對所服務的北大圖書館心存感激。我在讀研期間的專業是先秦思想史，整理胡適藏書的工作爲我打開了中國近現代學術文化史的大門，胡適廣博的學識、廣闊的交遊，使我的相關知識背景能夠如滚雪球般，不斷發現未知，不斷補充新知。

　　本書將在 2023 年末出版，距我主編的《胡適藏書目録》出版的 2013 年，整整十年。念及此時，突然想到，《北京大學圖書館藏胡適未刊書信日記》的出版會不會是在 2003 年呢？經查竟然真的是 2003 年，又一個十年！雖然《北京大學圖書館藏胡適未刊書信日記》編輯出版時，我不巧去法國巴黎第十大學圖書館交流兩個月，由校史館楊琥兄編輯成書，但早期的發現和簡單整理肯定是與我有關的。時光匆匆，每個人都不完全是時間的主人，因此能真正好好做事，且能夠做出點事情的機會並不多。這樣看來，我覺得自己還算幸運。

　　雖然這些書信都屬於北京大學圖書館，我只不過做了點整理和編輯的工作，但是在本書即將出版之際，我還是要對在本書編輯整理過程中給予幫助的師友表示感謝。他們是：哈佛燕京圖書館王繫老師，以及她聰明可愛的女兒王喬安，很多英文手寫體的釋讀得到她們熱情的幫助；我的同事，北京大學圖書館的張紅揚、吳政同、丁世良、周永喜、鄺俊琴、王錚等老師，他們在這些書信的發現、掃描、整理、釋讀方面給予我很多支持和幫助；北京大學外國語學院陳明教授，熱心幫助辨識英文手稿；原北大文庫負責人周家珍老師，爲北大文庫的文獻收集殫精竭慮，不辭辛勞，胡適卸任駐美大使後的美國各界名人的英文書信集，應該就是周老師調撥到北大文庫的；北大出版社的編輯吳冰妮老師，爲本書的出版費心費力，沒有她的大力支持，本書很難順利出版。

　　筆者2018年有幸加入歐陽哲生老師主持的"胡適年譜新編"這一國家社會科學基金重大項目，並由此得到不少支持和幫助，在此一併表示感謝。

　　本次出版的書信集除了影印原件，爲研究者提供一手文獻外，還嘗試對手稿進行釋讀，爲研究者提供便利。雖然筆者多年接觸手寫文字，但仍力有未逮，誤讀之處，敬請指正。

鄒新明

2023年3月4日

編輯體例

一、本書收録的胡適來往書信，根據來源分爲發現於胡適藏書之中的書信（包括中文書信與英文書信兩類）和胡適卸任駐美大使後美國各界名士致意信函兩部分。

二、中文書信按照作者姓名拼音排序，少量機關公函和日人書信按名稱拼音排入，不再另排。

三、英文書信和胡適卸任駐美大使後美國各界名士致意信函按照作者姓名（名在前，姓在後）分別排序。

四、本書對每位書信作者做了簡單介紹，少量未查到作者情況者，以"作者生平不詳"說明。

五、爲便於讀者閱讀，本書對手寫書信做了釋讀，並採取了影印件與釋讀文字左右對照的編排方式。印刷或打印書信不再重新録入。

六、書信中的衍文和個別拼寫問題，用"[ ]"加以標註。個別難以識讀的文字或單詞用"□"表示。

目　錄

發現於胡適藏書中的書信

中文書信

包鷺賓致胡適（一九二二年十月二十九日）……………………………… 3
蔡元培致胡適（一九三〇年十一月六日）………………………………… 9
蔡正中致胡適………………………………………………………………… 15
曹葆華致胡適………………………………………………………………… 19
陳榮捷致胡適（一九四二年四月二十六日）……………………………… 23
陳瑞祺致胡適（一九三四年六月三日）…………………………………… 27
陳廷璠致胡適………………………………………………………………… 33
陳萬里致胡適（一九四八年一月二十二日）……………………………… 37
程敷鍇致胡適………………………………………………………………… 41
戴堅致胡適…………………………………………………………………… 45
范振聲致胡適（一九三四年九月二十三日）……………………………… 49
馮叔蘭（馮沅君）致胡適…………………………………………………… 55
高夢旦致陶孟和、蔣夢麟（一九二〇年十月二十七日）………………… 59
高夢旦致胡適（一九二八年九月三十日）………………………………… 65

顧孟餘致胡適（一九三二年六月九日）……………………… 69

顧隨致胡適（一九三一—一九三六年十二月十二日）……… 73

顧頡剛致胡適（一九三五年五月十二日）…………………… 77

何天行致胡適（一九四八年五月三十一日）………………… 83

賀生樂致胡適…………………………………………………… 89

胡厚宣致胡適…………………………………………………… 91

胡適致高仲洽（一九三〇年九月二日）……………………… 95

胡適致皮宗石單不广（一九三三年四月十八日）…………… 99

胡先驌致胡適………………………………………………… 105

胡哲敷致胡適………………………………………………… 109

黃學周致胡適（一九三三年十一月以后）………………… 113

黃貽清致胡適（一九四七年三月十一日）………………… 115

黃毅民致胡適………………………………………………… 121

簡文致胡適…………………………………………………… 129

江紹原致胡適………………………………………………… 133

焦易堂致胡適（一九三四年六月—九月）………………… 137

金國珍致胡適（一九四七年四月二十二日）……………… 141

黎錦熙致胡適（一九二一年五月四日）…………………… 145

李大釗致胡適………………………………………………… 149

李振邦致胡適（一九四七年三月十九日）………………… 153

連橫致胡適…………………………………………………… 157

林語堂致胡適（一九三五年）……………………………… 161

劉半農致胡適………………………………………………… 165

劉文典致胡適………………………………………………… 169

劉蔭仁致胡適（一九四六年十二月二十五日）…………… 173

羅雄飛致胡適………………………………………………… 179

羅仲言致胡適（一九四八年七月一日）…………………… 187

馬衡致胡適（一九四八年五月十五日）	191
甯華庭致胡適	195
歐陽溙致胡適	199
青木正兒致胡適（一九二一年二月三日）	205
桑原騭藏致胡適	211
沈從文致胡適	215
孫次舟致胡適（一九四七年五月二十四日）	219
孫澤英致胡適	223
孫拯致胡適（一九三〇年三月二日）	227
唐世隆致胡適書信兩通（一九三一年七月二十一日，一九三一年九月十一日）	231
陶孟和致胡適（一九二〇年十一月十二日）	241
陶孟和致奚滇	245
汪敬熙致胡適（一九四四年十二月三日）	249
王季同致胡適（一九四三年十一月十八日）	255
王靜如致胡適	263
王世杰致胡適（一九三五年三月八日）	267
王小航致胡適（一九三一年春——一九三三年六月）	273
王孝魚致胡適（一九四五年——一九四八年）	289
王重民致胡適	299
王卓然致胡適（一九三二年十二月六日）	301
魏建功羅常培致胡適（一九三四年十一月二十日）	303
吳敬寰初若瑤致胡適	307
吳廷燮致胡適	309
吳虞致胡適（一九三三年十一月二十九日）	311
吳作民致胡適（一九四七年十二月四日）	315
向乃祺致胡適	323

蕭恩承致胡適（一九三二年）	327
蕭乾致胡適（一九四五年四月廿九日）	331
嚴璩致胡適	337
楊樂公致胡適	341
葉式欽致胡適（一九四八年四月七日）	345
伊見思致胡適（一九四八年三月十四日）	347
易熙吾致某根泰（一九四六年九月十四日）	351
袁同禮致胡適	359
章廷謙（川島）致胡適（一九三五年四月十三日）	365
張光祖致胡適	371
張國維致胡適（一九三三年五月十三日）	375
張君勱致胡適	379
張孟休致胡適	383
張頤致胡適	387
趙承信致胡適（一九四七年一月二十七日）	391
趙鳳喈致胡適（一九二八年五月二十六日）	395
趙貞信致胡適（一九四七年七月十一日）	399
智武致胡適	403
朱經農致胡適（一九一六年八月二十三日）	405
朱士嘉致胡適（一九四四年七月三十一日）	409
祝實明致胡適（一九四六年七月三十日）	415
國立北平故宮博物院總務處致胡適（一九四七年九月十三日）	421
國立編譯館致胡適	423
江蘇省立教育學院惠北普及民眾教育實驗區致胡適（一九三二年十二月一日）	427
開明書店致胡適	429
民族雜誌社致胡適（一九三六年三月十五日）	431

商務印書館致胡適……433

上海市公用局致胡適（一九四八年十一月二十二日）……465

行政院農村復興委員會秘書處致胡適（一九三五年五月二十一日）……467

興士團遠東部致胡適……469

張家口奮鬥日報致胡適（一九四七年十二月二十日）……473

中國教育電影協會致胡適（一九三五年六月）……481

中國物理學會致胡適……483

中國營造學社致胡適……485

中華職業教育社致胡適（一九三〇年四月二十五日）……487

中央研究院歷史語言研究所致胡適（一九三〇年三月二十四日）……489

發現於胡適藏書中的書信

英文書信

A. Douglas Rugh 致胡適（一九三五年六月十九日）……493

A. Y. Ching 致胡適（一九二七年六月一日）……495

Adelaide M. Anderson 致胡適（一九二六年十月八日）……497

Alan Macintosh 致胡適（一九三一年六月十九日）……503

Allen Churchill 致胡適（一九四一年十月十四日）……505

B. C. Bridges 致胡適（一九四二年六月八日）……507

B. H. Streeter 致胡適（一九二六年十二月九日）……511

Bernard Lightenberg 致胡適（一九四五年八月十七日）……515

Constance Warren 致胡適（一九三六年九月九日）……517

Edward C. Carter 致胡適（一九三九年一月三十日）……519

Evan Morgan 致 Rawlinson（一九三〇年四月二十五日），
　Robert F. Fitch 致胡適（一九三〇年五月二日，一九三〇年七月十五日）…… 521

Everett R. Clinchy 致胡適 ······ 529

Frances Carpenter Huntington 致胡適 ······ 531

G. W. Sheppard 致胡適（一九二九年十月二十二日）······ 537

George Catlin 致胡適（一九四八年八月七日）······ 539

H. J. Timperley 致胡適（一九三一年三月五日）······ 541

H. L. Huang 致胡適（一九一六年十二月六日）······ 543

Hamilton Fish Armstrong 致胡適（一九三六年十月十三日）······ 547

Henry W. Edgerton 致胡適（一九四一年三月二十六日）······ 549

Hu Shi 致某人 ······ 555

Irving Dilliard 致胡適 ······ 559

Joanna Scott 致胡適（一九四五年三月三十日）······ 561

John Dewey 致 Mr. William（一九二八年四月十日）······ 565

John Story Jenks 致胡適（一九四〇年九月二十四日）······ 567

Juliet Bredon Lauru 致胡適（一九三四年）······ 569

L. B. Juin 致胡適（一九四〇年十一月五日）······ 575

L. G. Morgan 致胡適（一九三五年五月一日）······ 579

L. P. Cookingham 致胡適（一九四二年五月十一日）······ 587

Lawrence Morris 致胡適（一九四一年八月十三日）······ 591

Leon Augustus Hausman 致胡適（一九四六年三月二十六日）······ 593

M. B. Schnapper 致胡適 ······ 595

Manley O. Hudson 致胡適（一九四三年十二月一日）······ 597

Manuel L. Quezon 致胡適（一九二七年八月十日）······ 599

Mary Mackay 致胡適（一九三六年十月二十七日）······ 601

Mary P. E. Nitobé 致胡適（一九三五年三月二十六日）······ 603

Paul Eldridge 致胡適（一九三一年五月十七日）······ 609

Robert □致胡適 ······ 611

Roger S. Greene 致胡適（一九三六年二月一日）······ 613

Victor K. Kwong 致胡適（一九三六年十月二十九日）…… 615

Vung Yuin Ting 致胡適（一九三六年九月十六日）…… 619

Walter Bosshard 致胡適（一九四七年十月二十七日）…… 625

William Fogg Osgood，Mrs. 致胡適 …… 627

Yung Kwai 致胡適（一九四二年九月五日）…… 631

附：AGENDA FOR ROUND TABLES ON CHINA …… 635

胡適卸任駐美大使後美國各界人士致意信劄

A. A. Mueller …… 641

Alan Valentine …… 645

Alfred Kohlberg …… 649

Alice Draper Carter …… 653

Allan Forbes …… 657

Arthur Capper …… 661

Arthur Hays Sulzberger …… 665

Arthur H. James …… 669

Arthur Judson Brown …… 673

Arthur V. Davis …… 677

B. A. Garside …… 681

Bayard M. Hedrick …… 687

Bernard Lichtenberg …… 691

Breckenridge Long …… 695

C. Andrade, 3rd …… 699

Charles A. Sprague …… 703

Charles K. Edmunds …… 707

Charles P. Taft，Mr. and Mrs. …… 711

Charles S. Pharis	715
Charles Merz	719
Charles Seymour	723
Charles Stewart Mott	727
Chester H. Rowell	729
Clarence E. Pickett	733
Clark H. Minor	737
Claude E. Forkner	741
Claude R. Wickard	747
Cordell Hull	751
Daniel W. Bell	755
Dave Hennen Morris	759
David O. Selznick	763
Donald D. Van Slyke	767
Dorothy Canfield Fisher	771
Douglas Auchincloss	775
Dwight H. Green	779
E. P. Carville	783
Edward C. Carter	787
Edward H. Hume	791
Edwin C. Lobenstine	795
Edwin M. McBrier	801
Elizabeth C. Morrow	807
Elizabeth Luce Moore	811
Eric M. North	817
Eugene E. Barnett	821
Felix Frankfurter	827

Fiorello H. LaGuardia	831
Francis S. Hutchins（何欽思）	835
Francis Biddle	839
Frank Co Tui	843
Frank T. Cartwright	847
Frank Knox	851
Frank Meleney	855
Franklin D. Roosevelt	859
Frederick H. Wood	863
G. Harold Welch	867
Galen M. Fisher	871
George T. Marchmont	875
H. E. Yarnell	879
H. R. Ekins	883
Harlan Fiske Stone	887
Harold E. Stassen	893
Harold L. Ickes	897
Harper Sibley, Georgiana Sibley	901
Harry B. Price	905
Harvey S. Firestone, Jr	909
Helen Rogers Reid	913
Henry R. Luce	917
Henry St. George Tucker	921
Henry W. Hobson	925
Henry Morgenthau, Jr	929
Herbert H. Lehman	933
Herbert Welch	937

Hugo L. Black	941
J. W. Decker	945
James G. Blaine	949
James L. McConaughy	953
James R. Angell	957
James V. Forrestal	961
Jesse D. Gard	965
Jesse H. Jones	969
John D. Rockefeller, 3rd	973
John E. Miles	979
John R. Mott	983
John Gunther	987
Julean Arnold	991
Julius Klein	995
Karl T. Compton	999
L. A. Weigle	1003
Lauchlin Currie	1007
Lenning Sweet	1011
Marion Fitch Exter	1015
Martha Finley (Mrs. John H.)	1021
Maurice William	1025
Mildred H. McAfee	1029
Mildred Hughes (Mrs. James E.)	1033
Myron C. Taylor	1037
Otis Peabody Swift	1043
Paul G. Hoffman	1047
Paul Monroe	1051

Pearl S. Buck	1055
Ralph A. Bard	1059
Ralph E. Diffendorfer	1063
Ralph L. Carr	1069
Ray Lyman Wilbur	1073
Raymond Clapper	1077
Richard J. Walsh	1081
Robert A. Millikan	1085
Robert Gordon Sproul	1089
Robert H. Jackson	1093
Robert L. Smith	1097
Robert P. Patterson	1101
Roy W. Howard	1105
Rufus M. Jones	1109
Sidney D. Gamble	1113
Sidney P. Osborn	1117
Silas H. Strawn	1121
Stanley Reed	1125
Sumner Welles	1129
Thomas J. Watson	1133
Thomas L. Sidlo	1137
Thomas W. Lamont	1141
W. R. Herod	1145
Walter B. Cannon	1149
Walter G. Hiltner	1153
Walter Parker	1157
Wayne Chatfield Taylor	1161

Wendell L. Willkie ……………………………………………… 1165

William D. Leahy ……………………………………………… 1169

William O. Douglas ……………………………………………… 1173

William Philip Simms ……………………………………………… 1177

William Green ……………………………………………… 1181

Wilson Compton ……………………………………………… 1185

Wynn C. Fairfield ……………………………………………… 1189

發現於胡適藏書中的書信
中文書信

包鷺賓致胡適（一九二二年十月二十九日）

　　此信發現於 *Selected Stories by Guy de Maupassant* 一書中。

　　包鷺賓（1899—1944），字漁莊，江西南城縣人。早年就讀於南昌省立中學。1920 年考入北京大學哲學系預科，1926 年北京大學哲學系本科畢業，先後任江西省立第一中學、省立第一女子中學、省立農業專門學校國文教員。曾任江西私立心遠大學教授。1931 年任武昌私立華中大學中文系主任，歷任國學講師、副教授、教授。其間曾得到美國哈佛燕京學社資助，與游國恩、傅懋勣等人研究西南少數民族文化。1944 年暑假，應邀去大理爲編寫縣志作實地考察，不幸染疾去世。

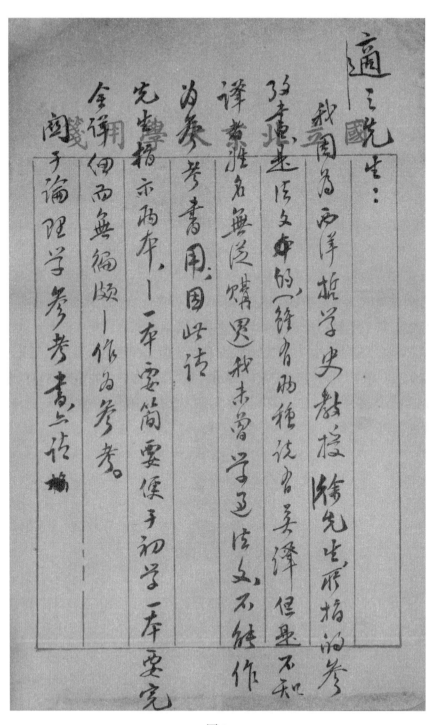

圖1

適之先生：

　　我因爲西洋哲學史教授徐先生，所指的參考書，是法文的，（雖有兩種説有英譯但是不知譯者姓名無從購買）我未曾學過法文，不能作爲參考書用；因此請

先生指示兩本，──一本要簡要便于初學一本要完全詳細而無偏頗──作爲參考。

　　關於論理學參考書，亦請

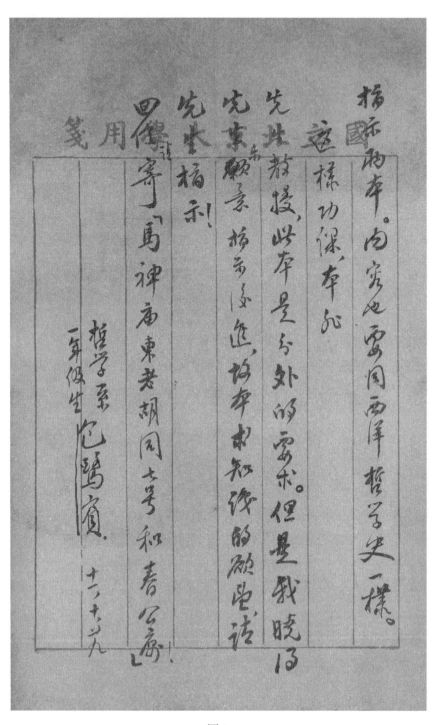

圖2

指示兩本。內容也要同西洋哲學史一樣。

　　這樣功課，本非先生教授，此本是分外的要求。但是我曉得先生樂意指示後進，故本求知識的欲望，請先生指示！

　　回信請寄"馬神廟東老胡同七號和春公寓"！

哲學系一年級生包鷺賓
十一，十，廿九

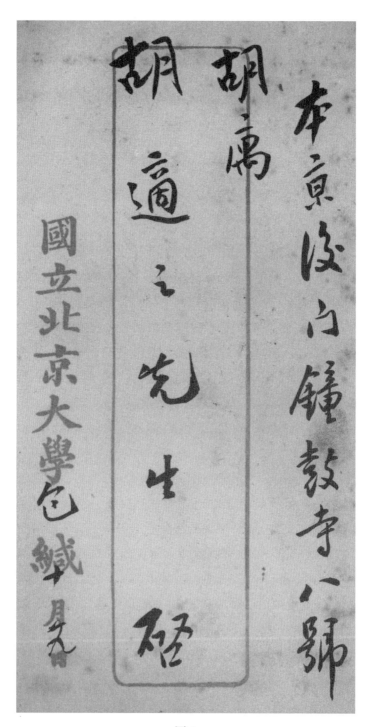

圖3

蔡元培致胡適（一九三〇年十一月六日）

　　此信發現於《尊聞録》一書中。該書出版於 1930 年，胡適當時還在上海，同年 11 月 28 日舉家遷往北平。故此信應寫於 1930 年。封面有蔡元培題字："熊十力先生屬轉贈胡適之先生。十九年十月卅一日蔡元培。"

　　蔡元培（1868—1940），字鶴卿，號子民，浙江紹興人。1883 年考中秀才，後在紹興古越藏書樓校書。1889 年中舉。1890 年取進士。1892 年授翰林院庶吉士。1894 年補翰林院編修。1898 年 9 月戊戌政變後返紹興，任中西學堂監督。1901 年赴上海，任南洋公學特班教員，參與創辦《外交報》。1902 年參與發起中國教育會，任事務長。同年秋與蔣智由等創辦愛國女學。1903 年，兼任商務印書館編譯所所長，參與創辦《俄事警聞》(後改爲《警鐘日報》)。1904 年秋，與龔寶銓等在上海成立光復會，被推爲會長。1907 年赴德國留學，入萊比錫大學研究哲學、文學、美學和心理學。1911 年辛亥革命爆發後歸國，1912 年 1 月，任南京臨時政府教育總長，3 月被任命爲唐紹儀內閣教育總長，同年 7 月辭職，9 月再赴德國。1916 年回國，同年底任北京大學校長。1920 年底到歐洲考察教育，次年 9 月回國。1923 年 1 月提出辭職，7 月出國考察。1926 年 1 月，當選爲國民黨第二屆中央監察委員，2 月回到國內。5 月在上海參加皖蘇浙三省聯合會，響應國民革命軍北伐。1927 年 "四一二" 政變後至南京，任國民政府教育行政委員會常務委員，同年先後任大學院院長、國民政府委員、中央特別委員會委員。1928 年 4 月，任中央研究院院長，10 月，被推舉爲監察院院長。1932 年 12 月，與宋慶齡等發起組織中國民權保障同盟，任副主席。

1933年10月，任全國經濟委員會委員。1935年11月，任國民黨第五屆中央監察委員。1937年抗日戰爭爆發，上海淪陷，移居香港。1940年3月5日在香港病逝。終年72歲。著有《中國倫理學史》《石頭記索隱》等，有《蔡元培全集》。

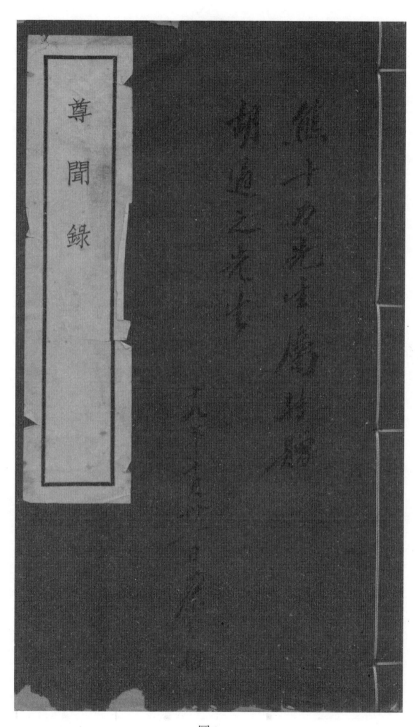

圖1

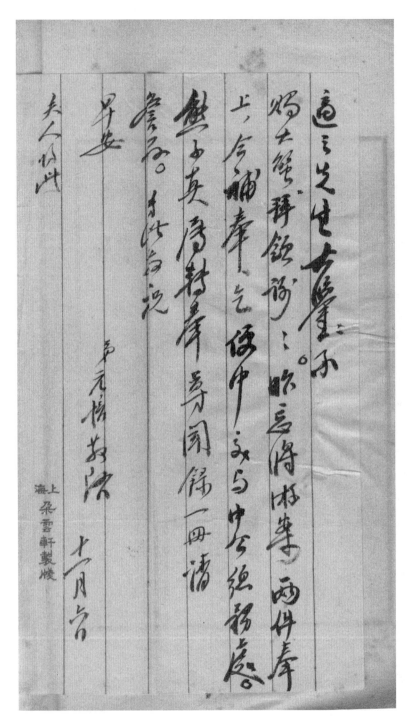

圖2

適之先生大鑒：
　　承
賜大蟹，拜領，謝謝！昨忘將游案兩件奉上，今補奉，乞便中交與中公總務處。熊子真屬轉奉《尊聞錄》一冊，請
詧存。專此，敬祝
早安
　　夫人均此。

弟元培敬啓
十一月六日

蔡正中致胡適

　　此信發現於《今後我國的出路及人類之將來》一書中。此書出版於1933 年。

　　蔡正中，疑即貴州郎岱人蔡正中（1891—1951），字心一，早年就讀於貴陽一中，後考入上海大夏大學政治經濟系，畢業後任教於福建師範學校。後曾任西南游擊幹部訓練班政治部少將主任。1945 年任貴州省榕江縣縣長。

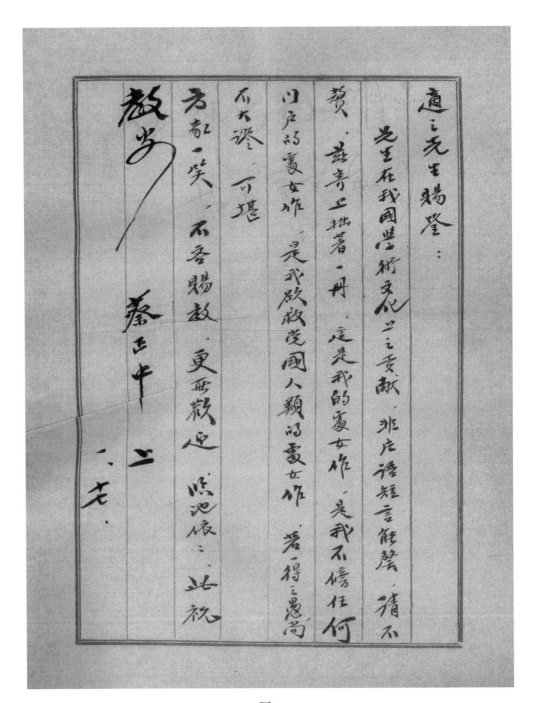

圖1

適之先生賜鑒：

　　先生在我國學術文化上之貢獻，非片語短言能罄，請不贅。茲寄上拙著一册，這是我的處女作，是我不傍任何門户的處女作，是我欲救黨國人類的處女作，若一得之愚，尚不大謬，可堪
方家一笑，不吝賜教，更所歡迎。臨池依依，此祝
教安

　　　　　　　　　　　　　　　　　　　　　　　蔡正中　上
　　　　　　　　　　　　　　　　　　　　　　　　一，十七

曹葆華致胡適

　　此信發現於《寄詩魂》一書中。《寄詩魂》出版於 1930 年 12 月，此信有可能寫於 1931 年 2 月 11 日。

　　曹葆華（1906—1978），原名曹寶華。筆名伊人、葆華等。四川樂山人。1931 年畢業於清華大學外國文學系，同年入清華大學研究院，1935 年畢業。讀書期間從事新詩創作，抗戰爆發後創作了一些宣傳抗日的詩。1939 年 11 月到延安，任魯迅藝術文學院文學系教員。1944 年起，在中共中央宣傳部俄文翻譯室工作，曾任該室主任。1962 年調中國科學院文學研究所（1964 年轉外國文學研究所，今屬中國社會科學院）任研究員，從事馬克思主義文藝理論的翻譯和研究工作。

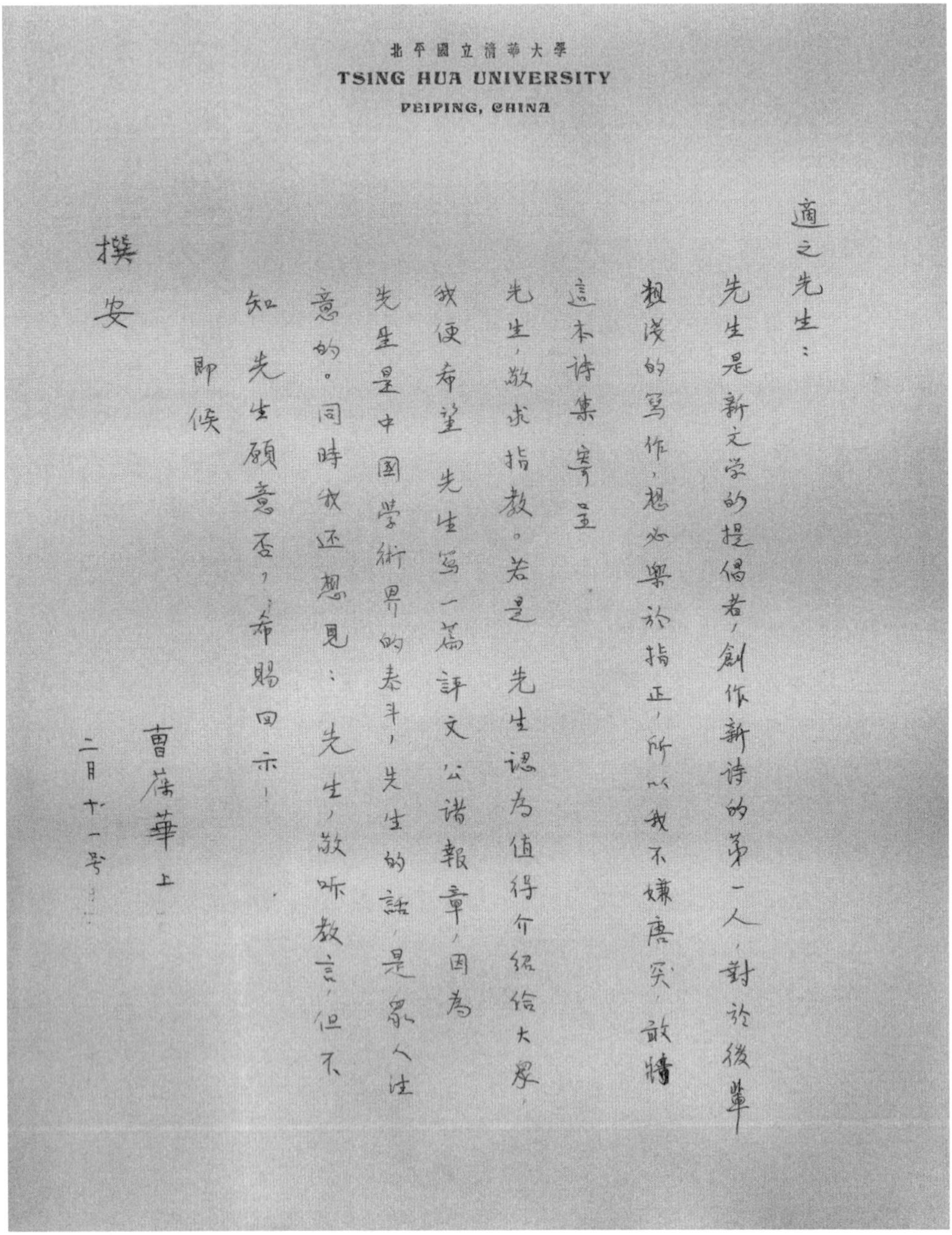
北平國立清華大學
TSING HUA UNIVERSITY
PEIPING, CHINA

適之先生：

先生是新文学的提倡者，創作新诗的第一人，對於後輩粗淺的寫作，想必樂於指正，所以我不嫌唐突，敢特這本诗集寄呈先生，敬求指教。若是先生認為值得介紹給大衆，我便希望先生寫一篇評文公諸報章，因為先生是中國学術界的泰斗，先生的話，是衆人注意的。同時我还想見：先生，敬听教言，但不知先生願意否？希賜回示！

即候

撰安

曹葆華 上

二月十一号

圖 1

適之先生：

　　先生是新文學的提倡者，創作新詩的第一人，對於後輩粗淺的寫作，想必樂於指正，所以我不嫌唐突，敢將這本詩集寄呈
先生，敬求指教。若是先生認爲值得介紹給大衆，我便希望先生寫一篇評文公諸報章，因爲
先生是中國學術界的泰斗，先生的話，是衆人注意的。同時我還想見見先生，敬聽教言，但不知先生願意否？希賜回示。
　　　即候
撰安

　　　　　　　　　　　　　　　　　　　　　　　　　曹葆華上
　　　　　　　　　　　　　　　　　　　　　　　　　二月十一號

陳榮捷致胡適（一九四二年四月二十六日）

此信發現於 Zen Buddhism and its Influence on Japanese Culture 一書中。

陳榮捷（1901—1994），中國哲學史家，廣東開平人。1916 年入廣州嶺南學堂，1924 年畢業於嶺南大學，旋即赴美留學，入哈佛大學，1927 年獲哲學碩士學位，1929 年獲哲學博士學位。同年歸國，任嶺南大學教授，次年出任教務長。1936 年再度赴美，先後執教於達慕思學院、夏威夷大學、匹茲堡徹含慕學院，並兼任哥倫比亞大學教授。1978 年當選台灣"中央研究院"院士。1980 年當選美國亞洲研究與比較哲學學會會長。1986 年任北美華裔學人協會副會長。1994 年在美國去世。1946 年爲麥克奈爾主編《中國》一書撰寫《新儒學》一章，爲戰後西方研究理學與朱熹思想專篇之始。1953 年出版《現代中國宗教之趨勢》一書，著力介紹以熊十力爲代表的現代新儒學。1966 年被聘爲《哲學百科全書》中國哲學主編。主要著作有《現代中國宗教之趨勢》《中國哲學歷史圖》《中國哲學資料書》等，譯著有《傳習錄》《老子》《六祖壇經》等。被歐美學界譽爲"介紹東方哲學文化思想最完備周詳之中國哲人"。

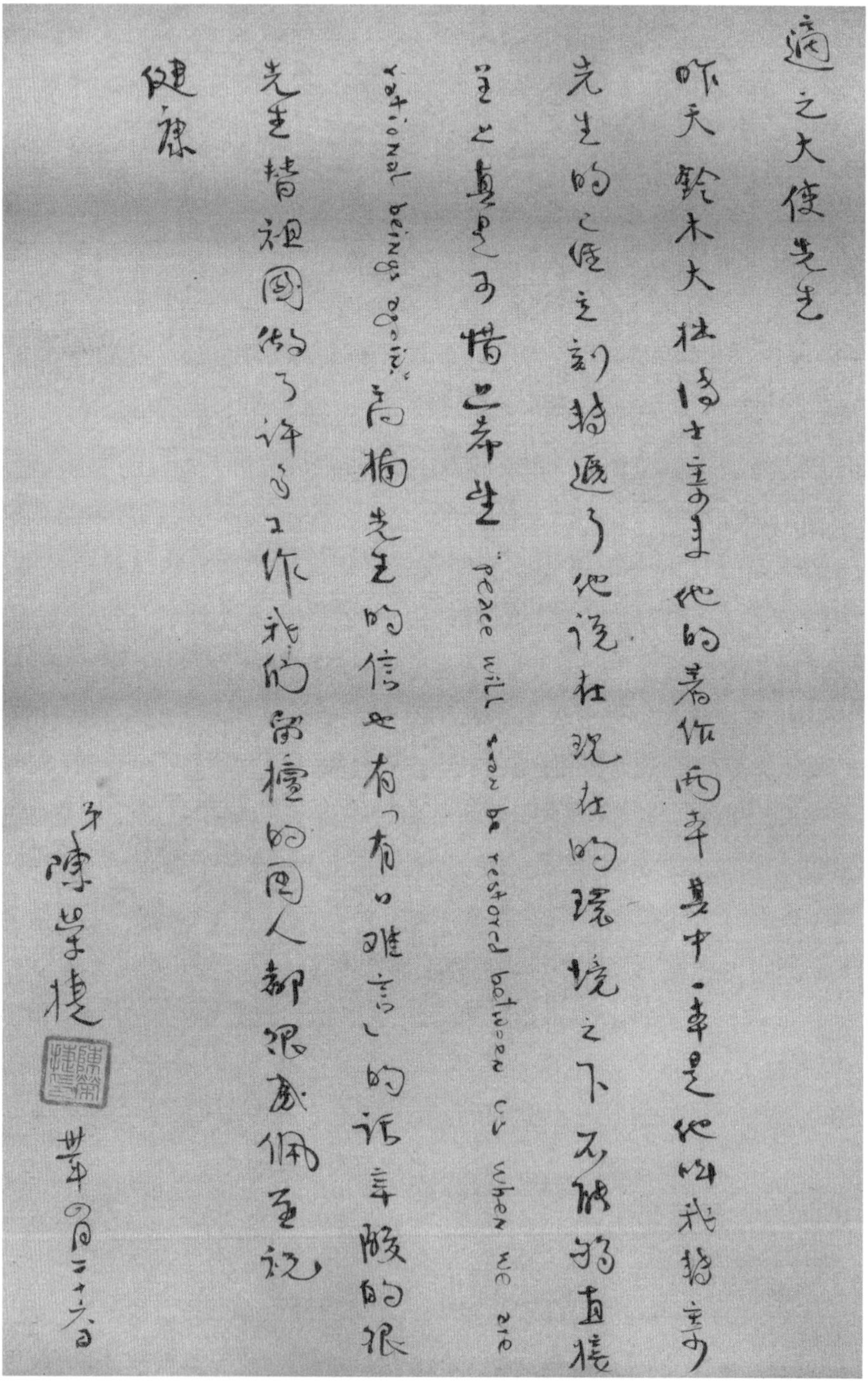

適之大使先生

昨天鈴木大拙博士來訪，他的著作兩年前寄來，是他以我指導先生的經之託特送了他。說在現在的環境之下不能有直接注之真是可惜之事生"peace will ever be restored between us when we are rational beings again." 高楠先生的信也有"有口難言"的話，幸勝的很

先生替祖國做了許多工作，我的同檀的同人都很感佩，並記

健康

弟 陳榮捷 [印]

卅年四月二十六日

圖1

適之大使先生：

　　昨天鈴木大拙博士寄來他的著作兩本，其中一本是他叫我轉寄先生的，已經立刻轉遞了。他說，在現在的環境之下不能夠直接呈上，真是可惜，只希望"Peace will soon be restored between us when we are rational beings again"。高楠先生的信也有"有口難言"的話，辛酸的很。先生替祖國做了許多工作，我們留檀的國人都很感佩。並祝
健康

　　　　　　　　　　　　　　　　　　　　　　　　　弟　陳榮捷
　　　　　　　　　　　　　　　　　　　　　　　　　卅一年四月二十六日

陳瑞祺致胡適（一九三四年六月三日）

此信發現於《道字初刊》一書中。

陳瑞祺（1885—1950），名禎祥，字文典，別號瑞祺。廣東新會人。早年在香港求學，18歲隨父從商，先後在香港、越南等地經營米業，成爲富商。從商之餘從事研究，曾與子女研製人造絲、人造棉、人造蔴等人造纖維，以及風熱油、風寒油、霍亂散等藥品。熱心公益事業，多次派員到國內災區賑濟災民，並在新會、香港、澳門等地創辦小學。在香港設立道字總社，與其子陳子民創造拼音"道字"，以期改良文字，普及教育。1950年在香港逝世，著有《瑞祺學説》等。

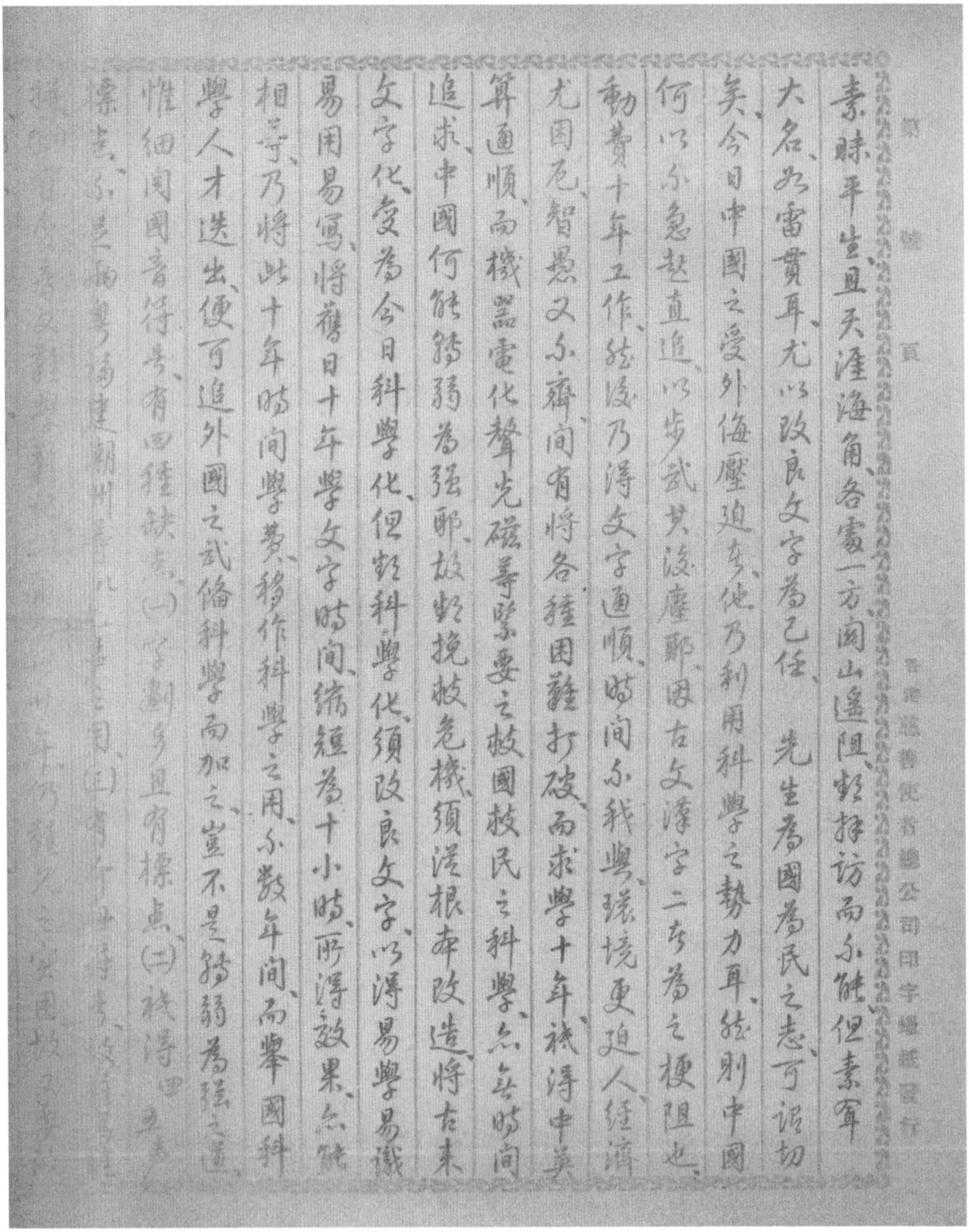

賀 穎 貞

素昧平生，且天涯海角各處一方，關山遙阻，難排訪而不識，但素聞大名，如雷貫耳。尤以改良文字為己任，先生為國為民之志可謂切矣。今日中國之受外侮壓迫者，他乃利用科學之勢力耳。然別中國何以不急起直追，以步武後塵耶？因古文漢字二者為之梗阻也。動費十年工作，然後乃得文字通順。時間不我與，環境更迫人經濟尤困危，智愚又不齊，間有將各種困難打破而求學十年被浮中美算通順、高機器電化聲先磁善緊要之敌國技民之科學，無每時間追求中國何能？猶弱為強耶？故欲挽救危機須從根本改造，將古來文字化變為今日科學化。但輕科學化，須改良文字以得易學易識易用易寫，將舊日十年時間縮短為十小時間。相等，乃將此十年時間學費移作科學之用，不數年間而舉國科學人才選出，便可追外國之武，倘科學而加之當不是猶弱為強之道。惟細閱國音符號，有四種缺憾：（一）秩序里立未標点不甚明，有將建朝州等（二）字劃多且有標点不

[remainder unclear]

素昧平生，且天涯海角，各處一方，關山遥阻，欲拜訪而不能，但素聞大名，如雷貫耳，尤以改良文字爲己任，先生爲國爲民之志，可謂切矣。今日中國之受外侮壓迫者，他乃利用科學之勢力耳。然則中國何以不急起直追，以步武其後塵耶？因古文漢字二者爲之梗阻也。動費十年工作，然後乃得文字通順，時間不我與，環境更迫人，經濟尤困厄，智愚又不齊，間有將各種困難打破，而求學十年，祇得中英算通順，而機器電化聲光磁等緊要之救國救民之科學，亦無時間追求，中國何能轉弱爲強耶？故欲挽救危機，須從根本改造，將古來文字化，變爲今日科學化。但欲科學化，須改良文字，以得易學易識易用易寫，將舊日十年學文字時間，縮短爲十小時，所得效果，亦能相等。乃將此十年時間學費，移作科學之用，不數年間，而舉國科學人才迭出，便可追外國之武備科學而加之，豈不是轉弱爲強之道？

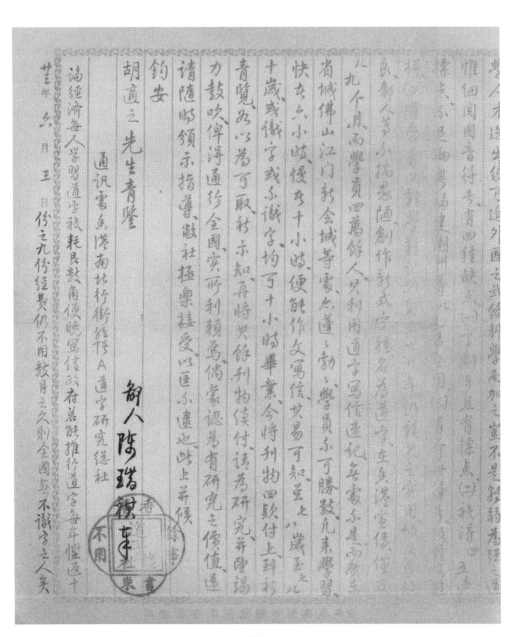

圖 2

惟細閱國音符號,有四種缺點:(一)字劃多且有標點,(二)祇得四五聲標點,不足兩粵福建潮州等八九聲之用,(三)有介母符號、故難寫難拼,(四)有變音又難學難記。故爾出世廿年,仍難見之實用,故又要改良。鄙人等不揣愚陋,創作新式字種,名爲道字,在香港宣傳,僅及八九個月,而學員四萬餘人,其利用道字寫信速記,無處不是,而廣東省城佛山江門新會城等處,亦蓬蓬勃勃,學員不可勝數。凡來學習,快者六小時,慢者十小時,便能作文寫信,其易可知。雖七八歲至七八十歲,或識字或不識字,均可十小時畢業。今將刊物四款付上,到祈青覽,如以爲可取,祈示知,再將其餘刊物續付,請爲研究,并望竭力鼓吹,俾得通行全國,實所利賴焉。倘蒙認爲有研究之價值,還請隨時頒示指導,敝社極樂接受,以匡不逮也。此上并候
鈞安
　　胡適之先生青鑒
　　　　　　　　　　　　　　　　　　　鄙人　陳瑞祺奉
　　　　　　　　　　通訊處香港南北行街五十八號A道字研究總社
　　　　　　　　　　　　　　　　　　　廿三年六月三日
　　論經濟每人學習道字祇耗銀數角,便曉寫信,政府若能推行道字,每年慳返十份之九份經費,仍不用數月之久,則全國無不識字之人矣。

陳廷璠致胡適

　　此信發現於《世界文化史》一書中。此書由陳廷璠翻譯，上册初版於 1930 年，即北大圖書館胡適藏書之本。1936 年中華書局再版，《改版序》稱："本書上册於民國十九年出版，然因出版倉卒，錯誤百出。廿年夏將下册譯竣後，又將上册重加修改……""本書在民國廿年下册譯竣，上册大加修正之後，即由胡適之先生介紹於新月書店，當新月正在排版之際，忽遭一二八事變……復因他事蹉跎，以致本書譯竣六年，除在中大印作講義之外，未能早日與一般讀者見面……"則此信當寫於上册出版之後、"一·二八"事變之前，即 1930 年或 1931 年的 11 月 19 日。

　　陳廷璠（1897—?），字空三。早年爲無政府主義者，1920 年與陳德榮主編《社會運動》雜誌，1923 年參與創辦北京世界語專門學校，後任教於暨南大學、中山大學。主要譯作有：《世界文化史》《俄國史》。

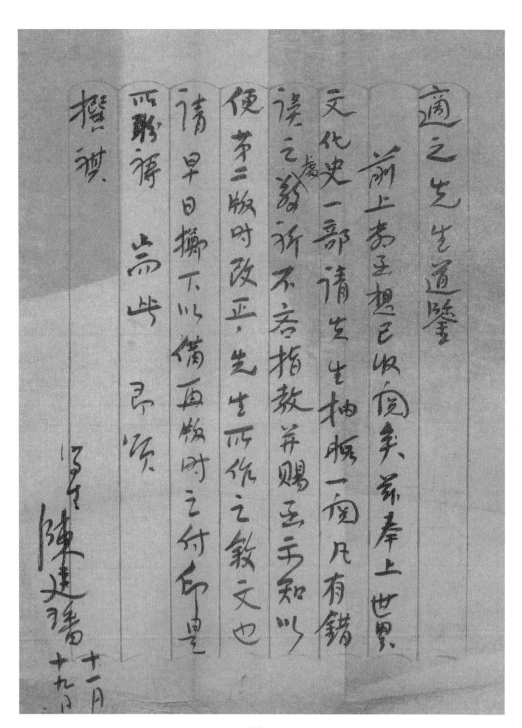

圖1

適之先生道鑒：

  前上教函想已收閱矣，茲奉上《世界文化史》一部，請先生抽暇一閱，凡有錯誤之處，敬祈不吝指教，并賜函示知，以便第二版時改正，先生所作之叙文也請早日擲下，以備再版時之付印，是所盼禱。耑此，即頌

撰祺

學生　陳廷璠

十一月十九日

陳萬里致胡適（一九四八年一月二十二日）

　　此信發現於《江蘇兩年來的衛生工作》一書中。此書出版於1948年，結合信中所述"弟勝利後爲桑梓服務，主持處務已屆兩年"等，此信或寫作於一九四八年一月二十二日。

　　陳萬里（1892—1969），名鵬，字萬里，以字行，江蘇吳縣人。1917年畢業於北京醫科專門學校，後任北京大學校醫。1919年開始鑽研攝影，1923年與黃振玉等發起組織中國最早的攝影藝術團體——藝術寫真研究會，後改稱光社。1924年，溥儀被逐出故宮，陳萬里參加清室善後委員會，拍攝了大量當時宮殿狀況照片。1926年隨美國考古隊到西北實地考察，次年出版《西行日記》。1926年任廈門大學考古學導師、講師。1928年起先後赴龍泉、紹興等地搜集瓷片標本。1930年赴歐洲考察。曾任浙江省立醫院院長、浙江衛生處處長。1941年起歷任衛生署視察、衛生署保健處處長等職，1946年去職，同年出版《瓷器與浙江》，開古窯址調查之先河。1950年調故宮博物院工作，歷任設計員、研究員。著有《中國青瓷史略》《陳萬里陶瓷考古文集》等。

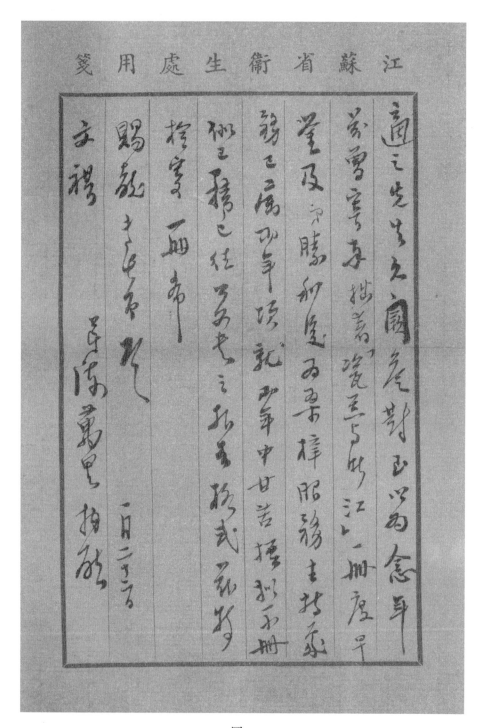

圖1

適之先生：

  久闕詹對，至以爲念。年前曾寄奉拙著《瓷器與浙江》一册，度早鑒及。弟勝利後爲桑梓服務，主持處務已屆兩年。頃就兩年中甘苦撰擬一小册，似已勝已往公文書之報告格式，兹特檢寄一册，希賜教。專此，即頌

文祺

弟　陳萬里
一月二十二日拜啟

程敷鍇致胡適

　　此信發現於《黃山遊覽指南》一書中。此書出版於 1935 年 1 月，署名程鐵華。故此信有可能寫於 1935 年。

　　程敷鍇（1877—？），字鐵華，安徽績溪人。早年畢業於南通高等師範，精於地圖之學。1904 年任教於績溪思誠兩等小學堂。1913 年與同鄉胡晉接創辦安徽省立五師（後更名爲二師），曾任文牘、地理教員。曾與胡晉接合編《中國四大交通圖》《中華民國地理新圖》等。

程豐源米棧用箋

適之先生道鑒 黃山風景多而且奇移步換形不能盡述不特為我國絕無僅有標準好山亦不為世界絕無僅有標準好山現我皖省政府經營建設先造毀屯汽車路繞經黃山之麓將來交通一便遊人必多毛溪新徽印書館欲便利遊覽參考起見囑子編輯黃山遊覽指南一書現已印成今由郵寄呈一部 先生將來進覽妨可作參考遇有此書中不對之處請 賜正示知以便再版更改是幸 出版時呈社 代為序言不勝盼切之至此上奉候

近安

弟程敷錩頓上

程鐵華緘事

通訊處屯溪對河陽湖或由屯溪科學書館轉

適之先生道鑒：

　　黃山風景多而且奇，移步換形，不能盡述。不特爲我國絕無僅有標準好山，亦即爲世界絕無僅有標準好山。現我皖省政府經營建設，先造殷屯汽車路繞經黃山山麓，將來交通一便，遊人必多。屯溪新徽印書館欲便利遊覽各界起見，囑予編輯《黃山遊覽指南》一書，現已印成，今由郵寄呈一部，先生將來遊覽斯山，可作參考。遇有與書中不對之處，請即惠函示知，以便再版更改是幸。得暇時還祈代爲序言，不勝盼切之至。此上，并候
近安

　　　　　　　　　　　　　　　　　　　　　　　　弟　程敷鍇頓上

戴堅致胡適

此信發現於《兵學研究綱要》一書中，此書出版於 1947 年 1 月，則此信當寫於之後。

戴堅（1907—1999），別號鐵肩，湖南長沙人。早年畢業於中央陸軍軍官學校武漢分校第七期、陸軍大學第十三期。曾任教導、預備第二師參謀長、第一〇三師團長、第五軍高參兼幹訓班教育長、軍令部第一廳第一處處長、第五十三軍榮譽第二師師長、第六十七師師長、整編第四十四旅旅長。1947 年任陸軍大學將官班乙級第三期主任。1948 年 9 月 22 日授少將銜。1948 年任駐美參謀團首席團員。1949 年任國防部高參。後經香港到美國定居。著有《抗日戰爭及赴日本受降回憶記》《兵學研究綱要》。

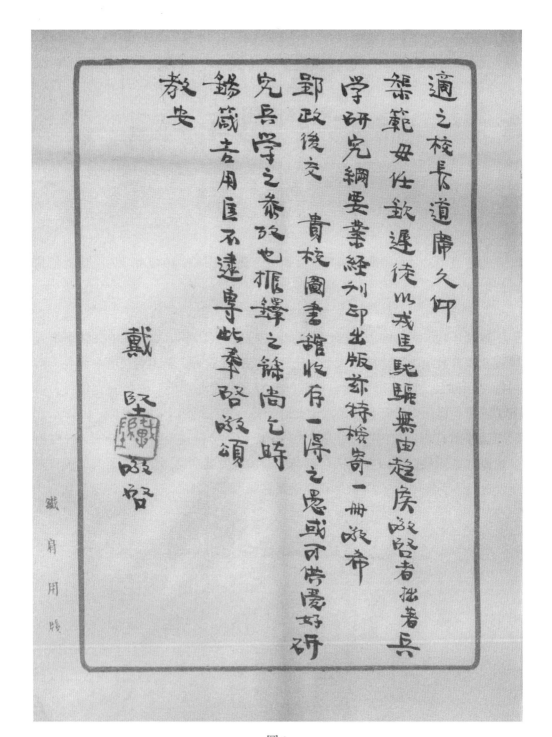

圖1

適之校長道席：

久仰榘範，毋任欽遲，徒以戎馬馳驅，無由趨侯，敬啓者，拙著《兵學研究綱要》業經刊印出版，茲特檢寄一冊，敬希
郵政後交貴校圖書館收存，一得之愚，或可供愛好研究兵學之參攷也。振鐸之餘，尚乞時
錫箴言，用匡不逮。專此奉啓，敬頌
教安

戴堅敬啓

范振聲致胡適（一九三四年九月二十三日）

此信發現於《章實齋年譜》一書中。

范振聲，河北定縣人。早年就讀於保定志存中學，1936年畢業於北京大學史學系。

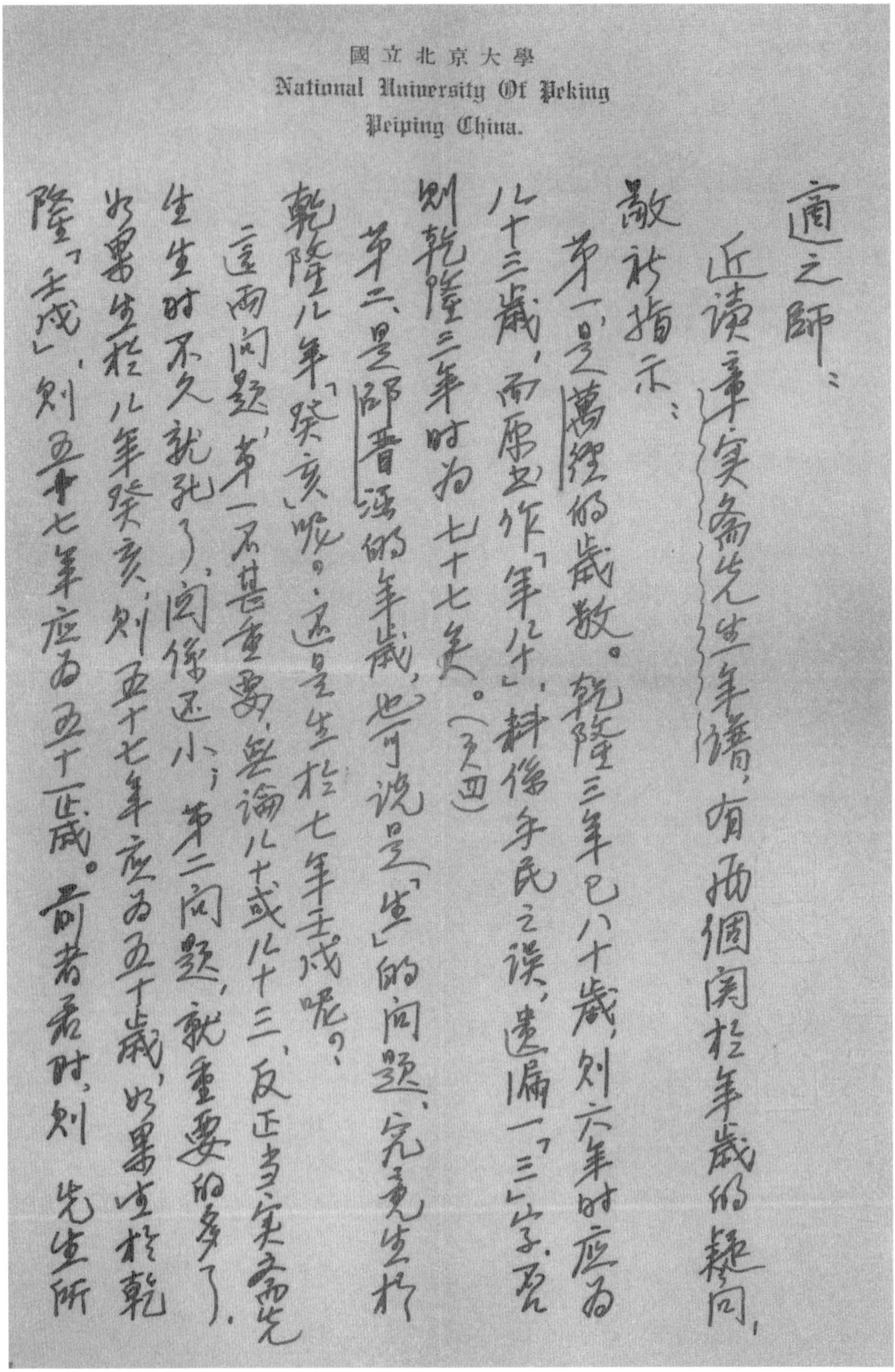

適之師：

近讀年實齋先生年譜，有兩個關於年歲的疑問，敬祈指示。

第一是「萬經的歲數」。乾隆三年已八十歲，列六年時應為八十三歲，而原書作「年八十」，耕愫手民之誤，遺漏一「三」字耳。則乾隆三年時为七十七矣。(页四)

第二是邵晉涵的年歲，也可說是「生」的問題，究竟生於乾隆几年癸亥呢，还是生於七年壬戌呢？

這兩問題，第一不甚重要，無論八十三、反正考實齋先生生時不久就死了，闗係還小；第二問題，就重要的多了，如果生於乾几年癸亥，列五十七年癸亥，如男先生於乾隆「壬戌」，列五十七年應為五十歲。前者若時，列先生所隆「壬戌」，列五十七年應為五十一歲。

圖 1

適之師：

　　近讀《章實齋先生年譜》，有兩個關於年歲的疑問，敬祈指示：

　　第一，是萬經的歲數。乾隆三年已八十歲，則六年時應爲八十三歲，而原書作"年八十"，料係手民之誤，遺漏一"三"字，否則乾隆三年時爲七十七矣。（頁四）

　　第二，是邵晉涵的年歲，也可說是"生"的問題，究竟生於乾隆八年"癸亥"呢？還是生於七年壬戌呢？

　　這兩問題，第一不甚重要，無論八十或八十三，反正當實齋先生生時不久就死了，關係還小；第二問題，就重要的多了。如果生於八年癸亥，則五十七年應爲五十歲，如果生於乾隆"壬戌"，則五十七年應爲五十一歲。前者若對，則先生所

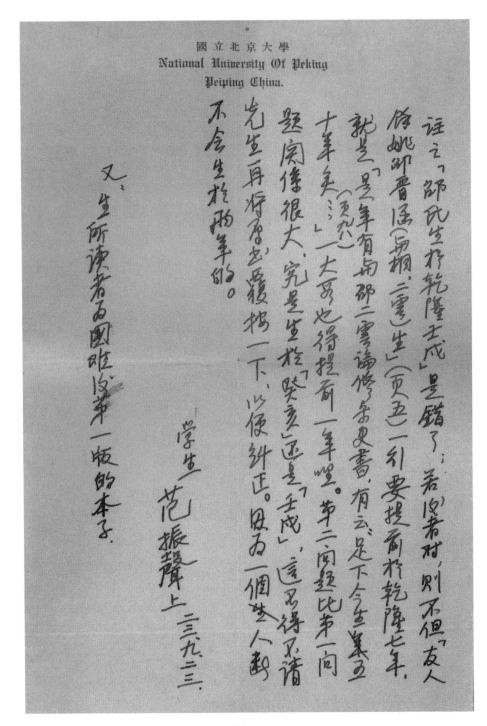

圖2

注之"邵氏生於乾隆壬戌"是錯了；若後者對，則不但"友人餘姚邵晉涵（與相，二雲）生"（頁五）一行要提前於乾隆七年，就是"是年有與邵二雲論修宋史書，有云：足下今生五十矣……"（頁九八）一大段也得提前一年哩。第二問題比第一問題關係很大，究是生於"癸亥"還是"壬戌"，這不得不請先生再將原書覆按一下，以便糾正。因為一個人斷不會生於兩年的。

學生　范振聲　上
二三．九．二三

又：生所讀者為國難後第一版的本子。

馮叔蘭（馮沅君）致胡適

　　此信發現於 *A Short History of Science* 一書中。信中提及之陸侃如《宋玉》一書出版於 1929 年 8 月。則此信當寫於 1929 年之後。

　　馮叔蘭，即馮沅君（1900—1974）原名淑蘭，字德馥，河南唐河縣人，馮友蘭之妹。1922 年畢業於北京女子高等師範學校，同年入北京大學研究所國學門，1925 年畢業，任教於南京金陵大學。次年回北京，任教於中法大學，同時在北京大學研究所國學門從事研究。1927 年任教於上海中國公學，1929 年與陸侃如結婚。1932 年與陸侃如赴法留學，入巴黎大學，1935 年獲文學博士學位。同年歸國，任教於天津河北女子師範學院。抗戰期間任教於輾轉遷徙的中山大學、武漢大學、東北大學。抗戰勝利後，隨東北大學復員到瀋陽。1947 年任教於青島山東大學。新中國成立後仍任山東大學中文系教授，1963 年任山東大學副校長。曾任第一至第三屆全國人大代表、山東省文聯副主席。著有《中國詩史》《中國文學史》《中國文學史簡編》，論文收入《馮沅君古典文學論文集》。

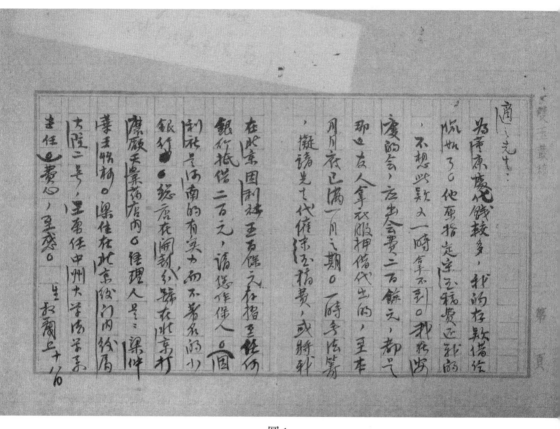

圖1

適之先生：

　　爲董康處代錢較多，我的存款借給侃如了。他原指定《宋玉》稿費還我的，不想此款又一時拿不到。我在安慶的會，應出會費二百餘元，都是那邊友人拿衣服押借代出的，至本月月底已滿一月之期。一時無法籌，擬請先生代催《宋玉》稿費，或將我在北京因利社五百餘元存摺至任何銀行抵借二百元，請您作保人。（因利社是河南的有實力而不著名的小銀行，總店在開封，分號在北京打磨廠天彙藥店內。經理人是：梁仲華王怡柯。梁住在北京後門內後局大院二號，王曾任中州大學法學系主任。）費心，至感。

生叔蘭上
十八日

高夢旦致陶孟和、蔣夢麟
（一九二〇年十月二十七日）

此信發現於 Hilda Lessways 一書中。

高夢旦（1870—1936），福建長樂人，名鳳謙，字夢旦。秀才出身，1896年赴杭州協助創辦求是書院，1901年該書院改名浙江大學堂，任總教習。次年率學生留學日本，任留日學生總監督。1903年回國，入商務印書館，任國文部主任，主編小學國文教科書，1908年倡議編纂《辭源》並參與編輯。1918年任商務印書館編譯所所長，1921年改任出版部部長。晚年提出"簡字方案""度量衡方案"等多項改革建議。

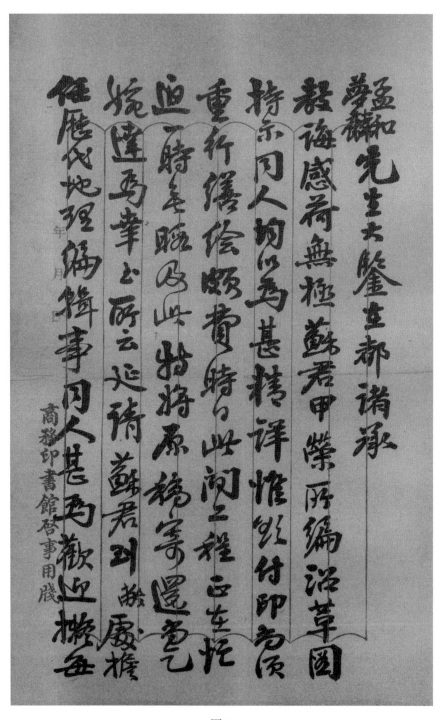

圖1

孟和、夢麟先生大鑒：

  在都諸承

教誨，感荷無極。蘇君甲榮所編沿革圖，持示同人，均以爲甚精詳，惟欲付印尚須重行繕繪，頗費時日。此間工程正在忙迫，一時無暇及此，特將原稿寄還，尚乞

婉達爲幸。至所云延請蘇君到敝處擔任歷代地理編輯事，同人甚爲歡迎，擬每

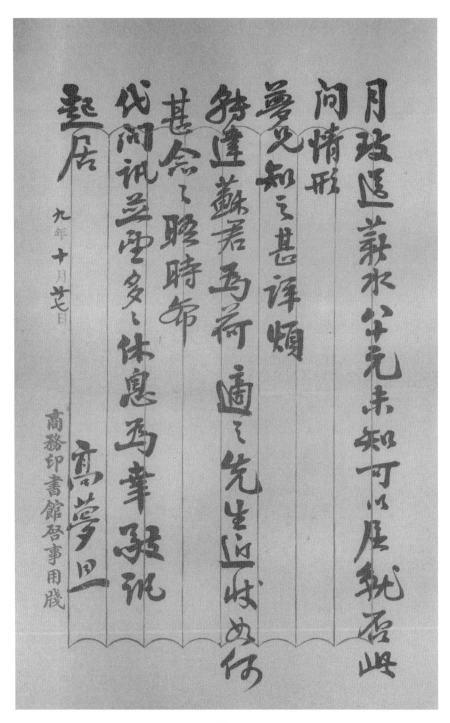

圖2

月致送薪水八十元。未知可以屈就否？此間情形
夢兄知之甚詳，煩
轉達蘇君爲荷。適之先生近狀如何？甚念念，晤時希
代問訊，並望多多休息爲幸。敬訊起居。

　　　　　　　　　　　　　　　　　　　　高夢旦
　　　　　　　　　　　　　　　　　　九年十月廿七日

高夢旦致胡適（一九二八年九月三十日）

　　此信發現於《一九二八年全國教育會議案及報告書》。信中所述曆法改革似與其書《十三月新曆法》有關。《十三月新曆法》商務印書館初版於1931年6月，後於1933年12月收入王雲五主編的《萬有文庫》第一集一千種叢書中。但書中第一章第五頁有云："民國十七年（一九二八）五月，南京大學院召集全國教育會議，徵求議案。余因將舊作重加整理，名爲週曆議案，提出該會如下……"則此信蓋爲提出議案時爲徵求胡適意見而作，當作於1928年9月30日。

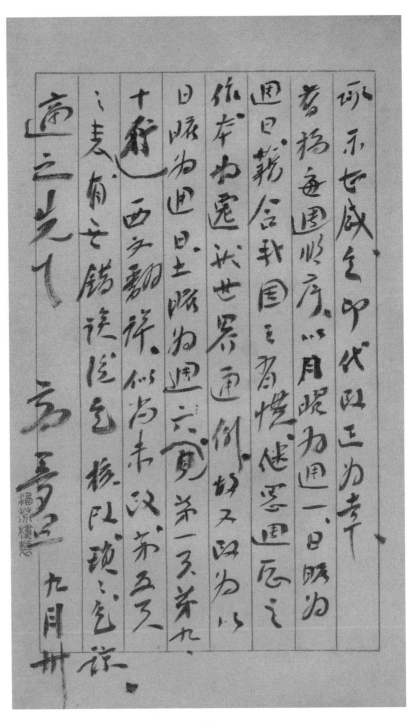

圖1

承示甚感，乞即代改正爲幸。

舊稿每週順序，以月曜爲週一，日曜爲週日，藉合我國之習慣，繼思週曆之作，本爲遷就世界通例，故又改爲以日曜爲週日，土曜爲週六（見第一頁第九、十行）。西文翻譯，似尚未改。第五頁之表，有無錯誤，還乞核改，瑣瑣，乞諒。

適之先生

高夢旦

九月卅

顧孟餘致胡適（一九三二年六月九日）

　　此信發現於《包寧綫包臨段經濟調查報告書》中。據此書"總述"，此次調查進行於 1931 年 5 月間，而信中提及"曾于去夏組織經濟調查隊前赴包頭、臨河一帶實地調查"，則此信應寫於 1932 年 6 月 9 日。

　　顧孟餘（1888—1973），原名兆雄、兆熊，別字夢漁、夢餘，原籍浙江上虞，生於順天府宛平。早年就讀於北京譯學館，後留學德國萊比錫大學電機工程系、柏林大學政治經濟學系，其間加入同盟會。1911 年回國，參加武昌起義。同年留學法國。1917 年回國，任北京大學教授，兼德文門主任，後兼經濟系主任、教務長。1924 年任國民黨北京特別市黨部籌備主任。1925 年任國立廣東大學校長。1926 年任黃埔軍校政治講師、國立中山大學校務委員會副委員長、國民黨中央宣傳部代理部長。1927 年任武漢國民政府教育部長。寧漢分裂後，到上海創辦《前進》，以反對軍事獨裁爲名反蔣。1931 年任國民黨第四屆中央執行委員會常務委員。1932 年任南京國民政府鐵道部長。後任國民黨中央宣傳部長、中央政治委員會秘書長、國民參政員。1941 年任中央大學校長，1943 年辭職。後任行政院高等考試典試委員會委員長。1945 年當選國民黨中央執行委員。1948 年任國民政府顧問。1949 年後定居美國加州，曾任加州大學中國問題研究所顧問，並被臺灣當局聘爲"總統府"資政。1969 年去臺灣，1972 年在臺北病逝。

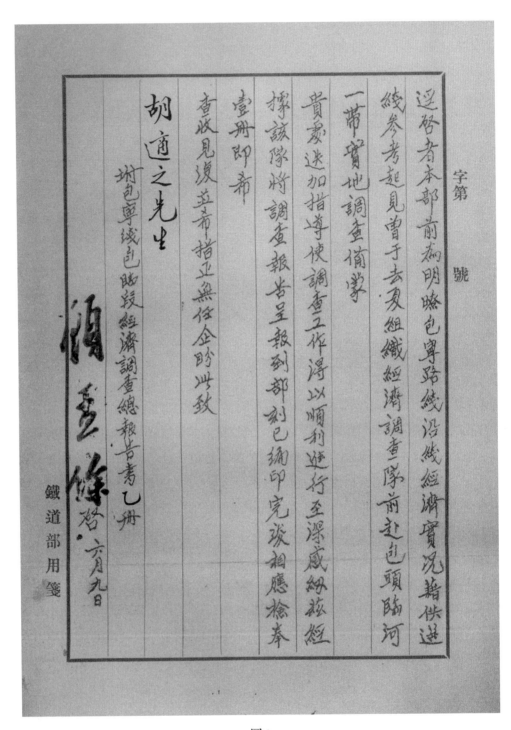

逕啓者本部前為明瞭包寧路線沿線經濟實況藉供選線參考起見曾于去夏組織經濟調查隊前赴包頭臨河一帶實地調查備案

貴處迭加指導使調查工作得以順利進行至深感紉茲經擬該隊將調查報告呈報到部刻已繕印完竣相應檢奉壹冊即希

查收見復並希指正無任企盼此致

胡適之先生

附包寧線包臨段經濟調查總報告書乙冊

顧毓瑔啓 六月九日

鐵道部用箋

圖 1

逕啓者：

　　本部前爲明瞭包寧路綫沿綫經濟實況，藉供選綫參考起見，曾于去夏組織經濟調查隊前赴包頭、臨河一帶實地調查，備蒙貴處迭加指導，使調查工作得以順利進行，至深感紉，茲經據該隊將調查報告呈報到部，刻已編印完竣，相應檢奉壹册，即希查收見復，並希指正，無任企盼。此致
胡適之先生

　　坿《包寧綫包臨段經濟調查總報告書》乙册。

顧孟餘　啓
六月九日

顧隨致胡適（一九三一——一九三六年十二月十二日）

此信發現於《石湖居士詩集》一書中。信中提及之《稼軒年譜》當爲鄭騫《辛稼軒年譜》，此書於一九三八年五月出版，書前有顧隨序，書末後記稱"予爲此譜及稼軒詞校注，始於民國二十年秋日"，而胡適於一九三七年九月已赴美，則此信當作於一九三一年至一九三六年間。

顧隨（1897—1960），原名寶隨，後更名隨，字羨季，別號苦水，河北清河人。1910年入廣平府中學堂。1915年考入天津北洋大學英語系預科。1917年轉入北京大學文科英文門。1920年畢業，任山東青州中學國文、英語教員。次年任濟南《民治日報》記者。後任教於濟南女子職業學校、山東省立第一女子中學、青島膠澳中學。1924年在上海參加淺草社。1926年任教於天津女子師範學院。1929年任燕京大學國文系講師，後升任教授。曾在輔仁大學、中法大學等校兼課。1941年至輔仁大學任教，1949年兼國文系主任。1953年任天津師範學院中文系教授。1960年9月6日逝世。著有《稼軒詞說》《東坡詞說》《元明殘劇八種》等。

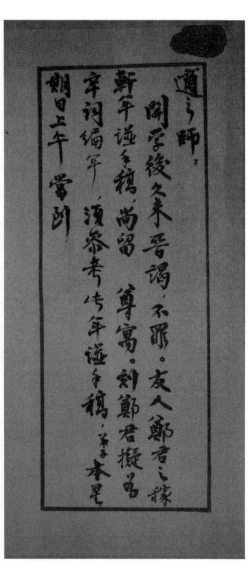 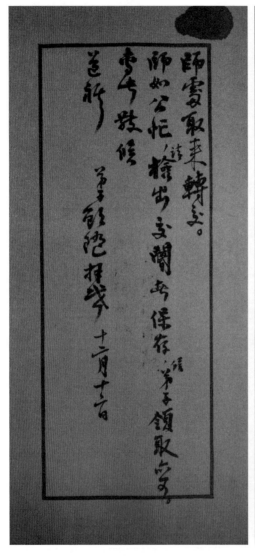

圖2　　　　　　　　圖1

適之師：

　　開學後久未晉謁，不罪。友人鄭君之《稼軒年譜》手稿，尚留尊寓。刻鄭君擬爲《辛詞編年》，須參考《年譜》手稿，弟子本星期日上午當到師處取來轉交。

師如公忙，請檢出交閽者保存，候弟子領取亦可。

耑此，敬候

道祺。

弟子 顧隨拜啓
十二月十二日

顧頡剛致胡適（一九三五年五月十二日）

　　此信發現於《論字喃之組織及其與漢字之關涉》一文中。此文作者聞宥，發表於《燕京學報》1933 年第 14 期。據學者考證，此信應寫於 1935 年 5 月 12 日。參見季琳超《關於顧頡剛著述的文獻學劄記（四則）》，《文匯報》2018 年 5 月 25 日《文匯學人》第 12—13 版。

　　顧頡剛（1893—1980），原名誦坤，字誠吾，號銘堅。江蘇吳縣（今蘇州）人。1913 年考入北京大學預科，1916 年入北京大學本科哲學門，1920 年畢業，留北大圖書館任助教，從事編目工作，次年任北大研究所國學門助教。1922 年到商務印書館編纂中學歷史教科書。1923 年底回北京大學，在研究所編輯《歌謠》周刊。同年提出"層累地造成的中國古史"觀，成為古史辨派創始人。1926 年被聘為廈門大學文科教授，翌年任中山大學文史教授，後兼任語言歷史研究所主任。1929 年任燕京大學歷史系教授，同年兼任北平研究院史學研究會歷史組主任。1931 年在北京大學兼課。1934 年創辦禹貢學會，任《禹貢》半月刊主編。1936 年創建邊疆研究會。1937 年兼任北平研究院史學研究所研究員。抗戰爆發後，到甘、青、寧考察教育。1938 年任雲南大學文學系教授。1939 年任成都齊魯大學史學教授、國學研究所主任。1941 年 10 月任第三屆國民參政會參政員，同年底任教於中央大學。1943 年 2 月與傅斯年等發起組織中國史學會，任常務理事。1944 年任復旦大學史地系教授。1946 年任蘇州社會學院教授。1948 年 3 月當選為中央研究院院士；6 月任蘭州大學教授兼歷史系主任；9 月被舉為北平研究院學術會議會員。中華人民共和國成立後，先後任誠明文學院、上海學院、復旦大學教授。1954年任中國科學院哲學社會科學部研究員。1977年任中國社會科學院歷史研究室研究員、學術委員。1980年12月25日在北京病逝。著有《漢代學術史略》《秦漢的方士與儒生》《五德終始説下的政治和歷史》等。

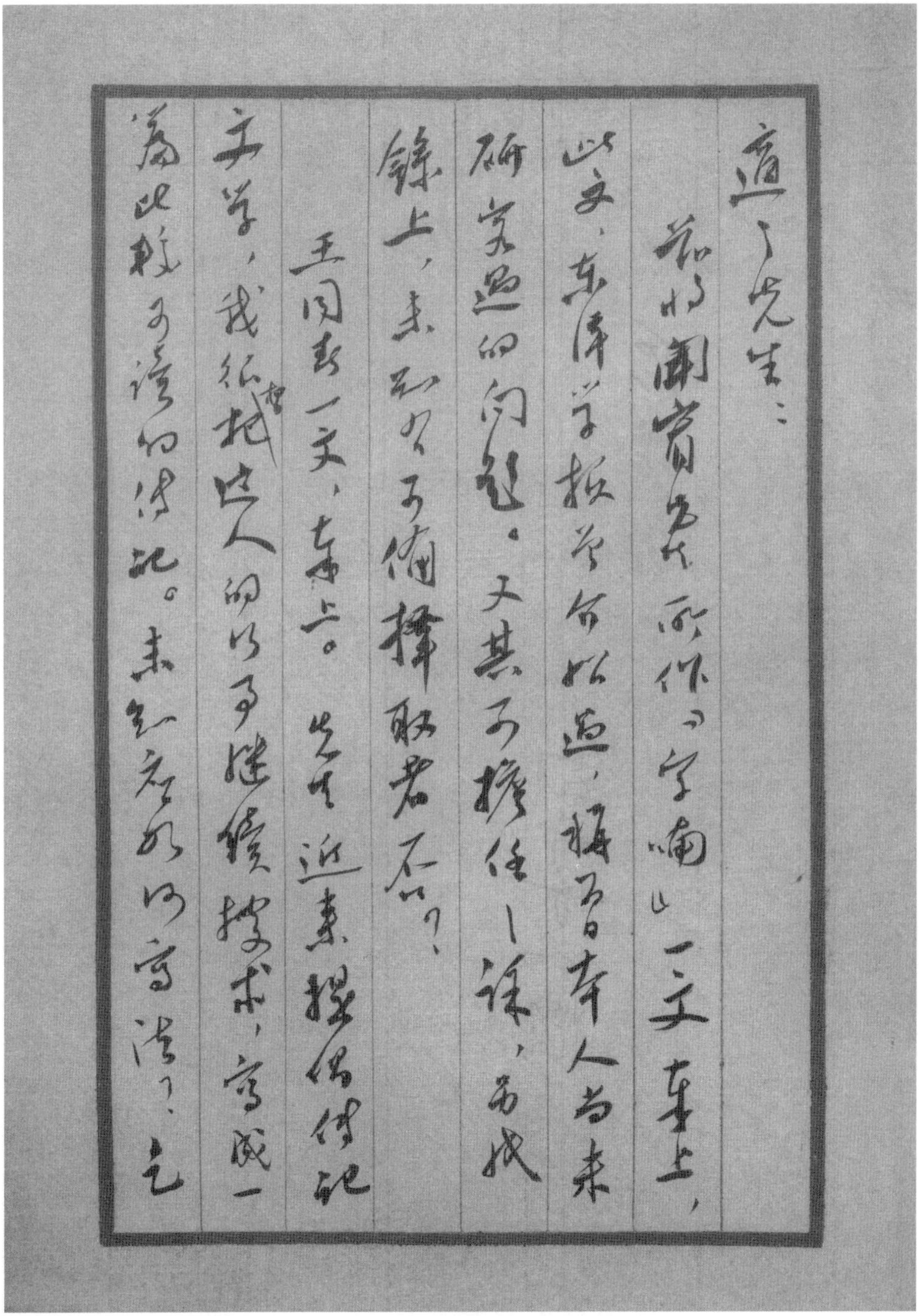

適之先生：
前將閻[illegible]所作之[illegible]一文奉上，
此文，東洋學報[illegible]過，[illegible]人尚未
研究過的問題。又其[illegible]，為我
錄上，未知可否備擇取者否？
王國維一文，奉上。先生近來提倡傳記
文學，我很想找近人的行事繼續搜求，寫成一
篇比較可讀的傳記。未知[illegible]以為何如？[illegible]

圖 1

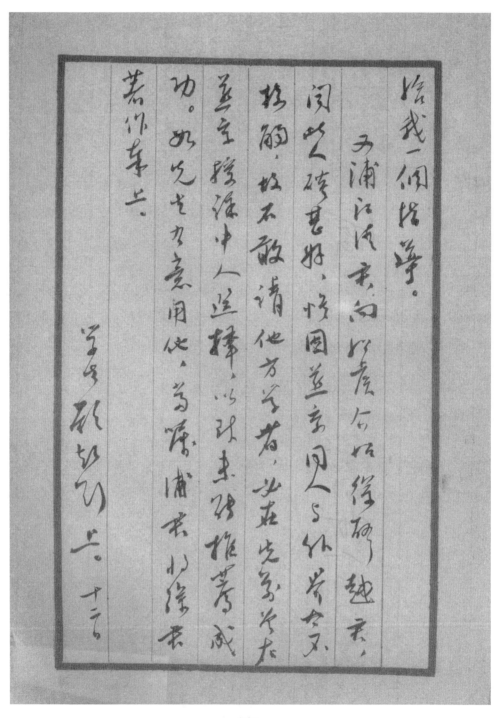

圖2

給我一個指導。

子浦兄近來為何不肯給我信？頃趙元任來，閒談極善好，惜回蕪去見不到兄等，不然，極願邀他來請他方去考者，必在先家此去菡室鈴選中人送擇，以致未能推薦成功。如先生有意用他，當囑浦東小徐表若作來上。

弟適 九、十二

適之先生：

　　茲將聞宥先生所作《字喃》一文奉上，此文，《東洋學報》曾介紹過，稱爲日本人尚未研究過的問題。又其可擔任之課，另紙錄上，未知有可備擇取者否？

　　王同春一文，奉上。先生近來提倡傳記文學，我很想把這人的行事繼續搜求，寫成一篇比較可讀的傳記。未知應如何寫法？乞給我一個指導。

　　又浦江清君向紹虞介紹徐聲越君，聞此人確甚好，惟因燕京同人與外界太不接觸，故不敢請他方學者，必在先前曾在燕京授課中人選擇，以致未能推薦成功。如先生有意用他，當囑浦君將徐君著作奉上。

　　　　　　　　　　　　　　　　　　　　　　學生　顧頡剛　上
　　　　　　　　　　　　　　　　　　　　　　　　十二日

何天行致胡適（一九四八年五月三十一日）

此信發現於《楚辭作於漢代考》一書中。此書出版於 1948 年 4 月，故此信當寫於 1948 年 5 月 31 日。

何天行（1913—1986），生於浙江杭州。1926 年入杭州梅東高橋鹽務中學讀書，學名扶桑。1929 年投考上海大同大學預科，改名天行，字摩什。1931 年入中國公學經濟系，後改入文學系。1935 年轉學至復旦大學，1936 年畢業，同年任職於浙江省財政廳，參加吳越史地研究會。1937 年 6 月任上海滬江大學商學院國文教師兼代大學部講師，至 1942 年。1944 年任雲和聯立中學文史地教員。1945 年任西湖博物館歷史部主任。1948 年兼任國立藝術專科學校圖書館主任。1949 年任浙江大學人類學古器物學兼職教授、西湖博物館專門委員，加入中國人類學會、中國史學會。1950 年任浙江博物館歷史文化部主任。1952 年任職於上海市文化局。1956 年任職於東北人民大學圖書館，後因病在家休養著述。1986 年 1 月病故。著有《杭縣良渚鎮之石器與黑陶》《楚辭作於漢代考》等。

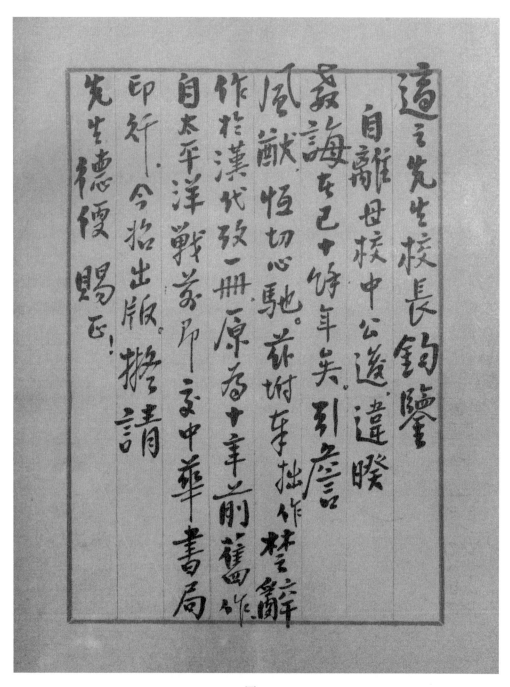

圖1

適之先生校長鈞鑒：

　　自離母校中公後，違睽
教誨者已十餘年矣。引詹
風猷，恒切心馳。茲坿奉拙作《楚辭作于漢代攷》一册，原爲十年前舊作，自太平洋戰前即交中華書局印行，今始出版，擬請
先生德便賜正！

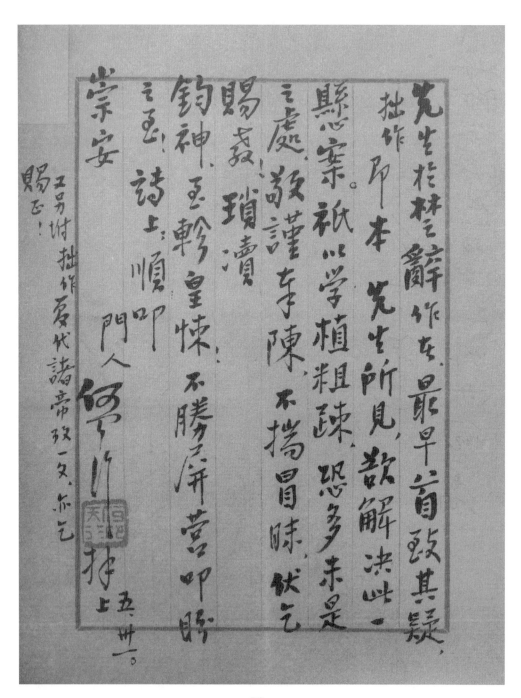

圖2

先生於楚辭作者，最早首致其疑，拙作即本先生所見，欲解決此一懸案。祇以學植粗疏，恐多未是之處，敬謹奉陳，不揣冒昧，伏乞賜教！瑣瀆
鈞神，至軫皇悚！不勝屏營叩盼之至！薄上，順叩
崇安

門人　何天行拜上
五，卅一

又另坿拙作《夏代諸帝攷》一文，亦乞賜正！

賀生樂致胡適

此信發現於《平民新字說》一書中。

賀生樂，山西臨汾人。致力於漢字改革，著有《平民新字說》《平民新字原》《平民新字彙》《系全易建名字》《生樂新字》等。

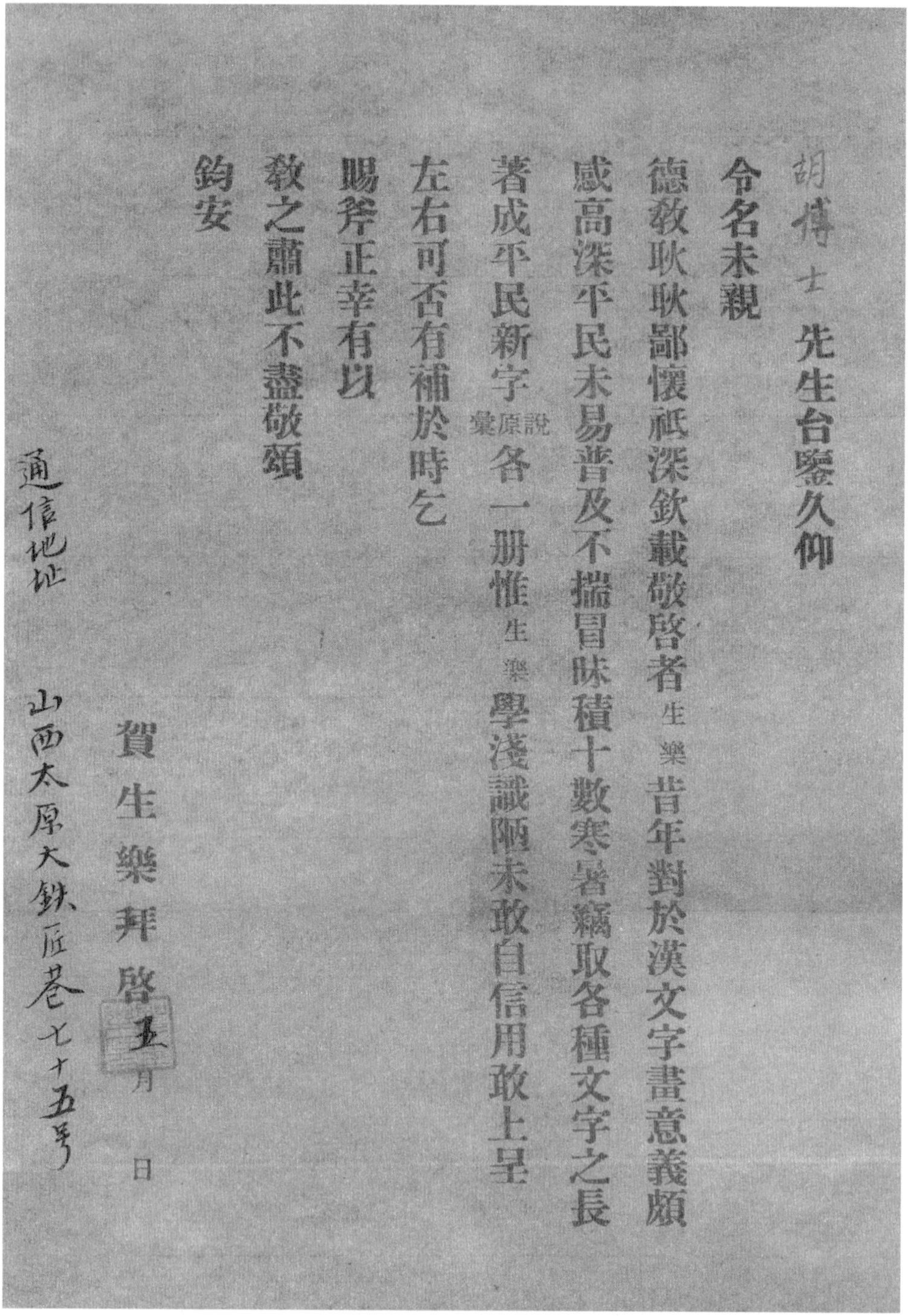

胡博士 先生台鑒久仰

令名未親

德教耿耿鄙懷祇深欽載敬啟者 生樂昔年對於漢文字畫意義頗

感高深平民未易普及不揣冒昧積十數寒暑竊取各種文字之長

著成平民新字彙原說各一冊惟生樂學淺識陋未敢自信用敢上呈

左右可否有補於時乞

賜斧正幸有以

教之蕭此不盡敬頌

鈞安

　　　　　　　　　　　賀生樂拜啟　五月　　日

通信地址　山西太原大鐵匠巷七十五号

圖 1

胡厚宣致胡適

此信發現於《卜辭同文例》中。《卜辭同文例》發表於 1947 年《中研院史語所集刊》第九本上。

胡厚宣（1911—1995），幼名福林。河北望都人。1934 年畢業於北京大學史學系，畢業後任職於中央研究院歷史語言研究所。1940 年至 1946 年任成都齊魯大學國學研究所研究員、教授，1947 年任上海復旦大學歷史系教授，1956 年調任中國科學院歷史研究所（現屬中國社會科學院）研究員，直到 1995 年去世。主要從事甲骨文、商史研究，著有《甲骨六錄》《戰後平津新獲甲骨集》《戰後寧滬新獲甲骨集》《戰後南北所見甲骨錄》《戰後京津新獲甲骨集》《甲骨續存》《古代研究的史料問題》等。主編《甲骨文合集》。

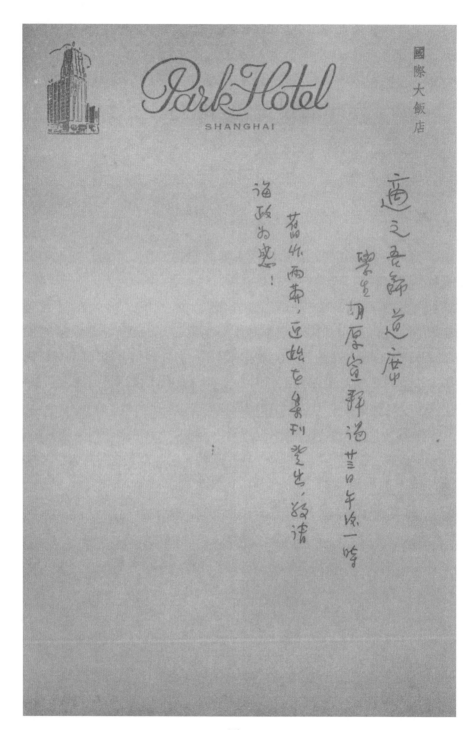

圖1

適之吾師道席：

　　學生胡厚宣拜謁，廿三日午後一時。

　　舊作兩篇，近始在《集刊》登出，敬請
誨政爲感！

胡適致高仲洽（一九三〇年九月二日）

此信發現於 *Houdini, His Life-Story* 一書中。

高仲洽（1902—？），福建長樂人。高夢旦之子。1924 年畢業於復旦大學，獲文學士學位。曾譯有《羅馬小史》。中國歷史研究院藏胡適檔案（以下簡稱"北京檔"）藏有高仲洽致胡適書信三通。

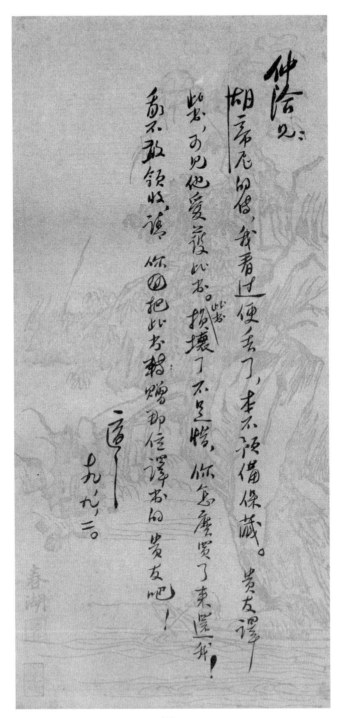

圖 1

仲洽兄：

　　胡帝尼的傳，我看過便丟了，本不預備保藏。貴友譯此書，可見他愛護此書。此書損壞了不足惜，你怎麼買了來還我！我不敢領收，請你把此書轉贈那位譯書的貴友吧！

適之
十九,九,二。

胡適致皮宗石單不广（一九三三年四月十八日）

此信發現於《念菴羅先生集》一書中。

皮宗石（1887—1967），字皓白，號海帆，湖南長沙人。早年就讀於長沙城南書院。1903 年留學日本東京帝國大學，1905 年加入同盟會，1912 年回國，參與創辦漢口《民國日報》。次年因反對袁世凱遭到通緝，留學英國。1920 年回國，任長沙法政專門學校教員，後任北京大學政治學教授，1922 年兼北京大學圖書館館長。1927 年任國民政府中央法制委員會委員，次年任司法部秘書長，同年八月參與籌辦國立武漢大學，歷任武漢大學教授、法學院院長、教務長等職。1937 年—1941 年任國立湖南大學校長。1942 年 7 月當選第三屆國民參政會參議員。1945 年 5 月任國民政府教育部教育研究委員會委員。新中國成立後，歷任中南軍政委員會財經委員會委員、中南行政委員會參事、湖北省政協常委等職。1954 年將 1512 册藏書捐贈湖南師範學院。

單不广（1877—1929），初名恭修，字詒孫，號伯寬，祖籍浙江蕭山，生於海寧。1906 年留學日本半年，後任雙山學堂堂長，旋任嘉興秀水學堂教習。先後任教於開智學堂、浙江第一師範學校、嘉興浙江省立第二中學。曾兩度受聘爲浙江省圖書館編輯。1920 年任北京大學國文系講師，後兼任北京大學圖書館中文部主任。1924 年任浙江省立二中教員，旋任浙江省圖書館中文部主任。後應蔡元培之邀到中央研究院襄理院事。著有《宋儒年譜》《宋代哲學思想史》等。

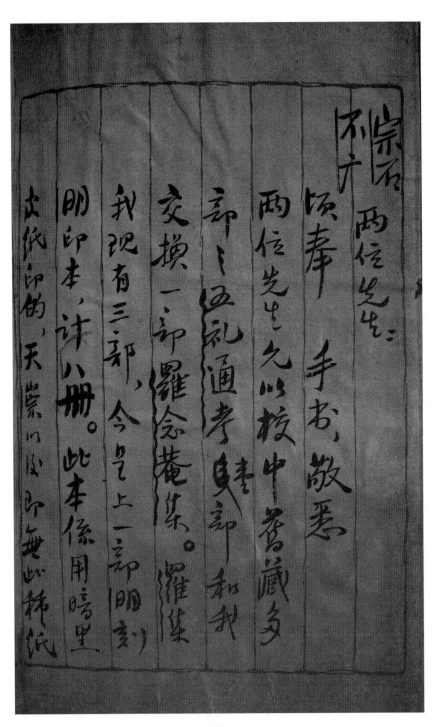

圖1

宗石、不广兩位先生：

　　頃奉　手書，敬悉

兩位先生允以校中舊藏多部之《五禮通考》壹部和我交換一部《羅念菴集》。《羅集》我現有三部，今呈上一部明刻明印本，計八冊。此本係用暗黑皮紙印的，天、崇以後即無此種紙

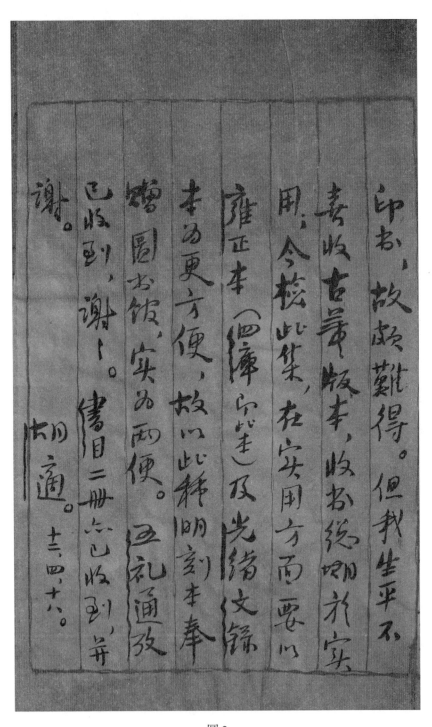

圖 2

印書，故頗難得。但我生平不喜收古董版本，收書總期於實用；今檢此集，在實用方面要以雍正本（《四庫》即此本）及光緒《文錄》本爲更方便，故以此種明刻本奉贈圖書館，實爲兩便。《五禮通攷》已收到，謝謝。《書目》二册亦已收到，并謝。

胡適
十二，四，十八。

胡先驌致胡適

　　此信發現於 *My Country and My People* 一書中。此版本出版於 1935 年，故此信應寫於 1935 年之後。

　　胡先驌（1894—1968），字步曾，號懺庵，江西新建人。1908 年入京師大學堂預科，1912 年底赴美留學，次年入加州大學伯克利分校農學院。1914 年 6 月與胡適、任鴻雋、趙元任等人發起成立"中國科學社"。1916 年獲植物學碩士，同年回國，任江西省廬山森林局副局長。1918 年任南京高等師範學校教授。1922 年與吳宓、梅光迪等創辦《學衡》雜誌，以"昌明國粹，融化新知"爲宗旨，提倡復古，反對新文化運動，成爲"學衡派"代表人物。1923 年南京高師併入東南大學，任生物學系主任。同年秋再度赴美留學，入哈佛大學，1925 年獲植物學博士學位。同年歸國，歷任東南大學、北京大學、北京師範大學等校教授，與秉志共同創辦中國科學社生物所和静生生物調查所，並創辦廬山植物院。1940 年 10 月任中正大學校長，1944 年 5 月辭職。當選中央研究院評議員、院士。新中國成立後，任中國科學院植物研究所研究員。

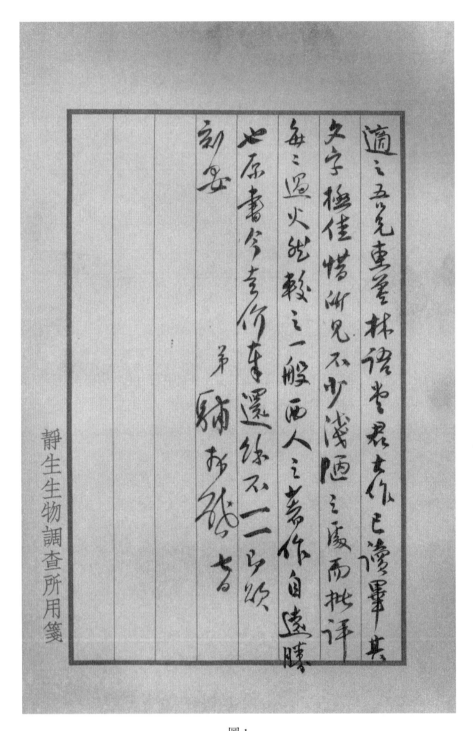

圖1

適之吾兄惠鑒：

　　林語堂君大作已讀畢，其文字極佳，惜所見不少淺陋之處，而批評每每過火，然較之一般西人之著作自遠勝也。原書今走价奉還，餘不一一。即頌

刻安

　　　　　　　　　　　　　　　　　　　　　　　弟驌拜啓
　　　　　　　　　　　　　　　　　　　　　　　　七日

胡哲敷致胡適

　　此信發現於《陸王哲學辨微》一書中。此書出版於 1930 年，則此信或寫於 1930 年 10 月 8 日。

　　胡哲敷（1898—？），安徽合肥人。曾任浙江大學中文系教授，國立浙江大學附屬中學校長。抗戰期間曾隨浙江大學西遷遵義、湄潭、永興等地。著有《史學概論》《老莊哲學》《曾國藩》《陸王哲學辨微》等。

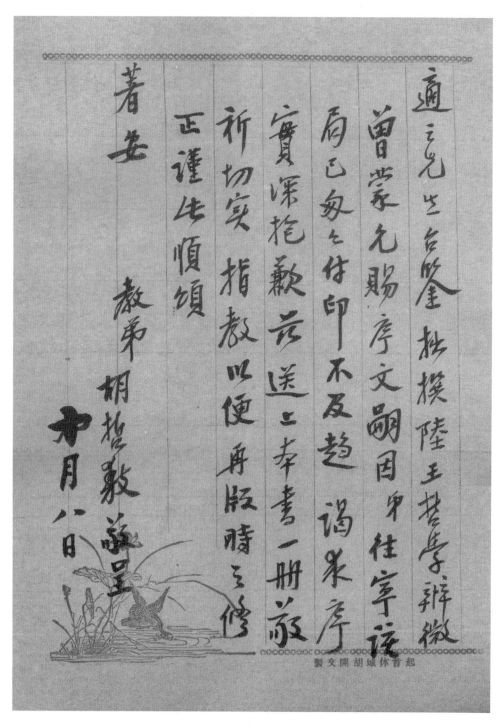

圖1

適之先生台鑒：

  拙撰《陸王哲學辨微》曾蒙允賜序文，嗣因弟往寧，該局已匆匆付印，不及趨謁求序，實深抱歉，茲送上本書一冊，敬祈切實指教，以便再版時之修正。謹此，順頌

著安

教弟 胡哲敷 敬呈
十月八日

黃學周致胡適（一九三三年十一月以後）

此信發現於《布丁》一書中，此書似出版於 1933 年 11 月，故此信大致寫於此後不久。

黃學周（1895—1956），字培泉，別字拙余，福建永定人。早年畢業於廣州法政專門學校，後肄業於廣東大學經濟科。1924 年任龍岩縣縣長。1926 年 12 月參加北伐，任國民革命軍東路軍總指揮部交通處設計股股長、交通處總務科科長。1927 年任津浦鐵路運輸公司司令部總務科中校科長、車務處中校主任。1930 年任隴、津兩路運輸司令部運輸處上校處長、上校參謀長兼隴海鐵路總務處副處長。1931 年任隴、津、平、道四路運輸司令部少將參謀長兼隴海鐵路總務處處長。抗戰中期離開鐵路部門經商。抗戰勝利後，在湖南晃縣創辦龍岡煙廠。1948 年回家鄉，1956 年病逝。曾任國語羅馬字促進會特委，並於 1934 年 9 月發起該會第一次全國代表大會，編有標準羅馬字拼音書籍多種。

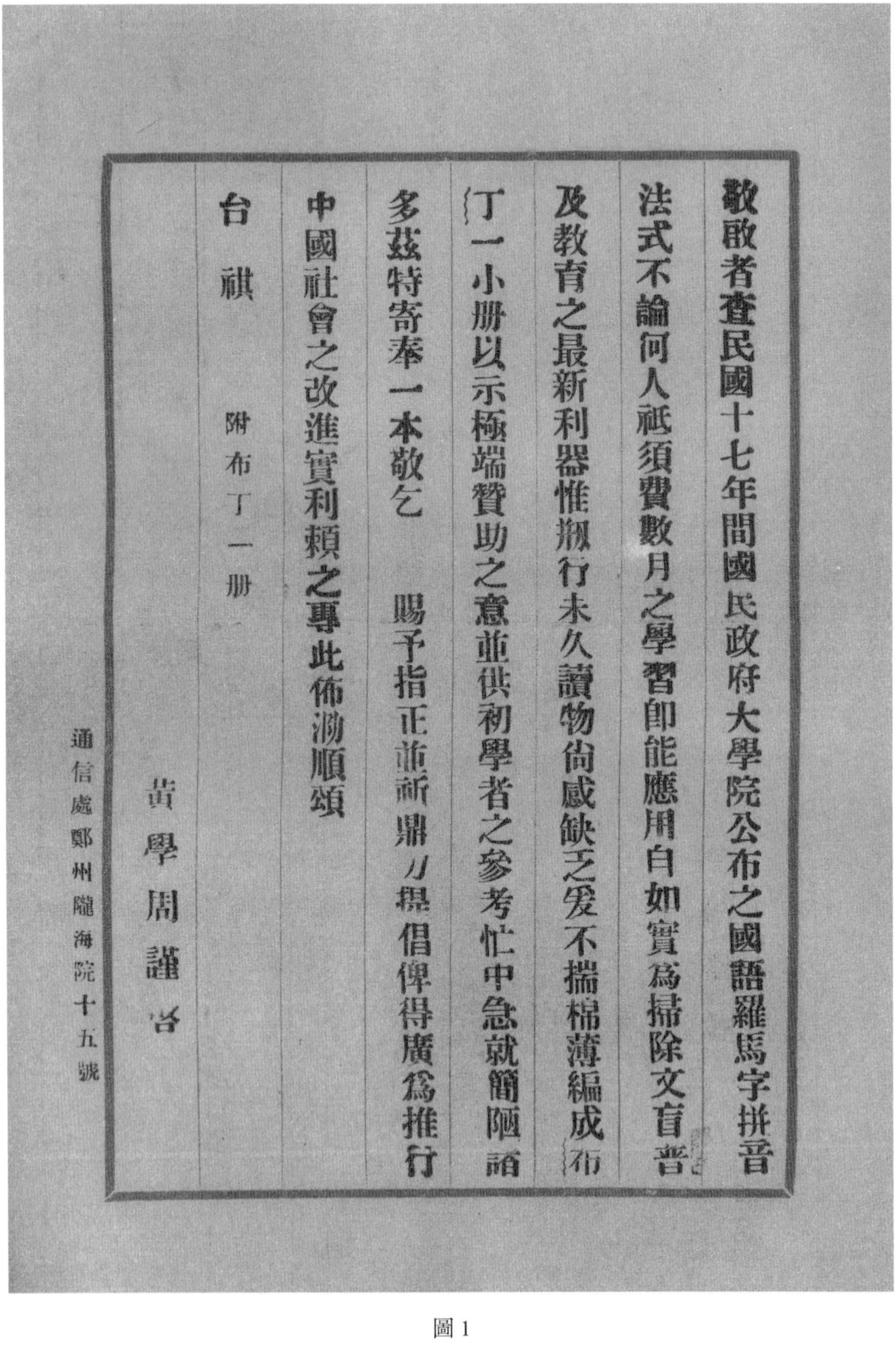

敬啓者查民國十七年間國民政府大學院公布之國語羅馬字拼音法式不論何人祇須費數月之學習卽能應用自如實爲掃除文盲普及教育之最新利器惟頒行未久讀物尚感缺乏爰不揣棉薄編成布丁一小册以示極端贊助之意並供初學者之參考忙中急就簡陋詒多茲特寄奉一本敬乞　賜予指正並祈鼎力提倡俾得廣爲推行中國社會之改進實利賴之專此佈泐順頌

台祺　附布丁一册

黄學周謹啓

通信處鄭州隴海院十五號

圖 1

黃貽清致胡適（一九四七年三月十一日）

此信發現於《寒季自我衛生》一書中。

黃貽清，1929 年任鐵道部衛生處事務員。曾任職於中華醫學會駐濟編譯部。主要從事衛生醫學著述，編有《中華醫學會創立二十年來大事記》《寒季自我衛生》等。譯有《西藥擇要》，與胡宣明翻譯《羅氏衛生學》，主編《南京市政府十九年年刊》。曾任《中華醫學》雜誌編輯，《衛生短波》主編。

適之先生：

點清是變了，胡宣明先生的講演一向把大部份的時間述事醫學衛生文字工作的。可是過去對於大學用書和醫學雜誌文字，還只是沿用那古言文，一字要自己對一般人宣傳衛生，才用語體文寫述。

最近讀先生回國時候給說者談話的新聞，知道您對某先生也用了語體寫過一本科學書很是頌慰，

適之先生：

　　貽清是受了胡宣明先生的誘掖，一向把大部份的時間從事醫學衛生文字工作的。可是過去對於大學用書和醫學雜誌文字，還只是沿用那文言文，一定要自己對一般人宣傳衛生，才用語體文寫述。

　　最近讀先生回國時候給記者談話的新聞，知道您對某先生也用了語體寫過一本科學書很是欣慰，

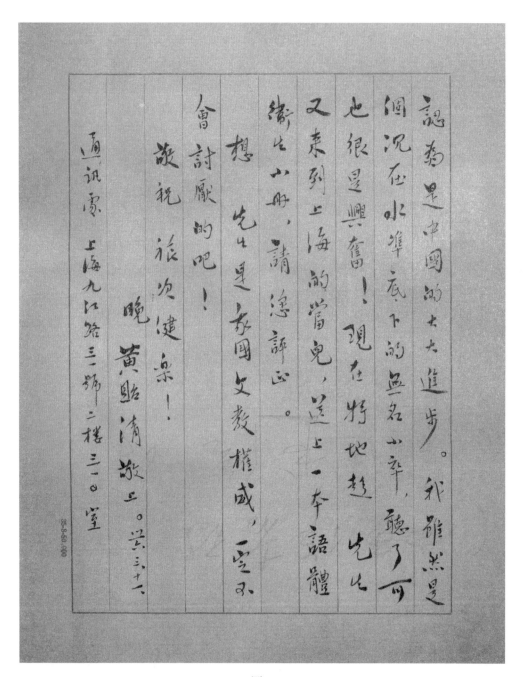

圖2

認爲是中國的大大進步。我雖然是個沉在水準底下的無名小卒，聽了可也很是興奮！現在特地趁先生又來到上海的當兒，送上一本語體衛生小册，請您評正。

想先生是我國文教權威，一定不會討厭的吧！

敬祝旅次健樂！

晚　黃貽清敬上

卅六，三，十一

通訊處　上海九江路三一號二樓三一〇室

黃毅民致胡適

　　此信件發現於《國學叢論》中,《國學叢論》最初由北平燕友學社出版,上冊出版於 1935 年 6 月,下冊出版於 1936 年 4 月。則此信最早寫於 1936 年 5 月 29 日。

　　黃毅民,燕京大學國文系畢業,後任教於北平慕貞女中、育英中學。

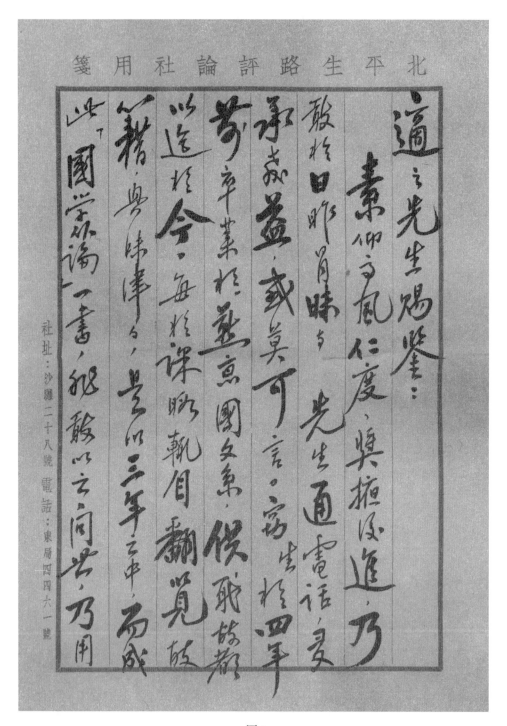

圖1

適之先生賜鑒：

　　素仰高風仁度，獎掖後進，乃敢於日昨冒昧與先生通電話，多承教益，感莫可言。竊生於四年前卒業於燕京國文系，供職故都以迄於今。每於課暇輒自翻覽故籍，興味津津，是以三年之中，而成此《國學叢論》一書，非敢以之問世，乃用

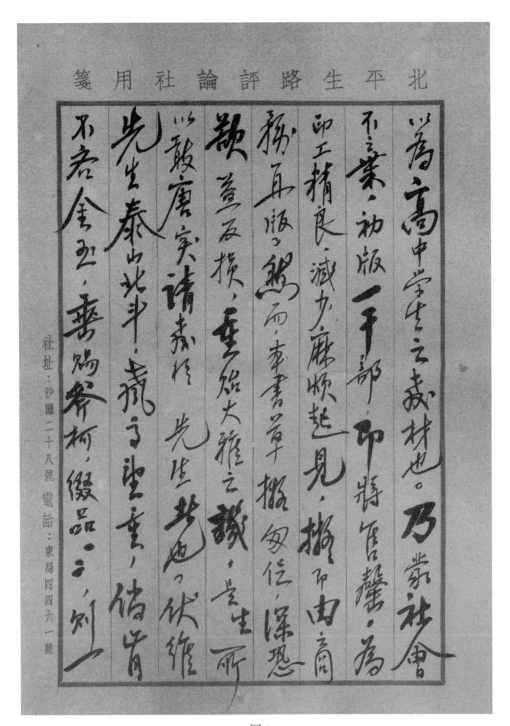

圖 2

以爲高中學生之教材也。乃蒙社會不棄，初版一千部，即將售罄。爲印工精良，減少麻煩起見，擬即由商務再版。然而本書草擬匆促，深恐欲益反損，重貽大雅之譏，是生所以敢唐突請教於先生者也。伏維先生泰山北斗，聲高望重，倘肯不吝金玉，垂賜斧柯，綴品一二，則一

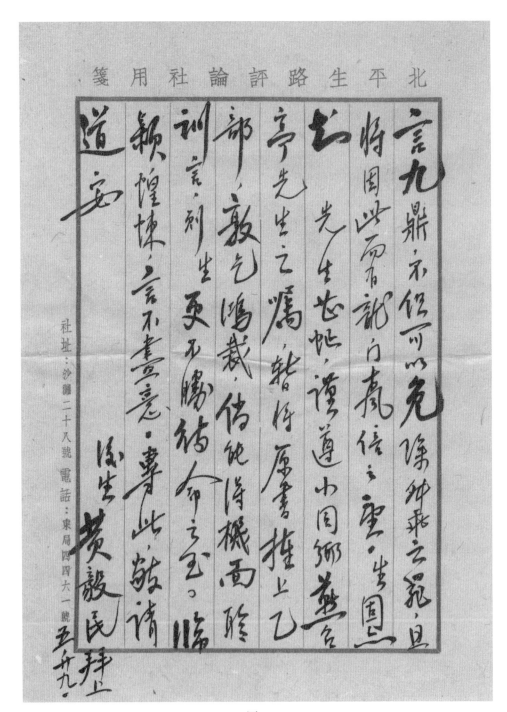

圖3

言九鼎,不但可以免除舛乖之罪,且將因此而有龍門聲倍之望。生固亦知先生甚忙,謹遵小同鄉燕台亭先生之囑,暫將原書捧上乙部,敦乞鴻裁,倘能得機面聆訓言,則生更不勝待命之至。臨穎惶悚,言不盡意。專此,敬請
道安

　　　　　　　　　　　　　　　　　　後生　黃毅民拜上
　　　　　　　　　　　　　　　　　　　　五,廿九

簡文致胡適

此信發現於《簡筆字彙稿本》一書中。

作者簡文,生平不詳。

敬肅者前呈"簡筆字彙稿本"一部，諒蒙賜閱。現在文感覺稿本內容頗為紛歧，須待整理。久仰

先生崇泰斗，敬懇不吝賜教誨，列更正方法數條，是否妥當或應補充與否，均待決于

高明，文未敢擅專也。特此敬叩

大安

通訊處：湖南長沙嶽雲中學校王殷凱君轉

簡文謹啟 十月二十五日

1、分類　稿本中除分別部首排列外，並以各字之某部分具有類似之形體者分為若干類。如"襄"改簡如"衣"，以"衰""袞""裏"列入此類；又如"堇""廑""謹"列入蓳類，以免筆畫歧異。

2、修改部首　如"竹"原改如"㣺"，茲作直線體之"⺈"，"足"原改為

1. 分類 稿本中除分別部首排列外,並以各字之某部分具有類似之形體者分為若干類。如「襄」改簡如「𧘇」,以「𧘇」「攘」列入此類;又如「䀗」「𤴼」以「𧘇」以免筆畫歧異。

2. 修改部首 如「竹」原改如「⺮」,茲作直線體之「⺮」;足原改為「⻊」,現改作「⻊」;又「⻌」作「⻍」;「片」作「片」;弓作「弓」等等。

3. 整理簡字 各字在十畫以內盡可改簡者仍改之。如是隊為是;徑改為径,旁改為旁,吾改為吾等等。

4. 劃一筆畫 組織相同之字如貝作贝,果作果,則以惻作惻而不照初改體之惻;裸裸踝則一律改為裸裸踝,更正原改式之「裸」「棵」「踝」。

5. 排列號碼 字彙稿本完成後,採用王雲五先生四角號碼撿字法排列,原有之部首方式一并撤消。

江紹原致胡適

此信發現於 *The Ramayana and the Mahabharata* 一書中。此書出版於 1910 年。信中提及之《最近代基督教義》爲作者發表於 1919 年 5 月《新潮》第 1 卷 5 期上的文章。

江紹原（1898—1983），安徽旌德人。1914 年畢業於上海滬江大學預科班。1915 年留美，就讀於加利福尼亞大學文學院，兩年後因病回國。1917 年入北京大學哲學系。1920 年再度赴美留學，先後就讀於芝加哥大學、伊利諾伊大學，獲哲學博士學位。1923 年回國，同年任教於北京大學哲學系，并擔任鋼和泰助手。1927 年任中山大學教授兼英國語言文學系代理系主任。不久辭職，1930 年回北京大學哲學系任教。1931 年至 1934 年，先後任教於北平女子文理學院、北平大學、中法大學、河南大學。1935 年任中法大學孔德研究院駐北平研究員。抗戰期間困留北平，閉户讀書。抗戰勝利後，先後任教於臨時大學、中國大學、西北大學。新中國成立後任山西大學英語系教授兼系主任。1956 年後，歷任科學出版社副編審、編審，商務印書館編審。主要著作有《中國古代旅行之研究》《髪鬚爪》等。

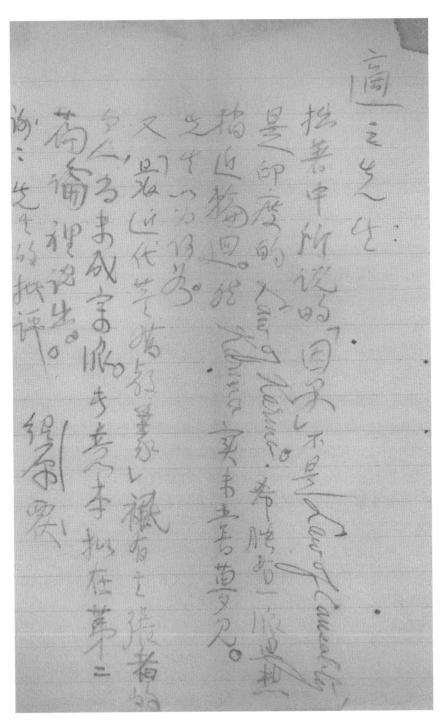

圖1

適之先生：

　　拙著中所說的"因果"不是 law of causality，是印度的 Law of Karma，希臘有一派思想稍近輪迴。然 Karma 實未嘗夢見。先生以為何如。

　　又《最近代基督教義》祇有主張者的個人，尚未成宗派。此意本擬在第二篇論裡說出。謝謝先生的批評。

　　　　　　　　　　　　　　　　　　　　　　　　　　紹原覆

圖 2

焦易堂致胡適（一九三四年六月—九月）

　　此信發現於《縣自治法草案縣自治法施行法草案》一書中。今國圖藏此書，封面題："徵求意見。對於四種草案如有意見請於九月三十日以前寄交立法院法制自治法委員會。"書首有《徵求意見啓事》，末尾所署時間爲"中華民國二十三年六月"，即 1934 年 6 月。則此信當寫於 1934 年 6 月—9 月間。

　　焦易堂（1880—1950），名希孟，字易堂，號稷山，陝西武功人。辛亥革命爆發後，陝西起義獨立，任都督府參謀。1913 年參加"二次革命"。1917 年赴廣州參加護法運動，任大元帥府參議、護法國會議員。1918 年任陝西勞軍使赴陝宣慰起義護法的陝西靖國軍。1921 年任大本營參議，次年任國民黨華北軍事黨務特派員、陝豫軍事特派員等職。1926 年北伐期間，任國民革命軍第二軍宣慰使。1928 年 11 月任國民政府立法院立法委員，兼法制委員會委員長，並與王用賓等創辦首都女子法政講習所。1930 年起兼任考試院考選委員會委員。1935 年 7 月任最高法院院長；11 月當選爲國民黨第五屆中央執行委員。1942 年任國民政府委員，1943 年 10 月任國民政府顧問。1945 年 5 月當選爲國民黨第六屆中央執行委員。1947 年當選爲行憲國民大會代表。1949 年 12 月去臺灣。1950 年 10 月病逝於臺北。著有《釋總理錢幣革命》《稷山文存》等。

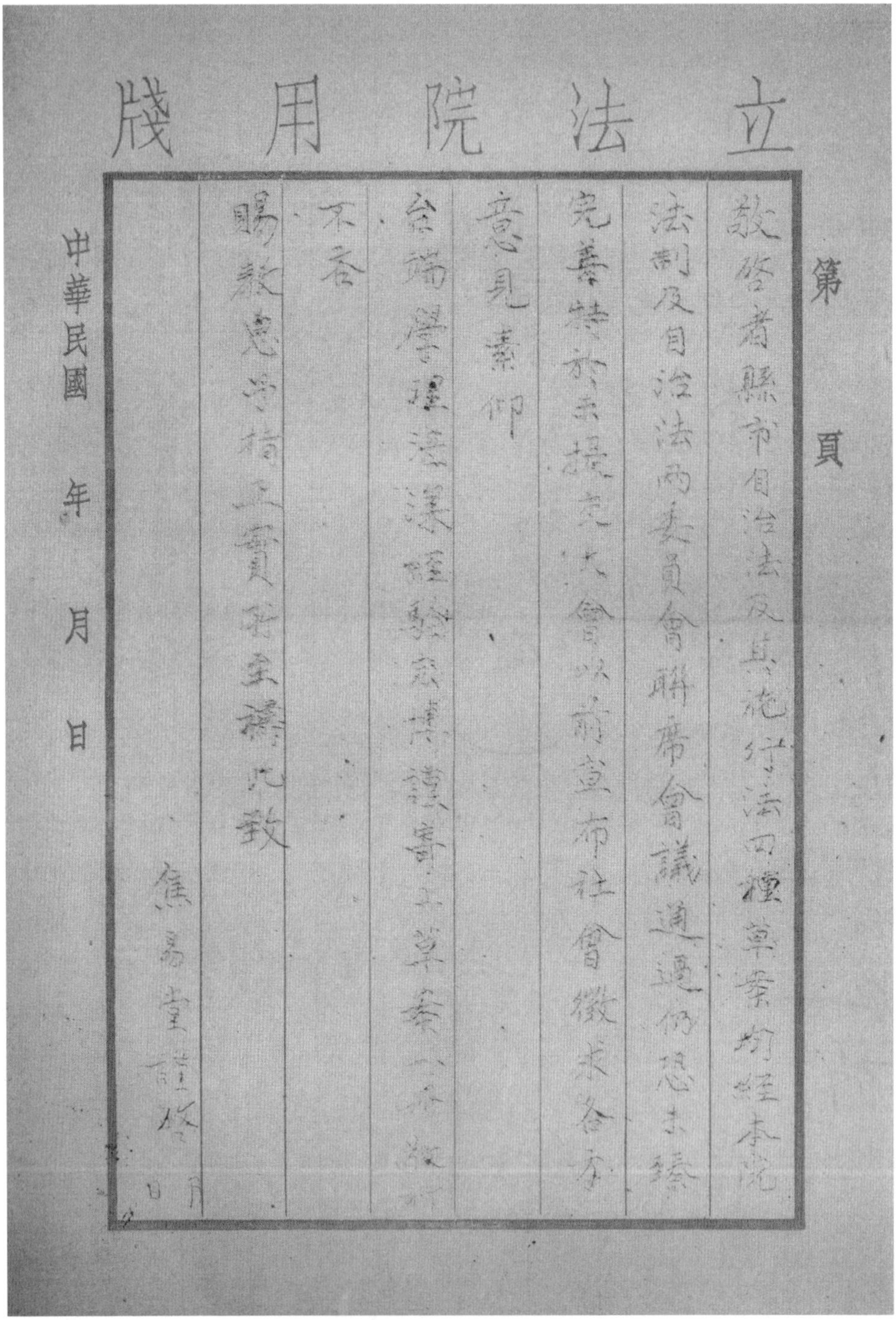

立法院用牋

敬啟者縣市自治法及其施行法四種草案均經本院法制及自治法兩委員會聯席會議通過惟恐未臻完善特於未提交大會以前宣布社會徵求各方意見素仰

台端學礫法漢經驗宏博讀寄上業奉一份敬祈

不吝

賜教惠示梢正實所至禱此致

焦易堂謹啓

中華民國　年　月　日

圖 1

敬啓者：

　　縣市自治法及其施行法四種草案均經本院法制及自治法兩委員會聯席會議通過，仍恐未臻完善，特於未提交大會以前宣布社會，徵求各方意見。素仰台端學理湛深，經驗宏博，謹寄上草案一册，敬祈不吝賜教，惠予指正，實所至禱。此致

焦易堂謹啓
　月　　日

金國珍致胡適（一九四七年四月二十二日）

　　此信發現於《市政概論》一書中。此書出版於 1941 年，此時胡適仍任駐美大使，至 1946 年 7 月返國抵滬，在上海、南京兩地逗留至七月底方至北平。信中稱"昨夏在申得晉謁尊顏"，又稱"頃因料理家務返平，不日即當南返"，則寫信時作者、胡適當皆在北平，則此信或寫於 1947 年 4 月 22 日。

　　金國珍，湖北咸寧人，1925 年畢業於北京大學經濟系。1935 年畢業於日本東京帝國大學，後入研究院專攻城市管理，獲碩士學位。曾任職於上海市社會局。著有《市公安》《市政概論》《中國財政論》等。

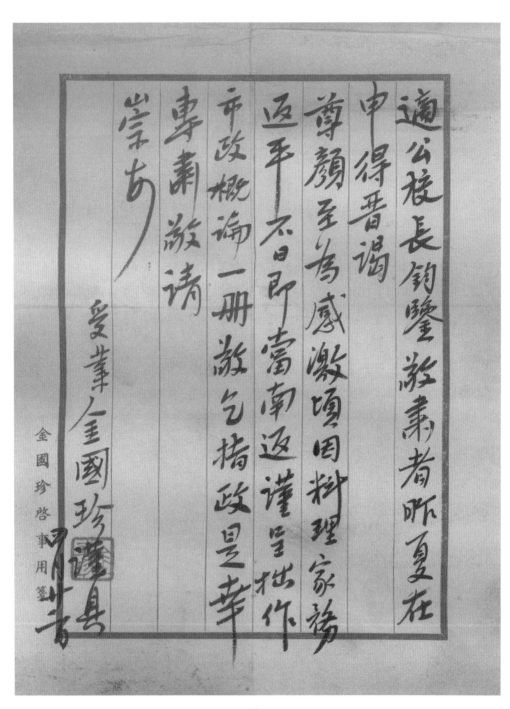

圖1

適公校長鈞鑒：
　　敬肅者，昨夏在申得晉謁
尊顏，至爲感激，頃因料理家務返平，不日即當南返。謹呈拙作《市政概論》一册，敬乞指政是幸。專肅，敬請
崇安
　　　　　　　　　　　　　　　受業　金國珍謹具
　　　　　　　　　　　　　　　　　四月廿二日

黎錦熙致胡適（一九二一年五月四日）

此信發現於《黎錦熙的國語講壇》一書中。

黎錦熙（1890—1978），字劭西、邵西，湖南湘潭人。清秀才，1911年畢業於湖南優級師範學堂。1913年任湖南第四師範學校歷史教員，次年該校合併爲湖南省立第一師範，仍任歷史教員。1915年到北京任教育部教科書特約編纂員。1916年參與發起組織國語研究會。1918年任國語統一籌備會委員，設立國語傳習所，任導師。1920年任北京高等師範學校國文系教員，1923年該校改爲北京師範大學，任教授，後兼任國文系主任，研究所副所長。抗戰爆發後，隨校西遷，任西北聯合大學教授兼國文系主任。1925年發起成立國語運動大會。後歷任北京師範大學、燕京大學、西北聯合大學、西北師院、湖南大學教授。1935年任教育部國語推行委員會常務委員。1936年任西北師範學院院長。1944年與許德珩等人發起組織民主科學社（九三學社前身）。1945年任西北師範學院院長。1946年九三學社正式成立，當選爲中央監事會監事。1947年任湖南大學國文系教授。1948年任北平師範大學國文系主任、文學院長。新中國成立後，任北京師範大學中文系主任，1955年當選爲中國科學院哲學社會科學部學部委員。曾任中國文字改革委員會委員，九三學社中央常委，政協第一、二、三屆全國委員。著有《新著國語文法》《國語運動史綱》《國語新文字論》等。

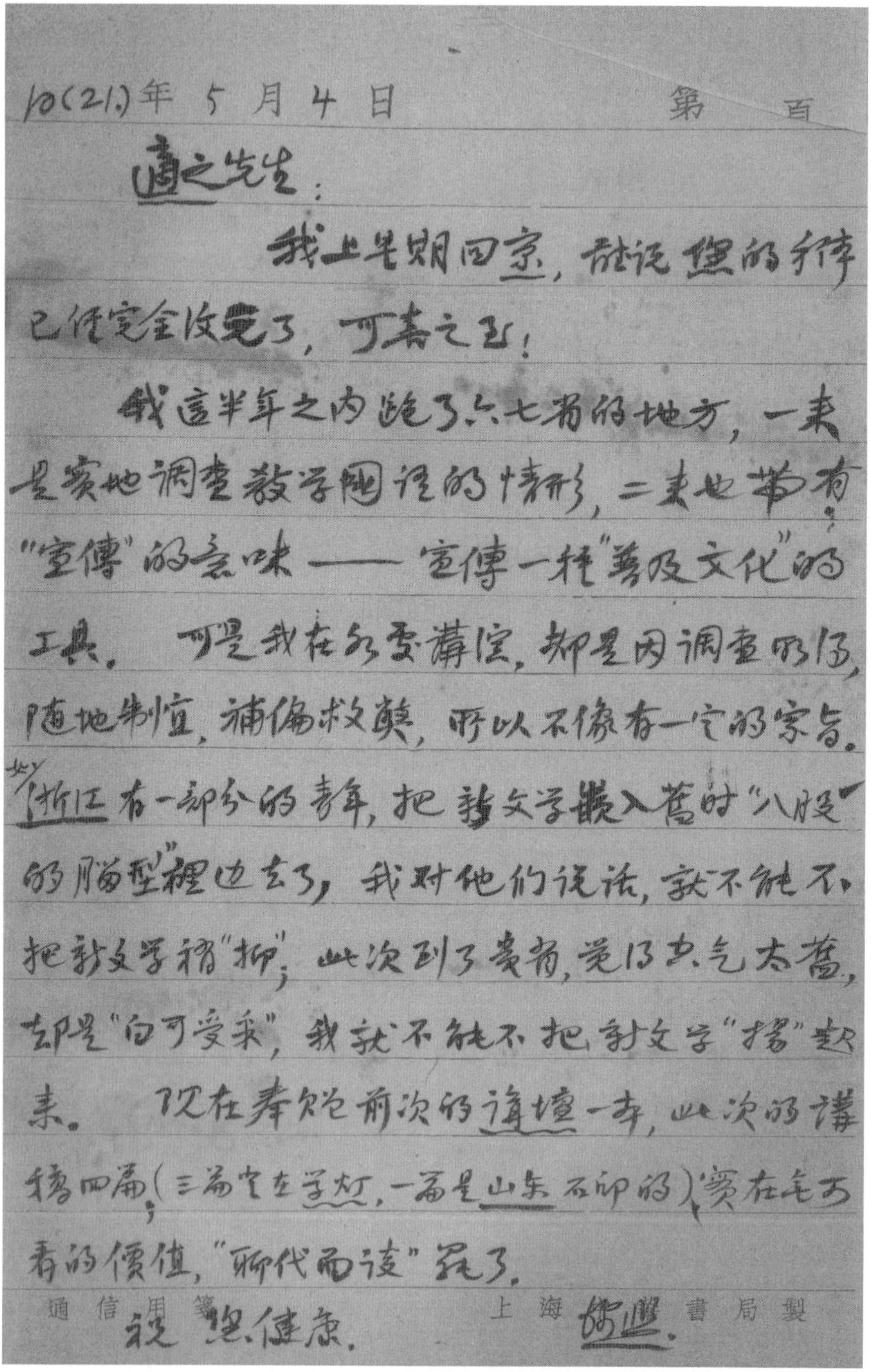

10(21)年 5 月 4 日

適之先生：

我上星期回京，就说您的行踪已经完全没定了，可恨之至！

我這半年之內跑了六七省的地方，一來是實地調查教學問題的情形，二來也帶有"宣傳"的意味——宣傳一種"普及文化"的工具。可是我在各處講演，却是因調查的結果，隨地制宜，補偏救弊，所以不像有一定的宗旨。浙江有一部分的青年，把新文學擺入舊的"八股"的腦型裡邊去了，我對他們說話，就不能不把新文學稍"抑"；此次到了貴州，覺得六氣太舊，却是"尚可受采"，我就不能不把新文學"揚"起來。現在奉上前次的講壇一本，此次的講稿四篇（三篇是在學校，一篇是山東石印的），實在无甚有的價值，"聊代面談"罷了。

祝您健康。

圖1

10（21）年5月4日

適之先生：

我上星期回京，聽說您的身體已經完全復元了，可喜之至！

我這半年之內跑了六七省的地方，一來是實地調查教學國語的情形，二來也帶有"宣傳"的意味——宣傳一種"普及文化"的工具。可是我在各處講演，都是因調查所得，隨地制宜，補偏救弊，所以不像有一定的宗旨。如浙江有一部分的青年，把新文學嵌入舊時"八股的腦型"裡邊去了，我對他們説話，就不能不把新文學稍"抑"；此次到了貴省，覺得空氣太舊，卻是"白可受采"，我就不能不把新文學"揚"起來。現在奉贈前次的《講壇》一本，此次的講稿四篇（三篇登在《學燈》，一篇是山東石印的），實在無可看的價值，"聊代面談"罷了。

祝您健康。

錦熙

李大釗致胡適

　　此信無日期。信件發現於信中提到的日本學者帆足理一郎的《哲學概論》中，該書出版於 1921 年，所提及的代轉人章洛聲，曾在北大出版部工作，住在胡適家中。1922 年胡適創辦《努力週報》，章洛聲積極參與編務工作，1923 年夏因病去世，故此信大致寫於 1921—1923 年間。

　　李大釗（1889—1927），河北樂亭人。1905 年考入永平府中學，1907 年考入天津北洋法政專門學校，1913 年畢業。同年底赴日留學，入東京早稻田大學，其間積極參加留日學生愛國運動。1916 年回國後，主編《晨鐘報》，後參與《憲法公言》《言治》《甲寅日刊》等的創辦編輯。1917 年 11 月任職北京大學，1918 年 1 月起任北大圖書館主任，1920 年起兼任政治系、史學系教授。1922 年 12 月辭去北大圖書館主任之職，任校長室秘書，曾連續四年當選校評議會評議員。1918 年 1 月，《新青年》改爲以北大教授爲主體的同人雜誌，李大釗爲主要編輯之一，1918 年底與陳獨秀創辦《每週評論》，積極領導和參與新文化運動。俄國十月革命後，發表《庶民的勝利》和《我的馬克思主義觀》等著名文章，率先在中國接受和傳播馬克思主義。1920 年 3 月指導成立"北京大學馬克思學說研究會"，10 月創建中共北京黨小組，全面參與中國共產黨的籌組。中國共產黨成立後，負責北京地委、北京區委、北方區委的工作，當選爲中共第三、四屆中央委員，是中國共產黨早期活動的重要領導者。1924 年協助孫中山改組國民黨、建立國共合作統一戰線，並在國民黨一大上當選爲國民黨中央執行委員。1927 年 4 月 6 日被奉系軍閥逮捕，4 月 28 日，英勇就義。

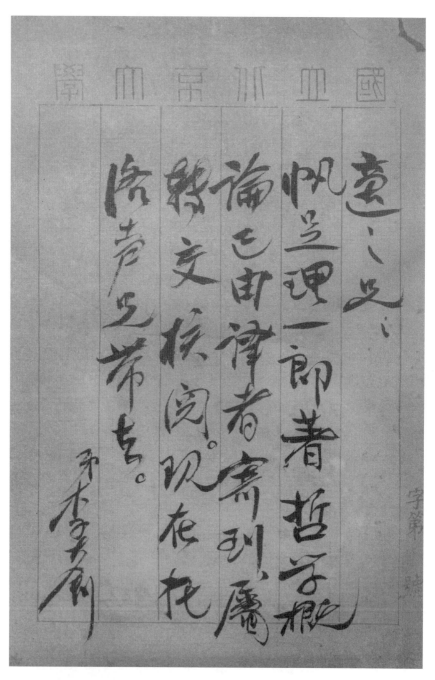

圖1

適之兄：

帆足理一郎著《哲學概論》已由譯者寄到，屬轉交核閱。現在托洛聲兄帶去。

弟 李大釗

李振邦致胡適（一九四七年三月十九日）

此信發現於《八年抗戰經過概要》一書中。

此信僅署三月十九日，信中説（三月）十六日星期天，查萬年曆，當爲 1947 年，另信中提到國民黨軍隊攻佔延安，此事在 1947 年 3 月 19 日，與信中所説"延安已於今日上午十時被我軍攻佔了"相合。故此信日期應爲 1947 年 3 月 19 日。

此信署名"振邦"，筆跡與"北京檔"館藏號 HS-JDSHSC-1173-007"李振邦致胡適函"一致，故可推定作者爲李振邦。

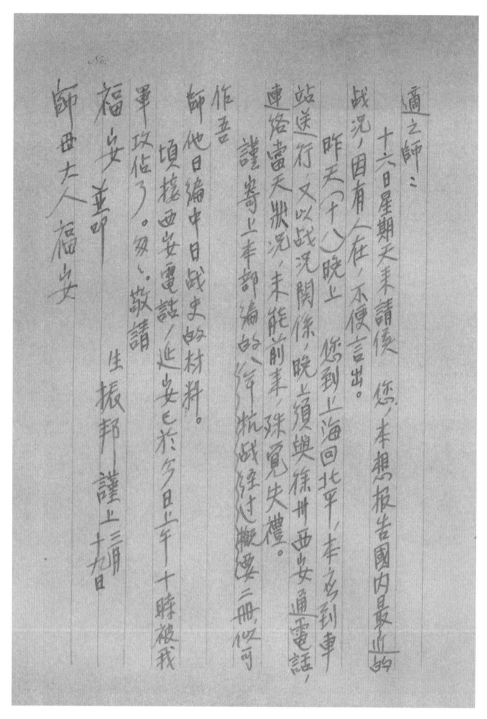

圖1

適之師：

　　十六日星期天來請侯您，本想報告國內最近的戰況，因有人在，不便言出。

　　昨天（十八）晚上您到上海回北平，本應到車站送行，又以戰況關係，晚上須與徐州、西安通電話，連絡當天狀況，未能前來，殊覺失禮。

　　謹寄上本部編的《八年抗戰經過概要》二册，似可作吾師他日編中日戰史的材料。

　　頃接西安電話，延安已於今日上午十時被我軍攻佔了。匆匆。敬請
福安，並叩
師母大人福安

生　振邦謹上
三月十九日

連横致胡適

此信發現於《臺灣通史》一書中。

連横（1878—1936），原名允斌，字武公，號葛陶、雅堂、劍花。國民黨榮譽主席連戰的祖父。臺灣省臺南人。原籍福建漳州。1897年入上海聖約翰大學學習俄文。1898年、1899年先後任《臺澎日報》《臺南新報》漢文部主筆。1904年到廈門與蔡佩香等籌資合辦《福州日日新報》，鼓吹排滿，不久報社爲當局查封，回臺，任《臺南新報》漢文部主編。1908年春從臺南移居臺中任《臺灣新聞》漢文部主筆。1911年經由日本旅遊至大陸各地，主編《華僑雜誌》。1913年春在北京以華僑身份選舉國會議員。後入《新吉林報》工作，不久任《邊聲社》主編。1914年返北京，任清史館名譽協修。同年冬回臺任《臺南新報》主筆。1918年完成《臺灣通史》。1919年，被華南銀行發起人林熊征禮聘爲秘書。1924年2月創辦《臺灣詩薈》雜誌。1927年開設"雅堂書局"，專賣漢文書籍，遭取締。1929年，爲保存臺灣方言，編寫《臺灣語典》四卷。1930年在臺南創辦《三六九小報》。1936年定居上海，同年6月28日病逝。其他著作有：《劍花室詩集》（即《甯南詩草》）《劍花室文集》《臺灣詩乘》《大陸詩草》等。

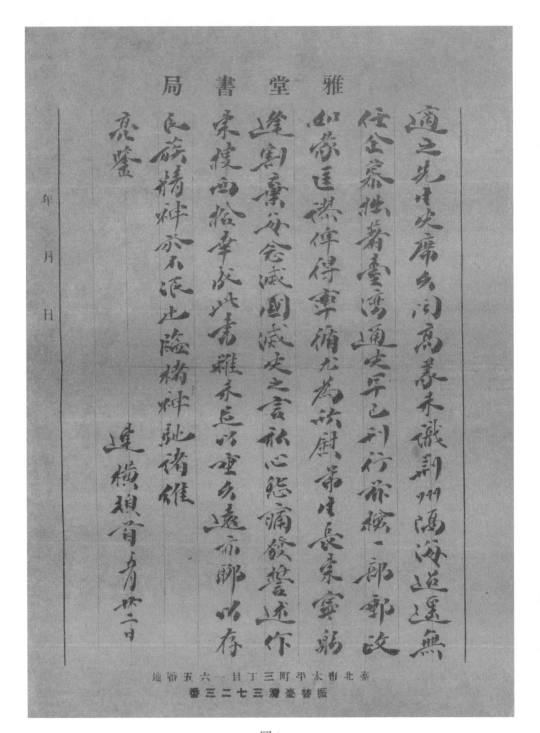

圖1

適之先生史席：

久聞高義，未識荊州，隔海迢遙，無任企慕。拙著《臺灣通史》早已刊行。茲檢一部郵政。如蒙匡謬，俾得率循，尤爲欣慰。弟生長東寧，躬逢割棄，每念滅國滅史之言，私心怨痛，發誓述作，東搜西拾，幸成此書。雖未足以垂久遠，亦聊以存民族精神於不泯也。臨楮神馳，諸維亮鑒。

連橫頓首
五月廿二日

林語堂致胡適（一九三五年）

　　此信發現於《五十年來百部佳作特輯》一書中。信中所說的《人間世》於1934年創刊，1935年10月20日出版第38期百部佳作特輯。則此信當寫於1935年。

　　林語堂（1895—1976），原名玉堂，福建龍溪人。1916年畢業於上海聖約翰大學，同年任清華學校英文教師。1919年赴美哈佛大學留學，1921年獲文學碩士學位。後入德國萊比錫大學研究語言學，獲哲學博士學位。1923年回國，任教於清華學校。1924年參加語絲社。1925年任北京大學英文系教授，後任北京女子師範大學英文系教授兼教務長。1926年任廈門大學文科主任、國學院總秘書。1927年任國民黨武漢政府外交部秘書。1928年任中央研究院出版品交換處處長。1929年任上海東吳大學英文教授。1930—1931年，繼續在中央研究院任職。1932年，創辦《論語》半月刊，1934年創辦《人間世》半月刊，1935年創辦《宇宙風》旬刊。1936年赴美從事寫作和宣傳中國文化。1939年回國。1940年再赴美，在紐約從事寫作。1947年出任聯合國教科文組織美術與文學組主任，不久辭職，繼續以寫作為業。1954年任新加坡南洋大學校長，次年辭職。1965年回香港，1966年定居臺灣。1967年去香港中文大學主持詞典編纂。1976年病逝於香港。主要著作有《剪拂集》《大荒集》《吾國與吾民》等。

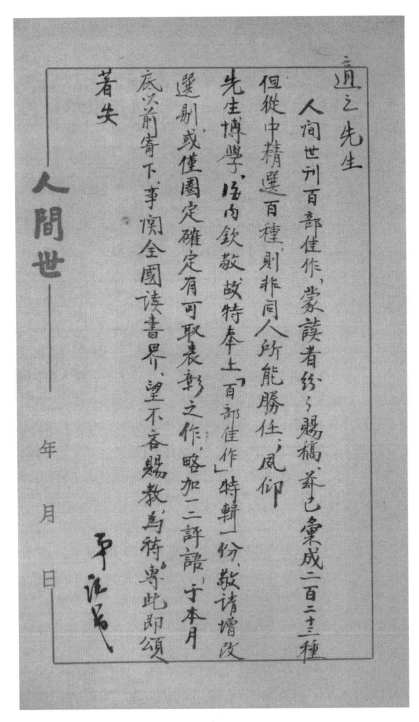

圖1

適之先生：

　　《人間世》刊百部佳作，蒙讀者紛紛賜稿，茲已彙成二百二十三種，但從中精選百種，則非同人所能勝任；夙仰先生博學，海內欽敬，故特奉上"百部佳作"特輯一份，敬請增改選剔，或僅圈定確定有可取表彰之作，略加一二評語，于本月底以前寄下，事關全國讀者界，望不吝賜教，爲禱。專此即頌
著安

弟　語堂

劉半農致胡適

此信發現於《新嘉量之校量及推算》一書中，出版於 1928 年 12 月，輔仁大學輔仁學誌編輯會印行。

劉半農（1891—1934），原名壽彭，後改名復，初字半儂，後改爲半農，號曲庵，江蘇江陰人。1907 年考入常州府中學堂。1912 年到上海，1913 年任中華書局編譯員，開始發表小說。1915 年任《中華新報》編譯員。1917 年任北京大學預科教授，積極參加新文化運動，爲《新青年》編輯之一。1920 年出國留學，1925 年獲法國國家文學博士學位。同年秋回國，任北京大學教授，兼任北大研究所國學門導師、中法大學國文系講師。1926 年秋，兼任中法大學國文系主任。1928 年被聘爲中央研究院歷史語言研究所特約研究員、北平古物保護委員會委員、國語統一籌備委員會委員。1929 年重返北京大學任教，同年被聘爲輔仁大學教務長。1934 年 7 月在北平病逝。主要著作有《中國文法通論》《四聲實驗錄》等。

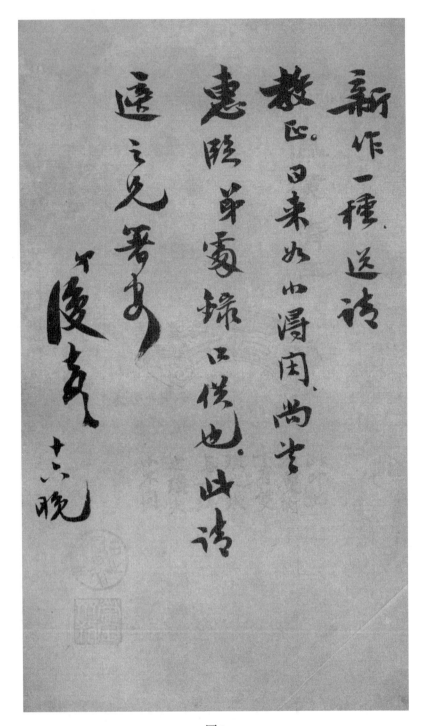

圖1

新作一種，送請教正。日來如小得閑，尚望惠臨弟處錄口供也。此請
適之兄箸安

　　　　　　　　　　　　　　　　　　　　　　　　弟復頓首
　　　　　　　　　　　　　　　　　　　　　　　　十六晚

劉文典致胡適

此信發現於《韋莊年譜》一書中。作者曲瀅生,出版於 1932 年 6 月,北平清華園我輩語叢刊社印行。封面爲胡適題。書首張昺仁序説:"書中關於韋莊的生年月日……他仍虛衷地請教胡適之先生,直至胡先生來信表示同意時,他心中纔覺粗安。"又説:"這書付梓問世的動機,是外界的,是由我們慫恿的。"與劉氏信中措辭相近,此信應寫於該書出版之後不久。

劉文典(1889—1958),原名文驄,字叔雅,安徽合肥人。1906 年入蕪湖安徽公學,後加入同盟會。1909 年赴日留學,入早稻田大學。1912 年回國,在上海參與主辦《民立報》。1913 年,"二次革命"失敗後,再度赴日,參加中華革命黨,任孫中山秘書處秘書。1916 年回國,次年應陳獨秀之聘,任北京大學文科預科教授。1927 年任安徽大學文學院預備主任,兼預科籌備主任,次年任預科主任,文法學院院長,主持校務。1928 年回北京大學任教。1929 年任清華大學中文系教授。1931 年代理中文系主任。1938 年任西南聯合大學教授。1943 年任雲南磨黑中學校長,同年被西南聯大解聘。1944 年任雲南大學文史系教授。新中國成立後,被評爲一級教授。曾當選全國政協委員。1958 年去世。主要著作有《淮南鴻烈集解》《莊子補正》等。

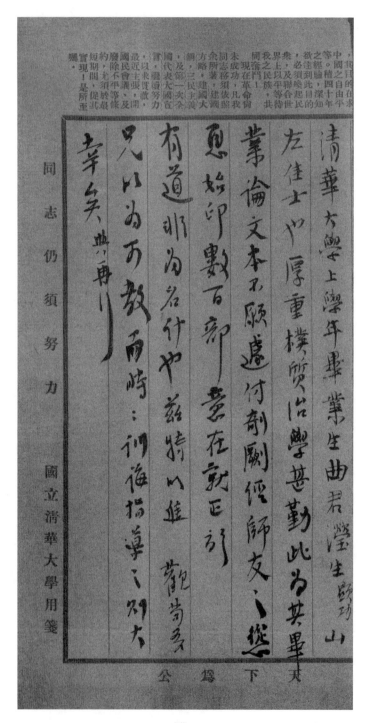

圖1

（前似有缺頁）清華大學上學年畢業生曲君瀅生顯功，山左佳士也，厚重樸質，治學甚勤，此爲其畢業論文，本不願遽付剞劂，經師友之慫恿，始印數百部，意在就正於有道，非爲名計也。茲特以進觀，苟吾兄以爲可教，而時時訓誨指導之，則大幸矣。

典再拜

劉蔭仁致胡適（一九四六年十二月二十五日）

　　此信發現於《說文中象形字分類簡譜》一書中，北京大學圖書館所藏手稿本完成於一九四六年。信中提及胡適"最近出席具有重大歷史意義的國大……"，並稱之爲"制憲的國大"，當指一九四六年十一月國民黨召開的"制憲國大"，則此信應寫作於一九四六年十二月二十五日。

　　劉蔭仁（1904—1957），湖南新化人。1926年在北京大學讀書期間加入中國共產黨，1927年輟學回新化從事革命活動，1928年被捕，1931年被保釋出獄，後回北京大學復學，1935年畢業於北京大學國文系，先後在長沙岳雲及省立五中等校任教。抗戰爆發後，經徐特立介紹到新四軍政治部工作。1939年因病返鄉，任中國工農合作社邵陽事務所合作金庫主任，並義務在新化女中授課，後又在縣男中教課。皖南事變後，轉移到桂林，在宋慶齡主辦的工農合作社任指導員。抗戰勝利後，任教於新化同大中學，1951年任同大中學校長。1957年12月去世。

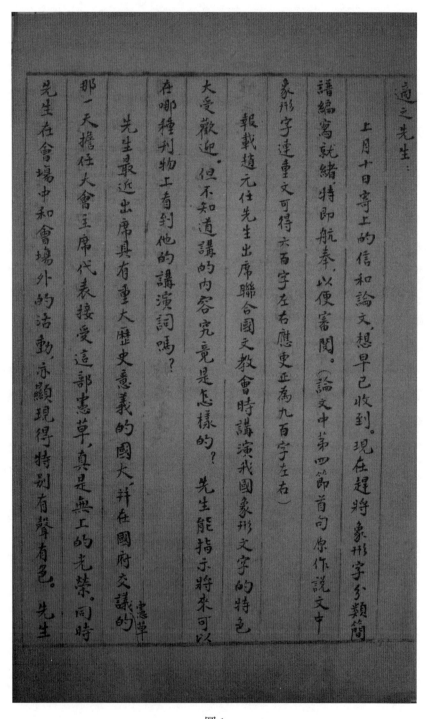

圖1

適之先生：

上月十日寄上的信和論文,想早已收到。現在趕將象形字分類簡譜編寫就緒,特即航奉,以便審閱。(論文中第四節首句原作說文中象形字連重文可得六百字左右應更正為九百字左右)

報載趙元任先生出席聯合國文教會時講演我國象形文字的特色大受歡迎,但不知道講的內容究竟是怎樣的?先生能指示將來可以在哪種刊物上看到他的講演詞嗎?

先生最近出席具有重大歷史意義的國大,并在國府交議的那一天擔任大會主席代表接受這部憲草,真是無上的光榮。同時先生在會場中和會場外的活動,亦顯現得特別有聲有色。先生

適之先生：

　　上月十日寄上的信和論文，想早已收到。現在趕將"象形字分類簡譜"編寫就緒，特即航奉，以便審閱。（論文中第四節首句原作"《說文》中象形字連重文可得六百字左右"，應更正爲"九百字左右"。）

　　報載趙元任先生出席聯合國文教會時講演我國象形文字的特色大受歡迎。但不知道講的内容究竟是怎樣的？先生能指示將來可以在哪種刊物上看到他的講演詞嗎？

　　先生最近出席具有重大歷史意義的國大，并在國府交議憲草的那一天擔任大會主席代表接受這部憲草，真是無上的光榮。同時先生在會場中和會場外的活動，亦顯現得特別有聲有色。先生

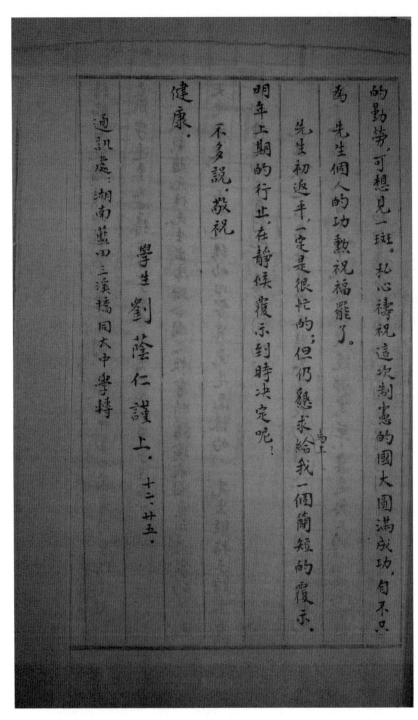

圖2

的勤勞，可想見一斑。私心禱祝這次制憲的國大圓滿成功，自不只爲先生個人的功勳祝福罷了。

先生初返平，一定是很忙的；但仍懇求馬上給我一個簡短的覆示。明年上期的行止，在靜候覆示到時決定呢！

不多說，敬祝

健康。

學生　劉蔭仁謹上
十二．廿五．

通訊處：湖南藍田三溪橋同大中學轉

羅雄飛致胡適

此信發現於《文藝說》一書中。作者生平不詳。

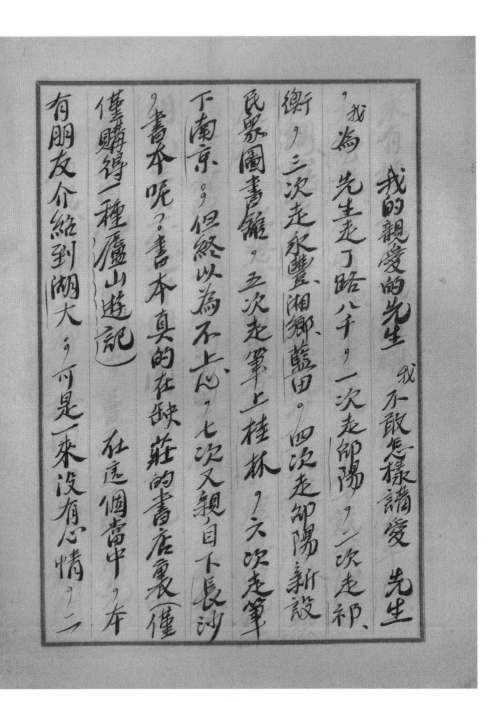

圖1

我的親愛的先生：

我不敢怎樣講愛先生，我爲先生走了路八千，一次走邵陽，二次走祁、衡，三次走永豐、湘鄉、藍田，四次走邵陽新設民衆圖書館，五次走筆上桂林，六次走筆下南京；但終以爲不上心，七次又親自下長沙，書本呢？書本真的在缺莊的書店裏（僅僅購得一種《廬山遊記》）。在這個當中，本有朋友介紹到湖大；可是一來沒有心情，二

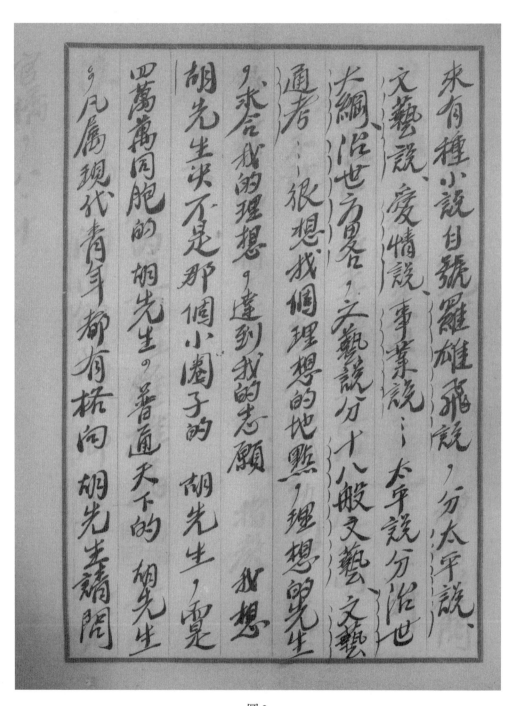

圖 2

來有種小說自號《羅雄飛說》，分《太平說》《文藝說》《愛情說》《事業說》……《太平說》分《治世大綱》《治世方畧》，《文藝說》分《十八般文藝》《文藝通考》……很想找個理想的地點，理想的先生，求合我的理想，達到我的志願。我想胡先生決不是那個小圈子的胡先生，而是四萬萬同胞的胡先生，普通天下的胡先生；凡屬現代青年都有格向胡先生請問，

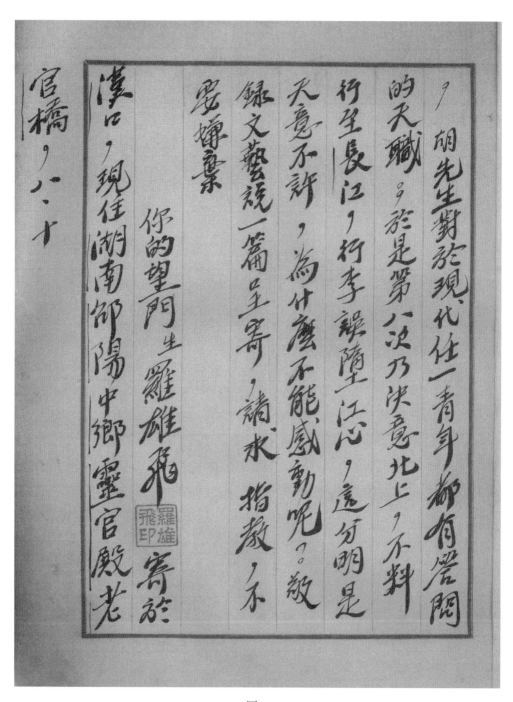

圖3

胡先生對於現代任一青年都有答問的天職；於是第八次乃決意北上，不料行至長江，行李誤墮江心，這分明是天意不許，爲什麼不能感動呢？敬錄《文藝説》一篇呈寄，請求指教，不要嫌棄。

  你的望門生羅雄飛寄於漢口，現住湖南邵陽中鄉靈官殿老官橋，八，十

羅仲言致胡適（一九四八年七月一日）

此信發現於《經濟史學原論》一書中。

羅仲言，即羅章龍（1896—1995），曾用名文虎，又名羅仲言，湖南瀏陽人。1912 年就讀於長沙第一中學，1918 年與毛澤東等發起組織新民學會，同年考入北京大學德語預科，次年積極投身"五四"運動。1920 年初參與發起組織"北京大學馬克思學說研究會"，後在李大釗指導下參與創建北京共產主義組織。中國共產黨成立後，曾任中共北京區委委員，先後參加領導 1921 年底的隴海鐵路大罷工和 1922 年長辛店大罷工、開灤煤礦大罷工。1923 年在中共三大上當選中央委員和中央局委員，會後到上海中共中央工作。此後在中共四大、五大、六大上，均當選爲中央委員。1926 年到武漢中央分局工作，兼任湖北省委委員、中共漢口市委書記。1931 年因反對王明被中央開除出黨。1933 年被捕，1934 年出獄後，任河南大學經濟系教授，次年兼經濟系主任。1938 年起先後在西北大學、華西協和大學和湖南大學任教。1953 年任教於武漢中南財經學院，後任教於湖北大學、湖北財經學院。1978 年調北京，任中國革命博物館顧問。1995 年在北京病逝。

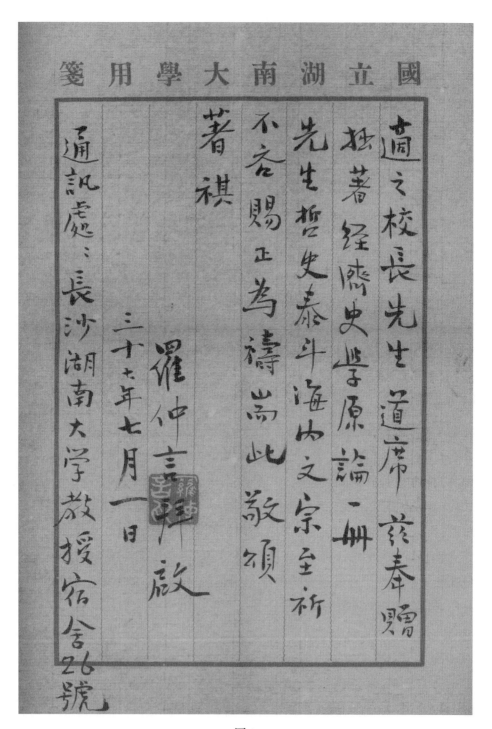

圖1

適之校長先生道席：

　　茲奉贈拙著《經濟史學原論》一册，先生哲史泰斗，海內文宗，至祈不吝賜正爲禱。耑此，敬頌

著祺

羅仲言拜啓
三十七年七月一日

　　　　通訊處：長沙湖南大學教授宿舍 26 號

馬衡致胡適（一九四八年五月十五日）

　　此信發現於何永懋《論語正》一書中。此書初版於一九四六年十一月，信中提及之《孝經正》，今北京大學圖書館藏有一本，首頁鈐"馬衡"藏書印，蓋即此本，而版權頁所記出版年月爲一九四七年八月，則此信最早或寫於一九四八年五月十五日。

　　馬衡（1881—1955），字叔平，別署無咎，號凡將齋主人，浙江鄞縣人。1901年畢業於上海南洋公學。1917年任北京大學國史編纂處徵集員，後受聘爲北大講師。1923年任北京大學史學系教授兼研究所國學門考古研究室主任、導師，後又兼任清華大學、北京師範大學、北京女子師範大學等校考古學教授。1925年9月任故宮博物院理事。1926年12月任故宮博物院維持會常務委員。1927年10月任故宮博物館管理委員會幹事兼古物館副館長。1929年3月任國立故宮博物院古物館副館長，同年兼任北京大學圖書館主任、國立北平研究院史學研究會會員。1934年9月任國立北平故宮博物院院長。1937年抗日戰爭爆發後，負責搶運故宮南京分院文物。中華人民共和國成立後，仍任故宮博物院院長，兼任全國文物保管委員會主任委員。1955年3月26日在北京病逝。主要著作有：《中國金石學概要》《漢石經集存》《凡將齋金石叢稿》等。

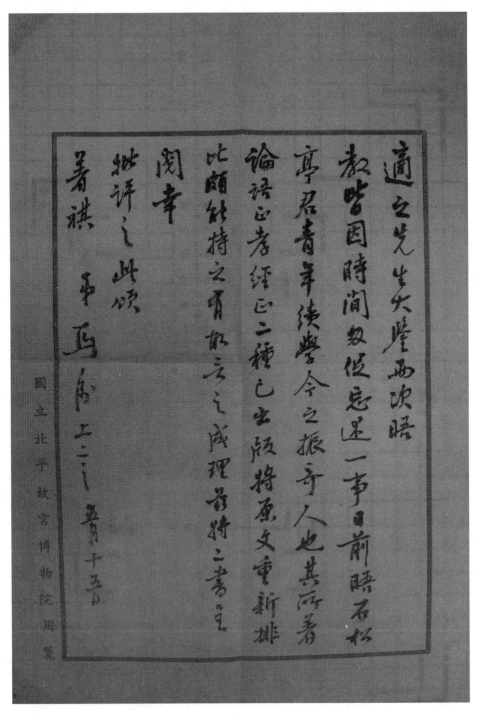

圖1

適之先生大鑒：兩次晤教，皆因時間匆促，忘述一事。日前晤石松亭君，青年績學，今之振奇人也。其所著《論語正》《孝經正》二種已出版，將原文重新排比，頗能持之有故，言之成理。茲將二書呈閱，幸
批評之。此頌
著祺！

　　　　　　　　　　　　　　　　　　　弟　馬衡　上言
　　　　　　　　　　　　　　　　　　　五月十五日

甯華庭致胡適

此信發現於《共鳴》創刊號中。此刊出版於 1930 年。

甯華庭（1903—1949），安徽青陽人。1925 年考入上海光華大學文學系，次年考入東吳大學法學系夜讀班，1930 年獲文學士和法學士學位。畢業後先後在東吳大學、上海法政學院、上海惠中中學任教。1925 年任上海律師事務所律師，曾主辦《共鳴》雜誌。後曾任國民政府第二十三集團軍中校秘書。1940 年起，先後任教於徽州中學、安徽省立池州師範。1945 年底任國民政府行政院最高經濟委員會經濟督察專員，1948 年秋辭職歸故里。1949 年 11 月病逝。

適之先生：

蒙賜題字，感謝得很！奉上一冊货（貨）幼稚錯誤并小有膀（膨）脹踢教否？我們出此刊物，因覺現下的改革，只在都市的地方，鄉間僻縣到了不管，故離幼稚，亦要來說幾句話，算不知及響妙㕘？

耑此敬請

著安

學生 宗舟華 十二度又月廿日元華

適之先生：

　　蒙賜題字，感謝得很！奉上一册，其幼稚錯誤，弗卜有暇能賜教否？

　　我們出此刊物，因覺現下的改革，只在都市的地方鬧，鄉間僻縣到可不管，故雖幼稚，亦要來說幾句話，第不知反響如何？

　　耑此，敬請

著安

學生　甯華庭
六月廿四日 光華

歐陽溇致胡適

此信發現於《簡體字之研究》一書中。此書出版於 1936 年，信中提及之《簡體字考證》，據國家圖書館文獻線上瀏覽，封面有"呈總裁賜正"字樣，其自序所署時間爲"中華民國二十五年雙十節"，但書末版權頁所注出版時間爲"中華民國二十五年六月初版"，因《簡體字考證》書末附錄《簡體字之研究》33 頁，故此出版時間或爲《簡體字之研究》之出版時間。又信中稱《簡體字考證》已有樣張、序文、凡例，則根據其序寫作時間，此信或寫於 1937 年 2 月 25 日。

歐陽溇，字幼濟，江西宜黃人。國語講習所第二期畢業，1926 年曾與余精一等人創辦三自大同社通訊社。

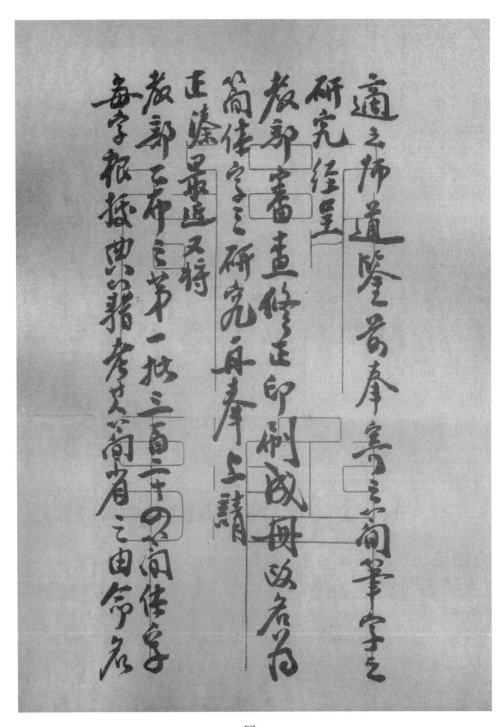

圖1

適之師道鑒：

前奉寄之《簡筆字之研究》經呈
教部審查修正，印刷成册，改名爲《簡體字之研究》，再奉上，請正。溱最近又將
教部公布之第一批三百二十四簡體字每字根據典籍，考其簡省之由，命名

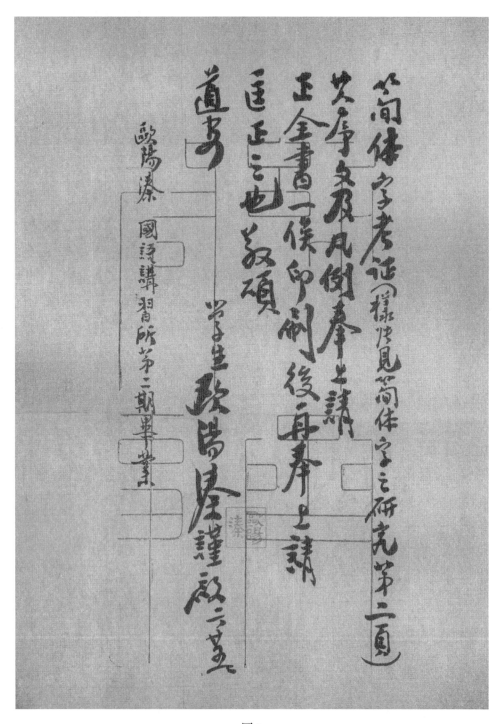

圖2

《簡體字考證》（樣張見《簡體字之研究》第二頁），其序文及凡例奉上請正。全書一俟印刷後，再奉上請匡正之也。敬頌

道安

            學生　歐陽溁謹啓
               二，廿五

歐陽溁，國語講習所第二期畢業。

青木正兒致胡適（一九二一年二月三日）

此信發現於《李卓吾先生批點忠義水滸傳》一書中。

青木正兒（1887—1964），字君雅，別號迷陽，生於日本山口縣下關，日本著名漢學家。1907年進入京都大學文學院，師事著名漢學家狩野直喜和鈴木虎雄，專攻中國文學。1911年畢業，1919年任同志社大學文學院教授。1920年與小島祐馬、木田成之等創辦《支那學》雜誌。1922年至1926年先後兩次訪問中國，遊覽名山大川，考察中華風物，遊學北京，求師訪友。1923年任仙台東北帝國大學助教。1935年獲文學博士學位。後歷任京都大學文學院教授，山口大學文理學院教授、院長，立命館大學文學院教授等職。爲日本學士院會員、日本中國學會會員。主要著作：《中國近世戲曲史》（初名爲《明清戲曲史》）、《中國文學概論》，有《青木正兒全集》十卷。

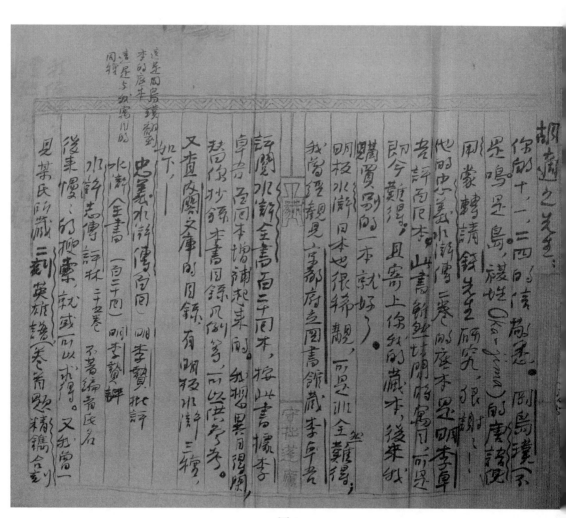

圖1

胡適之先生：

你的十，一，二四的信敬悉。岡島璞（不是鳴，是島，複姓 Oka-jima）的《唐語便用》蒙轉請錢先生研究，狠謝謝！

他的《忠義水滸傳》二卷的底本是明李卓吾評百回本。此書雖然坊間時寓目，可是即今難得；且寄上你我的藏本，後來我購買別的一本就好了。

明板《水滸》日本也很希覯，可是非全然難得；我曾經觀見京都府立圖書館藏李卓吾評閱《水滸全書》百二十回本，按此書據李卓吾百回本增補起來的。我想異日得閒，替你抄錄本書目錄凡例等，可以供參考。又查內閣文庫的目錄，有明板《水滸》三種，如下，——

《忠義水滸傳》（百回）明李贄批評（這是岡島璞翻刻本的底本）

《水滸全書》（百二十回）明李贄評（這是與我寓目的同種）

《水滸志傳評林》二十五卷 不著編者氏名

後來慢慢的搜索，就或可以求得。又我曾一見某氏所藏《二刻英雄譜》（卷首題《精鐫合刻

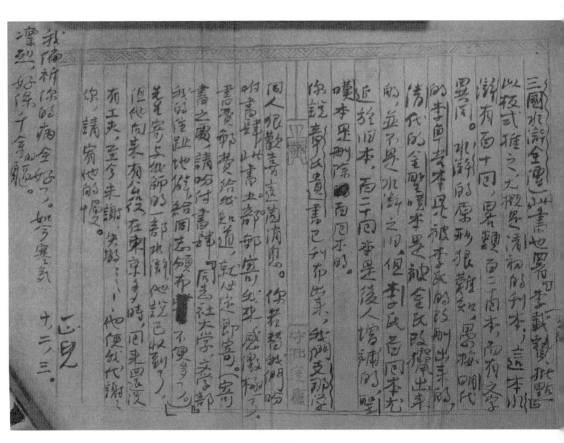

圖 2

三國水滸全傳》），此書也署"李載（恐衍）贊批點"，以板式推之，大概是清初的刊本；這本《水滸》有百十回，署類百二十回本，而有文字異同。《水滸》的原形狠難知，愚按明代的李卓吾本是被李氏的改删出來的，清代的金聖嘆本是被金氏改攛出來的，並不是《水滸》之舊，但李氏百回本尤近於舊本，百二十回本是後人增補的，聖嘆本是删除百回本的。

你說《章氏遺書》已刊布出來，我們支那學同人狠歡喜這箇消息。你若替我們吩咐書肆，此書五部郵寄我來，感激極了。書費郵費給我知道，就必定即寄。（寄書之處，請吩咐書肆"同志社大學，文學部"，我的住趾地僻，給同志頒布不便多了。）先生寄與我師的一部《水滸》，他說已收到了，但他向來有公役，在東京多時，回來還沒有工夫，至今未謝，失敬失敬！他使我代謝謝你，請宥他的慢。

我偏祈你的病全好了。如今寒氣凛烈，好保千金的軀。

正兒
十,二,三。

桑原騭藏致胡適

　　此信發現於《宋末の提舉市舶西域人蒲壽庚の事蹟》一書中。此書出版於 1923 年，作者於 1931 年 5 月去世，此信當寫於此數年間。

　　桑原騭藏（1870—1931），日本福井縣敦賀市人，日本京都學派代表人物，著名歷史學家。1896 年畢業於東京帝國大學文學系漢學科，同年入大學院專攻東洋史。1898 年任第三高等學校教授，次年改任東京高等師範學校教授。1907 年到中國留學，1909 年回國，任京都帝國大學教授。長期致力於東西交通史研究。主要著作有《蒲壽庚之事跡》《東西交通史論叢》等。

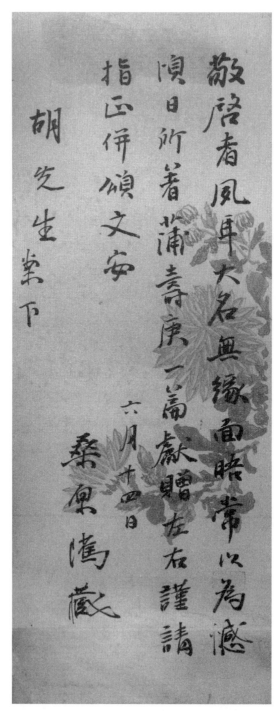

圖1

敬啓者：

夙聞大名，無緣面晤，常以爲憾。頃日所著蒲壽庚一篇獻贈左右，謹請指正。并頌文安。

六月十四日
桑原騭藏

胡先生　案下

沈從文致胡適

此信發現於《陶淵明批評》一書中。此書出版於 1947 年，作者蕭望卿，成資爲其字。《陶淵明批評》1947 年 7 月由開明書店初版，此信寫於三月，而胡適於 1948 年 12 月已經離開北平，故此信當寫於 1948 年 3 月 5 日。但信中稱"這同學目下還只二十六歲"，蕭望卿生於 1917 年，二十六歲則爲 1943 年，或"二十六歲"之説有誤。

沈從文（1902—1988），原名沈岳煥，湖南鳳凰人。1918 年隨本鄉部隊在沅水流域生活。1923 年到北京，曾在北京大學旁聽。1924 年開始在北京報刊上發表作品。1928 年到上海，與丁玲、胡也頻籌辦《紅黑》雜誌和出版社，同年參加新月社。次年在中國公學任教。1930 年任教於武漢大學，1933 年任教於青島大學。1934 年在北平編寫中小學國文教科書，同年及 1935 年先後在北平和天津編輯《大公報》文藝副刊。抗戰爆發後，於 1938 年任西南聯合大學中文系教授。抗戰勝利後，回北平任北京大學教授。新中國成立後，任職於中國歷史博物館。1978 年任中國社會科學院歷史研究所研究員。除小説創作外，著有《中國古代服飾研究》《龍鳳藝術》等。

适之先生：

有本小书呈给您，作者萧东资，辛苦西南联大，这本小书就是他的毕业论文。近来清华研究院读了两年书，研究论文也即日呈上批评。因来匆匆，这论文是要请您批评。他的长处都是印象好批评。这是西南联大、华中国文系中学生有文艺才能运用外国语文作批评比较的一位。他本是外文系学生，读金书甫一岛二先生鼓励才转系。现在已不想在学校里工作论文又会工作，不知您肯给他一些帮助没有？这同学目下医只二十四岁，将来一定是笔杆就。左传记和批评上都会对他有些批评，因为一枝笔特别好、人又极诚朴。专此并候安佳。

沈从文 敬启 三月五日

適之先生：

　　有本小書呈給您，作者蕭成資，畢業西南聯大，這本小書就是他的畢業論文。近在清華研究院讀了兩年書，研究論文題目是"李白批評"，未通過。（因爲照習慣，研究論文重考證，他的長處卻是印象的批評。）照我所知説來，這是西南聯大八年來國文系中學生有文彩又能運用外國語文作比較批評的一位，（他本是外文系學生，得金甫一多二先生鼓勵才轉系。）現在已不想在學校重作論文，又無工作，不知您能給他一點幫助沒有？這同學目下還只二十六歲，將來一定有成就，在傳記和批評上都有新的成就可望，因爲一枝筆特別好，人又極誠樸。敬此，并頌安佳。

　　　　　　　　　　　　　　　　　　　　　生　從文敬啓
　　　　　　　　　　　　　　　　　　　　　三月五日

孫次舟致胡適（一九四七年五月二十四日）

　　此信發現於《嵩縣唐墓所出剪銅尺及墓誌考釋》一文中。信中所稱《文史周刊》，當指胡適所創辦的《大公報·文史周刊》，創刊於 1946 年 10 月 16 日，終刊於 1947 年 11 月 14 日。故此信當寫於 1947 年 5 月 24 日。

　　孫次舟（1908—2000），原名孫志楫，山東即墨人。1933 年畢業於私立中國大學中國文學專業。曾任山東省立臨沂中學教員，省立圖書館編審。1937 年主編《歷史與考古》雜誌。抗戰爆發後，顧頡剛任齊魯大學國學研究所主任，聘請孫氏爲專任研究員，受顧氏指導，信守"疑古"。後任教於金陵女子大學。新中國成立後，任四川大學、南充師範學院歷史系教授。

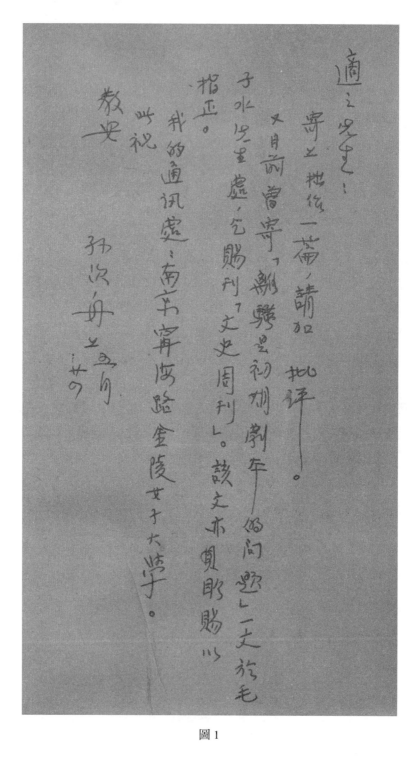

圖1

適之先生：

　　寄上拙作一篇，請加批評。

　　又日前曾寄《離騷是初期劇本的問題》一文於毛子水先生處，乞賜刊《文史周刊》。該文亦盼賜以指正。

　　我的通訊處：南京甯海路金陵女子大學。

　　此祝

教安

孫次舟上
五月廿四

孫澤英致胡適

　　此信發現於《獨裁政治之理論和實際》一書中，此書出版於 1934 年，故此信應寫於 1934 年之後。

　　作者生平不詳。

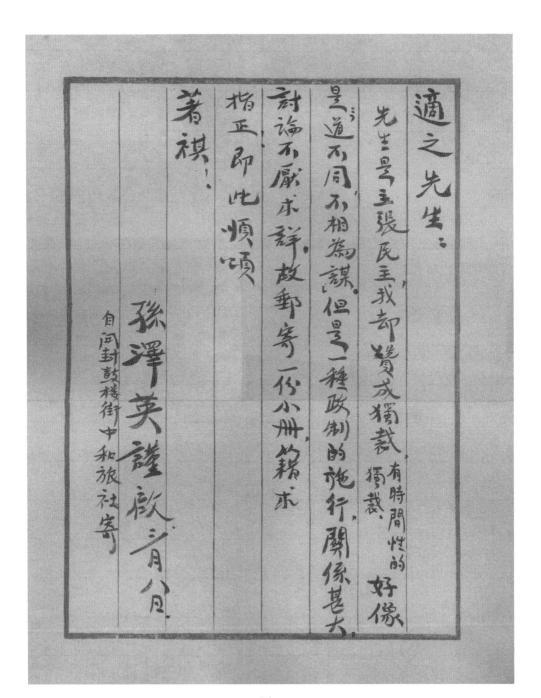

適之先生：

先生是主張民主，我卻贊成獨裁，有時間性的獨裁。好像是道不同不相為謀，但是一種政制的施行關係甚大，討論不厭求詳，故郵寄一份小冊籍求指正，即此順頌

著祺！

孫澤英謹啟 三月八日

自河封鼓樓街中和旅社寄

圖 1

適之先生：

　　先生是主張民主，我却贊成獨裁（有時間性的獨裁）。好像是："道不同，不相爲謀。"但是一種政制的施行，關係甚大，討論不厭求詳，故郵寄一份小册，藉求
指正！即此順頌
著祺！

孫澤英謹啓
三月八日
自開封鼓樓街中和旅社寄

孫拯致胡適（一九三〇年三月二日）

此信發現於《銀價之研究》一書中。

孫拯，字公度，曾任南京國民政府立法院統計處處長，1932年國防設計委員會成立後，任該委員會下統計處處長。1934年4月，國防設計委員會改隸軍事委員會，更名爲資源委員會，任經濟研究室主任，後曾任資源委員會委員、經濟研究所所長。曾任中國統計學社會員、中國經濟建設協會副總幹事。著有《銀價之研究》。

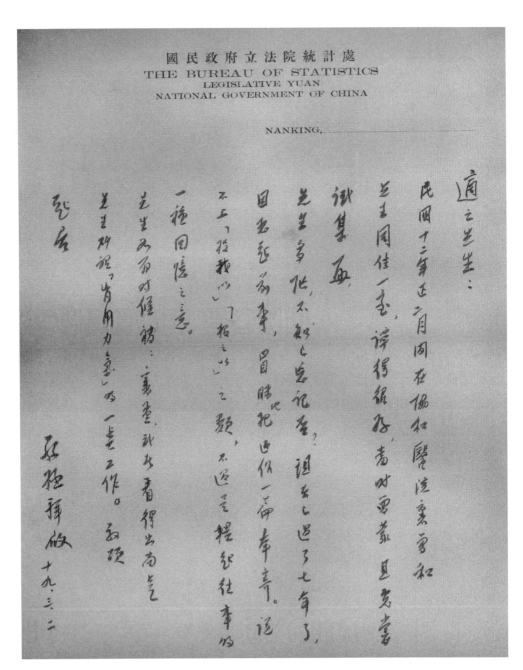

圖1

適之先生：

　　民國十二年正二月間在協和醫院裏曾和
先生同住一室，譚得很好，當時曾蒙見惠《嘗試集》一册，
先生多忙，不知已忘記否？現在已過了七年了，因想起前事，冒昧地把近作一篇奉寄。説不上"投我以""報之以"之類，不過是提起往事的一種回憶之意。
先生如有時候稍稍審查，或者看得出尚是
先生所謂"肯用力氣"的一點工作。敬頌
起居

孫拯拜啟

十九．三．二

唐世隆致胡適書信兩通（一九三一年七月二十一日，一九三一年九月十一日）

此二信發現於《民間疾苦詩》一書中。據北京大學圖書館所藏此書之著錄，此書爲油印本一函二册，而第二册爲第一册的删改本，出版於一九三一年。或可推知，第一信中所附詩稿即第一册，後據胡適所提意見修訂爲第二册，即第二信信封所稱"坿書一本"。則此二信當寫於一九三一年。

唐世隆（1901—？），初名唐煜隆，號光晉，字次虎，筆名唐突，四川威遠人。早年就讀於嘉定府中學，畢業後從軍，曾在劉文輝川軍歷任排長、連長、副官、參謀等職。後入北平陸軍大學第九期，畢業後回川軍任職，歷任上校參謀長，成都衛戍司令部少將參謀長等職。抗戰爆發後，任川軍某軍少將參謀長，後任重慶中央大學少將軍事主任教官、國民政府軍事委員會少將高級參謀。抗戰勝利後，任"重慶行轅復原委員會軍事組"中將副組長、國民政府西南長官公署軍運指揮部指揮官等職。新中國成立後以中醫行醫。

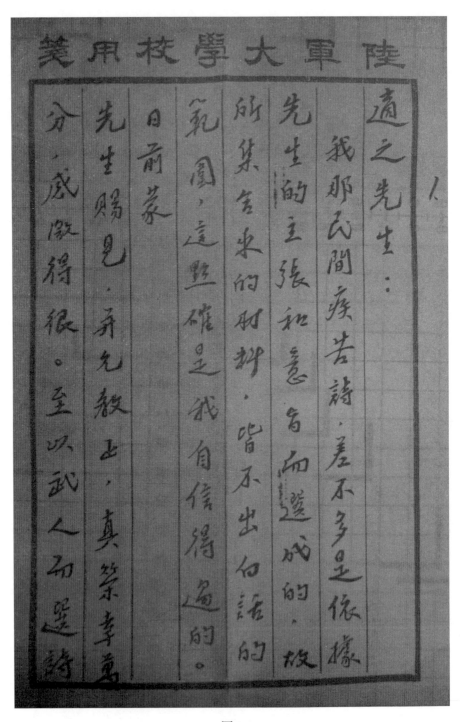

適之先生：

我那民間疾苦詩，差不多是依據先生的主張和意旨而選成的，故所集舍來的材料，皆不出白話的範圍，這點確是我有信得過的。

日前蒙先生賜見，弄兄教正，真榮幸萬分，感激得很。至以武人而選詩

圖1

适之先生：

我那《民间疾苦诗》，差不多是依据先生的主张和意旨而选成的，故所集合来的材料，皆不出白话的范围，这点确是我自信得过的。

日前蒙

先生赐见，并允教正，真荣幸万分，感激得很。至以武人而选诗，

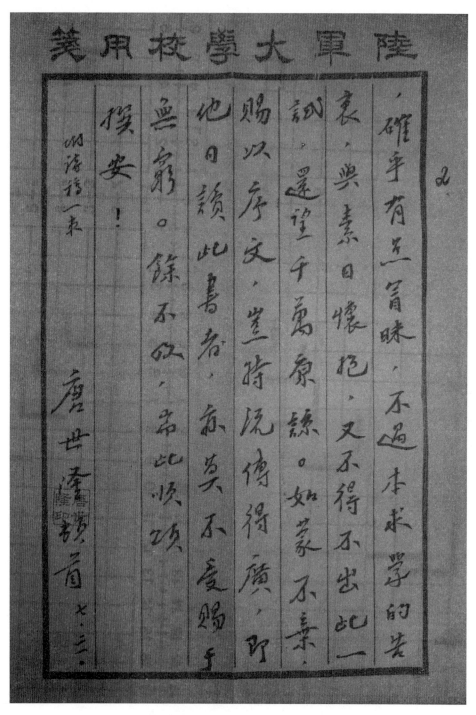

圖 2

確乎有點冒昧,不過本求學的苦衷,與素日懷抱,又不得不出此一試,還望千萬原諒。如蒙不棄,賜以序文,豈特流傳得廣,即他日讀此書者,亦莫不受賜于無窮。餘不及,耑此,順頌
撰安!
　　坿詩稿一束
唐世隆　頓首
七．二一．

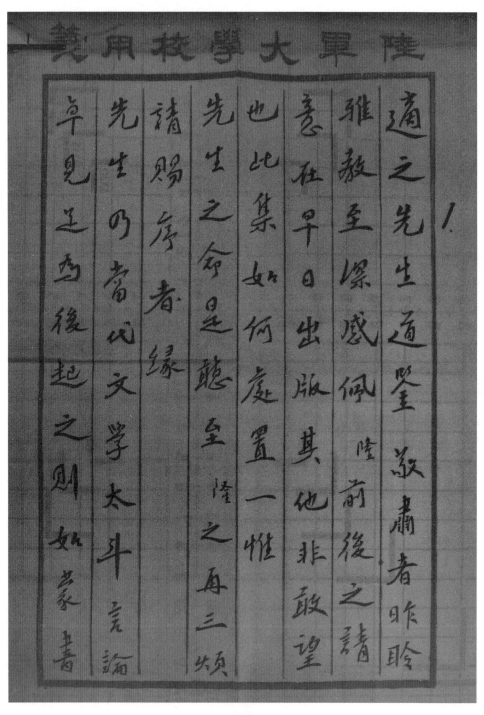

圖3

適之先生道鑒：

敬肅者，昨聆雅教，至深感佩。隆前後之請，意在早日出版，其他非敢望也。此集如何處置，一惟
先生之命是聽，至隆之再三煩請賜序言者，緣
先生乃當代文學太斗，言論卓見，足爲後起之則，如蒙書

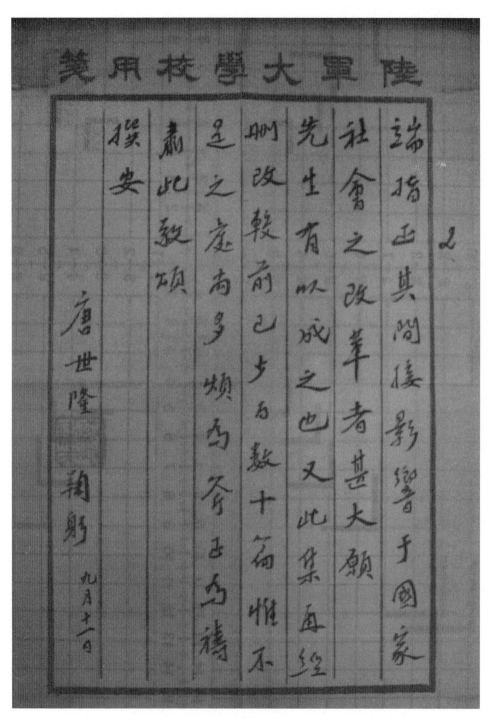

圖4

端指正，其間接影響于國家社會之改革者甚大，願
先生有以成之也。又此集再經刪改，較前已少百數十篇，惟不足之處尚多，煩
爲斧正爲禱。肅此，敬頌

  撰安。

唐世隆　鞠躬
九月十一日

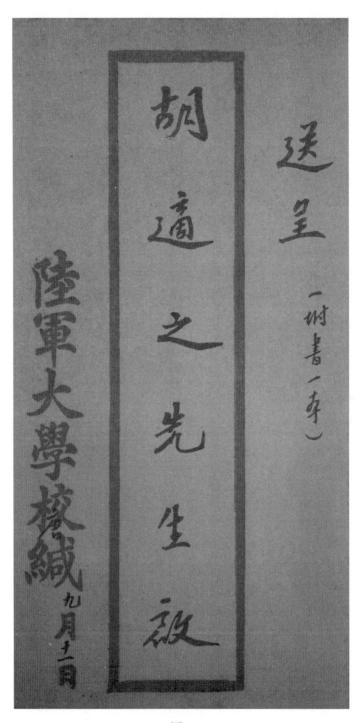

圖5

陶孟和致胡適（一九二〇年十一月十二日）

  此信發現於 *Hilda Lessways* 一書中，信末所署日期無年代，書中所夾另一封高夢旦致蔣夢麟、陶孟和書信（見本書第 59—63 頁），日期爲 1920 年 10 月 27 日，信中説："適之先生近狀如何？"此信中"病體如何"，胡適 1920 年 9 月曾生病，或同指此事，高夢旦致陶孟和、蔣夢麟那一封信或即此信所轉，故大致推定此信寫於 1920 年。

  陶孟和（1888—1960），原名陶履恭，祖籍浙江紹興，生於天津。幼年就讀於嚴氏家塾。1904 年家塾英文館改爲敬業中學堂，爲該中學師範班學生。1906 年，敬業中學堂建新校於南開，改稱南開學校，爲南開學校第一屆師範班畢業生。不久以官費留學日本東京高等師範學校，1909 年畢業後赴英國倫敦大學留學，專攻社會學。1914—1926 年任北京大學教授，曾任教務長。1926 年創建社會調查所，任所長。1930 年與孫本文等發起成立中國社會學社。1934 年該所與中央研究院社會科學研究所合併，任所長。1949 年參加新政協，中華人民共和國成立後任中國科學院副院長兼聯絡局局長、社會研究所所長。著有《社會與教育》《北平生活費之分析》等。

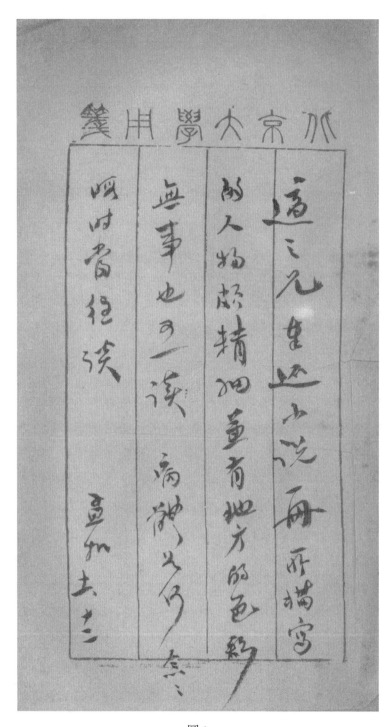

圖 1

適之兄：

奉還小説一册，所描寫的人物頗精細，兼有地方的色彩，無事也可一讀。病體如何，念念。暇時當往談。

孟和

十一，十二

陶孟和致奚湞

此信發現於 *The New Motherhood* 一書中。此書出版於 1922 年，則此信應寫於 1922 年之後。

奚湞（1899—？），字沅君，江蘇南匯人。1919 年入協和女子大學英文系，次年 3 月與王蘭等成爲北京大學一批旁聽生。1923 年畢業於北京大學英文系。曾加入寰球中國學生會。

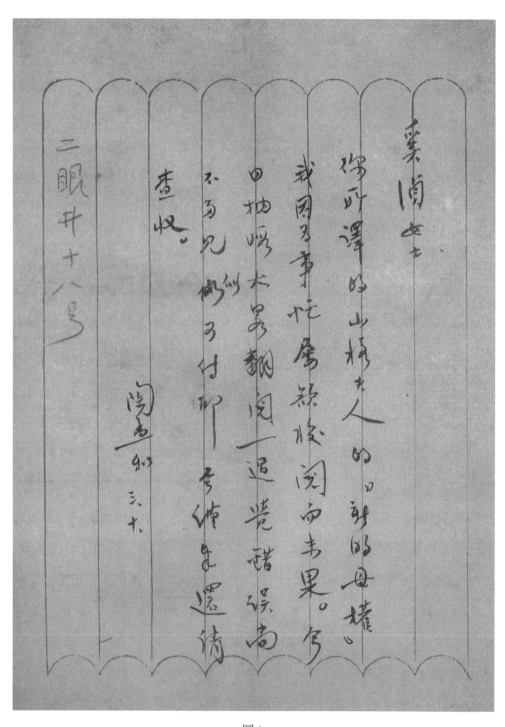

圖1

奚湞女士：

　　你所譯的山格夫人的《新的母權》，我因爲事忙，屢欲校閱而未果。今日抽暇大略翻閱一過，覺錯誤尚不多見，似可付印，今謹奉還，請查收。

　　　　　　　　　　　　　　　　　　　　　　　　　　　陶孟和
　　　　　　　　　　　　　　　　　　　　　　　　　　　三,十

汪敬熙致胡適（一九四四年十二月三日）

此信發現於 Men of Science in America 一書中。

汪敬熙（1893—1968），字緝齋，山東濟南人。1919 年畢業於北京大學經濟系，在校期間曾參加新潮社。次年爲穆藕初資助留學的六位北大畢業生之一，赴美國約翰·霍普金斯大學，攻讀心理學和生理學，1923 年獲博士學位。次年回國，任河南中州大學心理學教授。一年後赴美繼續研究，1927 年回國，任廣州中山大學心理學教授。1931—1934 年任北京大學心理學教授，主持建立神經生理學實驗室。1934 年任中央研究院心理研究所專任研究員兼所長。1946 年任北京大學動物系主任，次年任聯合國文教組織自然科學處國際科學合作組主任。1948 年當選中央研究院院士。1953 年赴美，先後任約翰·霍普金斯大學、威斯康星大學教授。1968 年病逝於麥迪遜。

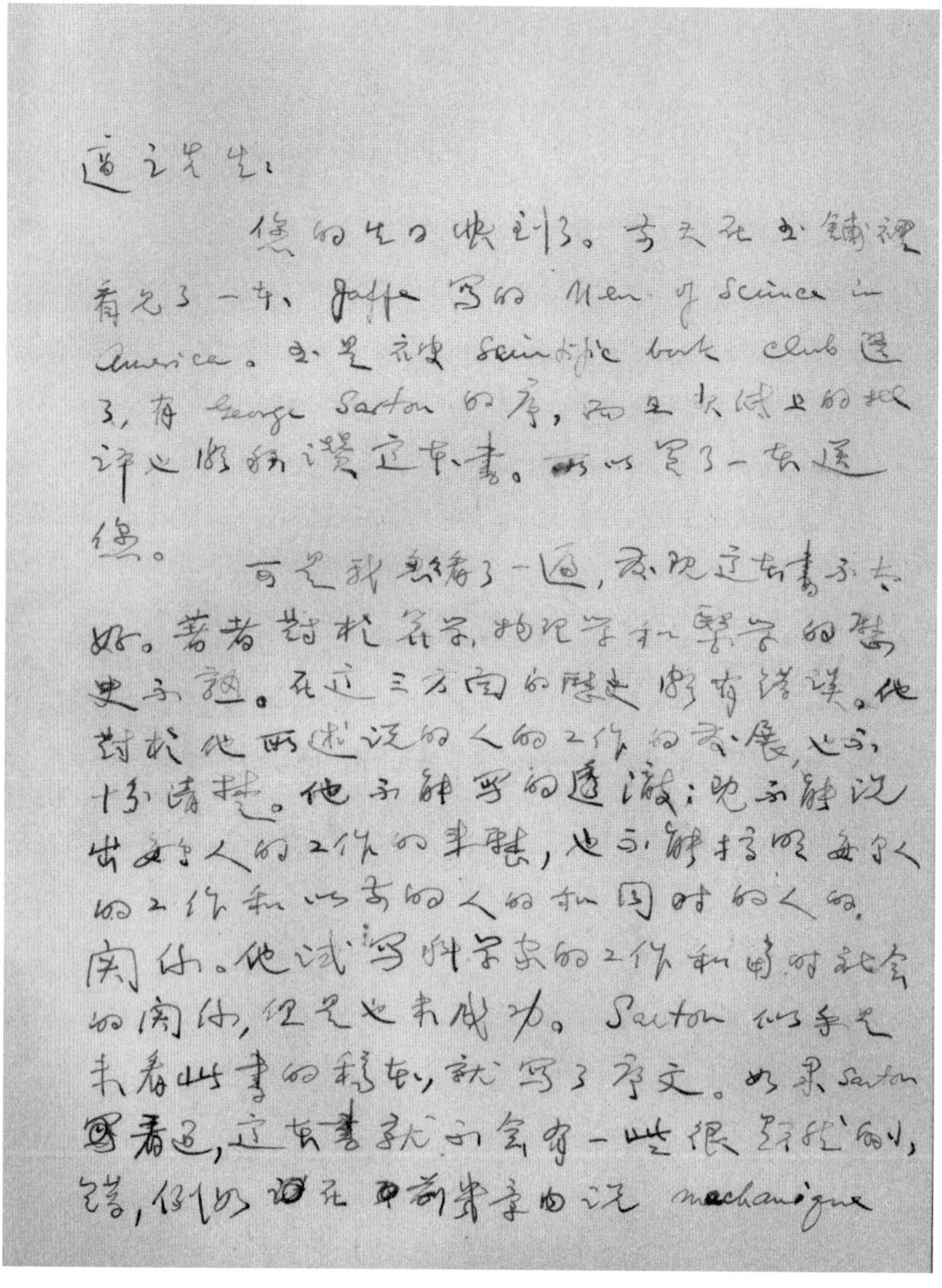

適之先生：

您的七日收到了。方才在书铺裡看见了一本 Jaffe 写的 Men of Science in America。这是被 Scientific book club 选了，有 George Sarton 的序，而且封底上的评也很热心讚这本书。所以买了一本送您。

可是我急读了一遍，不觉这本书不大好。著者对於名字，地名字和数字的历史不熟。在这三方面的历史都有错误。他对於他所述说的人的工作的发展，也不十分清楚。他不能写的透澈；也不能说出好人的工作的丰裕，也不能搪明每个人的工作和以前的人和同时的人的关係。他试写科学家的工作和同时社会的关係，但是也未成功。Sarton 似乎是未看此书的稿初，就写了序文。如果 Sarton 要看这，这本书就不会有一些很明显的例，错，例如书中常常写的话 mechanique

图1

適之先生：

您的生日快到了。前天在書鋪裡看見了一本 Jaffe 寫的 *Men of Science in America*。書是被 Scientific Book Club 選了，有 George Sarton 的序，而且報紙上的批評也頗稱讚這本書。所以買了一本送您。

可是我匆匆看了一遍，發現這本書不太好。著者對於算學、物理學和醫學的歷史不熟。在這三方面的歷史頗有錯誤。他對於他所述說的人的工作的發展，也不十分清楚。他不能寫的透澈：既不能說出每個人的工作的來歷，也不能搞明每個人的工作和以前的人的和同時的人的關係。他試寫科學家的工作和當時社會的關係，但是也未成功。Sarton 似乎是未看此書的稿本，就寫了序文。如果 Sarton 看過，這本書就不會有一些很顯然的小錯，例如在前幾章內說 *Machanique*

Celestin 之 Lagrange 為作的，而孔後享盛名，说出这书的真著者，Laplace。其他類似的，差是這种重要的錯誤不少。

不過由这本書可以看出，美國的科學先有 descriptive 科學，而後有 experimental 科學。並且也可以看出，美國西部科學之发達。Jaffe 舉的四了现在的美國科學家都是在 California。Morgan 和 Hubble 在 Pasadena 附近；Evans 和 Lawrence 在 Berkeley。

國内战事情形，報上消息，均不好。日來甚為關心之。在此地工作再做到一月，下月即須去 Chicago。

您在岭仲講演，此否？元任林人二兄處請先问？見林人二时，請代为致意。

敬頌 道安

廿三，十二，三

書不及另上。

Celeste 是 Lagrange 作的，而在後幾章內說出這書的真著者，Laplace。其他類似的，並且更重要的錯頗不少。

　　不過由這本書可以看出，美國的科學是先有 descriptive 科學，而後有 experimental 科學。並且也可以看出，美國西部科學日見發達。Jaffe 舉的四個現在的美國科學家都是在 California。Morgan 和 Hubble 在 Pasadena 附近；Evans 和 Lawrence 在 Berkeley。

　　國內戰事消息，政治消息，均不好。日來苦悶之至。在此地工作正做到一半，下月即須去 Chicago。

　　您在哈佛講演，忙不？元任、樹人二兄想常見面？見樹人兄時，請代爲致意。

敬熙謹上
卅三，十二，三

書另包寄上。

王季同致胡適（一九四三年十一月十八日）

此信發現於《因明入正理論摸象》一書中。

王季同（1875—1948，一説生年不詳），又名季鍇，字孟晉，號小徐，江蘇吳縣人。1895 年畢業於京師同文館，1903 年隨蔡元培組織拒俄同志會，主編《俄事警聞》。1904 年任教於上海愛國女學。後任同文館算學教習。1909 年被清政府派赴英國任駐歐洲留學生監督署隨員，後轉入英吉利電器公司和德國西門子電機廠研究實習。回國後曾任職於鎮江大照電氣公司、吳淞中國鐵工廠，在上海創辦大效機器廠。曾任教於北京大學。曾任中國教育會董事。在電機工程理論與製造方面均有很多成績。1928 年任中央研究院工學研究所專任研究員。1929 年出席日本東京萬國工業會議、世界動力會議東京會議。晚年研究佛學，著有《佛法與科學之比較》《佛法省要》《因明入正理論摸象》等。

適之先生道鑒久濶為悵小兒守競返國詢悉
國故學史大綱下編理十餘年未竟之件起人遽聞同深快慰惟聞十餘
年前足下為寫中國哲學史大綱下編而讀佛書讀不得要領於
是佛教與禪宗乃至受禪宗影響而產生之宋明諸儒哲學遂皆無從寫起而
不得不擱筆今事過十數年又提筆續寫意旨
頗會歉然尚未久曾副足下左駐美大使任上用遊駐之國之都會應彼邦之圓
倩之請屢作種: 公開演講惟宣言拒絕演講佛法與辦學之時此足下既不能
把握佛法綱要旨則大著下編帳有滿紙敷衍文章以清代應奉此第三場之
之不知佛法玅無於十三年前序批著佛法與辦學之一場文字六減色不少矣示左崔眉發
此等一發不中前功畫棄之文字李勸足下還是不寫為妙若足下決計完成
此大箸則請放棄具西學格歐美入為主之惟物成見一依弟之勸則不可保
證足下寫一兩最有精彩之中國哲學史大綱下編也蓋一切成見即佛法政謂我
法二執非但為一切有情流轉生死不得解脱不成佛道之障礙亦為一切學共
做其門傍戶穿鑿附會對於一切學術思想但如隨聲附和亦如未有真知灼見之谟
聯其實十餘年前弟寫佛法與科學等篇時於佛法如減六甚幼稚故獵涉佛書
遠不逮足下之博真至今上六高未必能與足下之抗衡惟弟夙生薰習得禪宗根
發清季又受楊仁老鉗鎚故能寫佛法與科學及針對
序等顛撲不破之弘法文字然其時第尚未正式
做過久宗工夫即於尊序詁足下證適這種真現量沒有第因尚未證適
不敢犯妄言之戒惟近做宗門工夫兩年來確有所得者龍于逭禪即有

適之先生道鑒：

久闊爲悵。小兒守競返國，詢悉足下稅駕紐約，繼續寫《中國哲學史大綱》下編，理十餘年未竟之緒。故人遙聞，同深快慰。惟聞十餘年前，足下爲寫《中國哲學史大綱》下編而讀佛書。讀佛書不得要領，於是佛教與禪宗，乃至受禪宗影響而產生之宋明諸儒哲學，皆無從寫起，而不得不擱筆。今事逾十稔，重又捉筆續寫，意者足下之於佛法近年有所領會歟？然未久曾聞足下在駐美大使任上，周遊駐在國各都會，應彼邦各團體之請，屢作種種公開演講，惟宣言拒絕演講佛法云云。果爾，則足下今日之不知佛法，殆猶無殊於十三年前序拙箸《佛法與科學》之時也。足下既不能把握佛法要旨，則大箸下編惟有滿紙敷衍文章，如清代應舉者第三場之五道空策而已，非但毫無精彩，且恐帶累頭二場文字亦減色不少矣。忝在舊友，此等一發不中，前功盡棄之文字，奉勸足下還是不寫爲妙。若足下決計完成此大箸，則請放棄其西學於歐美先入爲主之唯物成見，一依弟勸，則弟可保證足下寫一冊最有精彩之《中國哲學史大綱》下編也。蓋一切成見，即佛法所謂"我法二執"，非但爲一切有情流轉生死，不得解脫，不成佛道之障礙，亦爲一切學者依門傍戶，穿鑿附會，對於一切學術思想但知隨聲附和，未有真知灼見之障礙。其實十餘年前弟寫《佛法與科學》等篇時，於佛法知識亦甚幼稚，所涉獵佛書遠不逮足下之博。直至今日亦尚未必能與足下抗衡。惟弟夙生薰得禪宗根器，清季又受楊仁老鉗鎚，故能寫《佛法與科學》，及針對尊序咄咄逼人之自序等顛撲不破之弘法文字。然其時弟雖篤信佛法是真理，却尚未正式做過各宗工夫。即如尊序詰弟證過這種真現量沒有，弟固尚未證過，不敢犯妄言之戒。惟近做宗門工夫兩年來，確有所得。昔龍牙遁禪師有

頌曰學道如鑽火逢煙未可休直待金星現歸家始到頭後來神秀禪師別
前頌曰山僧即不然學道如鑽火逢煙便可休莫待金星現燒殺令勤
維未臻前頌空星現後頌便休之境界但確已如鑽火逢煙因此書於春節援
筆寫佛傳省要一小冊裝滿弘法因願寫出後常不愜意再三修改今年
六月將勒出版牟又因近來國内出版事業非常擁擠正分上所刷中歲尾年
頸感能出版耳足下試閱此批著可知吾真語實語而佛傳禪道之為學
宙間唯一真理鐵案難翻也此書價值不知其奧郎一般讀者大概
不免漢共蓋多數人未讀佛書未習科學不知吾所論已少數共能讀佛
書知批著於說忠與大乘佛傳符合和未習科學理論絕對正確而未讀
有此何關係別有少數出堆習科學引證科學理論究
佛書不知佛傳果否如此臉念且當有其先入為主不信佳佛傳之成見反疑
批著為穿鑿附會惟足下飽讀佛書薰習精神此必修德識批著之真德
羅齋滑稽皆印度人等捕風捉影衞鑿空楔之說且根據批著别而佛之
以寫大者不偏必修在學術界故異彩也若足下常不以一見批著為滿之更願
與弟作進一步之切磋則弟之為欽近蓋此也
記誦故今生思想深刻目謂過人而學問淵博不逮足下甚
世多事記誦而少做參究工夫故今生學問淵博過人而思想深刻遜弟一籌
若交接知識兩人皆有裨益也又弟自見楊仁老臨知唯物論似是而非佛傳
確是真理因思當今科學時代學此為不遇楊仁老等大善知識未有不墜

頌曰："學道如鑽火，逢煙未可休，直待金星現，歸家始到頭。"後來神鼎諲禪師別前頌曰："山僧即不然，學道如鑽火，逢煙便可休，莫待金星現，燒額又燒頭。"今弟雖未臻前頌"金星現"、後頌"便休"之境界，但確已如鑽火逢煙。因此去春即援筆寫《佛法省要》一小冊，冀滿弘法夙願。寫出後尚不愜意，再三修改。今年六月始勒成定本。又因近來國內出版事業非常擠軋，至今在印刷中，歲尾年頭或能出版耳。足下試閱此拙箸，可知句句真語、實語，而佛法禪道之爲宇宙間唯一真理，鐵案難翻也。然此書價值，弟雖自知甚審，而一般讀者大都不免漠然。蓋多數人未讀佛書，未習科學，不知所云無論已。少數讀者雖讀佛書，知拙箸所說悉與大乘佛法符合，而未習科學，不知其與近代科學理論究有如何關係；別有少數讀者，雖習科學，知其所引證科學理論絕對正確，而未讀佛書，不知佛法果否如此脗合。且尚有其先入爲主，不信任佛法之成見，反疑拙箸爲穿鑿附會。惟足下飽讀佛書，兼精科學，必能認識拙箸之真價值，知其絕不類古人楊德祖言武王伐紂以妲己賜周公，近人胡懷琛言墨翟、禽滑釐皆印度人等捕風捉影、嚮壁虛構之談。且根據拙箸引而伸之，以寫大箸下編，必能在學術界放異彩也。若足下尚不以一見拙箸爲滿足，更願與弟作進一步之切磋，則弟尤爲歡迎。蓋弟夙世多做宗門參究工夫，而少事記誦，故今生思想深刻自謂過人，而學問淵博不逮足下遠甚。足下則夙世多事記誦，而少做參究工夫，故今生學問淵博過人，而思想深刻遜弟一籌。若交換知識，兩人皆有裨益也。又弟自見楊仁老，始知唯物論似是而非，佛法確是真理。因思當今科學時代學者，苟不遇楊仁老等大善知識，未有不蹉過唯一真理之佛法希誤信似是而非之唯物論故發願專對科學家弘揚佛法然年不善外國語文偶以英語寫教理之科論文尚可敷衍至於文哲等科論文不得不敬謝不敏且老夫耄矣弘法之作亦不復能多做故亟擬將自己心得傳諸年富力強之知友朋輩中能以英語從事著作比雅足下與林語堂先生命足下於佛家言已有根柢尤適合弟之理想倘足下不對此發生興趣則弟之愉快匪可言喻也又拙著佛法省要雖為未出版但近年曾著因明入正理論撰像山由商務印書館出版此書雖於佛法教理未有詳悉之討論然概括佛法之方法論由此可見佛法談非異於一切宗教是真理而非迷信非無因巴話附呈一冊乞指教並請撰安

弟周〇啟

卅二、二、十八

過唯一真理之佛法，而誤信似是而非之唯物論者，故發願專對科學家弘揚佛法。然弟不善外國語文，偶以英語寫數理工科論文尚可敷衍，至於文哲等科論文，不得不敬謝不敏。且老夫耄矣，弘法工作亦不復能多做，故亟擬將自己心得傳諸年富力強之知友。朋輩中能以英語從事箸作者，推足下與林語堂先生，而足下於佛家言已有根柢，尤適合弟之理想。倘足下能對此發生興趣，則弟之愉快匪可言喻也。又拙箸《佛法省要》雖尚未出版，但近年曾箸《因明入正理論摸象》，已由商務印書館出版。此書雖於佛法教理未有詳悉之討論，然實概括佛法之方法論，由此可見佛法所以異於一切宗教，是真理而非迷信，非無因也。茲附呈一冊，乞指教，並請
撰安

弟同手啟
卅二, 十一, 十八

王静如致胡適

此信發現於《河西字藏經雕版考》中，但此文發表於史語所單刊甲種之八《西夏研究》第一輯中，1932年出版，而非信中所説第三輯，《西夏研究》第三輯爲史語所單刊甲種之十三，1933年出版。因王静如1933年已至歐洲訪學，故此信有可能寫於1932年12月18日。

王静如（1903—1990），原名振宇，號静之，筆名菲烈，河北深澤人。1923年畢業於直隸第六中學，旋考入北京民國大學語文系。1927年考入清華大學研究院，師從趙元任，1929年畢業，同年任中央研究院歷史語言研究所助理研究員。1933年赴歐洲，在法、英、德等國學習研究語言學和漢學。1936年回國，任國立北平研究院史學研究所研究員、中法大學教授兼文史系主任，並兼任輔仁大學史學系、燕京大學中文系、中國大學文學院教授。1950年任中國科學院考古研究所研究員。1953年任中央民族學院研究部教授。1958年任中國科學院民族研究所研究員兼學術委員。1978年任中國社會科學院民族研究所研究員、學術委員。曾任國家文物局歷史文物咨議委員會委員、中國民族研究會常務委員、中國語言學會理事等職。著有《西夏研究》（三輯，1936年獲法國院士會銘文學院東方學"茹蓮獎金"）、《西夏文漢藏譯音釋略》等。

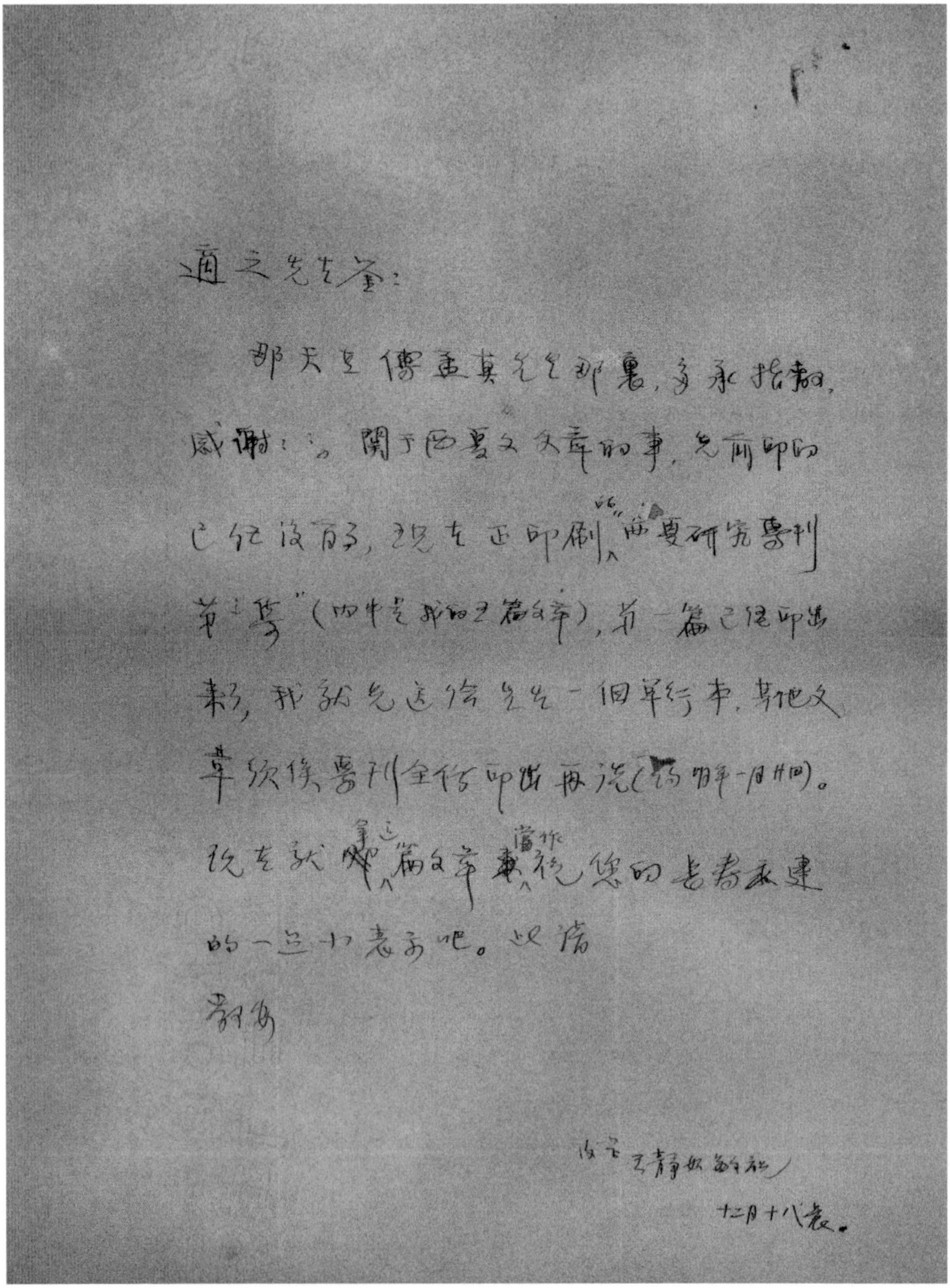

適之先生鑒：

那天在傅孟真先生那裏，多承指教，感謝！關于西夏文文章的事，先前印的已忘沒有了，現在正印倒"西夏研究專刊第二号"（四中是我的三篇文章），第一篇已經印出來了，我就先送給先生一個單行本，其他文章須俟專刊全印出再送（约卅一日出版）。現在就以這篇文章來作當作祝您的壽來達的一點小意思吧。此請

釣安

後學 王靜如敬上
十二月十八夜。

圖1

適之先生鑒：

　　那天在傅孟真先生那裏，多承指教，感謝感謝。關於西夏文文章的事，先前印的已經沒有了，現在正印刷的"西夏研究專刊第三集"（內中是我的五篇文章），第一篇已經印出來了，我就先送給先生一個單行本，其他文章須俟專刊全份印出再說（約明年一月廿四）。現在就拿這篇文章當作祝您的長壽永建的一點小表示吧。此請

教安

後學　王靜如敬祝
十二月十八晨

王世杰致胡適（一九三五年三月八日）

此信發現於《改進中國農業計劃草案》一書中。

王世杰（1891—1981），初名躞廷，字雪艇。湖北崇陽人。1910年考入天津北洋大學採礦冶金科。辛亥革命爆發後，返武昌任都督府秘書。1913年赴英國留學，入倫敦政治經濟學院，1917年獲法學學士學位，同年轉入巴黎大學，1920年獲法學博士學位。同年回國，任北京大學法科教授，1924年與胡適等人創辦《現代評論》。1927年任南京國民政府法制局局長。1928年任武漢大學校長，1932年兼任湖北省教育廳廳長。1933年出任南京國民政府教育部長，1938年改任中央政治委員會外交專門委員會主任委員，名列國防最高會議委員。後任軍事委員會參事室主任、國民黨中央宣傳部長、國民參政會秘書長等職。1945年任南京國民政府外交部長，1948年12月辭職。1948年3月當選中央研究院院士。1949年末去臺灣，歷任臺灣國民黨"總統府"秘書長、"行政院政務委員"、"中央研究院"院長、"總統府資政"等職。1981年4月在臺北病逝。著有《比較憲法》《中國奴婢制度史》等。

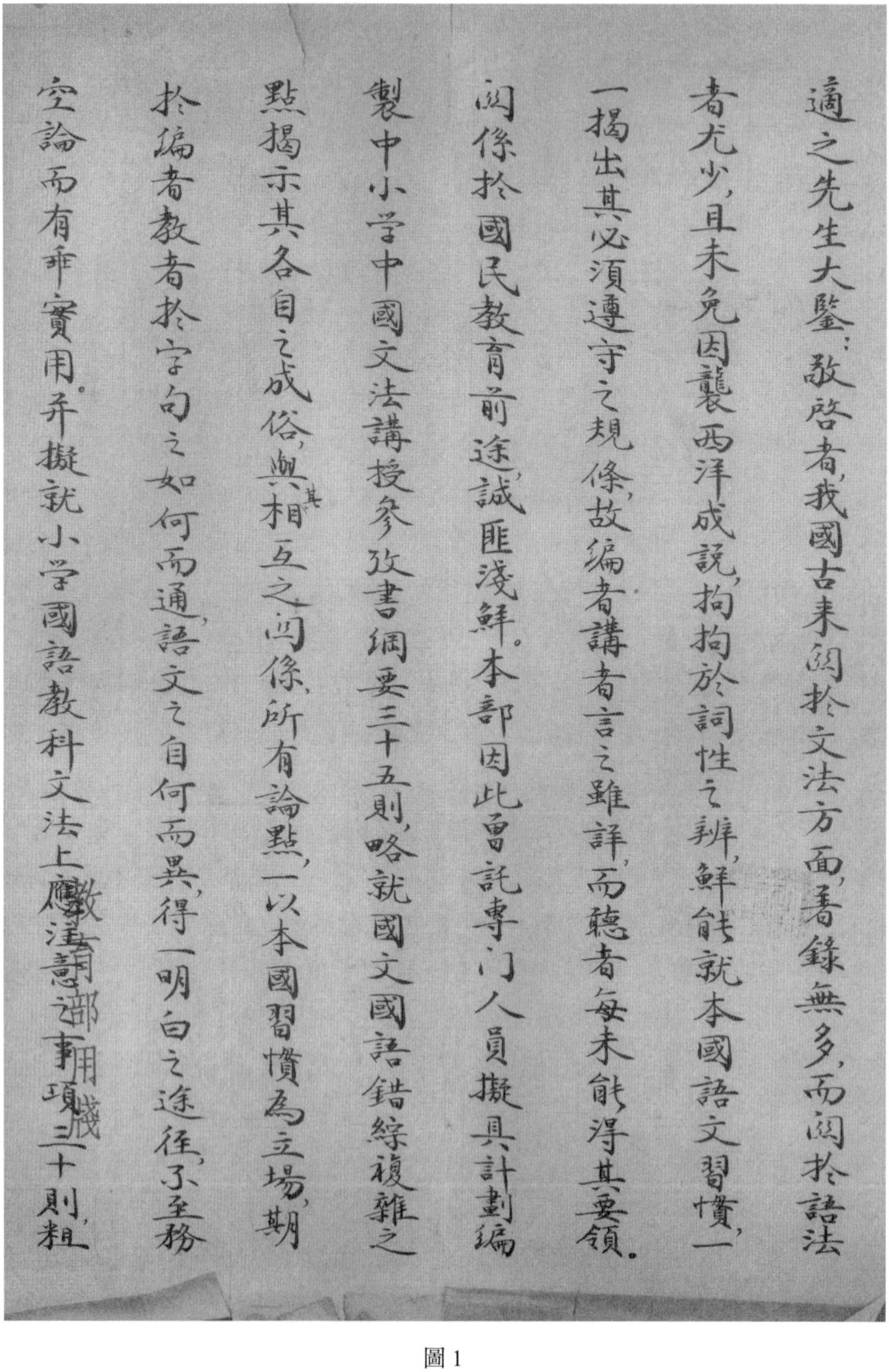

適之先生大鑒：敬啓者，我國古來關於文法方面，著錄無多，而關於語法者尤少，且未免因襲西洋成說，拘拘於詞性之辨，鮮能就本國語文習慣一一揭出其必須遵守之規條，故編者講者言之雖詳，而聽者每未能得其要領。關係於國民教育前途誠匪淺鮮。本部因此曾託專門人員擬具計劃編製中小學中國文法講授參攷書綱要三十五則，略就國文國語錯綜複雜之點揭示其各自之成俗，與其相互之關係，所有論點一以本國習慣為立場，期於編者教者於字句之如何而通語文之自何而異，得一明白之途徑，不至務空論而有乖實用。并擬就小學國語教科文法上酌注意事項三十則，粗

圖1

適之先生大鑒：

敬啓者，我國古來關於文法方面，著録無多，而關於語法者尤少，且未免因襲西洋成説，拘拘於詞性之辨，鮮能就本國語文習慣，一一揭出其必須遵守之規條，故編者講者言之雖詳，而聽者每未能得其要領。關係於國民教育前途，誠匪淺鮮。本部因此曾託專門人員擬具計劃編製中小學中國文法講授參攷書綱要三十五則，略就國文國語錯綜複雜之點揭示其各自之成俗，與其相互之關係。所有論點，一以本國習慣爲立場，期於編者教者於字句之如何而通，語文之自何而異，得一明白之途徑，不至務空論而有乖實用。并擬就小學國語教科文法上應注意之事項三十則，粗

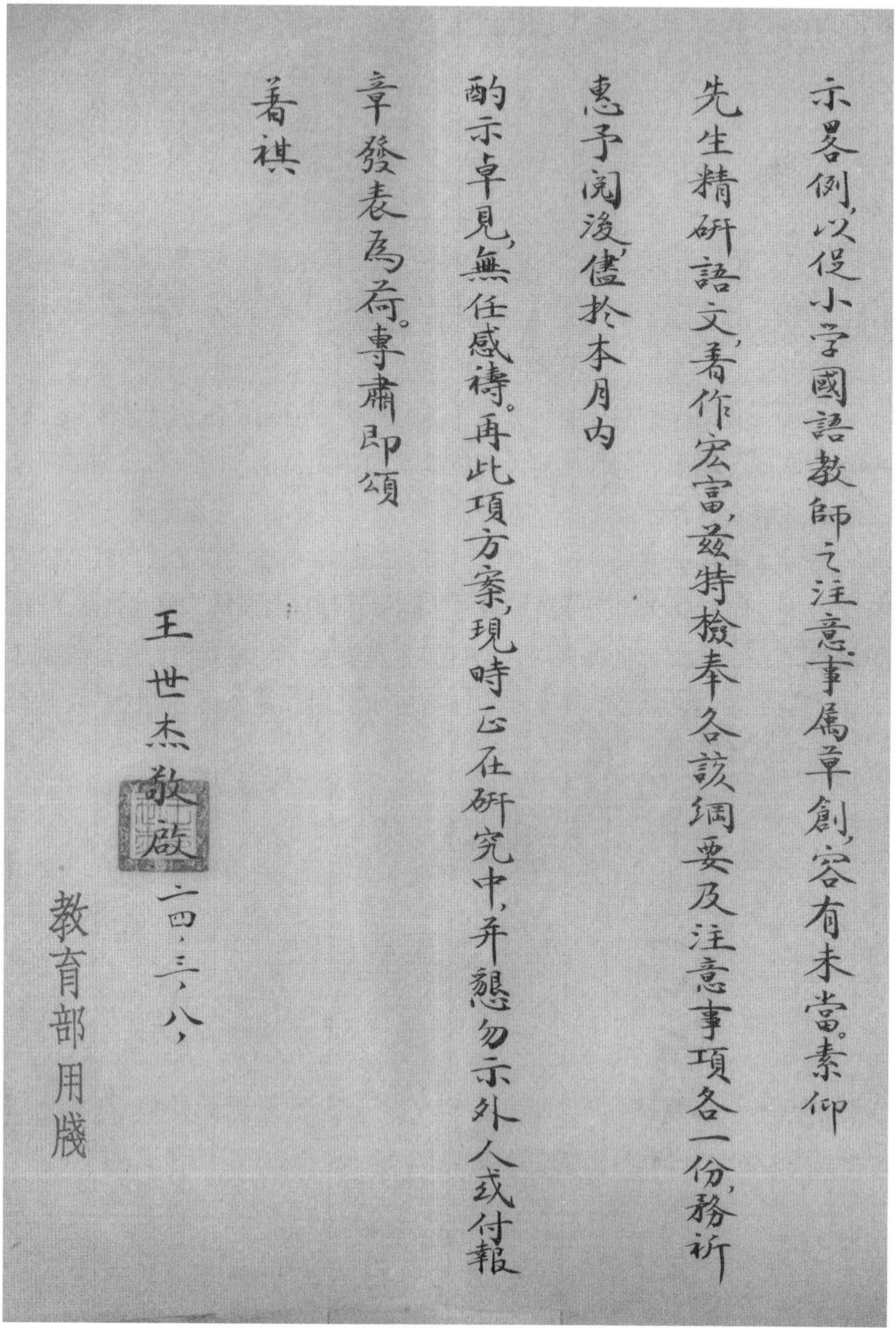

示器例，以促小學國語教師之注意事項，草創容有未當，素仰

先生精研語文，善作宏言，茲特檢奉各該綱要及注意事項各一份，務祈

惠予閱後儘於本月內

酌示卓見，無任感禱。再此項方案，現時正在研究中，并懇勿示外人或付報章發表為荷。專肅即頌

著祺

王世杰 敬啟 一四·三·八

教育部用牋

圖 2

示暑例，以促小學國語教師之注意。事屬草創，容有未當。素仰先生精研語文，著作宏富，茲特檢奉各該綱要及注意事項各一份，務祈惠予閱後，儘於本月內酌示卓見，無任感禱。再此項方案，現時正在研究中，并懇勿示外人或付報章發表爲荷。專肅即頌
著祺

              王世杰敬啓
              二四,三,八

王小航致胡適（一九三一年春——一九三三年六月）

此組信件發現於三種書籍之中，皆不署時間。其中圖1—圖4發現於《小航文存》（北京大學圖書館典藏號SB/817.87/1092），圖5發現於另一部《小航文存》（北京大學圖書館典藏號SB/817.87/1092/C2），圖6—圖8發現於《增訂三體石經時代辨誤》一書中。兩種《小航文存》皆爲朱印本，即信中所稱"紅樣本"，當爲正式印刷之前的校對樣本。

據《小航文存》前胡適序，其於1930年9月至北平後借住羊宜賓胡同任叔永家中，"十月八日，有一位白頭老人來訪"，即王小航，則二人相識於1930年10月。1930年11月28日，胡適舉家遷至北平，寓居於米糧庫胡同。據信中所述，並參徐一士《談王小航》一文，圖1圖2之信或爲徐氏代轉，又"久擬赴米糧庫未遂也"，則時間應在胡適一家遷居北平之後，或在1931年春。圖3信中小字曰："託徐一士時尚不知米糧庫住址也。"則時間當在圖1圖2信件之後。又"乞題跋數語"，而胡適序末所署時間爲"民國二十年五月三十一日夜"，即1931年5月31日，則此信或寫於1931年5月31日之前。圖4信件內容與"米糧庫"相關，故繫於其後。圖5信中稱"天氣奇熱"，又稱"《小航文存》卷二後添一篇"，則隨信所附之《小航文存》或爲再作修訂後的另一樣稿，故此信或寫於1931年夏天。

發現於《增訂三體石經時代辨誤》中之信件，稱"此類書弟原看作沒用的緒餘，所以未肯呈正"，或寫於贈其他著作之後，姑繫於此。

王小航（1859—1933），原名照，字黎青，號小航，又號水東，河北寧河人。10 歲從塾師學詩文。1877 年入書院。1891 年中舉人。1894 年取進士，授翰林院庶吉士。適逢中日甲午戰爭，在家鄉蘆臺辦鄉團。1895 年赴北京應散館試，改授禮部主事。1897 年回蘆臺創辦小學堂，同年冬，回京供職。翌年 3 月，與徐世昌、李石曾等在北京設立八旗奉直第一號小學堂。1898 年戊戌變法期間，積極參與維新活動，多次上書言事，得光緒帝讚賞，擢四品京堂候補。戊戌變法失敗後，與康有爲等逃亡日本。1900 年春潛行歸國，回天津隱居，仿日本片假名創"官話字母"，著《官話合聲字母》，得吳汝綸讚賞。1903 年在北京設立官話字母義塾，出版注音《三字經》《百家姓》《千字文》和《官話字母義塾叢書》。1904 年春，以戊戌餘黨向提督衙門投案自首，不久獲赦出獄。1905 年在保定創辦拼音官話書報社，出版供新軍學習字母用的《對兵説話》，次年遷北京，並舉辦官話字母第一號義塾，共辦 24 號，創辦《拼音官話報》。1910 年攝政王載澧嚴禁官話字母傳習，封閉官話書報社，遂被迫避往江蘇。1913 年，北京政府教育部召開讀音統一會，被選爲副會長，不久辭職。段祺瑞當政時，一度入幕，不久離去。1923 年後從事著述。1927 年撰《方家園雜咏紀事》，揭露清廷内幕。1933 年 6 月 1 日病逝。著作大部分收在《水東集》中，另有《小航文存》。

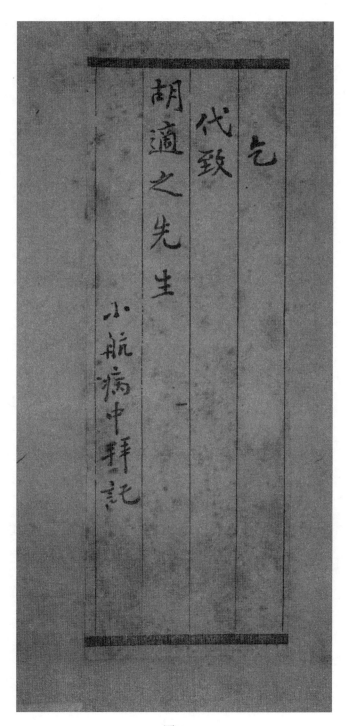

圖1

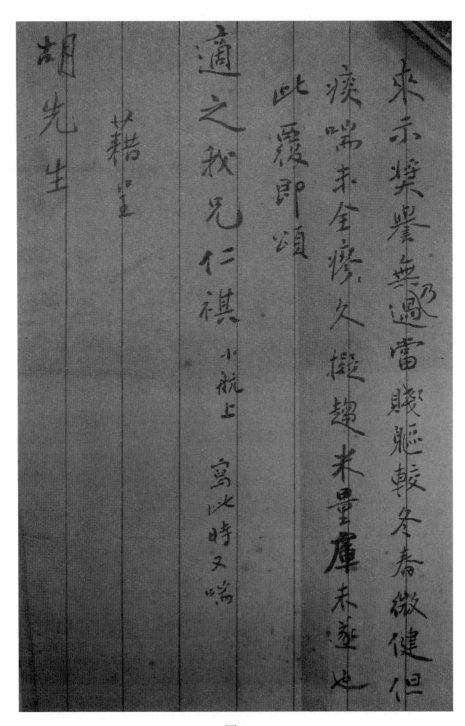

圖 2

乞
　　　代致
胡適之先生
　　　　　　　　　　　　　　　　　小航病中拜託

　　來示獎譽無乃過當。賤軀較冬春微健，但痰喘未全瘳。久擬趨米量庫未遂也。
　　此覆，即頌
適之我兄仁祺
　　　　　　　　　　　　　　　　　　　　小航上
　　　　　　　　　　　　　　　　　　　寫此時又喘

　　藉呈
胡先生

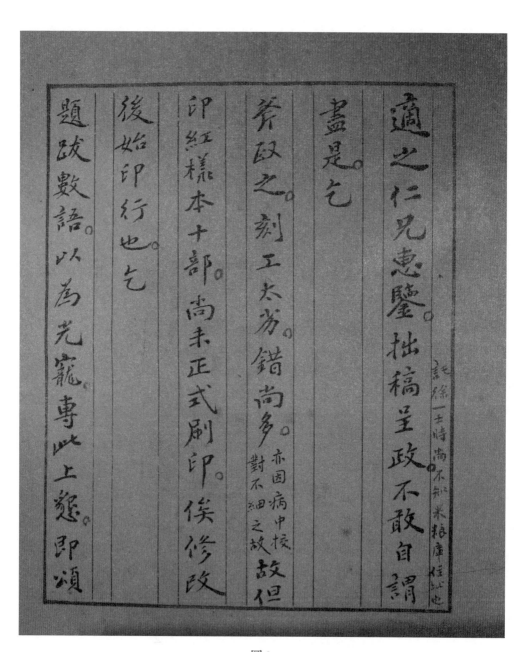

圖 3

適之仁兄惠鑒：

　　拙稿呈政（託徐一士時尚不知米糧庫住址也），不敢自謂盡是。乞斧政之。刻工太劣，錯尚多。（亦因病中校對不細之故。）故但印紅樣本十部，尚未正式刷印。俟修改後始印行也。乞題跋數語，以爲光寵。專此上懇，即頌

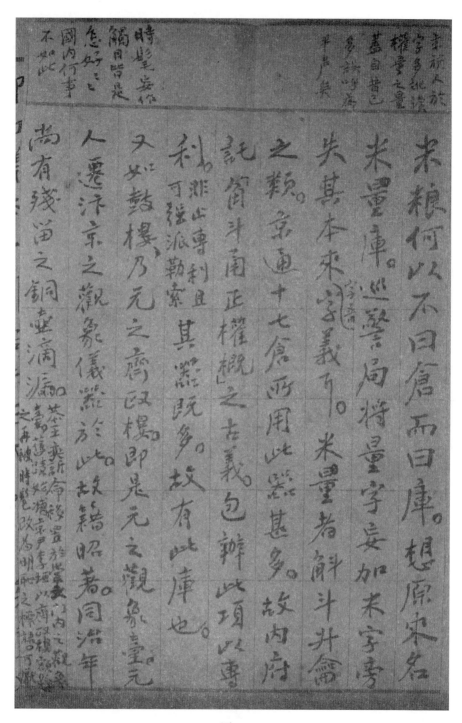

圖4

米糧何以不曰倉而曰庫，想原來名米量庫，巡警局將量字妄加米字旁，失其本來字音字義耳。（京旗人於字多訛讀，權量之量蓋自昔已多誤呼爲平聲矣。）米量者，斛斗升龠之類。京通十七倉所用此器甚多。故內府託"角斗甬正權概"之古義，包辦此項以專利。（非止專利，且可強派勒索。）其器既多，故有此庫也。

又如鼓樓，乃元之齊政樓，即是元之觀象臺。元人遷汴京之觀象儀器於此，故籍昭著。同治年尚有殘留之銅壺滴漏。（恭王奕訢命移置於崇文門內之觀象臺，舊蹟始滅。京尹李垣以齊政樓額懸之，再被時髦，改爲明恥之標語，可厭。）（時髦妄作觸目皆是，怎好怎好。國內何事不如此。）

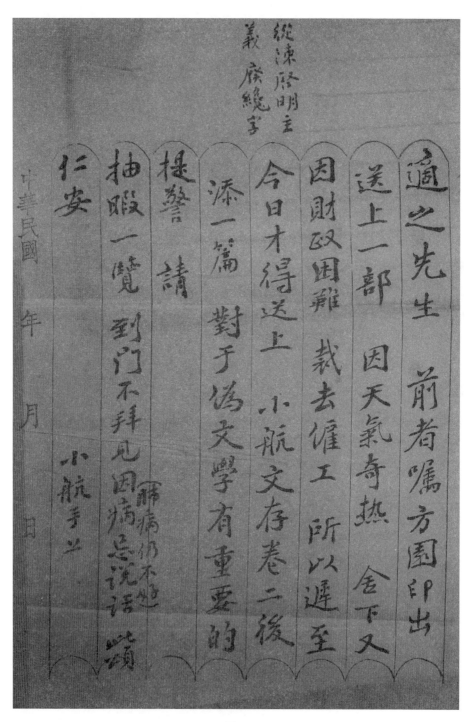

圖5

適之先生：

　　前者囑方園印出，送上一部。因天氣奇熱，舍下又因財政困難，裁去傭工，所以遲至今日才得送上（從陳啓明主義，廢纔字）。《小航文存》卷二後添一篇，對于偽文學有重要的提警。請
抽暇一覽。到門不拜見，因病忌説話（肺病仍不好）。此頌
仁安！

小航手上

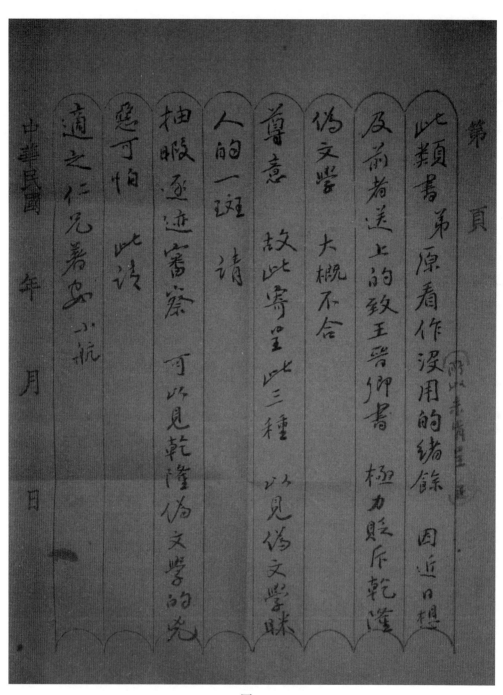

圖6

此類書弟原看作沒用的緒餘（所以未肯呈正）。因近日想及前者送上的致王晉卿書，極力貶斥乾隆僞文學，大概不合
尊意，故此寄呈此三種，以見僞文學眯人的一斑。請
抽暇逐迹審察，可以見乾隆僞文學的兇惡可怕。此請
適之仁兄著安！

小航

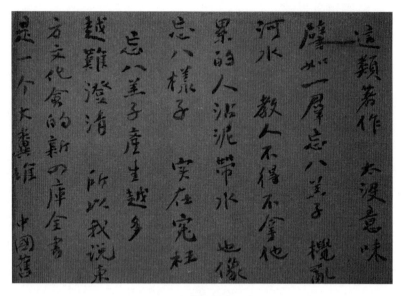

圖 7

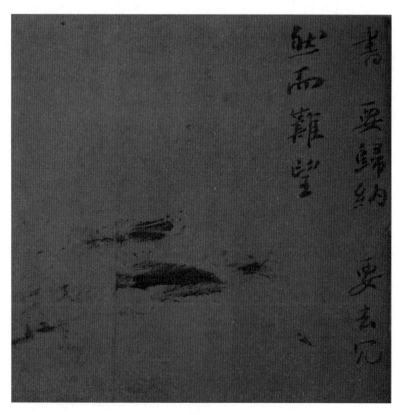

圖 8

這類著作，太没意味。譬如一群忘八羔子，攪亂河水，教人不得不拿他，累的人沾泥帶水，也像忘八樣子，實在冤枉。忘八羔子產生越多，越難澄清，所以我説東方文化會的《新四庫全書》是一個大糞堆，中國舊書，要歸納，要去冗，然而難望。

王孝魚致胡適（一九四五年——一九四八年）

　　此信發現於《老子微》一書中。據信中所述及作者、胡適生平，此信當寫於 1945 年—1948 年間。

　　王孝魚（1900—1981），原名王永祥，字孝魚，以字行，山西榆次人。1917 年考取清華留美預備學校，次年因病輟學，後轉入南開中學。1925 年畢業於南開大學哲學系。次年在張學良部下任文職。1927 年任東北大學歷史系、哲學系講師，後升任教授，同年兼任遼寧省教育廳編輯主任。1932 年任南京中山文化教育館編輯及特約研究員。抗戰時期隱居北平，潛心研究老莊哲學。抗戰勝利後，任東北大學教授，瀋陽《中央日報》主編，瀋陽《和平日報》文史周刊副主編。新中國成立後，任北京蒙藏學院講師。1954 年任中共中央馬列編譯局編審。1958 年後任中華書局哲學組編審。1962—1963 年在北京大學古典文獻專業和中國人民大學哲學系短期講學。"文革"期間受到不公正待遇，被遣返故里。1979 年任職於山西省社會科學院哲學所。主要著作有：《船山學譜》《莊子通疏證》《老子微》等。

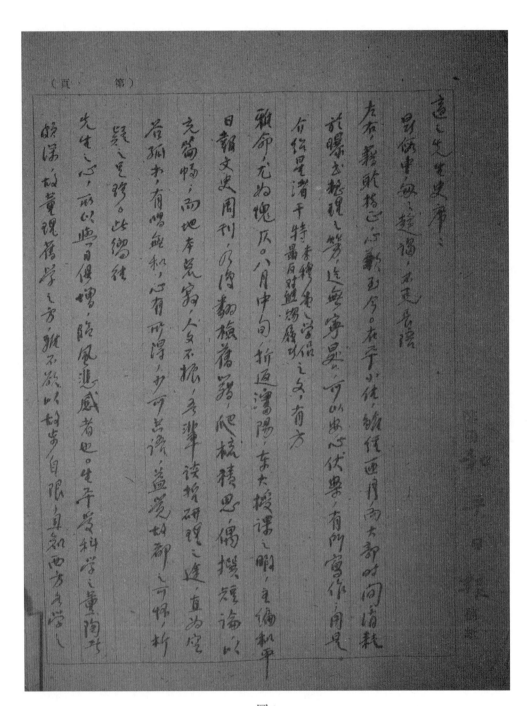

圖1

適之先生史席：

　　暑假中匆匆趨謁，不克長陪
左右，藉聆指正，心歉至今。在平小住，雖經匝月，而大部時間消耗於曝書整理之勞，迄無寧晷，可以安心伏案，有所寫作；用是介紹星渚干特（李穆堂之學侶，最反對熊賜履者）之文，有方
雅命，尤爲愧仄。八月中旬，折返瀋陽，東大授課之暇，主編《和平日報》"文史周刊"，乃復翻檢舊籍，爬梳積思，偶撰短論，以充篇幅；而地本荒寂，人文不振，吾輩談哲研理之途，直爲空谷孤木，有唱無和，心有所得，少可共語，益覺故都之可懷，析疑之足珍。此嚮往
先生之心，所以與日俱增，臨風悲感者也。生平受科學之熏陶者頗深，故董理舊學之方，雅不欲以故步自限，且知西方各學之

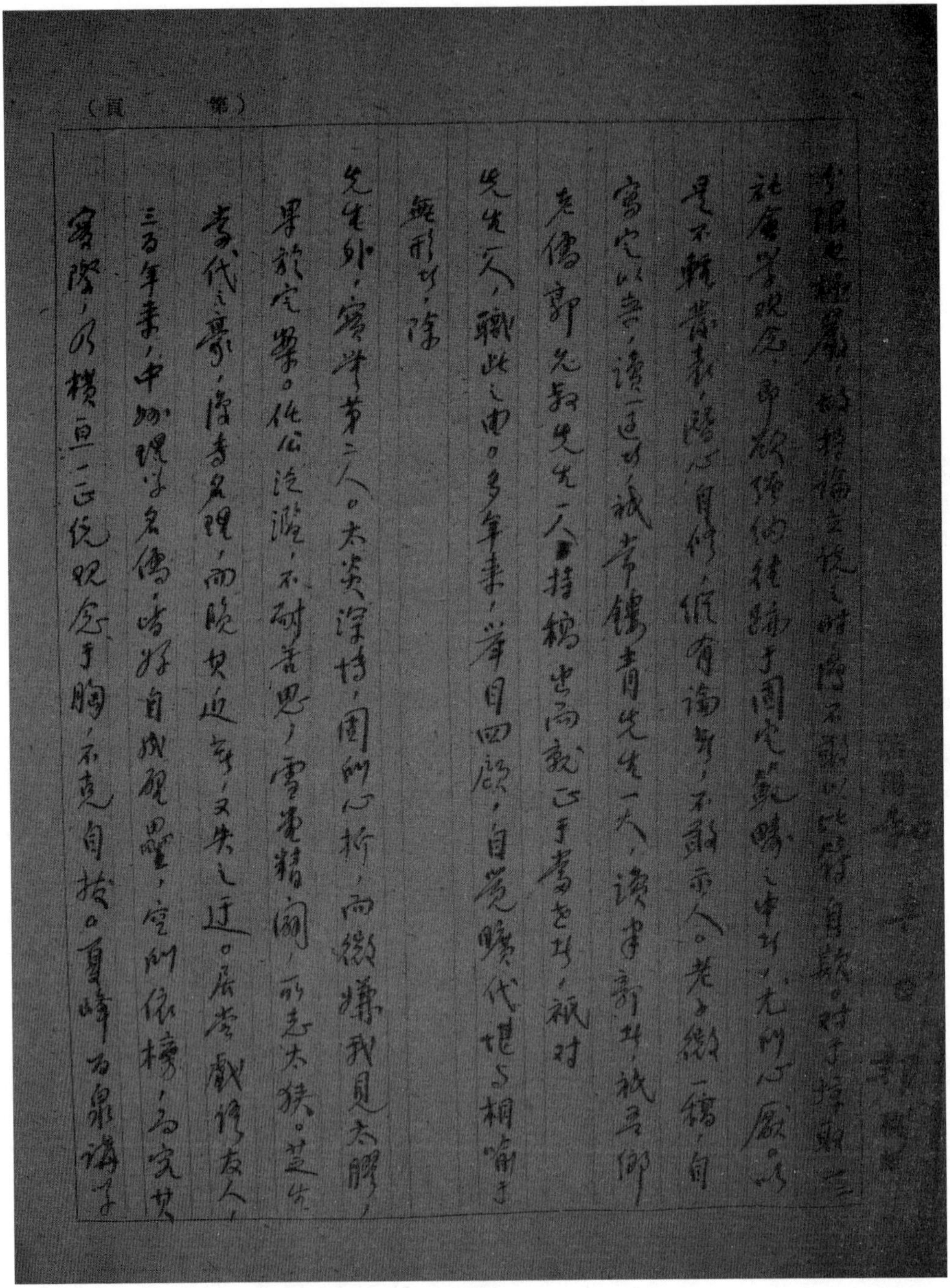

圖2

分限也極嚴，故持論立說之時，復不敢以比符自欺。對於掠取一二社會學觀念，即欲強納往跡于固定範疇之中者，尤所心厭。以是不輕發表，潛心自修，縱有論者，不敢示人。《老子微》一稿，自寫定以來，讀一過者，祇常鏤青先生一人，讀半部者，祇吾鄉老儒郭允叔先生一人，持稿出而就正于當世者，祇對先生一人，職此之由。多年來，舉目四顧，自覺曠代堪與相喻于無形者，除先生外，實無第二人。太炎深博，固所心折，而微嫌我見太膠，果於定案。任公泛濫，不耐苦思；雪堂精闓，所志太狹。芝生當代之豪，復專名理，而覽其近著，又失之迂。居嘗戲語友人，三百年來，中州理學名儒，皆好自成壁壘，空所依榜，而究其實際，乃橫亘一正統觀念于胸，不克自拔。夏峰百泉講學

之廠，未能暢所欲言。果于河北、向日未能不同于此。對於之近世皆澹陽吾吾辛 曰 剪寄呈

以数美之外訪之年，浮夜我望，懷念

先生，新晉其雄，以專門時附。近日草成甘苦之心境于其中

的心得稍已寫，私謂或不遠于專家所謂十分之見地。欽附錄副

寄呈

芋正之外，考成四更施之意于正文，稿紙粗具，而文字猶長，實待

實係逗平时，真為躬持

凡家，而論得失。老之徽一稿，楷義完寫，自覺可以見以回江

代定聯絡一定葉，但序倒著凡，湧色待正，為多有待審意

欲再研討方，草成就子獨已，一並另，而鑽研氣久，念覺

研究莊之難，不知何日方了此心願也！李大釗低，仍在年

月之末，相見匪遙，對此先達。澤涵兄想早已到美，文稿

之風，未能收碩果于河洛之間者，未始不因于此。特今之迂者，飾以歐美之外衣已耳。深夜獨坐，懷念

先生，聊發其狂，以當晤對。近日草成"孟子心性之説與管子中的心術篇"一文，私謂或不遠于東原所謂十分之見者，兹特録副，寄呈

斧正。此外，尚成"惠施與孟子"一文，稿雖粗具，而文字稍長，容待寒假返平時，再爲躬持

几前，面論得失。《老子微》一稿，精義宏旨，自覺可以懸諸國門，代老聃作一定案；但序例發凡，潤色修正，尚多有待。蓄意欲再鼓餘力，草成《莊子微》後，一並爲之，而鑽研愈久，愈覺研治莊子之難。不知何日方可了此心願也！東大放假，約在本月之末，相見匪遥，特此先達。澤涵兄想早已到美，又棖

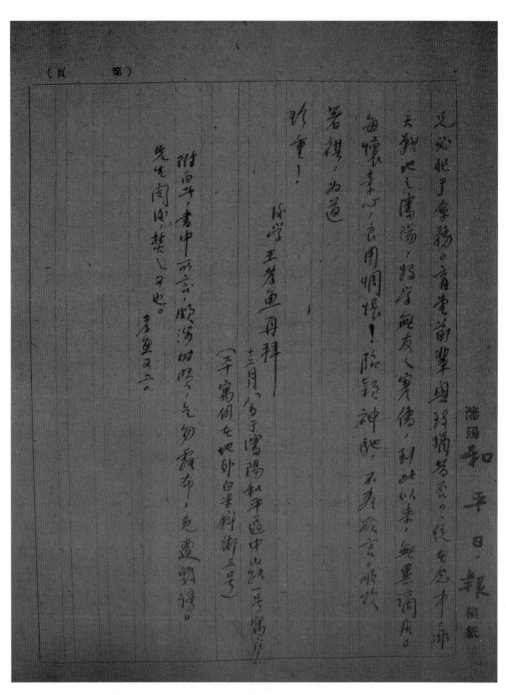

圖4

兄必忙于系務。育堂前輩興致猶昔否？統在念中。冰天戰地之瀋陽，獨學無友之寒儒，到此以來，無異謫居。每懷素心，良用惆悵！臨穎神馳，不盡欲言。順頌
著祺，爲道
珍重！
後學 王孝魚再拜
十二月八日于瀋陽和平區中山路一號寓廬
（平寓仍在地外白米斜街三號）

附白者，書中所言，頗涉時賢，乞勿露布，免遭毀謗。先生閱後，焚之可也。
孝魚又上。

王重民致胡適

　　此贈書條發現於《金山國墜事拾零》一書中。據國家圖書館著錄，所藏此書爲北平圖書館館刊九卷六號抽印本，出版時間爲 1935 年 12 月。

　　王重民（1903—1975），字有三，號冷廬，河北高陽人。目錄學家，圖書館學家，敦煌學家。
　　1928 年畢業於北京高等師範學校國文系，旋供職於國立北平圖書館，任編纂委員兼索引組組長。1934 年以"交換館員"的身份赴法國巴黎國家圖書館工作，1938 年又被轉派英國倫敦大英博物館圖書館，致力於搜求流散海外珍貴文獻。1939 年受聘於美國國會圖書館，主要從事美國國會圖書館藏善本書和北平圖書館寄存美國國會圖書館善本書整理編目工作。1947 年回國，任北平圖書館參考部主任，兼北京大學中文系教授，並在該系創建圖書館學專修科。1949 年北平和平解放後，被任命爲北平圖書館副館長，同年 7 月建成獨立建制的北京大學圖書館學專修科，該專修科 1951 年 7 月升爲圖書館學系，招收了第一屆本科生。1952 年北京大學遷往西郊，專任北京大學圖書館學系教授、系主任。
　　王重民在文獻學和敦煌學領域取得了傑出的學術成就。有《中國善本書提要》《中國善本書提要補編》《敦煌古籍敘錄》《敦煌變文集》《敦煌曲子詞集》等著述。

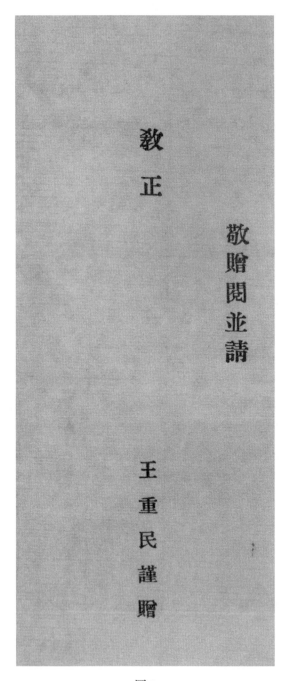

圖1

王卓然致胡適（一九三二年十二月六日）

此信發現於《東北與日本之法的關係》一書中。此書出版於 1932 年 10 月，故此信應寫於 1932 年。

王卓然（1893—1975），字回波，遼寧撫順人。1911 年考入奉天兩級師範，兩年後考入該校英語專科，1917 年畢業後任奉天省立第四師範學校教育教員兼國文教員，次年改任安東商業中學學監兼英文教員。1919 年考入北京高等師範教育研究科，1922 年畢業後回奉天，任省教育廳視學。次年公費留學美國哥倫比亞大學教育學院，1927 年獲碩士學位。次年回國，任東北大學教育學院教授，後擔任張學良的諮議兼家庭教師。1931 年 4 月，隨張學良至北平，7 月任北平師範大學教授。"九一八"事變後，被張學良任命爲東北外交研究會秘書主任。1933 年任國民政府行政院駐北平政務整理委員會委員，華北建設討論會會員，3 月，以東北大學秘書長名義代行校長職務，1936 年 8 月，免東大秘書長職務。1937 年抗日戰爭爆發後，在武漢加入東北救亡總會，並被推爲該會主席團成員。旋任軍事委員會第六部設計委員及民衆動員委員會委員。1938 年 6 月，當選爲第一屆國民參政會參政員。1940 年 12 月，當選爲第二屆參政員。1945 年底，加入中國民主同盟，並與許德珩等發起組織九三學社，任九三學社第一屆中央理事。1948 年 1 月，僑居日本。1951 年 5 月歸國，先後在津、京兩地開辦托兒所和少年兒童科學教育館。1955 年 5 月被任命爲國務院參事室參事，從事文字改革和科學普及工作。1975 年 1 月 31 日在北京病逝。終年 82 歲。

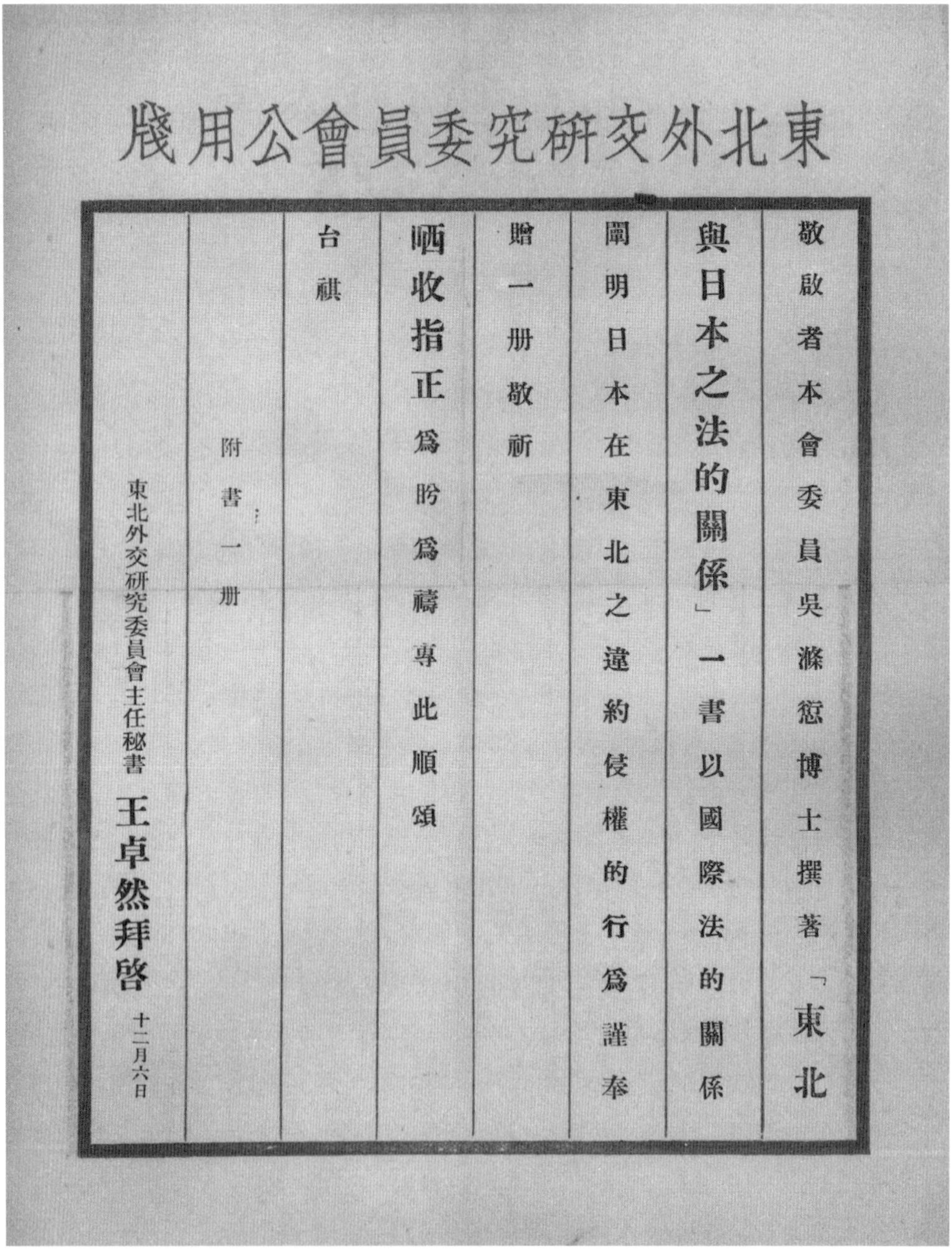

東北外交研究委員會公用牋

敬啟者本會委員吳潁慤博士撰著「東北與日本之法的關係」一書以國際法的關係闡明日本在東北之違約侵權的行爲謹奉贈一冊敬祈

　　晒收指正爲盼爲禱專此順頌

台祺

　　　　附書一冊

東北外交研究委員會主任秘書
王卓然拜啓
十二月六日

圖1

魏建功羅常培致胡適（一九三四年十一月二十日）

此信發現於《廣韻聲紐韻類之統計》一書中，作者爲白滌洲，即信中所稱"滌洲"，逝世於 1934 年 10 月。此信蓋亦寫於 1934 年。

魏建功（1901—1980），筆名天行、文狸、山鬼。江蘇海安縣人。1919 年秋考入北京大學預科，1921 年入中文系，1925 年畢業，任北大研究所國學門助教，隨錢玄同研習音韻訓詁學。1928 年任教育部國語統一籌備委員會委員，同年應邀至朝鮮京城大學講學。1929 年任北京大學助教，後升任副教授、教授。1935 年，教育部國語統一籌備委員會裁撤，改設國語推行委員會，任委員兼常務委員。1937 年全面抗戰爆發，任西南聯合大學教授，西南女子師範學院教授兼國語科主任及教務主任。1945 年 11 月到臺灣籌備設立臺灣省國語推行委員會。1946 年任臺灣省國語推行委員會主任委員。1948 年回北京大學，1951 年任新華辭書社社長，主編《新華字典》。1954 年任中國文字改革委員會委員。1956 年被評爲北京大學一級教授，1959 年任北京大學古典文獻教研室主任。1962 年任北京大學副校長。晚年曾任《中國語文》雜誌常務編委、文化部古籍整理規劃小組組員等職，曾任九三學社中央委員。1980 年在北京逝世。主要著作有《古音系研究》《中國文字改革問題》等。

羅常培（1899—1958），字莘田，號恬庵。北京人，滿族。1916 年畢業於北京市立第三中學，同年考入北京大學文科國文門，1919 年畢業，同年轉入北京大學哲學系學習，1921 年畢業，任南開中學國文教員。次年任京師第一中學國文教師兼總務長，旋代理校長。1923 年任西安國立西北大學教授兼國學專修科主任。1926 年與魯迅等人應聘到廈門大學任教，次年改任廣州中山大學中國語言文學系教授，1928 年任語言文學系主任。1929 年任中央研究院歷史語言研究所專職研究員。1934 年借聘到北京大學任中文系教授，次年兼任中文系主任。1937 年專任北京大學教職，任中央研究院通訊研究員，同年底任長沙臨時大學中國文學系教授。次年隨長沙臨時大學遷昆明，任教於改名後的國立西南聯合大學。1940 年任西南聯大中文系及師範學院國文系主任。1944 年赴美國講學，1948 年 7 月離美回國，仍任北京大學國文系教授，並兼任文科研究所所長。1949 年 10 月當選中國文字改革協會常務理事。1950 年 6 月任中國科學院語言研究所所長。1952 年任《中國語文》雜誌主編，1955 年 10 月當選中國科學院哲學社會科學部學部委員。1958 年 12 月因病去世。主要著作有《唐五代西北方音》《漢語音韻學導論》《語言與文化》等。

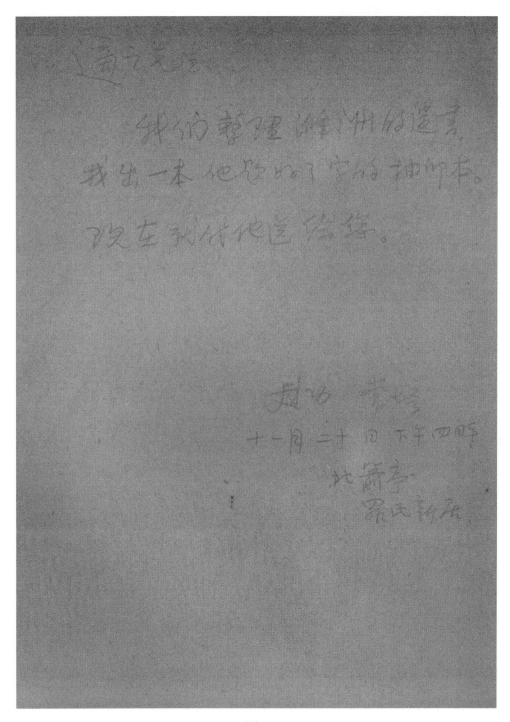

圖1

適之先生：

我們整理滌洲的遺書，找出一本他題好了字的抽印本。現在就代他送給您。

建功　常培
十一月二十日下午四時
北箭亭
羅氏新居

吳敬寰初若瑢致胡適

此賀年卡發現於《中國公學己巳級紀念冊》中。

吳敬寰（1902—1976），山東泰安人。1929 年畢業於燕京大學研究院，獲物理學碩士學位，爲國内最早被授予該學科碩士學位的學者之一。曾任清華大學研究院物理研究員，燕京大學物理系助教，濟南齊魯大學物理系講師、副教授兼無線電專修科主任，山東大學物理系副主任、教授，廣西大學、中山大學工學院教授。1952 年院系調整，調任華南工學院教授。1956 年隨華南工學院無線電有關專業調入成都電訊工程學院。

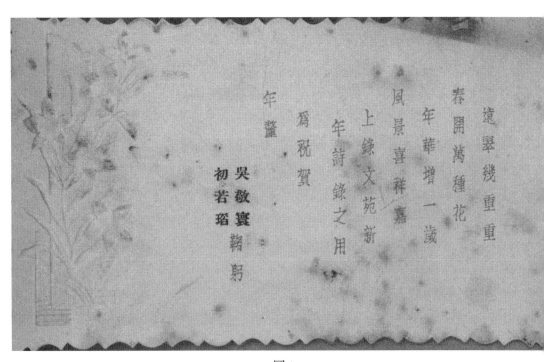

圖1

吴廷燮致胡适

  此信發現於《自治外蒙古》一書中，作者屈羲，出版於 1918 年。信中自稱"廷燮"，又據所著諸書，作者當爲吳廷燮。信中所提諸書，其中《明督撫年表》初版於 1918 年，爲五卷本，後收入二十五史補編本，增爲六卷。此信中稱"《明督撫年表》五卷"，則爲初印本，則此信或亦作於 1918 年。

歷代方鎮年表說略

竊維封建既廢，史置州鎮都督總管節度安撫行省督撫之類，名異實同，一方治亂視乎其長，得人與否，國家興亡往往隨之，軍民之治，或分或合，與時推移，廷爰弱冠從事於此，正史編年，實所根本，雜艾稗官文集，地志均勤搜采，數十年，許成漢方鎮年表二卷，三國方鎮年表一卷，晉方鎮年表二卷，宋齊梁陳方鎮年表各一卷，元魏方鎮年表二卷，西魏東魏北齊周隋方鎮年表各一卷，北宋方鎮經撫年表六卷，南宋制撫年表二卷，明督撫年表五卷，清督撫年表十二卷，方鎮行省廢置之由，用人得失政治隆替，均具於此，今重分權古制，所列可備參稽，茲先將印出明督撫年表五卷奉上，伏望察正

吳虞致胡適（一九三三年十一月二十九日）

此信發現於《吳虞文續別錄》一書中。此書出版於 1933 年。信中所說之胡適《四十自述》初刊亦在 1933 年，1931 年 1、2 月份曾在美國雜誌上發表部分英文。1933 年 6 月 18 日胡適啟程赴美，當年 10 月初乘船回國。此信當寫於 1933 年 11 月 29 日。

吳虞（1872—1949），原名姬傳、永寬，字又陵、幼陵，號愛智，四川新繁人。1891 年入成都尊經學院，曾從廖平遊學。戊戌變法後棄舉業求新學。1905 年赴日留學，入日本法政大學速成科，1907 年畢業後回國，先後任教於成都縣中學堂、嘉定府中學堂、通省法政學堂、官班法政學堂。辛亥革命爆發後，曾任四川省川西道公署顧問兼内務科長、《西成報》總編輯、《公論日報》主筆、四川《政治公報》主編等職。1917 年 1 月起在《新青年》上發表批判封建禮教的文章，著名一時。同年在四川法政學校任教員。1921 年任北京大學國文系教授，1925 年返回成都，先後任教於成都大學、四川大學中國文學院和外國文學院、省立第一師範學校、國立四川大學，1933 年被解聘，賦閑在家。1949 年 4 月在成都逝世。著有《吳虞文集》《吳虞文續錄別錄》等。

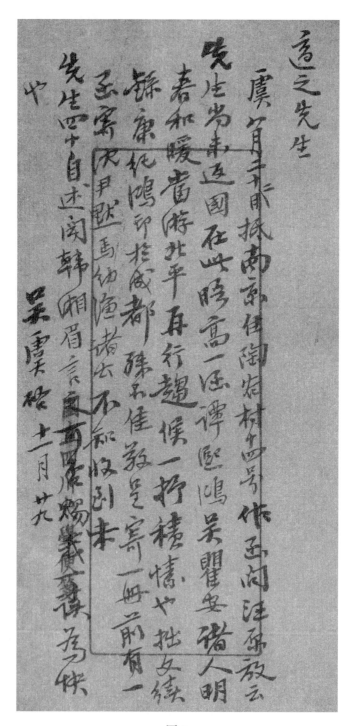

圖1

適之先生：

　　虞八月二十二日抵南京，住陶谷村十四號，作函問汪原放，云先生尚未返國。在此晤高一涵、譚熙鴻、吳瞿安諸人。明春和暖當游北平，再行趨候，一抒積悰也。拙文續録，康紀鴻印於成都，殊不佳，敬呈寄一册。前有一函寄沈尹默、馬幼漁諸公，不知收到未？

先生《四十自述》聞韓湘眉言之，可否賜我一讀爲快也？

　　　　　　　　　　　　　　　　　　　　　　　　吳虞　啓
　　　　　　　　　　　　　　　　　　　　　　　　十一月廿九

吳作民致胡適（一九四七年十二月四日）

此信發現於《事理學》一書中。

吳作民（1906—1974），別號盡我，安徽涇縣人。早年到北京勵群學院半工半讀，後考入南開大學，一年後轉入清華大學，1929年畢業於該校政治系。1930—1932年先後任教於山東臨清省立十一中、北平私立文治中學、上海私立青年中學。1935年前後任上海法政學院英語教授。1941年任教於貴陽大夏大學。抗戰勝利後，1946年任貴陽師範學院教授。新中國成立後，先後任貴陽師範學院和貴州大學外語系教授。1974年因病去世。著有《事理學》等。

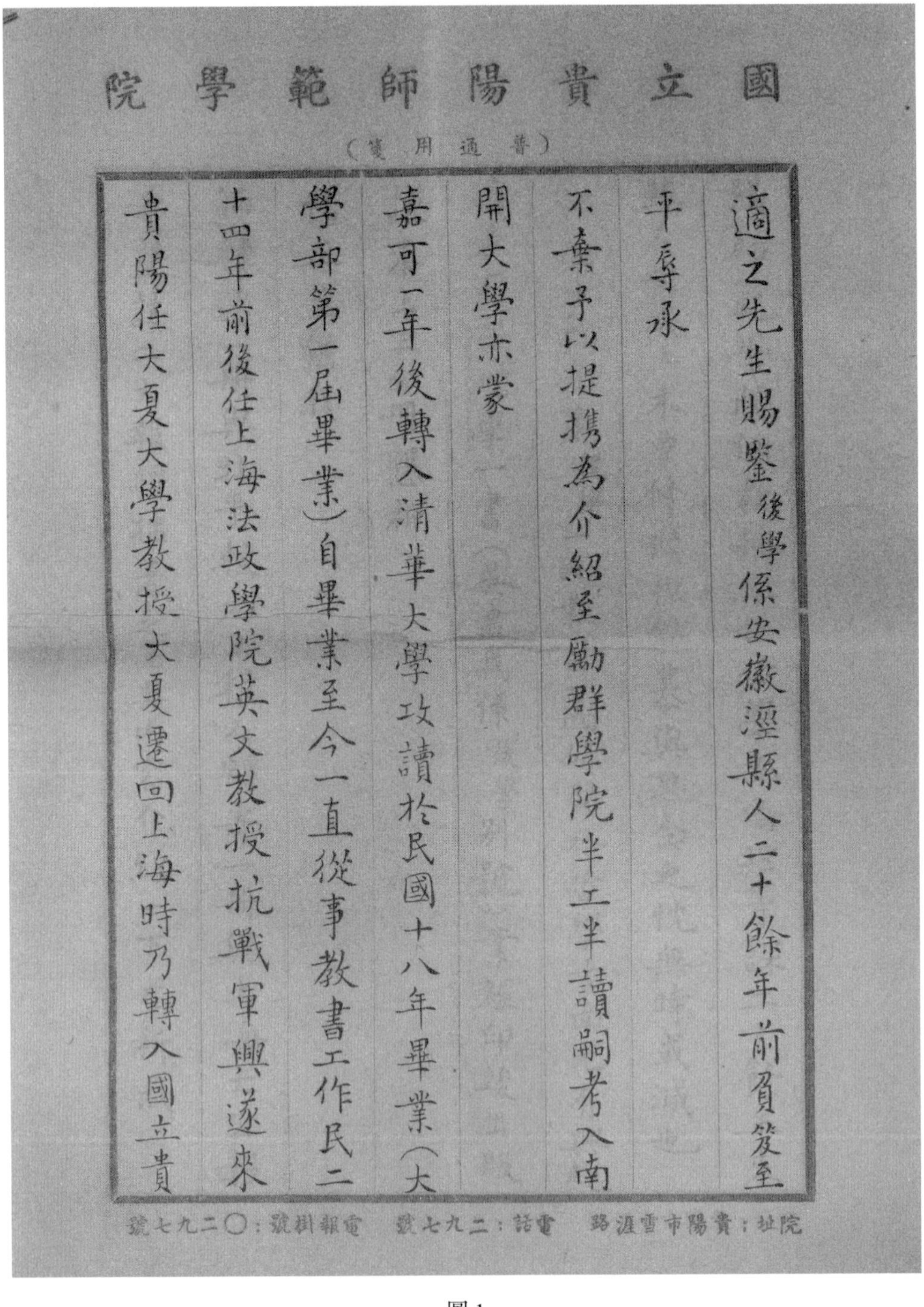
國立貴陽師範學院

（普通用箋）

適之先生賜鑒後學係安徽涇縣人二十餘年前負笈至
平辱承
不棄予以提携為介紹至勵群學院半工半讀嗣考入南
開大學亦蒙
嘉可一年後轉入清華大學攻讀於民國十八年畢業（大
學部第一屆畢業）自畢業至今一直從事教書工作民二
十四年前後任上海法政學院英文教授抗戰軍興遂來
貴陽任大夏大學教授大夏遷回上海時乃轉入國立貴

院址：貴陽市雪涯路　電話：二九七號　電報掛號：〇二九七號

圖 1

適之先生賜鑒：

　　後學係安徽涇縣人，二十餘年前負笈至平，辱承
不棄，予以提携，爲介紹至勵群學院，半工半讀，嗣考入南開大學，亦蒙
嘉可。一年後轉入清華大學攻讀，於民國十八年畢業（大學部第一屆畢業）。自
畢業至今一直從事教書工作，民二十四年前後任上海法政學院英文教授。抗戰
軍興，遂來貴陽任大夏大學教授。大夏遷回上海時，乃轉入國立貴

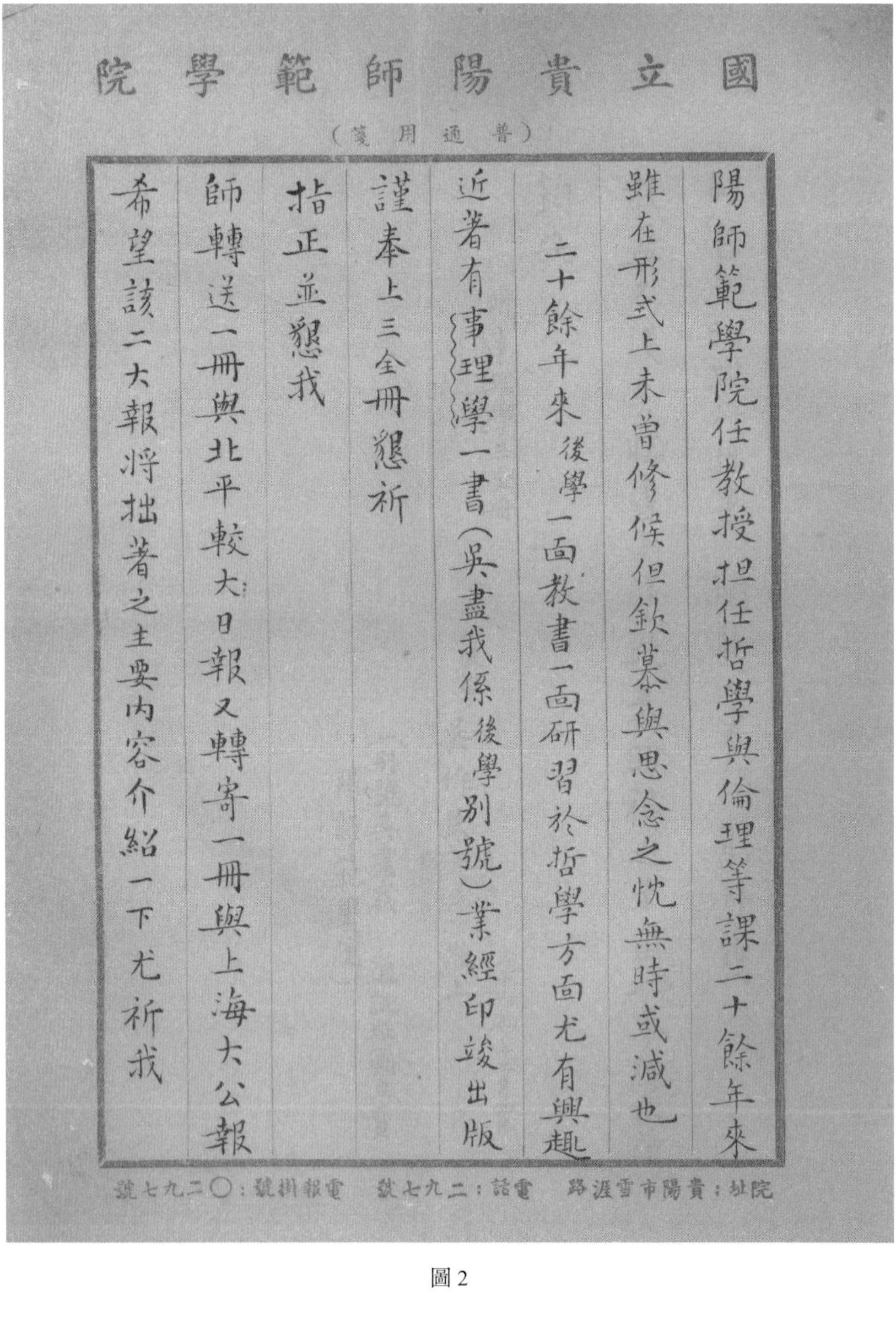

國立貴陽師範學院
（普通用箋）

陽師範學院任教授擔任哲學與倫理等課二十餘年來雖在形式上未曾修候但欽慕與思念之忱無時或減也

二十餘年來後學一面教書一面研習於哲學方面尤有興趣

近著有事理學一書（吳盡我係後學別號）業經印竣出版

謹奉上三全冊懇祈

指正並懇我

師轉送一冊與北平較大日報又轉寄一冊與上海大公報

希望該二大報將拙著之主要內容介紹一下尤祈我

院址：貴陽市雪涯路　電話：二九七號　電報掛號：〇二九七號

圖2

陽師範學院任教授，擔任哲學與倫理等課。二十餘年來，雖在形式上未曾修候，但欽慕與思念之忱，無時或減也。

　　二十餘年來，後學一面教書，一面研習，於哲學方面尤有興趣，近著有《事理學》一書（吳盡我係後學別號）業經印竣出版，謹奉上三全冊，懇祈指正，并懇我

師轉送一册與北平較大日報，又轉寄一册與上海《大公報》，希望該二大報將拙著之主要内容介紹一下，尤祈我

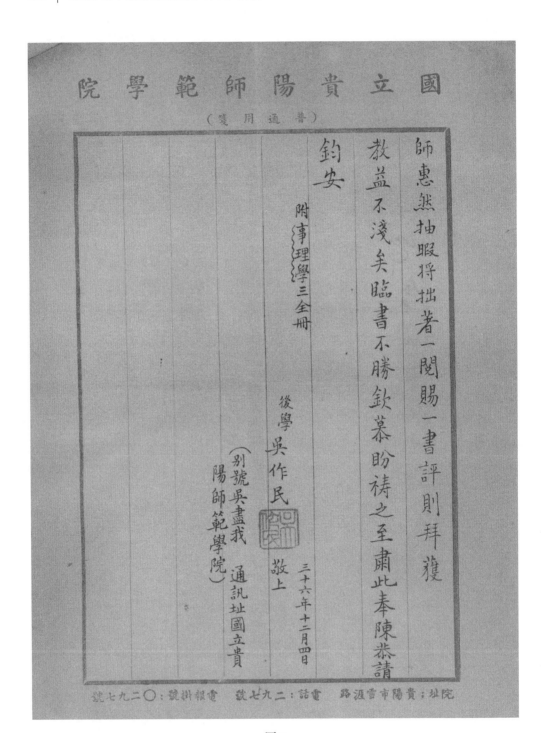

圖 3

師惠然抽暇將拙著一閱，賜一書評，則拜獲
教益不淺矣。臨書不勝欽慕盼禱之至。肅此奉陳，恭請
鈞安

　　附《事理學》三全册。

後學吳作民 敬上
三十六年十二月四日
（別號吳盡我　通訊址國立貴陽師範學院）

向乃祺致胡適

此信發現於《土地問題》一書中。此書出版於 1931 年。

向乃祺（1884—1954），字伯祥，湖南永順人，土家族。1901 年入長沙高等學堂，1904 年畢業，同年赴日本留學，入早稻田大學本科政治經濟科。1912 年畢業，獲政治學士學位。歸國後，加入國民黨，曾任湖南省財政司科長。1913 年當選爲參議院議員，憲法起草委員會委員。1914 年，袁世凱解散國會，避走成都。1916 年黎元洪重開國會，入京復議員職。1923 年曹錕賄選總統，棄職赴滬。1925 年起，歷任北京大學、朝陽大學教授，民國大學教務長。後曾先後任貴州省、湖北省縣政人員訓練所教育長。抗戰爆發後，曾任湖南建設委員會委員、省臨時參議會參議、第九戰區經委駐常德辦事處主任。1943 年去重慶，參加憲政運動。抗戰勝利後，任國大代表。1947 年當選爲監察院監察委員。新中國成立後，歷任湖南省人民政府救災委員、湖南軍政委員會參事室參事等職。1954 年病逝於長沙。

適之先生賜鑒敬啓者拙著土地問題從法律經濟制度歷史立場研究其癥結之所在及其解決之方問於中國井田法些先生在建設雜誌所發表之意見微有出入自知淳爾操觚不無疵繆先生著述等身眾流仰鏡謹檢拙著一份就正於大雅之前倘荷惠賜品題籍增聲價則幸甚耑此祗頌著安 弔向乃祺謹啓四月三日

適之先生賜鑒：

　　敬啓者，拙著《土地問題》從法律經濟制度歷史立場研究其癥結之所在，及其解決之方。關於中國井田法與
先生在《建設》雜誌所發表之意見，微有出入，自知率爾操觚，不無疵繆，
先生著述等身，衆流仰鏡，謹檢拙著一份，就正於
大雅之前。倘荷
惠賜品題，藉增聲價，則幸甚。專此，祇頌
著安

　　　　　　　　　　　　　　　　　　弟　向乃祺謹啓
　　　　　　　　　　　　　　　　　　　四月三日

蕭恩承致胡適（一九三二年）

　　此信發現於《教育哲學》一書中，此書出版於 1926 年。信中提及之 The History of Modern Education in China，今北京大學圖書館所藏胡適藏書本爲 1932 年出版，則此信或寫於 1932 年 4 月之前。

　　蕭恩承（1898—？），字鐵笛，江西永新人。1921 年畢業於長沙雅禮大學。1922 年赴美留學，1924 年獲哥倫比亞大學碩士學位，1925 年獲紐約大學博士學位。歸國後任滬江大學教授，1926 年 9 月任廈門大學教育系教授。1930 年代任北京大學教育系教授。1935 年任南京國民政府外交部湘鄂二省視察專員。曾任南京國民政府外交部秘書擴大會議國際宣傳主任，立法院編譯處處長、立法院立法委員兼軍事委員會委員長。著有《教育哲學》《兒童心理學》等。

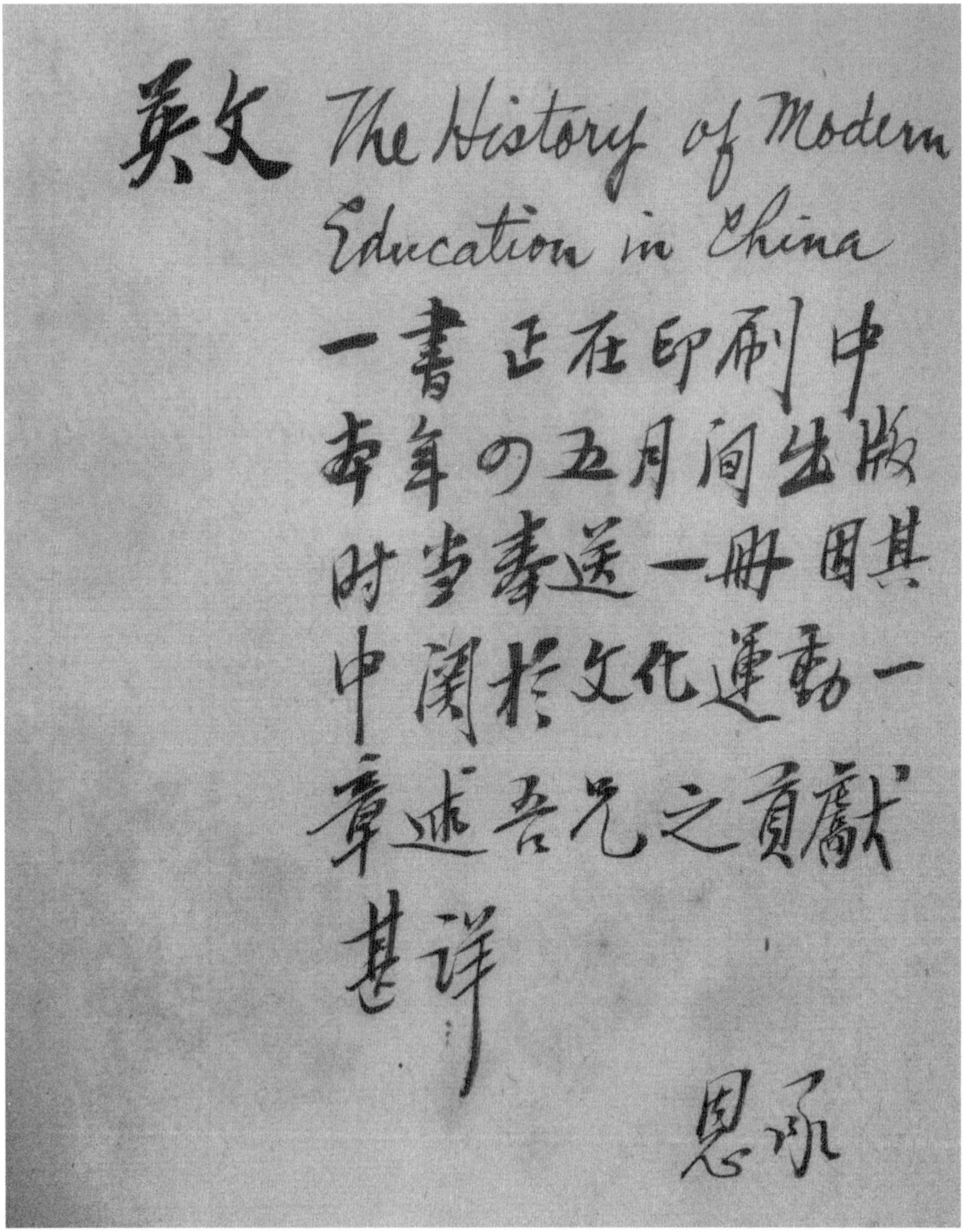

英文 The History of Modern Education in China 一書正在印刷中 本年の五月間出版 時當奉送一册 其中關於文化運動一章述吾兄之貢獻甚詳

恩承

圖1

英文 *The History of Modern Education in China* 一書正在印刷中，本年四五月間出版時當奉送一册，因其中關於文化運動一章，述吾兄之貢獻甚詳。

恩承

蕭乾致胡適（一九四五年四月廿九日）

此信發現於 *The spinners of silk* 一書中。此書出版於 1944 年。另據信中所述"大會"等事宜及信箋上所印旅館地址，此信或寫於 1945 年 4 月底胡適作爲中國代表團成員出席在舊金山召開的聯合國會議期間。

蕭乾（1910—1999）原名蕭秉乾，筆名蕭乾。蒙古族，生於北京。早年在北新書局當學徒，1931 年考入燕京大學，1933 年開始在《水星》《國聞週報》《大公報·文藝》上發表作品，1935 年畢業。先後主編津、滬、港《大公報·文藝》。1939—1942 年，任英國倫敦大學東方學院講師，兼《大公報》駐英記者。1942 年至 1944 年在劍橋大學英國文學系讀研究生。1944 年任《大公報》駐英國特派員兼戰地記者。新中國成立後，歷任英文版《人民中國》副總編輯、《譯文》編輯部副主任、《文藝報》副總編、人民文學出版社編輯、中央文史館館長等職。

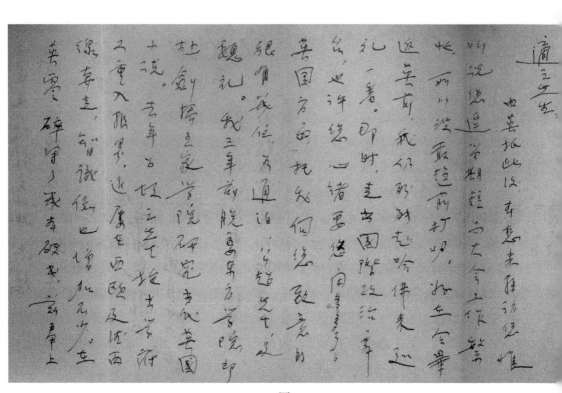

圖1

適之先生：

　　由英抵此後，本想來拜訪您，惟聽說您逗留期短，而大會工作繁忙，所以沒敢趨前打叨。好在會畢返英前，我仍盼能赴哈佛來巡禮一番。那時，走出國際政治舞臺，也許您心緒要悠閑多多了。英國方面，托我向您致意的很有幾位，如通伯、公超先生，及魏禮。我三年前脫離東方學院，即赴劍橋王家學院研究當代英國小說。去年爲政之先生拖出學府，又重入報界，近屢在西歐及德西綫奔走，智識倒也增加不少。在英零碎寫了幾本破書，茲奉上

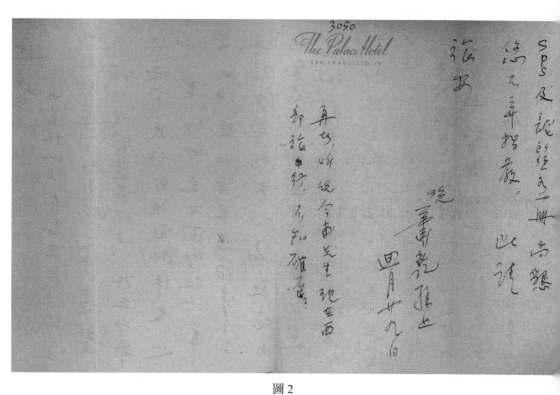

圖 2

SPS及《龍鬚》各一册，尚懇您不棄指教。此請
旅安

晚蕭乾拜上
四月廿九日

再者，聽說今甫先生現在西部旅行，不知確否？

嚴璩致胡適

此信發現於《客音情歌集》一書中，作者鍾敬文。信與書應無關。信末署名"璩"，結合信中所述，應即嚴璩，嚴復長子，嚴復有《政治講義》，1906年商務印書館出版。

嚴璩（1874—1942），字伯玉，福建閩侯人，嚴復長子。早年就讀於天津北洋水師學堂，1896年留學英國倫敦大學，1900年畢業。後任清廷駐英國、法國公使館隨員。回國後任廣東洋務局局長。民國二年（1913）任長蘆鹽務稽核所經理，後歷任北京政府鹽務署參事，財政部次長兼鹽務署署長、鹽務稽核總所總辦、華俄道勝銀行清理處督辦等職。1942年病逝於上海。編著《侯官嚴先生年譜》《越南視察報告》。

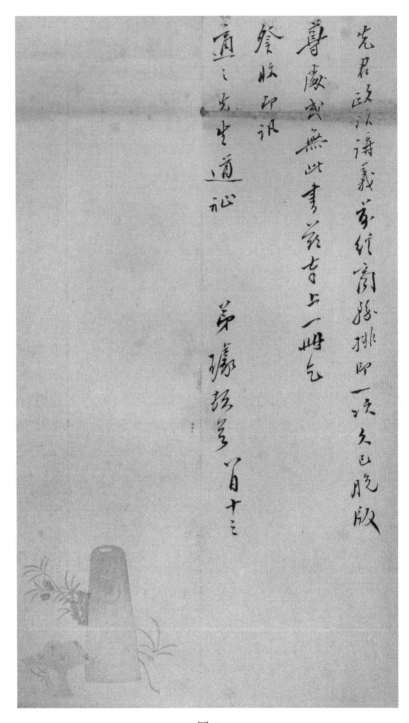

圖1

先君《政治講義》前經商務排印一次，久已脫版，
尊處或無此書，茲奉上一冊，乞
晉收，即訊
適之先生道祉

弟璩頓首
八月十三

楊樂公致胡適

此信發現於 *The Philosophy of William James* 一書中。此書出版於 1914 年。

楊樂公，生平不詳。

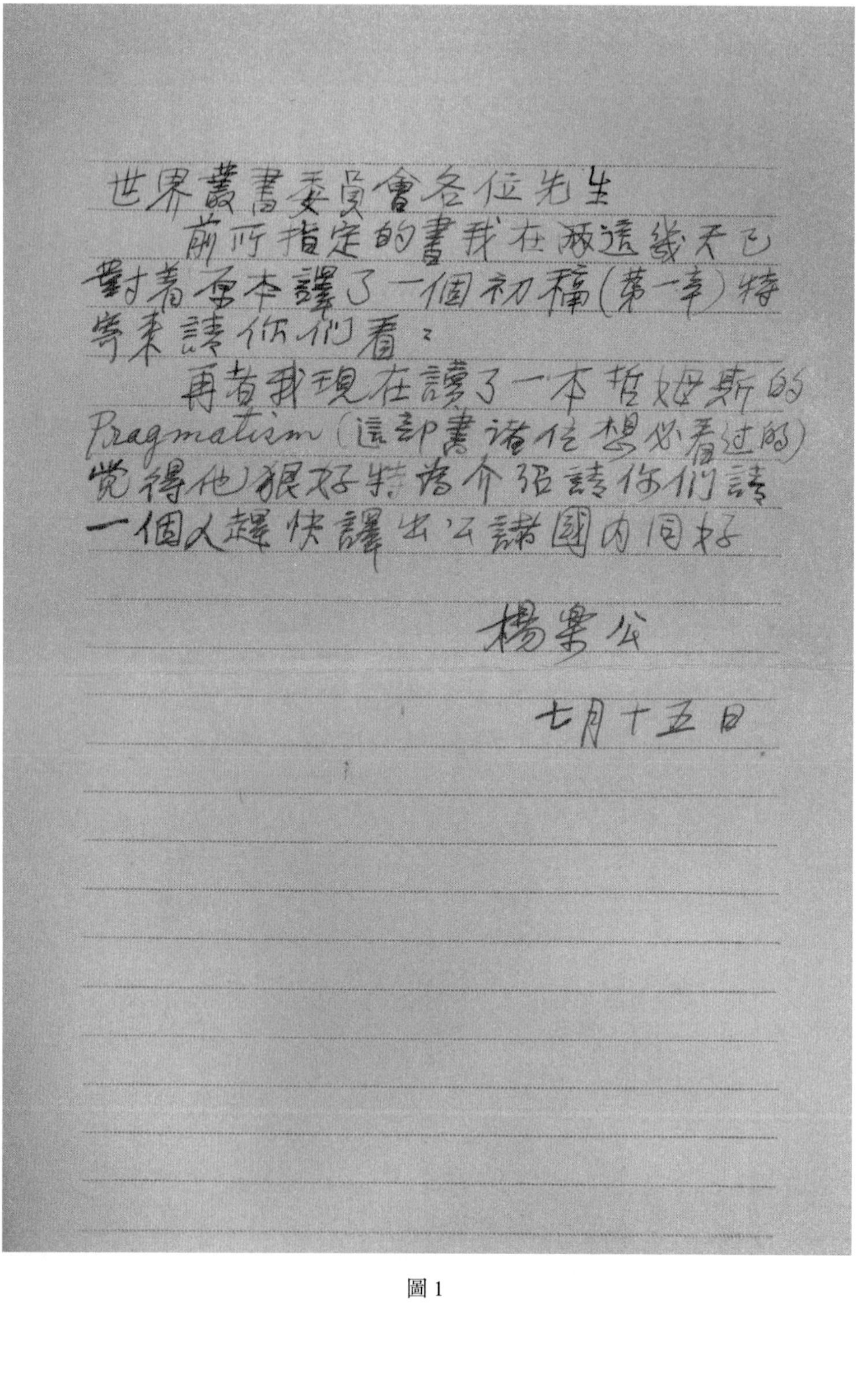

世界叢書委員會各位先生

　前所指定的書我在前這幾天已對着畜本譯了一個初稿（第一章）特寄來請你們看。

　再者我現在讀了一本哲姆斯的 Pragmatism（這部書諸位想必看過的）覺得他很好特為介紹請你們請一個人趕快譯出以諸國内同好

楊壽公

七月十五日

圖1

世界叢書委員會各位先生：

　　前所指定的書我在這幾天已對着原本譯了一個初稿（第一章），特寄來請你們看看。

　　再者，我現在讀了一本哲姆斯的 *Pragmatism*（這部書諸位想必看過的）覺得他狠好，特爲介紹，請你們請一個人趕快譯出，公諸國內同好。

楊樂公
七月十五日

葉式欽致胡適（一九四八年四月七日）

此信發現於《助產學報》創刊號中。

葉式欽，生平不詳，1948年代理國立北平高級助產職業學校校長。

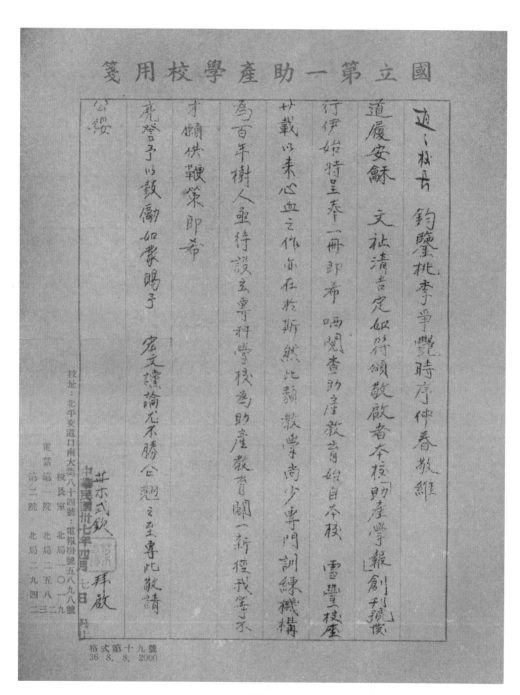

圖1

伊見思致胡適（一九四八年三月十四日）

此信發現於《民主與設計》一書中。

作者生平不詳。

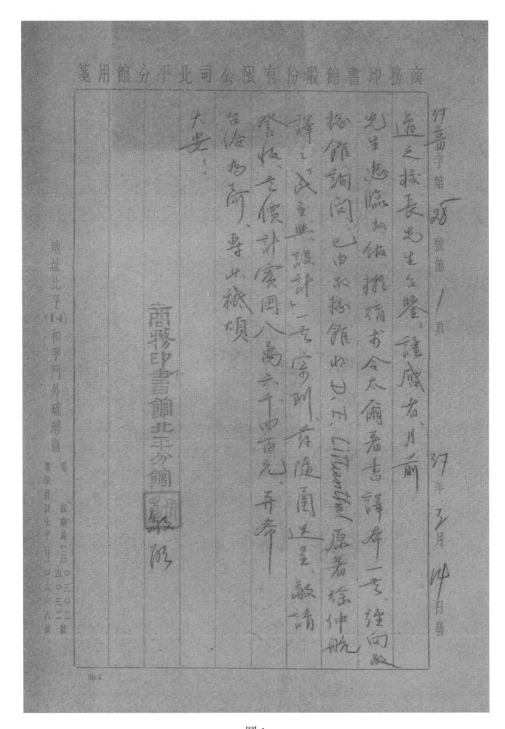

圖1

適之校長先生台鑒：
　　謹啓者，月前
先生惠臨敝館，擬購李令太爾著書譯本一書，經向敝捴館詢問，已由敝捴館將 D. E. Lillienthal 原著、徐仲航譯之《民主與設計》一書寄到，兹隨函送呈，敬請
詧收。書價計實圃八萬六千四百元，并希
台洽爲荷。專此，祗頌
大安！

　　　　　　　　　　　　　　　　　　商務印書館北平分館伊見思敬啓

易熙吾致某根泰（一九四六年九月十四日）

此數紙發現於《常用字源》一書中。

作者生平可參考信中所述。

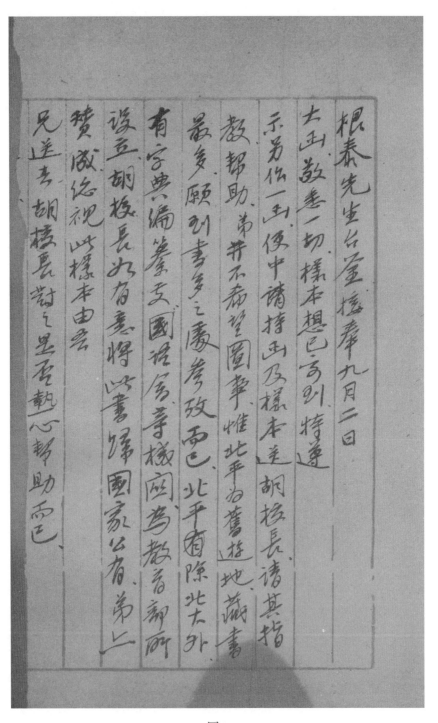

圖1

根泰先生台鑒：

　　接奉九月二日
大函，敬悉一切。樣本想已寄到，特遵
示另作一函，便中請持函及樣本送胡校長，請其指教幫助。弟并不希望圖事，惟北平爲舊遊地，藏書最多，願到書多之處參攷而已。北平除北大外，有字典編纂處、國語會等機關，爲教育部所設立，胡校長如有意將此書歸國家公有，弟亦贊成。總視此樣本由吾
兄送去，胡校長對之是否熱心幫助而已。

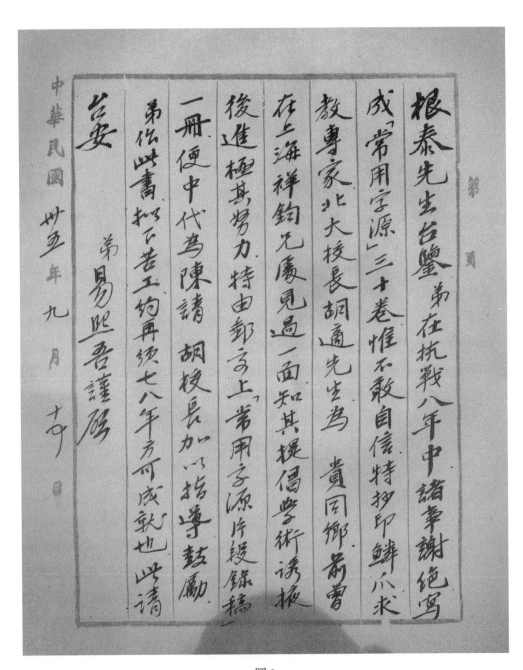

圖2

根泰先生台鑒：

　　弟在抗戰八年中諸事謝絕，寫成"常用字源"三十卷，惟不敢自信，特抄印鱗爪，求教專家。北大校長胡適先生爲貴同鄉，前曾在上海祥鈞兄處見過一面，知其提倡學術，誘掖後進，極其努力，特由郵寄上"常用字源片段錄稿"一冊，便中代爲陳請胡校長加以指導鼓勵。弟作此書，擬下苦工，約再須七八年方可成就也。此請
台安

　　　　　　　　　　　　　　　　　　　　　　　弟易熙吾謹啓
　　　　　　　　　　　　　　　　　　　　　中華民國卅五年九月十四日

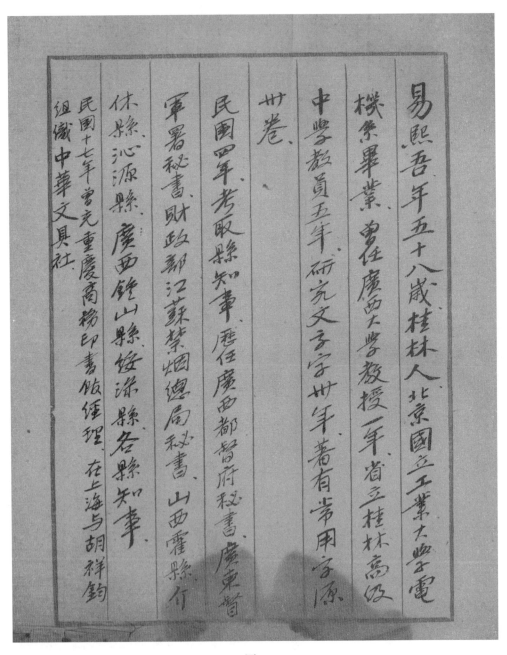

易熙吾年五十八歲桂林人北京國立工業大學電機系畢業、曾任廣西大學教授一年、省立桂林高級中學教員五年、研究文字廿年、著有常用字原卅卷、

民國四年考取縣知事、歷任廣西都督府秘書、廣東督軍署秘書、財政部江蘇菸烟總局秘書、山西霍縣、休縣、沁源縣、廣西鍾山縣、鎔涤縣各縣知事、

民國十七年曾充重慶商務印書館經理、在上海与胡祥鈞組織中華文具社

圖 3

易熙吾，年五十八歲，桂林人，北京國立工業大學電機系畢業，曾任廣西大學教授一年，省立桂林高級中學教員五年，研究文字學卅年，著有《常用字源》卅卷。

民國四年，考取縣知事，歷任廣西都督府秘書，廣東督軍署秘書，財政部江蘇禁烟總局秘書，山西霍縣、介休縣、沁源縣、廣西鍾山縣、綏淥縣各縣知事。

民國十七年曾充重慶商務印書館經理，在上海與胡祥鈞組織中華文具社。

袁同禮致胡適

　　此信件發現於《漢書藝文志講疏》一書中。此書於 1924 年、1925 年、1927 年、1929 年、1933 年皆有出版，核北大圖書館所藏胡適藏書中此本出版於 1925 年。

　　袁同禮（1895—1965），字守和，原籍河北徐水，生於北京。1913 年考入北京大學預科，1916 年預科畢業，到清華大學圖書館參考部工作，曾代理圖書館主任。1919 年加入少年中國學會。1920 年赴美留學，1922 年獲哥倫比亞大學文學士學位，次年入紐約州立圖書館專科學校，畢業後曾在美國國會圖書館從事中文編目工作。1923 年到英、法考察學習。1924 年回國，任廣東嶺南大學圖書館館長，次年改任北京大學圖書館主任。1927 年任京師圖書館圖書部主任，1929 年升任館長。同年京師圖書館與北海圖書館合併爲國立北平圖書館，任副館長，1942 年任館長。1949 年赴美，曾任斯坦福大學研究所編纂主任。1957 年任職於美國國會圖書館編目部。1962 年 2 月病逝於美國。著有《西文漢學書目》《中國留美同學博士論文目錄》等。

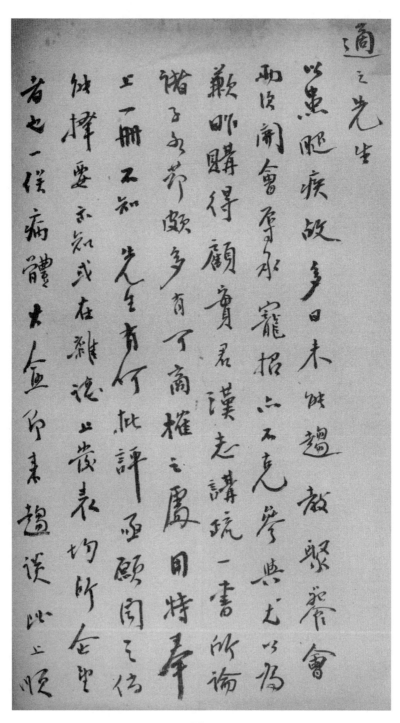

圖1

適之先生：

　　以患腿疾，故多日未能趨教。聚餐會兩次開會，辱承寵招，亦不克參與，尤以爲歉。昨購得顧實君《漢志講疏》一書，所論諸子各節，頗多有可商榷之處，用特奉上一册，不知先生有何批評，亟願聞之，倘能擇要示知，或在雜誌上發表，均所企望者也。一俟病體大愈，即來趨談。此上，順

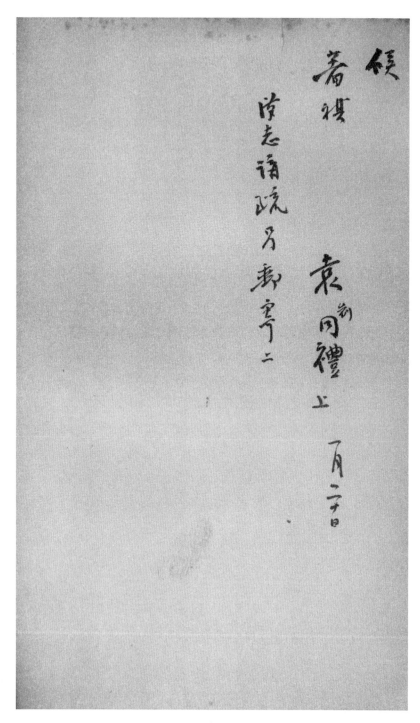

圖2

候

著祺

　　　　　　　　　　　　　　　　　　　　　袁制同禮　上
　　　　　　　　　　　　　　　　　　　　　　一月二十日

《漢志講疏》另郵寄上

章廷謙（川島）致胡適（一九三五年四月十三日）

此信發現於《游仙窟》一書中。扉頁有作者題記：適之先生教正，生廷謙呈。一九三五，四，十三。

章廷謙（1901—1981），字矛塵，筆名川島、侔塵，浙江紹興人。1915年隨父西去太原，入太原第一中學，後入山西大學預科。1916年2月升讀山西大學哲學系。1919年10月轉入北京大學哲學系。1922年6月畢業留校，任校長室外交秘書，兼哲學系助教。1924年11月與魯迅、周作人、顧頡剛等創辦《語絲》週刊。1926年2月任北京中俄大學教授兼註冊組主任，同年12月任廈門大學國學研究院出版部幹事。次年任職於國民黨浙江省黨部宣傳部，旋任杭州《民國日報》編輯，同年8月改任浙江大學農學院教授，兼浙江省立高級中學教員。1930年11月任南京國民政府教育部編審。1931年7月回北京大學，仍任校長辦公室秘書，兼任講師。次年兼北平大學女子文理學院講師。抗戰爆發後，於1937年11月任長沙臨時大學校長室秘書。1938年5月長沙臨時大學遷昆明，更名爲西南聯合大學，仍任校長室秘書。抗戰勝利後，北大復員，於1946年8月隨校返北平，任中文系副教授。1949年10月加入中國民主促進會。1956年8月任民進中央委員會委員。1957年3月兼民進北京大學支部主任委員；同年加入中國作家協會。1958年12月任民進五屆中央委員會委員。1981年5月12日病逝。終年80歲。有散文集《月夜》《川島選集》等，曾校點《游仙窟》。

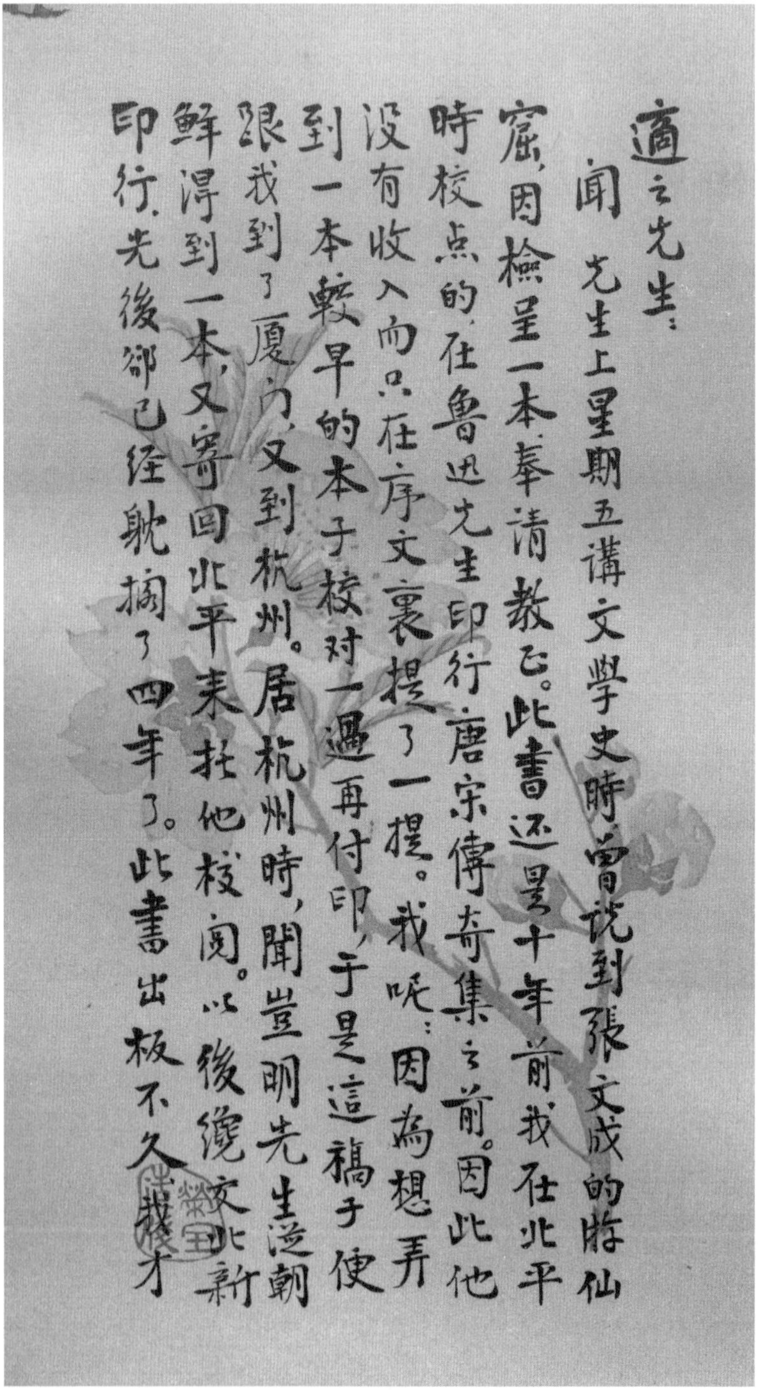

適之先生：
聞 先生上星期五講文學史時，曾說到張文成的游仙窟，因檢呈一本，奉請教正。此書还是十年前我在北平時校点的，在魯迅先生印行唐宋傳奇集之前。因此他没有收入，而只在序文裏提了一提。我呢，因為想弄到一本較早的本子校对一遍再付印，于是這稿子便跟我到了廈门，又到杭州。居杭州時，聞豈明先生從朝鮮得到一本，又寄回北平來托他校閱。以後纔交北新印行。先後卻已經耽擱了四年了。此書出板不久，我才

圖 1

適之先生：

　　聞先生上星期五講文學史時曾説到張文成的《游仙窟》，因檢呈一本，奉請教正。此書還是十年前我在北平時校點的，在魯迅先生印行《唐宋傳奇集》之前。因此他沒有收入，而只在序文裏提了一提。我呢，因爲想弄到一本較早的本子校對一過再付印，于是這稿子便跟我到了廈門，又到杭州。居杭州時，聞豈明先生從朝鮮得到一本，又寄回北平來托他校閲。以後纔交北新印行。先後卻已經耽擱了四年了。此書出板不久，我才

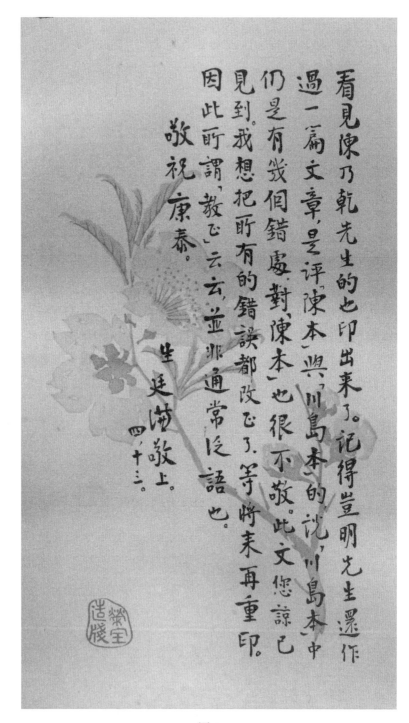

看見陳乃乾先生的也印出來了。記得豈明先生還作過一篇文章,是評〝陳本〞與〝川島本〞的,沈,川島本中仍是有幾個錯處,對〝陳本〞也很不敬。此文您諒已見到。我想把所有的錯誤都改正了,等將來再重印。因此所謂〝敎正〞云云,並非通常泛語也。

敬祝康泰。

生 廷沛敬上。
四、十三。

圖2

看見陳乃乾先生的也印出來了。記得豈明先生還作過一篇文章，是評"陳本"與"川島本"的，説"川島本"中仍是有幾個錯處，對"陳本"也很不敬。此文您諒已見到。我想把所有的錯誤都改正了，等將來再重印。因此所謂"教正"云云，並非通常泛語也。

敬祝康泰。

生 廷謙敬上。
四，十三。

張光祖致胡適

此信發現於《墨辯新詁質疑》一書中。此書出版於 1946 年。

張光祖,曾任職於交通部電信總局電信人員北平訓練所,餘不詳。

交通部電信總局電信人員北平訓練所

適之先生大鑒：頃接友人萬崇一君來函附所著墨辯新詁質疑囑即轉投教正並謂前曾由豫寄平一本恐因郵局關係未能到達左右故特檢附該書一卷希查收是幸如有賜教逕寄開封中山路中段二九六號萬君即可專肅並請
教安

張光祖拜啓 七月卅日

適之先生大鑒：

  頃接友人萬宗一君來函，附所著《墨辯新詁質疑》，囑即轉投
教正，並謂前曾由豫寄乎一本，恐因郵遞關係，未能到達
左右，故特檢附該書一卷，希
查收是幸。如有
賜教，逕寄開封中山路中段二九六號萬君即可。專肅，並請
教安

                張光祖拜啓
                七月卅一日

張國維致胡適（一九三三年五月十三日）

此信發現於《新創中國公年》一書中。

作者生平不詳。

中國科學化運動協會用箋

適之先生

茲奉呈拙著中「新刊中國公年」一文對於中國歷史紀年方法有所建議其末尾兩位數字可與西曆紀年完全相符極便於比較中西年代及計算年代等堪稱為合於科學化之方法於中國社會及歷史尚不無小補敬懇詳閱加以指正及批評並希代為宣傳介紹為感此頌

台綏

後學 張國維 謹啟

中華民國二十二年 ３月 十三日

適之先生：

　　茲奉呈拙著《新創中國公年》一册，對於中國歷史紀年方法有所建議，其末尾兩位數字可與西曆紀年完全相符，極便於比較中西年代及計算種種年代等，堪稱爲合於科學化之方法，於中國社會及歷史上不無小補。敬懇
詳閱，加以指正及批評，尤希代爲宣傳介紹爲感。此頌
台綏！

　　　　　　　　　　　　　　　　　　　　後學張國維謹啓
　　　　　　　　　　　　　　　　　　　　中華民國二十二年五月十三日

張君勱致胡適

此信發現於《國聯調查團報告書之批評》中，作者署名夢蝶，即信中所稱"伍憲子"之號。其書出版於 1932 年 12 月美國三藩市，則此信最早寫於 1933 年 1 月 30 日。

張君勱（1887—1969），本名嘉森，字君勱，又字士林，號立齋，江蘇寶山縣（今屬上海市）人。早年入上海廣方言館學習西學，1902 年考中秀才。1903 年先後入上海震旦學院和南京高等學堂學習。1906 年公費留學日本，入早稻田大學政治經濟科，其間曾於 1909 年創辦《憲政新志》雜誌，1910 年畢業，獲政治學學士學位。同年回國，授翰林院庶吉士。辛亥革命後，曾任寶山縣議會議長。1913 年赴德柏林大學留學。1915 年底回國，任上海《時事新報》主筆。1917—1918 年間任北京大學哲學系教授。1918 年末隨梁啟超遊歷歐洲。1920 年到德國從倭鏗學習哲學，並到法國求教於柏格森。1922 年 1 月回國，回國後宣傳柏格森的生命哲學，為科玄論戰中玄學派的主將。1923 年任上海國立自治學院院長，兩年後國立自治學院更名為"國立政治大學"，任校長。1929 年去德國耶納大學講授中國哲學，1931 年回國。1930 年代，曾先後任燕京大學、中山大學哲學系教授。1934 年在北平與張東蓀組建中國國家社會黨，創辦《再生》雜誌，當選為國家社會黨總務委員和總秘書。抗戰爆發後，被聘為國防參議會參議員，後國防參議會改為國民參政會，當選為國民參政會參政員。1939 年在雲南大理創辦民族文化學院，並任院長。1941 年與梁漱溟等人發起成立中國民主政團同盟。1945 年以中國代表團成員身份出席聯合國成立大會，1946 年回國，出席在重慶召開的政治協商會議，同年 8 月，將國家社會黨與民主憲政黨合併爲中國民主社會黨，任主席。1949 年 11 月由澳門流亡到印度、印尼、澳大利亞等國，講授孔孟哲學。1951 年到美國，撰寫《理學的發展》，極力宣揚宋明理學，自稱"二十世紀之新儒家"。1958 年，與唐君毅、徐復觀、牟宗三等聯合發表《中國文化宣言》。1969 年病逝於美國舊金山。

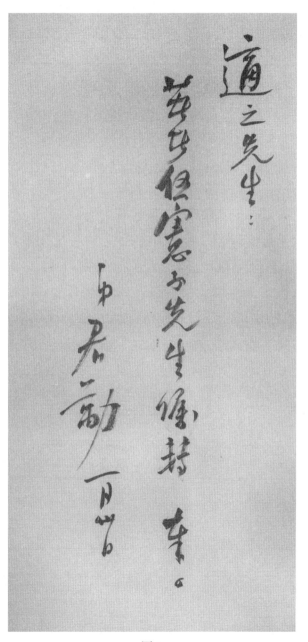

圖 1

適之先生：
　　著者伍憲子先生囑轉奉。
　　　　弟　君勱
　　　一月卅日

張孟休致胡適

　　此信發現於《國立北京大學重慶同學會同學錄》中，此書出版於 1944 年，此信當寫於 1944 年之後。

　　張孟休，四川南溪人，1935 年畢業於北京大學教育系，曾任北京大學教育系副教授。

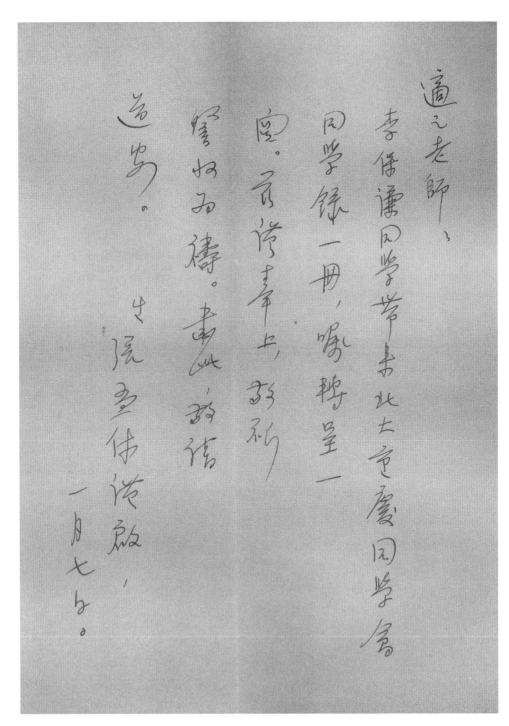

圖1

適之老師：

　　李保謙同學帶來《北大重慶同學會同學錄》一册，囑轉呈一閱。茲謹奉上，敬祈
詧收爲禱。肅此，敬請
道安。

　　　　　　　　　　　　　　　　　　　　生　張孟休謹啓
　　　　　　　　　　　　　　　　　　　　　　一月七日。

張頤致胡適

　　此信發現於 *The Development, Significance and Some Limitation of Hegel's Ethical Teaching* 一書中。信中提及"Lasson 的短評見 *Kant-Studien* 大約 1927—28",經核查,短評應發表於 1928 年 *Kant-Studien* 的第 33 卷,則此信應寫於 1928 年之後。

　　張頤(1887—1969),現代哲學家。字真如,又名唯識,別號丹崖。生於四川永寧(今敘永)。1906 年考入永寧中學堂,次年加入同盟會。1908 年考入四川省立高等學堂,與謝持、熊克武等共組乙辛學社。1911 年積極投身保路運動。1913 年考取四川省公費留學資格,入美國密歇根大學,1919 年獲哲學博士學位。同年秋轉入英國牛津大學,1923 年獲該校哲學博士學位。1924 年回國,任北京大學教授。1926 年南下任廈門大學副校長。1929 年重返北京大學,任哲學系主任。1935 年夏赴歐美考察。1936 年回國,任四川大學文學院院長,次年代理校長。1939 年改任武漢大學教授。1946 年重返北京大學,任哲學系教授。新中國成立後,任四川省文史館研究員,1957 年任全國政協委員。1969 年 6 月 23 日病逝於北京。主要著作有《黑格爾倫理研究》《黑格爾與宗教》等。

適之先生：

昨日談次，穩足下哲學意見毫不偏執佩甚。

昨晚在北海曾言及將以拙作就正蒸特送上請不吝氣以指教，為盼。實則其中有些地方我亦覺得不安，特啟所餘尚多，恐無機會修改耳。J.S. Mckenzie及 Pring Jaxon 均曾有短評發表，但他們都是赫格爾派其言不免有偏蔽處，足下別派眼光觀之其瑕疵當較易見此所由極欲就正於足下耳。手此順頌

譚祺 外書一冊

弟 張頤拜 七月廿七

(日) Jaxon 11.11.11 Kant-Studien Bd. 1927–28
(日) Mckenzie 的評在英國 International Journal of Ethies Oct. 1926

適之先生：

　　昨日談次，稔足下哲學意見毫不偏執，佩甚佩甚！

　　昨晚在北海曾言及將以拙作就正，茲特送上，請不客氣地指教爲盼。實則其中有些地方我亦覺得不妥，特二版所餘尙多，一時恐無機會修改耳。J. S. McKenzie 及 Georg Lasson 均曾有短評發表，但他們都是赫格爾派，其言不免有偏蔽處，足下以別派眼光觀之，其瑕疵當較易見，此所由極欲就正於足下也。手此順頌

譚祺　外書一册

弟　張頤　拜
七月廿七

　　再 McKenzie 的短評見 *International Journal of Ethics*, Oct. 1926，Lasson 的短評見 *Kant-Studien* 大約 1927—28。

趙承信致胡適（一九四七年一月二十七日）

　　此信發現於《獄中雜記》一書中。原無年代，所贈《獄中雜記》爲《大中》第一卷第四期至第八九合期抽印本，其中第八九合期出版於 1946 年 8 月，故推測此信可能寫於 1947 年 1 月 27 日。

　　趙承信（1907—1959），廣東新會縣人。1926 年畢業於廣州培英中學後，同年保送燕京大學社會學系，1930 年畢業，獲學士學位。同年赴美留學，入芝加哥大學，次年轉密歇根大學，專攻都市社會學和人口學，1933 年畢業，獲博士學位。同年回國，任燕京大學社會學系教授，後兼社會學系主任、法學院院長。1941 年太平洋戰争爆發後，曾被日軍逮捕入獄。1945 年負責燕京大學法學院復建，1948 年曾赴美考察一年。1952 年院系調整，先後任教於中央財經學院、中國人民大學。1957 年因建議在大學恢復社會學課程而被錯劃爲"右派"。主要著作有：《派克與人文區位學》《中國人口論》《社區人口研究》《家族制度作爲中國人口平衡的一個因素》《獄中雜記———一個社會學的解釋》等。

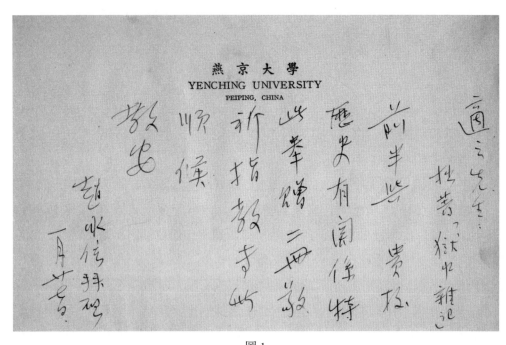

圖 1

適之先生：

　　拙著《獄中雜記》前半與貴校歷史有關係，特此奉贈二冊，敬祈指教。專此，順候

教安

趙承信拜啓

一月廿七日

趙鳳喈致胡適（一九二八年五月二十六日）

此信發現於《中國婦女在法律上之地位》一書中。此信原署日期爲五月廿六日，題名頁有胡適題記：著者送我的，適。十七,五,十八。作者信中說："頃以拙著——《中國婦女在法律之地位》——就正左右，蒙加校正，極感！"說明此信寫於胡適收到書之後，故此信大致應寫於 1928 年 5 月 26 日。

趙鳳喈（1896—1970），字鳴岐，安徽和縣人。1925 年畢業於北京大學法律系，任教於安徽法政專門學校，1927 年前後回北京大學，後留學法國巴黎大學，獲法學碩士。歸國後曾任中央大學講師。1933 年受聘於正在籌建的清華大學法律學系，後轉入政治學系任教授。抗戰爆發後，任西南聯大教授。抗戰勝利後，隨清華大學復員北平，任法律系主任，兼任清華大學研究院法學研究所政治學部主任。1949 年初北平解放後，辭去法律系主任。1952 年院系調整，清華大學法律系併入北京大學，賦閒在家。著有《中國婦女在法律上之地位》《民法親屬編》等。

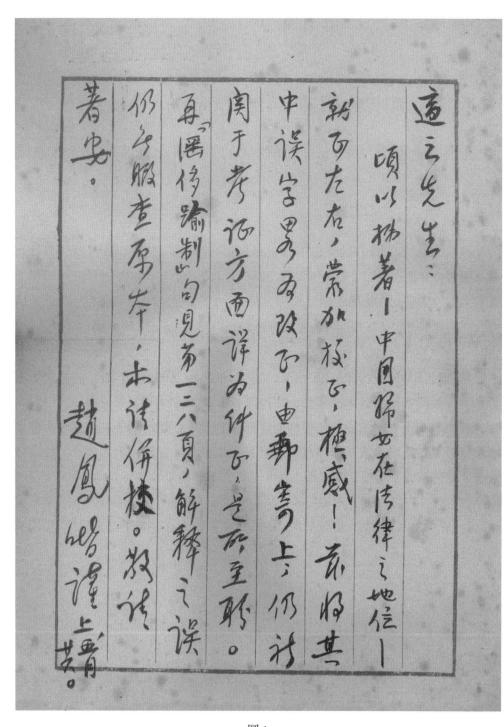

圖1

適之先生：

　　頃以拙著——《中國婦女在法律之地位》——就正左右，蒙加校正，極感！茲將其中誤字畧爲改正，由郵寄上；仍祈關於考證方面詳爲糾正，是所至盼。再"淫侈踰制"句見第一二八頁，解釋之誤仍無暇查原本，求請併校。敬請
著安。

趙鳳喈謹上
五月廿六。

趙貞信致胡適（一九四七年七月十一日）

　　此信發現於《論語堯曰作於墨者考》一書中。信中稱"後學于三十二年春始得由平繞道豫陝來蓉……于今已及四年"，則此信當寫於 1947 年 7 月 11 日。

　　趙貞信（1902—1989），原名雲端，字肖甫，浙江富陽人。自學成才，在顧頡剛、陳垣的影響提攜下從事考據學。曾任職於燕京大學引得編纂處。1937 年任北平中國大學國學系講師，兼禹貢學會編輯。抗戰期間任四川大學副教授。後任教於輔仁大學。新中國成立後，任北京師範大學歷史系教授，兼《光明日報·歷史教學》編輯。主要編注有《論語辨》《封氏聞見記校注附引得》《諸史然疑校訂》。

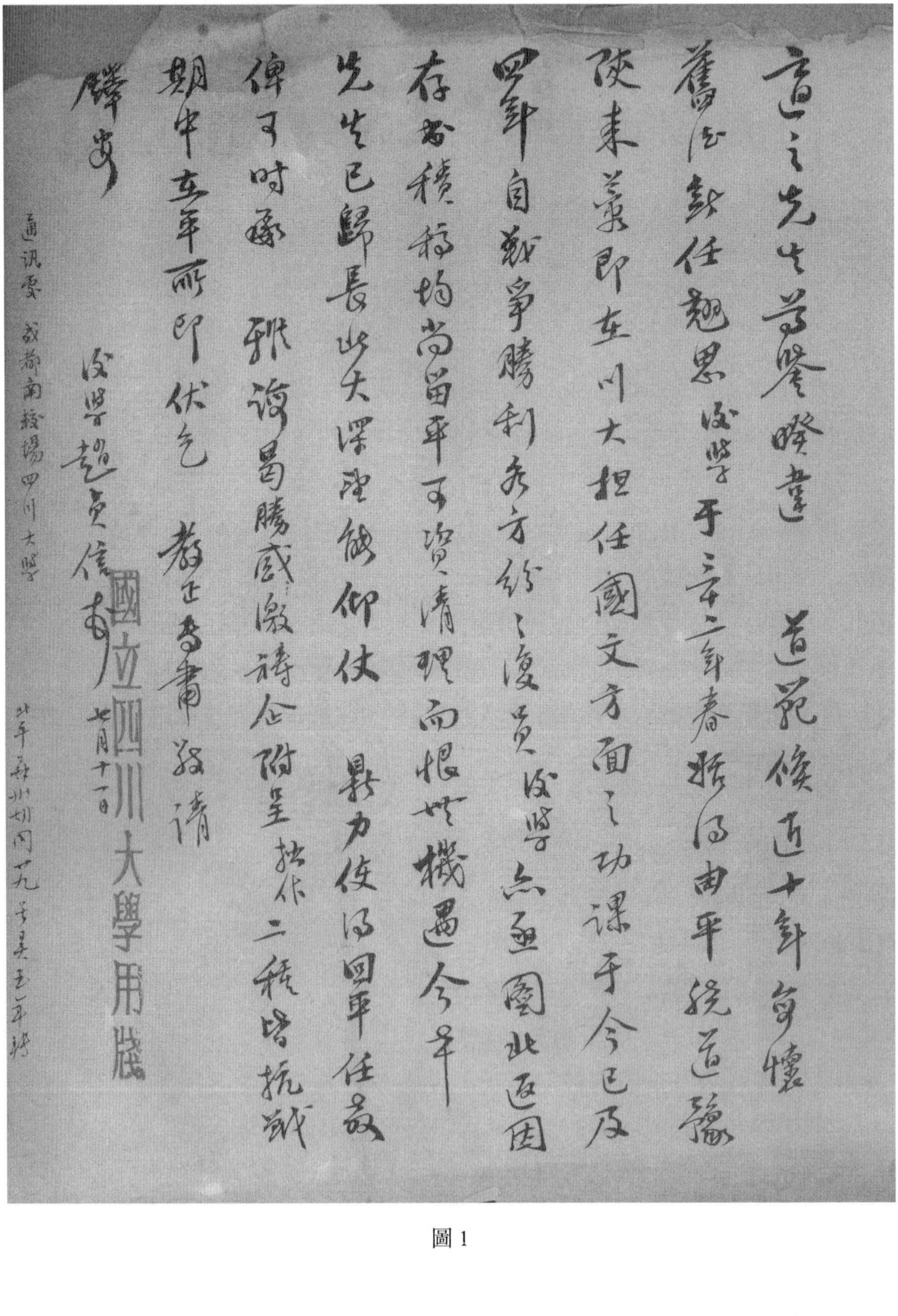

適之先生學譽晼邐 道範俊邁十年勞懷

舊法敦任魁恩發學于三十二年春轉回由平晓道轎

陝來蓉即左川大担任國文方面之功課于今已及

四年自就爭勝利來方紹之後發學点盈回此區因

歷年積稿均當出平可資清理而根掂機遇今年

先生巳歸長此天澤歷能仰仗暴力使阿回平任教

俾了時蹗 雅誼昌勝感激禱企附呈拙作二種皆抗戰

期中忝年所即伏乞 教正专肅致请

騫安

後學趙京信上 七月十日 國立四川大學用箋

通訊處 成都南較楊四川大學

北平新卅七同九号吳玉萍转

圖1

適之先生尊鑒：

　　暌違道範倏近十年，每懷
舊德，無任翹思，後學于三十二年春始得由平繞道豫陝來蓉，即在川大擔任國文方面之功課，于今已及四年。自戰爭勝利，各方紛紛復員，後學亦亟圖北返，因存書積稿均尚留平，可資清理，而恨無機遇。今幸
先生已歸長北大，深望能仰仗鼎力，使得回平任教，俾可時承雅誨，曷勝感激禱企。附呈拙作二種，皆抗戰期中在平所印，伏乞教正。專肅，敬請
鐸安

　　　　　　　　　　　　　　　　　　　　後學　趙貞信 拜
　　　　　　　　　　　　　　　　　　　　　　七月十一日
通訊處　成都南較場四川大學　　北平蘇州胡同廿九號吳玉年轉

智武致胡適

此信發現於《援世寶鑒》一書中，出版於 1947 年。

作者生平不詳。

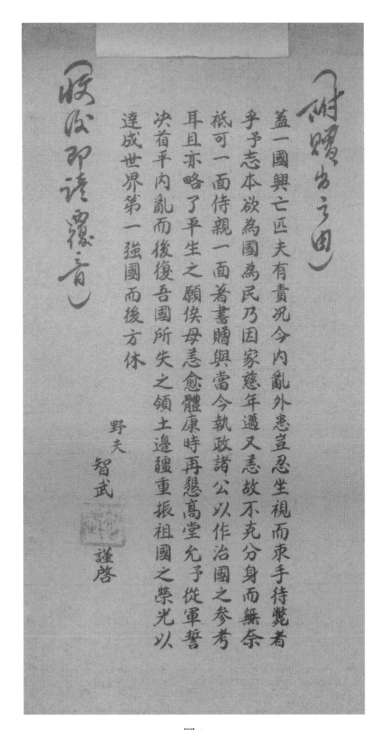

圖1

朱經農致胡適（一九一六年八月二十三日）

此信發現於 Towards an Enduring Peace 一書中。此信僅署星期三，郵戳爲 1916 年 8 月 24 日，信中提到廿六日（星期六），故此信當寫於 1916 年 8 月 23 日。

朱經農（1887—1951），原名有畇，改名經，字經農。祖籍江蘇寶山，生於浙江浦江。1903 年考入常德府中學堂。1904 年留學日本，次年加入同盟會，同年冬回上海，參與創辦中國公學。1912 年到北京，任《民主報》編輯，後兼《亞東新聞》總編輯。1913 年曾在北京政府農商部任職。1916 年任留美學生監督處書記，業餘入華盛頓大學聽課。1920 年辭職，入哥倫比亞大學，獲碩士學位。1921 年回國，任北京大學教授。1923 年赴上海任商務印書館編輯。1924 年秋兼任滬江大學國文系主任，並講授教育學。1925 年任光華大學教務長。1927 年，北伐軍攻佔上海，國民黨上海市政府成立，被任命爲教育局局長。1928 年任大學院普通教育處處長。同年秋，大學院改組爲教育部，任普通教育司司長。1930 年任教育部常務次長，同年冬辭職。1931 年春任中國公學代理校長。同年夏，任齊魯大學校長。1932 年 9 月任湖南省政府委員兼教育廳廳長。1943 年 3 月任中央大學教育長，實際主持中央大學。1944 年 3 月任教育部政務次長。1946 年 10 月繼王雲五任商務印書館總經理，兼任光華大學校長。1946 年 11 月、1948 年 3 月兩次當選爲制憲國民大會代表。1948 年 11 月 以中國首席代表身份出席聯合國文教會議，後留在美國。1950 年在康涅狄格州哈特福德神學院任教。1951 年 3 月 9 日病逝。主編《教育大辭書》，著有《教育思想》《愛山廬詩鈔》等。

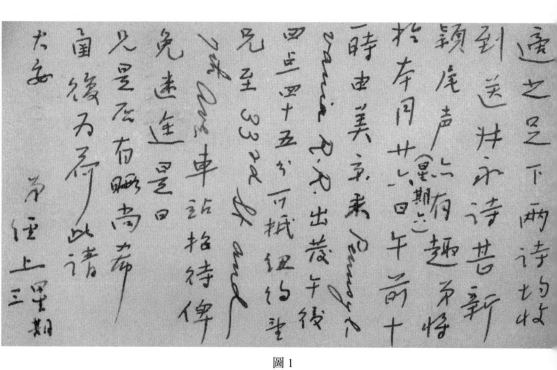

圖1

適之足下：

　　兩詩均收到，送叔永詩甚新穎，尾聲亦有趣。弟將於本月廿六日（星期六）午前十一時由美京乘 Pennsylvania R. R. 出發，午後四點四十五分可抵紐約，望兄至 33rd St. and 7th Ave 車站招待，俾免迷途。是日兄是否有暇，尚希函復爲荷。此請
大安

弟　經　上
星期三

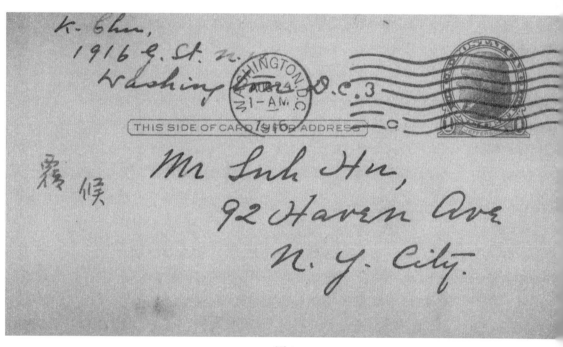

圖2

朱士嘉致胡適（一九四四年七月三十一日）

　　此信發現於《國會圖書館藏中國方志目錄》中，此書出版於 1942 年。據學者考證，朱士嘉 1942 年 9 月入哥倫比亞大學讀博士，1946 年 6 月畢業離校。其間按中日文系富路德教授的建議，整理和鑒定哥倫比亞大學東亞圖書館地方志館藏，並與國會地方志館藏作對比研究。他將這一重要研究工作的成果，以"哥倫比亞大學地方志"爲題發表在《哈佛亞洲研究學刊》上，時間爲 1944 年第 2 期 vol.8。其中細節與此信中所載吻合，例如數目爲一千三百來種，山東方志有兩百餘種，以及《桐溪記略》《弘治上海志》等，信中又稱"富先生打算把它開一書目單，在哈佛亞細亞學報發表"，"這一個書目單大約在下星期以內可以開完"，可見寫此信時朱士嘉對於哥倫比亞大學所藏中國方志的研究已粗具成果，與後來發表的文章區別不大，故此信距文章發表時間或許不長，很可能就寫於 1944 年。可參考《中美關係歷史大潮和個人學術追求——以哥倫比亞大學博士朱士嘉爲例》，天津師範大學學報（社會科學版），2021 年第 1 期。另朱士嘉《哥倫比亞大學地方誌》一文曾轉載於《國際漢學研究通訊》第四期，北京大學出版社 2011 年 12 月出版。

　　朱士嘉（1905—1989），字蓉江，江蘇無錫人。1920 年入江陰勵實中學，中學畢業後入杭州之江大學，後入燕京大學，1928 年獲學士學位，1932 年獲碩士學位。先後任輔仁大學講師、燕京大學圖書館中文編目部主任，並主編《史學年報》和《燕京大學圖報》。1939 年赴美，在國會圖書館整理中國方志。1942 年 9 月入哥倫比亞大學研究院，1946 年獲博士學位。1947 年任美國西雅圖華盛頓大學遠東系副教授。1950年歸國，任武漢大學歷史系教授。次年兼任武漢大學圖書館館長。1953年8月，調中國科學院歷史研究所第三所工作。1958年8月從北京調回武漢，先後任職於武昌中國科學院中南分院圖書館、湖北科技大學圖書館、中國科學院武漢辦事處。1975年7月借調北京中國科學院北京天文臺工作。1979年任湖北省文史館副館長。曾任湖北大學教授、中國地名委員會顧問、中國地方志協會副會長等職。編著有《中國地方志綜錄》《美國國會圖書館藏中國地方志目錄》等。

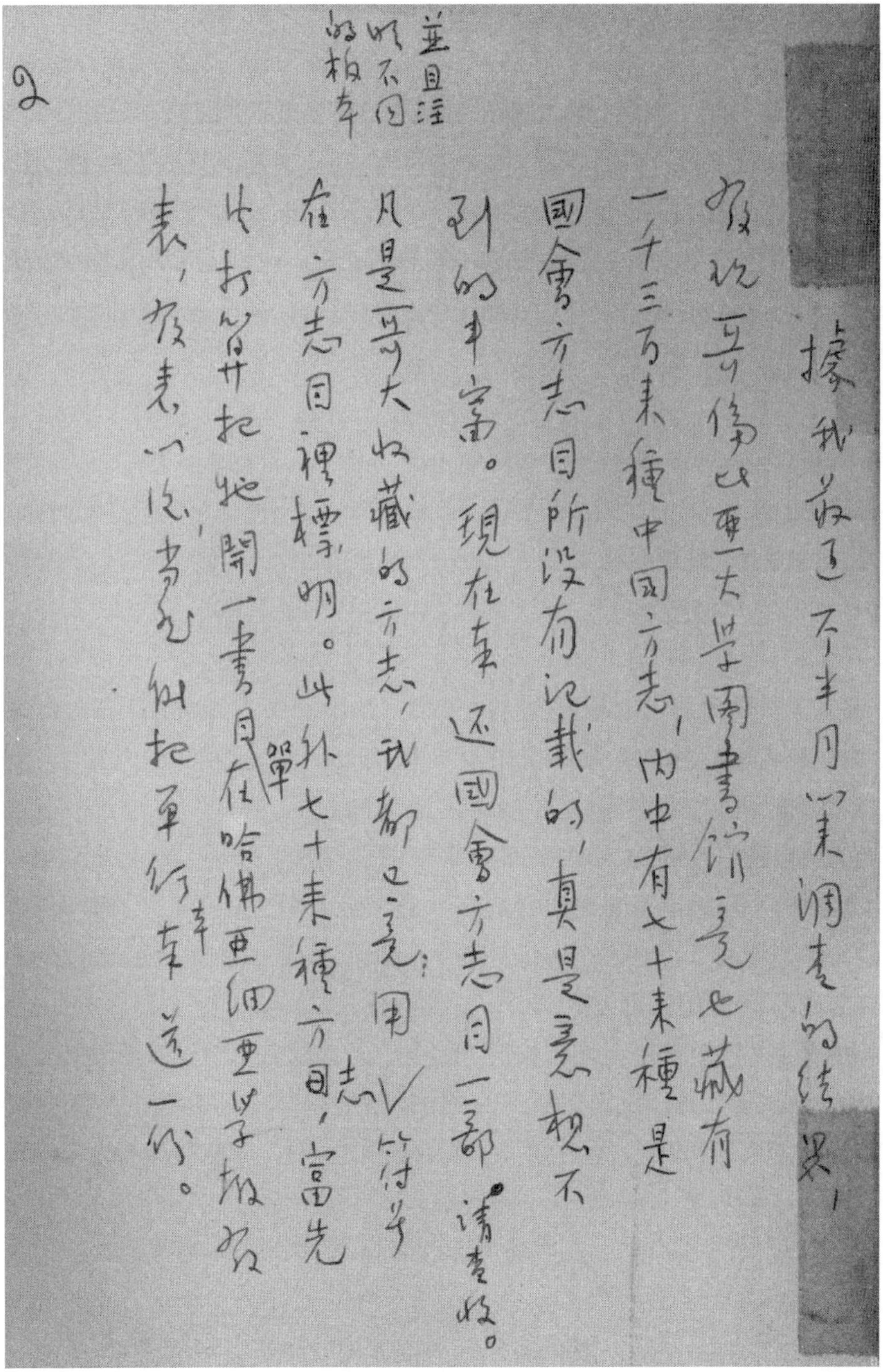

據我做了不少月來調查的結果，發現哥倫比亞大學圖書館竟也藏有一千三百來種中國方志，內中有七十來種是國會方志目所沒有記載的，真是意想不到的丰富。現在柔還國會方志目一部請查收。凡是哥大收藏的方志，我都已憑V符號在方志目裡標明。此外七十來種方志，富先生替廿把地開一書目放在哈佛燕大學報發表，發表以後，考凡仙把單行本送一份。

並且注明不同的板本

圖1

這一個書目單方存在下午託人以
開完，當時我再把家裡的一份給
先生送閱。馬大所藏山東方志居
然有二百零四種，數目竟在望衡
此外請他未葉和民國以來所修的
浙學未富。浙江的桐溪記男三卷，
十卷之三年程鵬程修的仁本是極力見
極有寄到的志了。桐鄉是桐鄉的別名。一五〇〇。
年宗切的私淑上海志之紀子歡。

校對的事不敢說我為閩今編的
方志目完也有不少錯誤的地方。將來如
趙和恆先生再商議或者在閩今的初步書
(字報)裡附上一個「勘誤表」。先生以為如
何？

有什麼事情的書信隨時告訴
我。有什麼要我的材料也請告訴我。敬
祝
先生安好！

後學 王嘉 敬上 七月廿一日

（前缺）

據我最近一個半月以來調查的結果，發現哥倫比亞大學圖書館竟也藏有一千三百來種中國方志，內中有七十來種是國會方志目所沒有記載的，真是意想不到的豐富。現在奉還國會方志目一部，請查收。凡是哥大收藏的方志，我都已竟用 V 符號在方志目裡標明（並且註明不同的板本）。此外七十來種方志，富先生打算把牠開一書目單，在哈佛亞細亞學報發表，發表以後，當然能把單行本奉送一份。

這一個書目單大約在下星期以內可以開完，當時我再把富裕的一份給先生送上存閱。哥大所藏山東方志居然有二百零四種，數目實在驚人！此外清代末葉和民國以來所修的也非常豐富。浙江的《桐溪記畧》六卷，嘉慶二年程鵬程（私人）修的，似乎是極少見極有條例的本子。桐溪是桐鄉的別名。一九四〇年景印的《[弘治]上海志》也很可觀。

校對的結果發現我為國會編輯的方志目竟也有不少錯誤的地方。將來我想和恒先生商議，或者在國會的報告書（年報）裡坿上一個"勘誤表"，先生以為如何？

有什麼要借的書，請隨時告訴我。有什麼要找的材料也請告訴我。暫時恕我不多寫了。敬祝
先生安好！

後學　士嘉敬上
七月卅一日

祝實明致胡適（一九四六年七月三十日）

此信發現於《不時髦的歌》一書中。

祝實明，生卒年不詳，原名祝世德，筆名祝笑我的、拾名、夏留仁、惠流芳等。1927年任四川萬縣某中學國文教師，曾在《語絲》上發表作品，後在《新時代》上發表新詩，作品受新月詩派影響。1931年前後任教於江西省璧山縣某中學。有《明季哀音錄》《白的悲哀》等短篇小說集，《不時髦的歌》《墾殖集》《影像集》等詩集。另著有《新詩的理論基礎》等。

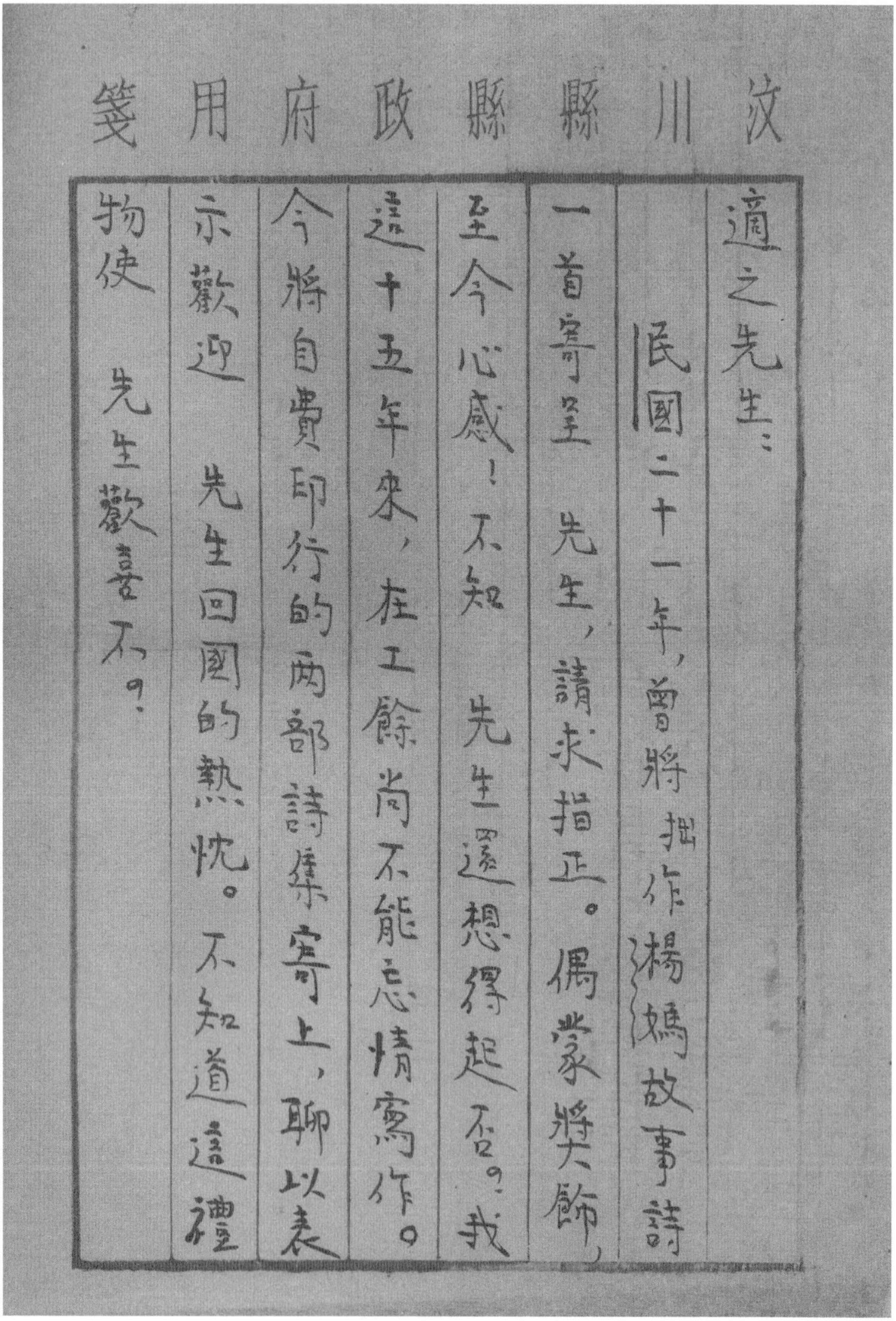

汶川縣縣政府用箋

適之先生：

民國二十一年，曾將拙作渴媽故事詩一首寄呈先生，請求指正。偶蒙獎飾，至今心感！不知先生還想得起否。我這十五年來，在工餘尚不能忘情寫作。今將自費印行的兩部詩集寄上，聊以表示歡迎先生回國的熱忱。不知道這禮物使 先生歡喜不。

圖1

適之先生：

　　民國二十一年，曾將拙作《楊媽》故事詩一首寄呈先生，請求指正。偶蒙獎飾，至今心感！不知先生還想得起否？我這十五年來，在工餘尚不能忘情寫作。今將自費印行的兩部詩集寄上，聊以表示歡迎先生回國的熱忱。不知道這禮物使先生歡喜不？

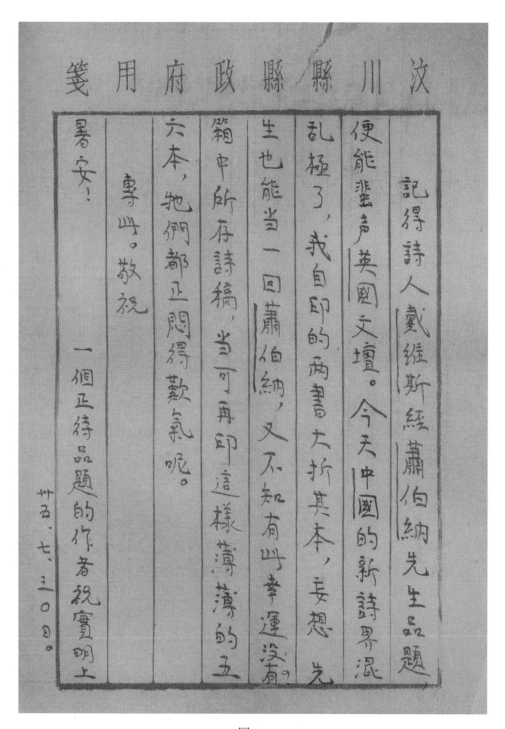

汶川縣縣政府用箋

記得詩人戴維斯經蕭伯納先生品題，便能蜚声英國文壇。今天中國的新詩界混乱极了，我自印的兩書大折其本，妄想先生也能当一回蕭伯納，又不知有此幸運沒有？

箱中所存詩稿，当可再印這樣薄薄的五六本，牠們都正悶得歎氣呢。

專此。敬祝

暑安！

一個正待品題的作者祝實明上

廿五、七、三〇日。

圖 2

記得詩人戴維斯經蕭伯納先生品題，便能蜚聲英國文壇。今天中國的新詩界混亂極了，我自印的兩書大折其本，妄想先生也能當一回蕭伯納，又不知有此幸運沒有？箱中所存詩稿，當可再印這樣薄薄的五六本，牠們都正悶得嘆氣呢。

　　專此。敬祝
暑安！

一個正待品題的作者祝實明上
卅五，七，三〇日。

國立北平故宮博物院總務處致胡適
（一九四七年九月十三日）

此信發現於《國立北平故宮博物院三十五年度工作報告》中。

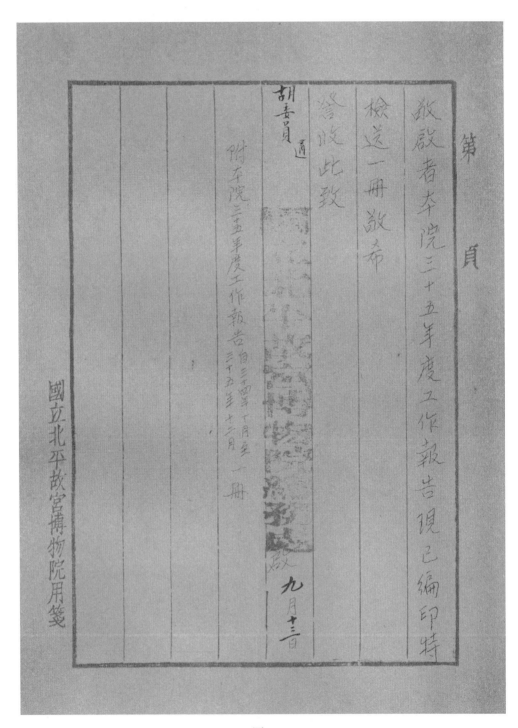

圖1

國立編譯館致胡適

此信發現於《全宋詞草目》中。此書出版於 1934 年。

謹啟者本館頃擬印行唐君圭璋近編之全宋詞一書為力求完備起見特將草目奉請
台覽唐君編輯是書係由(一)綜合諸家所刻叢集(二)搜求集部附詞(三)彙列選集所錄(四)增補諸書遺佚而成然遺漏要所不免如四庫存目所著錄之宋伯仁煙波漁隱詞張德瀛詞徵所著錄之闕刻本李元伯大觀昇平詞唐君即深以未得廣目為憾海內藏書家或竟有其書未可知也又如零篇斷簡散見於永樂大典及金石地志諸書為唐君所未留意者恐尚有遺漏風仰
先生詞學湛深見聞廣博幸乞　贊助俾臻完善其有裨

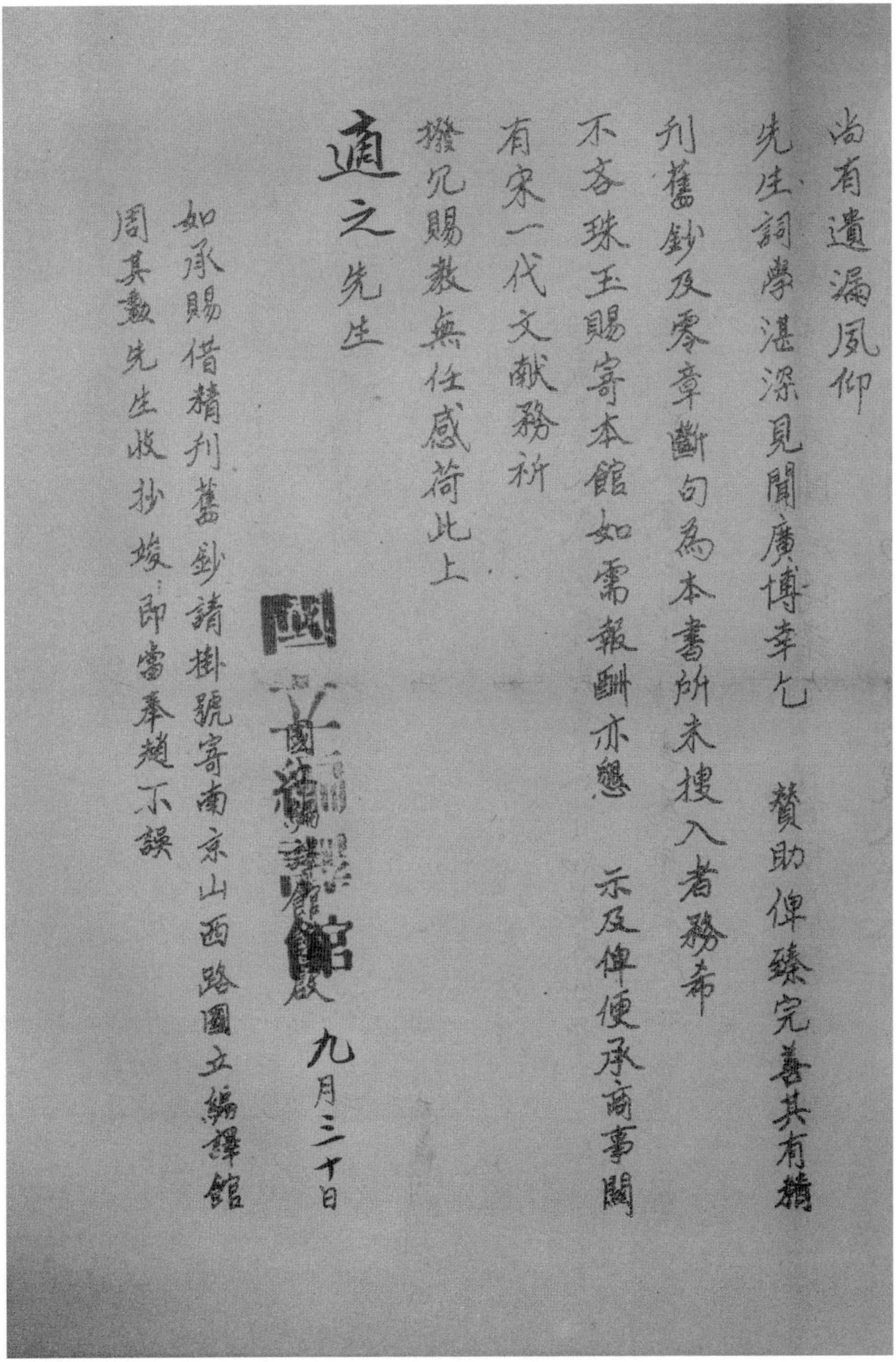

適之先生：

先生詞學湛深，見聞廣博，幸乞贊助，俾臻完善。其有搞刊舊鈔及零章斷句為本書所未搜入者，務希不吝珠玉，賜寄本館。如需報酬，亦懇示及，俾便承商。事關有宋一代文獻，務祈撥冗賜教，無任感荷。此上

適之先生

尚有遺漏，馮仰

如承賜借精刊舊鈔，請掛號寄南京山西路國立編譯館周其勳先生收，抄竣即當奉趙不誤。

國立編譯館啟 九月三十日

圖2

江蘇省立教育學院惠北普及民眾教育實驗區
致胡適（一九三二年十二月一日）

　　此函發現於江蘇省立教育學院惠北普及民眾教育實驗區所呈該區概況及進行計劃中。

江蘇省立教育學院惠北普及民眾教育實驗區

第　號

逕啟者敝院為適應時勢需要於本年八月在無錫惠山之北敝院附近劃定高長岸等三十餘村莊籌設惠北普及民眾教育實驗區（與敝院附設之北夏普及民教實驗區同時設立）從事試驗於一定年限內普及一區鄉村民眾教育以期達到完成地方自治發展鄉村經濟並改進農民生活之目的敝區自成立以來雖形式粗具而一切進行辦法尚乏南針素仰

先生熱心民教對於鄉村建設尤具

卓見為此專函奉懇隨時

駕臨敝區俯予

指導一切無任公感附呈敝區概況及進行計劃一份並祈

指正是幸此上

公鑒

江蘇省立教育學院惠北普及民眾教育實驗區啟　二十一年十二月一日

本區
總辦事處　無錫江蘇省立教育學院
第一分區辦事處　張家橋
第二分區辦事處　高長岸
第三分區辦事處　高涇橋

中華民國　年　月　日

總辦事處無錫省立教育學院內

開明書店致胡適

此信發現於《二十五史補編》一書中。此書首册印行於 1936 年 3 月。

開明書店股份有限公司用牋

敬啓者:「二十五史補編」第一册遲至現在始克送達台端,抱歉良深。其所以不能如期趕出之故,實緣校印時每有徵引舛錯必須逐細查對原書者(詳見各校記)工作遂不免延長。嗣後各册正在力求迅速進行,以冀稍減愆期之咎。然仍不敢掉以輕心上負雅望。每册出書距離誠恐或有差池,尚望明達鑒諒爲幸!

開明書店二十五史刊行委員會謹啓

圖1

民族雜誌社致胡適（一九三六年三月十五日）

此信發現於《民族》第四卷第一期中。

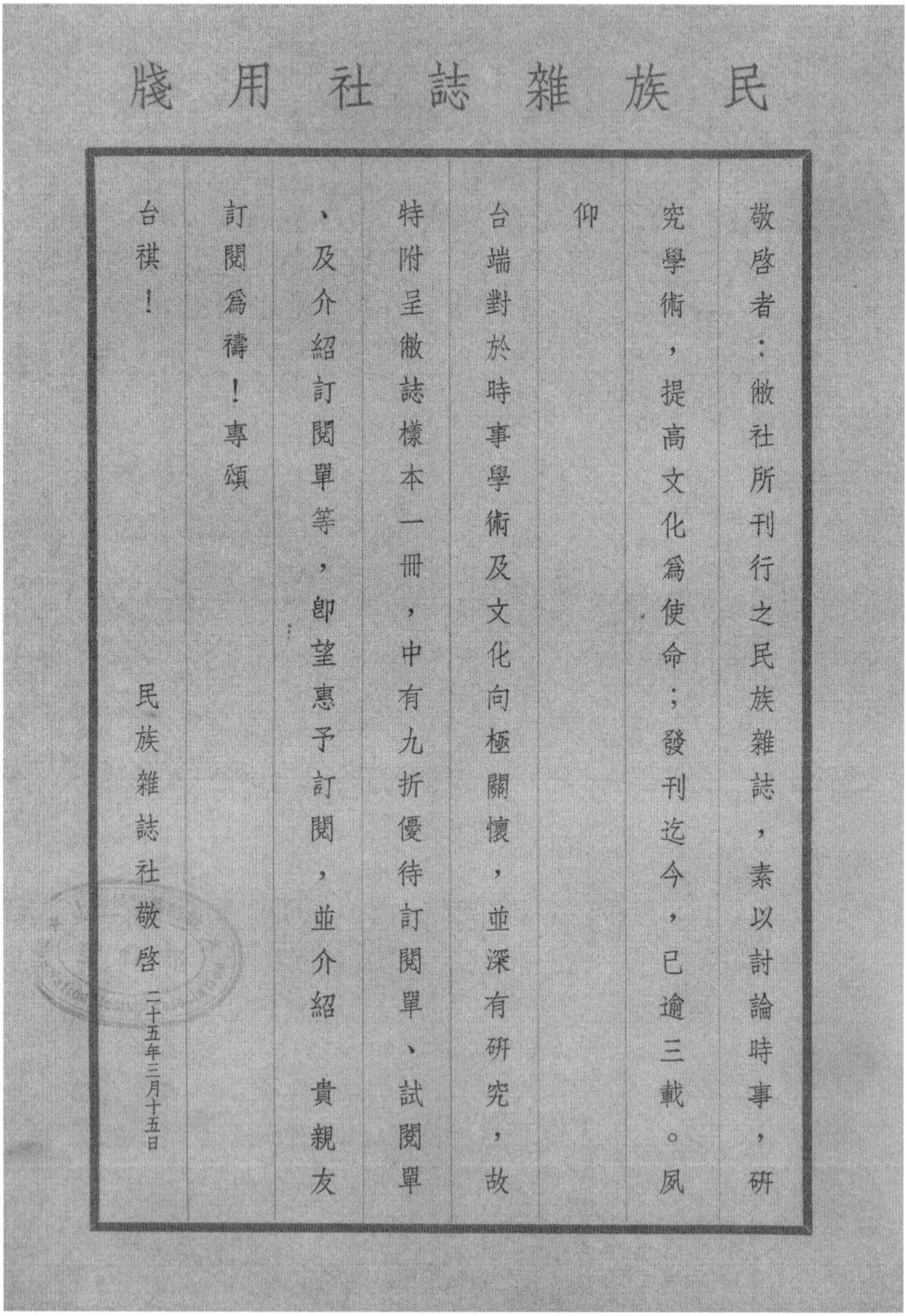

民族雜誌社用牋

敬啓者：敝社所刊行之民族雜誌，素以討論時事，研究學術，提高文化爲使命；發刊迄今，已逾三載。凤仰

台端對於時事學術及文化向極關懷，並深有研究，故特附呈敝誌樣本一冊，中有九折優待訂閱單、試閱單、及介紹訂閱單等，卽望惠予訂閱，並介紹 貴親友訂閱爲禱！專頌

台祺！

民族雜誌社敬啓 二十五年三月十五日

圖1

商務印書館致胡適

以下信件皆爲商務印書館歷年致胡適之公函,發現於各封信函所提及之相關書籍中。

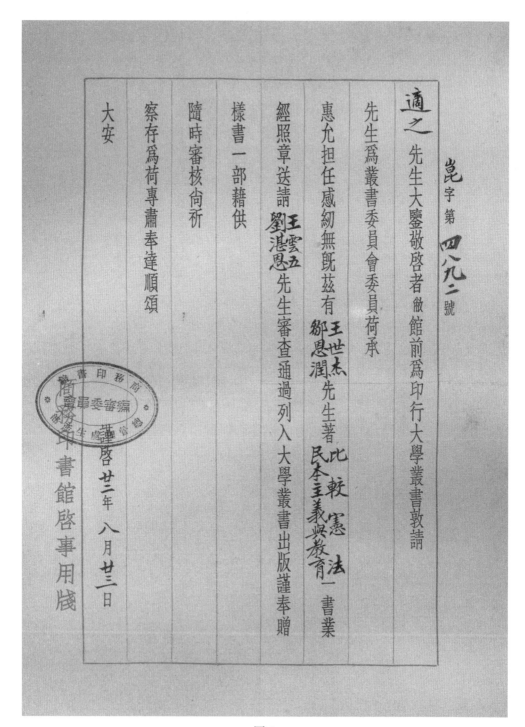

圖 1

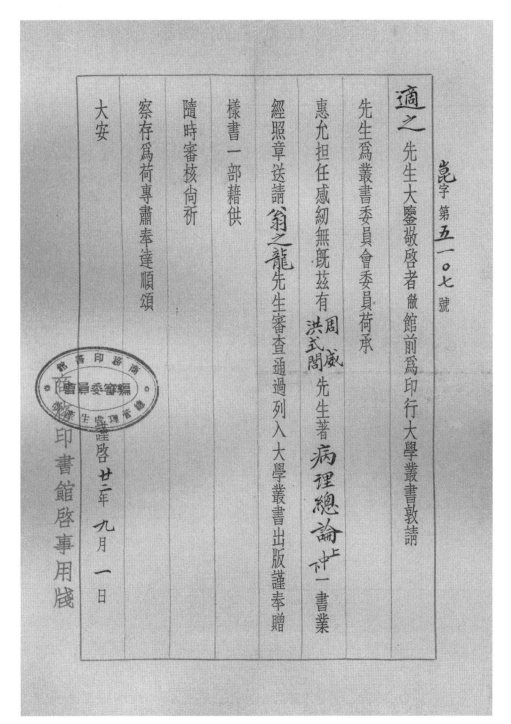

崑字第五一〇七號

適之先生大鑒敬啟者敝館前為印行大學叢書敬請

先生為叢書委員會委員荷承

惠允擔任感紉無既茲有周威 洪式閭先生著病理總論中一書業

經照章送請翁之龍先生審查通過列入大學叢書出版謹奉贈

樣書一部藉供

隨時審核尚祈

察存為荷專肅奉達順頌

大安

商務印書館啟事用箋 謹啟廿二年九月一日

圖2

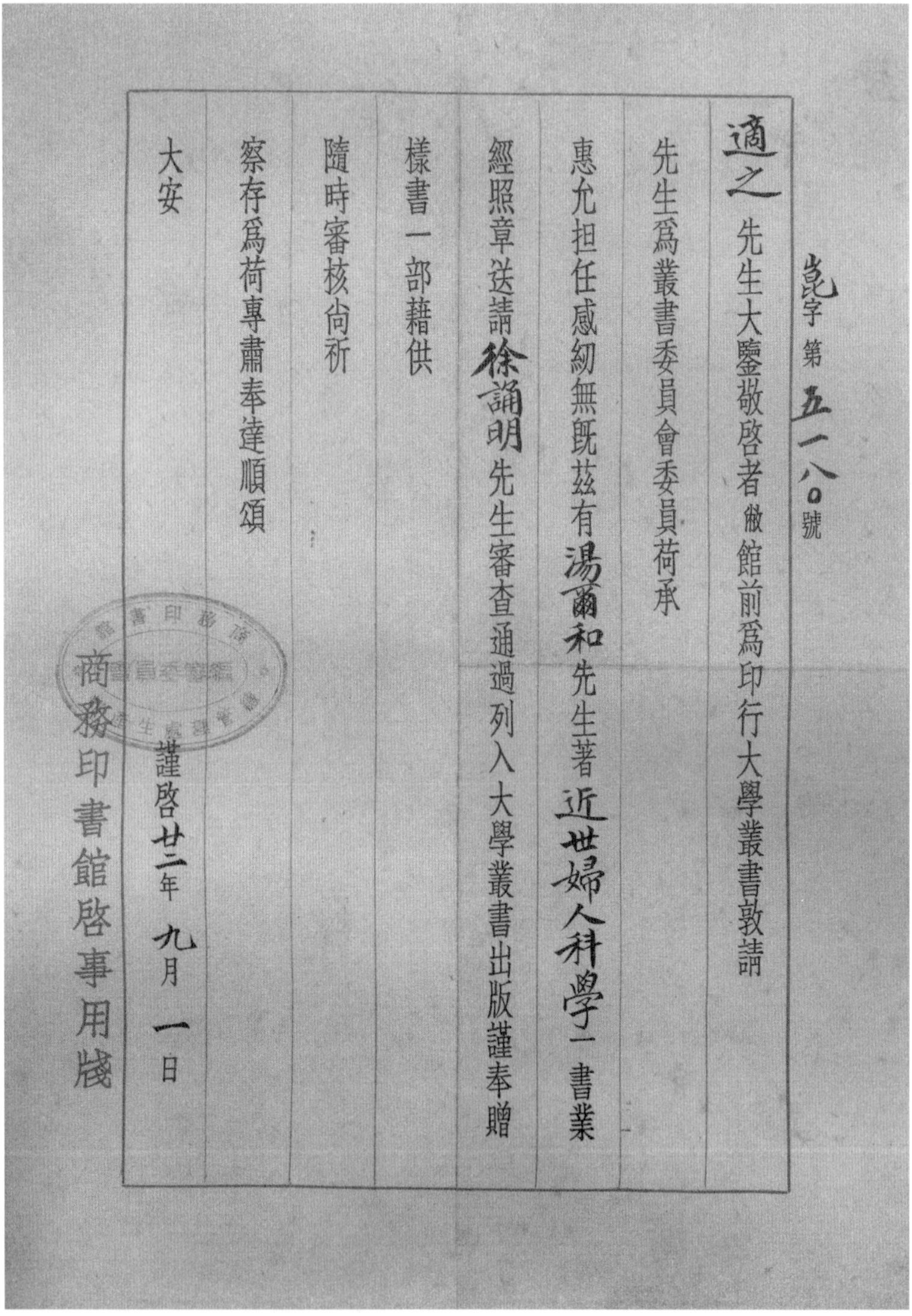

[illegible]字第五一八〇號

適之先生大鑒敬啓者敝館前爲印行大學叢書敦請
先生爲叢書委員會委員荷承
惠允担任感紉無既茲有湯爾和先生著近世婦人科學一書業
經照章送請徐誦明先生審查通過列入大學叢書出版謹奉贈
樣書一部藉供
隨時審核尚祈
察存爲荷專肅奉達順頌
大安

商務印書館
編審委員會

謹啓廿二年九月一日

商務印書館啓事用牋

圖 3

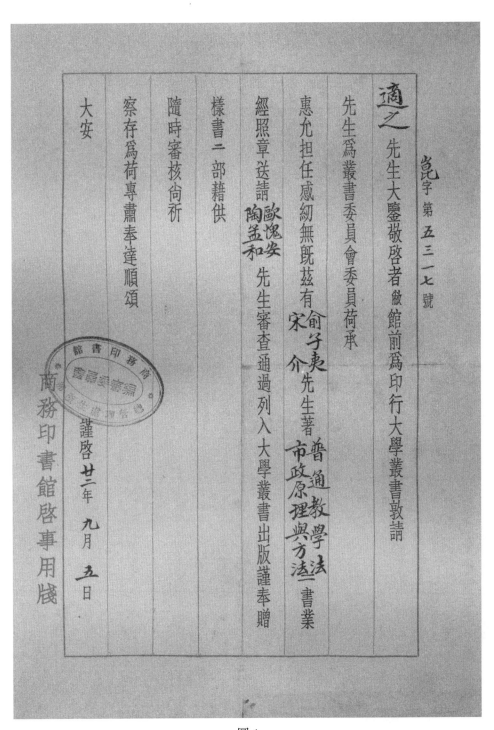

圖4

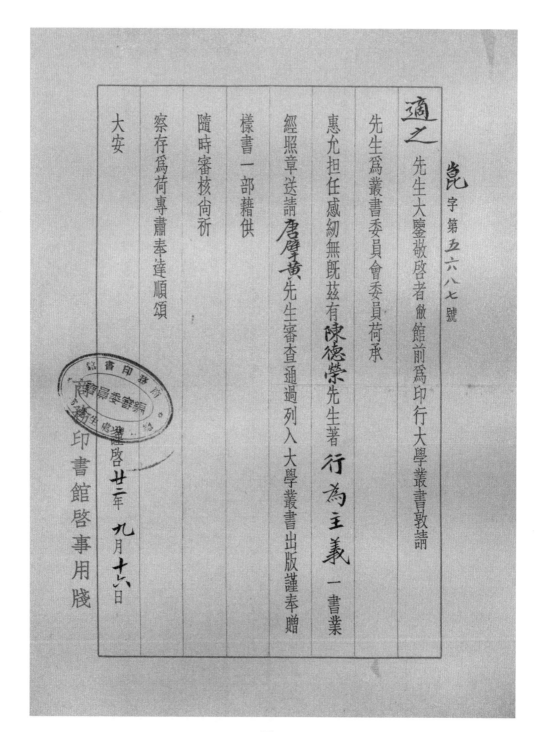

圖 5

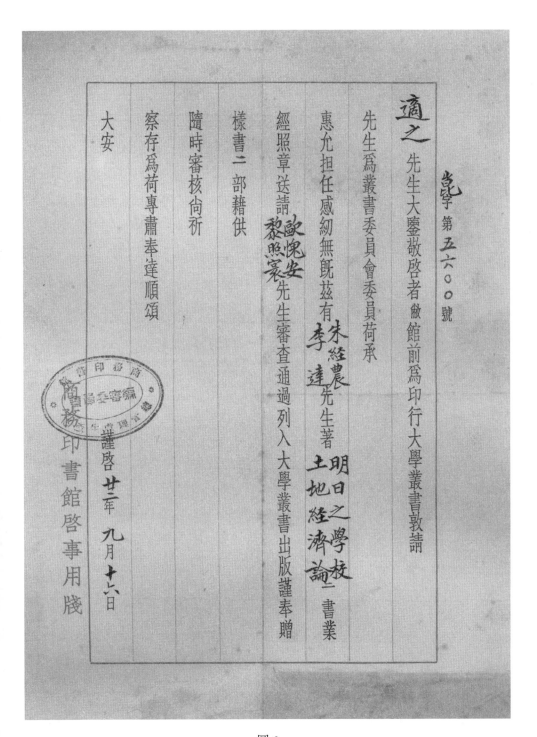

图6

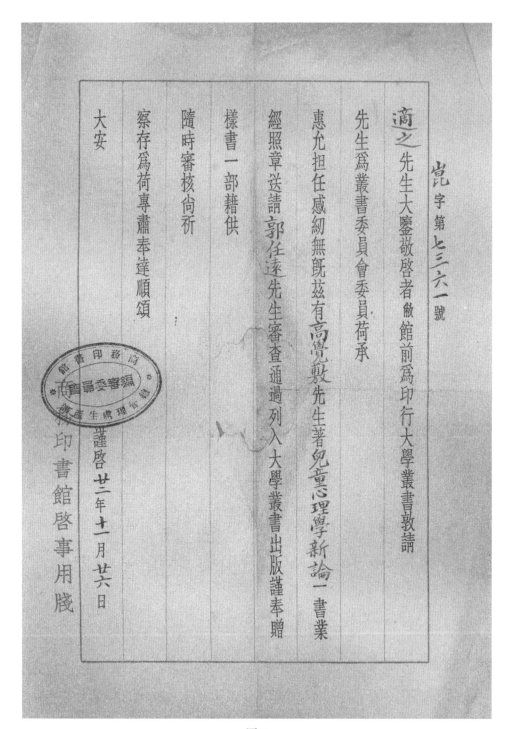

圖7

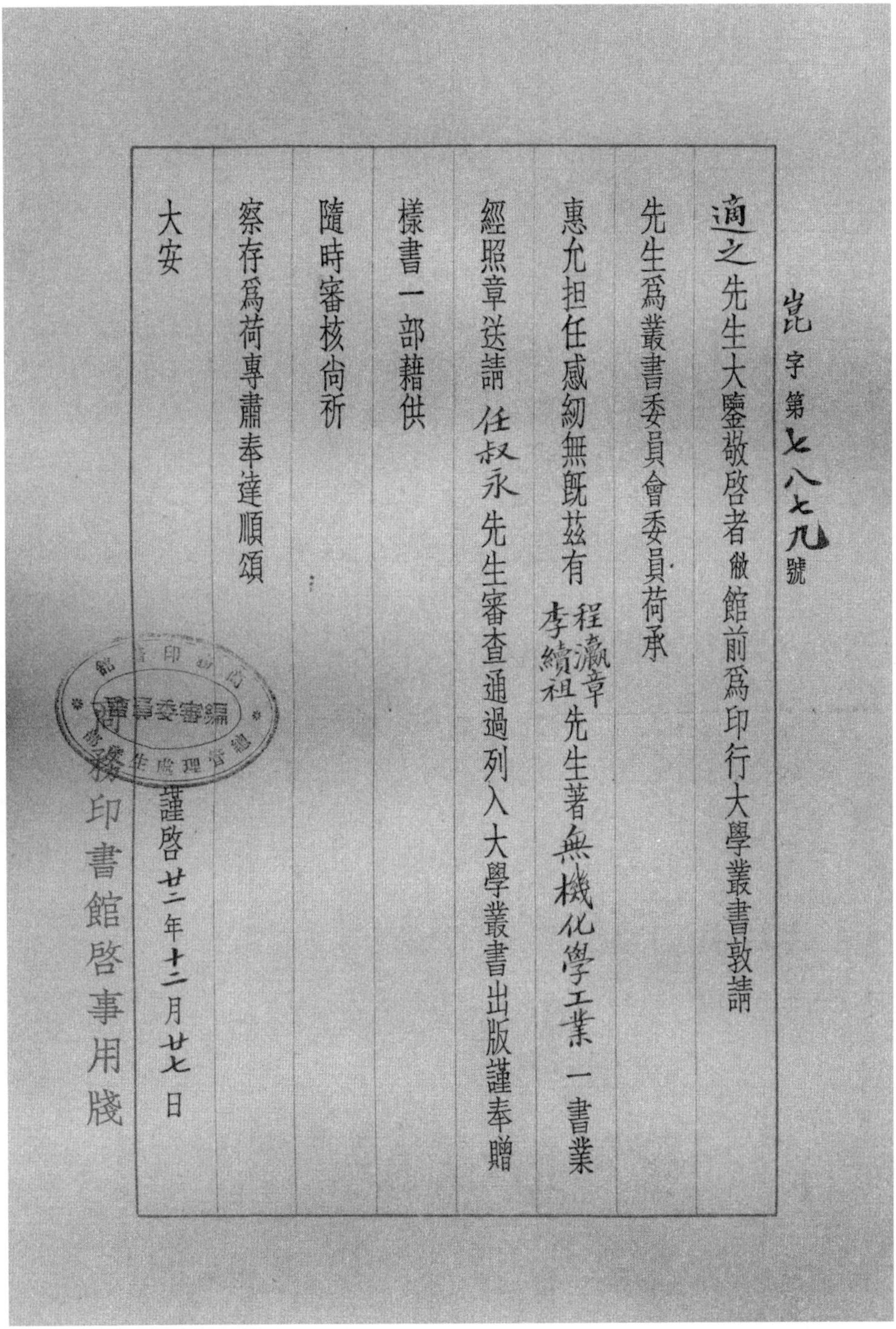

崑字第七八七九號

適之先生大鑒敬啟者敝館前為印行大學叢書敬請
先生為叢書委員會委員荷承
惠允擔任感紉無既茲有 程瀛章 先生著無機化學工業一書業
　　　　　　　　　　李續祖
經照章送請 任叔永先生審查通過列入大學叢書出版謹奉贈
樣書一部藉供
隨時審核尚祈
察存為荷專肅奉達順頌
大安

　　　　　　謹啟廿二年十二月廿七日
商務印書館啟事用牋

圖 8

虞字第一〇五號

適之先生大鑒敬啓者敝館前爲印行大學叢書敬請
先生爲叢書委員會委員荷承
惠允担任感紉無既茲有雍家源先生著**中國政府會計論**一書業
經照章送請馬寅初先生審查通過列入大學叢書出版謹奉贈
樣書一部藉供
察存爲荷專肅奉達順頌
大安

商務印書館啓事用牋

謹啓廿三年一月十三日

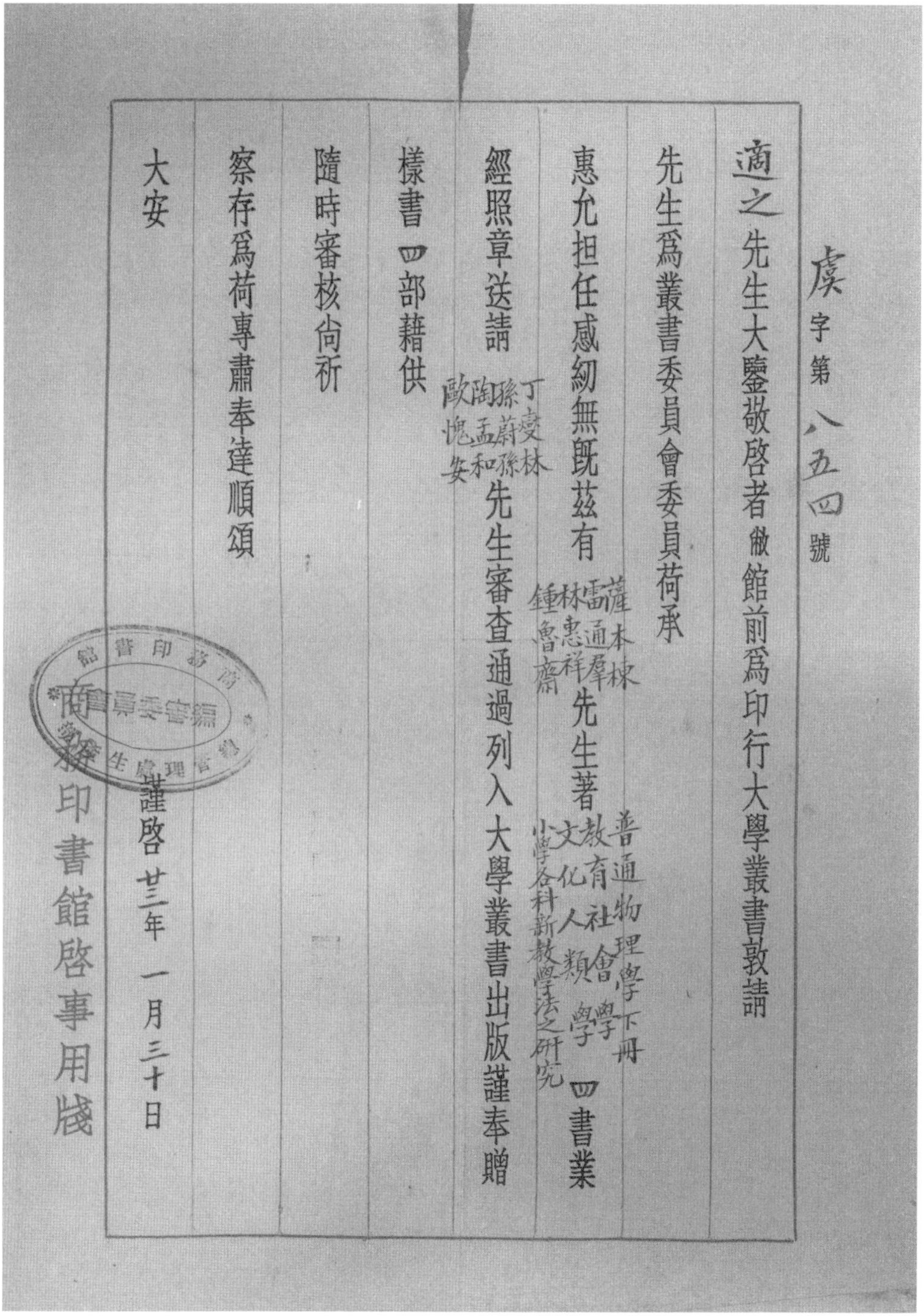

虞字第八五四號

適之先生大鑒敬啟者敝館前為印行大學叢書敬請

先生為叢書委員會委員荷承

惠允擔任感紉無既茲有

薩本棟

雷通羣

林惠祥　先生著

鍾魯齋

丁燮林

孫蕷孫

陶孟和

歐愧安

普通物理學下冊
教育社會學
文化人類學
小學各科新教學法之研究
四書業

經照章送請

先生審查通過列入大學叢書出版謹奉贈

樣書四部藉供

隨時審核尚祈

察存為荷專肅奉達順頌

大安

商務印書館啟事用箋

謹啟 廿三年 一月 三十日

圖10

虞字第 3015 號

適之先生大鑒敬啓者敝館前爲印行大學叢書敦請
先生爲叢書委員會委員荷承
惠允擔任感紉無既茲有 王撫洲 先生著 工業組織與管理
　　　　　　　　　　錢端升 先生著 德國的政府 三書業
經照章送請 胡春藻 先生審查通過列入大學叢書出版謹奉贈
　　　　　陶孟和
樣書三部藉供
隨時審核尚祈
察存爲荷專肅奉達順頌
大安

商務印書館啓 廿三年 五月 十二日
圖書館啓事用牋

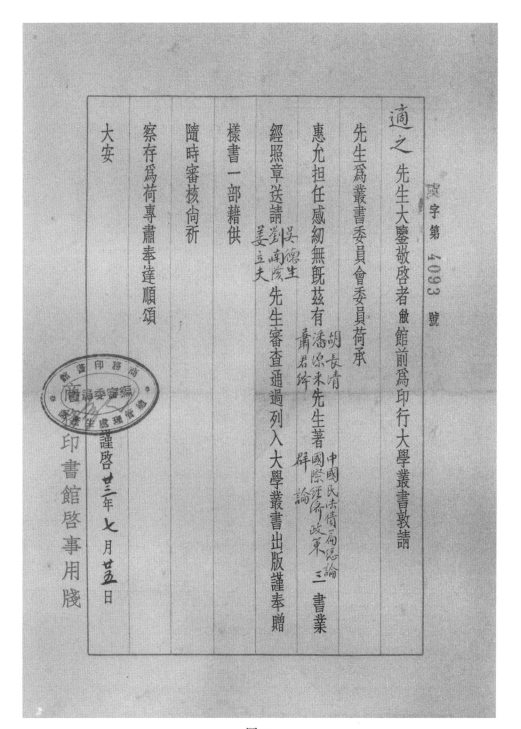

圖12

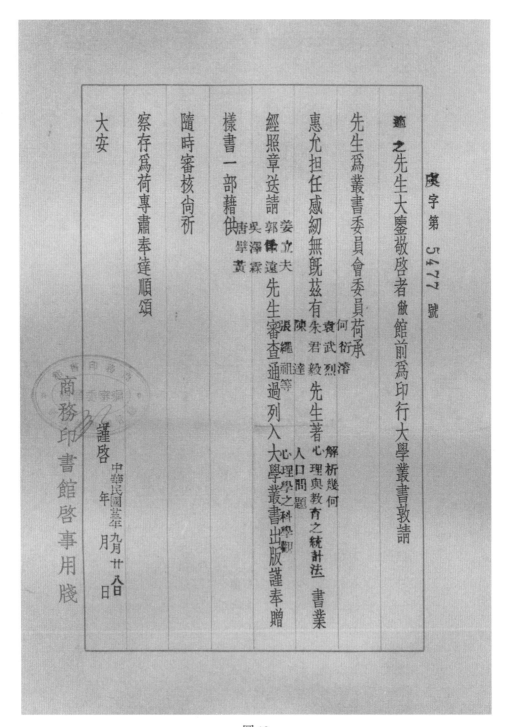

庚字第 5477 號

適之先生大鑒敬啓者敝館前為印行大學叢書敬請

先生為叢書委員會委員荷承

　　　　　　何衍濬　袁武烈　朱君毅

惠允担任感紉無既茲有　先生著 解析幾何　心理與教育之統計法　人口問題　心理學之科學觀 一書業

經照章送請　姜立夫　陳繩祖　郭德遠　吳澤霖　張達等　唐擘黃　先生審查通過列入大學叢書出版謹奉贈

樣書一部藉供

察存為荷專肅奉達順頌

大安

　　　　　　　　　　商務印書館啓事用牋

　　　　謹啓

中華民國　　年　九　月　廿八　日

圖 13

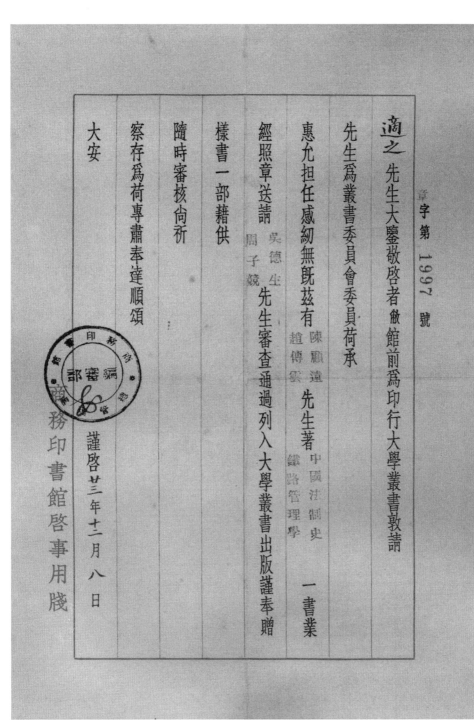

圖 14

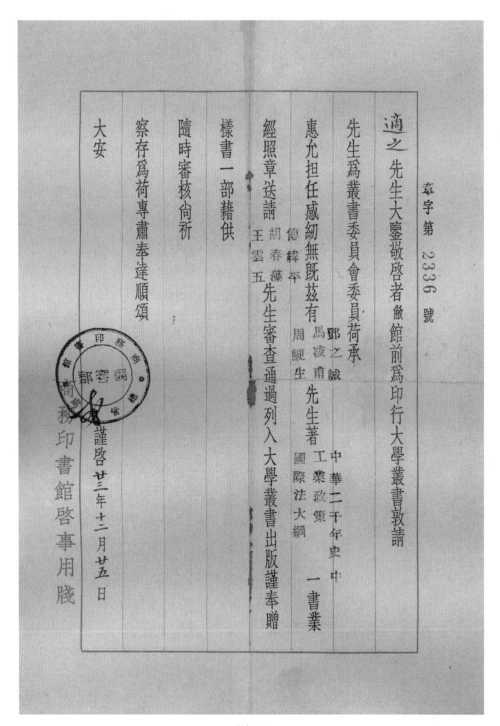

章字第 2336 號

適之先生大鑒敬啟者敝館前為印行大學叢書敦請
先生為叢書委員會委員荷承

惠允擔任感紉無既茲有

鄧之誠	中華二千年史
馬凌甫	工業政策
周鯁生	國際法大綱

   傅緯平

先生著　　　　　　一書業

經照章送請　胡春藻　先生審查通過列入大學叢書出版謹奉贈
　　　　　　王雲五

樣書一部藉供

隨時審核尚祈

察存為荷專肅奉達順頌

大安

商務印書館啟事用牋

謹啟 廿三年十二月廿五日

圖 15

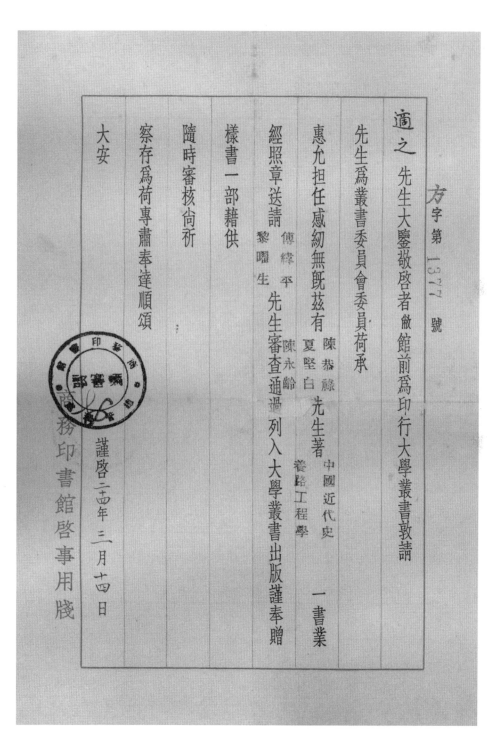

方字第1377號

適之先生大鑒敬啓者敝館前爲印行大學叢書敦請
先生爲叢書委員會委員荷承
惠允担任感紉無既茲有 陳恭祿 先生著 中國近代史 一書業
　　　　　　　　　夏堅白　　　　　養路工程學
經照章送請 傅緯平 先生審查通過列入大學叢書出版謹奉贈
　　　　　陳永齡
　　　　　黎曙生
樣書一部藉供
隨時審核尚祈
察存爲荷專肅奉達順頌
大安

商務印書館啓事用牋

謹啓二十四年三月十四日

圖16

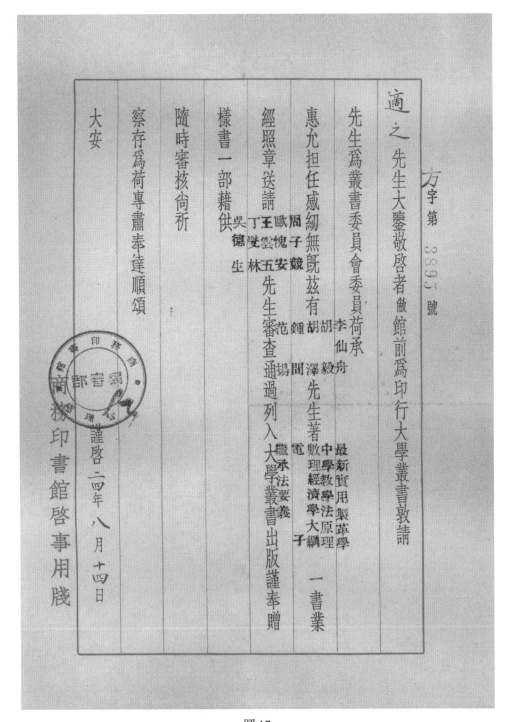

圖 17

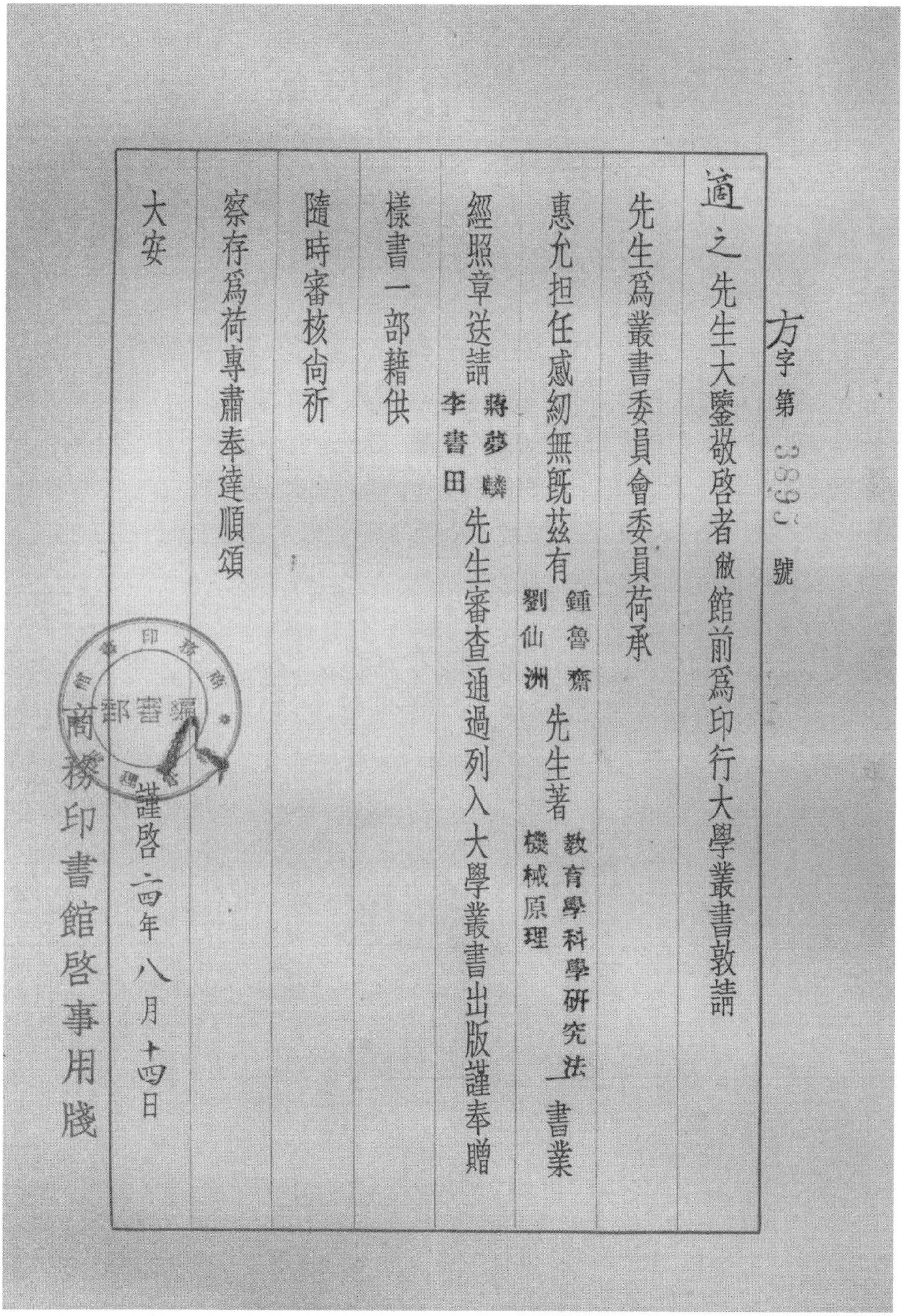

方字第3895號

適之先生大鑒敬啟者敝館前為印行大學叢書敬請

先生為叢書委員會委員荷承

惠允擔任感紉無既茲有 鍾魯齋 先生著 教育學科學研究法 書業
　　　　　　　　　劉仙洲　　　　機械原理

經照章送請 蔣夢麟 先生審查通過列入大學叢書出版謹奉贈
　　　　　李蓉田

樣書一部藉供

隨時審核尚祈

察存為荷專肅奉達順頌

大安

　　　　　商務印書館謹啟 二四年八月十四日

商務印書館啟事用箋

圖 18

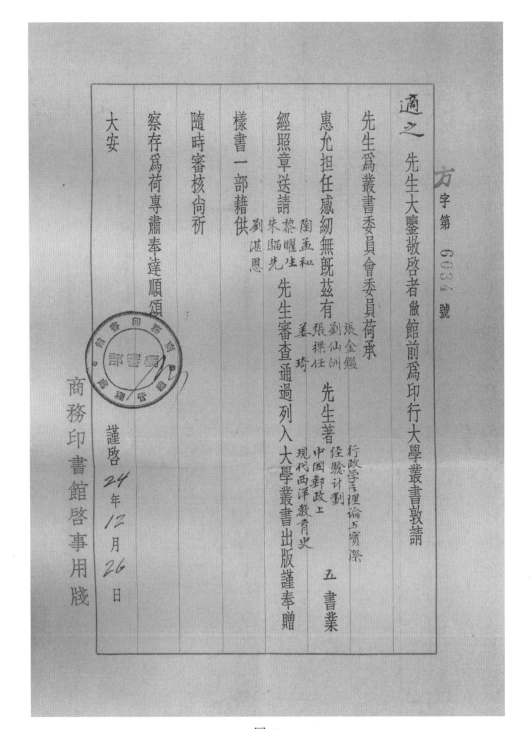

圖 19

方字第6034號

適之 先生大鑒敬啓者敝館前為印行大學叢書敬請

先生為叢書委員會委員荷承

惠允擔任感紉無既茲有 葉崇勳 中國鐵路會計學
張慶泰 歐洲政府
劉以祥 先生著 近世眼科學
黎曜生
李聖五 五書業
李相勖 訓育論

經照章送請 顏任光 先生審查通過列入大學叢書出版謹奉贈
蔣夢麟

樣書一部藉供

隨時審核尚祈

察存為荷專肅奉達順頌

大安

商務印書館啓事用牋 謹啓 24年12月26日

圖20

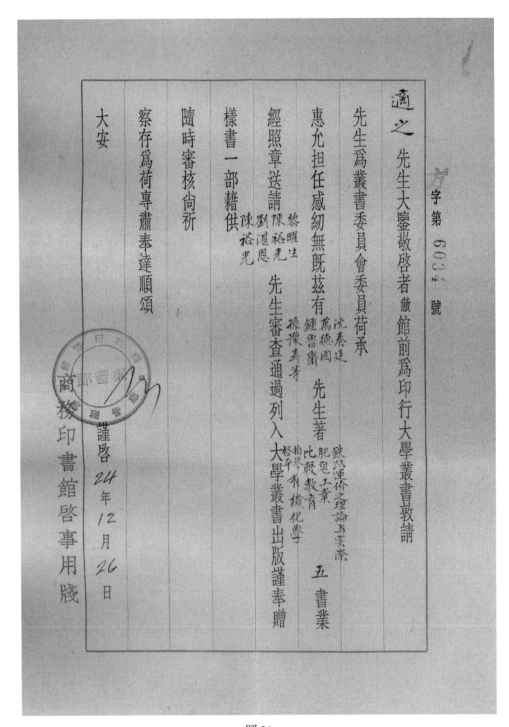

方字第 6034 號

適之 先生大鑒敬啟者敝館前為印行大學叢書敦請
先生為叢書委員會委員荷承
惠允擔任感紉無既茲有 鍾魯齋 先生著 比較教育
沈秉廷 萬德鼎
孫璟壽等 先生著 肥皂工業
耘芹 有機化學
鐵路運價之理論與實際
五書業
經照章送請 陳裕光 劉湛恩 黎曜生 先生審查通過列入大學叢書出版謹奉贈
樣書一部藉供
隨時審核尚祈
察存為荷專肅奉達順頌
大安

商務印書館啟 事用牋 謹啟 24年12月26日

圖 21

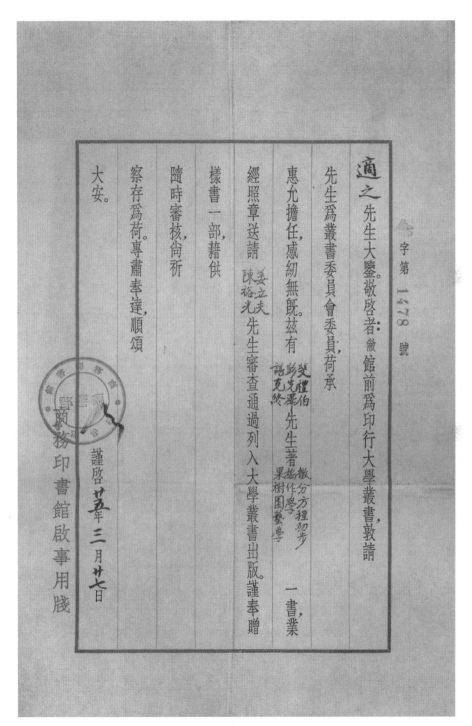

令字第1478號

適之先生大鑒。敬啓者：敝館前為印行大學叢書，敦請
先生為叢書委員會委員，荷承
惠允擔任，感紉無既。茲有 樊體伯 徵分方程初步
彭光澤先生著 作物學 一書，業
諾克終 果樹園藝學
經照章送請 姜立夫
陳裕光 先生審查通過列入大學叢書出版。謹奉贈
樣書一部，藉供
隨時審核。尚祈
察存為荷。專肅奉達。順頌
大安。

商務印書館啟事用牋

謹啓 廿五年三月廿七日

圖22

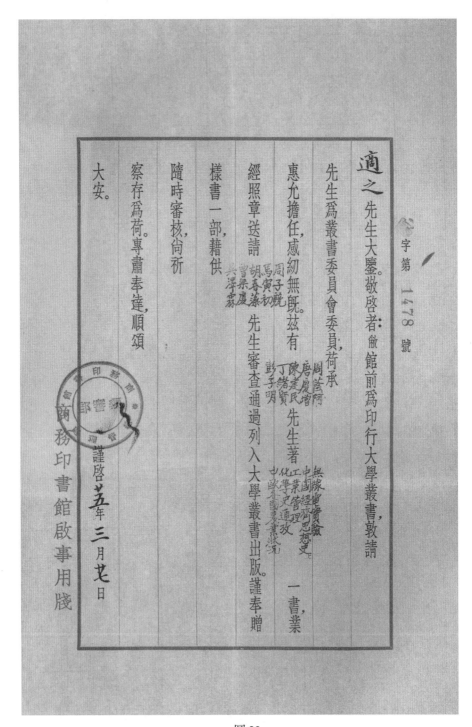

字第 1478 號

適之先生大鑒。敬啟者：敝館前為印行大學叢書，敦請
先生為叢書委員會委員，荷承
惠允擔任，感紉無既。茲有
　　周鯁生　無機實驗
　　厲鼎熚　中國經濟思想史
　　陳廈民　工業管理
　　丁緒寶　化學通改
　　彭子明　古歐史（？）
　　馬寅初
　　胡春藻
　　曾繁（大學叢書）
先生著一書，業經照章送請
先生審查通過列入大學叢書出版。謹奉贈
樣書一部，藉供
隨時審核，尚祈
察存為荷。專肅奉達，順頌
大安。

商務印書館啟事用牋
謹啟 廿五年三月廿日

圖 23

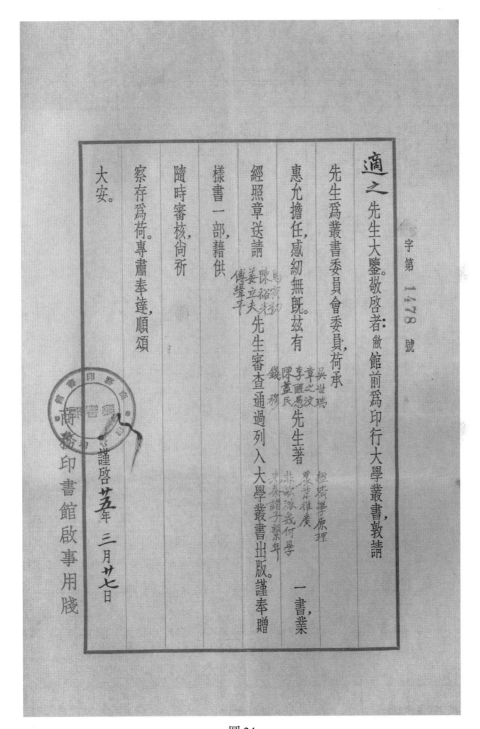

圖 24

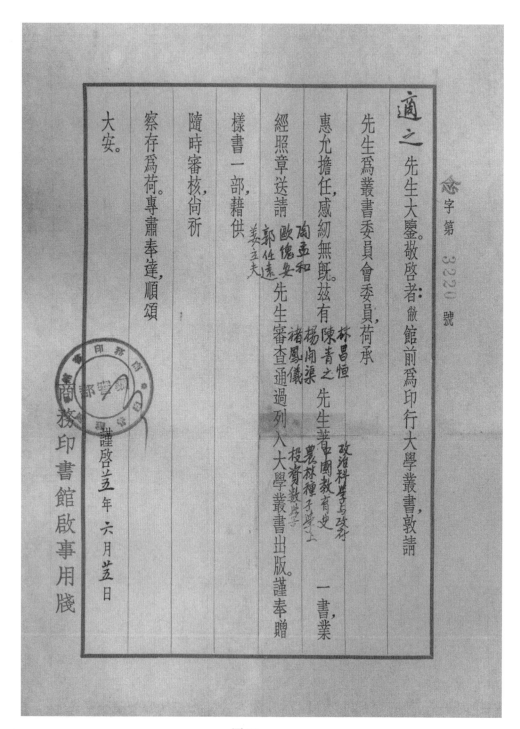

图 25

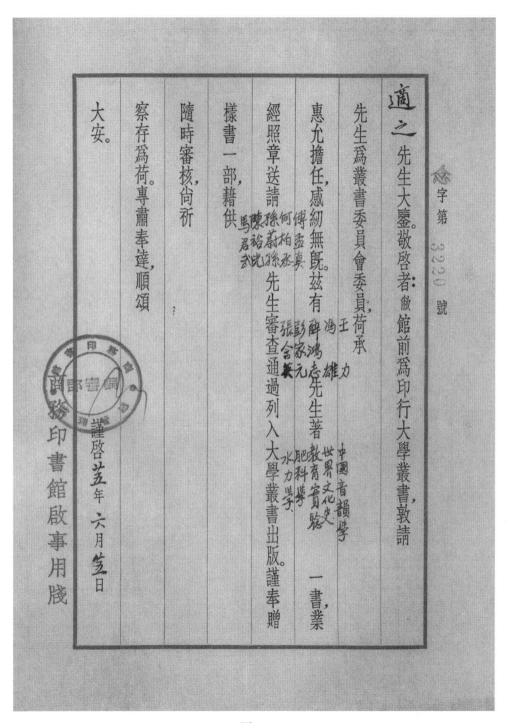

圖26

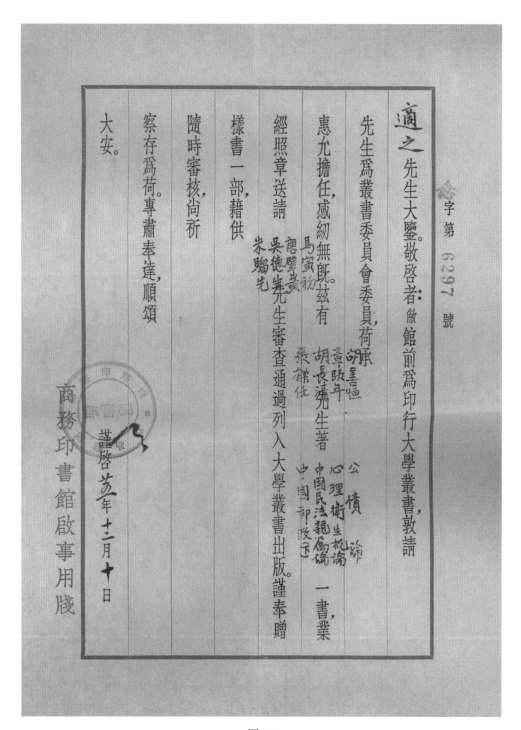

圖 27

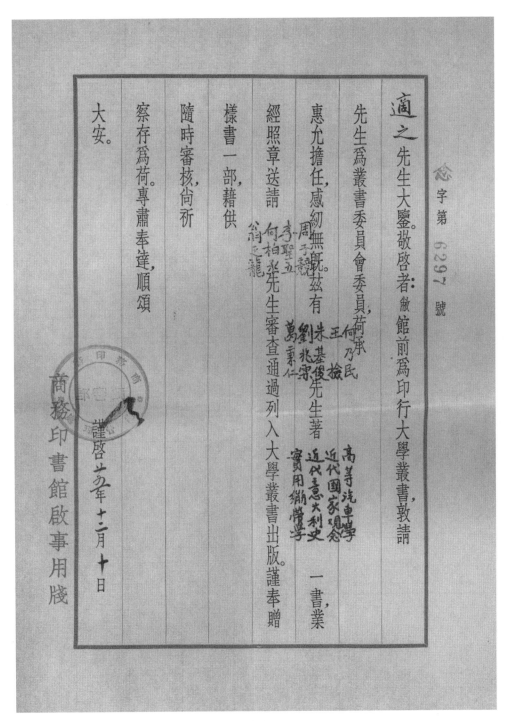

圖28

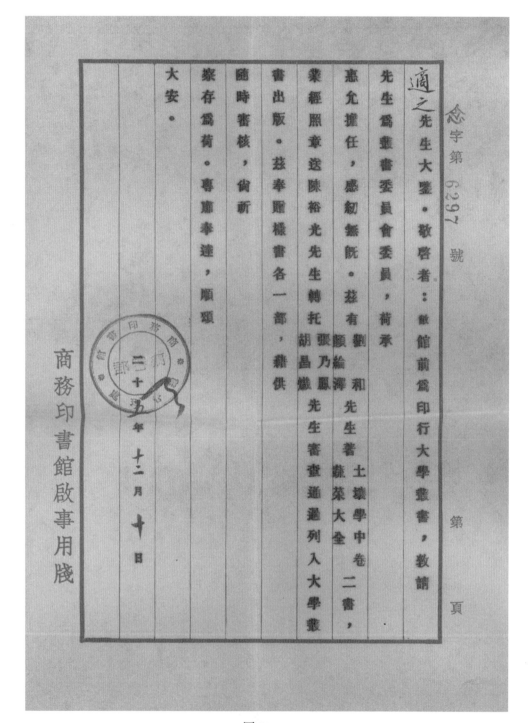

圖 29

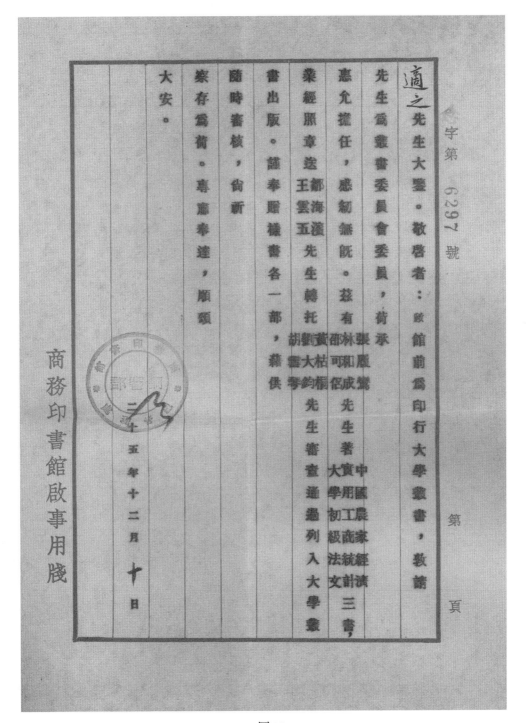

適之先生大鑒。敬啟者：敝館前為印行大學叢書，敬請先生為叢書委員會委員，荷承惠允擔任，感紉無既。茲有張鷹成先生著《中國農家經濟》，林和民先生著《工商統計》，邵可侶先生著《大學用初級法文》三書，黃桐先生著《書目》，胡明復先生著《大學叢書》（待查）擬列入大學叢書出版。謹奉贈樣書各一部，並乞原章逕郵海濱先生轉托王雲五先生審查蓬呈列入大學叢書，隨時審核，尚祈察存為荷。專肅奉達，順頌

大安。

商務印書館啟事用箋

十五年十二月十日

圖 30

上海市公用局致胡適（一九四八年十一月二十二日）

此信發現於《上海市公用事業統計年報》中。

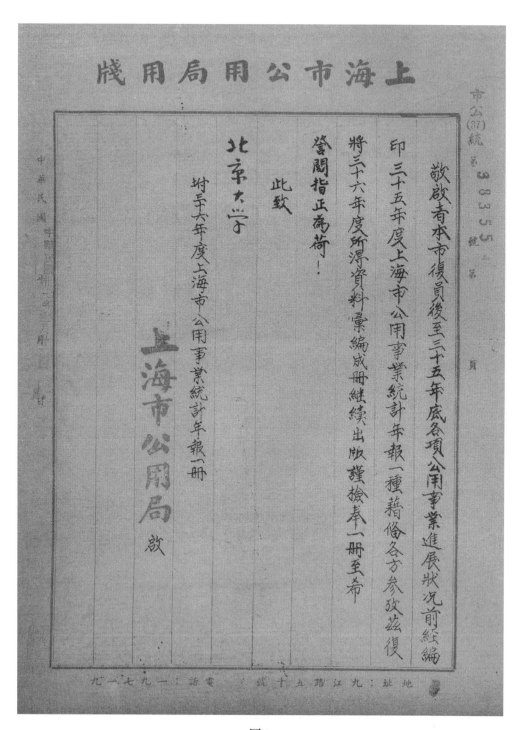

圖1

行政院農村復興委員會秘書處致胡適
（一九三五年五月二十一日）

此信發現於《雲南省農村調查》一書中。

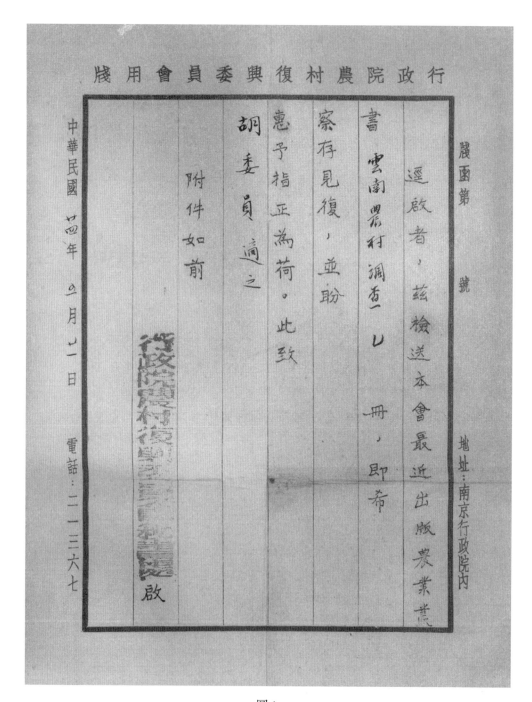

圖 1

興士團遠東部致胡適

　　此信發現於《興士團約法》一書中。"興士團"爲韓國人安昌浩倡導成立的民族獨立運動團體,遠東部,1918—1935在上海活動。

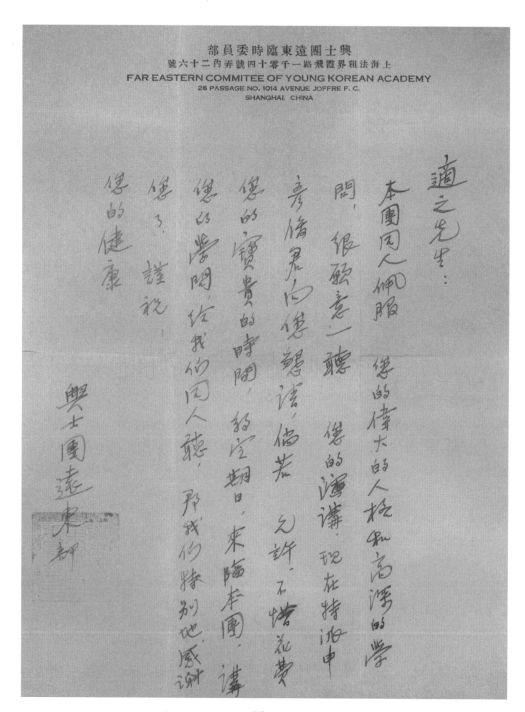

圖 1

適之先生：

　　本團同人佩服您的偉大的人格和高深的學問，很願意一聽您的演講，現在特派申彥俊君向您懇請，倘若允許，不惜花費您的寶貴的時間，約定期日，來臨本團，講您的學問，給我們同人聽，那我們特別地感謝您了。謹祝
您的健康

興士團遠東部

張家口奮鬥日報致胡適（一九四七年十二月二十日）

　　此信發現於《我們是怎樣成長的——奮斗日報九周年紀念册》中。據學者考查，《奮鬥日報》創刊於 1938 年初，九周年則爲 1947 年，1946 年 11 月至張家口辦報。對照此信中"去年冬天，我們儘力辦了張垣版"，可知"今年"爲 1947 年，與前述相合，故此信寫於 1947 年 12 月 20 日。參劉映元《傅作義將軍的喉舌——奮鬥日報》，《新聞研究資料》1981 年第 5 期。

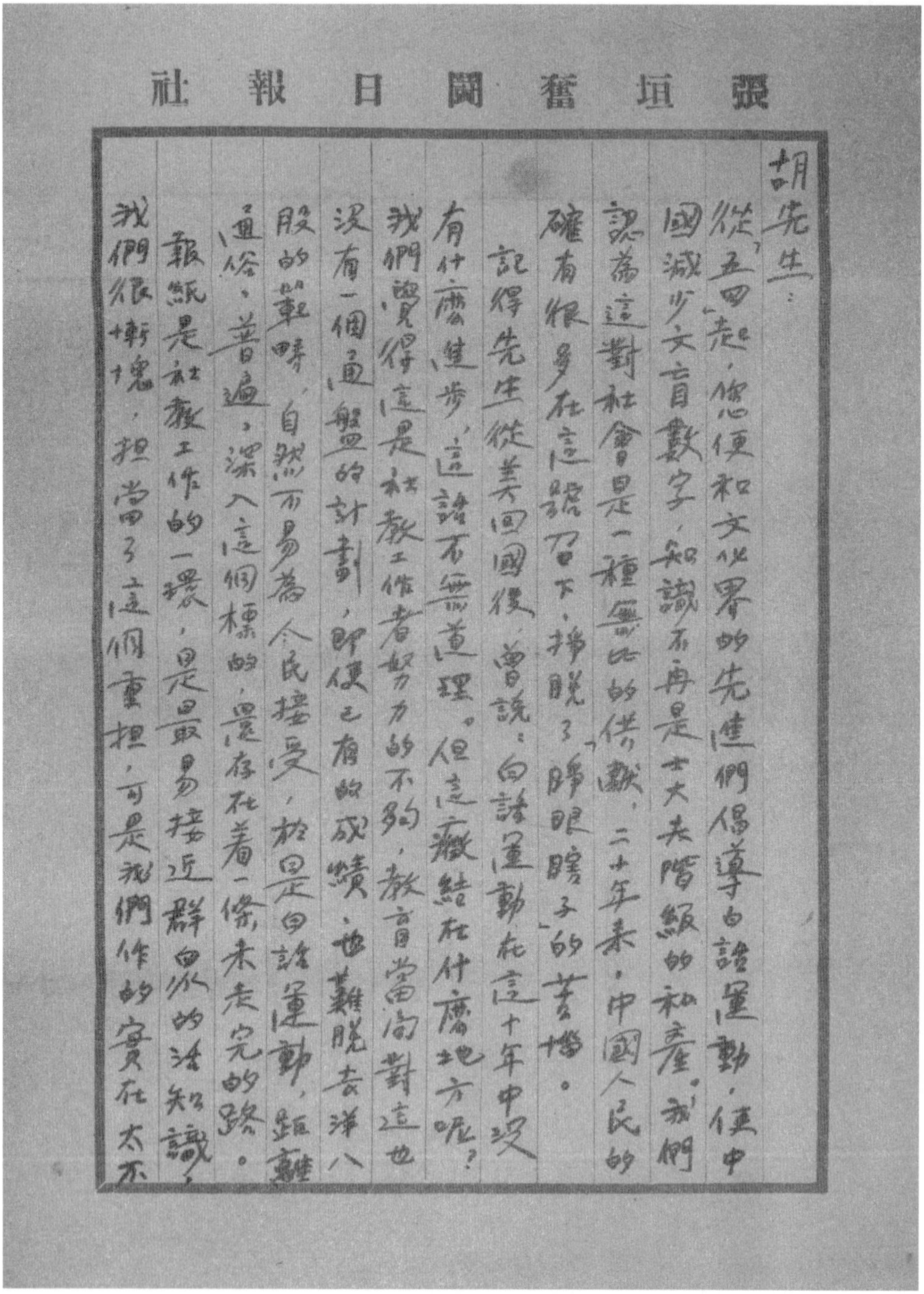

張垣舊聞日報社

胡先生：

從五四起，您便和文化界的先進們倡導白話運動，使中國減少文盲數字，知識不再是士大夫階級的私產，我們認為這對社會是一種無比的供獻，二十年來，中國人民的確有很多在這路習下，掙脫了"睜眼瞎子"的苦惱。

記得先生從美國回來，曾說：白話運動在這十年中沒有什麼進步，這話不無道理。但這癥結在什麼地方呢？我們覺得這是社教工作者努力的不夠，教育當局對這也沒有一個通盤的計劃，即便已有的成績，也難脫去洋八股的觀睛，自然而易為全民接受，於是白話運動，距離通俗、普遍，深入這個標的，還存在着一條未走完的路。

報紙是社教工作的一環，是最易接近群眾的知識股，自然而易接受，於是白話運動，距離通俗、普遍，深入這個標的，還存在着一條未走完的路。

我們很慚愧，擔當了這個重擔，可是我們作的實在太不

圖1

胡先生：

　　從"五四"起，您便和文化界的先進們倡導白話運動，使中國減少文盲數字，知識不再是士大夫階級的私產。我們認爲這對社會是一種無比的供獻，二十年來，中國人民的確有很多在這號召下，掙脱了"睜眼瞎子"的苦惱。

　　記得先生從美國回國後，曾説：白話運動在這十年中没有什麼進步，這話不無道理。但這癥結在什麼地方呢？我們覺得這是社教工作者努力的不夠，教育當局對這也没有一個通盤的計劃，即使已有的成績，也難脱去洋八股的範疇，自然不易爲人民接受，於是白話運動，距離通俗、普遍、深入這個標的，還存在着一條未走完的路。

　　報紙是社教工作的一環，是最易接近群衆的活知識，我們很慚愧，擔當了這個重擔，可是我們作的實在太不

適之:

奮鬥日報是抗戰期間在晉西北前線創刊的一個油印小報,起初僅供給軍中新聞消息,後來移到緩西以十六開鉛印姿態出現在軍民面前,勝利後東進而有歸緩四開報,去年冬天我們儘力辦了張垣版,從今年秋天我們開始改寫現在流行的新聞八股為使小學生、車夫、農民、工人能看懂的白話文。這是我們多年的願望,直到今天才敢作大膽的嘗試,雖然我們有這熱誠,但總限於人力缺乏,不能達到理想的地步,然而我們並不因此氣餒,假如要努力下去,相信這工作做一時期,便可以起些影響,新聞同業都能這樣做做,也不失為白話運動中的一個小小的力量。

現在我們把報紙寄給先生一份,請您在授教之餘,給夠了。

　　《奮鬥日報》是抗戰期間在晉西北前綫創刊的一個油印小報，起初僅供給軍中新聞消息，後來移到綏西以十六開鉛印姿態出現在軍民面前，勝利東進而有歸綏四開報，去年冬天，我們儘力辦了張垣版，從今年秋天我們開始改寫現在流行的新聞八股爲使小學生、車夫、農民、工人能看懂的白話文，這是我們多年的願望，直到今天才敢作大膽的嚐試，雖然我們有這熱誠，但總限於人力缺乏，不能達到理想的地步，然而我們並不因此氣餒，仍舊要努力下去，相信這工作做一時期，便可以起些影響，假如新聞同業都能這樣做做，也不失爲白話運動中的一個小小的力量。

　　現在我們把報紙寄給先生一份，請您在授教之餘，給

張垣奮鬬日報社

我們些應該改善的措葉，我相信更可加遠我們的里程，也就是使先生所倡導的白話運動，早日得到預期的效果，我們不期待，我們祇感謝。敬祝

教安

（附本奮鬬日報九週年紀念冊一本）

十二月二十日

我們些應該改善的指導，我相信更可加速我們的里程，也就是使先生所倡導的白話運動，早日得到預期的效果，我們在期待，我們在感謝。敬祝

教安

　　（附《奮鬥日報九週年紀念册》一本）

張家口奮鬥日報社
十二月二十日

中國教育電影協會致胡適（一九三五年六月）

此信發現於《中國之教育電影運動》一書中。

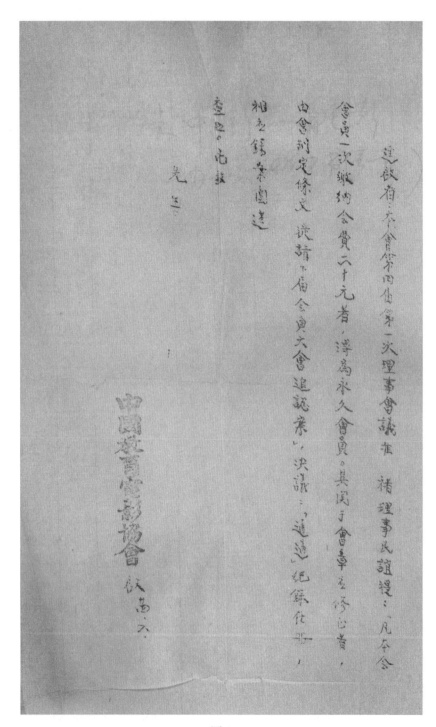

圖1

中國物理學會致胡適

此信件發現於中國物理學會呈請政府改定度量衡單位名稱的呈文中。信中所稱"第三屆年會"召開於 1934 年 8 月,故此函應在此之後發出。

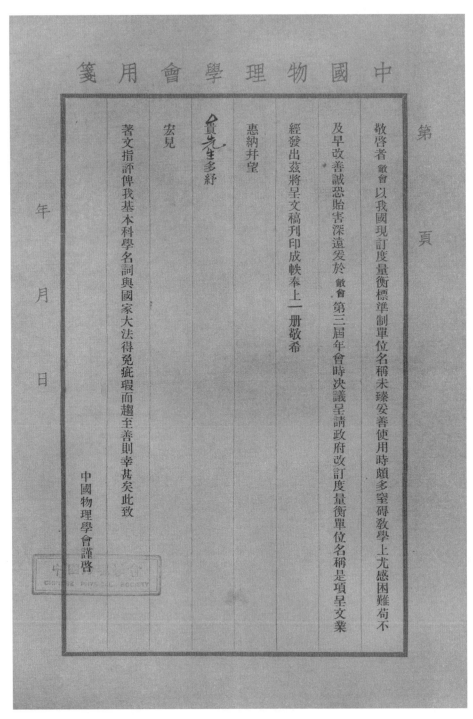

圖1

中國營造學社致胡適

此信發現於《清式營造則例》一書中。此書出版於 1934 年。

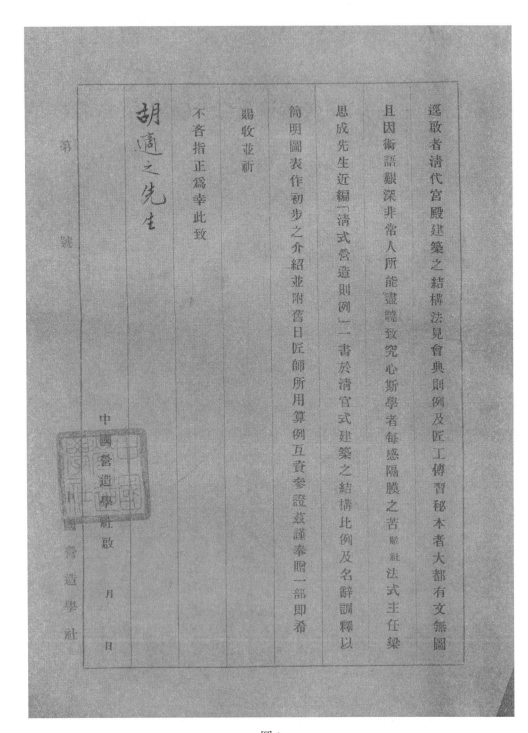

逕啟者清代宮殿建築之結構法見會典則例及匠工傳習秘本者大都有文無圖且因術語艱深非常人所能盡曉致究心斯學者每感隔膜之苦鄙社法式主任梁思成先生近編「清式營造則例」一書於清官式建築之結構比例及名辭訓釋以簡明圖表作初步之介紹並附舊日匠師所用算例互資參證茲謹奉贈一部即希

賜收並祈

不吝指正為幸此致

胡適之先生

第　　號

中國營造學社啟　　月　　日

中國營造學社

圖1

中華職業教育社致胡適（一九三〇年四月二十五日）

此信發現於《民國十八年之中華職業教育社》一書中。

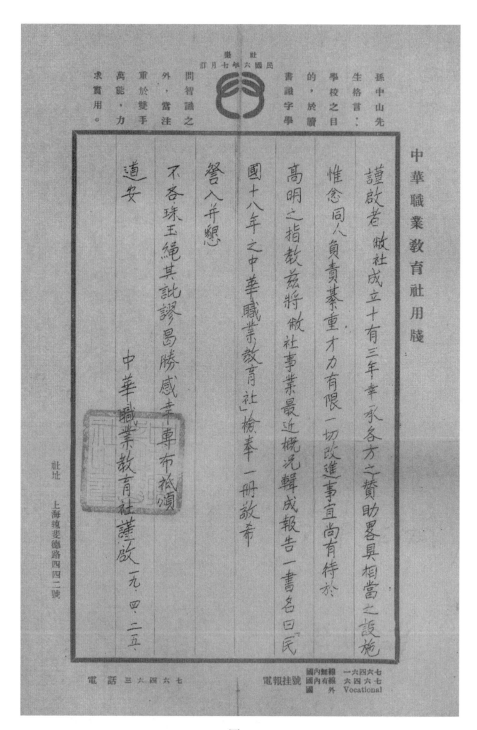

圖1

中央研究院歷史語言研究所致胡適
（一九三〇年三月二十四日）

此信發現於《宋元以來俗字譜》一書中。

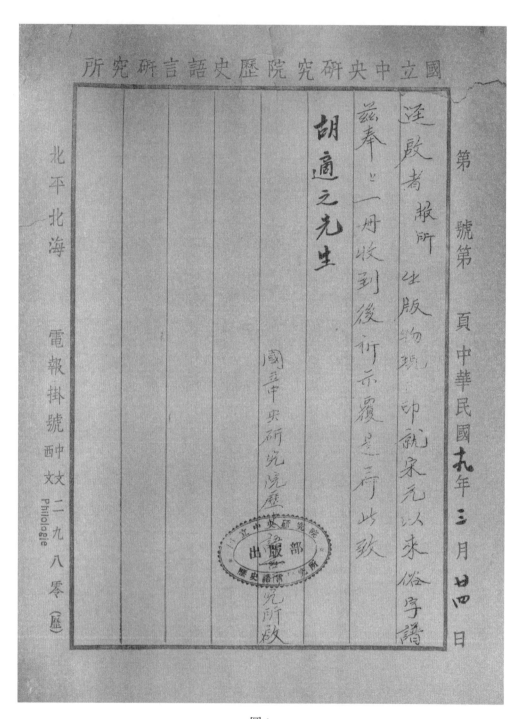

圖 1

發現於胡適藏書中的書信
英文書信

A. Douglas Rugh 致胡適（一九三五年六月十九日）

此信件發現於 Yenching Windows 一書中。

A. Douglas Rugh, 即 Arthur Douglas Rugh（1907—1969），1907 年生於上海，父親任國際基督教青年會秘書，1910 年隨父母回美國，1916 年隨父母再返上海，高中畢業後，返美就讀於歐柏林學院，1929 年畢業，後入哥倫比亞大學，畢業後到黎巴嫩貝魯特美國大學（American University）任教三年。1934 年任教於燕京大學，講授英文及新聞學，並兼任燕大學生刊物 Yenching Windows 的指導教授。1937 年抗戰爆發後回美，後獲得西雅圖華盛頓大學博士學位，應聘紐約大學。抗戰期間到昆明，任美國紅十字會軍隊服務處戰地指揮官，抗戰勝利後到北平繼續工作，1946 年返美，任教於康州中康學院（Central Connecticut State College），並先後擔任註冊部主任、心理系主任。其間曾於 1955 年被聯合國經濟社會委員會派往中東協助處理阿拉伯難民事務；1963—1965 年再赴黎巴嫩，任貝魯特美國大學外國學生顧問。1969 年 12 月 14 日在康州去世。

YENCHING UNIVERSITY
PEIPING, CHINA.

DEPARTMENT OF ENGLISH

June 19, 1935

Dr. Hu Shih
Peking National University

Dear Dr. Hu,

    I thought you might be interested in seeing a copy of "Yenching Windows", published by the class in advanced English composition here at Yenching, and am mailing you a copy under separate cover.

    In order that you will not mistake the nature and purpose of this magazine, let me say that it represents only the work of this one class (fourteen students). The foreign students in Yenching are usually exempted from Freshman English and that explains why there are six in this course. However, of the 50 titles, 32 are by Chinese members of the class. This is the second year that this class has published a magazine of their own work and we feel that it not only is a real stimulus for them but also reveals to some extent the quality of undergraduate ability in creative writing.

    I would be very pleased to receive your critical comment on this year's effort if you have time to look it over.

Sincerely yours,

A. Douglas Rugh

圖 1

A. Y. Ching 致胡適（一九二七年六月一日）

此信件發現於 *Japanese Poetry* 一書中。

作者生平不詳。

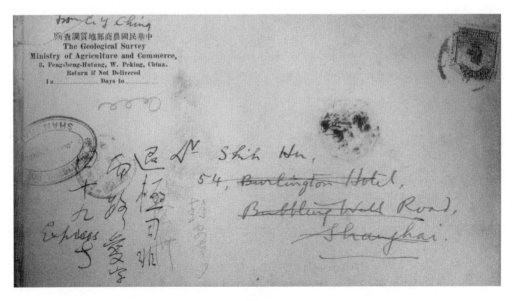

圖1

農商部地質調査所
The Geological Survey,
3, Feng-Sheng Hutung,
W. Peking, China.

1 June 1927

My dear Hu,

I have just received your letter of the 26th May, and have written to Ch'en asking him to have a talk with your wife about the house as I do not intend to stay here for any length of time. My sole object at present is to work up the scientific material I collected in Yunnan. I can write my report anywhere but the collection of rocks etc. must be studied here. Fortunately the work is nearly finished, and I may leave here any time this month.

I have written to Fox about your travelling expense, and as soon as I receive a reply I will let Mrs. Hu know.

C. C. has gone abroad and Yen will probably do the same soon, so the old question is no longer of any actuality.

Please do your best about my brother's property. Never mind about me. I do'nt care, but if they lose their property my burden will be hopelessly increased. Ask Hsu whether my friend Ch'en Yi can do anything. Chien and Huang might also be of use.

Yours sincerely,

V. K. Ting

P.S. The National Commercial Bank here will always know my address.

圖 2

Adelaide M. Anderson 致胡適（一九二六年十月八日）

此信件發現於 *Seven Ages* 一書中。

Adelaide Mary Anderson（1863—1936），英國人，生於澳大利亞墨爾本。1887年畢業於劍橋大學格頓學院。1894年成爲英國第一位女性工廠檢查員。1897年被聘爲女王陛下工廠檢查女官員。退休之後，1923年應上海公共租界工部局邀請來華，任工部局委派的委員，調查幼童勞動情況。調查結果以《人道與勞動》（*Humanity and Labour*）爲名發表。1925年以英國外交部庚款顧問委員會的身份再度來華。1930年曾到埃及調查當地童工情況。1931年，國際聯盟勞動局成立檢查中國工廠的委員會，被派爲委員。1932—1936年任英國中國大學委員會委員。北京檔藏 Anderson 1926年致胡適書信四封。

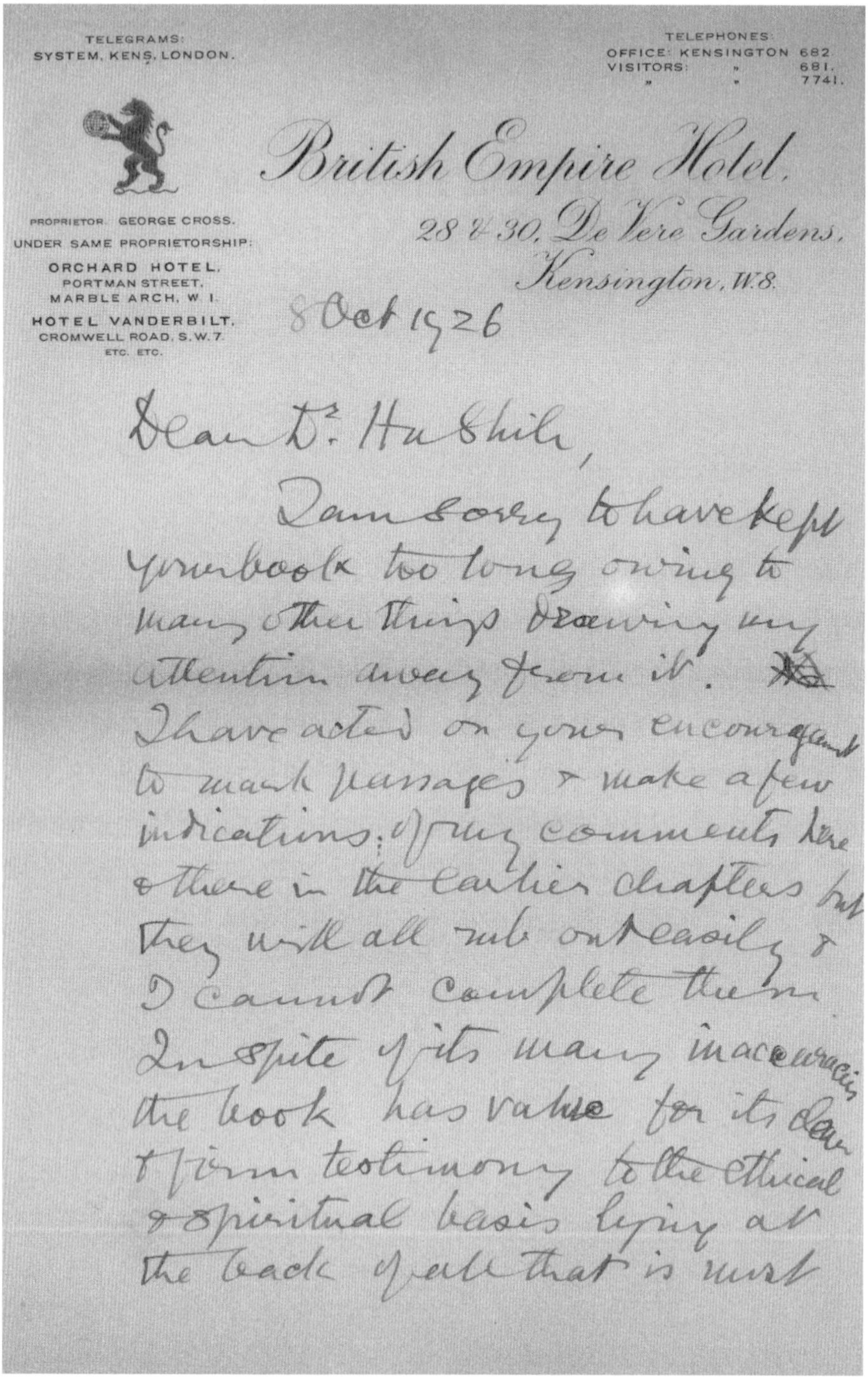

British Empire Hotel,
28 & 30, De Vere Gardens,
Kensington, W.8.

8 Oct 1926

Dear Dr. Hu Shih,

I am sorry to have kept your book too long owing to many other things drawing my attention away from it. I have acted on your encouragement to mark passages & make a few indications; of my comments here & there in the earlier chapters but they will all rub out easily, & I cannot complete them. In spite of its many inaccuracies the book has value for its clear & firm testimony to the ethical & spiritual basis lying at the back of all that is most

圖1

8 Oct. 1926

Dear Dr. Hu Shih,

I am sorry to have kept your book too long owing to many other things drawing my attention away from it.

I have acted on your encouragement to mark passages & make a few indications of my comments here & there in the earlier chapters but they will all rule out easily & I cannot complete them. In spite of its many inaccuracies the book has value for its clear & firm testimony to the ethical & spiritual basis lying at the back of all that is most worthy in European civilisation, & there are some fine clues to the guiding personalities in English history. One has but to go back to the original documents of catholic christianity as interpreted in the light of genuine modern criticism to see how uncritically dogmatic the writer of "Seven Ages" is about the claims made by Jesus and his disciples, & how inaccurate.

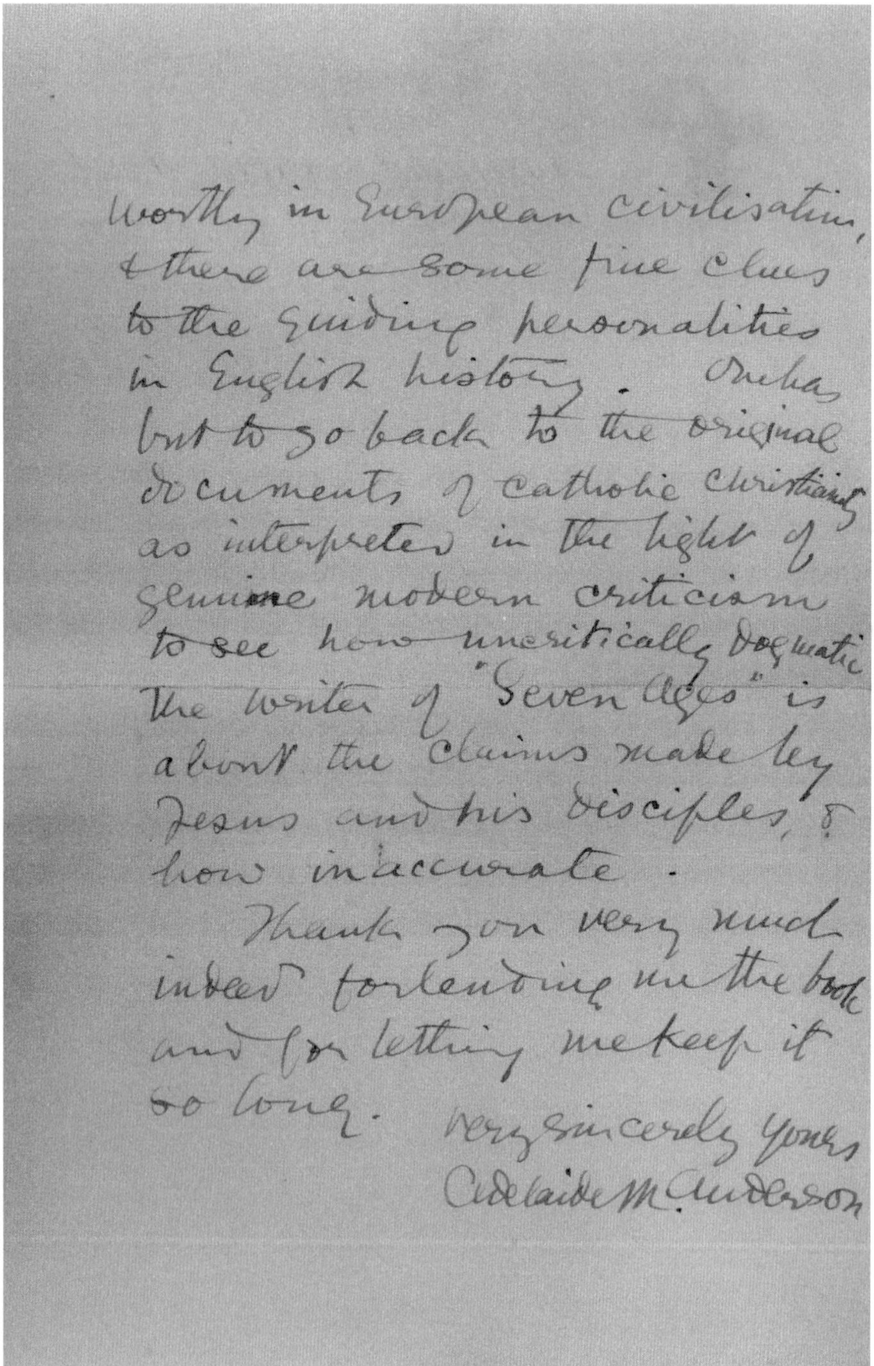

Thank you very much indeed for lending me the book and for letting me keep it so long.

Very sincerely yours
Adelaide M. Anderson

圖 2

worthy in European civilisation, & there are some fine clues to the guiding personalities in English history. One has but to go back to the original documents of Catholic Christianity as interpreted in the light of genuine modern criticism to see how uncritically Dogmatic the writer of *"Seven Ages"* is about the claims made by Jesus and his disciples, & how inaccurate.

Thank you very much indeed for lending me the book and for letting me keep it so long.

Very sincerely yours
Adelaide M. Anderson

Alan Macintosh 致胡適（一九三一年六月十九日）

此信發現於費唐提交上海公共租界工部局報告書第一卷摘要譯文中。

費唐即信中提及之 Mr.Justice Feetham，即 Richard Feetham，寫信人 Alan Macintosh 應爲費唐之工作人員。

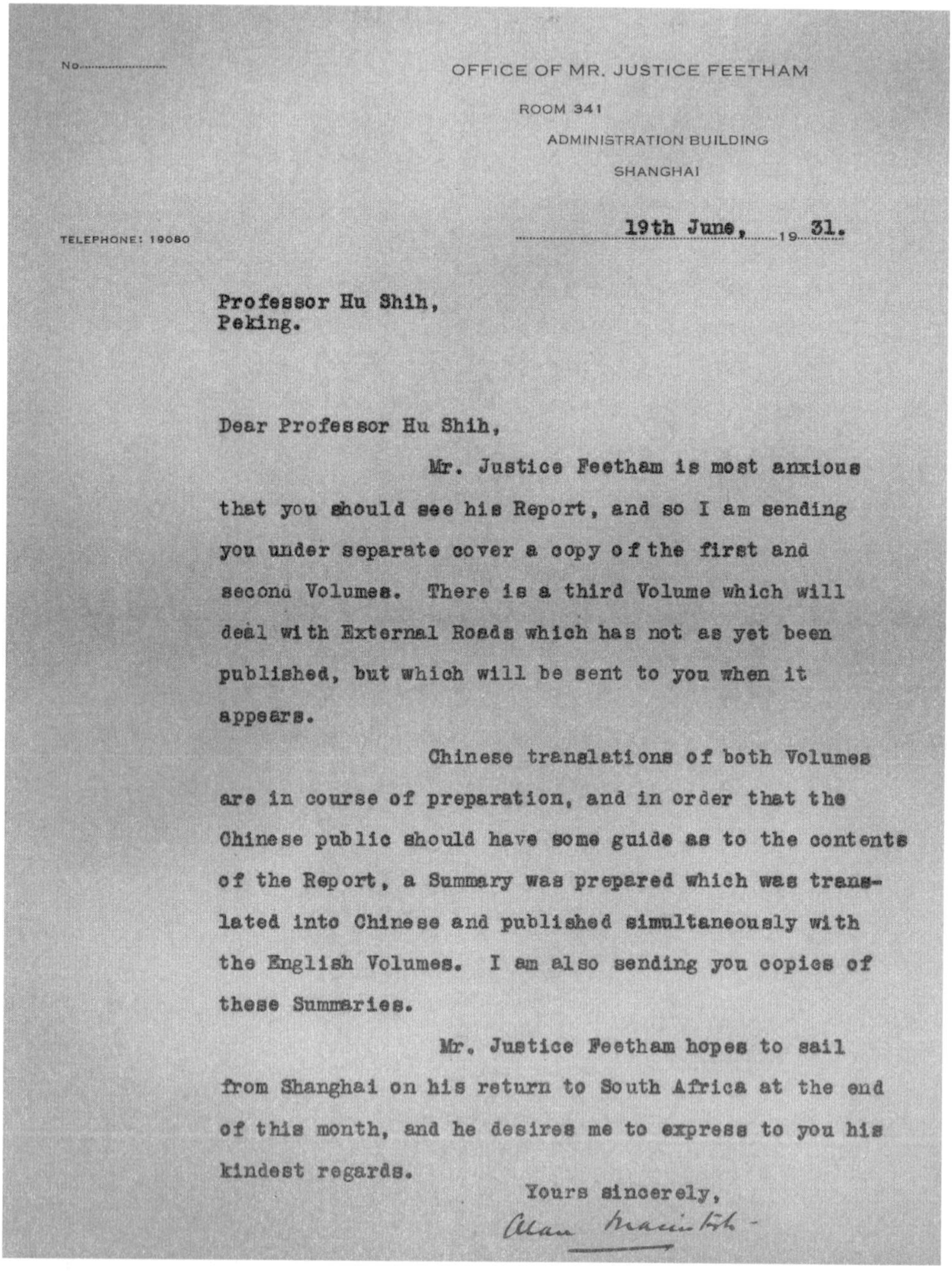

OFFICE OF MR. JUSTICE FEETHAM
ROOM 341
ADMINISTRATION BUILDING
SHANGHAI

TELEPHONE: 19080

19th June, 1931.

Professor Hu Shih,
Peking.

Dear Professor Hu Shih,

  Mr. Justice Feetham is most anxious that you should see his Report, and so I am sending you under separate cover a copy of the first and second Volumes. There is a third Volume which will deal with External Roads which has not as yet been published, but which will be sent to you when it appears.

  Chinese translations of both Volumes are in course of preparation, and in order that the Chinese public should have some guide as to the contents of the Report, a Summary was prepared which was translated into Chinese and published simultaneously with the English Volumes. I am also sending you copies of these Summaries.

  Mr. Justice Feetham hopes to sail from Shanghai on his return to South Africa at the end of this month, and he desires me to express to you his kindest regards.

        Yours sincerely,
        Alan Macintosh

圖 1

Allen Churchill 致胡適（一九四一年十月十四日）

此信件發現於 The End is not Yet 一書中。

Allen Churchill，時任職於美國紐約 Robert M. McBride & Company 出版公司。餘不詳。

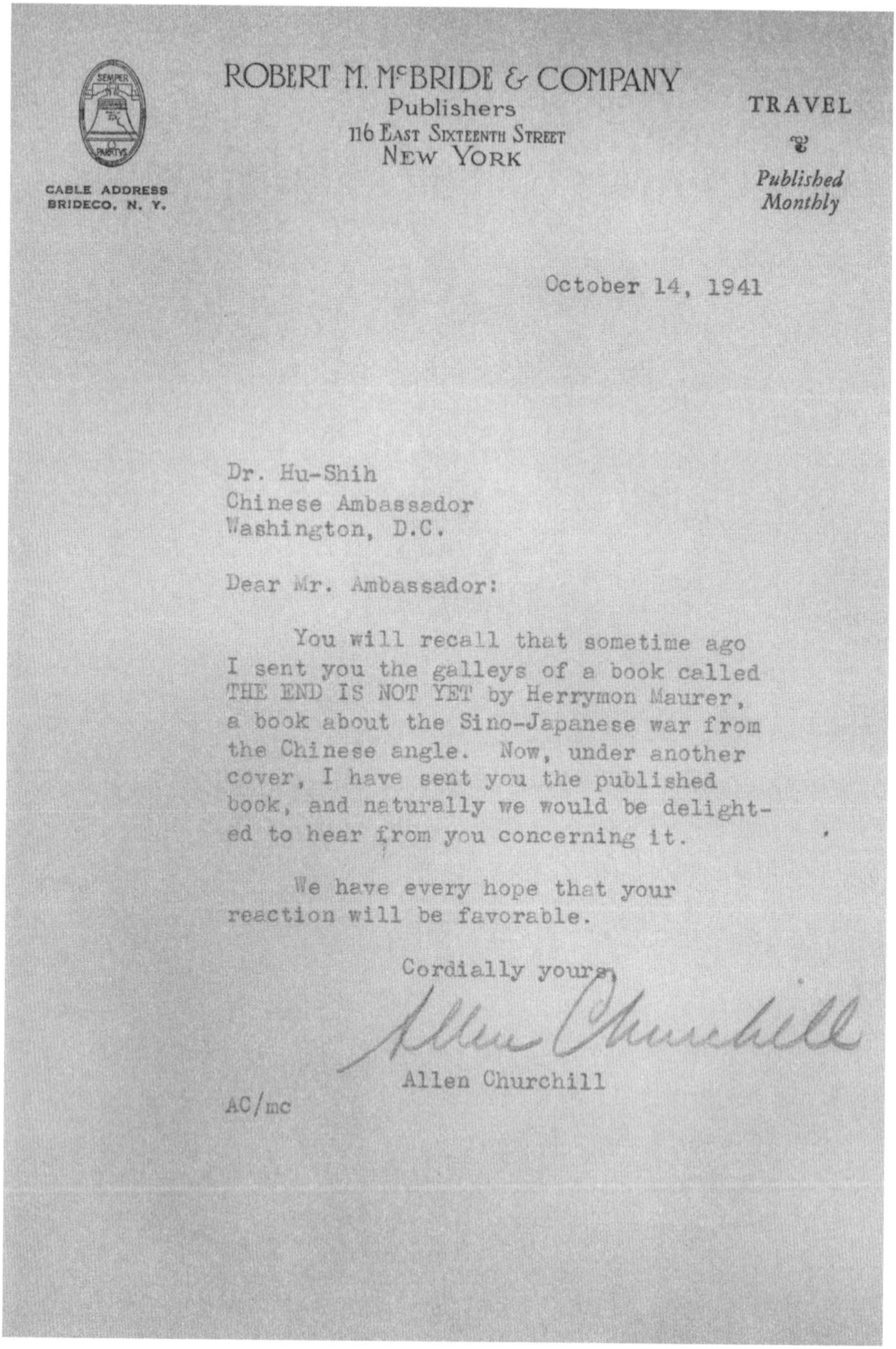

ROBERT M. McBRIDE & COMPANY
Publishers
116 EAST SIXTEENTH STREET
NEW YORK

CABLE ADDRESS
BRIDECO, N. Y.

TRAVEL

Published Monthly

October 14, 1941

Dr. Hu-Shih
Chinese Ambassador
Washington, D.C.

Dear Mr. Ambassador:

  You will recall that sometime ago I sent you the galleys of a book called THE END IS NOT YET by Herrymon Maurer, a book about the Sino-Japanese war from the Chinese angle. Now, under another cover, I have sent you the published book, and naturally we would be delighted to hear from you concerning it.

  We have every hope that your reaction will be favorable.

       Cordially yours,

       Allen Churchill

AC/mc

圖 1

B. C. Bridges 致胡適（一九四二年六月八日）

此信件發現於 *Practical Fingerprinting* 一書中，六月八日爲 B. C. Bridges 致胡適之信，六月十五日爲胡適秘書的回信。

B. C. Bridges，時任職於美國加州阿拉米達市警察局鑒定科，餘不詳。

June 8, 1942

Hon. Dr. Hu Shih
Ambassador of the Republic of China
Washington, D.C.

Hon. Sir:

  At the suggestion of our mutual friend, the Hon. Chi-Tsing Feng, Consul-General of the Republic of China, at San Francisco, I am sending you a complimentary copy of my latest work on fingerprinting, with the hope that it may offer some aid to Chinese police, and others.

  This book represents the result of two decades' study and experience in criminology, supplemented by much valuable cooperation from my students and confreres at the University of California and elsewhere. As you will note, the foreword was written by Professor August Vollmer, who is world-famous for his advancement in the field of law-enforcement.

  Personal identification is a subject of vital importance to society at all times, and with the advent of war, becomes a national necessity. In the recognition and apprehension of dangerous persons, and in the adjustment of numerous situations involving questioned identity, fingerprinting always has been an infallible ally.

  If my textbook can furnish any assistance to the Chinese people in their present courageous contest, I shall feel honored to have had an humble part in their ultimate achievement of victory.

          Sincerely yours,

          B. C. Bridges

          B. C. Bridges, Supt.
          Bureau of Identification
          Alameda Police Dept.

RECEIVED & RECORDED
JUN 12 1942
NO. 9838

圖1

June 15, 1942

Superintendent B. C. Bridges
Bureau of Identification
City of Alameda
California

Dear Sir:

    As the Ambassador was leaving for a number of speaking engagements, he asked me to write and thank you very sincerely for your kind letter of June 8th and the copy of your book, entitled PRACTICAL FINGERPRINTING. As soon as the pressure of his engagements lessens, he anticipates the pleasure of looking over your book with much interest.

                      Very truly yours,

                      Private Secretary

圖2

B. H. Streeter 致胡適（一九二六年十二月九日）

此信件發現於 *Reality: A New Correlation of Science and Religion* 一書中。

胡適 1926 年 12 月 10 日的日記中說："Oxford 的 Canon Burnet Hillman Streeter 寄贈他的近作 *Reality: A New Correlation of Science and Religion*。"

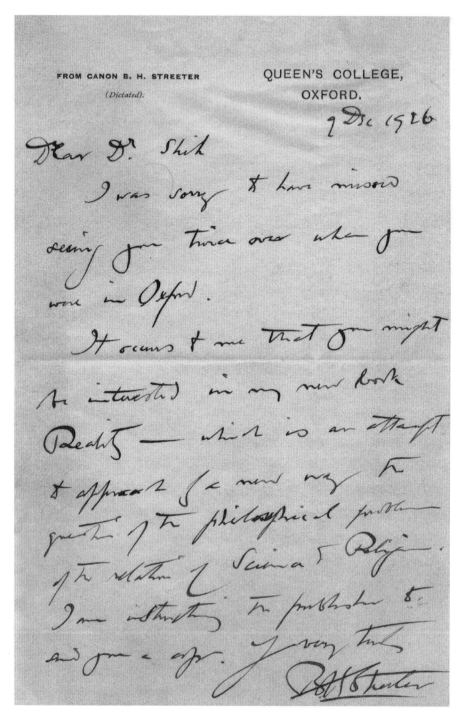

圖1

9 Dec 1926

Dear Dr. Shih

I was sorry to have missed seeing you twice over when you were in Oxford.

It occurs to me that you might be interested in my new book *Reality*— which is an attempt to approach of a new way the question of the philosophical problem of the relation of Science & Religion. I am instructing the publisher to send you a copy.

Yours truly
B. H. Streeter

Bernard Lightenberg 致胡適（一九四五年八月十七日）

此信件發現於 The Home Front 一書中。

Bernard Lichtenberg（1892—? ），生於奧地利。曾任紐約商業促進局（Better Business Bureau of New York）經理、國際會計師學會顧問組成員、全國廣告主協會主席、紐約公共關係學院院長。著有《廣告學原理》等。

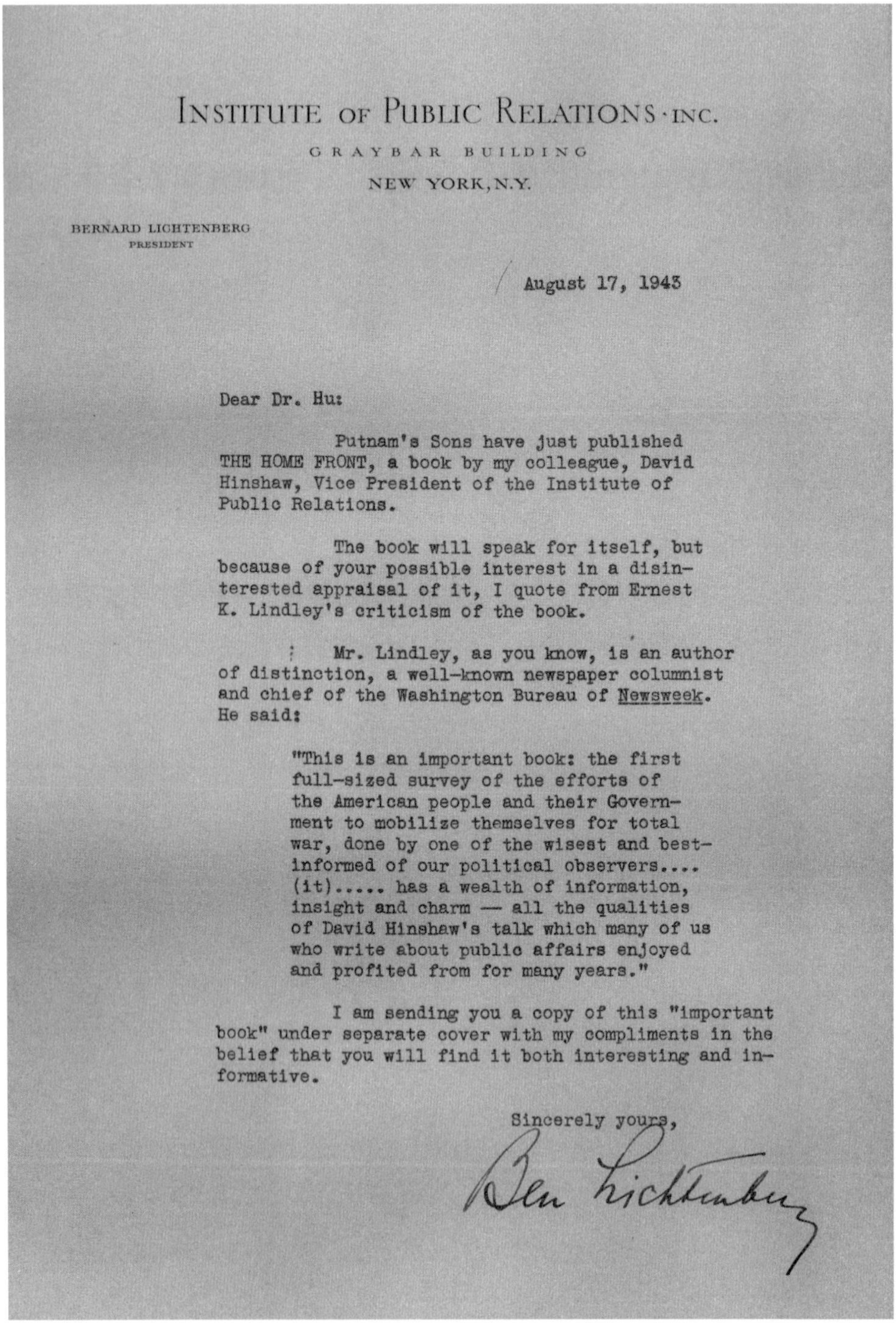

INSTITUTE OF PUBLIC RELATIONS · INC.

GRAYBAR BUILDING
NEW YORK, N.Y.

BERNARD LICHTENBERG
PRESIDENT

August 17, 1943

Dear Dr. Hu:

  Putnam's Sons have just published THE HOME FRONT, a book by my colleague, David Hinshaw, Vice President of the Institute of Public Relations.

  The book will speak for itself, but because of your possible interest in a disinterested appraisal of it, I quote from Ernest K. Lindley's criticism of the book.

  Mr. Lindley, as you know, is an author of distinction, a well-known newspaper columnist and chief of the Washington Bureau of Newsweek. He said:

> "This is an important book: the first full-sized survey of the efforts of the American people and their Government to mobilize themselves for total war, done by one of the wisest and best-informed of our political observers.... (it)..... has a wealth of information, insight and charm — all the qualities of David Hinshaw's talk which many of us who write about public affairs enjoyed and profited from for many years."

  I am sending you a copy of this "important book" under separate cover with my compliments in the belief that you will find it both interesting and informative.

Sincerely yours,

Ben Lichtenberg

圖 1

Constance Warren 致胡適（一九三六年九月九日）

此信件發現於 Handbook for the Sixth Conference of the Institute of Pacific Relations 一書中。

Constance Warren（1880—1970），1904 年獲瓦薩學院（Vassar College）文學士學位，1905 年獲哥倫比亞大學文學碩士學位。1929—1945 年任美國莎拉·勞倫斯學院院長。著有《女性教育的新思路》（A New Design for Women's Education），推廣莎拉·勞倫斯學院的個性化教育模式。

SARAH LAWRENCE COLLEGE
BRONXVILLE, NEW YORK

OFFICE OF THE PRESIDENT

TELEPHONE
BRONXVILLE 0700

September 9, 1936

Dr. Hu Shih
Harvard Tercentenary Conference of Arts and Sciences
Cambridge, Massachusetts

My dear Dr. Hu:

  It has long been my hope that some time when you were in the United States it would be possible for us to have you at Sarah Lawrence College. I wrote to you the last time you were here, for the Institute of Pacific Relations, but I think you had already left this country before I could get in touch with you.

  My old friend, Raymond Fosdick, has been visiting me this summer and tells me that you are here for the Harvard Tercentenary, and I am writing to ask, if you are going to be in the neighborhood of New York, whether it would be possible for you to speak before the students and faculty of Sarah Lawrence College. This is a very small college for girls, which has been in operation only eight years, carrying out a new plan of education on the college level in which I think you might be interested. Bronxville is half an hour by train from the Grand Central Station in New York. College opens on September 21st, and we have a visiting English lecturer from September 30th to October 2nd. Any time after that would be open, but preferably not on a week-end, as a great many of our students are likely to be away then. We have, for a small college, done a considerable amount of work in the understanding of Oriental civilization, and it is a subject in which I am very anxious that our students shall have an intelligent interest. Perhaps one other inducement for you to come might be that my closest childhood friend is Mrs. Schitze Wang, who is, I know, a friend of yours.

Very cordially yours,

Constance Warren
President

CW/M

圖 1

Edward C. Carter 致胡適（一九三九年一月三十日）

此信件發現於 When There is No Peace 一書中。

Edward C. Carter, 即 Edward Clark Carter（1878—1954），1900 年畢業於哈佛大學。一戰期間在印度和法國基督教國際青年會工作。後在太平洋學會工作，1926—1933 年任該會秘書，1933—1946 年任秘書長，1946—1948 年任副會長。1948 年離開太平洋學會，同年任紐約社會研究新學院副院長，後任院長。1940 年協助創立俄羅斯戰時救濟基金（1941—1945 年任主席）和美國援助中國協會（United States Service to China，1948 年任會長）。1940 年代曾任 Pacific Affairs 編輯。1948 年任聯合國亞洲及遠東經濟委員會顧問。Edward C. Carter 在太平洋學會任職期間即與胡適有交往，北京檔 Carter 最早致胡適書信時間爲 1929 年 10 月 20 日，主要內容爲關於在東京開會事宜。胡適日記中關於與 Carter 交往的最早記錄是 1934 年 4 月 25 日，當天到車站接 Carter 夫婦。Carter 在 1932 年與胡適書信往來較多，現存至少五封。曾於 1938 年 9 月 2 日致電胡適，祝賀他出任中國駐美大使。胡適任大使期間與其也有不少書信往來。

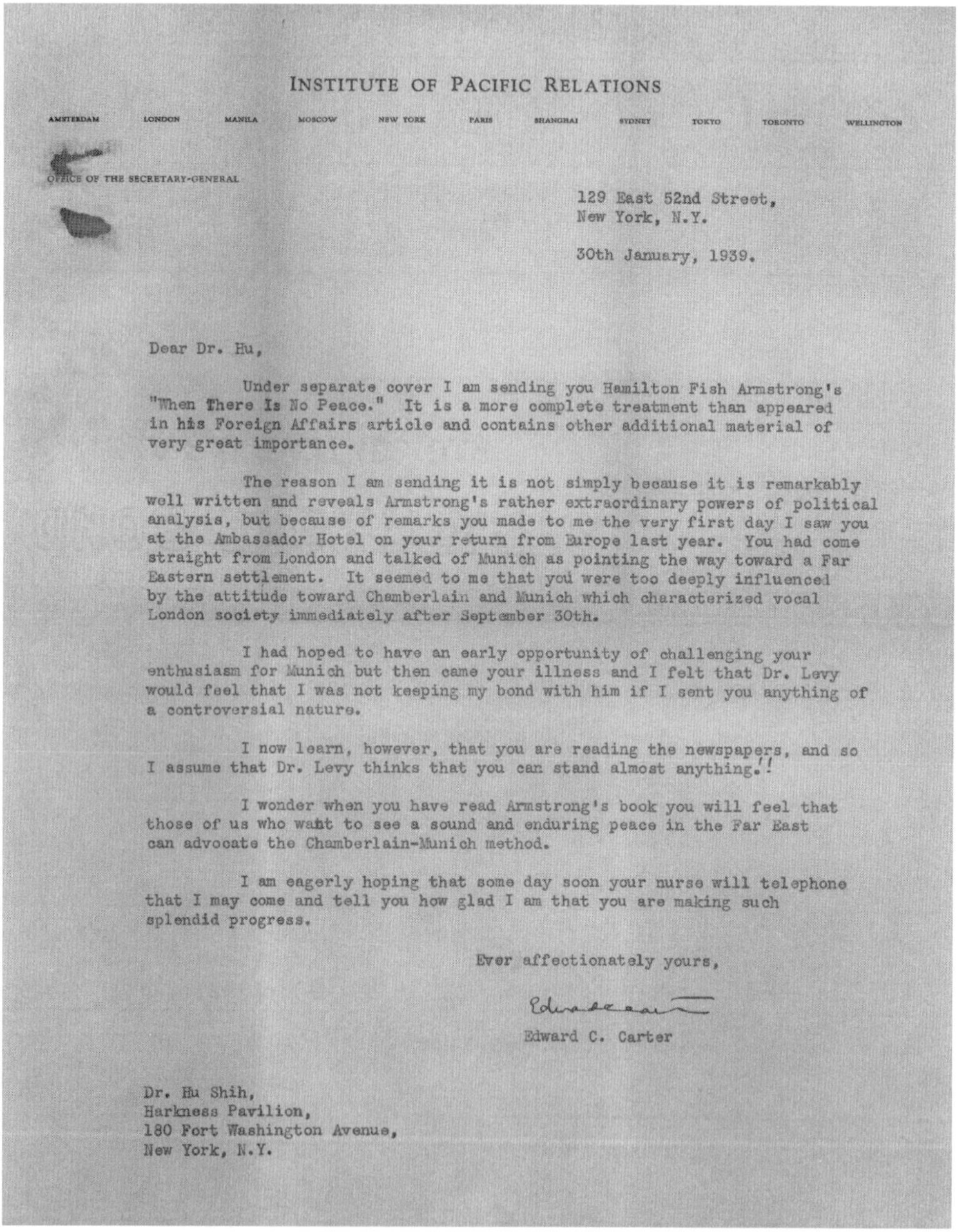

INSTITUTE OF PACIFIC RELATIONS

AMSTERDAM　LONDON　MANILA　MOSCOW　NEW YORK　PARIS　SHANGHAI　SYDNEY　TOKYO　TORONTO　WELLINGTON

OFFICE OF THE SECRETARY-GENERAL

129 East 52nd Street,
New York, N.Y.

30th January, 1939.

Dear Dr. Hu,

  Under separate cover I am sending you Hamilton Fish Armstrong's "When There Is No Peace." It is a more complete treatment than appeared in his Foreign Affairs article and contains other additional material of very great importance.

  The reason I am sending it is not simply because it is remarkably well written and reveals Armstrong's rather extraordinary powers of political analysis, but because of remarks you made to me the very first day I saw you at the Ambassador Hotel on your return from Europe last year. You had come straight from London and talked of Munich as pointing the way toward a Far Eastern settlement. It seemed to me that you were too deeply influenced by the attitude toward Chamberlain and Munich which characterized vocal London society immediately after September 30th.

  I had hoped to have an early opportunity of challenging your enthusiasm for Munich but then came your illness and I felt that Dr. Levy would feel that I was not keeping my bond with him if I sent you anything of a controversial nature.

  I now learn, however, that you are reading the newspapers, and so I assume that Dr. Levy thinks that you can stand almost anything.!!

  I wonder when you have read Armstrong's book you will feel that those of us who want to see a sound and enduring peace in the Far East can advocate the Chamberlain-Munich method.

  I am eagerly hoping that some day soon your nurse will telephone that I may come and tell you how glad I am that you are making such splendid progress.

Ever affectionately yours,

Edward C. Carter

Dr. Hu Shih,
Harkness Pavilion,
180 Fort Washington Avenue,
New York, N.Y.

圖 1

Evan Morgan 致 Rawlinson（一九三〇年四月二十五日），Robert F. Fitch 致胡適（一九三〇年五月二日，一九三〇年七月十五日）

此三封信件發現於 *A New Mind and Other Essays* 一書中。其中 4 月 28 日一封爲本書作者 Evan Morgan（莫安仁）請求 Dr. Rawlinson 爲其書寫書評。5 月 2 日一封爲本書編輯 Robert F. Fitch 請求胡適爲此書撰寫書評，並附此書簡介及約稿函。7 月 15 日一封則爲編輯給胡適的催稿函。

Evan Morgan（1860—1941），中文名莫安仁，英國浸禮會教士。1884 年來華，在西安傳教，一度調往山西任職。1918—1930 年任上海廣學會編輯。編有幾本學習漢語的書。

Frank Joseph Rawlinson（1871—1937），中文名樂靈生，美籍英人，1899 年赴美，1902 年取得美國國籍，同年來華，爲美國南浸信會傳道部教士。1921 年後加入美國公理會。1912 年任《教務雜志》副編輯，1915 年後任總編輯，其間曾任上海工部局中國學校部主任五年。1937 年 8 月 14 日日軍空襲上海公共租界，被炸死。著有 *Chinese Ideas of the Supreme Being* 和 *Naturalization of Christianity in China* 等。

Robert Ferris Fitch，中文名費佩德，美國北長老會傳教士，費啓鴻之子，生於上海。1898 年在美國大學畢業後回華，在寧波長老會所辦的中學任校長。後任杭州之江大學神學院教授兼名譽校長。著有 *Hangchow-Chekiang Itineraries* 和 *Pootoo Itineraries: Describing the Chief Places of Interest, with A Special Trip to Lo-Chia Shan*。

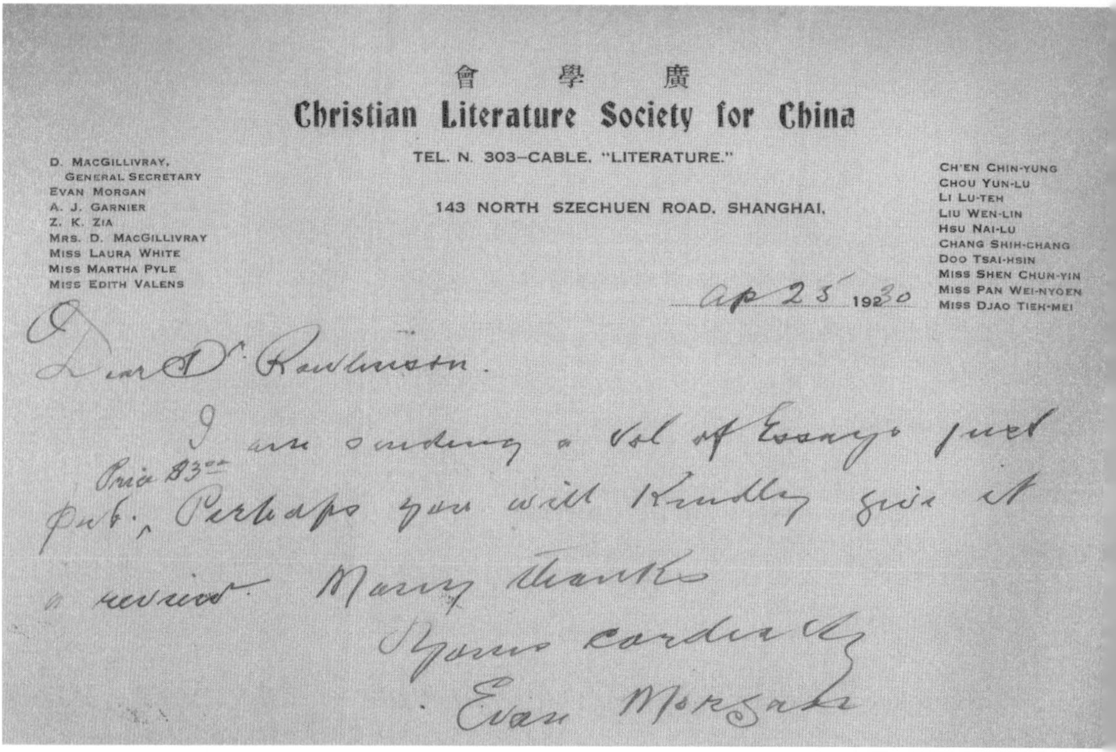

會　學　廣

Christian Literature Society for China

TEL. N. 303—CABLE. "LITERATURE."

143 NORTH SZECHUEN ROAD, SHANGHAI.

D. MACGILLIVRAY,
GENERAL SECRETARY
EVAN MORGAN
A. J. GARNIER
Z. K. ZIA
MRS. D. MACGILLIVRAY
MISS LAURA WHITE
MISS MARTHA PYLE
MISS EDITH VALENS

CH'EN CHIN-YUNG
CHOU YUN-LU
LI LU-TEH
LIU WEN-LIN
HSU NAI-LU
CHANG SHIH-CHANG
DOO TSAI-HSIN
MISS SHEN CHUN-YIN
MISS PAN WEI-NYOEN
MISS DJAO TIEH-MEI

Ap 25 1930

Dear Dr. Rawlinson.

I am sending a vol of Essays just pub., Price $3.00 Perhaps you will kindly give it a review. Many thanks

Yours cordially

Evan Morgan

圖 1

Apr. 25, 1930

Dear Dr. Rawlinson:

I am sending a Vol. of Essays just pub. Price $3.00. Perhaps you will kindly give it a review. Many thanks.

Yours Cordially
Evan Morgan

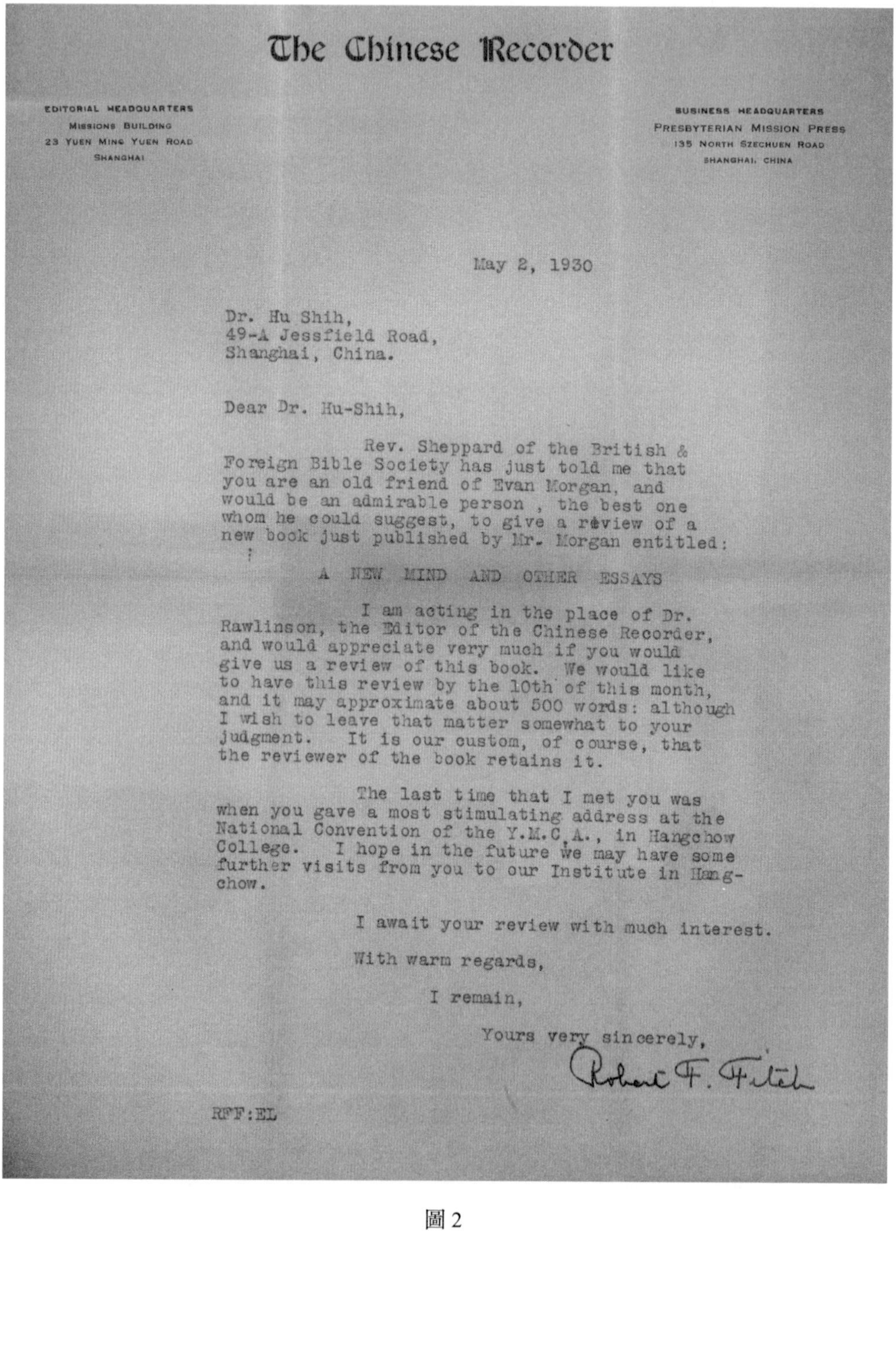

The Chinese Recorder

EDITORIAL HEADQUARTERS
MISSIONS BUILDING
23 YUEN MING YUEN ROAD
SHANGHAI

BUSINESS HEADQUARTERS
PRESBYTERIAN MISSION PRESS
135 NORTH SZECHUEN ROAD
SHANGHAI, CHINA

May 2, 1930

Dr. Hu Shih,
49-A Jessfield Road,
Shanghai, China.

Dear Dr. Hu-Shih,

  Rev. Sheppard of the British & Foreign Bible Society has just told me that you are an old friend of Evan Morgan, and would be an admirable person, the best one whom he could suggest, to give a review of a new book just published by Mr. Morgan entitled:

  A NEW MIND AND OTHER ESSAYS

  I am acting in the place of Dr. Rawlinson, the Editor of the Chinese Recorder, and would appreciate very much if you would give us a review of this book. We would like to have this review by the 10th of this month, and it may approximate about 500 words: although I wish to leave that matter somewhat to your judgment. It is our custom, of course, that the reviewer of the book retains it.

  The last time that I met you was when you gave a most stimulating address at the National Convention of the Y.M.C.A., in Hangchow College. I hope in the future we may have some further visits from you to our Institute in Hangchow.

  I await your review with much interest.

  With warm regards,

  I remain,

    Yours very sincerely,

    Robert F. Fitch

RFF:EL

圖 2

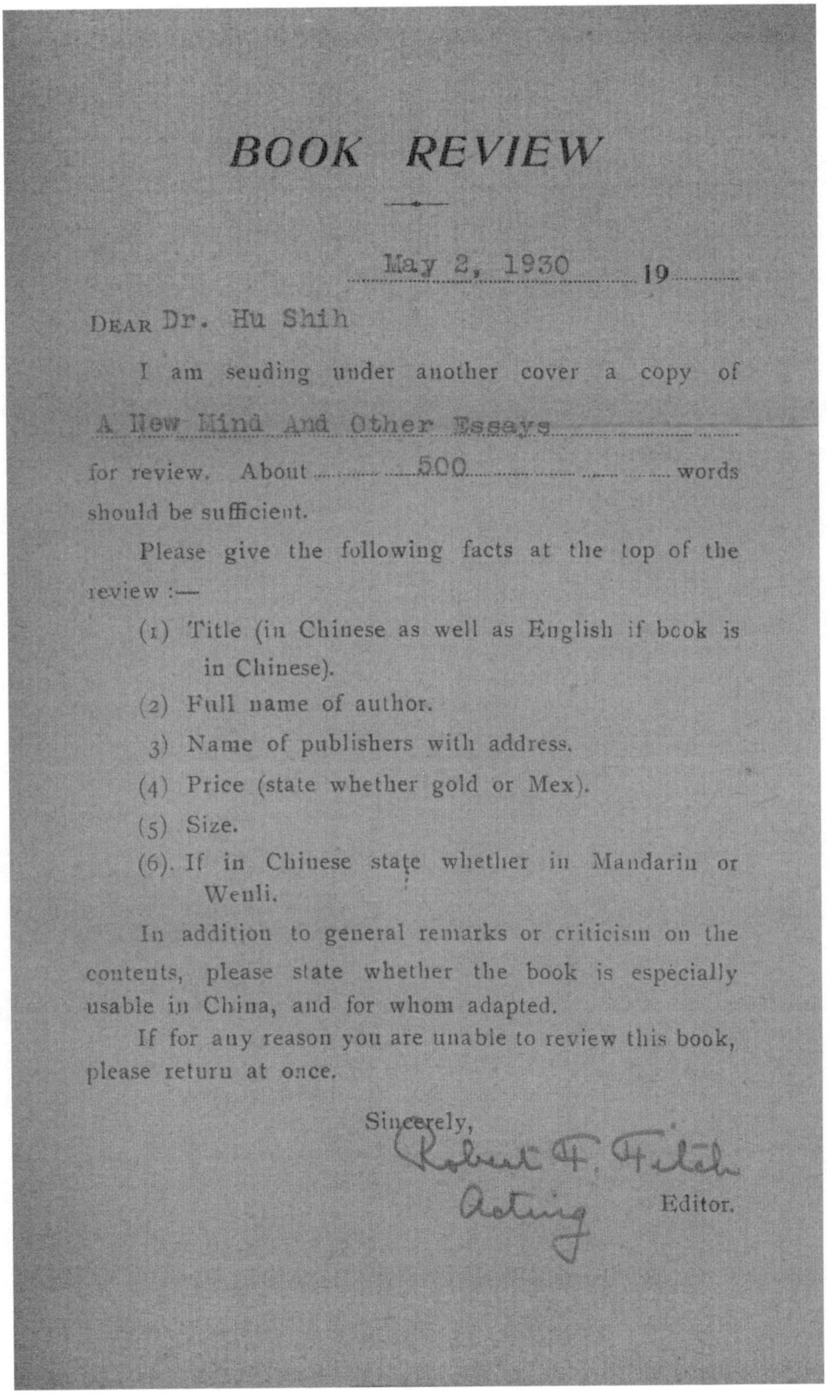

BOOK REVIEW

May 2, 1930   19......

DEAR Dr. Hu Shih

  I am sending under another cover a copy of A New Mind And Other Essays for review. About ......500...... words should be sufficient.

  Please give the following facts at the top of the review :—

  (1) Title (in Chinese as well as English if book is in Chinese).

  (2) Full name of author.

  3) Name of publishers with address.

  (4) Price (state whether gold or Mex).

  (5) Size.

  (6). If in Chinese state whether in Mandarin or Wenli.

  In addition to general remarks or criticism on the contents, please state whether the book is especially usable in China, and for whom adapted.

  If for any reason you are unable to review this book, please return at once.

Sincerely,

Robert F. Fitch
Acting Editor.

圖 3

A NEW MIND AND OTHER ESSAYS

by

EVAN MORGAN

Size. 8¼″ x 5¾″. Pp. 260. Price $3.00

The volume contains 28 essays. Some of the subjects are the following. The Lost Mind: The Perfect Life: The Taoist Superman: A Case of Ritualism: Imperialism: The Exclusive Spirit: Federation in Chinese Politics: China in History: The Yangtse: A League of Nations in Ancient China: The Committee Sense: Sanctity of Contract: Loyalty: Revenge: Potential Power of the Masses: Trend of Modern Chinese Literature: A New Mind.

More or less all the essays concern China. An attempt is made to understand the character of the Chinese as we see it shown in their religion: in the council chamber: in political life: in business and camp: in ancient ideal and modern practice. Examples are taken from ancient history and recent events. The subjects vary and the unitive thread is China.

These essays have been written at different times. Some of the subjects discussed were transient, but an element of permanency remains.

圖 4

The Chinese Recorder

EDITORIAL HEADQUARTERS
MISSIONS BUILDING
23 YUEN MING YUEN ROAD
SHANGHAI

BUSINESS HEADQUARTERS
PRESBYTERIAN MISSION PRESS
135 NORTH SZECHUEN ROAD
SHANGHAI, CHINA

July 15th, 1930

Dr. Hu Shih,
49-A, Jessfield Road,
Shanghai, China.

Dear Dr. Hu,

    On May 2, 1930, we sent you a book entitled: A NEW MIND AND OTHER ESSAYS, by Evan Morgan, requesting you to kindly send us a review for the Chinese Recorder, could you kindly forward us this review at your earliest convenience?

    Appreciating your cooperation in this matter,

    Very sincerely yours,

    Robert F. Fitch

    ROBERT F. FITCH,
    Acting-Editor.

RFF:EL

圖 5

Everett R. Clinchy 致胡適

此信件發現於 *Handbook for the Sixth Conference of the Institute of Pacific Relations* 一書中。

Everett R. Clinchy（189—1989），美國長老會傳道師，1929 年創辦（美國）全國基督教徒和猶太教徒聯合會（National Conference of Christians and Jews）。1958 年離開該會，致力於該會的分支機構世界兄弟會（World Brotherhood）推動全球種族、宗教和社會間理解的工作。

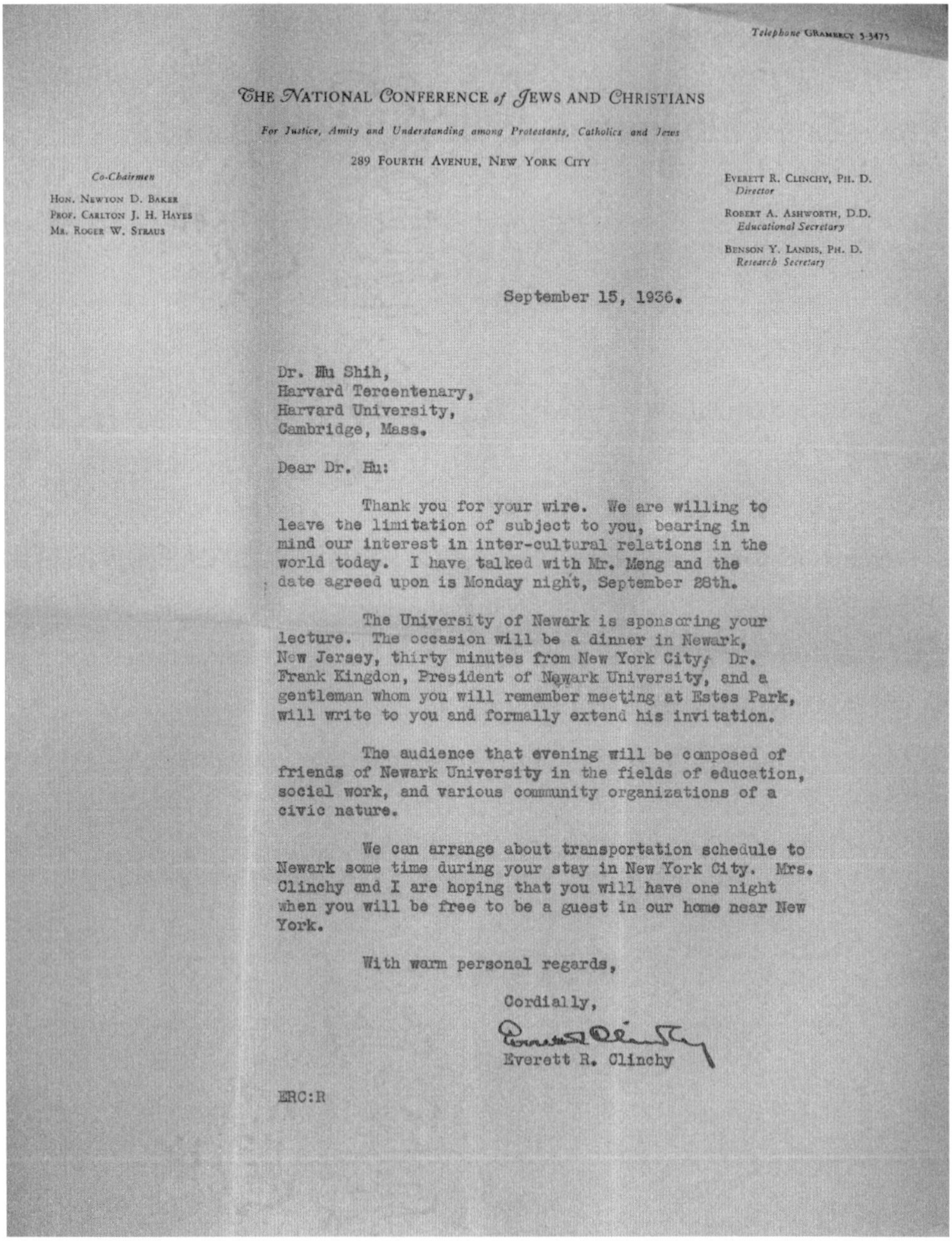

THE NATIONAL CONFERENCE of JEWS AND CHRISTIANS
For Justice, Amity and Understanding among Protestants, Catholics and Jews
289 FOURTH AVENUE, NEW YORK CITY

Co-Chairmen
HON. NEWTON D. BAKER
PROF. CARLTON J. H. HAYES
MR. ROGER W. STRAUS

EVERETT R. CLINCHY, PH. D.
Director
ROBERT A. ASHWORTH, D.D.
Educational Secretary
BENSON Y. LANDIS, PH. D.
Research Secretary

September 15, 1936.

Dr. Hu Shih,
Harvard Tercentenary,
Harvard University,
Cambridge, Mass.

Dear Dr. Hu:

Thank you for your wire. We are willing to leave the limitation of subject to you, bearing in mind our interest in inter-cultural relations in the world today. I have talked with Mr. Meng and the date agreed upon is Monday night, September 28th.

The University of Newark is sponsoring your lecture. The occasion will be a dinner in Newark, New Jersey, thirty minutes from New York City. Dr. Frank Kingdon, President of Newark University, and a gentleman whom you will remember meeting at Estes Park, will write to you and formally extend his invitation.

The audience that evening will be composed of friends of Newark University in the fields of education, social work, and various community organizations of a civic nature.

We can arrange about transportation schedule to Newark some time during your stay in New York City. Mrs. Clinchy and I are hoping that you will have one night when you will be free to be a guest in our home near New York.

With warm personal regards,

Cordially,

Everett R. Clinchy

ERC:R

圖 1

Frances Carpenter Huntington 致胡適

此信件發現於 *Tales of a Chinese Grandmother* 一書中。

Frances Carpenter Huntington（1890—1972），生於美國華盛頓特區，1912年畢業於史密斯學院（Smith College）。其父爲海外記者，曾作爲秘書和攝影師陪其父周遊世界各地，並出版多種圖書。曾任國際女地理學家學會副主席、英國皇家地理學會會員、史密斯學院校友會主席等職。

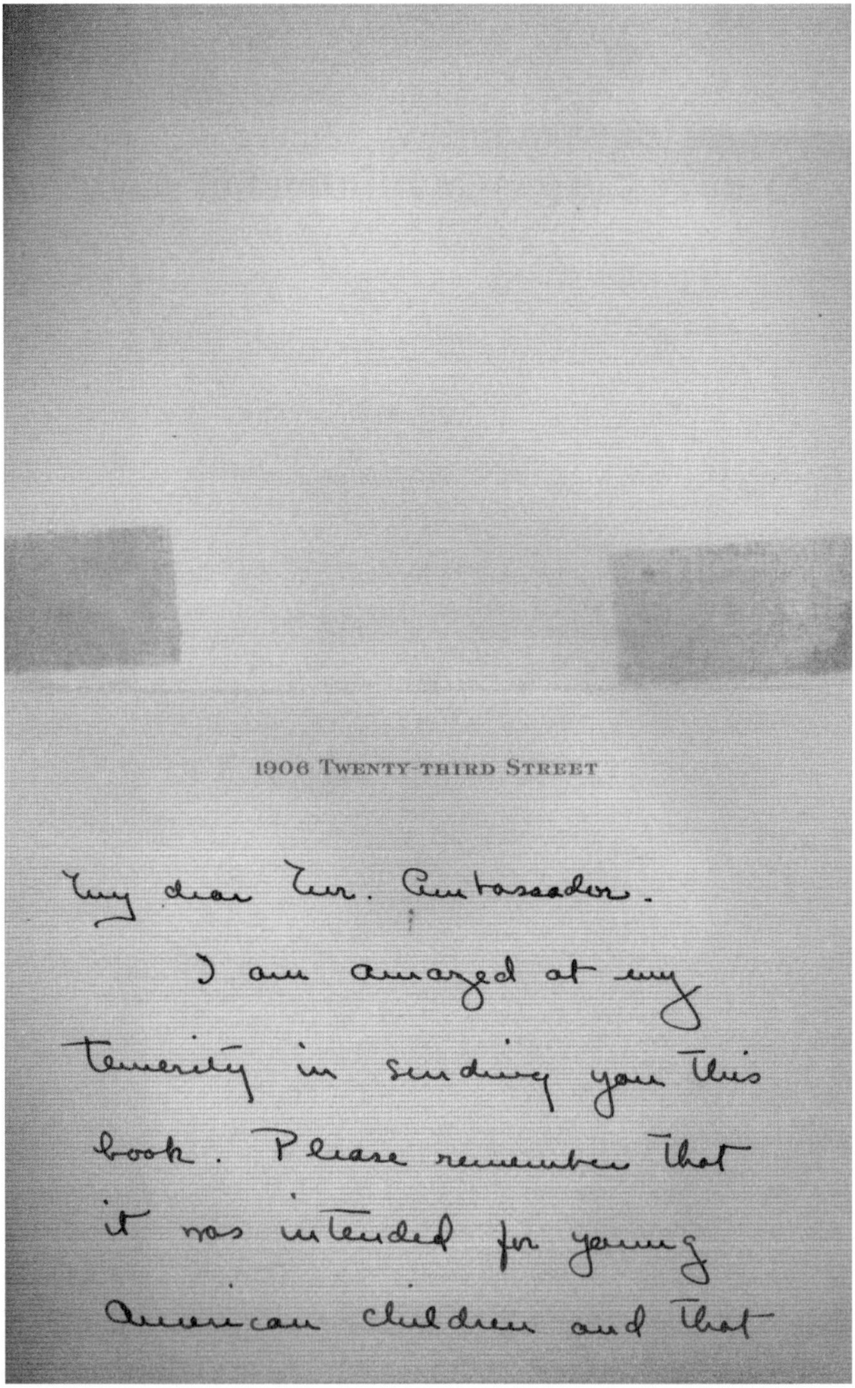

1906 TWENTY-THIRD STREET

My dear Mr. Ambassador.

I am amazed at my temerity in sending you this book. Please remember that it was intended for young American children and that

圖1

My dear Mr. Ambassador,

I am amazed at my temerity in sending you this book. Please remember that it was intended for young American children and that it was because of that, that I was forced to take certain liberties with my source material. The illustrations were made by a Danish artist in New York, who has made a speciality of ancient Chinese art study.

With the hope that you may have some young friend who will like to read the stories, I am

Sincerely yours,

Frances Carpenter Huntington

March 17th (Mrs. W. Chapin Huntington)

圖 2

it was because of that, that I was forced to take certain liberties with my source material. The illustrations were made by a Danish artist in New York, who has made a speciality of ancient Chinese art study.

With the hope that you may have some young friend who will like to read the stories, I am

Sincerely yours,
Frances Carpenter Huntington

March 17th   (Mrs. W. Chapin Huntington)

G. W. Sheppard 致胡適（一九二九年十月二十二日）

此信件發現於 *Portrait of a Chinese Lady* 一書中。

G. W. Sheppard，時任 British & Foreign Bible Society 駐中國機構秘書，餘不詳。

> TELEPHONE CENTRAL. 1872
>
> TELEGRAPHIC ADDRESS.
> "TESTAMENTS, SHANGHAI."
>
> CODES
> A.B.C. VIA EASTERN & C.I.M.
>
> SECRETARY
> REV. G.W. SHEPPARD
>
> British & Foreign Bible Society,
> China Agency,
> 3 Hongkong Road, Shanghai.
>
> 22nd October, 1929.
>
> Dr. Hu Shih,
>   49A Jessfield Road,
>   SHANGHAI.
>
> Dear Dr. Hu,
>
>   Herewith I have pleasure in forwarding a letter from Oxford for you, presumably from our mutual friend Professor Soothill.
>
>   Will you kindly remember to let me have the manuscript of your lecture recently given before the Royal Asiatic Society, or such part of it as you would like to be published in the next issue of the Journal?
>
>   With kind regards,
>   Yours sincerely,
>
>   G W Sheppard
>
> A

圖 1

George Catlin致胡適（一九四八年八月七日）

此信發現於 *In the Path of Mahatma Gandhi* 一書中。

作者生平不詳。

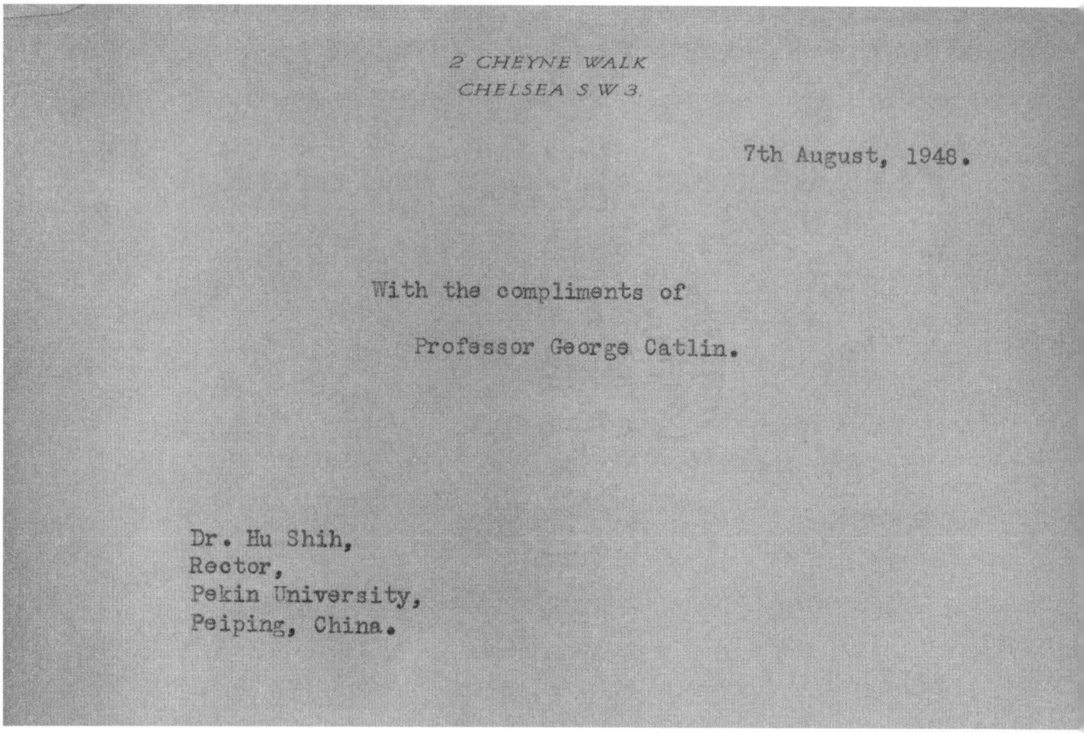

2 CHEYNE WALK
CHELSEA S.W.3.

7th August, 1948.

With the compliments of
Professor George Catlin.

Dr. Hu Shih,
Rector,
Pekin University,
Peiping, China.

圖 1

H. J. Timperley 致胡適（一九三一年三月五日）

此信件發現於 The Beginnings of Jourlism in China 一書中。

H. J. Timperley（1898—1954），即 Harold John Timperley，中文名田伯烈，澳大利亞人，一戰後來華，任路透社駐北京記者，後任《曼徹斯特衛報》（Manchester Guardian）及美國《聯合報》駐北京記者。曾任北平公理會教堂主席，1936年在北平創辦社區文化活動中心。1936年遷居上海，成爲"中國華洋義賑救灾總會"成員。不久被《曼徹斯特衛報》派往西班牙採訪西班牙内戰。1937年抗戰全面爆發後，被調派回中國。後任國民黨中央宣傳部顧問。編有《日人在華的恐怖》（The Japanese Terror in China）。1943年任聯合國情報官員。1947年2月在南京戰犯審判軍事法庭指證谷壽夫唆使日軍進行大屠殺的罪行。1948年在聯合國教科文組織巴黎總部工作。1950年到印尼，擔任印尼外交部技術顧問。1954年11月26日病逝。北京檔藏田伯烈致胡適書信四封，時間從1924年到1938年。

田伯烈

英國滿徹斯德保衛
日報特約駐平訪員

32 Ch'un Shu Hutung

H. J. TIMPERLEY
Telephone: East 3315

Peking, March 5, 1931.

Dear Dr. Hu:

    Somewhat belatedly but with my best wishes I am sending you a "Leader" reprint of the modest paper on "The Beginnings of Journalism in China" which I read before the "Things Chinese" Society last November. From a reference to pages 6 and 7 you will note that I have borrowed rather heavily from the introduction to your "Development of the Logical Method in Ancient China" though I hope you will feel I have made an adequate acknowledgment of the source. I had planned to consult you before using these references but unfortunately you were away in Shanghai at the time.

    I know that you are a very busy man but I should like to give myself the pleasure of calling upon you for a chat some day soon. Is there any special time at which you are usually at home and prepared to submit to intrusions?

                   Sincerely yours,

                    H. J. Timperley

圖 1

H. L. Huang 致胡適（一九一六年十二月六日）

　　此明信片發現於 *The Law Business or Profession* 一書中。據明信片上所印地址"哥倫比亞大學"，結合寫信人、收信人同在哥倫比亞大學的時間，以及信中"12月8日星期五"的日期，此明信片當寫於1916年，又據信末所署"Wednesday"，具體時間或爲1916年12月6日。

　　黃漢梁（1892—1974），福建思明（今廈門）人。早年畢業於清華學校，1911年作爲第三批庚子賠款留美生前往美國，入密歇根大學，1915年獲普林斯頓大學學士學位。1916年獲哥倫比亞大學文學碩士學位。1918年獲哥大經濟學博士學位。同年歸國，任上海銀行國外匯兑處主任，後到新加坡、菲律賓等地從事銀行職業。1923年任和豐銀行香港分行行長，兩年後任上海分行行長。1924年與商務印書館創辦人之一夏瑞芳的長女夏瑪琍結婚。後曾任浙江實業銀行、中國國貨銀行監察，實豐保險公司董事。1929年，任國民政府鐵道部經濟顧問。1930年出任鐵道部常務次長，兼整理招商局委員會委員、英國庚子賠款委員會委員。1931年12月至1932年1月曾署理財政部部長。後曾任中興銀行董事。1948年底前後赴菲律賓，後到美國。

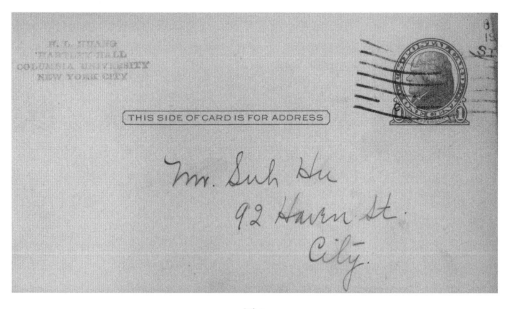

圖1

圖2

Dear Mr. Hu:

Professor Missay has consented to speak at our next Club meeting, Friday, Dec. 8.

My sincerely yours,

H. L. Huang

Wednesday

Hamilton Fish Armstrong 致胡適
（一九三六年十月十三日）

此電報發現於 *University of Iowa Studies* 一書中，另有信件一，日程表一，節目單一，電話記錄一。其中信件（見本書第 615—617 頁）可與此電報相互參看。

胡適 1936 年 7 月從上海赴美參加太平洋國際學會第六屆常會，以及哈佛大學三百周年紀念會等活動，11 月自舊金山回國。此後其文章 "The Changing Balance of Power in the Pacific" 發表於 *Foreign Affairs*（《外交》雜志）1937 年第 1 期。此電報與書信即涉及文章發表事宜。

Hamilton Fish Armstrong（1893—1973），《外交》雜志編輯。

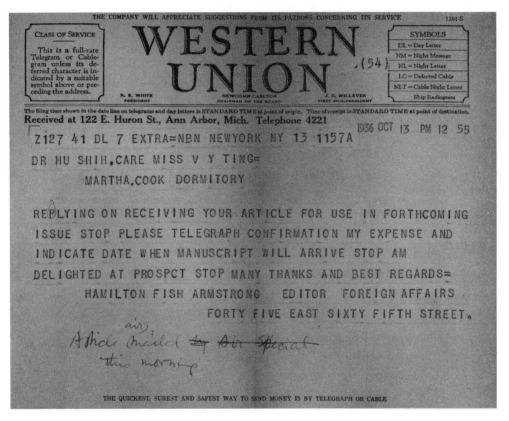

圖 1

Henry W. Edgerton 致胡適（一九四一年三月二十六日）

此信件發現於 The Life and Times of William Howard Taft 一書中，另有剪報一份。

Henry W. Edgerton，即 Henry White Edgerton（1888—1970），1910 年獲康奈爾大學文學學士學位，1914 年獲哈佛大學法學學士學位。1916—1918 年，任康奈爾大學法學院教授。1921—1928 年，任喬治華盛頓大學教授。1928—1937 年任康奈爾大學教授。1934—1935 年任美國司法部長特別助理。1938 年 12 月被羅斯福總統提名爲美國哥倫比亞特區聯邦巡迴上訴法院聯邦法官。1955—1958 年，任首席法官。北京檔藏有 Edgerton 1943 年 1 月 2 日致胡適書信一封。

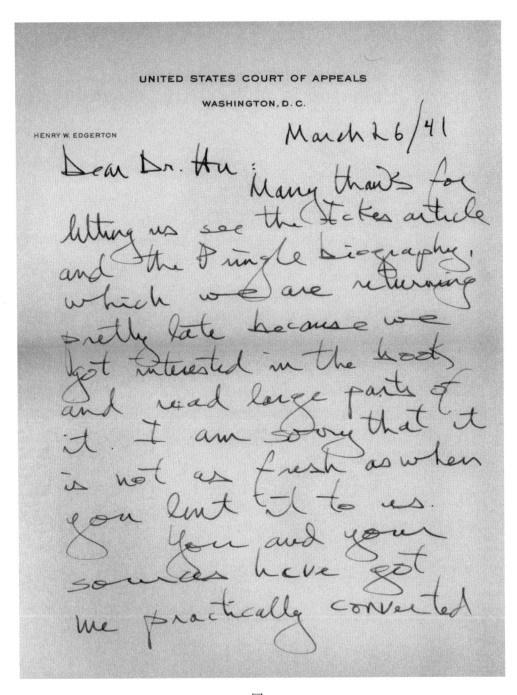

圖1

March 26, 1941

Dear Dr. Hu:

Many thanks for letting us see the Ickes article and the Pringle biography, which we are returning pretty late because we got interested in the book and read large parts of it. I am sorry that it is not as fresh as when you lent it to us.

You and your sources have got me practically converted

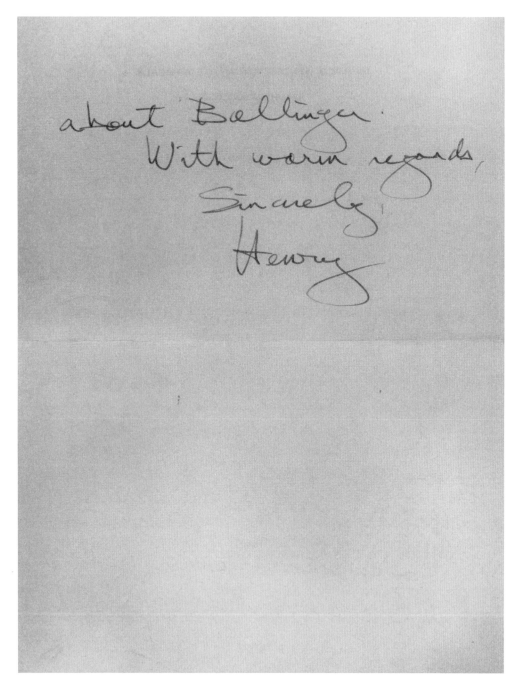

圖 2

about Bellinger.

With warm regards,
Sincerely,
Henry

Hu Shi 致某人

　　此信件發現於 The Establishment of Confucianism as a State Religion During the Han Dynasty 一文中，並附論文打印複寫件。此論文發表於 Journal of the North-China Branch of the Royal Asiatic Society，1929 年第 60 卷第 20—41 頁。收信人不詳。

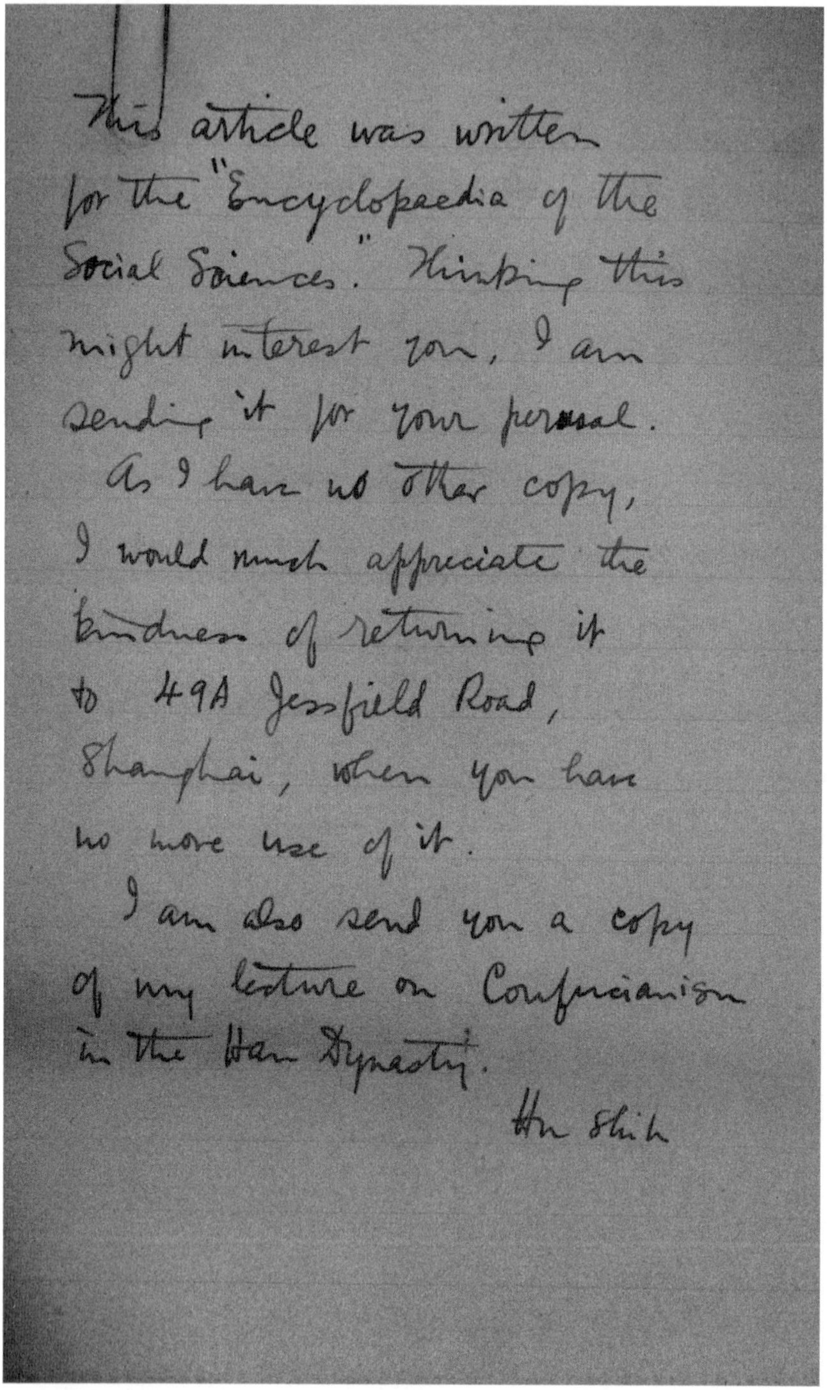

This article was written for the "Encyclopaedia of the Social Sciences." Thinking this might interest you, I am sending it for your perusal. As I have no other copy, I would much appreciate the kindness of returning it to 49A Jessfield Road, Shanghai, when you have no more use of it.

I am also send you a copy of my lecture on Confucianism in the Han Dynasty.

Hu Shih

圖1

This article was written for the "Encyclopedia of the Social Sciences." Thinking this might interest you, I am sending it for your perusal. As I have no other copy, I would much appreciate the kindness of returning it to 49A Jessfield Road, Shanghai, when you have no more use of it.

I am also send you a copy of my lecture on Confucianism in the Han Dynasty.

Hu Shih

Irving Dilliard 致胡適

  此信件發現於 *Mr. Justice Brandeis: Great American* 一書中。此書出版於 1941 年，根據信中所提到的 bill of rights day 及大法官布蘭德斯去世日期等信息，此信或寫於 1941 年。

  Irving Lee Dilliard（1899—2002），美國作家、編輯及憲法專家。1923 年開始擔任《聖路易斯郵報》當地通訊員。1927 年畢業於伊利諾伊大學香檳分校，後在哈佛大學讀研究生一年。1927 年成爲《聖路易斯郵報》記者。1943 年參加二戰。戰後任《聖路易斯郵報》主筆，1960 年退休。胡適任駐美大使期間與其有交往，北京檔藏有與其往來書信 8 封，主要時間在 1941 年。

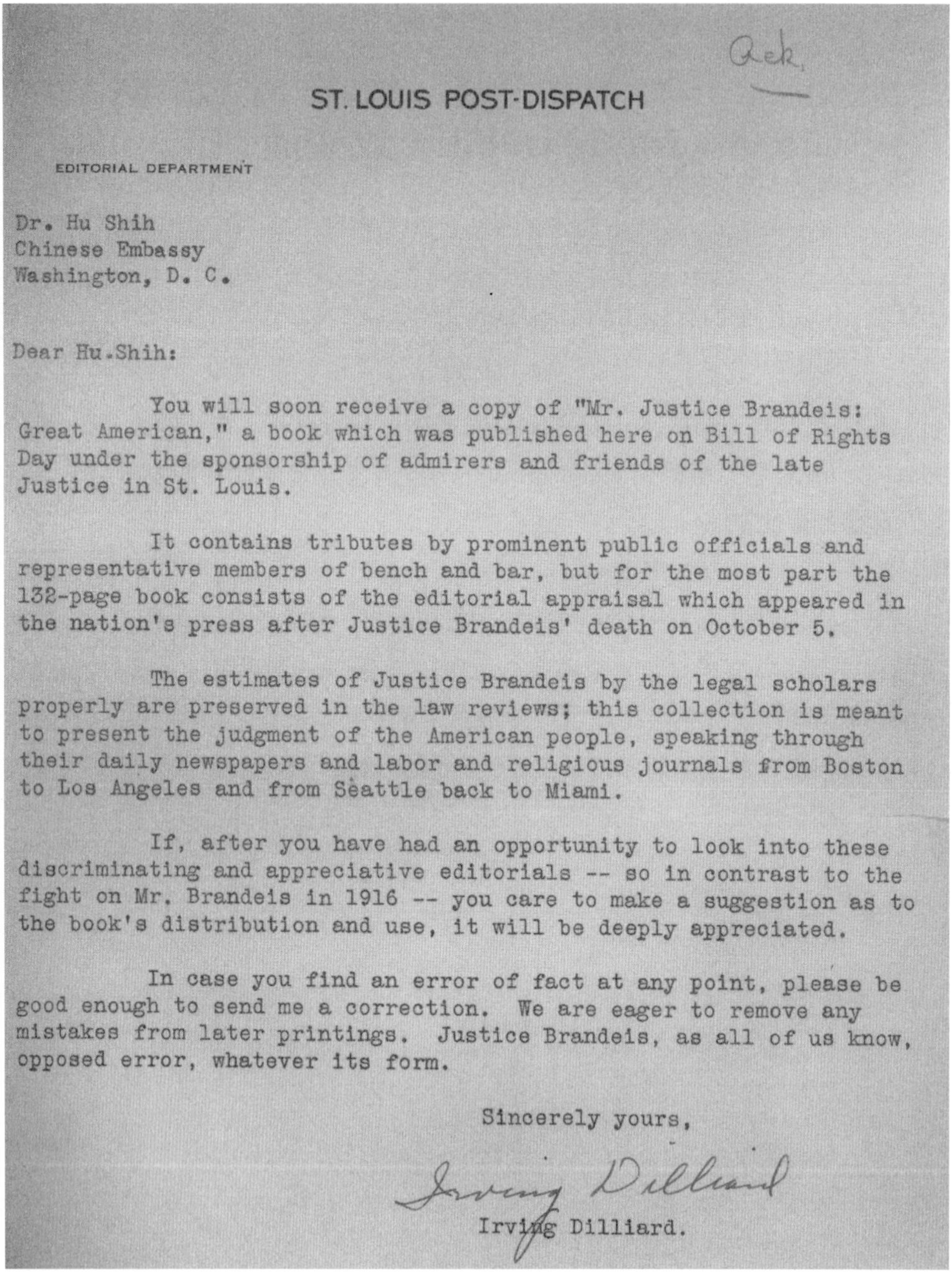

ST. LOUIS POST-DISPATCH

EDITORIAL DEPARTMENT

Dr. Hu Shih
Chinese Embassy
Washington, D. C.

Dear Hu Shih:

You will soon receive a copy of "Mr. Justice Brandeis: Great American," a book which was published here on Bill of Rights Day under the sponsorship of admirers and friends of the late Justice in St. Louis.

It contains tributes by prominent public officials and representative members of bench and bar, but for the most part the 132-page book consists of the editorial appraisal which appeared in the nation's press after Justice Brandeis' death on October 5.

The estimates of Justice Brandeis by the legal scholars properly are preserved in the law reviews; this collection is meant to present the judgment of the American people, speaking through their daily newspapers and labor and religious journals from Boston to Los Angeles and from Seattle back to Miami.

If, after you have had an opportunity to look into these discriminating and appreciative editorials -- so in contrast to the fight on Mr. Brandeis in 1916 -- you care to make a suggestion as to the book's distribution and use, it will be deeply appreciated.

In case you find an error of fact at any point, please be good enough to send me a correction. We are eager to remove any mistakes from later printings. Justice Brandeis, as all of us know, opposed error, whatever its form.

Sincerely yours,

Irving Dilliard.

圖 1

Joanna Scott 致胡適（一九四五年三月三十日）

此信發現於 *Europe: A New Picture* 一書中，隨函另附此系列書簡介。

Joanna Scott, *Europe: A New Picture* 的作者，餘不詳。

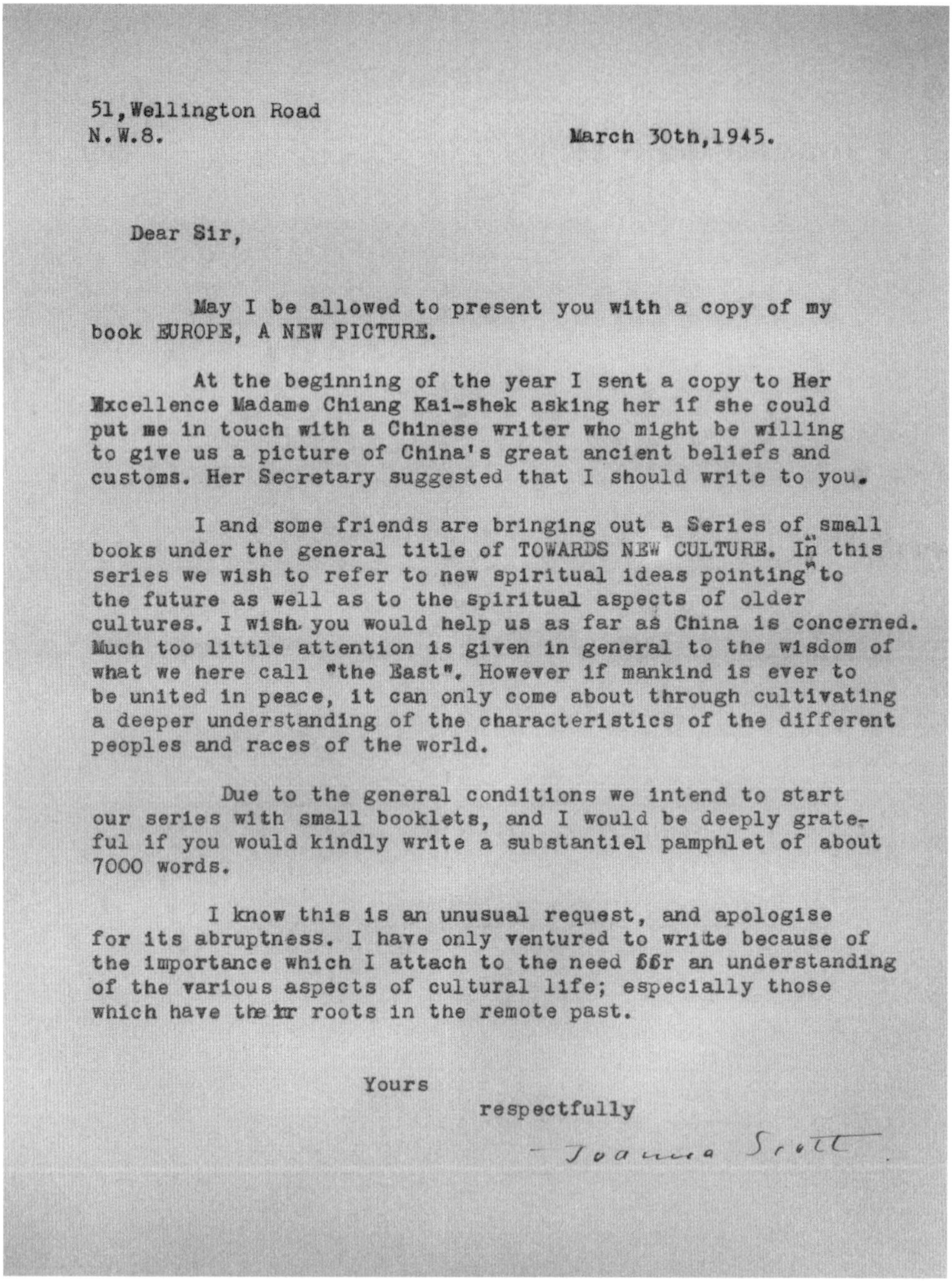

51,Wellington Road
N.W.8.   March 30th,1945.

Dear Sir,

    May I be allowed to present you with a copy of my book EUROPE, A NEW PICTURE.

    At the beginning of the year I sent a copy to Her Excellence Madame Chiang Kai-shek asking her if she could put me in touch with a Chinese writer who might be willing to give us a picture of China's great ancient beliefs and customs. Her Secretary suggested that I should write to you.

    I and some friends are bringing out a Series of small books under the general title of TOWARDS NEW CULTURE. In this series we wish to refer to new spiritual ideas pointing to the future as well as to the spiritual aspects of older cultures. I wish you would help us as far as China is concerned. Much too little attention is given in general to the wisdom of what we here call "the East". However if mankind is ever to be united in peace, it can only come about through cultivating a deeper understanding of the characteristics of the different peoples and races of the world.

    Due to the general conditions we intend to start our series with small booklets, and I would be deeply grateful if you would kindly write a substantiel pamphlet of about 7000 words.

    I know this is an unusual request, and apologise for its abruptness. I have only ventured to write because of the importance which I attach to the need for an understanding of the various aspects of cultural life; especially those which have their roots in the remote past.

                      Yours respectfully

                            — Joanna Scott

圖 1

Publication of a Series
TOWARDS NEW CULTURE

A SMALL group of people have set before themselves the task of publishing a series of books called *Towards New Culture*. They think that it is vital to see how new cultural ideas can be fruitfully applied in different spheres of actual practical life and to understand the true relationship between old and new values. They are interested in the various cultures of the world, and feel that every effort should be attempted to enhance the appreciation of other races as well as their own. The mentality of humanity in the Eastern and Southern parts of the World is spiritual in its essence and can be understood as such; on the other hand, modern Western development tends towards spiritual experiences of a new and not yet fully realised kind.

More and more the tendency will prevail in the near future to consider nations and continents as markets only. This, together with the imminent poverty of great zones of the world will of necessity lead to moral devaluation of cultural impulses.

The awakening of greater understanding for spiritual values can be a healing factor in this situation and can help to kindle the enthusiasm for the good in mankind.

Already many writers have agreed to collaborate in the suggested publications.

To sustain this work, free gifts from those interested, and unpaid contributions from the writers, will be needed. All proceeds from sales will be used for further publications.

FRANCIS H. WALL, *Secretary*,
51, Wellington Road,
London, N.W. 8.

圖 2

John Dewey 致 Mr. William（一九二八年四月十日）

此信件發現於 The Social Interpretation of History 一書中，貼於封底內頁。

John Dewey（1859—1952），即杜威，美國哲學家、教育學家，實驗主義代表。生於美國佛蒙特州。1879 年畢業於佛蒙特大學。1884 年獲約翰霍普金斯大學博士學位。後任教於密歇根大學、明尼蘇達大學、芝加哥大學。1896 年創辦芝加哥大學實驗學校。1904 年任哥倫比亞大學哲學系教授。胡適留美期間曾師從杜威，受其影響很大。1919 年 5 月來華演講，1921 年歸國。主要著作有《我的教育信條》《明日之學校》等。

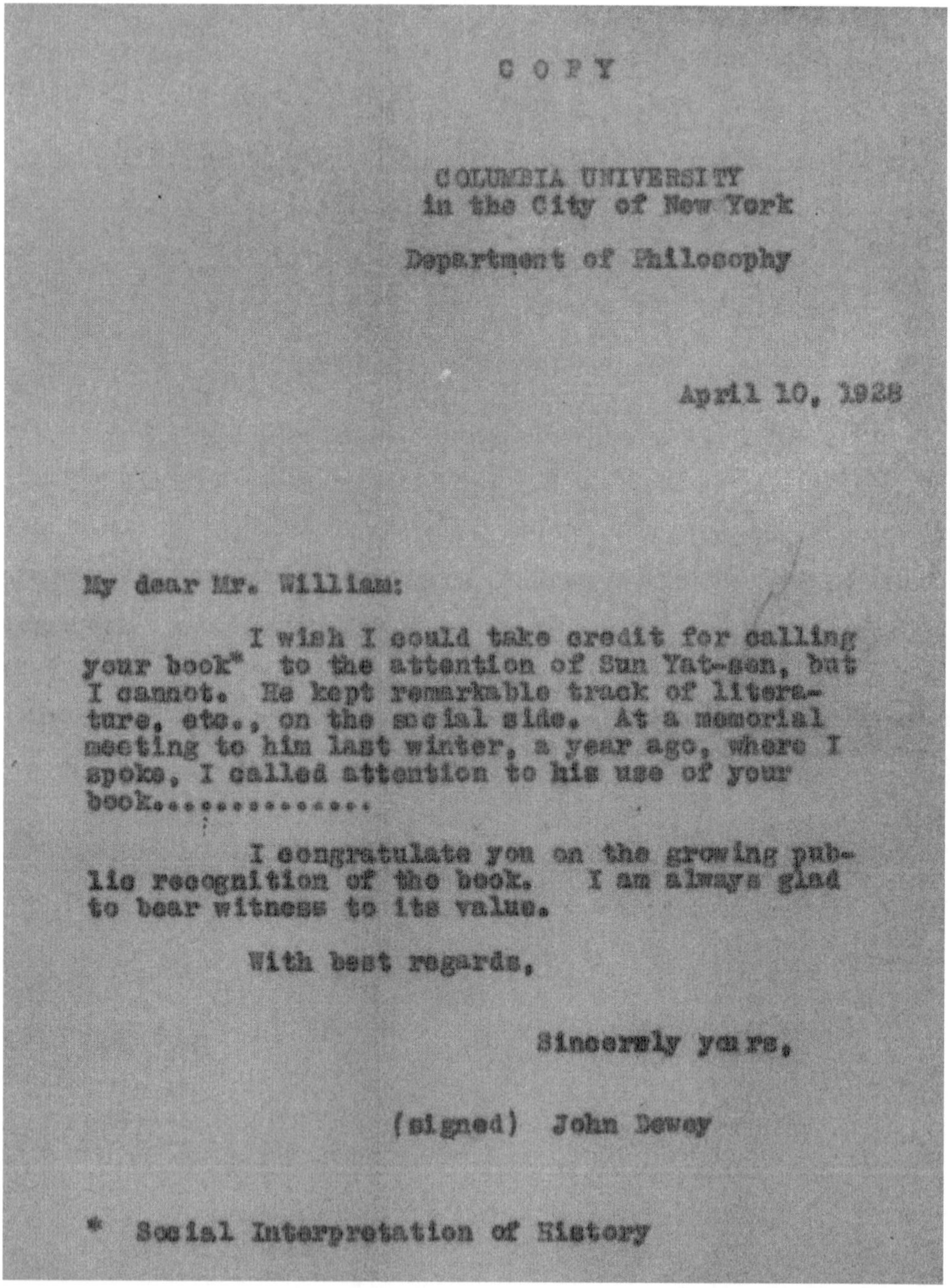

COPY

COLUMBIA UNIVERSITY
in the City of New York

Department of Philosophy

April 10, 1928

My dear Mr. William:

    I wish I could take credit for calling your book* to the attention of Sun Yat-sen, but I cannot. He kept remarkable track of literature, etc., on the social side. At a memorial meeting to him last winter, a year ago, where I spoke, I called attention to his use of your book...............

    I congratulate you on the growing public recognition of the book. I am always glad to bear witness to its value.

    With best regards,

Sincerely yours,

(signed) John Dewey

* Social Interpretation of History

圖1

John Story Jenks 致胡適（一九四〇年九月二十四日）

此信夾於 *A Dissertation on the Nature and Character of the Chinese System of Writing* 一書中。

John Story Jenks（1876—1946），生於美國費城，1896 年畢業於哈弗福德學院，銀行家，美國哲學學會成員。據胡適日記，胡適任大使期間與其有交往。1940 年 9 月 19 日，胡適到賓夕法尼亞大學宣讀論文後，與 Jenks 夫婦吃飯。此信寫於同月 24 日，信中説"很高興在費城與您再次見面"，應即指 9 月 19 日的會面。

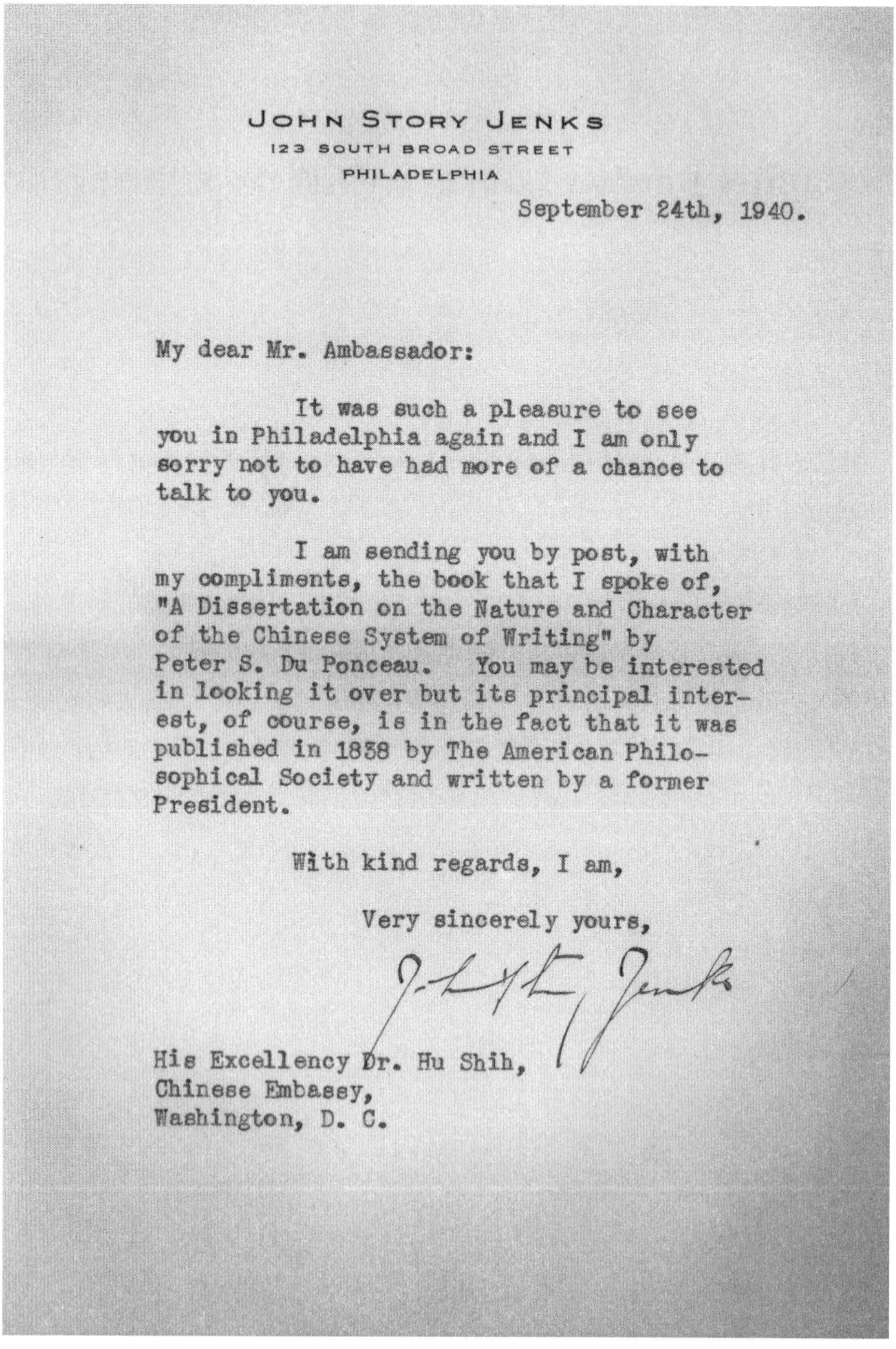

JOHN STORY JENKS
123 SOUTH BROAD STREET
PHILADELPHIA

September 24th, 1940.

My dear Mr. Ambassador:

    It was such a pleasure to see you in Philadelphia again and I am only sorry not to have had more of a chance to talk to you.

    I am sending you by post, with my compliments, the book that I spoke of, "A Dissertation on the Nature and Character of the Chinese System of Writing" by Peter S. Du Ponceau. You may be interested in looking it over but its principal interest, of course, is in the fact that it was published in 1838 by The American Philosophical Society and written by a former President.

    With kind regards, I am,

    Very sincerely yours,

    John Story Jenks

His Excellency Dr. Hu Shih,
Chinese Embassy,
Washington, D. C.

圖1

Juliet Bredon Lauru 致胡適（一九三四年）

此信件發現於 Hundred Altars 一書中，信中未注明時間。Hundred Altars 最早出版於 1934 年，是年胡適曾去南京，信中説寄至南京地址，故此信可能寫於 1934 年。

Juliet Bredon Lauru，中文名裴麗珠。英國女作家。中國海關代理總稅務司裴式楷之女，總稅務司赫德的内侄女，其夫爲法國人羅爾瑜（Charles Henry Lauru），曾在中國海關工作，後任鹽務稽核總所財務秘書。著有《赫德爵士傳奇》（Sir Robert Hart, the Romance of a Great Career），《北京紀勝》（Peking: A Historical and Intimate Description of its Chief Places of Interest），《中國風俗節日記》（The Moon Year: A Record of Chinese Customs and Festivals）等。

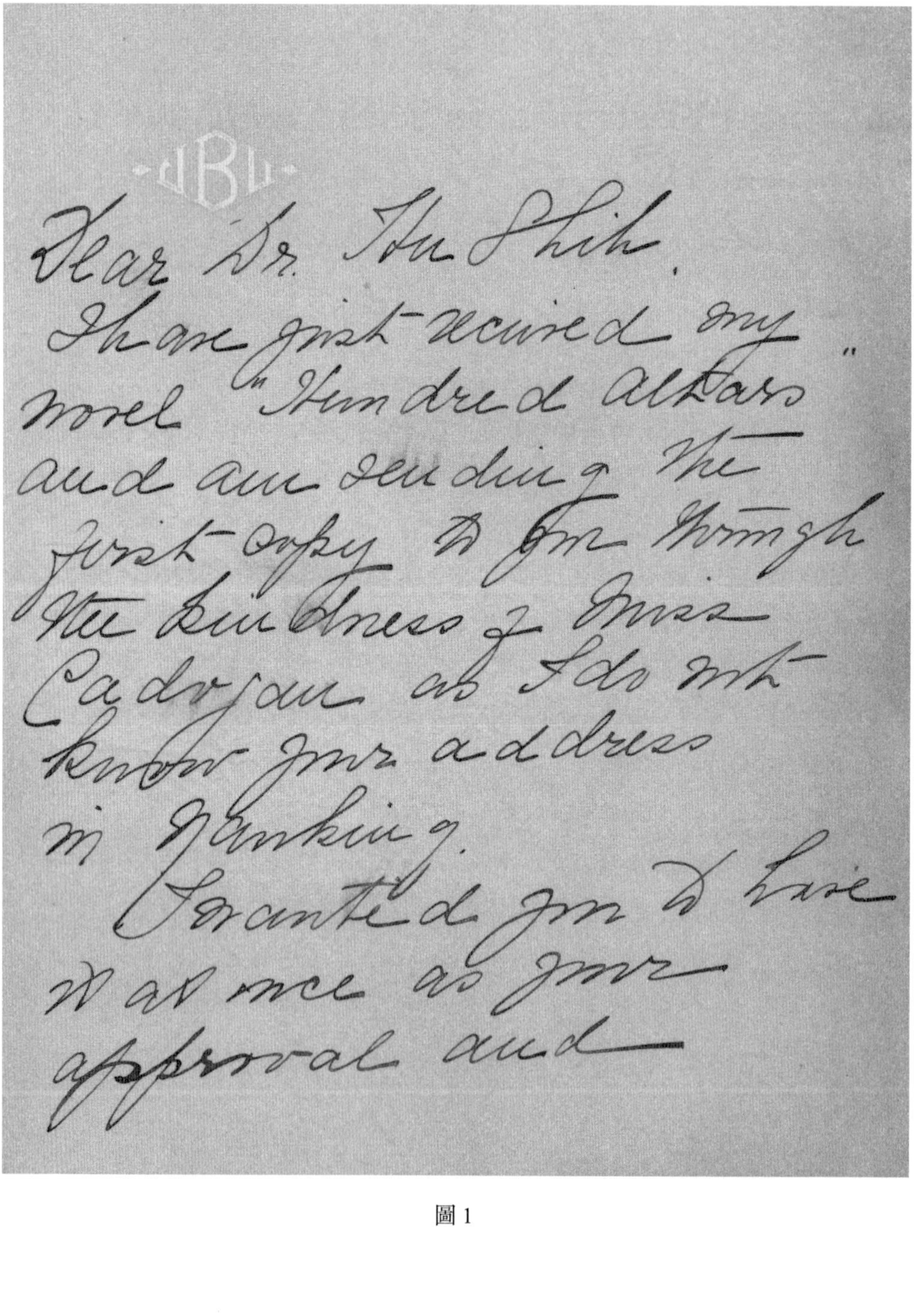

Dear Dr. Hu Shih,

I have just received my novel "Hundred Altars" and am sending the first copy to you through the kindness of Miss Cadogan as I do not know your address in Nanking.

I wanted you to have it at once as your approval and

圖 1

Dear Dr. Hu Shih,

I have just received my novel "Hundred Altars" and am sending the first copy to you through the kindness of Miss Cadogan as I do not know your address in Nanking.

I wanted you to have it at once as your approval and

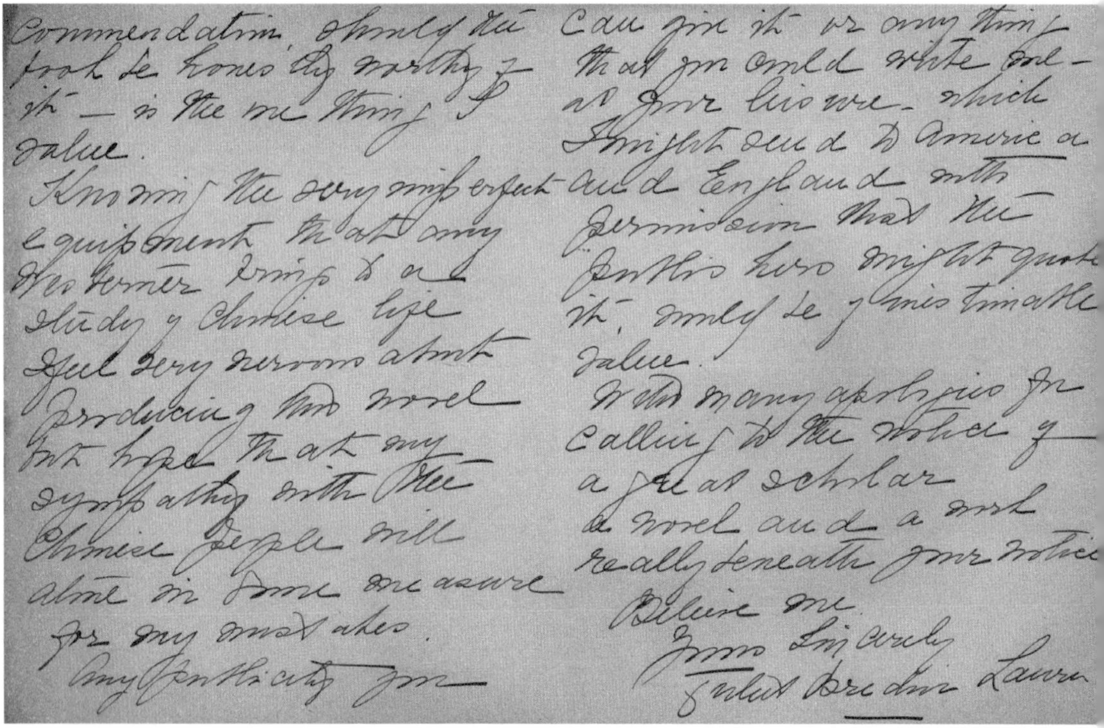

commendation, simply the fact he knows the worthy of it — is the one thing I value.

Knowing the very imperfect equipment that any Westerner brings to a study of Chinese life I feel very nervous about producing this novel but hope that my sympathy with the Chinese people will atone in some measure for my most obvious —

Any Publicity you

can give it or anything that you could write me — of your own — which I might send to America and England with permission that the authors here might quote it, would be of immense value.

With many apologies for calling to the notice of a great scholar a novel and a work really beneath your notice

Believe me
Yours Sincerely
Juliet Bredon Laura

圖 2

commendation, should the book be honestly worthy of it— is the one thing I value.

Knowing the very imperfect equipment that any Westerner brings to a study of Chinese life I feel very nervous about producing this novel but hope that my sympathy with the Chinese people will atone in some measure for my mistakes.

Any publicity you can give it or anything that you could write me— at your leisure—which I might send to America and England with permission that the public hero might quote it, would be of inestimable value.

With many apologies for calling to the notice of a great scholar a novel and a work really beneath your notice.

Believe me

Yours sincerely
Juliet Bredon Lauru

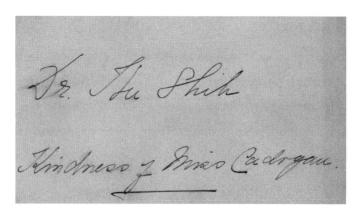

圖 3

L. B. Juin 致胡適（一九四〇年十一月五日）

此信發現於 *From Many Lands* 一書中。

L. B. Juin，生平不詳。

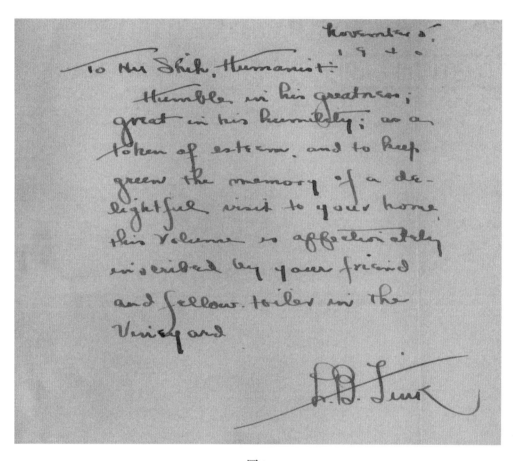

圖1

November 5, 1940

To Hu Shih, Humanist:

    Humble in his greatness; great in his humility; as a token of esteem, and to keep green the memory of a delightful visit to your home, this volume is affectionately inscribed by your friend and fellow toiler in the vineyard.

L. B. Juin

L. G. Morgan 致胡適（一九三五年五月一日）

此信件發現於 The Teaching of Science to the Chinese 一書中。

L. G. Morgan，早年畢業於倫敦大學，獲科學學士、文學碩士學位。1947 任香港皇后書院院長。

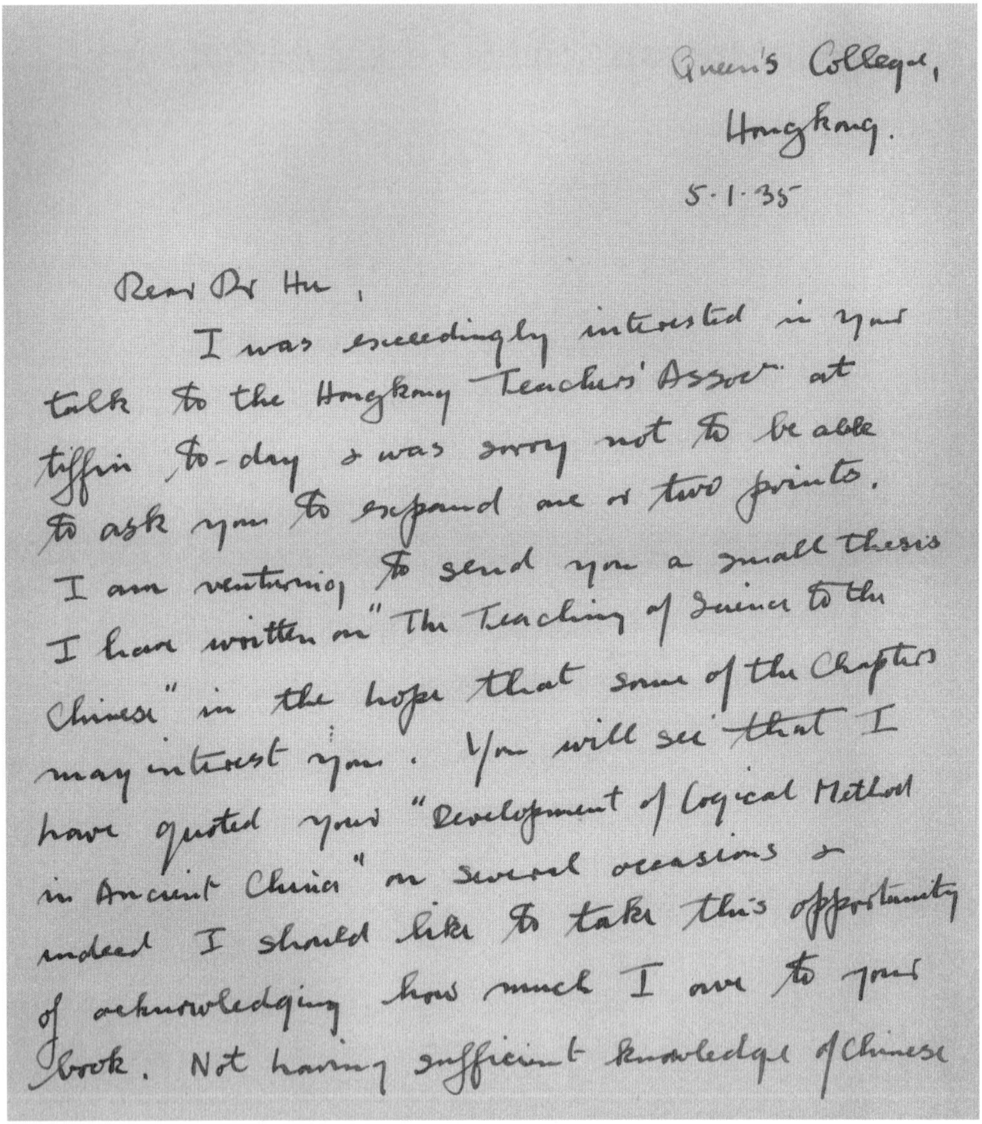

> Queen's College,
> Hongkong.
> 5.1.35
>
> Dear Dr Hu,
>
> I was exceedingly interested in your talk to the Hongkong Teachers' Assocⁿ at tiffin to-day & was sorry not to be able to ask you to expand one or two points. I am venturing to send you a small thesis I have written on "The Teaching of Science to the Chinese" in the hope that some of the chapters may interest you. You will see that I have quoted your "Development of Logical Method in Ancient China" on several occasions & indeed I should like to take this opportunity of acknowledging how much I owe to your book. Not having sufficient knowledge of Chinese

圖 1

Queen's College
Hongkong
5. 1. 35

Dear Dr. Hu,

I was exceedingly interested in your talk to the Hongkong Teachers' Assoc. at tiffin to-day & was sorry not to be able to ask you to expand one or two points. I am venturing to send you a small thesis I have written on *"The Teaching of Science to the Chinese"* in the hope that some of the chapters may interest you. You will see that I have quoted your *"Development of Logical Method in Ancient China"* on several occasions & indeed I should like to take this opportunity of acknowledging how much I owe to your book. Not having sufficient knowledge of Chinese to be able to go to original sources I was forced to rely on translations & the writings of noted sinologues & I certainly found your book of inestimable value.

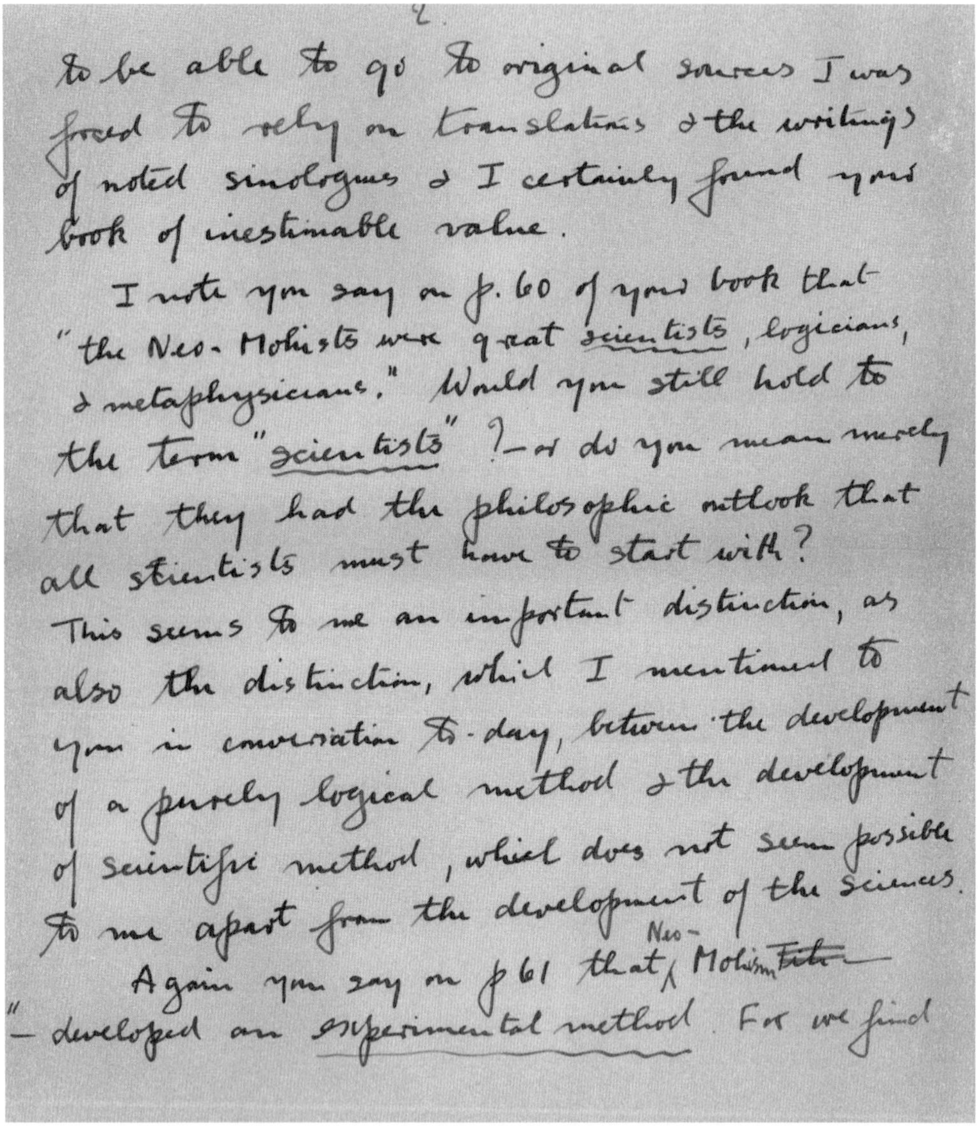

I note you say on p. 60 of your book that "the Neo-Mohists were great scientists, logicians, & metaphysicians." Would you still hold to the term "scientists"? — or do you mean merely that they had the philosophic outlook that all scientists must have to start with? This seems to me an important distinction, as also the distinction, which I mentioned to you in conversation to-day, between the development of a purely logical method & the development of scientific method, which does not seem possible to me apart from the development of the sciences.

Again you say on p 61 that Neo-Mohism "developed an experimental method. For we find

圖 2

to be able to go to original sources I was forced to rely on translations & the writings of noted sinologues & I certainly found your book of inestimable value.

I note you say on p. 60 of your book that "the Neo-Mohists were great scientists, logicians, & metaphysicians." Would you still hold to the term "scientists"? or do you mean merely that they had the philosophic outlook that all scientists must have to start with? This seems to me an important distinction, as also the distinction, which I mentioned to you in conversation to-day, between the development of a purely logical method & the development of scientific method, which does not seem possible to me apart from the development of the sciences.

Again you say on p. 61 that Neo-Mohism "–developed an experimental method. For we find

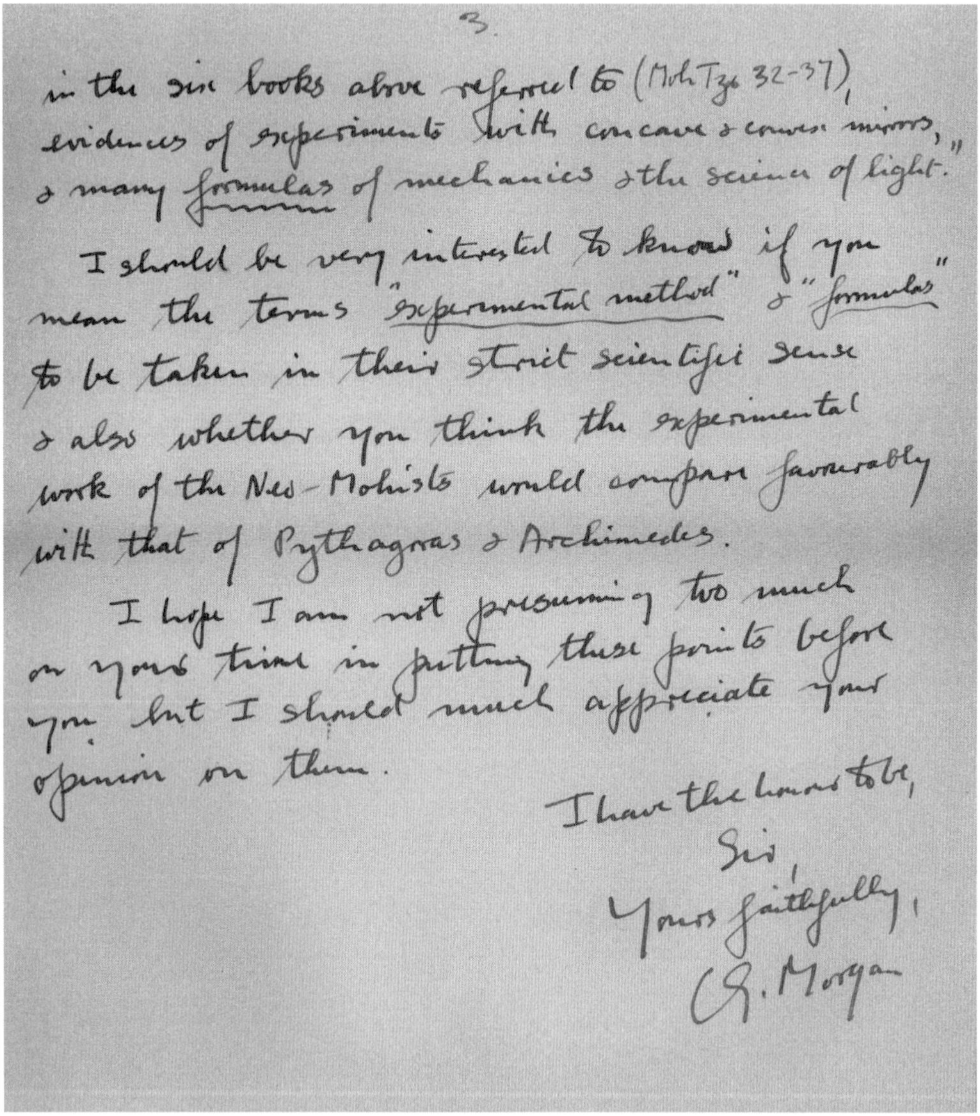

3.

in the six books above referred to (Moh Tze 32-37), evidences of experiments with concave & convex mirrors, & many formulas of mechanics & the science of light."

I should be very interested to know if you mean the terms "experimental method" & "formulas" to be taken in their strict scientific sense & also whether you think the experimental work of the Neo-Mohists would compare favourably with that of Pythagoras & Archimedes.

I hope I am not presuming too much on your time in putting these points before you, but I should much appreciate your opinion on them.

I have the honor to be, Sir, Yours faithfully, R. Morgan

圖 3

in the six books above referred to (Moh Tzi 32—37), evidences of experiments with concave & convex mirrors, & many formulas of mechanics & the science of light."

I should be very interested to know if you mean the terms "experimental method" & "formulas" to be taken in their strict scientific sense & also whether you think the experimental work of the Neo-Mohists would compare favourably with that of Pythagoras & Archimedes.

I hope I am not presuming too much on your time in putting these points before you but I should much appreciate your opinion on them.

I have the honor to be,

sir

Yours faithfully,

L. G. Morgan

L. P. Cookingham 致胡適（一九四二年五月十一日）

此信件發現於 *City Manager Government in the United States* 一書中，包括五月十一日 L. P. Cookingham 致胡適的書信，以及五月十八日胡適私人秘書的回信。

L. P. Cookingham，即 Laurie Perry Cookingham（1896—1992），生於美國芝加哥市，參加過第一次世界大戰，畢業於底特律理工學院。1926 年任密歇根州克勞森市（Clawson）市政執行官，1931 年任該州普利茅斯市市政執行官。1940 年任密蘇里州堪薩斯市市政執行官，前後達 19 年。此後又任堪薩斯州沃斯堡市（Fort Worth）市政執行官四年，之後退休。胡適 1942 年 4 月 26 日曾應邀在 The Municipal Air Terminal 發表演講，並與 Cookingham 合影。

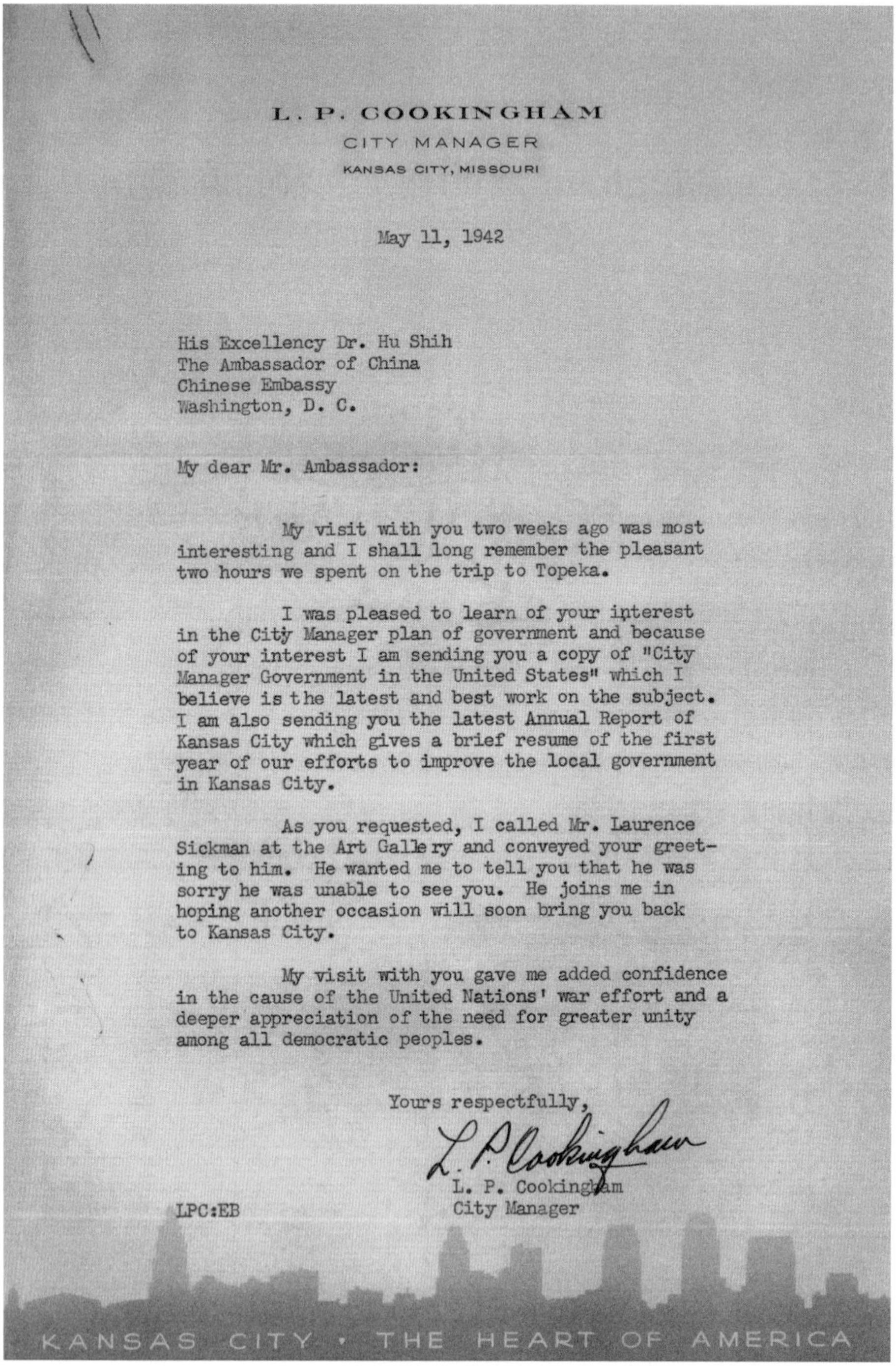

L. P. COOKINGHAM
CITY MANAGER
KANSAS CITY, MISSOURI

May 11, 1942

His Excellency Dr. Hu Shih
The Ambassador of China
Chinese Embassy
Washington, D. C.

My dear Mr. Ambassador:

  My visit with you two weeks ago was most interesting and I shall long remember the pleasant two hours we spent on the trip to Topeka.

  I was pleased to learn of your interest in the City Manager plan of government and because of your interest I am sending you a copy of "City Manager Government in the United States" which I believe is the latest and best work on the subject. I am also sending you the latest Annual Report of Kansas City which gives a brief resume of the first year of our efforts to improve the local government in Kansas City.

  As you requested, I called Mr. Laurence Sickman at the Art Gallery and conveyed your greeting to him. He wanted me to tell you that he was sorry he was unable to see you. He joins me in hoping another occasion will soon bring you back to Kansas City.

  My visit with you gave me added confidence in the cause of the United Nations' war effort and a deeper appreciation of the need for greater unity among all democratic peoples.

Yours respectfully,

L. P. Cookingham
City Manager

LPC:EB

KANSAS CITY · THE HEART OF AMERICA

圖 1

May 18, 1942

Mr. L. P. Cookingham
City Manager
Kansas City, Missouri

Dear Sir:

  In the absence of the Ambassador I am taking the liberty of acknowledging the receipt of your kind letter of May 11th and a copy each of the ANNUAL REPORT – KANSAS CITY, MISSOURI, 1940-1941 and CITY MANAGER GOVERNMENT IN THE UNITED STATES. Your letter and the two publications will be brought to the attention of the Ambassador as soon as possible after his return to Washington.

         Very truly yours,

         Private Secretary

圖2

Lawrence Morris 致胡適（一九四一年八月十三日）

此信件發現於 *Man and Society* 一書中。

Lawrence Morris（1903—1967），美國外交官 Dave Hennen Morris 之子，曾在羅斯福總統政府工作，胡適任駐美大使期間與其有交往。

49 WALL STREET

August 13, 1941.

Dear Doctor Hu:

    As I promised, I am sending you a copy of Mannheim's book about which we spoke the other day. I will be interested to hear your reactions to it when next we meet.

    It was good to see you again.

    Very sincerely,

Lawrence Morris

His Excellency, Dr. Hu Shih,
The Chinese Ambassador at Washington,
Chinese Embassy,
3225 Woodley Road, N. W.,
Washington, D. C.

圖1

Leon Augustus Hausman 致胡適
（一九四六年三月二十六日）

此信件發現於 The Illustrated Encyclopedia of American Birds 一書中。

Leon Augustus Hausman（1888—1966）生於美國紐黑文市，1914 年獲康奈爾大學文學學士學位，胡適留學康奈爾時的校友，1919 年獲該校哲學博士學位。1922—1925 年任羅格斯大學動物學講師。1925—1955 年任羅格斯大學新澤西女子學院動物學教授。其中 1941—1942 年曾任康奈爾大學生物學講師。北京檔藏有 Hausman 致胡適書信兩封，時間分別爲 1942 年 3 月 9 日和 9 月 28 日，第二封信爲胡適卸任駐美大使表示遺憾。

Leon Augustus Hausman, M.A., Ph.D.
Professor of Zoology, New Jersey College for Women
Consulting Ornithologist, New Jersey State Experiment Station, and *Lecturer in Ornithology*, New Jersey State Agricultural College.
(Rutgers University)

Department of Zoology
New Jersey College for Women
New Brunswick, N. J.

March 26, 1946

Dear Hu Shih,

    This book is offered as a slight token of my friendship and high esteem,- and in memory of days at Cornell, where, in the old COSMOPOLITAN CLUB, we boys marvelled at your abilities of thought and powers of expression! ALL of your very many friends are glad and happy that you are now increasingly to exert so strong an influence in the continued development of Eastern education. We, with you, will do all we can further to unite into a common body of sympathy and love, the Brothers of the East and West!

                    Sincerely your friend,

                        Leon

圖 1

M. B. Schnapper 致胡適

　　此信件發現於 *British Policy in Palestine* 一書中。此書似出版於 1942 年，作者 Paul L. Hanna。則此信或寫於 1942 年之後。

　　M. B. Schnapper，曾任美國公共關係學會執行秘書，餘不詳。

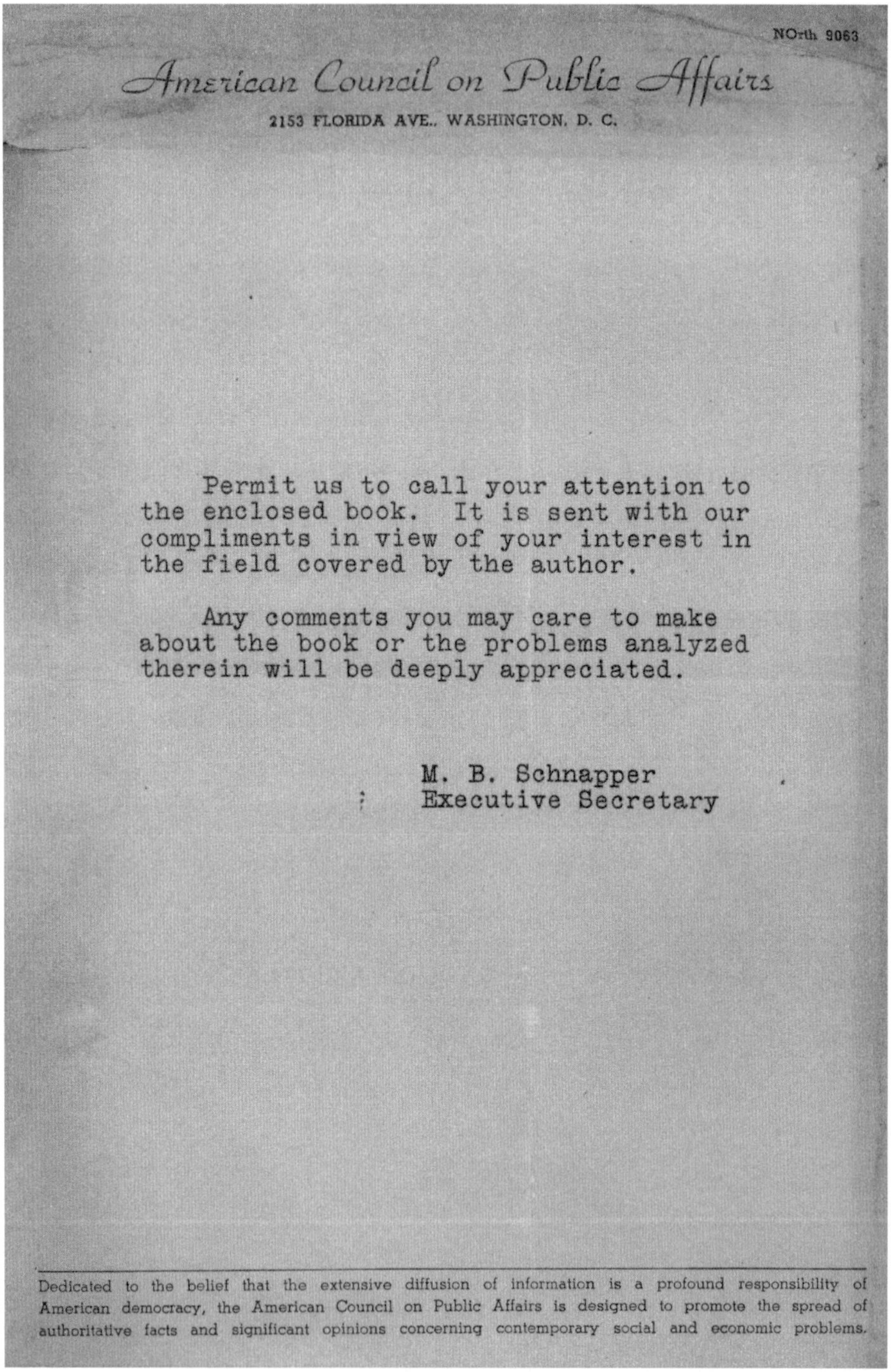

American Council on Public Affairs
2153 FLORIDA AVE., WASHINGTON, D. C.

NOrth 9063

    Permit us to call your attention to the enclosed book. It is sent with our compliments in view of your interest in the field covered by the author.

    Any comments you may care to make about the book or the problems analyzed therein will be deeply appreciated.

                                        M. B. Schnapper
                                        Executive Secretary

Dedicated to the belief that the extensive diffusion of information is a profound responsibility of American democracy, the American Council on Public Affairs is designed to promote the spread of authoritative facts and significant opinions concerning contemporary social and economic problems.

圖 1

Manley O. Hudson 致胡適（一九四三年十二月一日）

此信件發現於 *International Law of the Future* 一書中。

Manley O. Hudson，即 Manley Ottmer Hudson（1886—1960），生於美國密蘇里州，先後於 1906 和 1907 年在密蘇里州威廉朱厄爾學院（William Jewell College）獲得學士和碩士學位，1917 年獲哈佛大學哲學博士學位。1919 年任哈佛大學教授。曾擔任國聯、美國政府顧問或法律機構成員。曾兩次獲得諾貝爾和平獎提名。曾任 The Federation of International Polity Clubs 主席。

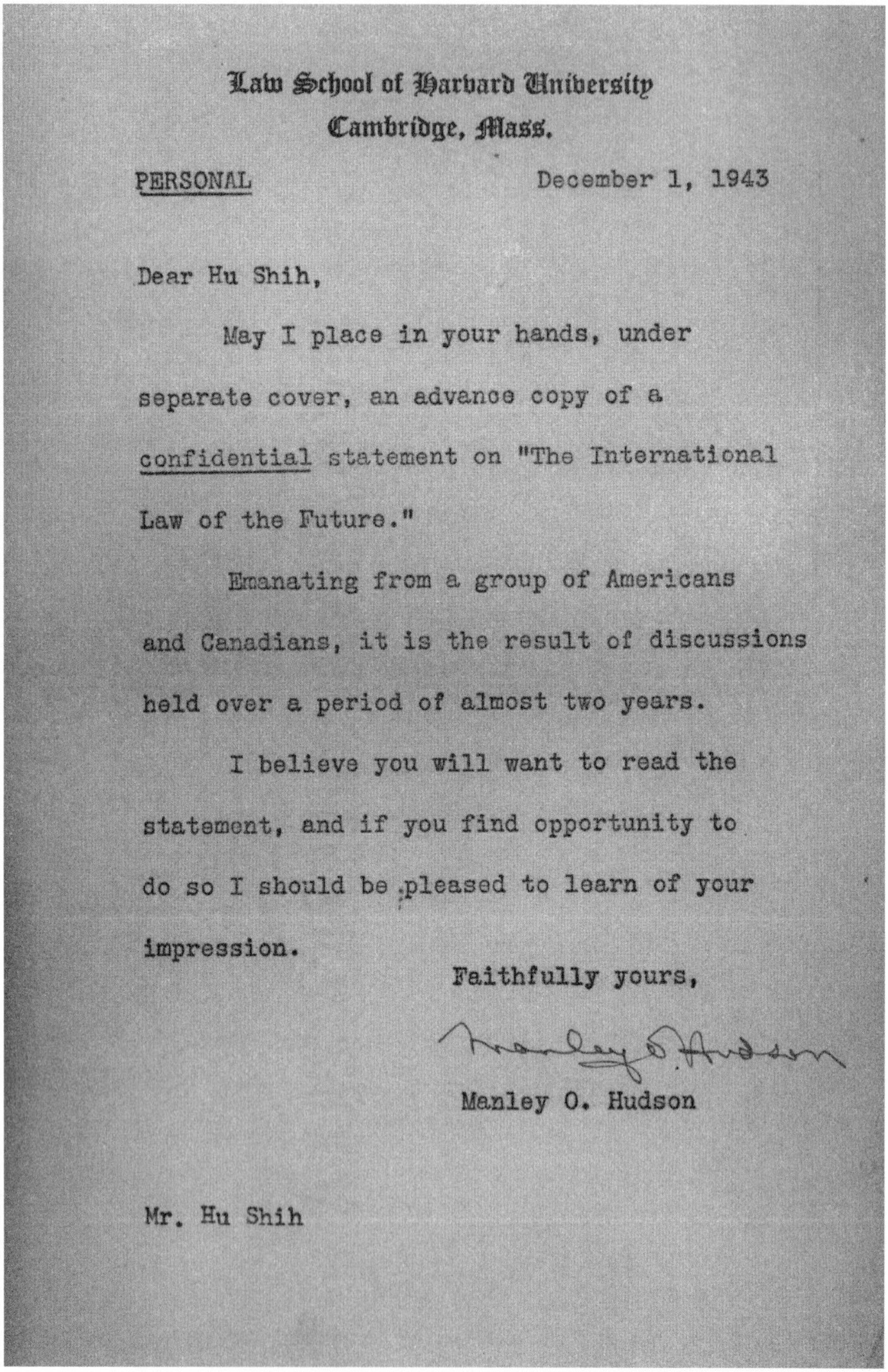

Law School of Harvard University
Cambridge, Mass.

PERSONAL   December 1, 1943

Dear Hu Shih,

   May I place in your hands, under separate cover, an advance copy of a confidential statement on "The International Law of the Future."

   Emanating from a group of Americans and Canadians, it is the result of discussions held over a period of almost two years.

   I believe you will want to read the statement, and if you find opportunity to do so I should be pleased to learn of your impression.

                       Faithfully yours,

                       Manley O. Hudson

Mr. Hu Shih

圖 1

Manuel L. Quezon 致胡適（一九二七年八月十日）

此信件發現於 *Joint Legistive Committee Report on Education* 一書中。

Manuel L. Quezon（1878—1944），曼努埃爾·路易·奎松，美治時期菲律賓著名領袖，被譽爲"菲律賓國父"。生於菲律賓呂宋島的巴勒，1893年聖胡安文學院畢業。1899年參加阿奎納多領導的反美獨立鬥爭。1903年畢業於聖托馬斯大學，同年獲律師資格。1905年開始參加政治活動，曾任檢察官和塔亞巴斯省省長、菲律賓派往美國國會的常駐專員和菲律賓參議院議長。1934年美國承認菲律賓"自治"，次年當選總統，1941年連任。日本侵占菲律賓時期，曾在澳大利亞和美國先後組織流亡政府。1944年8月1日在紐約病逝。北京檔藏有奎松1943年11月29日致胡適書信一封。

P. S. FORM No. 42.

PHILIPPINE SENATE
MANILA

OFFICE OF THE PRESIDENT

August 10, 1927

My dear Dr. Shih:

  I take great pleasure in presenting to you Mr. Camilo Osias who is the Official Representative of the Government of the Philippine Islands and the Head of the Philippine Delegation to the Eighth Far Eastern Championship Games to be held in China. Mr. Osias is one of the leading men of the Philippines. He is actively connected with all national movements of moment. He is an educator having served the Government Bureau of Education for several years and is now the President of the National University. He has been actively interested in athletics like myself for many years. At present he is the First Vice-President of the Philippine Amateur Athletic Federation and has been chosen to head the Philippine Delegation to Shanghai before this and also to Osaka, Japan. He is also a member of the Philippine Senate representing the Second Senatorial District and in the Philippine Legislature, he is not only Chairman of the Committee on Public Instruction and the Committee on Civil Service but a member of the most important committees. I believe you will enjoy meeting him and I know he will enjoy knowing you.

          Yours sincerely,

          MANUEL L. QUEZON

Dr. Hu Shih
49 A Jessfield Road
Shanghai, China

圖 1

Mary Mackay 致胡適（一九三六年十月二十七日）

此信件發現於 *Can China Survive?* 一書中，此書出版於 1936 年。

Mary Mackay，時任職於美國 Ives Washburn 出版社，餘不詳。

IVES WASHBURN, INC.
PUBLISHER
411 EAST 57TH STREET
NEW YORK

TELEPHONE: PLAZA 3-6130

October 27th, 1936.

Dr. Hu Shih
S.S. President Hoover,
San Francisco, Calif.

My dear Sir:

We are sending you today, via air mail, a copy of CAN CHINA SURVIVE? by Hallett Abend and Anthony Billingham, who, as you know, are the New York Times Far East correspondents.

We trust that you will find this book interesting and that it will help to make your crossing pleasurable. Should you care to send us, on your arrival in China, any comment on this book which we might use, we shall be most appreciative.

We have found that, in the short space of time since this book was published, it has stimulated more interest and greater friendliness - in the average person - than almost any other book on the subject. It seems to us that in the promotion of friendly relations between our country and China, it is important to arouse the interest and enlist the sympathies of the average intelligent American -(not just the reader with specialized interest in the Far East)- and this book seems to be doing just that. We shall await with much interest, your personal opinion.

We extend our cordial good wishes for a smooth crossing.

Very sincerely,

Mary Mackay

Mary Mackay

圖 1

Mary P. E. Nitobé 致胡適（一九三五年三月二十六日）

此信件發現於 *Reminiscences of Childhood* 一書中。

Mary P. E. Nitobé，Marry Patterson Elkinton Nitobé（1857—1938），美國費城人，1891 年與日本新渡户稻造（Inazo Nitobé）結婚，同年一起到日本北海道札幌生活，並在當地建立學校，生活工作了六年。後協助新渡户稻造完成《武士道》一書，並於 1899 年出版。1905 年因此書與其夫受到明治天皇的接見。1920 年新渡户稻造被任命爲國際聯盟事務局副局長，隨夫到日内瓦居住六年。1933 年，新渡户稻造去世後，繼續整理其夫的著作和日記，出版了《童年回憶》。1938 年 9 月 23 日在日本去世。

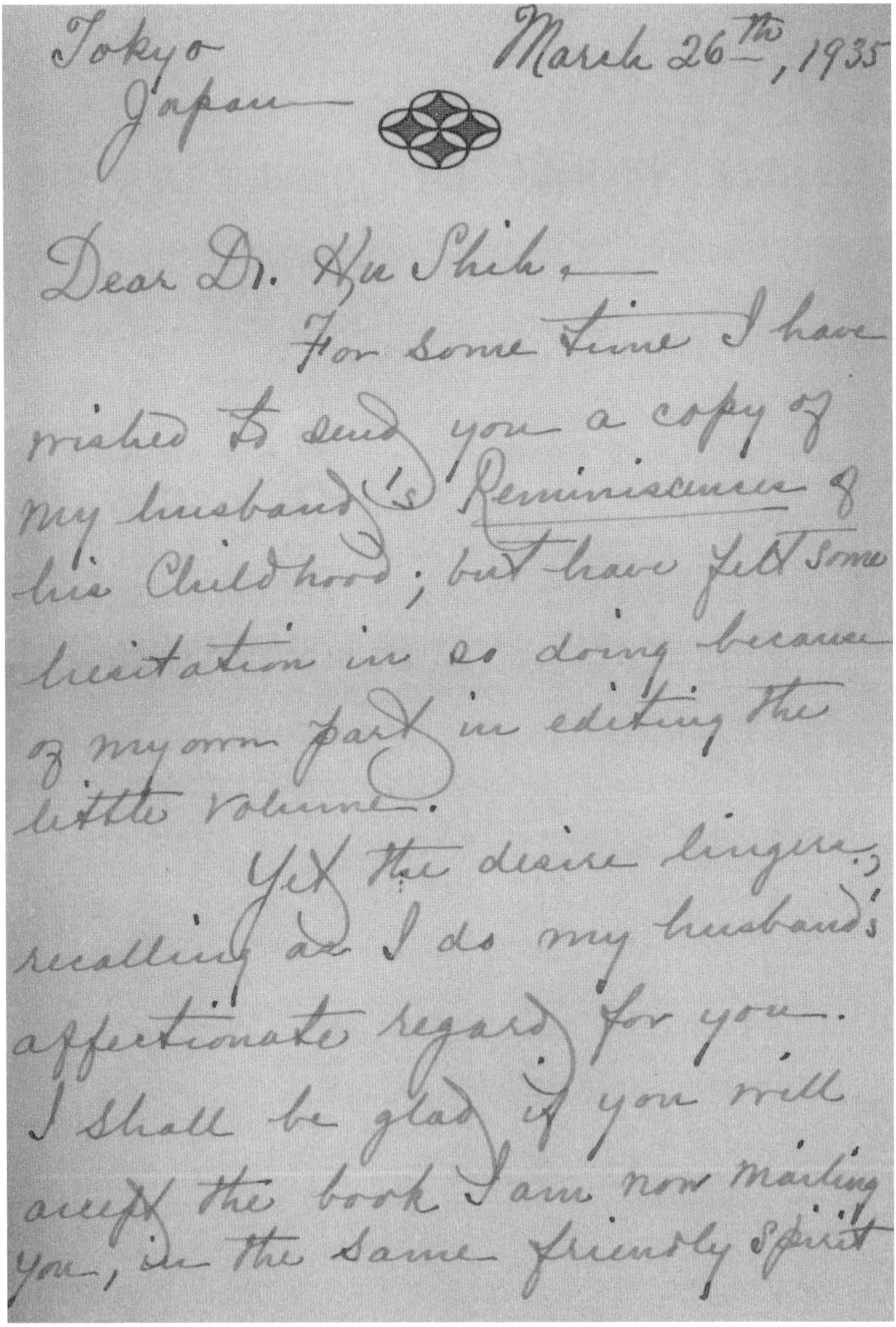

Tokyo, Japan
March 26th, 1935

Dear Dr. Hu Shih,

For some time I have wished to send you a copy of my husband's Reminiscences of his Childhood; but have felt some hesitation in so doing because of my own part in editing the little volume.

Yet the desire lingers, recalling as I do my husband's affectionate regard for you. I shall be glad if you will accept the book I am now mailing you, in the same friendly spirit

圖 1

Tokyo

Japan   March 26th, 1935

Dear Dr. Hu Shih,

For some time I have wished to send you a copy of my husband's Reminiscences of his Childhood; but have felt some hesitation in so doing because of my own part in editing the little volume.

Yet the desire lingers, recalling as I do my husband's affectionate regard for you. I shall be glad if you will accept the book I am now mailing you, in the same friendly spirit in which it is sent.

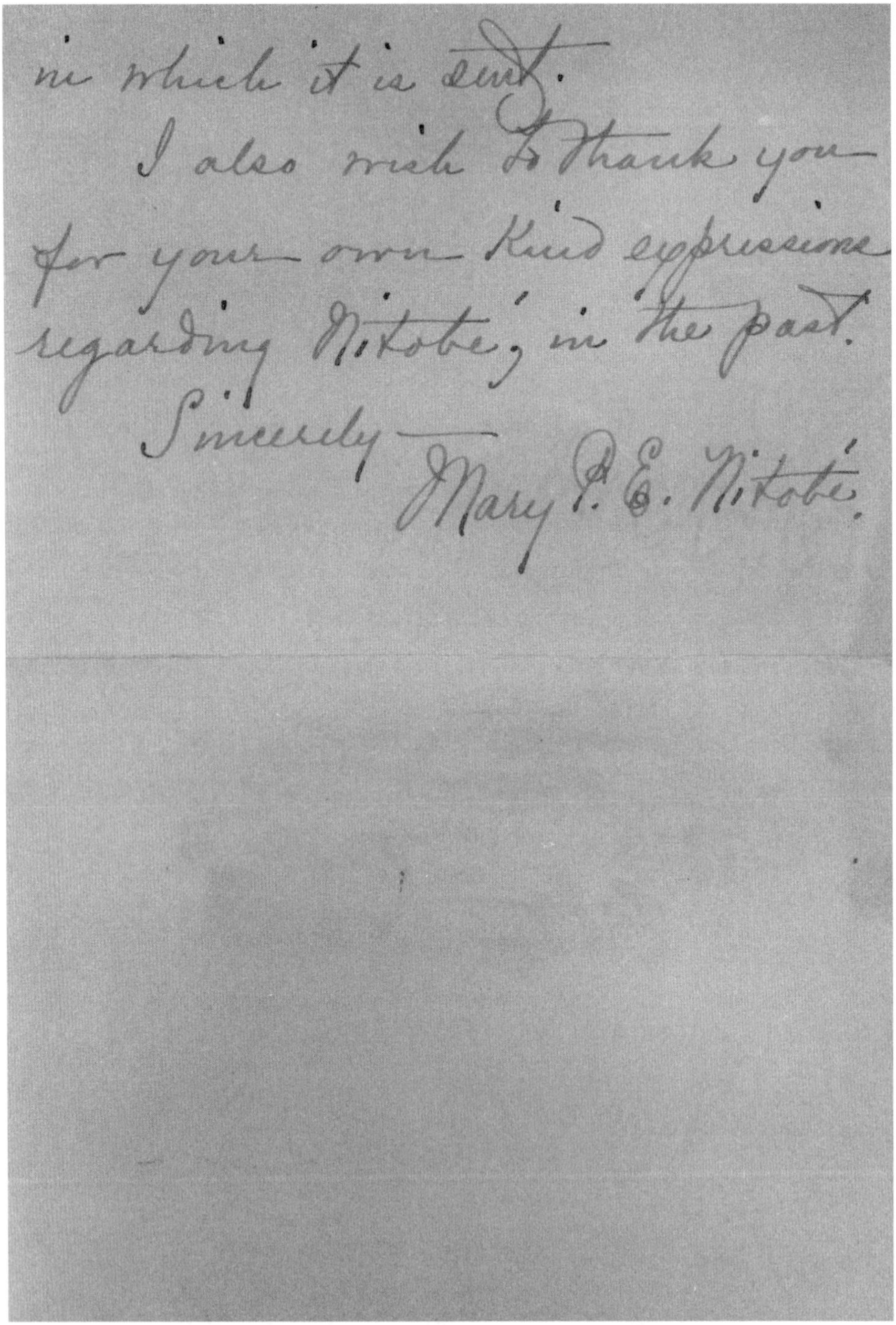

I also wish to thank you for your own kind expressions regarding Nitobe, in the past.

Sincerely—
Mary P. E. Nitobe.

圖 2

in which it is sent.

I also wish to thank you for your own kind expressions regarding Nitobé, in the past.

Sincerely
Mary P. E. Nitobé

Paul Eldridge 致胡適（一九三一年五月十七日）

此信發現於 *Cobwebs and Cosmos* 一書中。

Paul Eldridge（1888—1982），美國詩人、小說家。生於費城。1911 年獲賓州大學碩士學位，1913 年獲巴黎大學博士學位。主要在紐約的中學從事羅曼諸語言教學，直到 1945 年退休。1913 年、1923 年曾先後在巴黎索邦大學和意大利佛羅倫薩大學擔任美國文學講師。

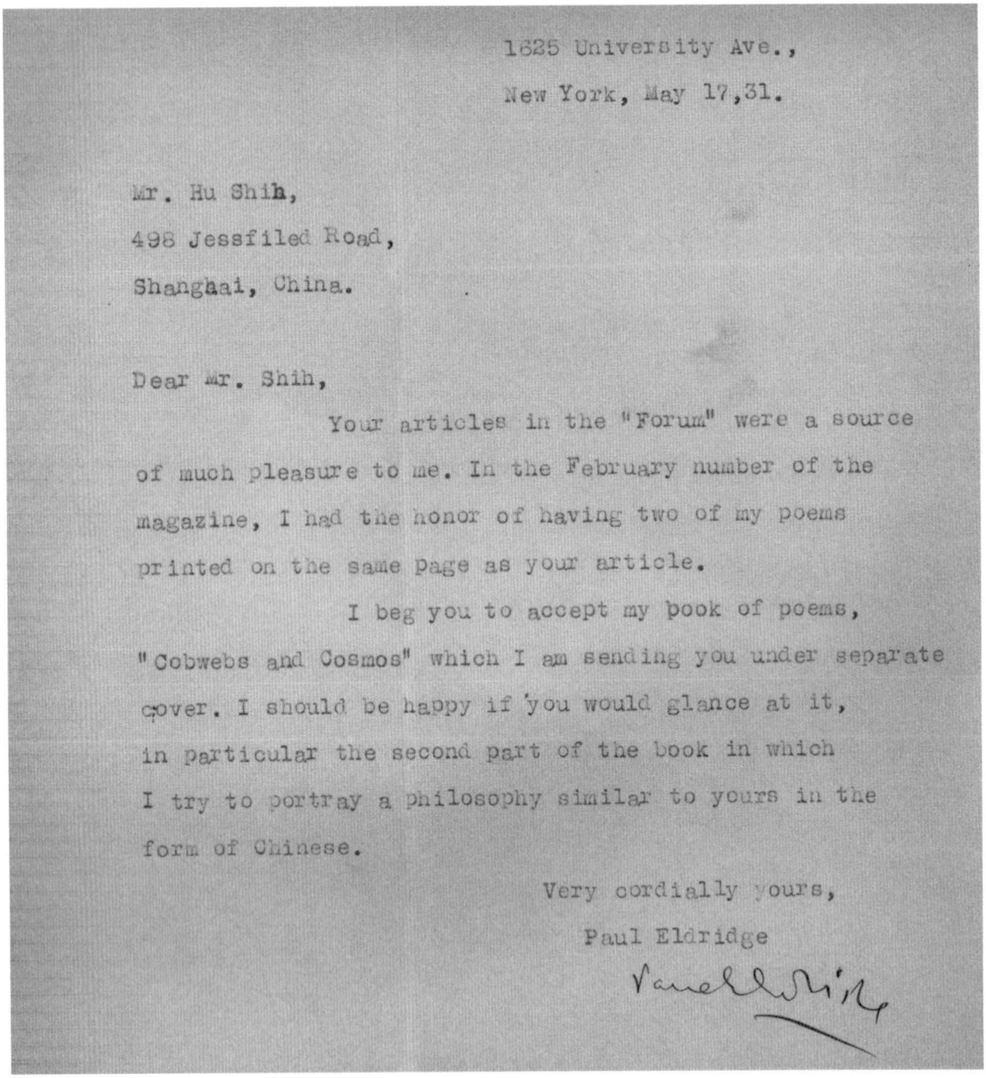

1625 University Ave.,
New York, May 17, 31.

Mr. Hu Shih,
498 Jessfiled Road,
Shanghai, China.

Dear Mr. Shih,

    Your articles in the "Forum" were a source of much pleasure to me. In the February number of the magazine, I had the honor of having two of my poems printed on the same page as your article.

    I beg you to accept my book of poems, "Cobwebs and Cosmos" which I am sending you under separate cover. I should be happy if you would glance at it, in particular the second part of the book in which I try to portray a philosophy similar to yours in the form of Chinese.

Very cordially yours,
Paul Eldridge

圖 1

Robert □致胡適

此信件發現於 *Handbook for the Sixth Conference of the Institute of Pacific Relations* 一書中。

信末作者簽名，只能辨認出名字爲"Robert"，姓氏難以識別。

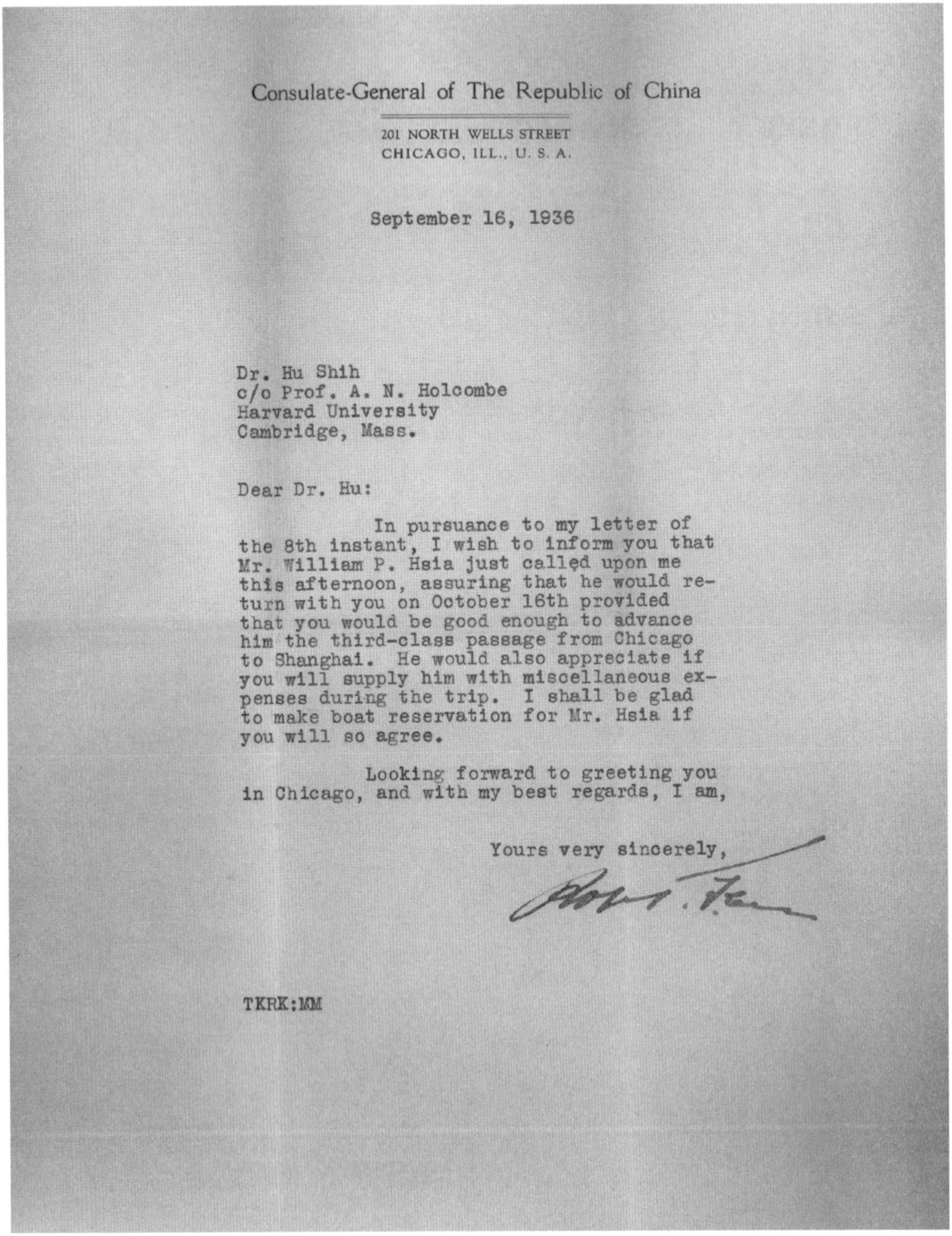

Consulate-General of The Republic of China

201 NORTH WELLS STREET
CHICAGO, ILL., U. S. A.

September 16, 1936

Dr. Hu Shih
c/o Prof. A. N. Holcombe
Harvard University
Cambridge, Mass.

Dear Dr. Hu:

  In pursuance to my letter of the 8th instant, I wish to inform you that Mr. William P. Hsia just called upon me this afternoon, assuring that he would return with you on October 16th provided that you would be good enough to advance him the third-class passage from Chicago to Shanghai. He would also appreciate if you will supply him with miscellaneous expenses during the trip. I shall be glad to make boat reservation for Mr. Hsia if you will so agree.

  Looking forward to greeting you in Chicago, and with my best regards, I am,

Yours very sincerely,

TKRK:MM

圖 1

Roger S. Greene 致胡適（一九三六年二月一日）

此信件發現於《農業經濟學》一書中。

Roger S. Greene，即 Roger Sherman Greene（1881—1947），顧臨。1901 年哈佛大學畢業，獲文學士學位，次年獲哈佛碩士學位。1902 年任職於美國駐外領事界，1907 年來華，任美國駐大連領事，後任駐哈爾濱領事。1911 年任美國駐漢口總領事，兼駐宜昌總領事。1914 年任洛克菲勒基金會駐華醫社代表，推動創辦醫學院和醫院，參與創辦北京協和醫學院。1922 年任北京協和醫學院董事會秘書。1928 年任北京協和醫學院代理校長，曾任中華教育文化基金董事會董事，1935 年辭職返美。抗戰期間曾任"美國不參加日本侵略委員會"主席，參與美國民間支援中國抗戰活動。

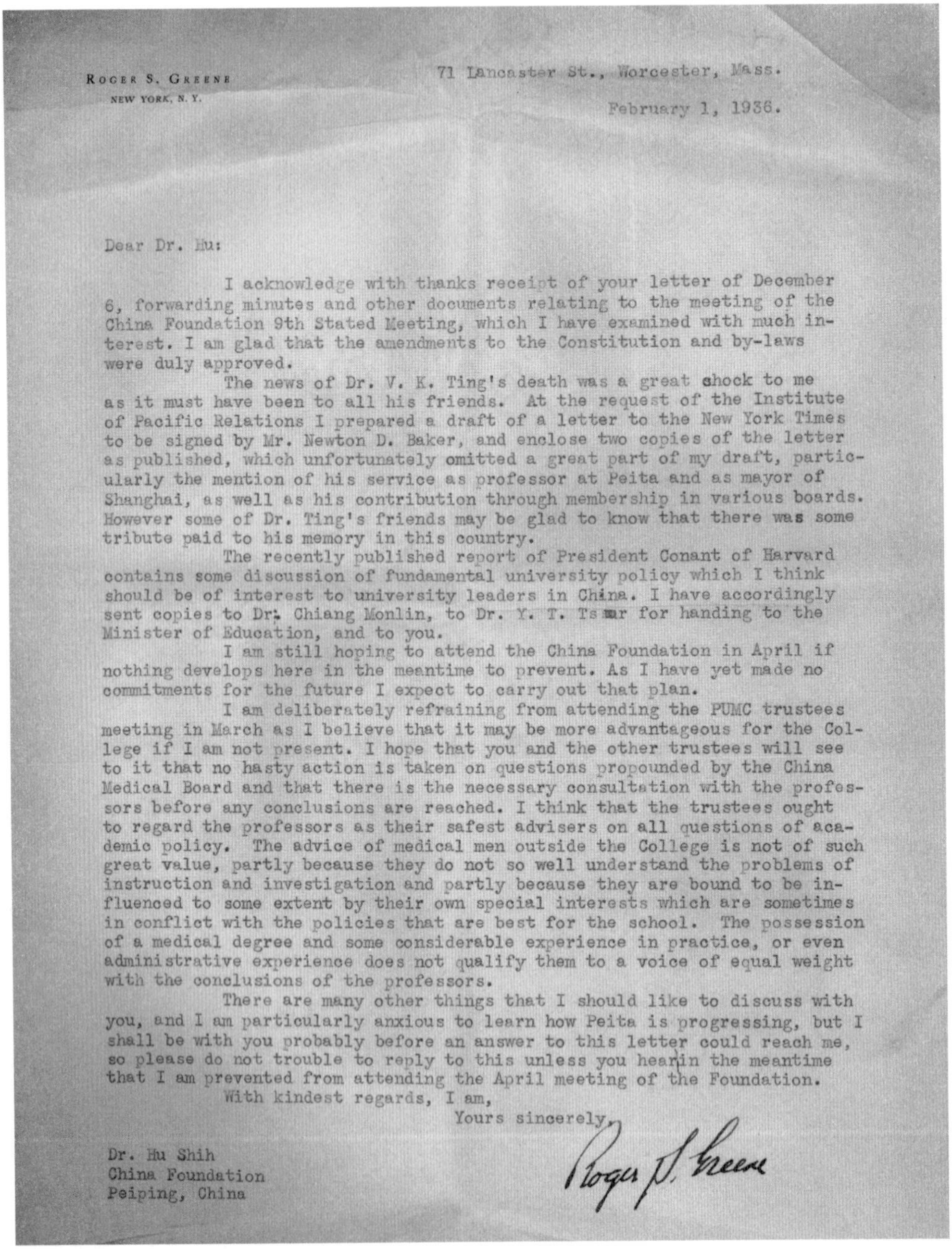

ROGER S. GREENE
NEW YORK, N.Y.

71 Lancaster St., Worcester, Mass.

February 1, 1936.

Dear Dr. Hu:

    I acknowledge with thanks receipt of your letter of December 6, forwarding minutes and other documents relating to the meeting of the China Foundation 9th Stated Meeting, which I have examined with much interest. I am glad that the amendments to the Constitution and by-laws were duly approved.

    The news of Dr. V. K. Ting's death was a great shock to me as it must have been to all his friends. At the request of the Institute of Pacific Relations I prepared a draft of a letter to the New York Times to be signed by Mr. Newton D. Baker, and enclose two copies of the letter as published, which unfortunately omitted a great part of my draft, particularly the mention of his service as professor at Peita and as mayor of Shanghai, as well as his contribution through membership in various boards. However some of Dr. Ting's friends may be glad to know that there was some tribute paid to his memory in this country.

    The recently published report of President Conant of Harvard contains some discussion of fundamental university policy which I think should be of interest to university leaders in China. I have accordingly sent copies to Dr. Chiang Monlin, to Dr. Y. T. Tsur for handing to the Minister of Education, and to you.

    I am still hoping to attend the China Foundation in April if nothing develops here in the meantime to prevent. As I have yet made no commitments for the future I expect to carry out that plan.

    I am deliberately refraining from attending the PUMC trustees meeting in March as I believe that it may be more advantageous for the College if I am not present. I hope that you and the other trustees will see to it that no hasty action is taken on questions propounded by the China Medical Board and that there is the necessary consultation with the professors before any conclusions are reached. I think that the trustees ought to regard the professors as their safest advisers on all questions of academic policy. The advice of medical men outside the College is not of such great value, partly because they do not so well understand the problems of instruction and investigation and partly because they are bound to be influenced to some extent by their own special interests which are sometimes in conflict with the policies that are best for the school. The possession of a medical degree and some considerable experience in practice, or even administrative experience does not qualify them to a voice of equal weight with the conclusions of the professors.

    There are many other things that I should like to discuss with you, and I am particularly anxious to learn how Peita is progressing, but I shall be with you probably before an answer to this letter could reach me, so please do not trouble to reply to this unless you hear in the meantime that I am prevented from attending the April meeting of the Foundation.

    With kindest regards, I am,

        Yours sincerely,

        Roger S. Greene

Dr. Hu Shih
China Foundation
Peiping, China

圖1

Victor K. Kwong 致胡適（一九三六年十月二十九日）

此信件發現於 *University of Iowa Studies* 一書中，另有電報一，日程表一，節目單一，電話記錄一。

Victor K. Kwong，即 K. L. Kwong，鄺光林（1898—？），字籍三。廣東臺山人，生於澳大利亞墨爾本。早年入哥倫比亞大學學習，一戰時赴英國任英軍青年會幹事兼中國勞工團秘書，戰後入哈佛大學，獲商學碩士學位。1922 年歸國，曾任商務印書館編輯兼上海總商會英文秘書，上海商科大學、光華大學、持志大學教授，國民政府外交部情報司駐滬主任，外交部情報處歐洲科科長等職。曾組織中國足球隊訪問澳大利亞。1930 年任外交部典職科科長，1931 年任駐馬尼拉總領事，1934 年任駐舊金山總領事。北京檔藏有鄺氏致胡適書信一封，時間爲 1944 年 5 月 23 日。

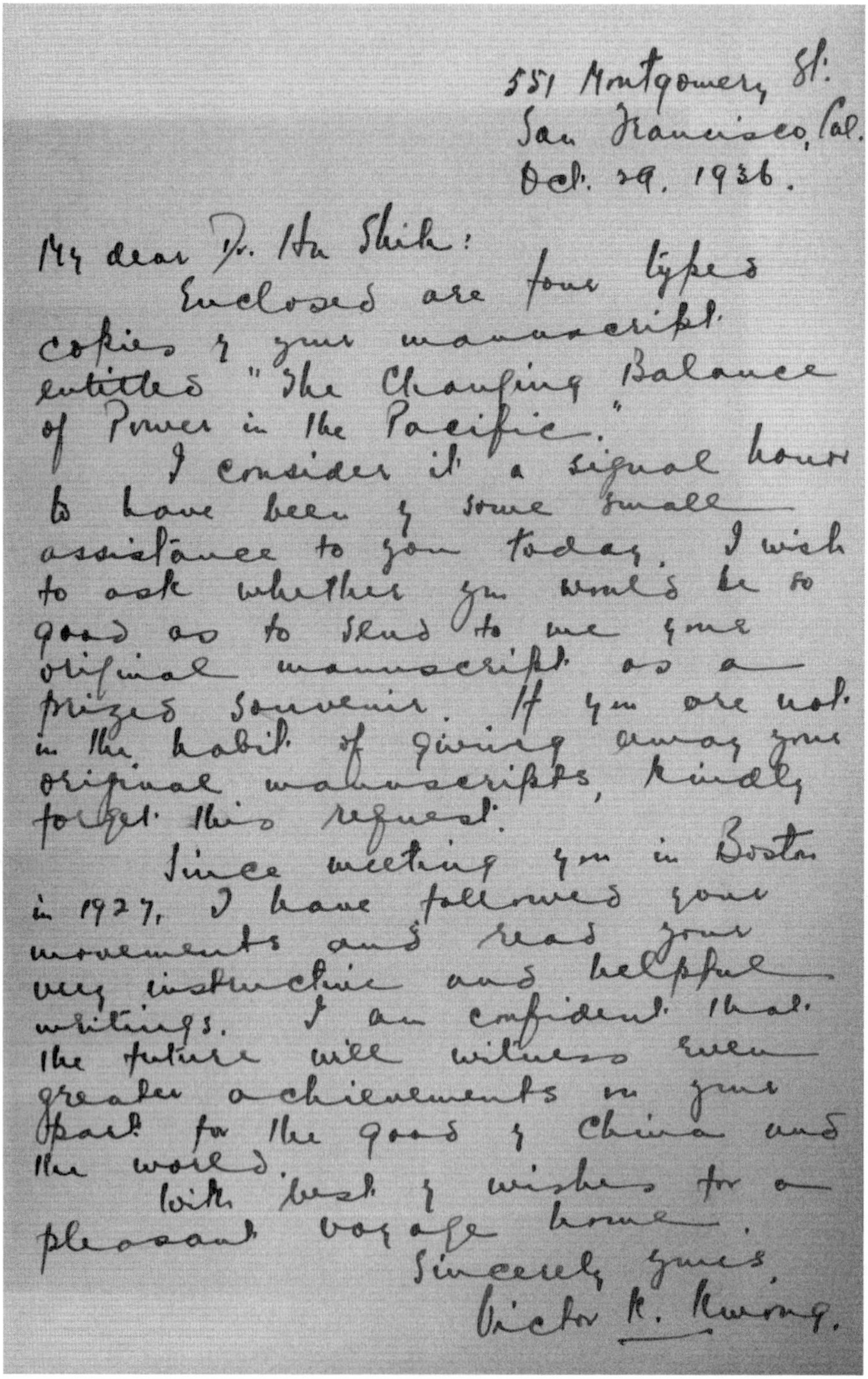

551 Montgomery St.
San Francisco, Cal.
Oct. 29, 1936.

My dear Dr. Hu Shih:

Enclosed are four typed copies of your manuscript entitled "The Changing Balance of Power in the Pacific."

I consider it a signal honor to have been of some small assistance to you today. I wish to ask whether you would be so good as to send to me your original manuscript as a prized souvenir. If you are not in the habit of giving away your original manuscripts, kindly forget this request.

Since meeting you in Boston in 1927, I have followed your movements and read your very instructive and helpful writings. I am confident that the future will witness even greater achievements on your part for the good of China and the world.

With best of wishes for a pleasant voyage home.

Sincerely yours,
Victor K. Kwong

圖 1

551 Montgomery St.
San Francisco, Cal.
Oct. 29, 1936

My dear Dr. Hu Shih:

Enclosed are four typed copies of your manuscript entitled *"The Changing Balance of Power in the Pacific."*

I consider it a signal honor to have been of some small assistance to you today. I wish to ask whether you would be so good as to send to me your original manuscript as a prized souvenir. If you are not in the habit of giving away your original manuscripts, kindly forget this request.

Since meeting you in Boston in 1927, I have followed your movements and read your very instructive and helpful writings. I am confident that the future will witness even greater achievements on your part for the good of China and the world.

With best of wishes for a pleasant voyage home.

Sincerely yours,
Victor K. Kwong

Vung Yuin Ting 致胡適（一九三六年九月十六日）

此信件發現於 *Handbook for the Sixth Conference of the Institute of Pacific Relations* 一書中。

Vung Yuin Ting，時爲美國密歇根大學中國留學生，中文名待考。

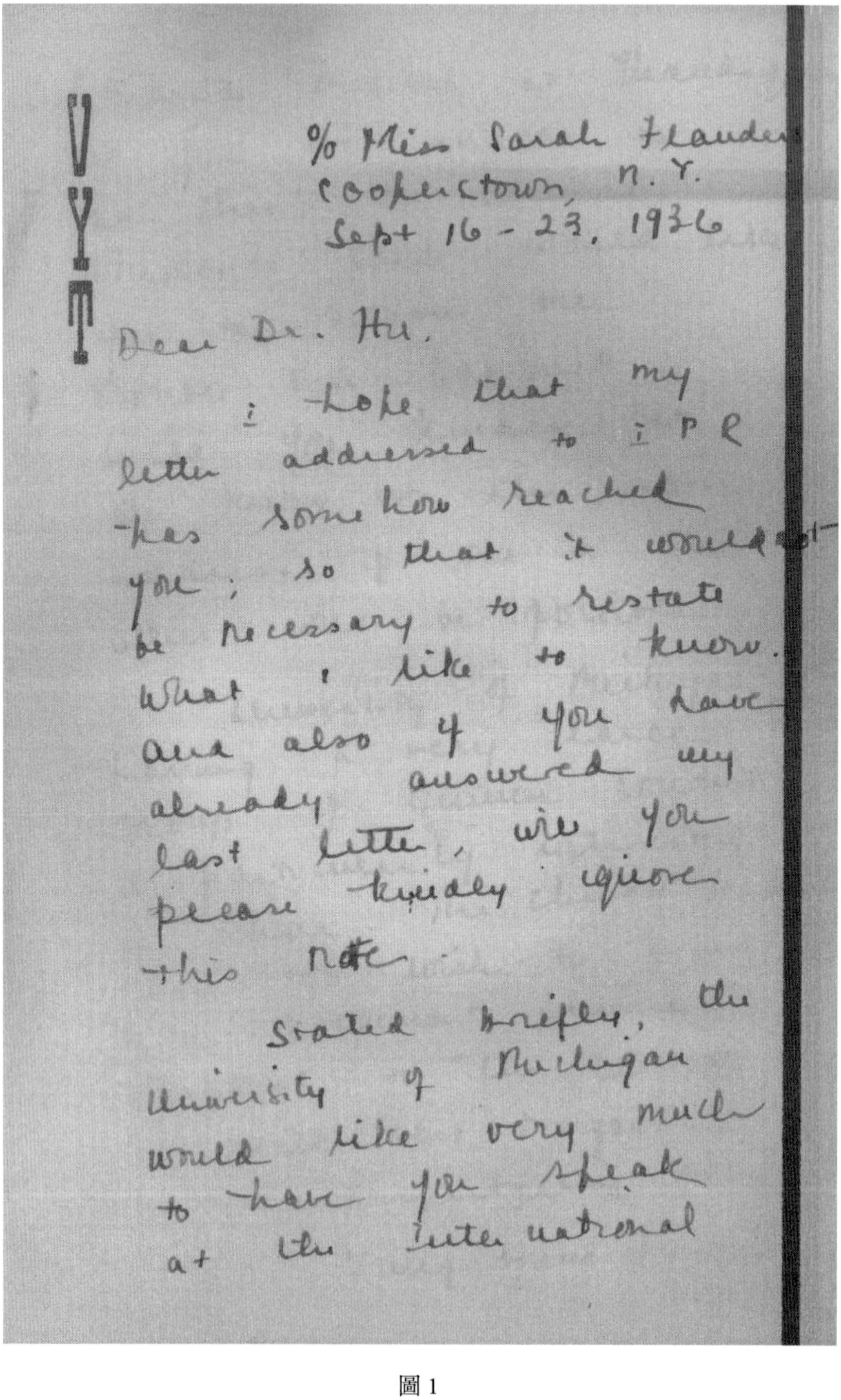

％ Miss Sarah Flanders
Cooperstown, N.Y.
Sept 16-23, 1936

Dear Dr. Hu,

i hope that my letter addressed to IPR has somehow reached you; so that it would not be necessary to restate what i like to know. and also if you have already answered my last letter, will you please kindly ignore this note.

Stated briefly, the University of Michigan would like very much to have you speak at the international

圖 1

O/O Miss Sarah Flanders
Cooperstown, N. Y.
Sept. 16-23, 1936

Dear Dr. Hu,

I hope that my letter addressed to IPR has somehow reached you; so that it would not be necessary to restate what I like to know and also if you have already answered my last letter, will you please kindly ignore this note.

Stated briefly, the University of Michigan would like very much to have you speak at the International

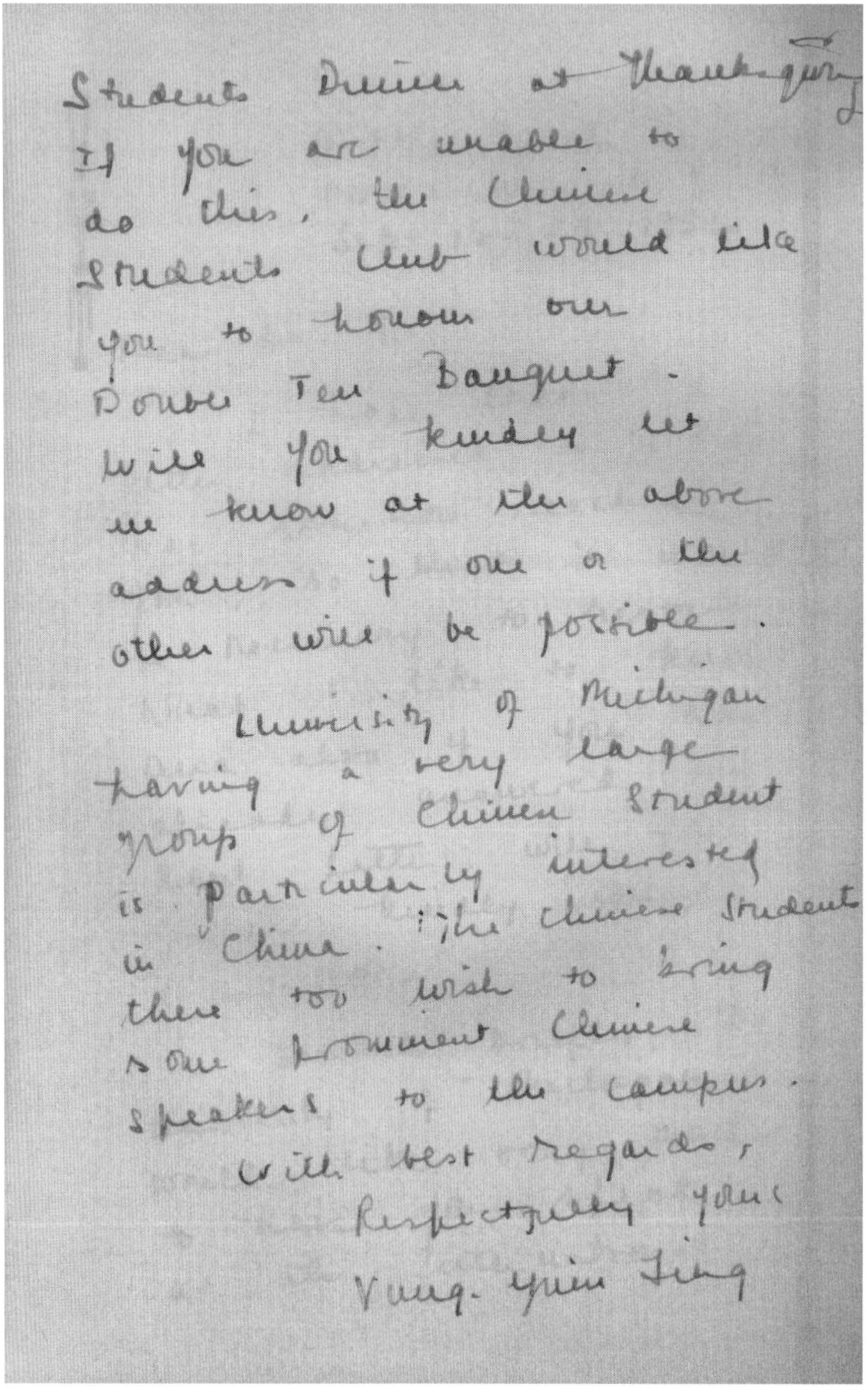

Students Dinner at Thanksgiving. If you are unable to do this, the Chinese Students Club would like you to honour our Double Ten Banquet. Will you kindly let me know at the above address if one or the other will be possible.

University of Michigan having a very large group of Chinese students is particularly interested in China. The Chinese Students there too wish to bring some prominent Chinese speakers to the campus.

With best regards,
Respectfully yours
Vung-Yuin Ting

圖 2

Students Dinner at Thanksgiving. If you are unable to do this, the Chinese Students Club would like you to honour our Double Ten Banquet. Will you kindly let me know at the above address if one or the other will be possible.

University of Michigan having a very large group of Chinese student is particularly interested in China. The Chinese students there too wish to bring some prominent Chinese speakers to the campus.

With best regards,
Respectfully yours,
Vung Yuin Ting

圖 3

Walter Bosshard 致胡適（一九四七年十月二十七日）

此信件發現於 *Werden und Wirken der BuchergildGutenberg* 一書中。

Walter Bosshard（1892—1975），博斯哈，瑞士攝影師、新聞記者。1920 年代開始發表關於中國和東南亞的照片。1928 年來華任新聞攝影師。1929 年隨斯文赫定率領的西北科學考查團赴新疆。1930 年曾出版甘地影集。1930 年後任瑞士《蘇黎世報》駐華通訊員。1942—1945 年任駐華盛頓記者。1946—1949 年任駐華盛頓記者。新中國成立後，曾來華訪問。

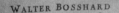

圖 1

William Fogg Osgood，Mrs. 致胡適

此名片發現於 Handbook for the Sixth Conference of the Institute of Pacific Relations 一書中。信中未標注時間。

Mrs. William Fogg Osgood，美國數學家 William Fogg Osgood 的夫人，其夫曾於 1918—1922 年任哈佛大學數學系主任。

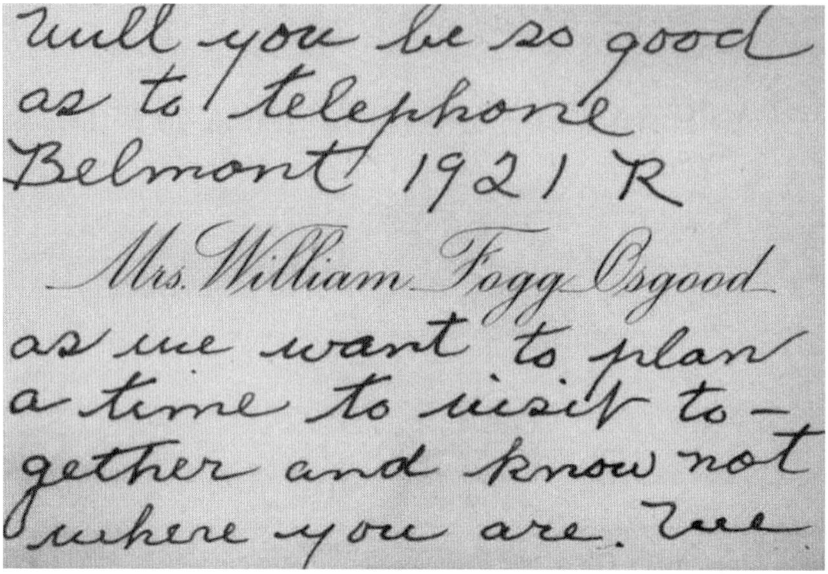

> Will you be so good as to telephone Belmont 1921 R
> Mrs. William Fogg Osgood
> as we want to plan a time to visit together and know not where you are. We

圖1

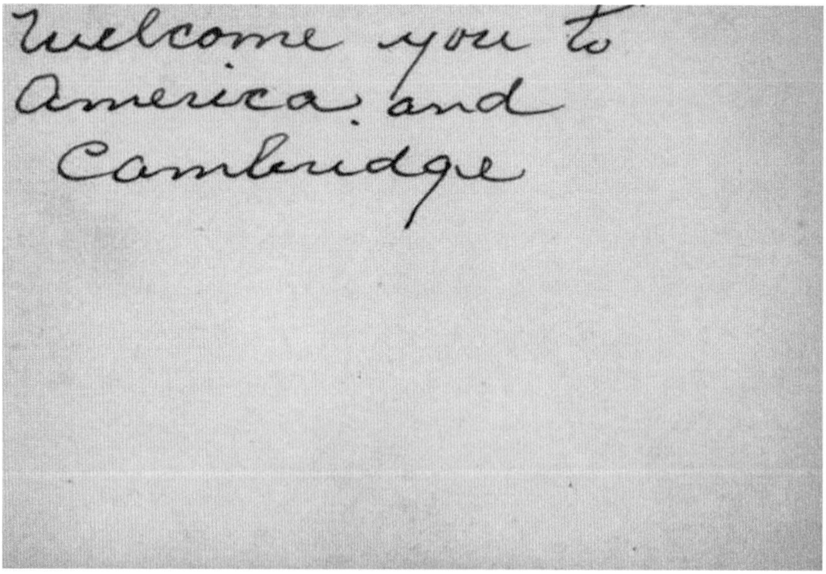

> welcome you to America, and Cambridge

圖2

Will you be so good as to telephone Belmont 1921 R as we want to plan a time to visit together and know not where you are. We welcome you to America and Cambridge.

Yung Kwai 致胡適（一九四二年九月五日）

此信件發現於 *Autobiography of Andrew Dickson White* 一書中。

Yung Kwai，即容揆（1860—1943），字贊虞。廣東新寧人，容閎之侄。1872年赴美留學。1884年畢業於美國耶魯大學，後入哥倫比亞大學礦業學院學習。1897年任職於中國駐美使館。1908年曾短暫回國，同年重回駐美使館工作。歷任駐美使館翻譯官，駐美國、墨西哥、丹麥使館書記官，留美學生監督。民國成立後，任駐美使館參事，一等秘書，代理駐美公使。

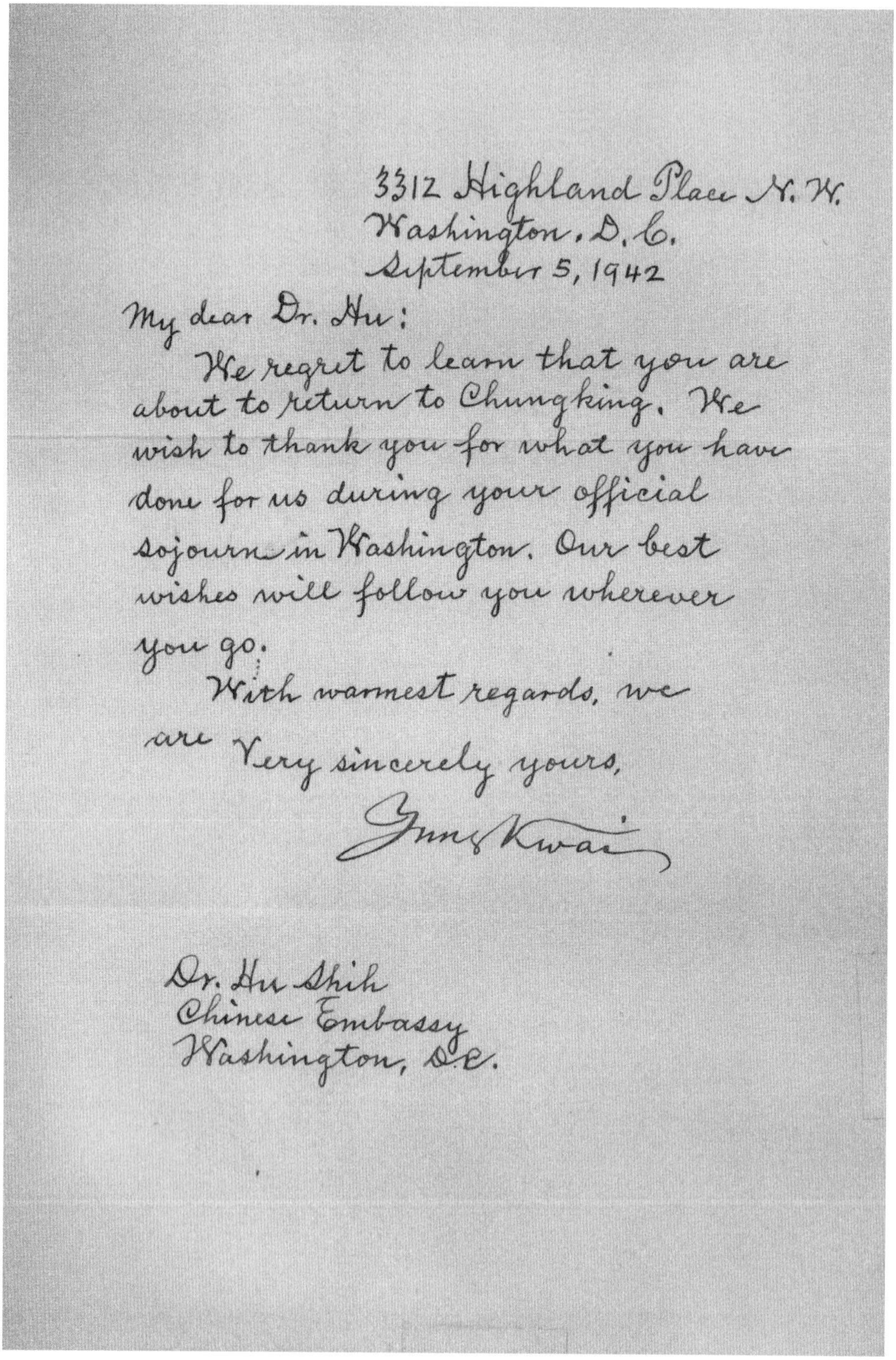

3312 Highland Place N. W.
Washington, D. C.
September 5, 1942

My dear Dr. Hu:

We regret to learn that you are about to return to Chungking. We wish to thank you for what you have done for us during your official sojourn in Washington. Our best wishes will follow you wherever you go.

With warmest regards, we are

Very sincerely yours,

Jung Kwai

Dr. Hu Shih
Chinese Embassy
Washington, D.C.

圖 1

3312 Highland Place N. W.

Washington, D. C.

September 5, 1942

My dear Dr. Hu:

    We regret to learn that you are about to return to Chungking. We wish to thank you for what you have done for us during your official sojourn in Washington. Our best wishes will follow you wherever you go.

    With warmest regards, we are

    Very sincerely yours,

Yung Kwai

Dr. Hu Shih
China Embassy
Washington, D. C.

附：AGENDA FOR ROUND TABLES ON CHINA

此二頁文件發現於 *Handbook for the Sixth Conference of the Institute of Pacific Relations* 一書中。

Secretariat 1936
Document 9

AGENDA FOR ROUND TABLES ON CHINA

Some of the questions found in the printed agenda for round table topic IV are re-grouped below in accordance with suggestions made by the China round table officers. The latter believe that such re-grouping will facilitate the discussions of these subjects.

I. Chinese Reconstruction: Aims and Achievements.

    a. What are the main features in the reconstruction program of the National Government today? What important changes in the original program have been made since 1933? (Consider here: road and railway construction; rural rehabilitation; control of opium production and trade; reforms in land tenure and taxation; flood protection works.)

    b. What concrete benefits can be attributed since 1931 to the reconstruction measures of the National Government? How has the economic life of rural China been affected thus far by the development of roads?

    c. In fostering the development of rural cooperatives, what changes in Chinese agricultural organization does the Government aim to bring about? Will the development of cooperatives provide a means for city banks to extend their influence over rural districts and to supplant the village money-lender?

    d. To what extent is China's economic reconstruction dependent on the assistance of the large city banks? How far have these banks already been persuaded or compelled to absorb the Government's deficit bonds? How far can large-scale measures of reconstruction be carried out without foreign capital?

    e. What are the principal obstacles now hindering the progress of the Government's reconstruction plans? To what extent will a successful fulfillment of these plans consolidate the political and military position of the Government?

II. The Communist Movement in China.

    a. What program of economic development and reconstruction is offered by the Chinese Communist Movement? In what respect does such a program run counter to the work of the present administration.

    b. What are the immediate and ultimate aims of the Government in its schemes of rural rehabilitation for the former Communist regions of Kiangsi and Fukien? How far has it been possible to carry out the announced plans of radical reforms in land tenure, taxation and usury?

圖 1

2.

III. International Implications of Chinese Reconstruction.

    a. What are the larger international implications of Chinese economic and social reconstruction, (a) as regards Far Eastern diplomatic relations, (b) as regards foreign trade and investment in China?

    b. What are the specific objections of the Japanese Government to foreign help in schemes for Chinese reconstruction? Does this attitude of the Japanese Government preclude all possibility of assistance to China from other nations? Along what lines would the Japanese Government finance, or participate directly in, projects for the economic development of China? Would such action on the part of Japan require the threat or the use of force, or could it be carried out as a result of diplomatic agreement with the Chinese Government?

    c. What are the possibilities of the National Government cooperating with the Left groups in the near future for the purpose of opposing Japanese penetration and paving the way for carrying out their respective programs? In the case of such a united front what would be the attitude of the foreign powers other than Japan?

    d. How far could Japan obtain her economic demands, e.g. for raw cotton, without the necessity for military action in North China?

    e. How far has the National Government been hindered in carrying out its reconstruction program by the existence of extraterritorial rights, the foreign concessions and foreign banks in China?

北京大學圖書館特藏文獻叢刊

北京大學圖書館藏
胡適未刊來往書信 下

鄒新明 編著

北京大學出版社
PEKING UNIVERSITY PRESS

胡適卸任駐美大使後
美國各界人士致意信劄

A. A. Mueller

作者生平不詳。

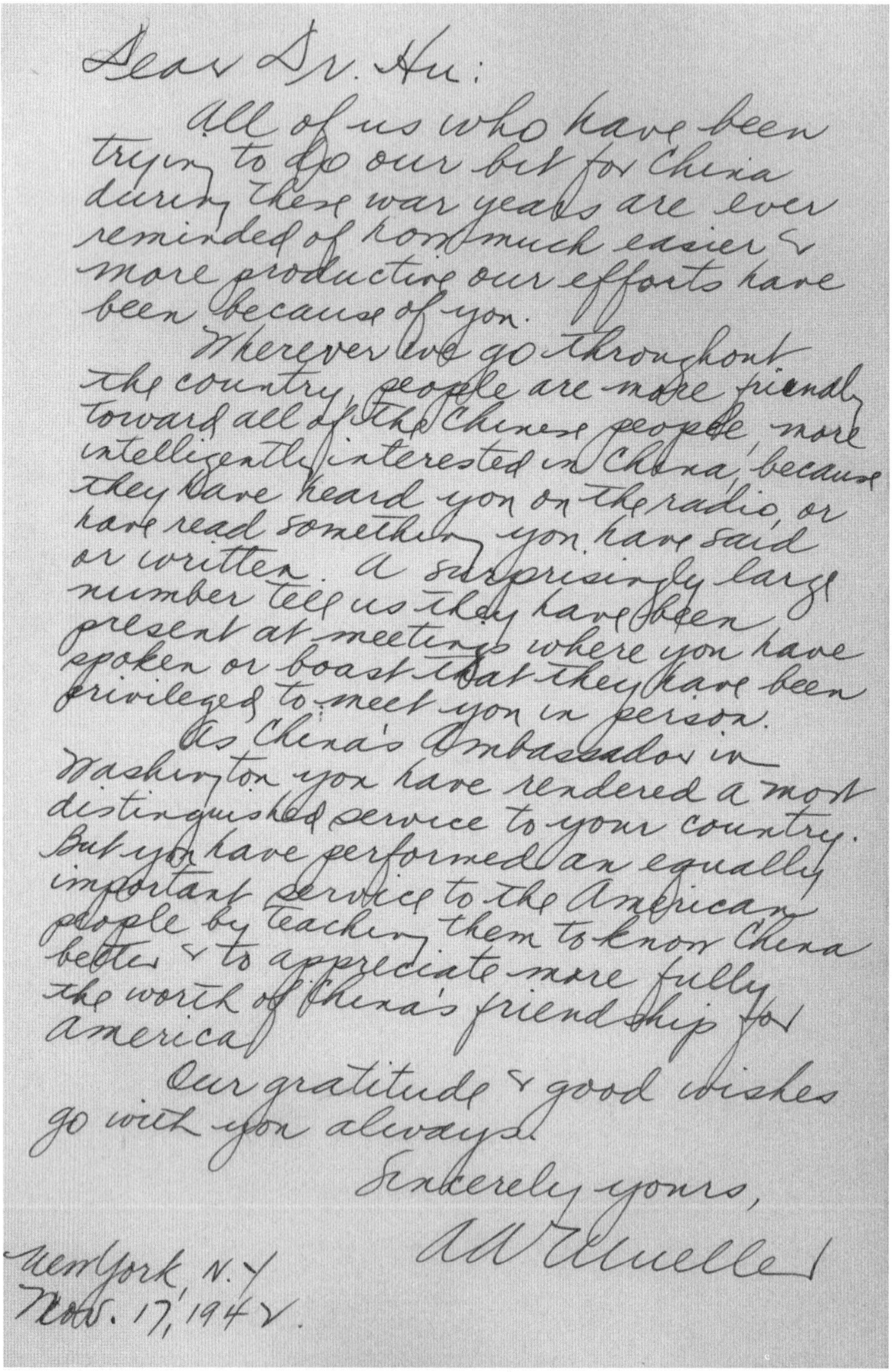

Dear Dr. Hu:

All of us who have been trying to do our bit for China during these war years are ever reminded of how much easier & more productive our efforts have been because of you.

Wherever we go throughout the country, people are more friendly toward all of the Chinese people, more intelligently interested in China, because they have heard you on the radio, or have read something you have said or written. A surprisingly large number tell us they have been present at meetings where you have spoken or boast that they have been privileged to meet you in person.

As China's Ambassador in Washington you have rendered a most distinguished service to your country. But you have performed an equally important service to the American people by teaching them to know China better & to appreciate more fully the worth of China's friendship for America.

Our gratitude & good wishes go with you always.

Sincerely yours,

AW Alluelle[?]

New York, N.Y.
Nov. 17, 1942.

图 1

Dear Dr. Hu:

All of us who have been trying to do our bit for China during these war years are ever reminded of how much easier & more producting our efforts have been because of you.

Wherever we go throughout the country, people are more friendly toward all of the Chinese people, more intelligently interested in China, because they have heard you on the radio, or have read something you have said or written. A surprisingly large number tell us they have been present at meetings where you have spoken or boast that they have been privileged to meet you in person.

As China's Ambassador in Washington you have rendered a most distinguished service to your country. But you have performed an equally important service to the American people by teaching them to know China better & to appreciate more fully the worth of China's friendship for America.

Our gratitude & good wishes go with you always.

Sincerely yours,
A. A. Mueller

New York, N. Y.
Nov. 17, 1942

Alan Valentine

Alan Valentine（1901—1980），生於美國紐約州格倫科夫。先後在斯沃斯莫爾學院和牛津大學貝利奧爾學院獲學士和碩士學位。1924 年代表美國隊參加奧運會橄欖球比賽。後到母校斯沃斯莫爾教英文，曾任教於耶魯大學皮爾森學院。1935—1950 年任羅徹斯特大學校長。北京檔有胡適與 Valentine 往來書信 15 封，時間範圍從 1941 年 1 月到 1942 年 4 月，包括 1941 年 6 月 6 日胡適接受羅徹斯特大學授予名譽法學博士學位等內容。另有胡適致 Valentine 電報稿兩份。

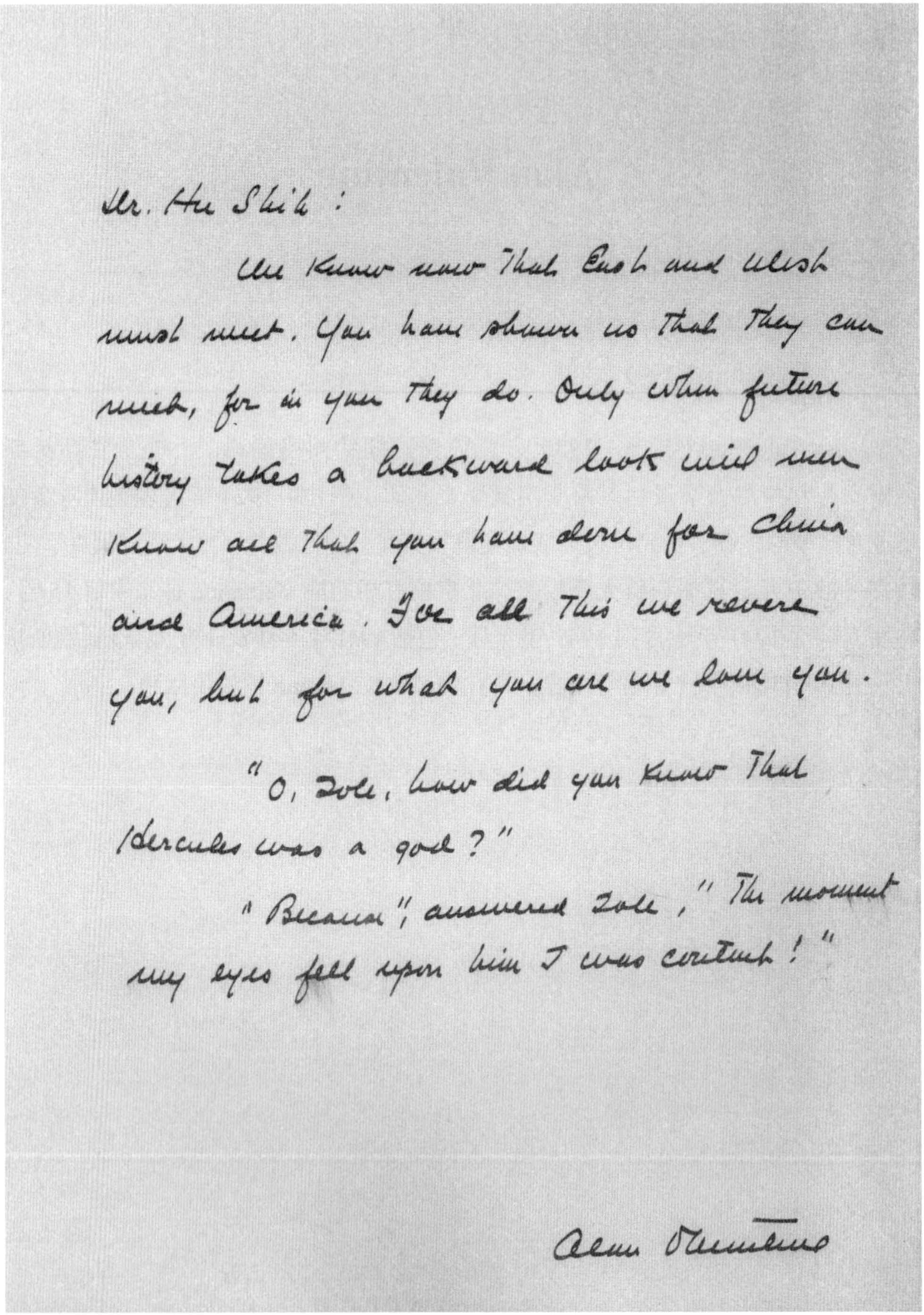

Mr. Hu Shih:

We know now that East and West must meet. You have shown us that they can meet, for in you they do. Only when future history takes a backward look will men know all that you have done for China and America. For all this we revere you, but for what you are we love you.

"O, Iole, how did you know that Hercules was a god?"

"Because", answered Iole, "the moment my eyes fell upon him I was content!"

Alan Valentine

图 1

Dr. Hu Shih:

We know now that East and West must meet. You have shown us that they can meet, for in you they do. Only when future history takes a backward look will men know all that you have done for China and America. For all this we revere you, but for what you are we love you.

"O, Iole, how did you know that Hercules was a god?"

"Because", answered Iole, "The moment my eyes fell upon him I was content!"

Alan Valentine

Alfred Kohlberg

　　Alfred Kohlberg（1887—1960），生於美國舊金山市。美國紡織品進口商，因業務關係經常到中國，支持蔣介石政府，爲太平洋學會董事會成員。北京檔收藏有 Kohlberg 致胡適書信三封，臺北胡適紀念館收藏有 Kohlberg 致胡適書信兩封。Kohlberg 1960 年去世後，胡適曾發去唁電，並在底稿上自譯中文："他一生是時時留意國際問題，每發現他認爲錯誤的思想，就用嬉笑挖苦的文字駁斥他們。這是他的'愛的工作'，這世間沒有別人能繼續這種工作了。"

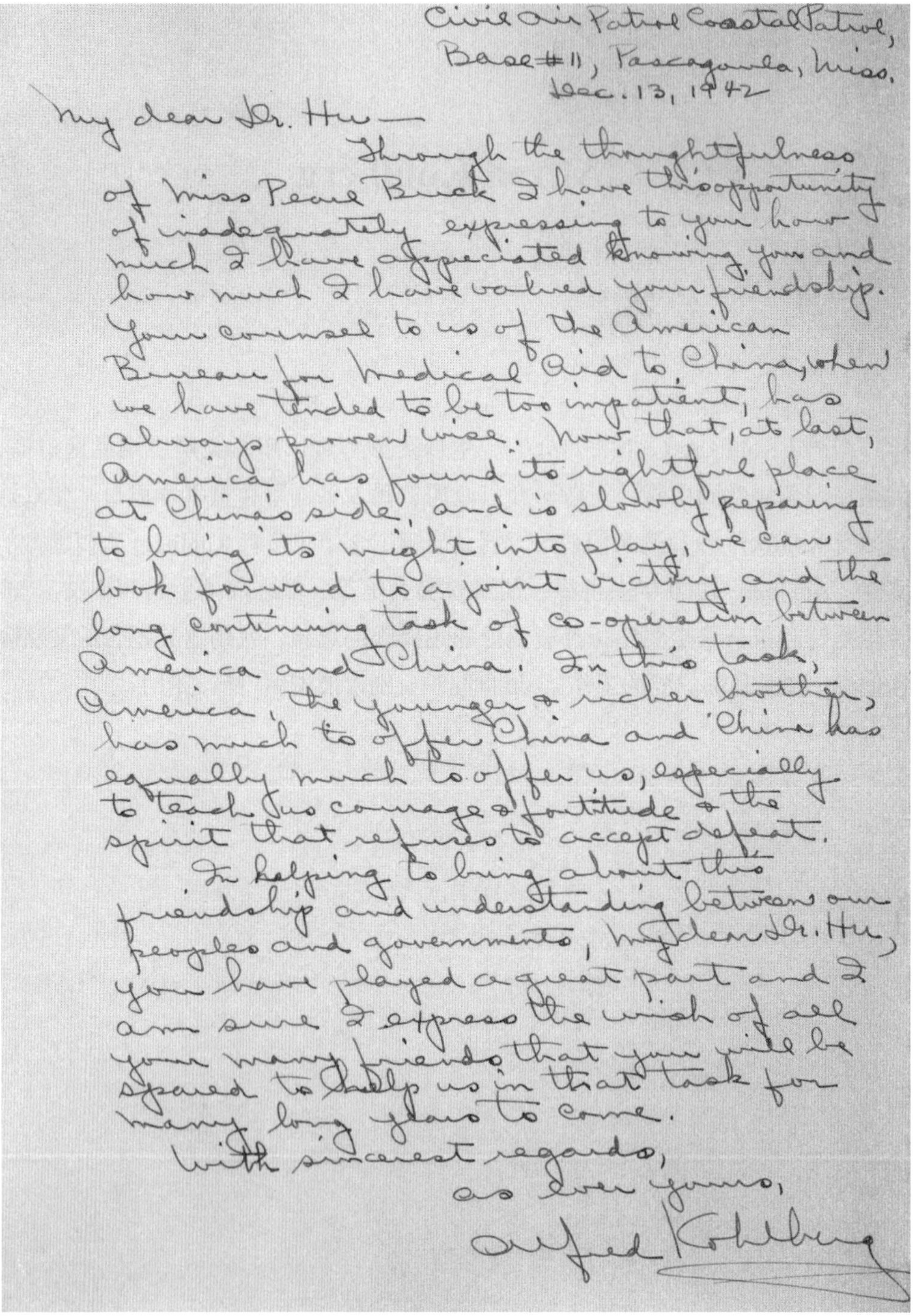

Civil Air Patrol Coastal Patrol,
Base #11, Pascagoula, Miss.
Dec. 13, 1942

My dear Dr. Hu —

Through the thoughtfulness of Miss Pearl Buck I have this opportunity of inadequately expressing to you how much I have appreciated knowing you and how much I have valued your friendship. Your counsel to us of the American Bureau for Medical Aid to China, when we have tended to be too impatient, has always proven wise. Now that, at last, America has found its rightful place at China's side, and is slowly preparing to bring its might into play, we can look forward to a joint victory and the long continuing task of co-operation between America and China. In this task, America, the younger & richer brother, has much to offer China and China has equally much to offer us, especially to teach us courage & fortitude & the spirit that refuses to accept defeat.

In helping to bring about this friendship and understanding between our peoples and governments, my dear Dr. Hu, you have played a great part and I am sure I express the wish of all your many friends that you will be spared to help us in that task for many long years to come.

With sincerest regards,
as ever yours,
Alfred Kohlberg

图 1

Civil Air Patrol Coastal Patrol

Base #11, Pascagoula, Miss.

Dec. 13, 1942

My dear Dr. Hu—

Through the thoughtfulness of Miss Pearl Buck I have this opportunity of inadequately expressing to you how much I have appreciated knowing you and how much I have valued your friendship. Your counsel to us of the American Bureau for Medical Aid to China, when we have tended to be too impatient, has always proven wise. Now that, at last, America has found its rightful place at China's side, and is slowly preparing to bring its might into play, we can look forward to a joint victory and the long continuing task of co-operation between American and China. In this task, America, the younger & richer brother, has much to offer China and China has equally much to offer us, especially to teach us courage & fortitude & the spirit that refuses to accept defeat.

In helping to bring about this friendship and understanding between our peoples and governments, my dear Dr. Hu, you have played a great part and I am sure I express the wish of all your many friends that you will be spared to help us in that task for many long years to come.

With sincerest regards,

As ever yours,

Alfred Kohlberg

Alice Draper Carter

　　Alice Draper Carter，Edward C. Carter 夫人。生平不詳，曾任美國救助中國戰時孤兒委員會（The American Committee for Chinese War Orphans）副主席。北京檔有 Alice Carter 致胡適書信五封，時間從 1939 年 3 月到 1940 年 3 月。涉及邀請胡適於 1940 年 3 月爲美國救助中國戰時孤兒委員會演講中國的文藝復興等內容。另有胡適致 Alice Carter 電報稿四通，主要內容爲上述演講的有關準備等。

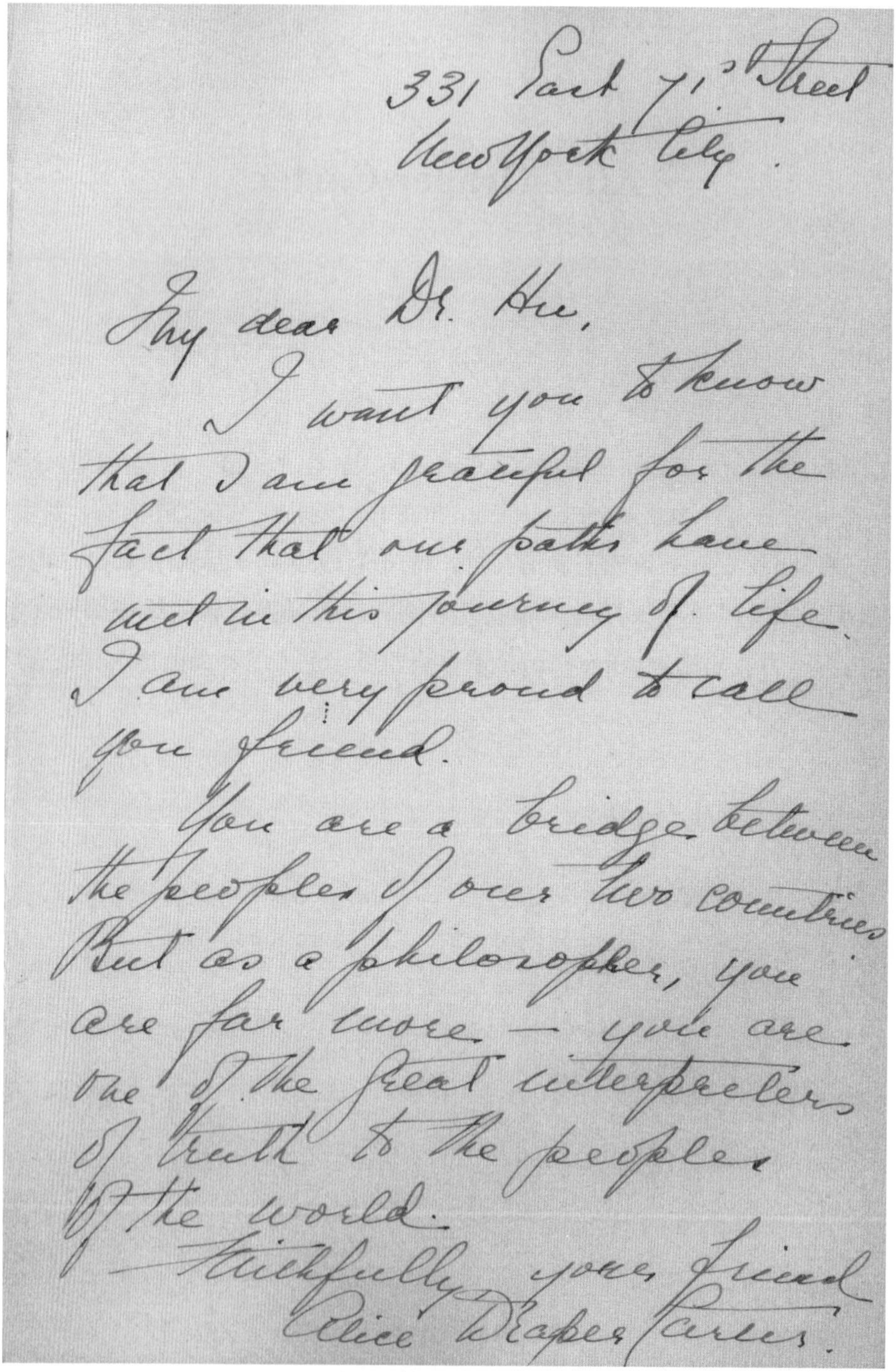

331 East 71st Street
New York City.

My dear Dr. Hu,

I want you to know that I am grateful for the fact that our paths have met in this journey of life. I am very proud to call you friend.

You are a bridge between the peoples of our two countries. But as a philosopher, you are far more — you are one of the great interpreters of truth to the peoples of the world.

Faithfully your friend
Alice Draper Parker.

图 1

331 East 71st Street
New York City

My dear Dr. Hu,

I want you to know that I am grateful for the fact that our paths have met in this journey of life. I am very proud to call you friend.

You are a bridge between the peoples of our two countries. But as a philosopher, you are far more—you are one of the great interpreters of truth to the peoples of the world.

Faithfully your friend
Alice Draper Carter

Allan Forbes

　　Allan Forbes（1874—1955），時任波士頓 State Street Trust Company 總裁。北京檔有胡適 1945 年 4 月 11 日致 Forbes 書信一封，大意爲感謝其贈送 1910 年考取庚子賠款留學生 70 人合影，並感謝其創造的讓自己發表重要演講的機會。

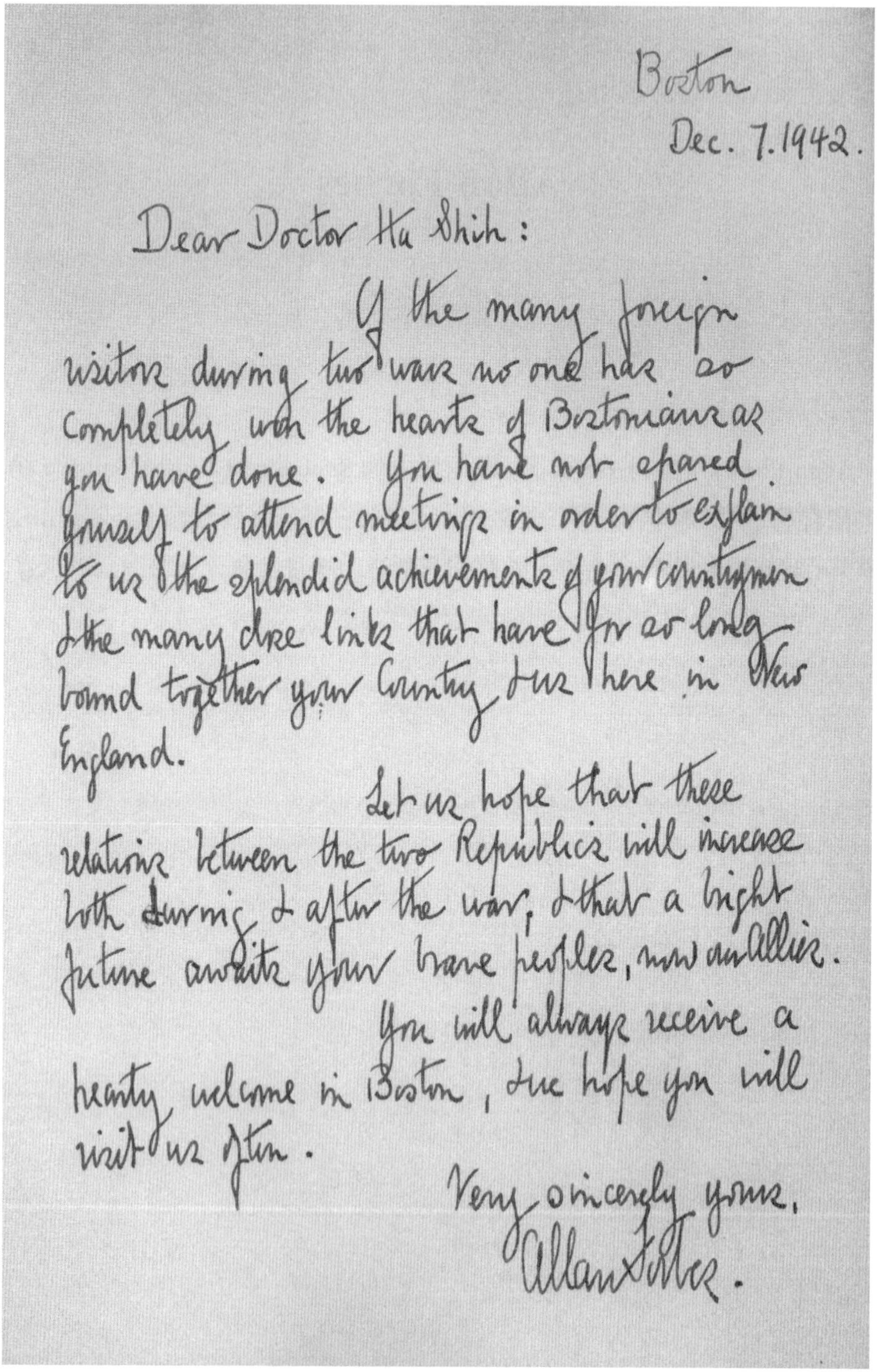

Boston
Dec. 7. 1942.

Dear Doctor Hu Shih:

Of the many foreign visitors during the wars no one has so completely won the hearts of Bostonians as you have done. You have not spared yourself to attend meetings in order to explain to us the splendid achievements of your countrymen & the many dear links that have for so long bound together your Country & us here in New England.

Let us hope that these relations between the two Republics will increase both during & after the war, & that a bright future awaits your brave peoples, now our allies.

You will always receive a hearty welcome in Boston, & we hope you will visit us often.

Very sincerely yours,
Allan Forbes.

图 1

Boston
Dec. 7, 1942

Dear Doctor Hu Shih:

Of the many foreign visitors during two wars no one has so completely won the hearts of Bostonians as you have done. You have not spared yourself to attend meetings in order to explain to us the splendid achievements of your countrymen & the many close links that have for so long bound together your country & us here in New England.

Let us hope that these relations between the two Republics will increase both during & after the war, & that a bright future awaits your brave peoples, now our Allies.

You will always receive a hearty welcome in Boston, & we hope you will visit us often.

Very sincerely yours,
Allan Forbes

Arthur Capper

　　Arthur Capper（1865—1951），生於美國堪薩斯州，時任美國參議院議員。早年從事新聞業，擁有幾家報紙和兩個廣播電臺。1915—1919 年任堪薩斯州州長，是擔任州長的首位本地人。1919—1949 年任美國參議院議員。1946 年任美國參議院農業委員會主席。北京檔有 Capper1941 年寫給胡適的書信兩封，以及胡適秘書代回復的書信一封。

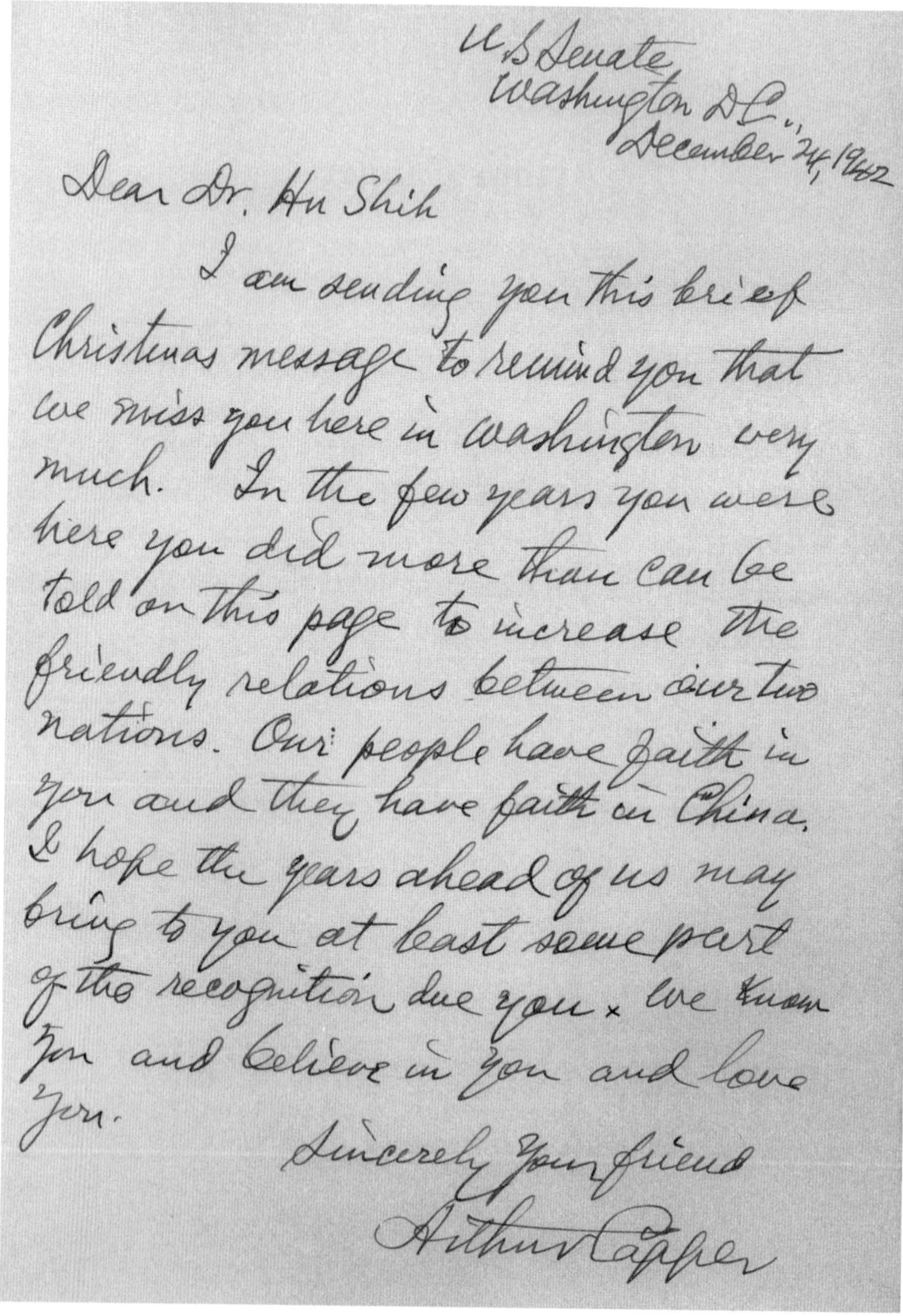

U.S. Senate
Washington D.C.,
December 24, 1942

Dear Dr. Hu Shih

I am sending you this brief Christmas message to remind you that we miss you here in Washington very much. In the few years you were here you did more than can be told on this page to increase the friendly relations between our two nations. Our people have faith in you and they have faith in China. I hope the years ahead of us may bring to you at least some part of the recognition due you. We know you and believe in you and love you.

Sincerely your friend
Arthur Capper

圖 1

U. S. Senate
Washington D. C.
December 24, 1942

Dear Dr. Hu Shih

    I am sending you this brief Christmas message to remind you that we miss you here in Washington very much. In the few years you were here you did more than can be told on this page to increase the friendly relations between our two nations. Our people have faith in you and they have faith in China. I hope the years ahead of us may bring to you at least some part of the recognition due you. We know you and believe in you and love you.

Sincerely your friend
Arthur Capper

Arthur Hays Sulzberger

Arthur Hays Sulzberger（1891—1968），1913 年畢業於哥倫比亞學院。1918 年開始在《紐約時報》工作，1935—1961 年任該報出版人。1944—1959 年任哥倫比亞大學董事。1939—1957 年任洛克菲勒基金會董事。1950 年當選美國人文與科學院院士。胡適曾於 1941 年 9 月 15 日致信 Sulzberger，祝賀《紐約時報》創刊九十周年。北京檔有 Sulzberger 致胡適書信四封，時間爲 1940 年 6 月到 1942 年 4 月，另有 1950 年 6 月、1953 年 5 月兩封。内容多爲約見或聚餐。

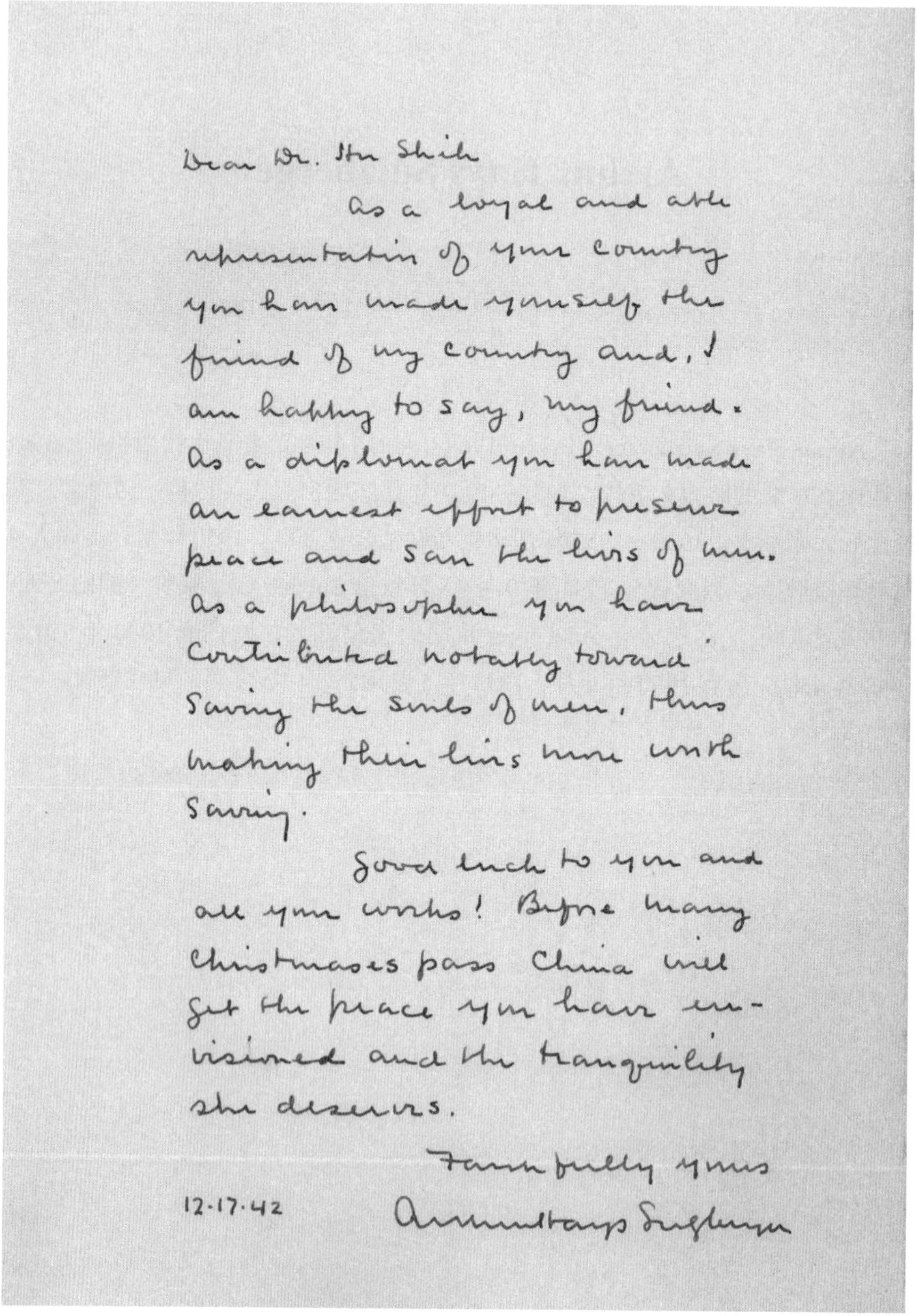

Dear Dr. Hu Shih

    As a loyal and able representative of your country you have made yourself the friend of my country and, I am happy to say, my friend. As a diplomat you have made an earnest effort to preserve peace and save the lives of men. As a philosopher you have contributed notably toward saving the souls of men, thus making their lives more worth saving.

    Good luck to you and all your works! Before many Christmases pass China will get the peace you have envisioned and the tranquility she deserves.

          Faithfully yours

12-17-42   Armstrong Ingham

圖 1

Dear Dr. Hu Shih

As a loyal and able representation of your country you have made yourself the friend of my country and, I am happy to say, my friend. As a diplomat you have made an earnest effort to preserve peace and save the lives of men. As a philosopher you have contributed notably toward saving the souls of men, thus making their lives more worth saving.

Good luck to you and all your works! Before many Christmases pass China will get the peace you have envisioned and the tranquility she deserves.

Faithfully yours
Arthur Hays Sulzberger

12. 17. 42

Arthur H. James

Arthur H. James（1883—1973），生於美國賓夕法尼亞州，時任該州州長。早年就讀於迪金遜法學院。1926年當選賓夕法尼亞州副州長。1931—1939年任賓州高級法院法官。1939—1943年任賓州州長。北京檔有Fred B. Trescher1942年4月3日致胡適書信一封，談及Arthur H. James將於5月16日出席The Westmoreland County Bar Association，並在會上授予胡適會員資格。

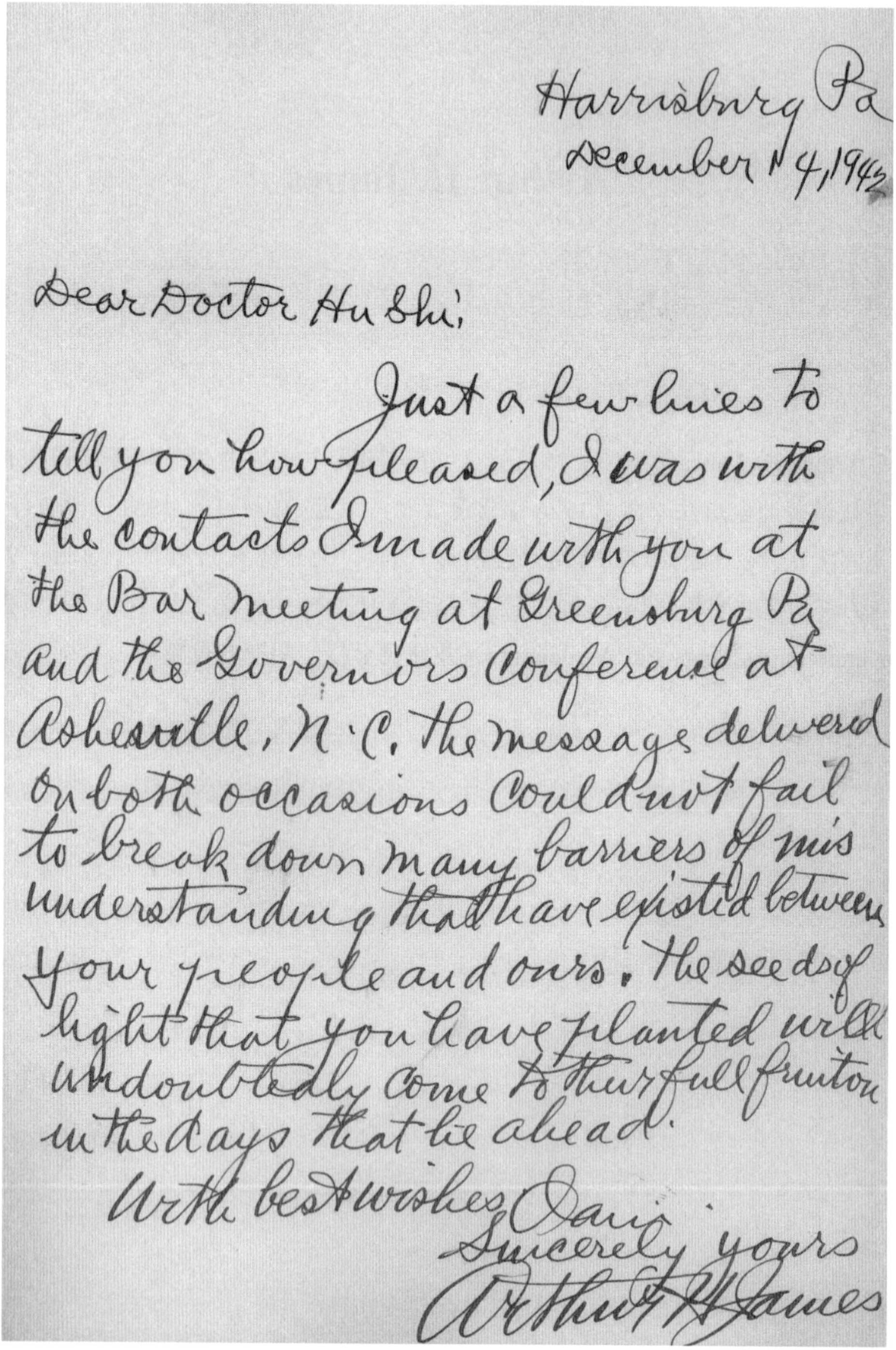

Harrisburg Pa
December 4, 1943

Dear Doctor Hu Shi;

Just a few lines to tell you how pleased I was with the contacts I made with you at the Bar meeting at Greensburg Pa and the Governors Conference at Asheville, N.C. The messages delivered on both occasions could not fail to break down many barriers of misunderstanding that have existed between your people and ours. The seeds of light that you have planted will undoubtedly come to their full fruition in the days that lie ahead.

With best wishes I am
Sincerely yours
Arthur H James

圖 1

Harrisburg Pa.
December 14, 1942

Dear Doctor Hu Shih:

Just a few lines to tell you how pleased, I was with the contacts I made with you at the Bar meeting at Greensburg Pa. and the Governor's Conference at Asheville, N.C. The messages delivered on both occasions could not fail to break down many barriers of misunderstanding that have existed between your people and ours. The seeds of light that you have planted will undoubtedly come to their full fruition in the days that lie ahead.

With best wishes. I am,

Sincerely yours
Arthur H. James

Arthur Judson Brown

　　Arthur Judson Brown（1856—1963），美國牧師、傳教士和作家，生於馬薩諸塞州，1883 年成爲美國長老會牧師，1883—1895 年到美國多地傳教。後到世界各地包括中國傳教。1914—1937 年任北京協和醫學院理事。曾任美國長老會海外傳教會幹事。北京檔有 Brown1938 年 5 月 14 日致胡適書信一封，信中談及對胡適演講的印象。

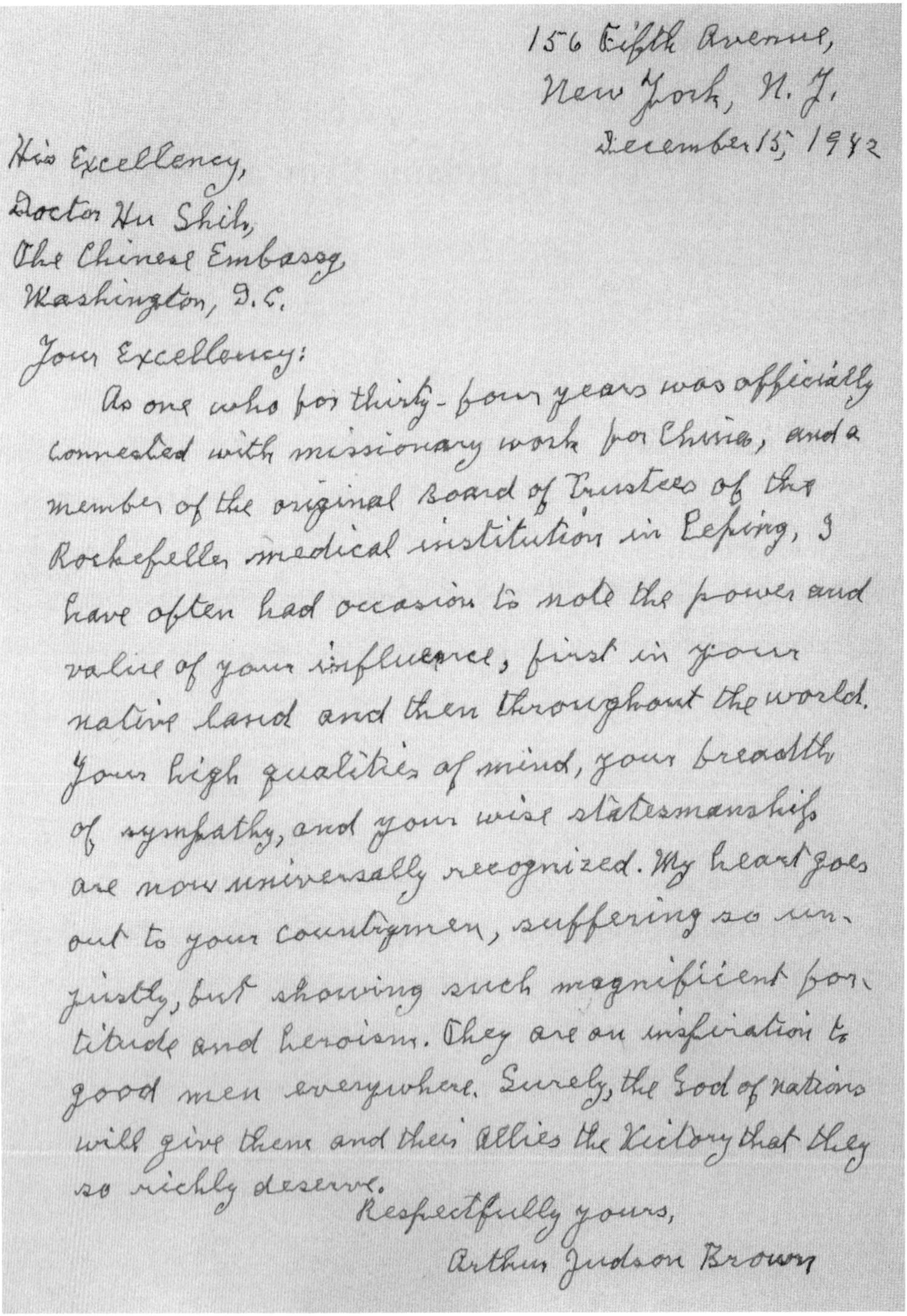

156 Fifth Avenue,
New York, N.Y.
December 15, 1942

His Excellency,
Doctor Hu Shih,
The Chinese Embassy,
Washington, D.C.

Your Excellency:

As one who for thirty-four years was officially connected with missionary work for China, and a member of the original Board of Trustees of the Rockefeller medical institution in Peping, I have often had occasion to note the power and value of your influence, first in your native land and then throughout the world. Your high qualities of mind, your breadth of sympathy, and your wise statesmanship are now universally recognized. My heart goes out to your countrymen, suffering so unjustly, but showing such magnificent fortitude and heroism. They are an inspiration to good men everywhere. Surely, the God of nations will give them and their Allies the Victory that they so richly deserve.

Respectfully yours,
Arthur Judson Brown

圖 1

156 Fifth Avenue,
New York, N. Y.
December 15, 1942

His Excellency,
Doctor Hu Shih,
The Chinese Embassy,
Washington, D. C.
Your Excellency:

 As one who for thirty-four years was officially connected with missionary work for China, and a member of the original Board of Trustees of the Rockefeller medical institution in Peking, I have often had occasion to note the power and value of your influence, first in your native land and then throughout the world. Your high qualities of mind, your breadth of sympathy, and your wise statesmanship are now universally recognized. My heart goes out to your countrymen, suffering so unjustly, but showing such magnificent fortitude and heroism. They are an inspiration to good men everywhere. Surely, the God of nations will give them and their allies the victory that they so richly deserve.

Respectfully yours,
Arthur Judson Brown

Arthur V. Davis

　　Arthur V. Davis（1867—1962），生於美國馬薩諸塞州，美國工業家、慈善家。1888年畢業於艾姆赫斯特學院。畢業後到匹兹堡冶金公司工作，1888年與美國鋁業大王霍爾合作完成廉價煉鋁法的試驗投産。1892年成爲匹兹堡冶金公司總經理，該公司於1907年更名爲美國鋁業公司，仍任總經理，1910年任該公司總裁，1928年任董事會主席，在該公司任職直到1958年。胡適任駐美大使期間，曾於1939年11月30日致信Earl H. Cressy，通知中國政府決定授予包括Arthur V. Davis在内四人"雙十"國慶榮譽勳章。Davis在12月8日致信胡適，表示感謝。

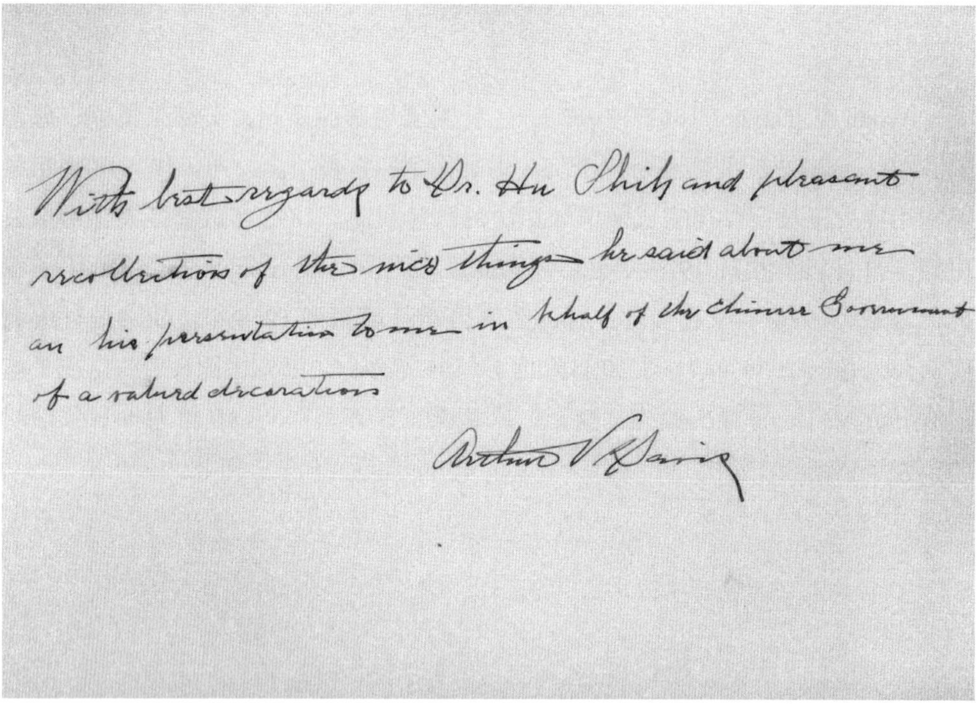

With best regards to Dr. Hu Shih and pleasant recollections of the nice things he said about me an his presentation to me in behalf of the Chinese Government of a valued decoration.

Arthur V. Davis

圖 1

With best regards to Dr. Hu Shih and pleasant recollections of the nice things he said about me on his presentation to me in behalf of the Chinese Government of a valued decoration.

Arthur V. Davis

B. A. Garside

  B. A. Garside（1894—1989），葛思德，生於美國俄克拉荷馬州，早年獲俄克拉荷馬大學學士學位，1922 年獲哥倫比亞大學碩士學位。1922—1926 年爲長老會在華傳教士，曾任齊魯大學教育學教授。返紐約後任中國基督教大學聯合董事會執行董事。爲 1941 年成立的美國援華救濟會以及後改組的美國援華聯合會的主要發起人之一。曾著有路思義傳記。胡適任駐美大使期間與其有交往。北京檔有 Garside 致胡適書信兩封，時間分別爲 1940 年 1 月 8 日和 1940 年 6 月 16 日。另有一封 1951 年 11 月 23 日致胡適書信。

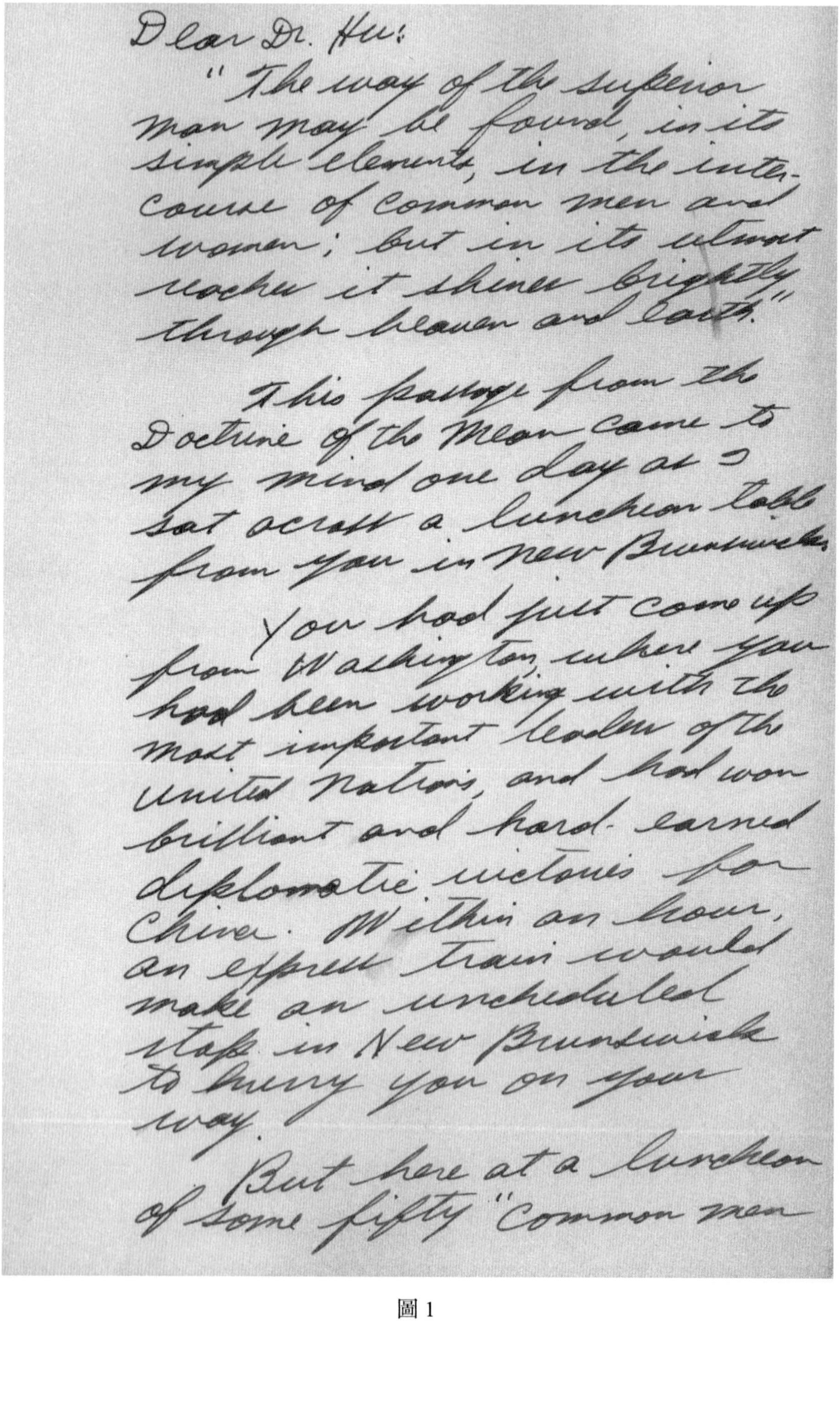

Dear Dr. Hu:

"The way of the superior man may be found, in its simple elements, in the intercourse of common men and women; but in its utmost reaches it shines brightly through heaven and earth."

This passage from the Doctrine of the Mean came to my mind one day as I sat across a luncheon table from you in New Brunswick.

You had just come up from Washington, where you had been working with the most important leaders of the United Nations, and had won brilliant and hard-earned diplomatic victories for China. Within an hour, an express train would make an unscheduled stop in New Brunswick to hurry you on your way.

But here at a luncheon of some fifty "common men

圖 1

Dear Dr. Hu:

"The way of the superior man may be found, in its simple elements, in the intercourse of common men and women; but in its utmost reaches it shines brightly through heaven and earth."

This passage from the *Doctrine of the Mean* came to my mind one day as I sat across a luncheon table from you in New Brunswick.

You had just come up from Washington, where you had been working with the most important leaders of the United Nations, and had won brilliant and hard-earned diplomatic victories for China. Within an hour, an express train would make an unscheduled stop in New Brunswick to hurry you on your way.

But here at a luncheon of some fifty "common men

and women." You let your lunch grow cold while you carried on an animated conversation with all those around you, and autographed in Chinese, the place cards of everyone present!

Historians will rank you among the most brilliant and successful of all the diplomats whom this global war has called forth. But by many hundreds of thousands of every-day Americans you will be best loved and most admired for the way you have won countless friends for yourself and for China by your sincerity and kindliness in intercourse with "common men and women."

Today, America and China are both heavily indebted to you for the superb service you have performed at a critical time for both countries. But we look to you for still greater accomplishments in the years ahead, both in scholarship and in statecraft.

Sincerely,
B. A. Garside

圖2

and women," you let your lunch grow cold while you carried on an animated conversation with all those around you, and autographed in Chinese the place cards of everyone present!

Historians will rank you among the most brilliant and successful of all the diplomats whom this global war have called forth. But by many hundreds of thousands of everyday Americans you will be best loved and most admired for the way you have won countless friends for yourself and for China by your sincerity and kindliness in intercourse with "common men and women."

Today, America and China are both heavily indebted to you for the superb service you have performed at a crucial time for both countries. But we look to you for still greater accomplishments in the years ahead, both in scholarship and in statecraft.

Sincerely,
B. A. Garside

Bayard M. Hedrick

作者生平不詳。

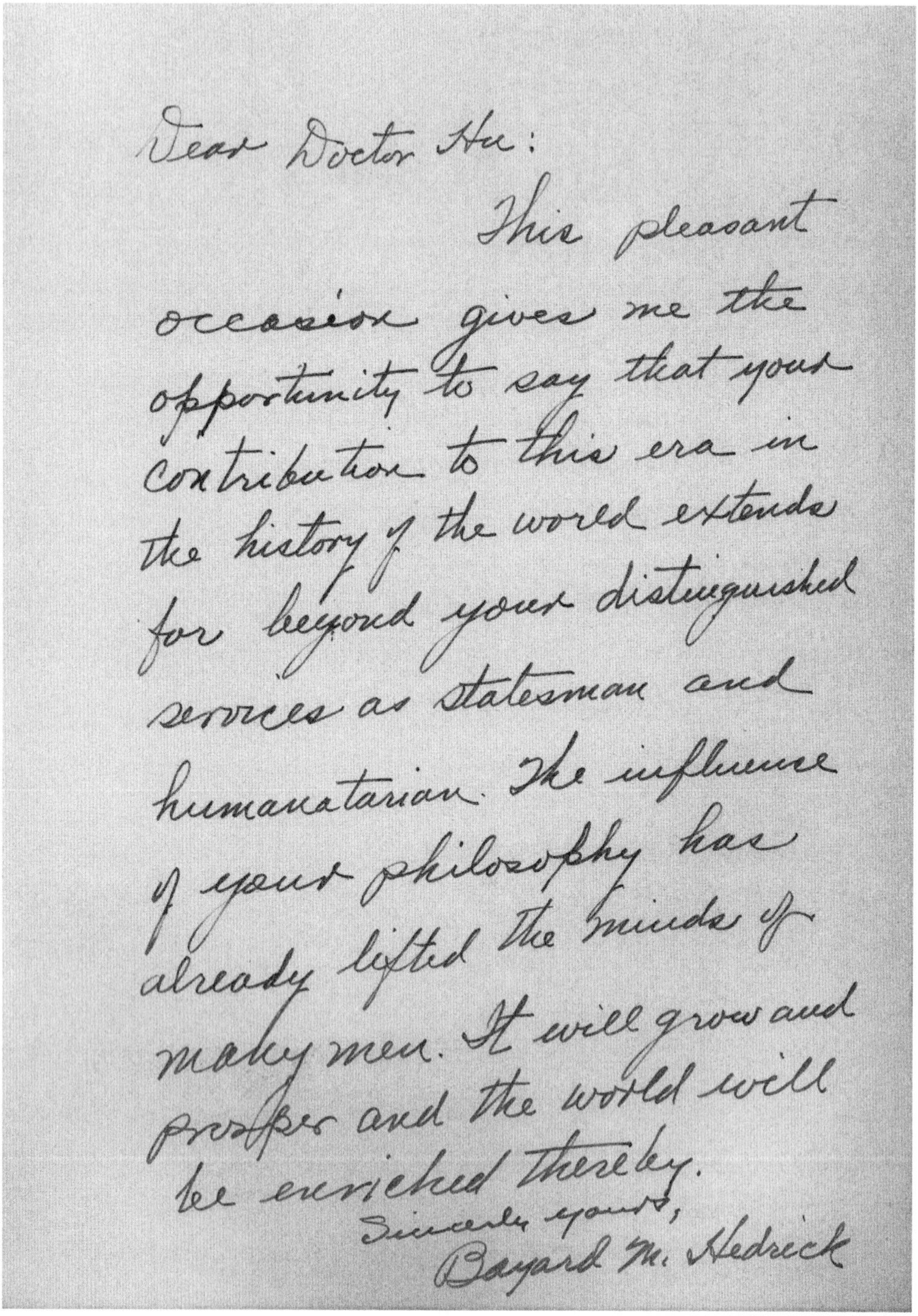

Dear Doctor Hu:

This pleasant occasion gives me the opportunity to say that your contribution to this era in the history of the world extends far beyond your distinguished services as statesman and humanatarian. The influence of your philosophy has already lifted the minds of many men. It will grow and prosper and the world will be enriched thereby.

Sincerely yours,
Bayard M. Hedrick

圖 1

Dear Doctor Hu:

This pleasant occasion gives me the opportunity to say that your contribution to this era in the history of the world extends far beyond your distinguished service as statesman and humanitarian. The influence of your philosophy has already lifted the minds of many men. It will grow and prosper and the world will be enriched thereby.

Sincerely yours,
Bayard M. Hedrick

Bernard Lichtenberg

　　Bernard Lichtenberg，曾任對外關係學院主席。北京檔有 Bernard Lichtenberg 1942 年 9 月 9 日致胡適書信一頁，主要內容是聽說胡適要卸任大使，對胡適的大使之職做了評價："You have been of inestimable help and value to your country here in United States and your Government should be appreciative and exceedingly grateful. From many different sources I have learned what a wonderful impression you have made here wherever you went. As for myself, it was a privilege to know you." 也許因爲已經私下給胡適寫了這封信，故 Bernard Lichtenberg 在應邀留言時寫得很簡短。

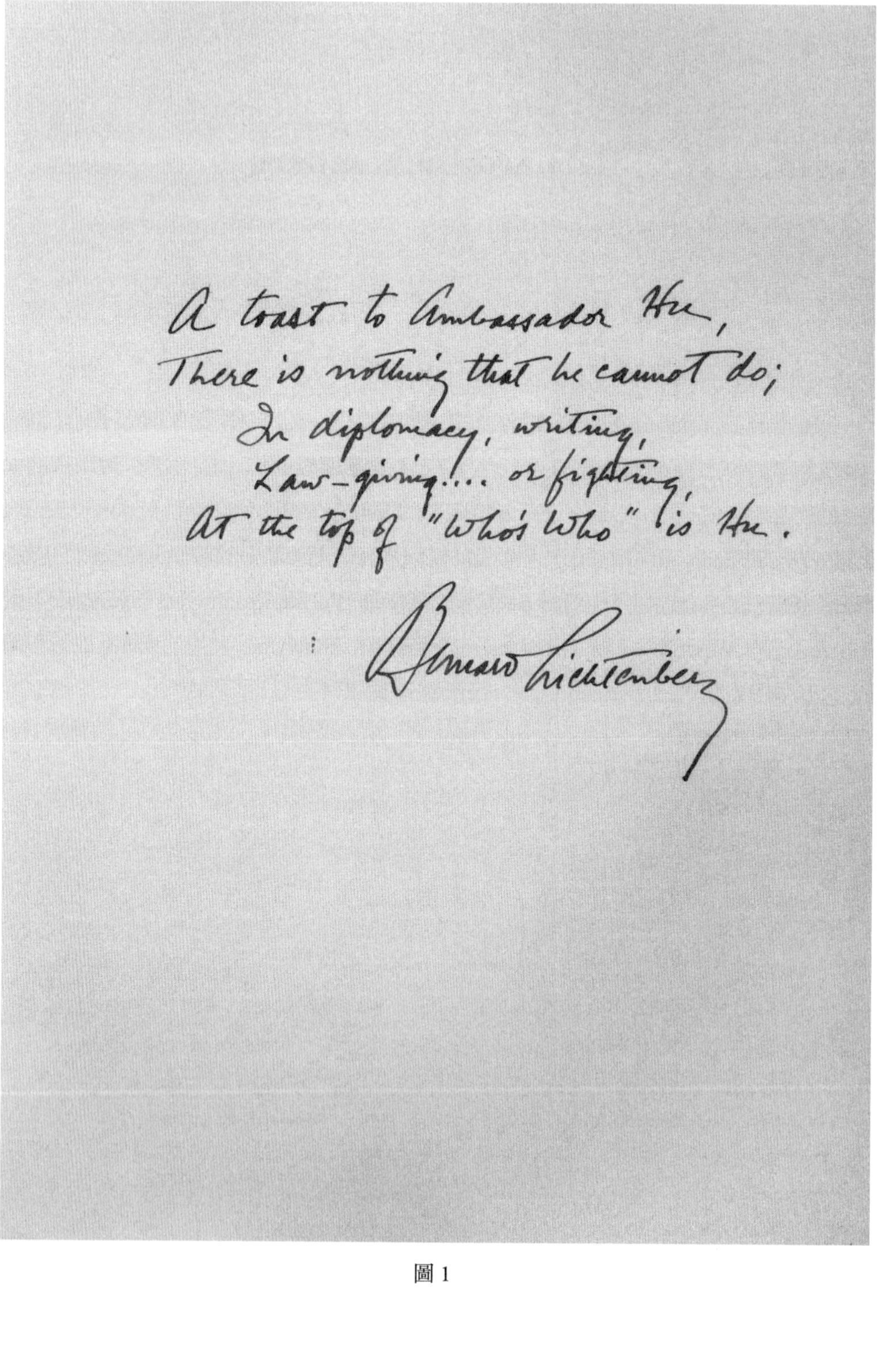

A toast to Ambassador Hu,
There is nothing that he cannot do;
In diplomacy, writing,
Law-giving.... or fighting,
At the top of "Who's Who" is Hu.

Bernard Lichtenberg

圖1

A toast to Ambassador Hu,
There is nothing that he cannot do;
In diplomacy, writing,
Law-giving... or fighting,
at the top of "Who's Who" is Hu.

Bernard Lichtenberg

Breckenridge Long

　　Breckenridge Long（1881—1958），生於美國密蘇里州，美國外交家、政治家，時任美國助理國務卿。1904年畢業於普林斯頓大學，1905—1906年在華盛頓大學法學院學習，1909年獲普林斯頓大學文學碩士學位。1917—1920年任第三助理國務卿。1933—1936年任美國駐意大利大使。1940—1944年任助理國務卿。

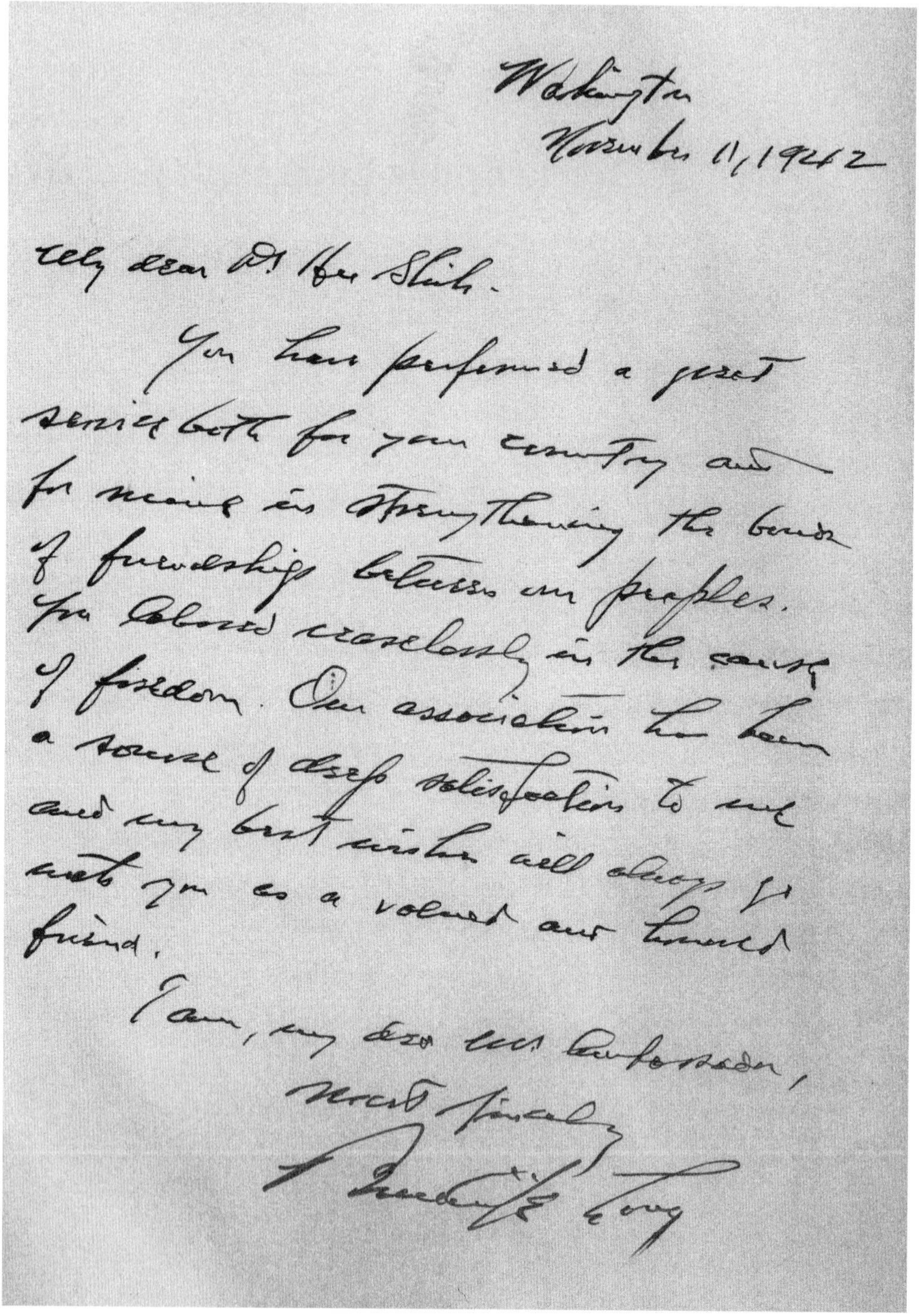

Washington
November 11, 1962

My dear Dr. Hu Shih:

You have performed a great service both for your country and for ours in strengthening the bonds of friendship between our peoples. You labored ceaselessly in the cause of freedom. Our association has been a source of deep satisfaction to me and my best wishes will always go with you as a valued and honored friend.

I am, my dear Ambassador,

Most sincerely,

Frederick ___

圖 1

Washington
November 11, 1942

My dear Dr. Hu Shih,

You have performed a great service both for your country and for mine in strengthening the bonds of friendship between our peoples.

You labored ceaselessly in the cause of freedom. Our association has been a source of deep satisfaction to me and my best wishes will always go with you as a valued and honored friend.

I am, my dear Mr. Ambassador,

Most Sincerely
Breckenridge Long

C. Andrade, 3rd

C. Andrade, 3rd,時任 Great state 石油公司總裁,餘不詳。

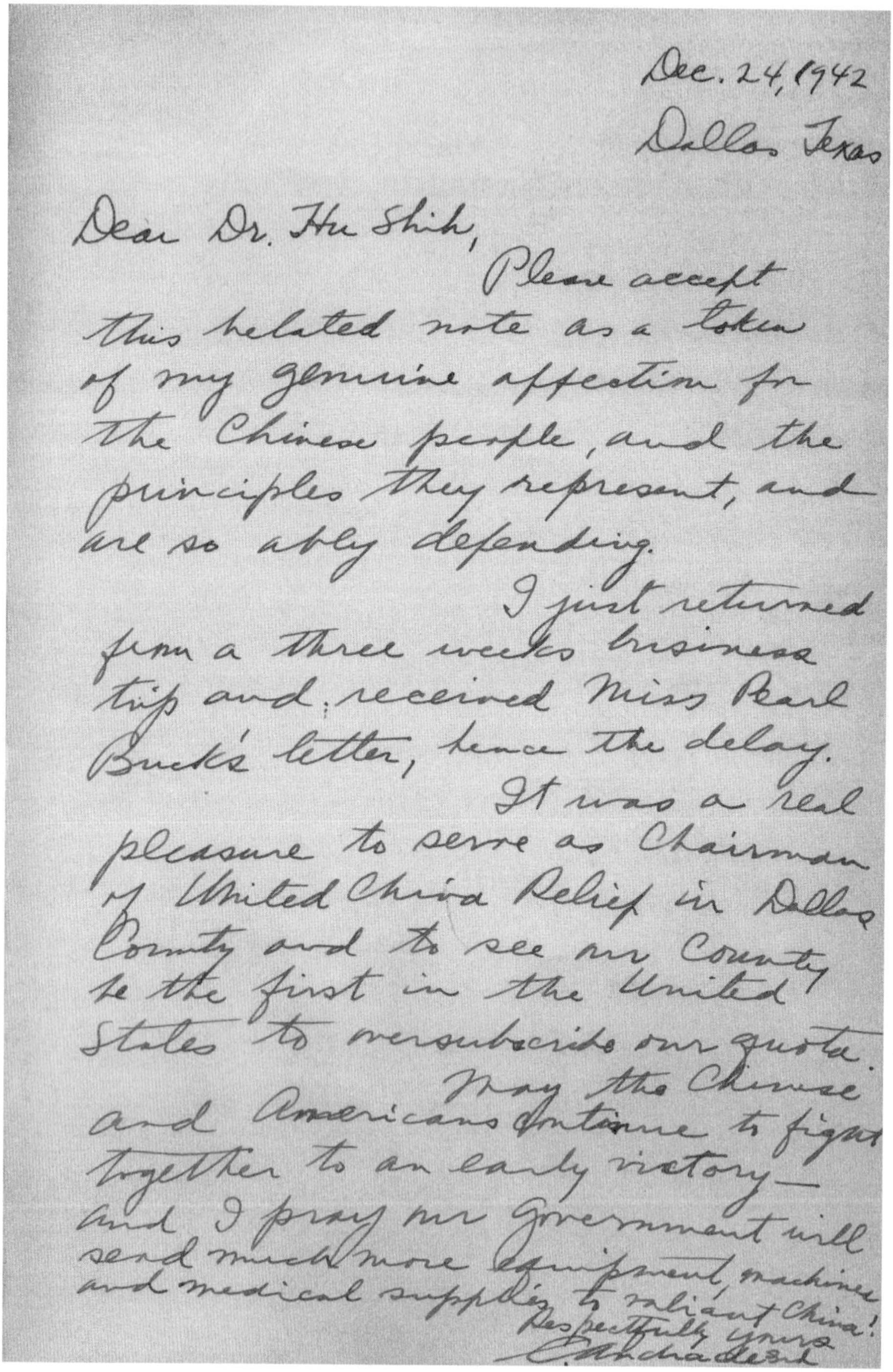

Dec. 24, 1942
Dallas, Texas

Dear Dr. Hu Shih,

Please accept this belated note as a token of my genuine affection for the Chinese people, and the principles they represent, and are so ably defending.

I just returned from a three weeks business trip and received Miss Pearl Buck's letter; hence the delay.

It was a real pleasure to serve as Chairman of United China Relief in Dallas County and to see our County be the first in the United States to oversubscribe our quota.

May the Chinese and Americans continue to fight together to an early victory — and I pray our government will send much more equipment, machines and medical supplies to valiant China!

Respectfully yours,
C. Andrade III

圖 1

Dec. 24, 1942
Dallas Texas

Dear Dr. Hu Shih,

Please accept this belated note as a token of my genuine affection for the Chinese people, and the principles they represent, and are so ably defending.

I just returned from a three weeks business trip and received Miss Pearl Buck's letter, hence the delay.

It was a real pleasure to serve as Chairman of United China Relief in Dallas County and to see our County be the first in the United States to oversubscribe our quota.

May the Chinese and Americans continue to fight together to an early victory—and I pray our government will send much more equipment, machines and medical supplies to valiant China!

Respectively yours
C. Andrade, 3rd

Charles A. Sprague

　　Charles A. Sprague（1887—1969），生於美國堪薩斯州，時任俄勒岡州州長。早年從事新聞業和教育，1910 年畢業於蒙莫斯學院。1939—1943 年任俄勒岡州州長。1955 年獲科爾比學院榮譽法學博士學位。北京檔有 Charles A. Sprague 1942 年 9 月 12 日致胡適書信一封，主要內容是很遺憾胡適卸任駐美大使，希望胡適留下，繼續在美國演講。

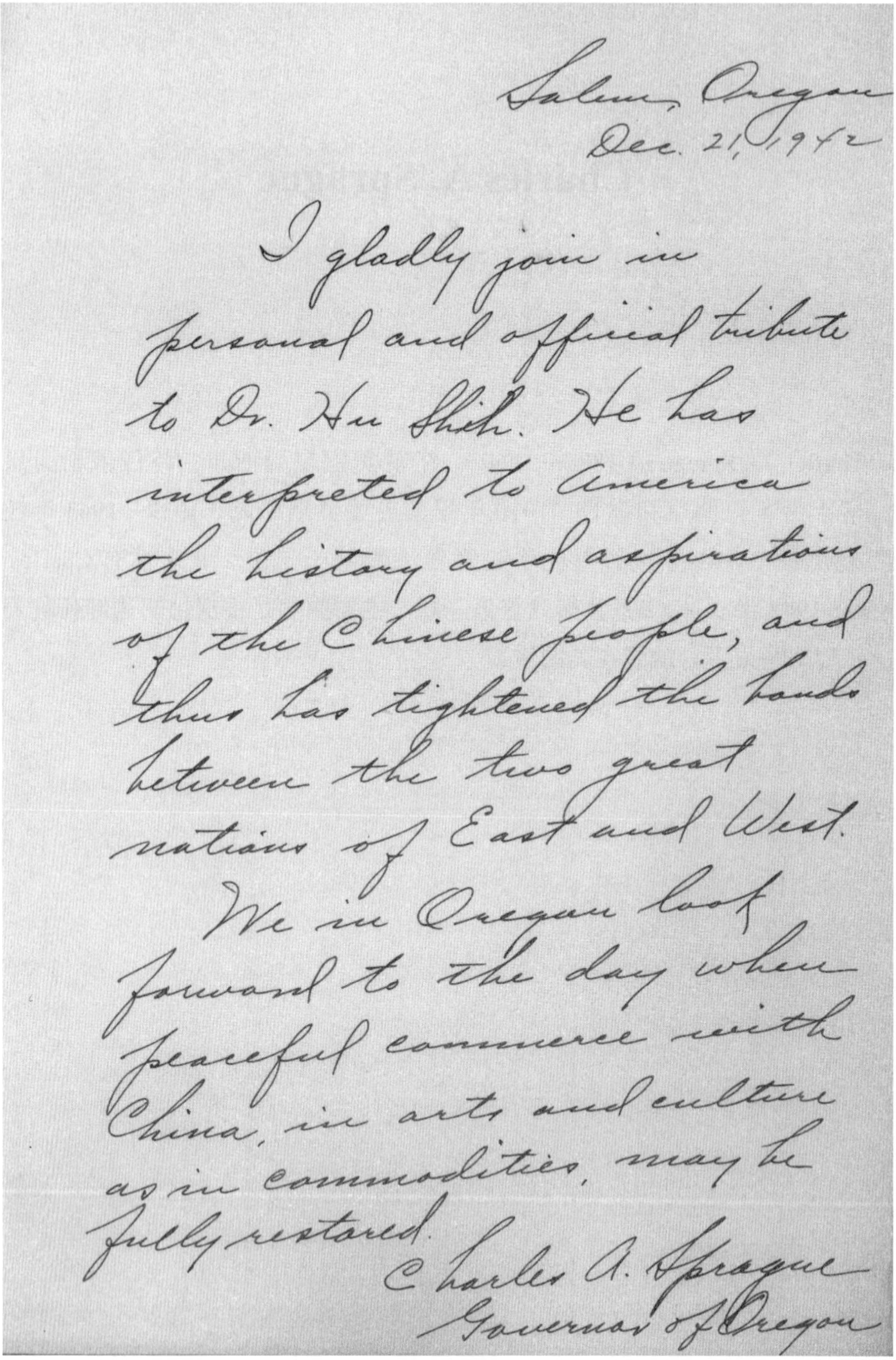

> Salem, Oregon
> Dec. 21, 1942
>
> I gladly join in personal and official tribute to Dr. Hu Shih. He has interpreted to America the history and aspirations of the Chinese people, and thus has tightened the bonds between the two great nations of East and West.
>
> We in Oregon look forward to the day when peaceful commerce with China, in arts and culture as in commodities, may be fully restored.
>
> Charles A. Sprague
> Governor of Oregon

圖1

Salem, Oregon
Dec. 21, 1942

I gladly join in personal and official tribute to Dr. Hu Shih. He has interpreted to America the history and aspirations of the Chinese people, and thus has tightened the hands between the two great nations of East and West.

We in Oregon look forward to the day when peaceful commence with China, in arts and culture as in commodities, may be fully restored.

Charles A. Sprague
Governor of Oregon

Charles K. Edmunds

　　Charles K. Edmunds（1876—1949），中文名晏文士，美國北長老會教士，物理學家。早年就讀於約翰·霍普金斯大學，主修物理學，獲哲學博士學位。1903年來華，在廣州傳教辦學。曾任嶺南學校物理學、電機工程學教授。1906—1917年任廣州嶺南學校（The Canton Christian College）校長。1928年任美國波莫納大學校長。著有 Science among the Chinese: Some Aspects of the Chinese Conception of the Universe as Compared with Modern Scientific Knowledge, Modern Education in China 等。北京檔有 Charles K. Edmunds 1942年12月28日致胡適書信一封，除了祝福胡適1943年好運外，還談到一起給胡適以書信方式留言之事，信中説："I hope my greeting which was intended for the group presented to you on the 26th really reached you..."

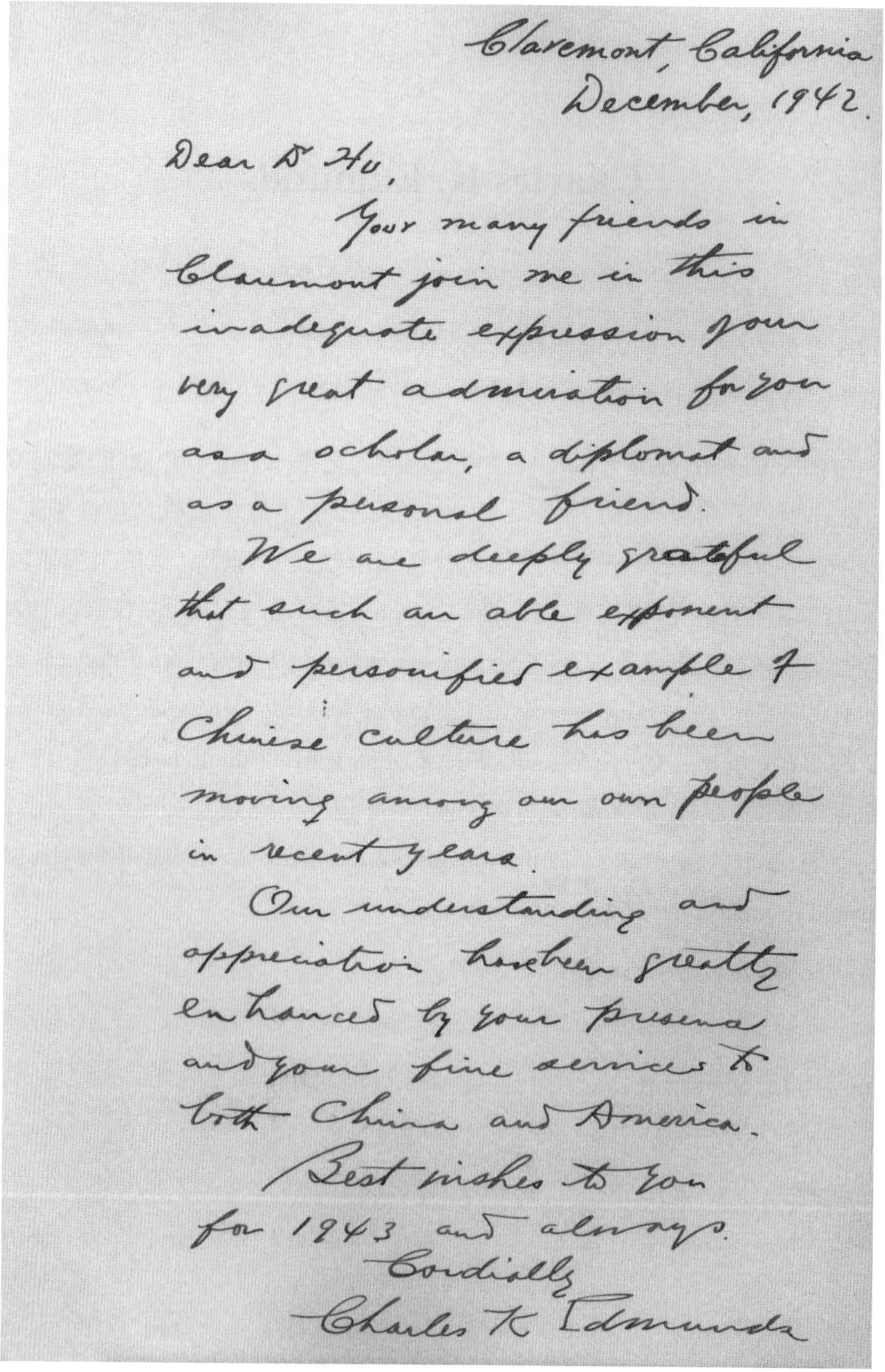

Claremont, California
December, 1942.

Dear Dr Hu,

Your many friends in Claremont join me in this inadequate expression your very great admiration for you as a scholar, a diplomat and as a personal friend.

We are deeply grateful that such an able exponent and personified example of Chinese culture has been moving among our own people in recent years.

Our understanding and appreciation has been greatly enhanced by your presence and your fine services to both China and America.

Best wishes to you for 1943 and always.

Cordially,
Charles K Edmunds

圖 1

Claremont, California
December, 1942

Dear Dr. Hu,

Your many friends in Claremont join me in this inadequate expression of our very great admiration for you as a scholar, a diplomat and as a personal friend.

We are deeply grateful that such an able exponent and personified example of Chinese culture has been moving among our own people in recent years.

Our understanding and appreciation have been greatly enhanced by your presence and your fine services to both China and America.

Best wishes to you
for 1943 and always
Cordially
Charles K. Edmunds

Charles P. Taft, Mr. and Mrs.

Charles P. Taft（1897—1983），生於美國俄亥俄州辛辛那提，美國第 27 任總統威廉·塔夫脫之子。1918 年畢業於耶魯大學，1921 年畢業於耶魯大學法學院。畢業後從事法律事務。1925 年任國際青年基督教聯合會主席。1955—1957 年任辛辛那提市長。

Eleanor Chase Taft（1894—1961），Charles P. Taft 之妻。胡適在任駐美大使前後與其有交往，北京檔藏有胡適與其往來函電十三通，時間從 1939 年 10 月到 1940 年 1 月。

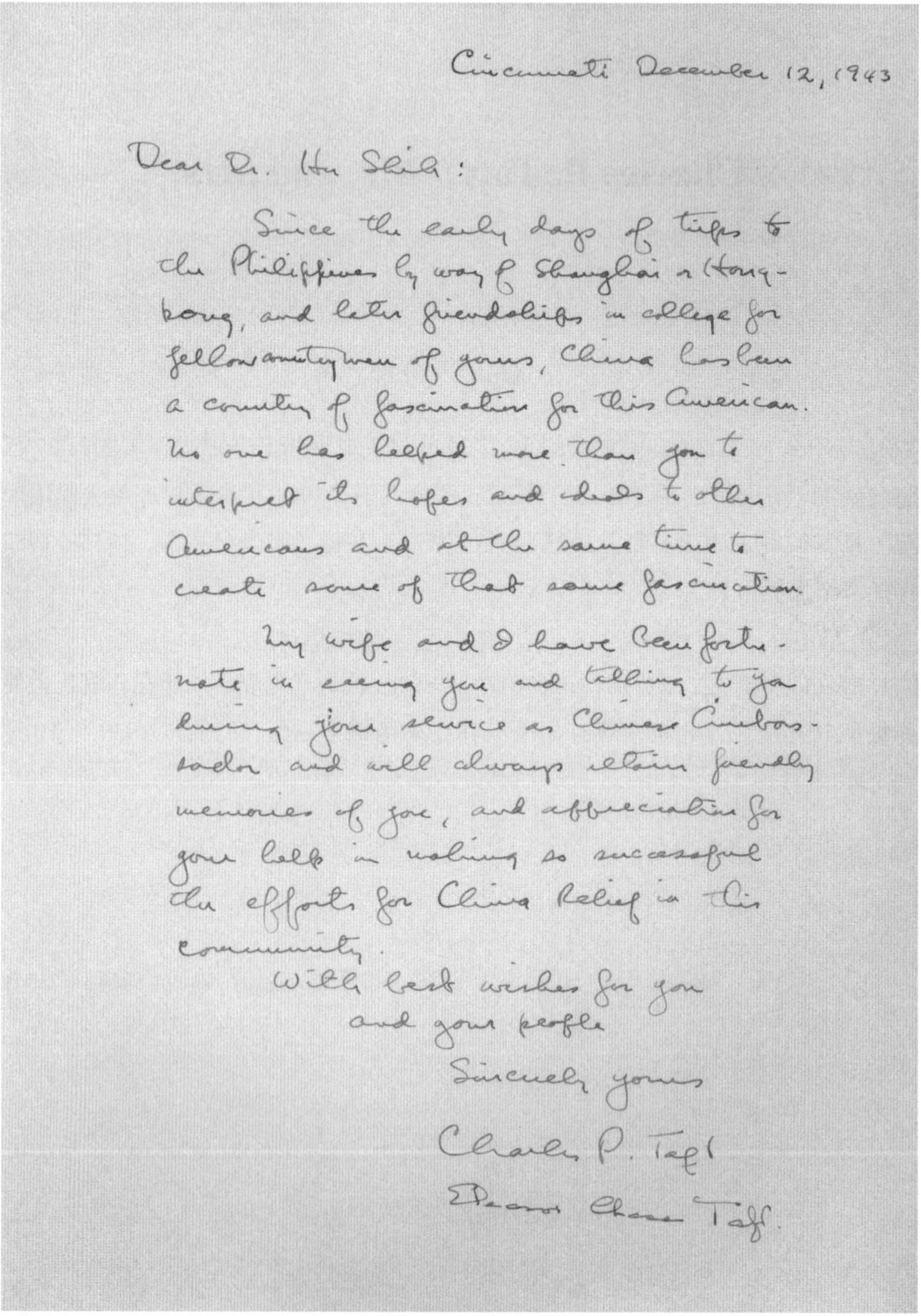

Cincinnati December 12, 1943

Dear Dr. Hu Shih:

Since the early days of trips to the Philippines by way of Shanghai & Hongkong, and later friendships in college for fellow countrymen of yours, China has been a country of fascination for this American. No one has helped more than you to interpret its hopes and ideals to other Americans and at the same time to create some of that same fascination.

My wife and I have been fortunate in seeing you and talking to you during your service as Chinese Ambassador and will always retain friendly memories of you, and appreciation for your help in making so successful the efforts for China Relief in this community.

With best wishes for you and your people

Sincerely yours
Charles P. Taft
Eleanor Chase Taft.

圖 1

Cincinnati December 12, 1943

Dear Dr. Hu Shih:

Since the early days of trips to the Philippines by way of Shanghai or Hong Kong, and later friendships in college for fellow countrymen of yours, China has been a country of fascination for this American. No one has helped more than you to interpret its hopes and ideals to other Americans and at the same time to create some of that same fascination.

My wife and I have been fortunate in seeing you and talking to you during your service as Chinese Ambassador and will always retain friendly memories of you, and appreciation for your help in making so successful the efforts for China Relief in this community.

With best wishes for you
and your people

Sincerely yours
Charles P. Taft
Eleanor Chase Taft

Charles S. Pharis

作者生平不詳。

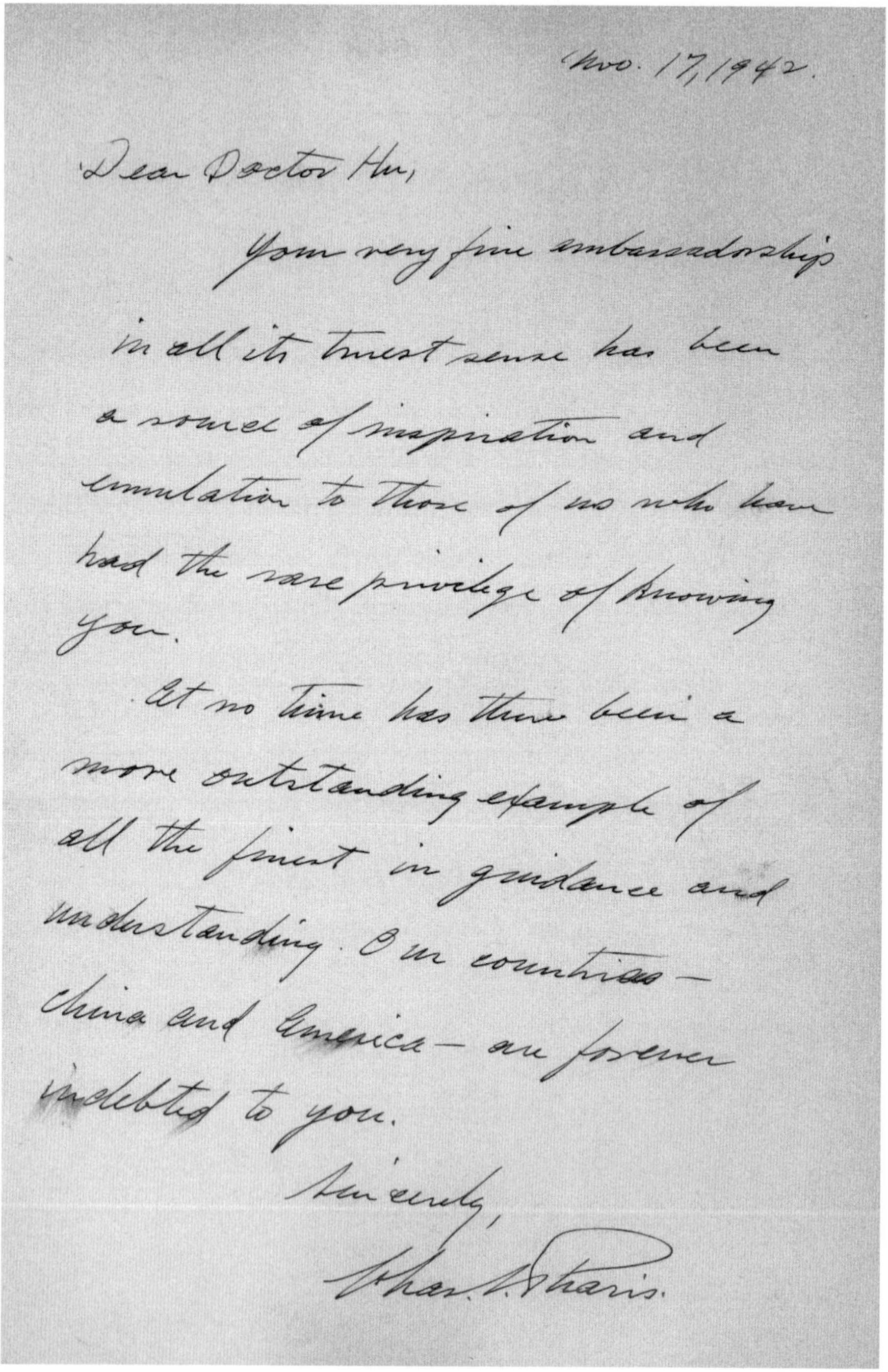

Nov. 17, 1942.

Dear Doctor Hu,

Your very fine embassadorship in all its truest sense has been a source of inspiration and emulation to those of us who have had the rare privilege of knowing you.

At no time has there been a more outstanding example of all the finest in guidance and understanding. Our countries — China and America — are forever indebted to you.

Sincerely,
Charles P. Tharis.

圖 1

Nov. 17, 1942

Dear Doctor Hu,

Your very fine ambassadorship in all its truest sense has been a source of inspiration and emulation to those of us who have had the rare privilege of knowing you.

At no time has there been a more outstanding example of all the finest in guidance and understanding. Our countries—China and America—are forever indebted to you.

Sincerely,
Charles S. Pharis

Charles Merz

　　Charles Merz（1893—1977），1938 年任《紐約時報》編輯，1961 年退休。胡適日記中有兩處提到 Merz，一處是 1939 年 6 月 20 日，提到"訪 Charles Merz"；一處是 1943 年 1 月 5 日，記錄到 Thomas Lamont 家晚飯，見到"美國人 Charles Merz 夫婦"。北京檔有 Merz 致胡適書信三封，時間爲 1942 年 11 月 6 日、1943 年 6 月 2 日、某年 11 月 25 日。

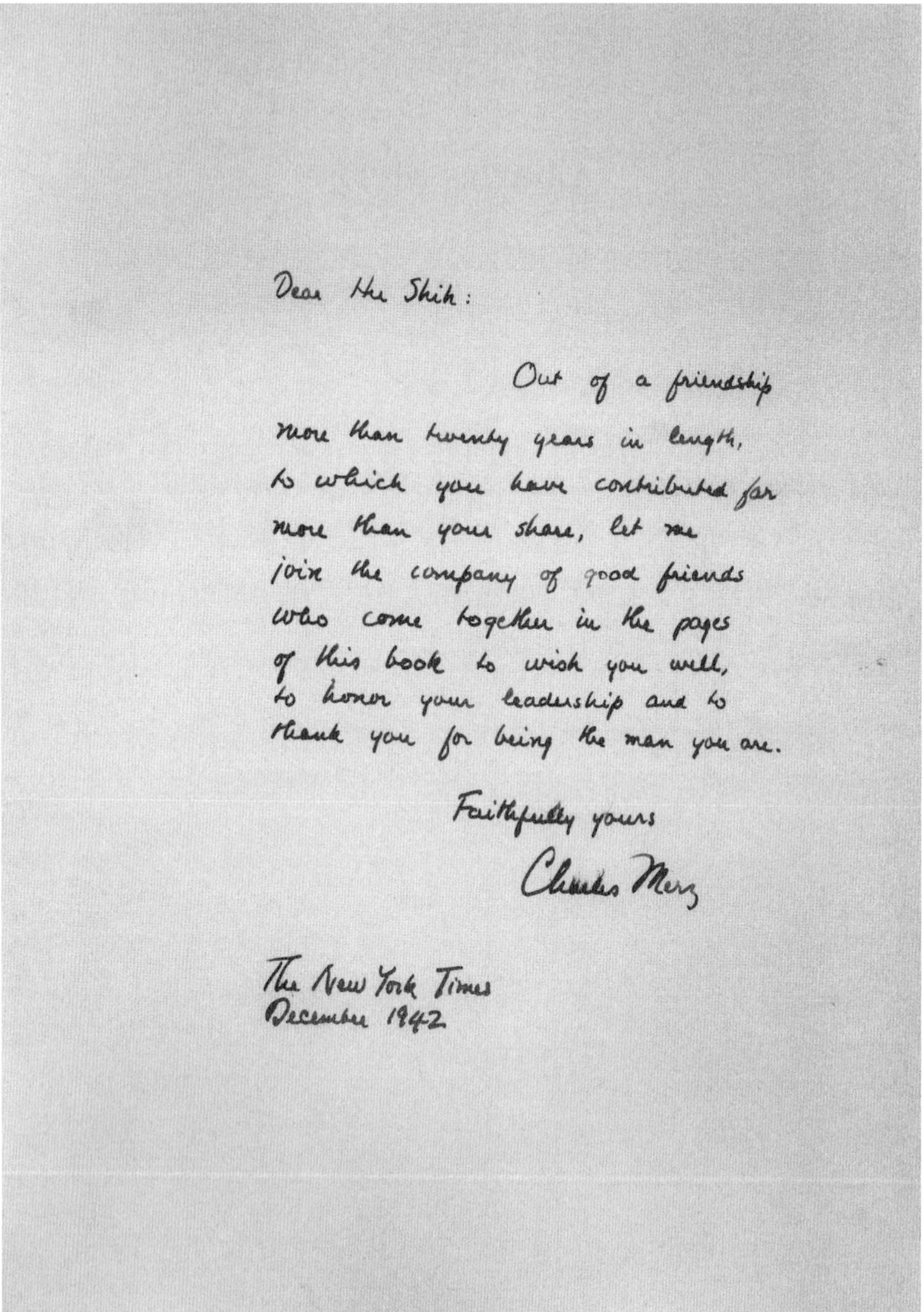

Dear Hu Shih:

　　Out of a friendship more than twenty years in length, to which you have contributed far more than your share, let me join the company of good friends who come together in the pages of this book to wish you well, to honor your leadership and to thank you for being the man you are.

　　　　　　　Faithfully yours
　　　　　　　Charles Merz

The New York Times
December 1942

圖 1

Dear Hu Shih:

Out of a friendship more than twenty years in length, to which you have contributed far more than your share, let me join the company of good friends who come together in the pages of this book to wish you well, to honor your leadership and to thank you for being the man you are.

Faithfully yours
Charles Merz

The New York Times
December 1942

Charles Seymour

  Charles Seymour（1885—1963），生於美國康涅狄格州紐黑文。1904年獲劍橋大學國王學院文學士學位，1908年獲耶魯大學文學士學位。1911年獲耶魯哲學博士學位。畢業後任教於耶魯大學，1918年任教授。1937—1951年任耶魯大學校長。北京檔有Charles Seymour與胡適往來書信電報及胡適私人秘書代復書信共五通，主要内容爲邀請胡適參加耶魯大學活動。

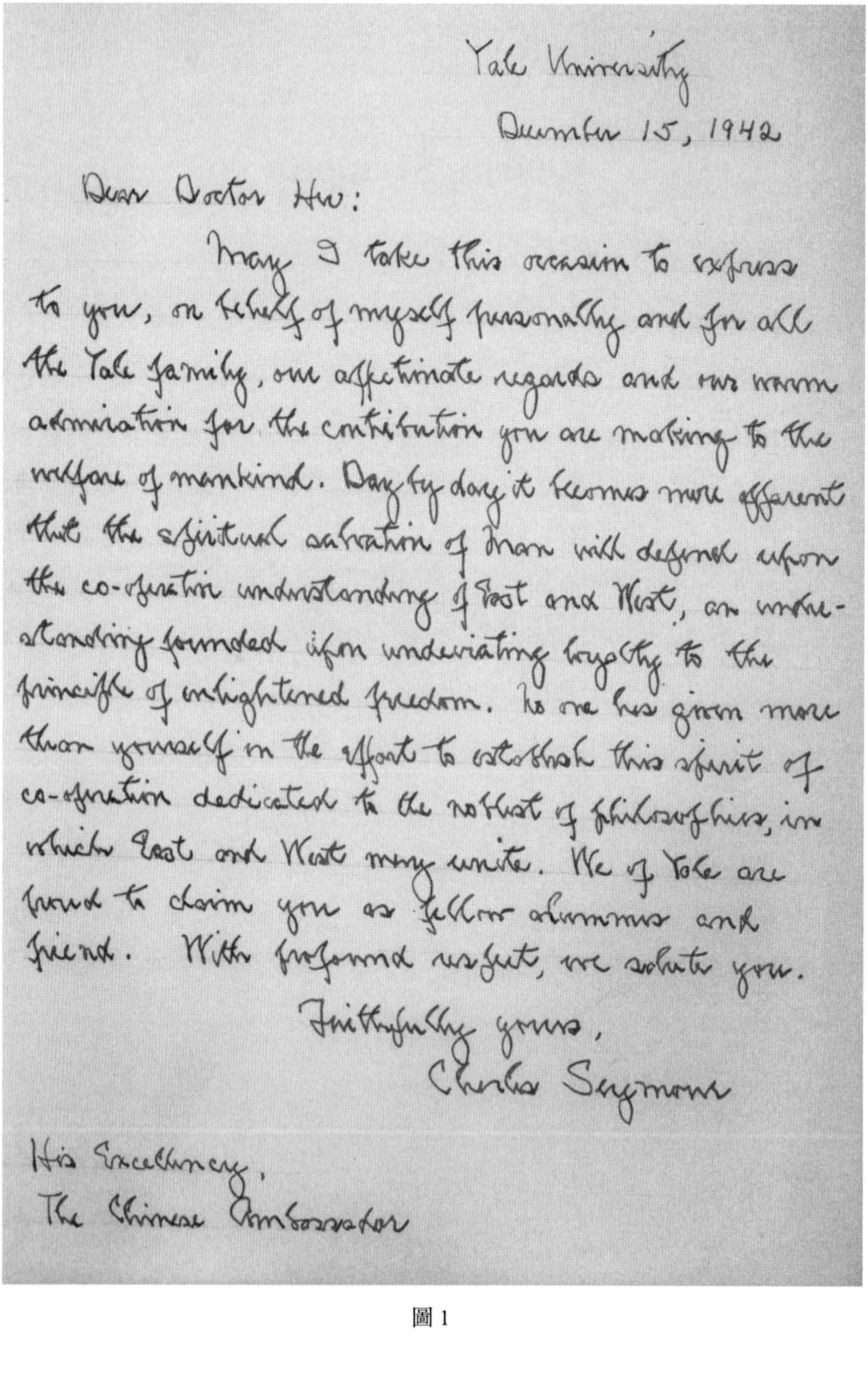

> Yale University
> December 15, 1942
>
> Dear Doctor Hu:
>
> May I take this occasion to express to you, on behalf of myself personally and for all the Yale family, our affectionate regards and our warm admiration for the contribution you are making to the welfare of mankind. Day by day it becomes more apparent that the spiritual salvation of man will depend upon the co-operative understanding of East and West, an understanding founded upon undeviating loyalty to the principle of enlightened freedom. No one has given more than yourself in the effort to establish this spirit of co-operation dedicated to the noblest of philosophies, in which East and West may unite. We of Yale are proud to claim you as fellow alumnus and friend. With profound respect, we salute you.
>
> Faithfully yours,
> Charles Seymour
>
> His Excellency,
> The Chinese Ambassador

圖 1

Yale University
December 15, 1942

Dear Doctor Hu:

May I take this occasion to express to you, on behalf of myself personally and for all the Yale family, our affectionate regards and our warm admiration for the contribution you are making to the welfare of mankind. Day by day it becomes more apparent that the spiritual salvation of man will depend upon the co-operative understanding of East and West, an understanding formed upon undeviation loyalty to the principle of enlightened freedom. No one has given more than yourself in the effort to establish this spirit of co-operation dedicated to the noblest of philosophies, in which East and West may unite. We of Yale are proud to claim you as fellow alumnus and friend. With profound respect, we salute you.

Faithfully yours,
Charles Seymour

His Excellency,
The Chinese Ambassador

Charles Stewart Mott

　　Charles Stewart Mott（1875—1973），生於美國新澤西州。1897年畢業於斯蒂文斯理工學院，美國通用汽車聯合創辦人。1912—1914年、1918—1919年兩度任密歇根州弗林特市市長。

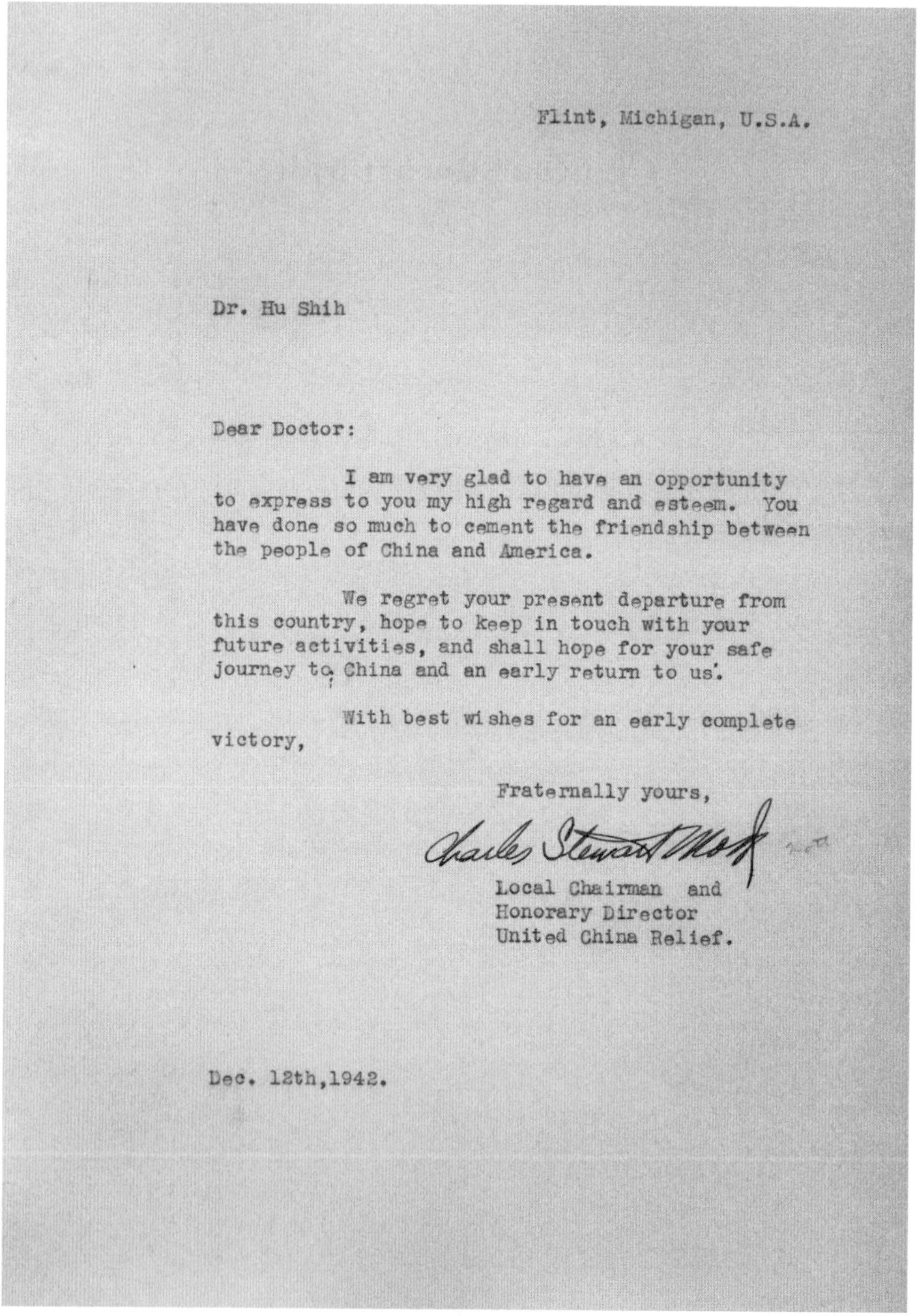

Flint, Michigan, U.S.A.

Dr. Hu Shih

Dear Doctor:

  I am very glad to have an opportunity to express to you my high regard and esteem. You have done so much to cement the friendship between the people of China and America.

  We regret your present departure from this country, hope to keep in touch with your future activities, and shall hope for your safe journey to China and an early return to us.

  With best wishes for an early complete victory,

        Fraternally yours,

        Charles Stewart Mott

        Local Chairman and
        Honorary Director
        United China Relief.

Dec. 12th, 1942.

圖 1

Chester H. Rowell

Chester H. Rowell（1867—1948），生於美國伊利諾伊州布盧明頓。1888 年畢業於密歇根大學。畢業後到柏林、巴黎、羅馬游學三年。1898 年任 *Fresno Morning Republican* 編輯和主管。1907 年任林肯 - 羅斯福聯盟合夥人和主席。1911 年任加州大學伯克利分校新聞學講師，1927—1934 年在斯坦福大學主講政治學。1932—1939 年任《舊金山紀事報》編輯。

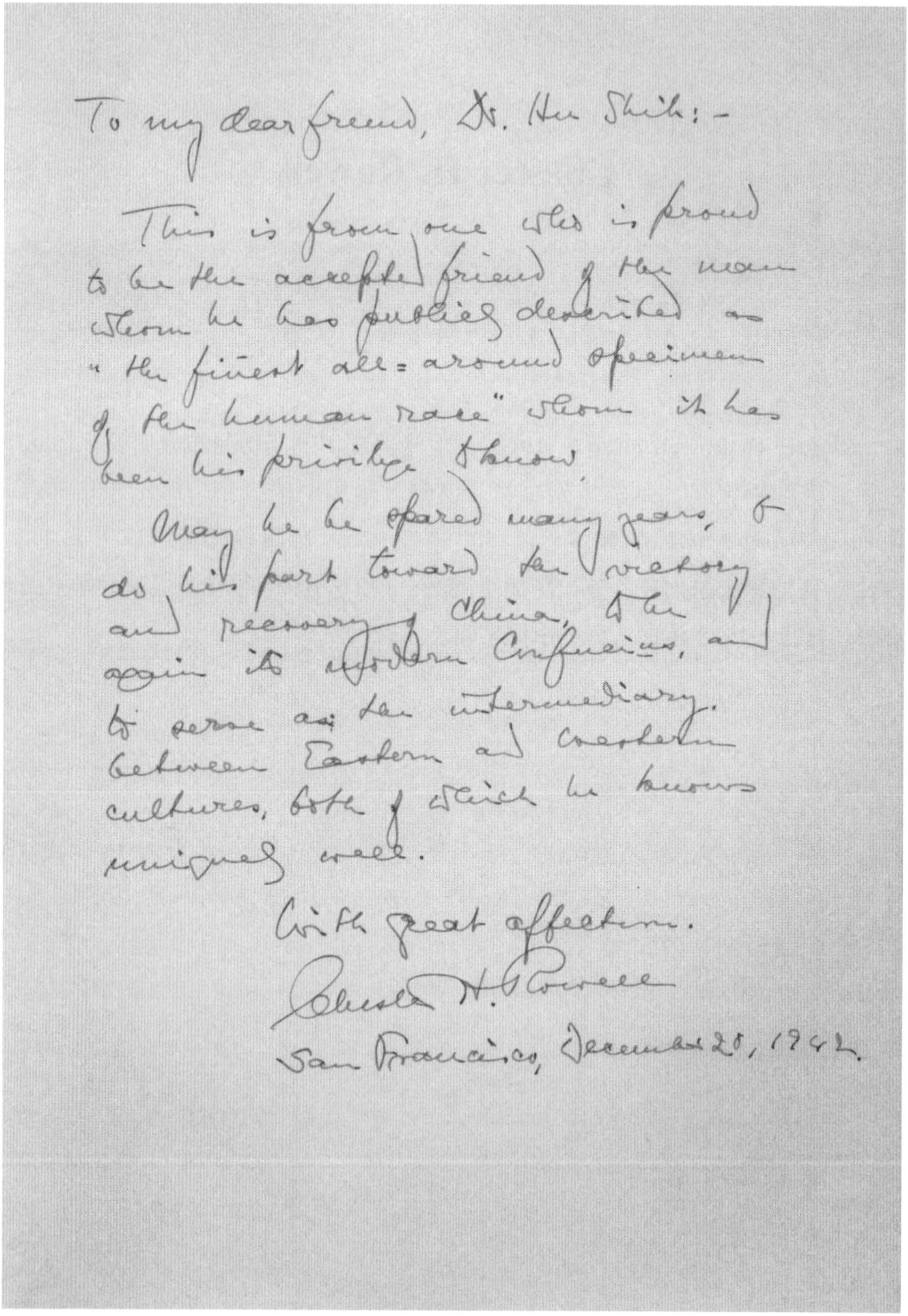

To my dear friend, Dr. Hu Shih:—

This is from one who is proud to be the accepted friend of the man whom he has publicly described as "the finest all-around specimen of the human race" whom it has been his privilege to know.

May he be spared many years, to do his part toward the victory and recovery of China, to be again its modern Confucius, and to serve as the intermediary between Eastern and Western cultures, both of which he knows uniquely well.

With great affection.

Chester H. Rowell

San Francisco, December 20, 1942.

圖 1

To my dear friend, Dr. Hu Shih:—

This is from one who is proud to be the accepted friend of the man whom he has publicly described as "the finest all-around specimen of the human race" whom it has been his privilege to know.

May he be spared many years, & do his part toward the victory and recovery of China, to be again its wisdom Confucius, and to serve as the intermediary between Eastern and Western cultures, both of which he knows uniquely well.

With great affection,
Chester H. Rowell
San Francisco, December 20, 1942.

Clarence E. Pickett

　　Clarence E. Pickett（1884—1965），生於貴格會家庭。早年就讀於哈佛神學院。後在多倫多和奧斯卡盧薩貴格會教區作牧師。1929—1950 年任美國教友會總幹事長。1947 年獲諾貝爾和平獎。

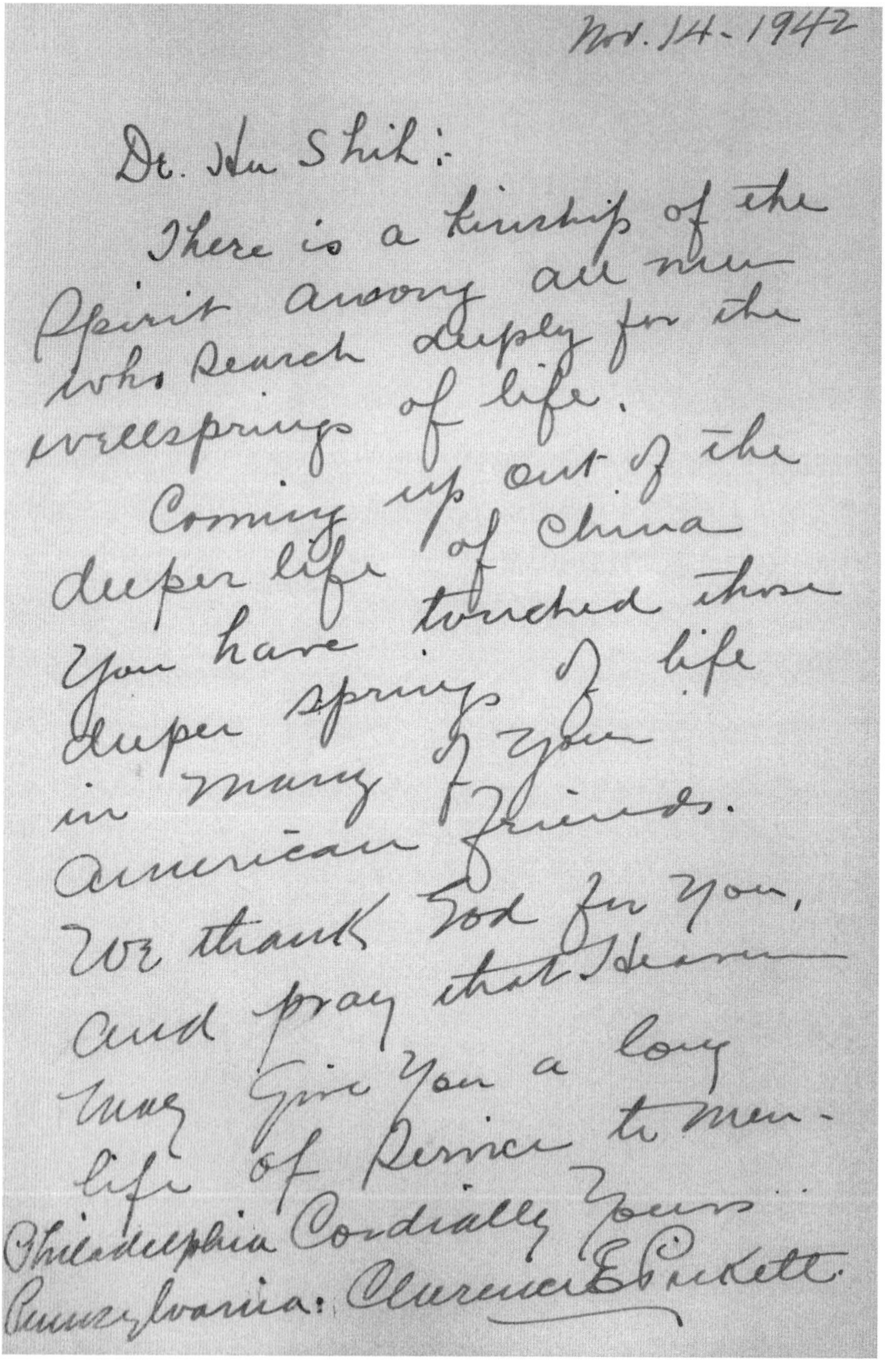

Nov. 14 - 1942

Dr. Hu Shih:

There is a kinship of the spirit among all men who search deeply for the wellsprings of life.

Coming up out of the deeper life of China you have touched those deeper springs of life in many of your American friends.

We thank God for you, and pray that Heaven may give you a long life of service to men.

Philadelphia Pennsylvania

Cordially Yours,
Clarence E. Pickett.

圖1

Nov. 14, 1942

Dr. Hu Shih:

There is a kinship of the spirit among all men who search deeply for the wellsprings of life.

Coming up out of the deeper life of China you have touched those deeper springs of life in many of your American friends.

We thank God for you, and pray that Heaven may give you a long life of service to men.

Cordially yours
Clarence E. Pickett

Philadelphia
Pennsylvania

Clark H. Minor

　　Clark H. Minor（？—1967），曾任美國通用電氣公司總裁，執行委員會主席，曾任"中美協進會"（China Society of America）榮譽會長。北京檔有 Clark H. Minor 致胡適書信兩封，時間分別爲 1942 年 9 月 3 日、1943 年 4 月 26 日，第一封信是對胡適卸任駐美大使的惋惜，以及對他的貢獻的評價等。第二封信主要是邀請胡適出席一個午宴並發表演講。臺北胡適紀念館藏有 Clark H. Minor 與 Mansfield Freeman 致胡適書信一封，報告"中美協進會"將於 1961 年底停止活動。

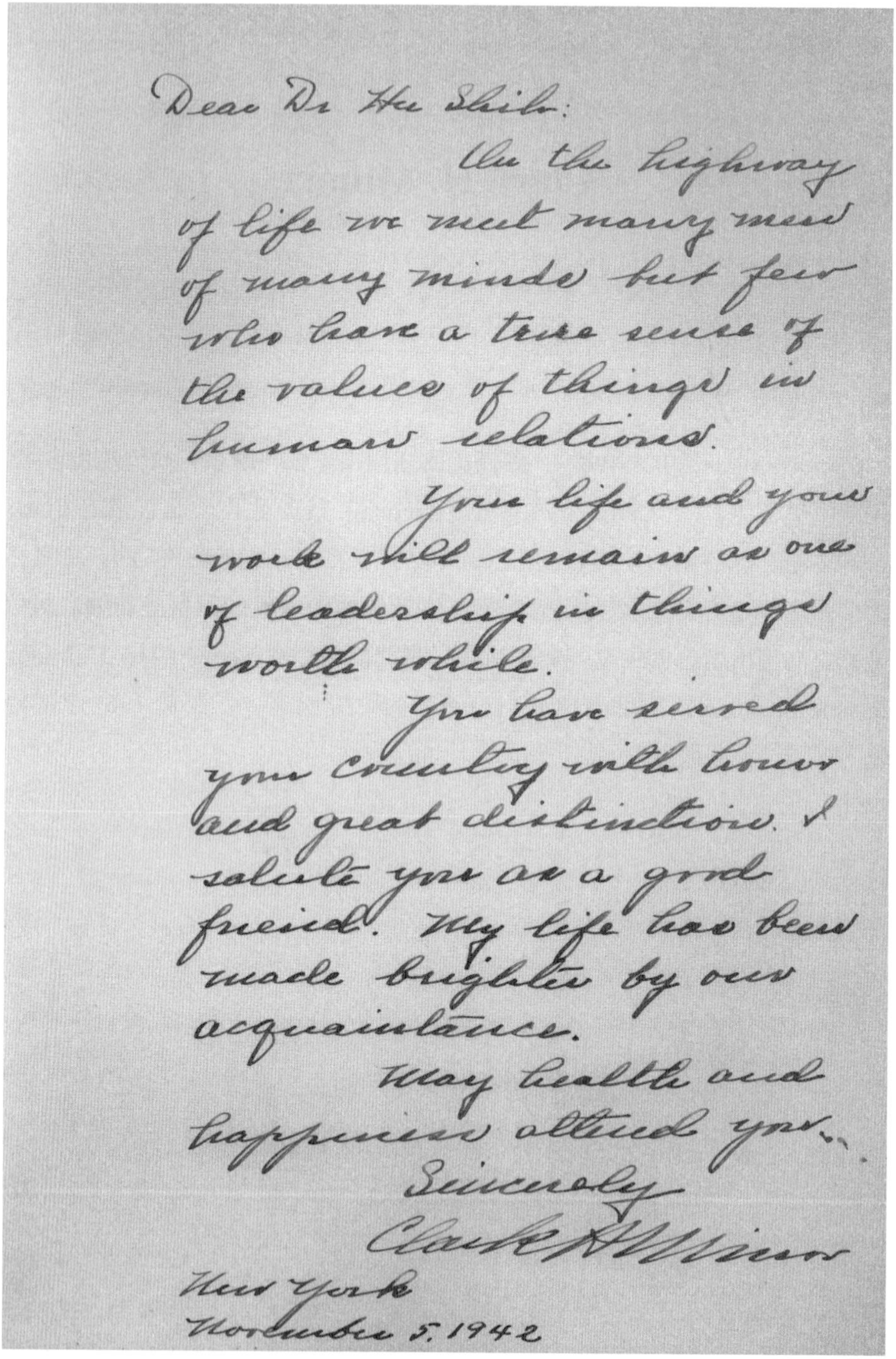

Dear Dr Hu Shih:

On the highway of life we meet many men of many minds but few who have a true sense of the values of things in human relations.

Your life and your work will remain as one of leadership in things worth while.

You have served your country with honor and great distinction. I salute you as a good friend. My life has been made brighter by our acquaintance.

May health and happiness attend you.

Sincerely
Clark Wissler

New York
November 5, 1942

圖1

Dear Dr. Hu Shih:

On the highway of life we meet many men of many minds but few who have a true sense of the values of things in human relations.

Your life and your work will remain as one of leadership in things worth while.

You have served your country with honor and great distinction. I salute you as a good friend. My life has been made brighter by our acquaintance.

May health and happiness attend you.

Sincerely
Clark H. Minor

New York
November 5, 1942

Claude E. Forkner

　　Claude E. Forkner（1900—1992），生於美國蒙大拿州，醫學博士。早年曾在北京協和醫學院任職五年。曾任泛美醫學會內科學部部長，康奈爾大學醫學院臨床醫學教授，紐約醫院主治醫師，哥倫比亞大學師範學院董事會成員。曾長期擔任伊朗沙阿穆罕默德·禮薩·巴勒維的私人醫生。北京檔有 Claude E. Forkner 致胡適書信一封，時間爲 1943 年 2 月 24 日，主要内容爲請胡適幫助起一個好的中文名字。

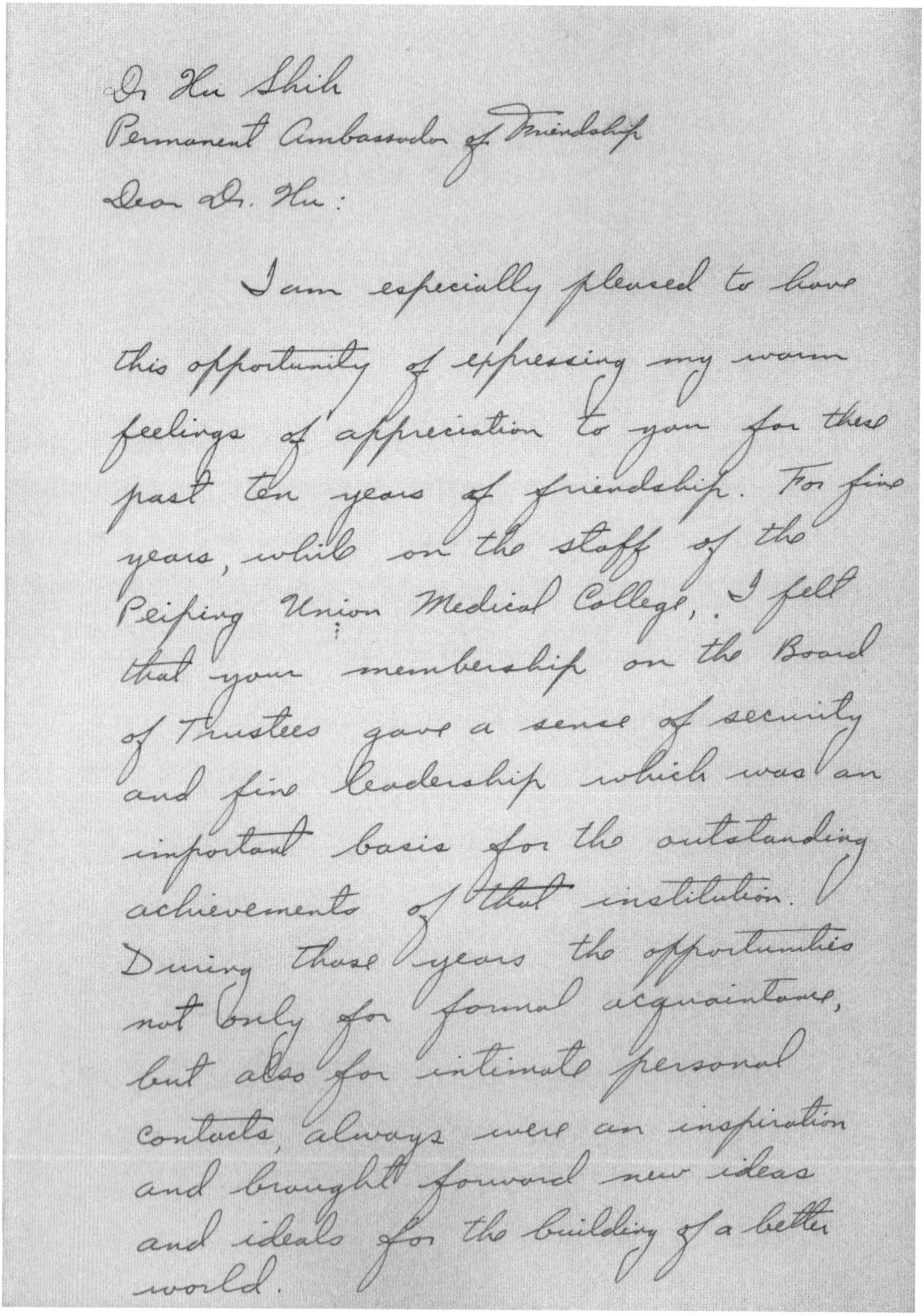

Dr Hu Shih
Permanent Ambassador of Friendship

Dear Dr. Hu:

I am especially pleased to have this opportunity of expressing my warm feelings of appreciation to you for these past ten years of friendship. For five years, while on the staff of the Peiping Union Medical College, I felt that your membership on the Board of Trustees gave a sense of security and fine leadership which was an important basis for the outstanding achievements of that institution. During those years the opportunities not only for formal acquaintance, but also for intimate personal contacts, always were an inspiration and brought forward new ideas and ideals for the building of a better world.

圖 1

Dr. Hu Shih

Permanent Ambassador of Friendship

Dear Dr. Hu:

I am especially pleased to have this opportunity of expressing my warm feelings of appreciation to you for these past ten years of friendship. For five years, while on the staff of the Peiping Union Medical College, I felt that your membership on the Board of Trustees gave a sense of security and fine leadership which was an important basis for the outstanding achievements of that institution. During these years the opportunities not only for acquaintance, but also for intimate personal contacts, always were an inspiration and brought forward new ideas and ideals for the building of a better world.

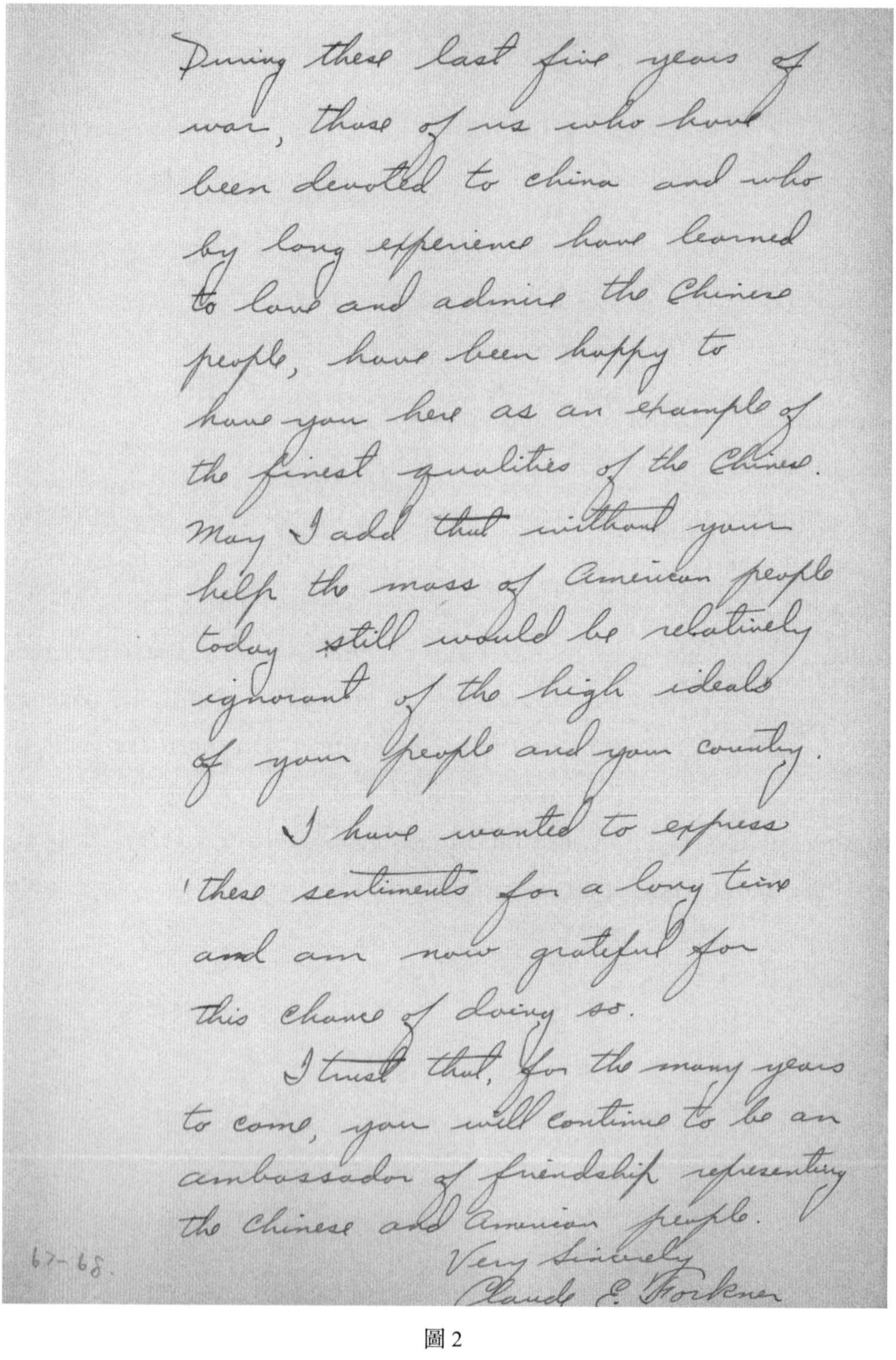

During these last five years of war, those of us who have been devoted to China and who by long experience have learned to love and admire the Chinese people, have been happy to have you here as an example of the finest qualities of the Chinese. May I add that without your help the mass of American people today still would be relatively ignorant of the high ideals of your people and your country.

I have wanted to express these sentiments for a long time and am now grateful for this chance of doing so.

I trust that, for the many years to come, you will continue to be an ambassador of friendship representing the Chinese and American people.

Very sincerely
Claude E. Forkner

圖 2

During these last five years of war, those of us who have been devoted to China and who by long experience have learned to love and admire the Chinese people, have been happy to have you here as an example of the finest qualities of the Chinese. May I add that without your help the mass of American people today still would be relatively ignorant of the high ideals of your people and your country.

I have wanted to express these sentiments for a long time and am now grateful for this chance of doing so.

I trust that, for the many years to come, you will continue to be an ambassador of friendship representing the Chinese and American People.

Very Sincerely
Claude E. Forkner

Claude R. Wickard

Claude R. Wickard（1893—1967），生於美國印第安那州卡羅爾，時任美國農業部部長。1915年畢業於普渡大學，獲農學士學位。1932年任美國農業部副部長，1940—1945年任部長。

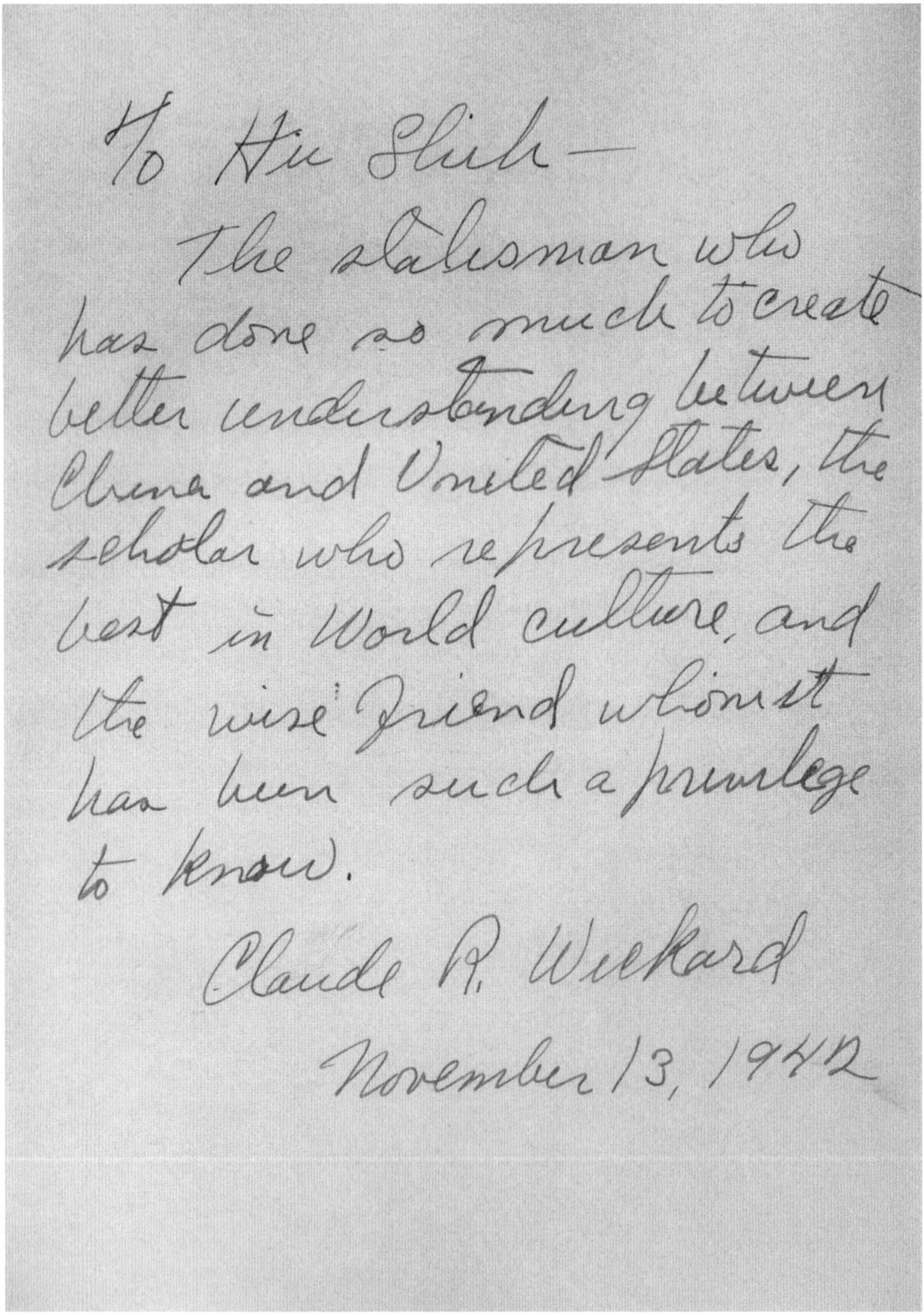

> To Hu Shih —
>
> The statesman who has done so much to create better understanding between China and United States, the scholar who represents the best in World culture, and the wise friend whom it has been such a privilege to know.
>
> Claude R. Wickard
> November 13, 1942

圖 1

To Hu Shih—

The statesman who has done so much to create better understanding between China and United States, the scholar who represents the best in world culture, and the wise friend whom it has been such a privilege to know.

Claude R. Wickard
November 13, 1942

Cordell Hull

　　Cordell Hull（1871—1955），生於美國田納西州，美國政治家，時任美國國務卿。1891 年畢業於美國坎伯蘭大學法學院。1907—1921、1923—1931 年任美國衆議院議員。1930 年當選參議員。1933 至 1944 年爲第 47 任美國國務卿，1945 年獲諾貝爾和平獎。胡適在任駐美大使前後與 Cordell Hull 有過交往，北京檔有胡適與 Cordell Hull 往來書信五封，時間跨度從 1939 年 7 月到 1942 年 9 月。

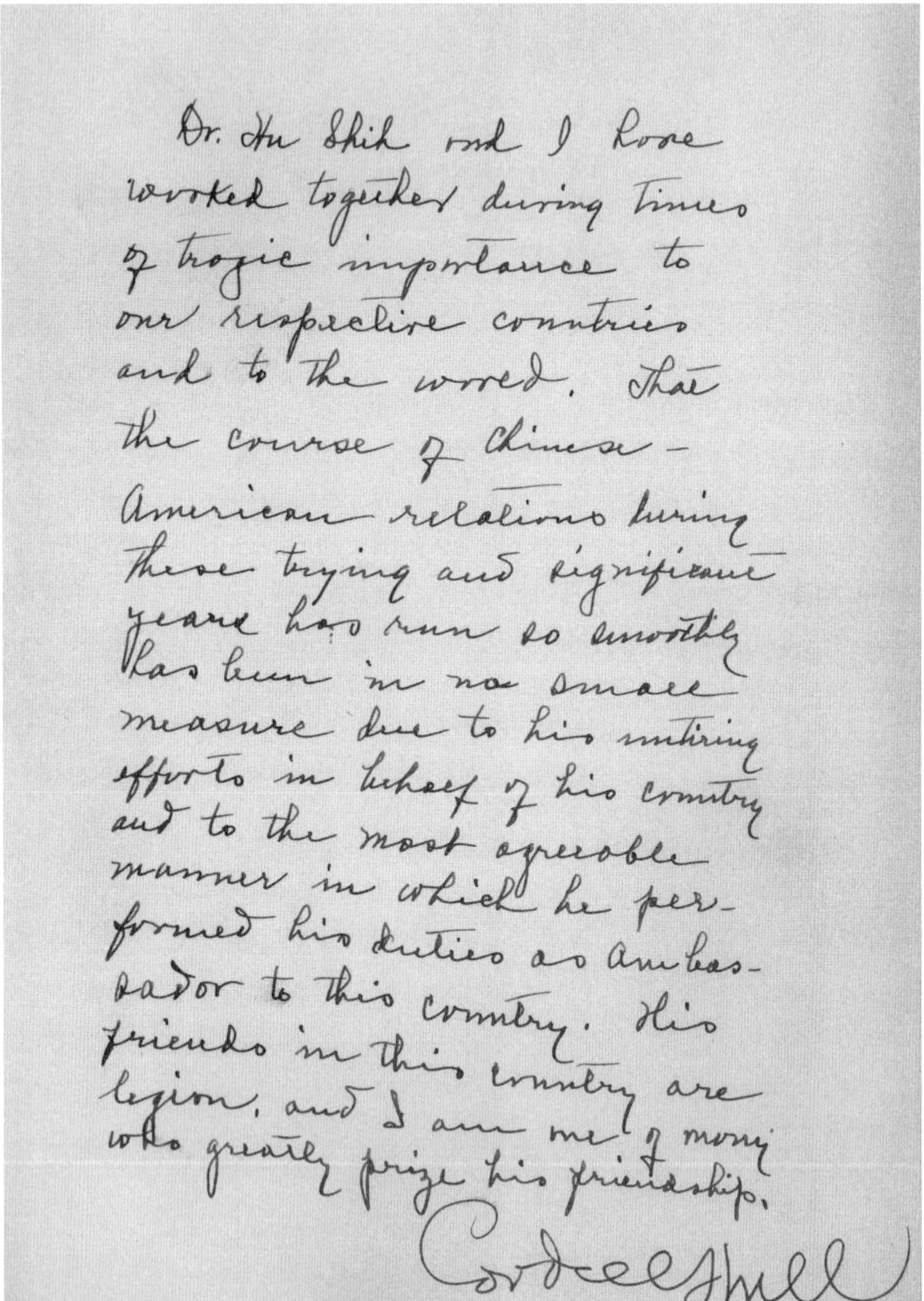

Dr. Hu Shih and I have worked together during times of tragic importance to our respective countries and to the world. That the course of Chinese-American relations during these trying and significant years has run so smoothly has been in no small measure due to his untiring efforts in behalf of his country and to the most agreeable manner in which he performed his duties as Ambassador to this country. His friends in this country are legion, and I am one of many who greatly prize his friendship.

Cordell Hull

圖 1

Dr. Hu Shih and I have worked together during times of tragic importance to our respective countries and to the world. That the course of Chinese-American relations during these trying and significant years has run so smoothly has been in no small measure due to his untiring efforts in behalf of his country and to the most agreeable manner in which he performed his duties as ambassador to this country. His friends in this country are legion, and I am one of many who greatly prize his friendship.

Cordell Hull

Daniel W. Bell

　　Daniel W. Bell（1891—1971），生於美國伊利諾伊州，早年獲傑姆城市學院文學學士、美國國家大學法學士、東南大學文學碩士學位，1934—1939年任美國預算局局長。時任美國財政部副部長。

> Washington, D.C., Nov. 17, 1942
>
> My dear Dr. Hu:
>
> I can not allow you to leave Washington without telling you that your retirement has left a sense of loss much deeper than the usual conventional regret at the departure of a respected and esteemed envoy. This sense of loss is tempered by the realization that you will continue, wherever you are, to be active in the cause of your great country.
>
> It must be a source of great satisfaction to you, as it is to your many friends, that your work here has resulted in such a true understanding between China and the United States, a relationship which, built upon the solid foundation of friendship, will continue and grow even stronger through the years to come.
>
> I hope that our paths may cross many times in the future.
>
> With best wishes, I remain
>
> Most sincerely yours,
>
> A.C.W.Bell

圖1

Washington, D. C., Nov. 17, 1942

My dear Dr. Hu:

I can not allow you to leave Washington without telling you that your retirement has left a sense of loss much deeper than the usual conventional regret at the departure of a respected and esteemed envoy. This sense of loss is tempered by the realization that you will continue, wherever you are, to be active in the cause of your great country.

It must be a source of great satisfaction to you, as it is to your many friends, that your work here has resulted in such a true understanding between China and the United States, a relationship which, built upon the solid foundation of friendship, will continue and grow even stronger through the years to come.

I hope that our paths may cross many times in the future.

With best wishes, I remain

Most sincerely yours,
D. W. Bell

Dave Hennen Morris

Dave Hennen Morris（1872—1944），生於美國路易斯安納州新奧爾良。1896年畢業於哈佛大學，1901年畢業於紐約法學院。1909年獲哥倫比亞大學法學碩士學位。曾任聖路易斯西南鐵路公司副總裁。1933—1937年任美國駐比利時大使。爲美國航空協會和美國汽車協會創立人。胡適任駐美大使前後與此人有交往，北京檔有其致胡適函電兩封，時間爲1942年10月和11月，內容均爲邀請胡適演講。

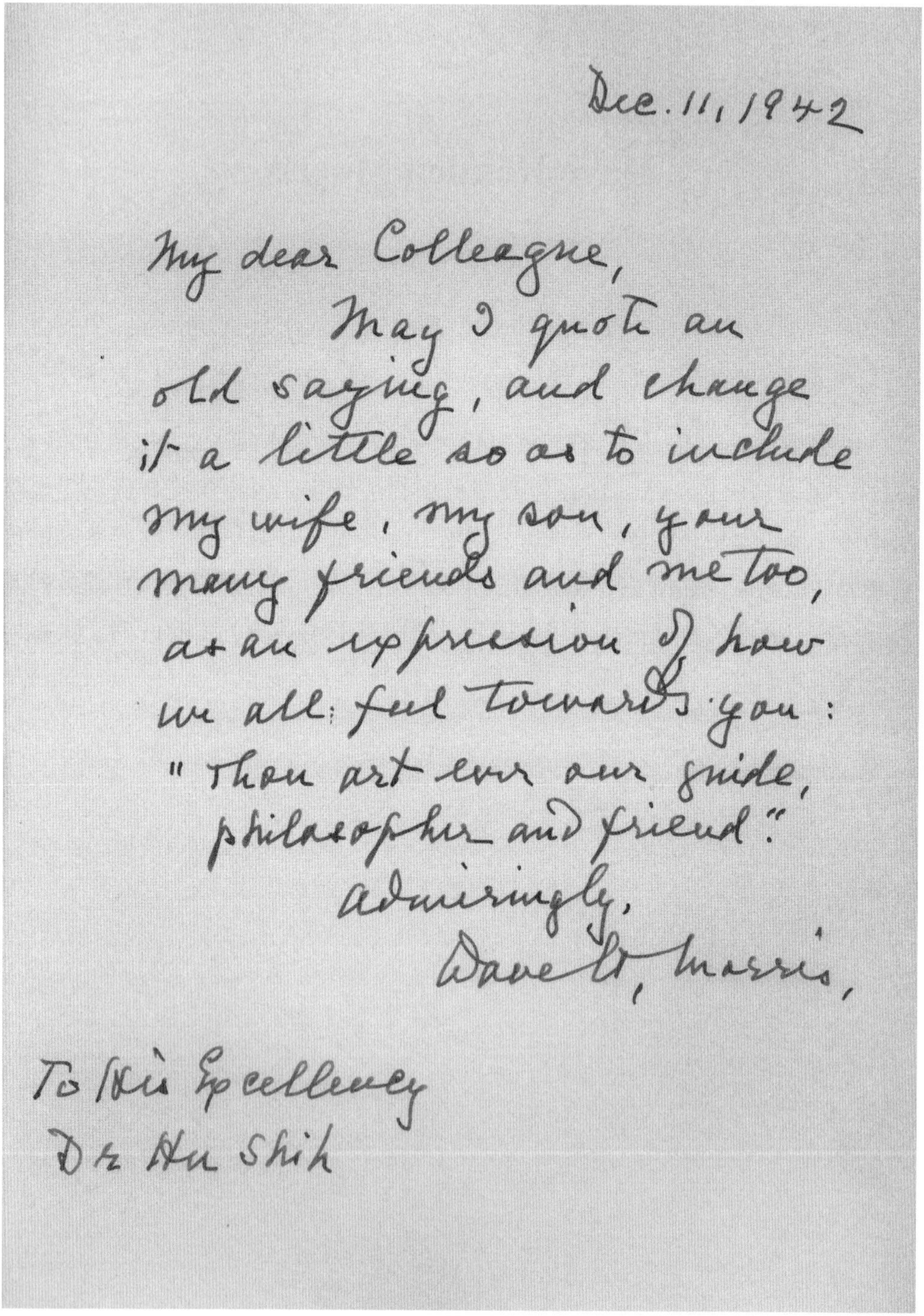

Dec. 11, 1942

My dear Colleague,

May I quote an old saying, and change it a little so as to include my wife, my son, your many friends and me too, as an expression of how we all feel towards you:

"Thou art ever our guide, philosopher and friend."

Admiringly,

Dave H. Morris,

To His Excellency
Dr. Hu Shih

圖 1

Dec. 11, 1942

My dear Colleague,

May I quote an old saying, and change it a little so as to include my wife, my son, your many friends and me too, at an expression of how we all feel towards you:

"Thou art ever our guide, philosopher and friend."

Admiringly,
Dave Hennen Morris

To His Excellency
Dr. Hu Shih

David O. Selznick

David O. Selznick（1902—1965），生於美國匹茲堡。著名電影製片人和劇本作家。早年就讀於哥倫比亞大學，後到好萊塢米高梅公司擔任故事編輯助理，1928—1931年轉到派拉蒙電影公司。1933年重回米高梅。以拍攝《飄》和《蝴蝶夢》而著名。

Dear Dr. Hu,

Your presence in America has been a source of inspiration to all who have had even remote contact with you. Few men from other lands have elicited such complete and unanimous admiration, in our times; fewer still have simultaneously won an enormously increased understanding of their own people.

Speaking for Hollywood, I can say that in your brief stays here you won the hearts of all, and the respect of the entire motion picture world — for both yourself and the great nation you so ably represented.

You have contributed nobly to the cause of the United Nations, and also to that even greater cause, the Brotherhood of Man.

It shall always be a source of pleasure to my future, as it has been of honour to my past, to have known you.

David O. Selznick

November, 1942.

圖 1

Dear Dr. Hu,

Your presence in America has been a source of inspiration to all who have had even remote contact with you. Few men from other lands have elicited such complete and unanimous admiration, in our times; fewer still have simultaneously won an enormously increased understanding of their own people.

Speaking for Hollywood, I can say that in your brief stays here you won the hearts of all, and the respect of the entire motion picture world—for both yourself and the great nation you so ably represented.

You have contributed nobly to the cause of the United Nations, and also to that even greater cause, the Brotherhood of Man.

It shall always be a source of pleasure to my future, as it has been of honour to my past, to have known you.

David O. Selznick

November, 1942

Donald D. Van Slyke

　　Donald D. Van Slyke（1883—1971），生於美國紐約州。1905 年、1907 年分別獲密歇根大學文學士和哲學博士學位。博士畢業後到洛克菲勒學院從事博士後研究，1911 年曾到柏林從事研究一年。1914 年被聘爲新成立的洛克菲勒學院附屬醫院首席化學家，主要從事人體組織中氣體和電解質的測量研究，爲血液定量化學的創始人之一。1948 年任新成立的布魯克海文國家實驗室生物學和醫學副主任。胡適任駐美大使前後與此人有交往，北京檔有胡適與其往來書信七封，時間從 1942 年 1 月到 1947 年 12 月。

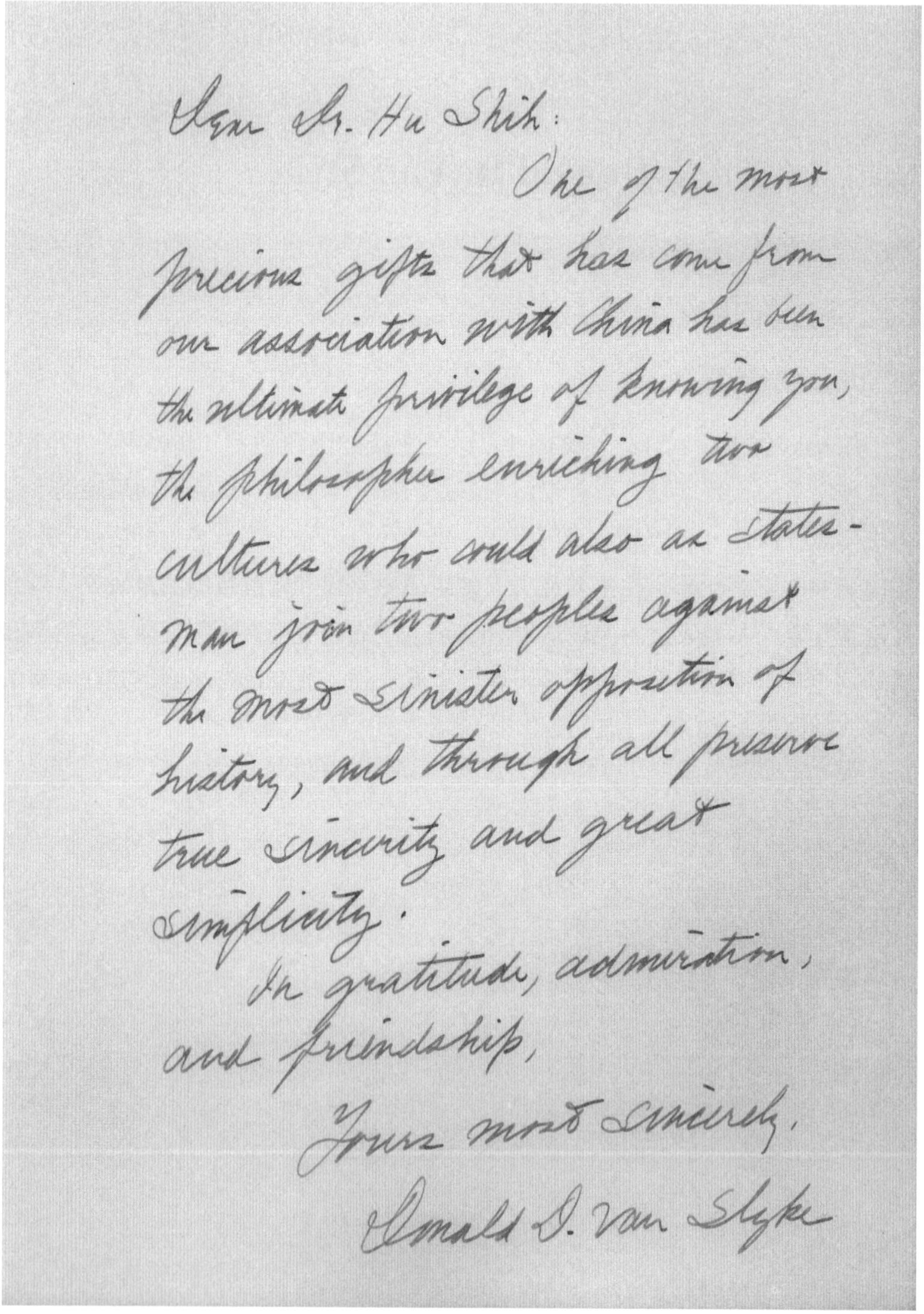

Dear Dr. Hu Shih:

One of the most precious gifts that has come from our association with China has been the ultimate privilege of knowing you, the philosopher enriching two cultures who could also as statesman join two peoples against the most sinister opposition of history, and through all preserve true sincerity and great simplicity.

In gratitude, admiration, and friendship,

Yours most sincerely,

Donald D. van Slyke

圖 1

Dear Dr. Hu Shih:

One of the most precious gifts that has come from our association with China has been the ultimate privilege of knowing you, the philosopher enriching two cultures who could also as statesman join two peoples against the most sinister opposition of history, and through all preserve true sincerity and great simplicity.

In gratitude, admiration, and friendship,

Yours most sincerely,
Donald D. Van Slyke

Dorothy Canfield Fisher

　　Dorothy Canfield Fisher（1879—1958），美國教育改革者、社會活動家、暢銷作家。生於美國堪薩斯州。1899 年畢業於俄亥俄州立大學，後到巴黎大學和哥倫比亞大學學習語言，1904 年獲哥倫比亞大學博士學位。曾獲達特茅斯學院、內布拉斯加大學等多所高校榮譽學位。一戰期間曾隨丈夫到巴黎，爲盲人老兵建立盲文印刷廠，並爲難民兒童建立療養院。曾廣泛參與教育和政治方面的社會活動。最著名的著作爲兒童讀物 *Understood Betsy*。

From
Dorothy Canfield Fisher
Arlington Vermont
November 12, 1942

The hurricane of calamity has beaten us out from old limits of race and nationality. Intelligent people no longer feel themselves members only of their own race, their own class, their own nationality. The solidarity we now feel is with the human race. We know that our fate depends on the survival of that part of humanity which deserves to survive.

Our hope —— it has been at times no more than a pale glimmer in the darkness —— is that our poor faulty race has enough nobility, intelligence, selflessness and endurance to outweigh its blackly evil qualities which have brought us to the present tragic crisis. Of this hope Dr. Hu Shih is one of the greatest bulwarks. We are his, and we give him the warmest gratitude for being a shining proof of human worth, one of our family circle whom we can present to Destiny as evidence that humanity deserves to go on living.

圖 1

From Dorothy Canfield Fisher

Arlington Vermont
November 12, 1942

The hurricane of calamity has beaten us out from old limits of race and nationality. Intelligent people no longer feel themselves member only of their own race, their own class, their own nationality. The solidarity we now feel is with the human race. We know that our fate depends on the survival of that part of humanity which deserves to survive.

Our hope—it has been at times no more than a pale glimmer in the darkness—is that our poor faulty race has enough nobility, intelligence, selflessness and endurance to outweigh its blackly evil qualities which have brought us to the present tragic crisis. Of this hope Dr. Hu Shih is one of the greatest bulwarks. We owe him, and we give him the warmest gratitude for being a shining proof of human worth, one of our family circle whom we can present to Destiny as evidence that humanity deserves to go on living.

Douglas Auchincloss

作者生平不詳。

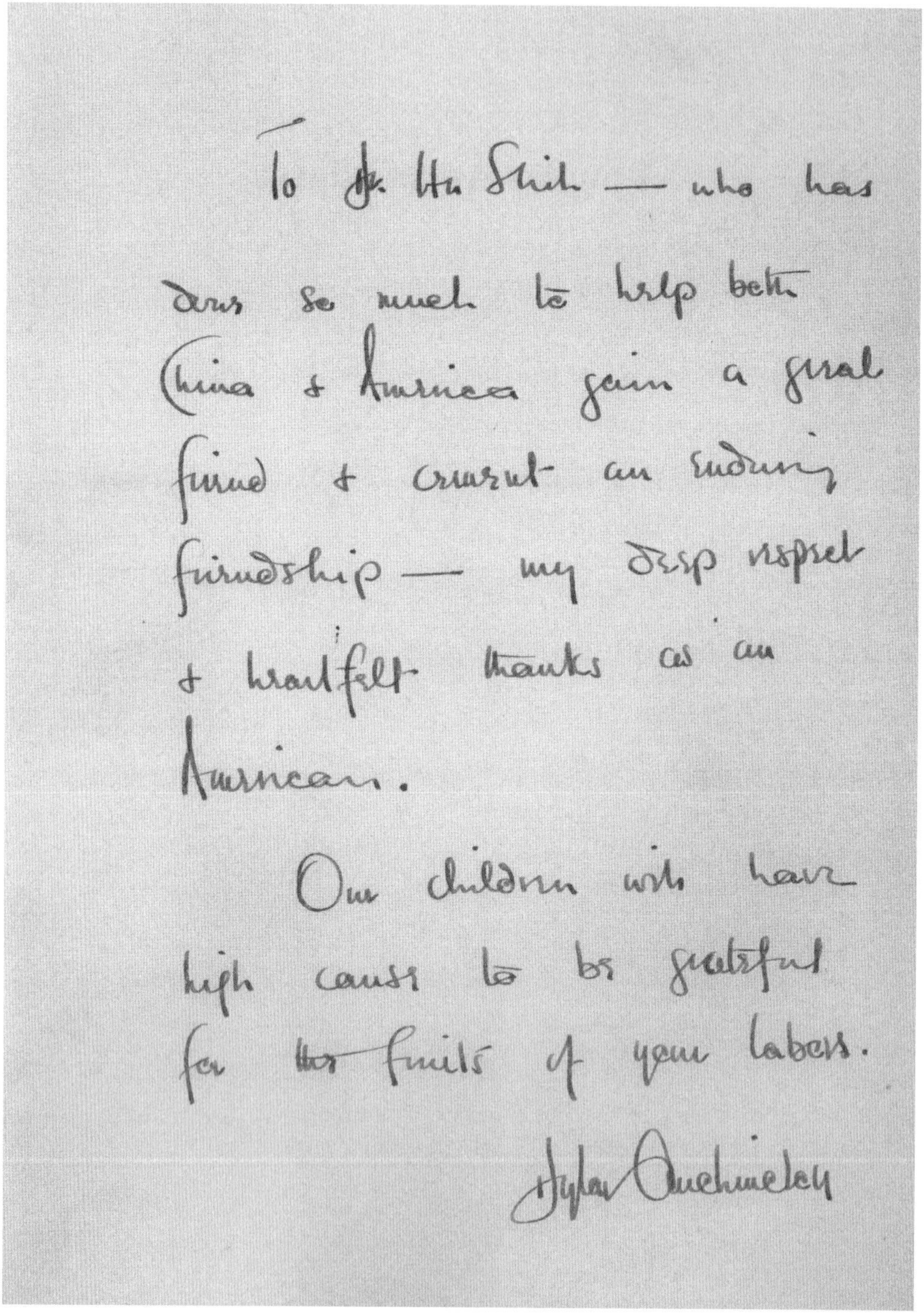

To Dr. Hu Shih — who has done so much to help both China & America gain a great friend & cement an enduring friendship — my deep respect & heartfelt thanks as an American.

Our children will have high cause to be grateful for the fruits of your labors.

Hugh Auchincloss

圖1

To Dr. Hu Shih—who has done so much to help both China & America gain a great friend and cement an enduring friendship—my deep respect & heartfelt thanks as an American.

Our children will have high cause to be grateful for the fruits of your labors.

Douglas Auchincloss

Dwight H. Green

　　Dwight H. Green（1897—1958），生於美國印第安那州，時任美國伊利諾伊州州長。早年就讀於瓦巴什學院，獲文學士學位，後畢業於芝加哥大學，獲法學博士學位。1941—1949年任美國伊利諾伊州州長。

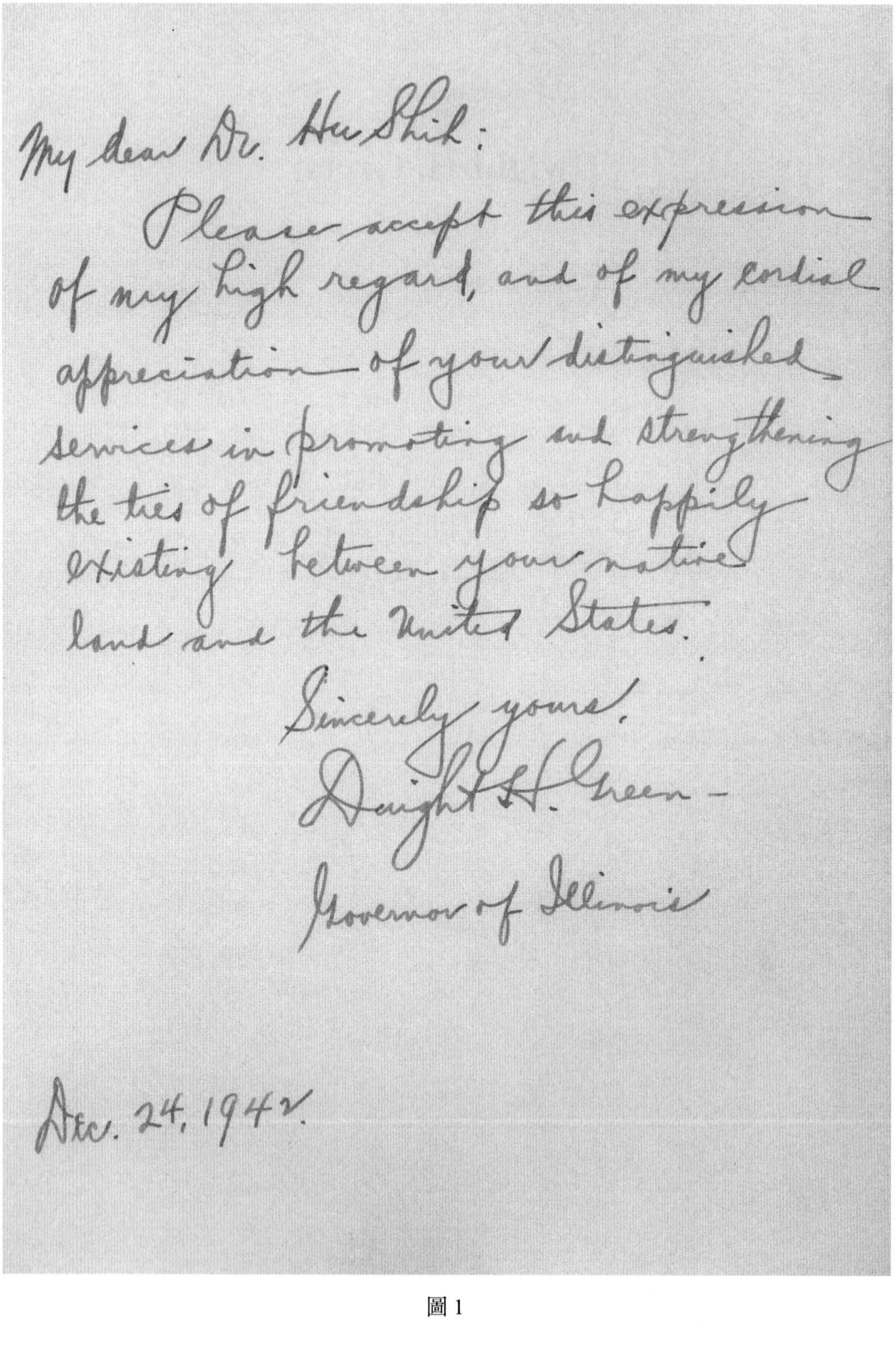

My dear Dr. Hu Shih:

Please accept this expression of my high regard, and of my cordial appreciation of your distinguished services in promoting and strengthening the ties of friendship so happily existing between your native land and the United States.

Sincerely yours,
Dwight H. Green —
Governor of Illinois

Dec. 24, 1942.

圖 1

My dear Dr. Hu Shih:

Please accept this expression of my high regard, and of my cordial appreciation of your distinguished services in promoting and strengthening the ties of friendship so happily existing between your native land and the United States.

Sincerely yours,
Dwight H. Green
Governor of Illinois

Dec. 24, 1942

E. P. Carville

E. P. Carville（1885—1956），生於美國內華達州，時任該州州長。1909 年獲聖母大學法學士學位。1939—1942 年任內華達州州長。1945 年任美國參議院議員。

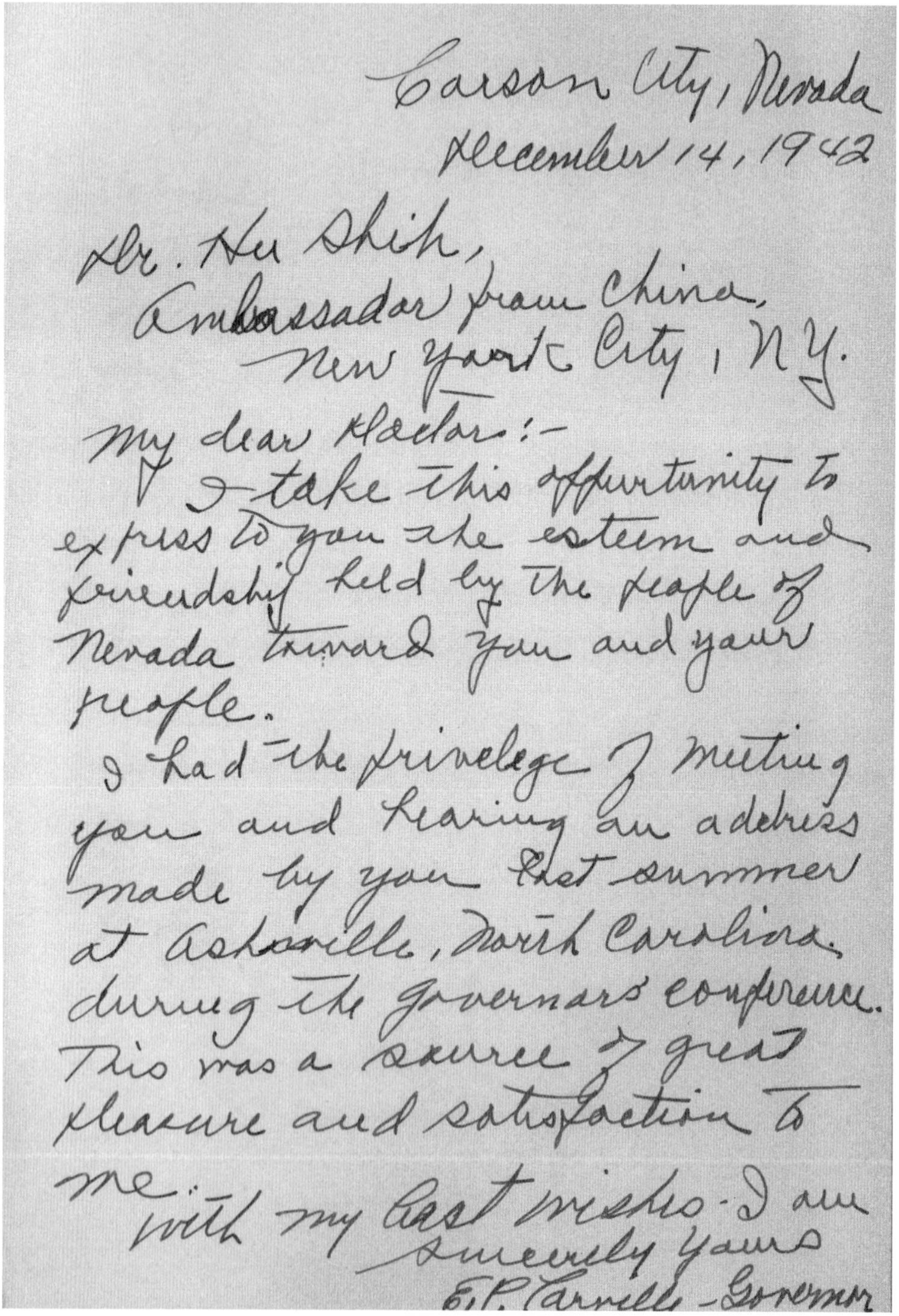

Carson City, Nevada
December 14, 1942

Dr. Hu Shih,
Ambassador from China,
New York City, N.Y.

My dear Doctor:-

I take this opportunity to express to you the esteem and friendship held by the people of Nevada toward you and your people.

I had the privilege of meeting you and hearing an address made by you last summer at Asheville, North Carolina, during the governors' conference. This was a source of great pleasure and satisfaction to me.

With my best wishes, I am
Sincerely yours
E.P. Carville - Governor

圖 1

Carson City, Nevada
December 14, 1942

Dr. Hu Shih,
    Ambassador from China,
        New York City, N.Y.

My dear Doctor:

I take this opportunity to express to you the esteem and friendship held by the people of Nevada toward you and your people.

I had the privilege of meeting you and hearing an address made by you last summer at Asheville, North Carolina during the governors' conference. This was a source of great pleasure and satisfaction to me.

With my best wishes, I am

                      Sincerely yours
                      E. P. Carville—Governor

Edward C. Carter

Edward C. Carter,簡介見前文。

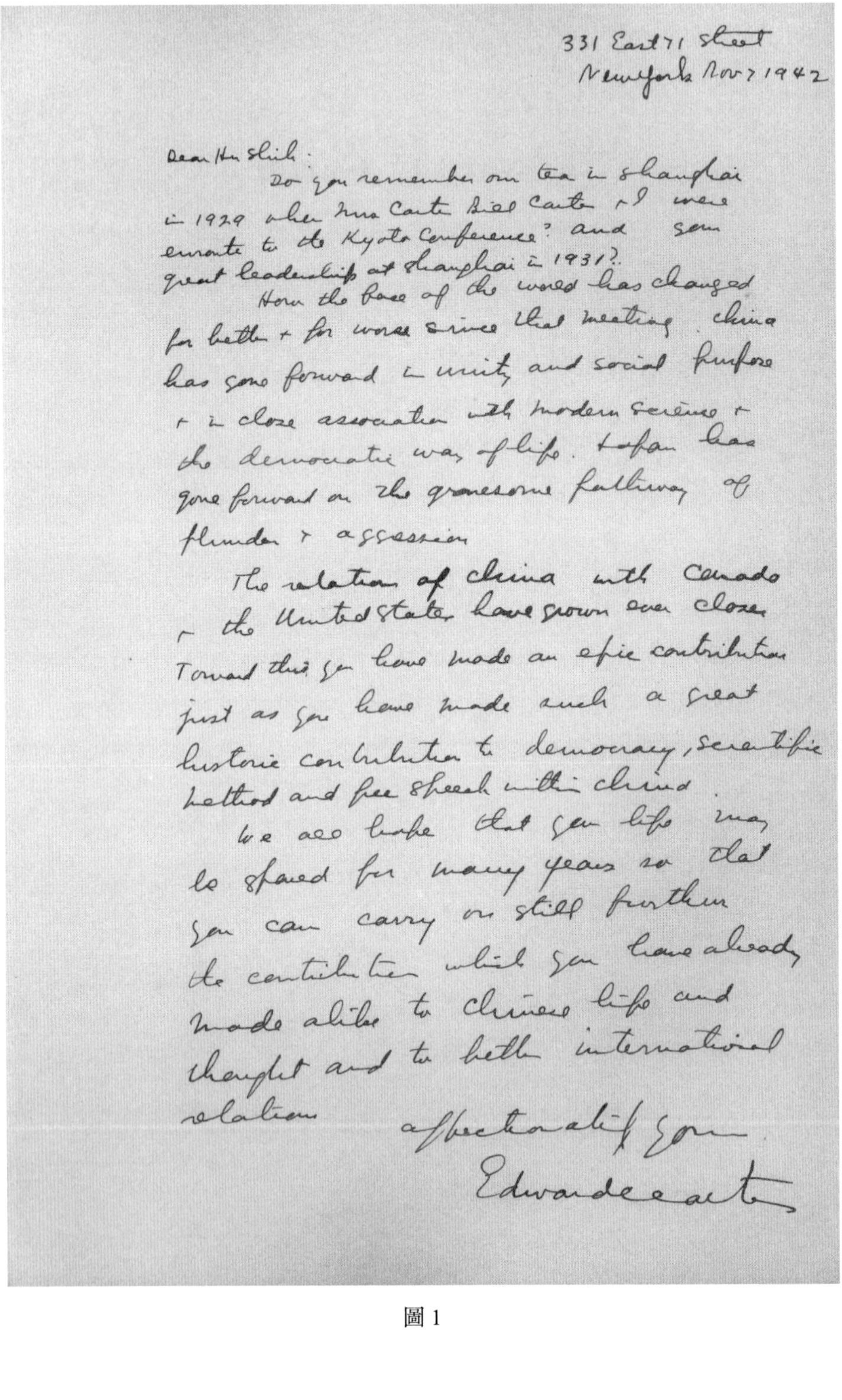

331 East 71 Street
New York Nov 7 1942

Dear Hu Shih:

Do you remember our tea in Shanghai in 1929 when Mrs Carter, Sidd Carter + I were enroute to the Kyoto Conference? and your great leadership at Shanghai in 1931?

How the face of the world has changed for better + for worse since that meeting. China has gone forward in unity and social purpose + in close association with modern science + the democratic way of life. Japan has gone forward on the gruesome pathway of plunder + aggression.

The relations of China with Canada + the United States have grown ever closer. Toward this you have made an epic contribution just as you have made such a great historic contribution to democracy, scientific method and free speech within China.

We all hope that your life may be spared for many years so that you can carry on still further the contribution which you have already made alike to Chinese life and thought and to better international relations.

affectionately yours,
Edward C Carter

圖1

331 East 71 Street

New York Nov. 7, 1942

Dear Hu Shih:

Do you remember our tea in Shanghai in 1929 when Mrs. Carter Bill Carter & I were enroute to the Kyoto Conference? And your great leadership at Shanghai in 1931?

How the face of the world has changed for better & for worse since that meeting. China has gone forward in unity and social purpose & in close association with modern science & the democratic way of life. Japan has gone forward on the gruesome pathway of plunder & aggression.

The relation of China with Canada & the United States have grown ever closer. Toward this you have made an epic contribution just as you have made such a great historic contribution to democracy, scientific method and free speech within China.

We all hope that your life may be spared for many years so that you can carry on still further the contribution which you have already made alike to Chinese life and thought and to better international relations.

Affectionately yours,

Edward C. Carter

Edward H. Hume

　　Edward H. Hume（1876—1957），生於印度艾哈邁德訥格爾，中文名胡美。1897 年畢業於耶魯大學，獲學士學位。1901 年獲約翰霍普金斯大學醫學院醫學博士學位。1903—1905 年在印度行醫。1909 年到中國長沙參加耶魯在中國項目，任長沙雅禮醫院主任醫師，1920—1923 年任雅禮會總幹事。1923—1926 年任湘雅醫學院院長。回國後曾任美國海外基督教醫學會（Christian Medical Council for Overseas）主任。胡適與胡美的書信往來至少自 1927 年胡適訪美期間就開始了。現存有胡美 1927 年 3 月 14 日致胡適書信。胡適卸任駐美大使時，胡美曾於 1942 年 9 月 3 日致信胡適，表示遺憾，並稱讚胡適是位優秀的文化大使。

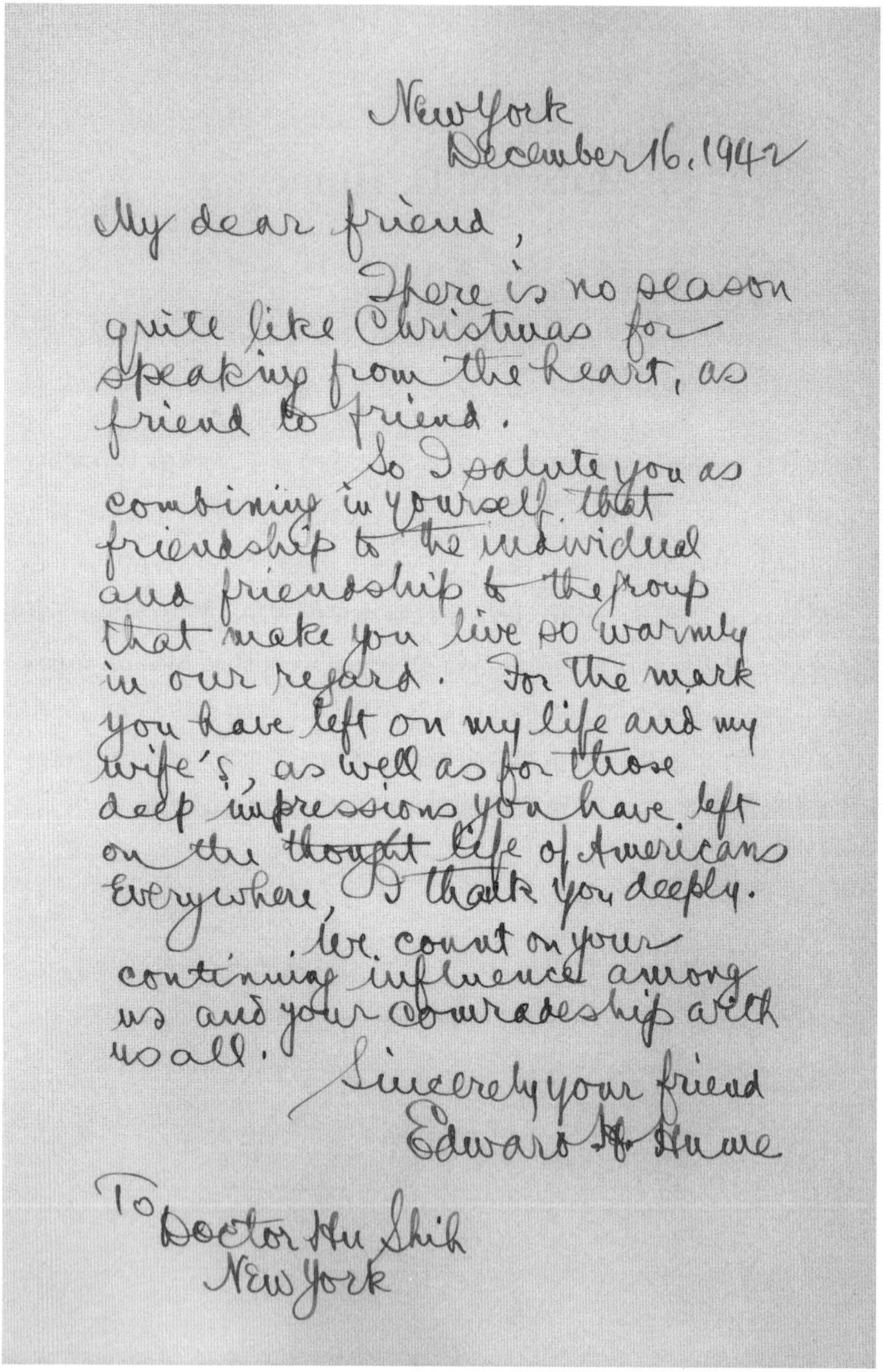

New York
December 16, 1942

My dear friend,

There is no season quite like Christmas for speaking from the heart, as friend to friend.

So I salute you as combining in yourself that friendship to the individual and friendship to the group that make you live so warmly in our regard. For the mark you have left on my life and my wife's, as well as for those deep impressions you have left on the thought life of Americans everywhere, I thank you deeply.

We count on your continuing influence among us and your comradeship with us all.

Sincerely your friend
Edward H. Hume

To Doctor Hu Shih
New York

圖 1

New York
December 16, 1942

My dear friend,

There is no season quite like Christmas for speaking from the heart, as friend to friend.

So I salute you as combining in yourself that friendship to the individual and friendship to the group that make you live so warmly in our regard. For the mark you have left on my life and my wife's, as well as for those deep impressions you have left on the thought life of Americans everywhere, I thank you deeply.

We count on your continuing influence among us and your comradeship with us all.

Sincerely yours friend
Edward H. Hume

To Doctor Hu Shih
New York

Edwin C. Lobenstine

　　Edwin C. Lobenstine（1872—1958），中文名羅炳生，美國北長老會教士。1898年來華，在上海、安徽一帶傳教。1924年後兼任中華全國基督教協進會名譽幹事。曾任中華醫學基金會主席。1935年退休回國。胡適與Lobenstine最早的書信往來是1928年7月14日Lobenstine致信胡適，想與胡適這樣一位非基督教自由派思想家討論中國的宗教。胡適在任駐美大使前後與Lobenstine也有交往，胡適卸任大使消息發佈後，Lobenstine於1942年9月3日致信胡適，表示遺憾。

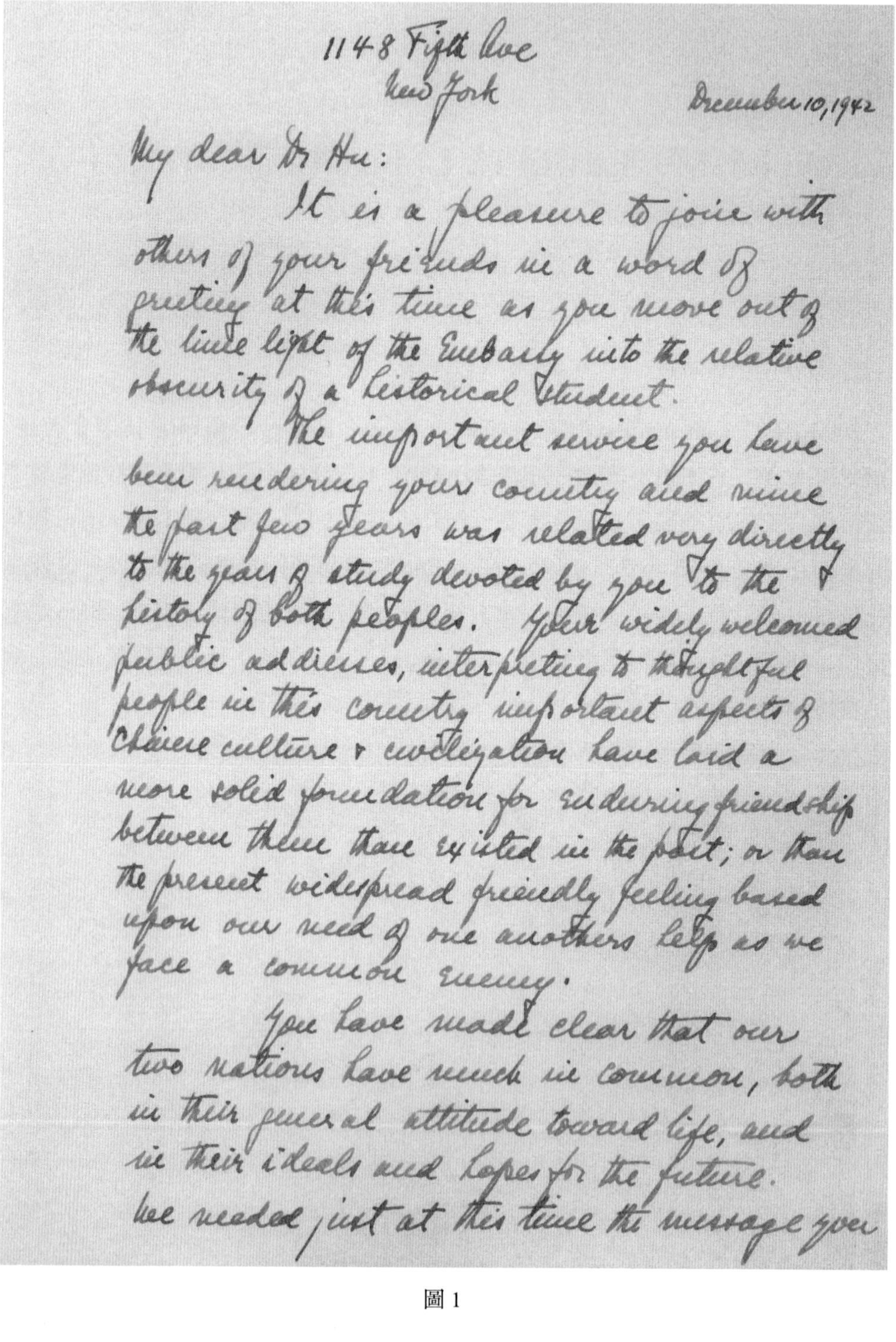

1148 Fifth Ave
New York
December 10, 1942

My dear Dr Hu:

It is a pleasure to join with others of your friends in a word of greeting at this time as you move out of the lime light of the Embassy into the relative obscurity of a historical student.

The important service you have been rendering your country and mine the past few years was related very directly to the years of study devoted by you to the history of both peoples. Your widely welcomed public addresses, interpreting to thoughtful people in this country important aspects of Chinese culture & civilization have laid a more solid foundation for enduring friendship between them than existed in the past; or than the present widespread friendly feeling based upon our need of one anothers help as we face a common enemy.

You have made clear that our two nations have much in common, both in their general attitude toward life, and in their ideals and hopes for the future. We needed, just at this time the message you

圖1

1148 Fifth Ave.
New York
December 10, 1942

My dear Dr. Hu:

It is a pleasure to join with others of your friends in a word of greeting at this time as you move out of the lime light of the Embassy into the relative obscurity of a historical student.

The important service you have been rendering your country and mine the past few years was related very directly to the years of study devoted by you to the history of both peoples. Your widely welcomed public addresses, interpreting to thoughtful people in this country important aspects of Chinese culture & civilization have laid a more solid foundation for enduring friendship between them than existed in the past; or than the present widespread friendly feeling based upon our need of one anothers help as we face a common enemy.

You have made clear that our two nations have much in common, both in their general attitude toward life, and in their ideals and hopes for the future. We needed just at this time the message you have brought and I, for one am thankful you had the opportunity to bring it, while representing your Government in Washington.

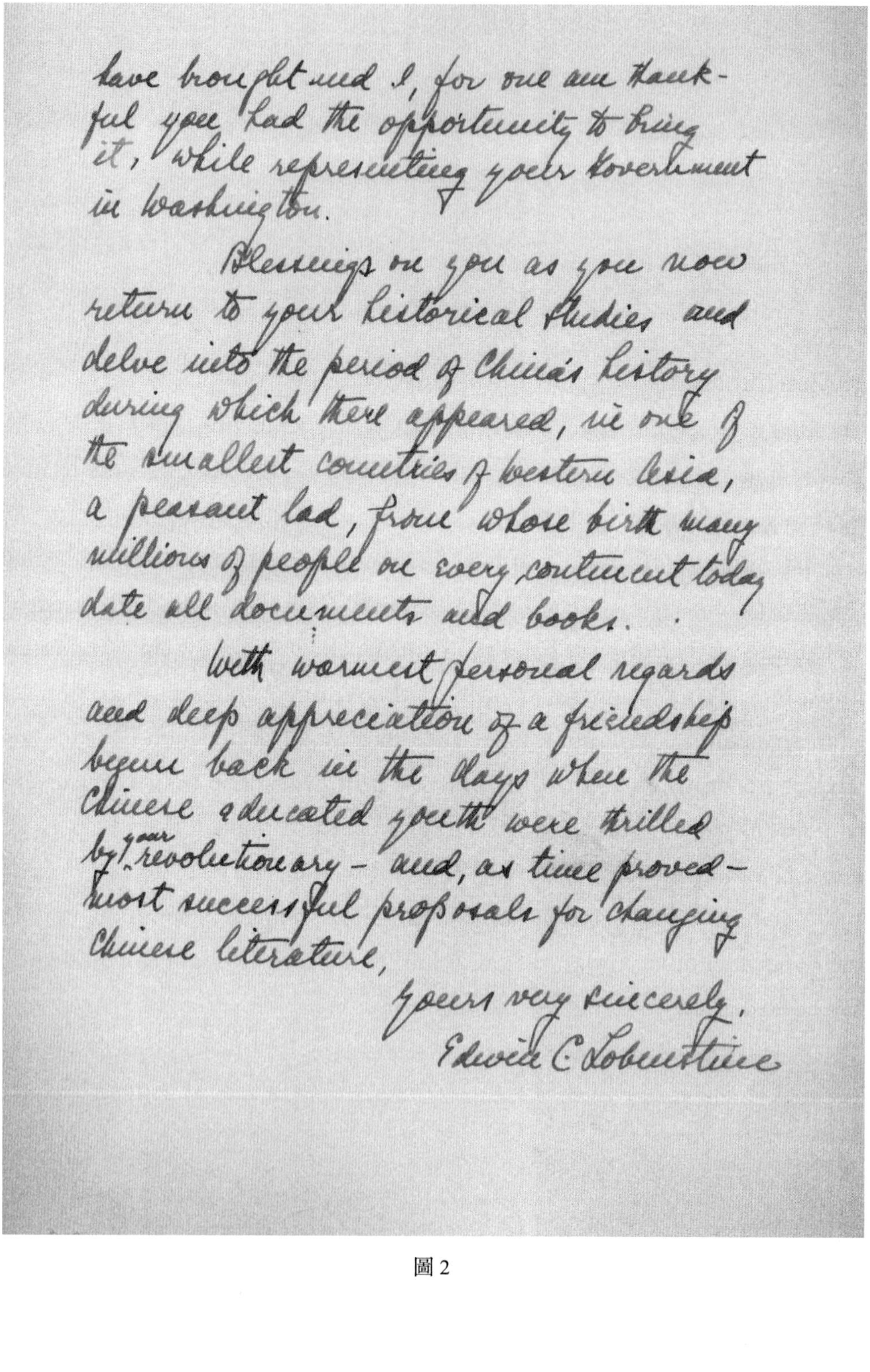

Blessings on you as you now return to your historical studies and delve into the period of China's history during which there appeared, in one of the smallest countries of western Asia, a peasant lad, from whose birth many millions of people on every continent today date all documents and books.

With warmest personal regards and deep appreciation of a friendship begun back in the days when the Chinese educated youth were thrilled by your revolutionary — and, as time proved — most successful proposals for changing Chinese literature,

Yours very sincerely,
Edwin C. Lobenstine

圖 2

have brought and I, for one am thankful you had the opportunity to bring it, while representing your Government in Washington.

Blessings on you as you now return to your historical studies and delve into the period of China's history during which there appeared, in one of the smallest countries of western Asia, a peasant lad, from whose birth many millions of people on every continent today date all documents and books.

With warmest personal regards and deep appreciation of a friendship begun back in the days when the Chinese educated youth were thrilled by your revolutionary—and as time proved—most successful proposals for changing Chinese literature,

Your very sincerely,
Edwin C. Lobenstine

Edwin M. McBrier

Edwin M. McBirer（1865—1956），生於美國紐約州。1884年畢業於赫蒙中學。曾爲F. W.伍爾沃斯公司總經理，美國衛理會海外傳教委員會執委會委員之一。

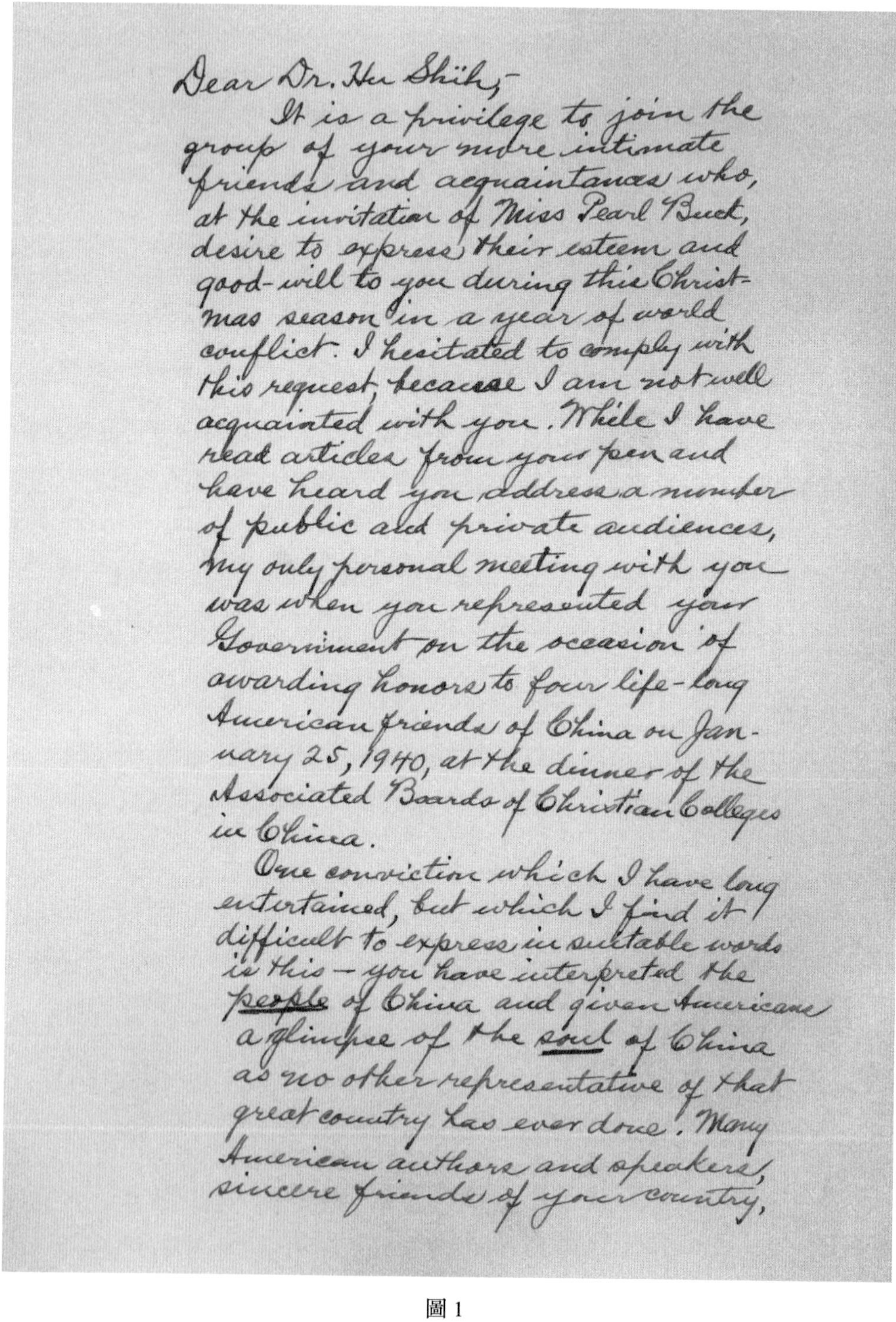

Dear Dr. Hu Shih,—

It is a privilege to join the group of your more intimate friends and acquaintances who, at the invitation of Miss Pearl Buck, desire to express their esteem and good-will to you during this Christmas season in a year of world conflict. I hesitated to comply with this request, because I am not well acquainted with you. While I have read articles from your pen and have heard you address a number of public and private audiences, my only personal meeting with you was when you represented your Government on the occasion of awarding honors to four life-long American friends of China on January 25, 1940, at the dinner of the Associated Boards of Christian Colleges in China.

One conviction which I have long entertained, but which I find it difficult to express in suitable words is this — you have interpreted the people of China and given Americans a glimpse of the soul of China as no other representative of that great country has ever done. Many American authors and speakers, sincere friends of your country,

圖1

Dear Dr. Hu Shih,

It is a privilege to join the group of your more intimate friends and acquaintances who, at the invitation of Miss Pearl Buck, desire to express their esteem and good-will to you during this Christmas season in a year of world conflict. I hesitated to comply with this request because I am not well acquainted with you. While I have read articles from your pen and have heard you address a number of public and private audiences, my only personal meeting with you was when you represented your Government on the occasion of awarding honors to four life-long American friends of China on January 25, 1940, at the dinner of the Associated Boards of Christian Colleges in China.

One conviction which I have long entertained, but which I find it difficult to express in suitable words is this—you have interpreted the people of China and given Americans a glimpse of the soul of China as no other representative of that great country has ever done. Many American authors and speakers, sincere friends of your country, have attempted to interpret China to us. They have lacked that which you possess — a background and a personality which is genuinely Chinese, coupled with a thorough knowledge of English literature, and an engaging frank and friendly spirit which captivates your audiences.

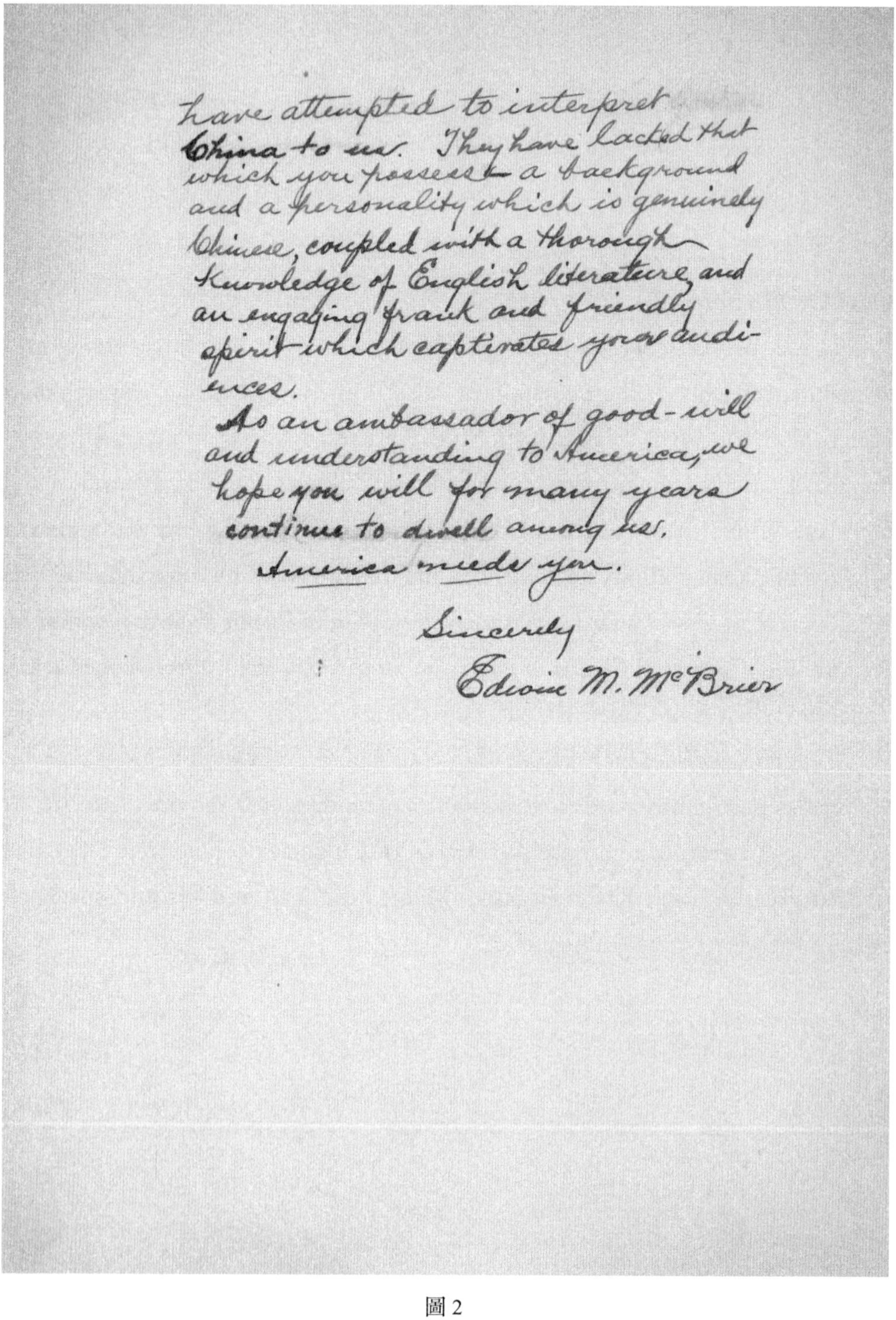

As an ambassador of good-will and understanding to America, we hope you will for many years continue to dwell among us. America needs you.

Sincerely
Edwin M. McBrier

圖 2

have attempted to interpret China to us. They have lacked that which you possess—a background and a personality which is genuinely Chinese, coupled with a thorough knowledge of English literature, and an engaging frank and friendly spirit—which captivates your audiences.

As an ambassador of good-will and understanding to America, we hope you will for many years continue to dwell among us.

America needs you.

Sincerely
Edwin M. McBirer

Elizabeth C. Morrow

　　Elizabeth C. Morrow，Mrs. Dwight W. Morrow，生平不詳，曾任美國某婦女團體榮譽主席。胡適任駐美大使期間與其有交往，北京檔中藏有 Morrow 致胡適函電五通，時間自 1939 年 8 月至 1940 年 11 月。

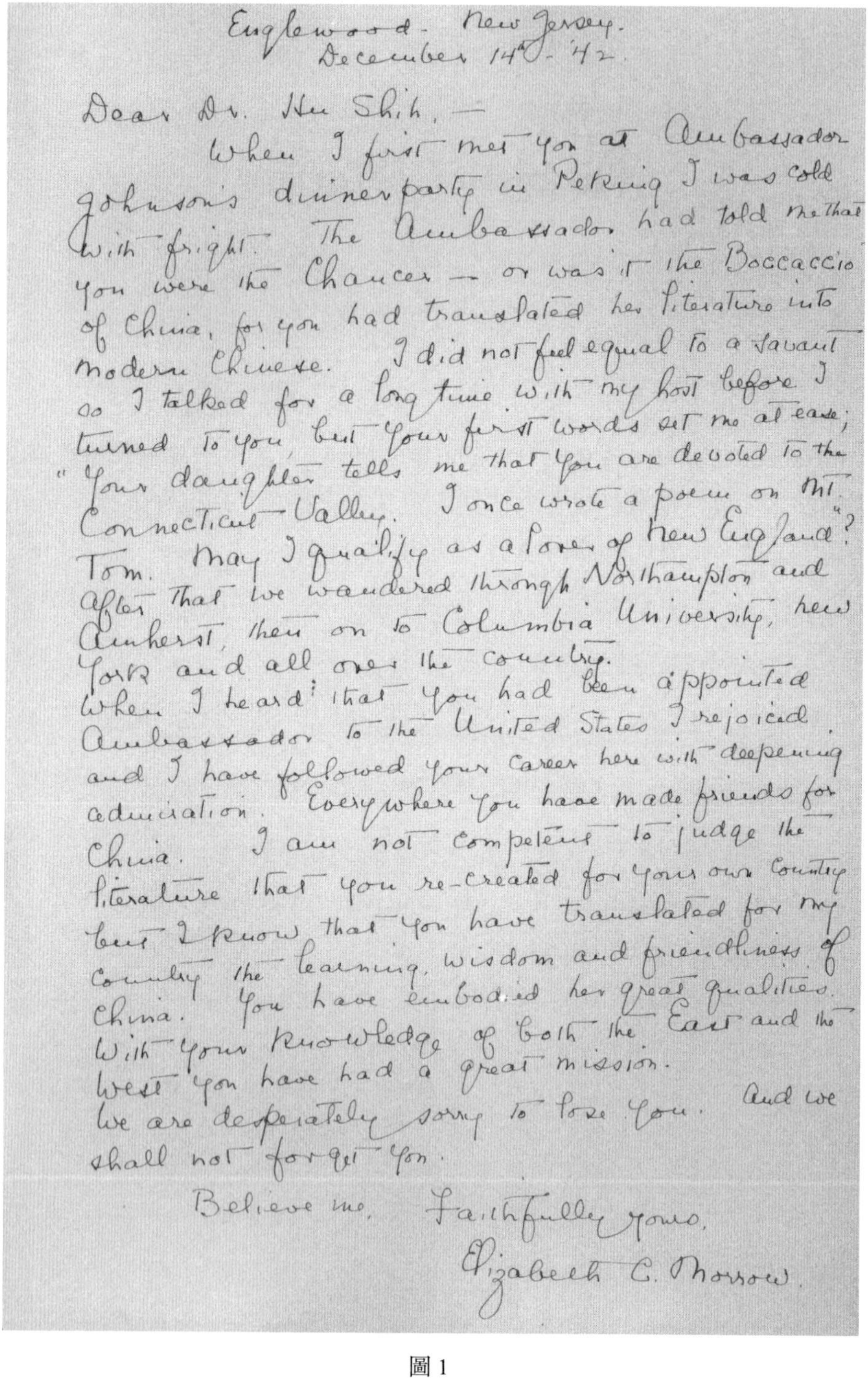

Englewood, New Jersey.
December 14th, '42.

Dear Dr. Hu Shih, —

When I first met you at Ambassador Johnson's dinner party in Peking I was cold with fright. The Ambassador had told me that you were the Chaucer — or was it the Boccaccio of China, for you had translated her literature into modern Chinese. I did not feel equal to a savant so I talked for a long time with my host before I turned to you, but your first words set me at ease: "Your daughter tells me that you are devoted to the Connecticut Valley. I once wrote a poem on Mt. Tom. May I qualify as a lover of New England"? After that we wandered through Northampton and Amherst, then on to Columbia University, New York and all over the country.

When I heard that you had been appointed Ambassador to the United States I rejoiced, and I have followed your career here with deepening admiration. Everywhere you have made friends for China. I am not competent to judge the literature that you re-created for your own country but I know that you have translated for my country the learning, wisdom and friendliness of China. You have embodied her great qualities. With your knowledge of both the East and the West you have had a great mission.

We are desperately sorry to lose you. And we shall not forget you.

Believe me,
Faithfully yours,
Elizabeth C. Morrow

圖 1

Englewood, New Jersey
December 14, '42

Dear Dr. Hu Shih,—

When I first met you at Ambassador Johnson's dinner party in Peking I was cold with fright. The Ambassador had told me that you were the Chaucer—or was it the Boccaccio of China, for you had translated her literature into modern Chinese. I did not feel equal to a savant as I talked for a long time with my host before I turned to you, but your first words set me at ease; "Your daughter tells me that you are devoted to the Connecticut-Valley. I once wrote a poem on MT. Tom. May I qualify as a lover of New England?" After that we wandered through Northampton and Amherst, then on to Columbia University, New York and all over the country.

When I heard that you had been appointed Ambassador to the United States I rejoiced and I have followed your career here with deepening admiration. Everywhere you have made friends for China. I am not competent to judge the literature that you re-created for your own country, but I know that you have translated for my country the learning, wisdom and friendliness of China. You have embodied her great qualities. With your knowledge of both the East and the West you have had a great mission.

We are desperately sorry to lose you, and we shall not forget you.

Believe me, faithfully yours,
Elizabeth C. Morrow

Elizabeth Luce Moore

　　Elizabeth Luce Moore（1904—2002），生於中國，1924 年畢業於韋爾斯利學院，後任《時代》《財富》雜誌編輯。其兄魯斯爲《時代》雜誌聯合創辦人、主編。1948—1966 年任韋爾斯利學院董事會董事。曾任紐約州立大學董事會主席，華美協進社董事會董事。胡適任大使期間與其有交往，北京檔中有胡適與 Moore 來往電報三通。

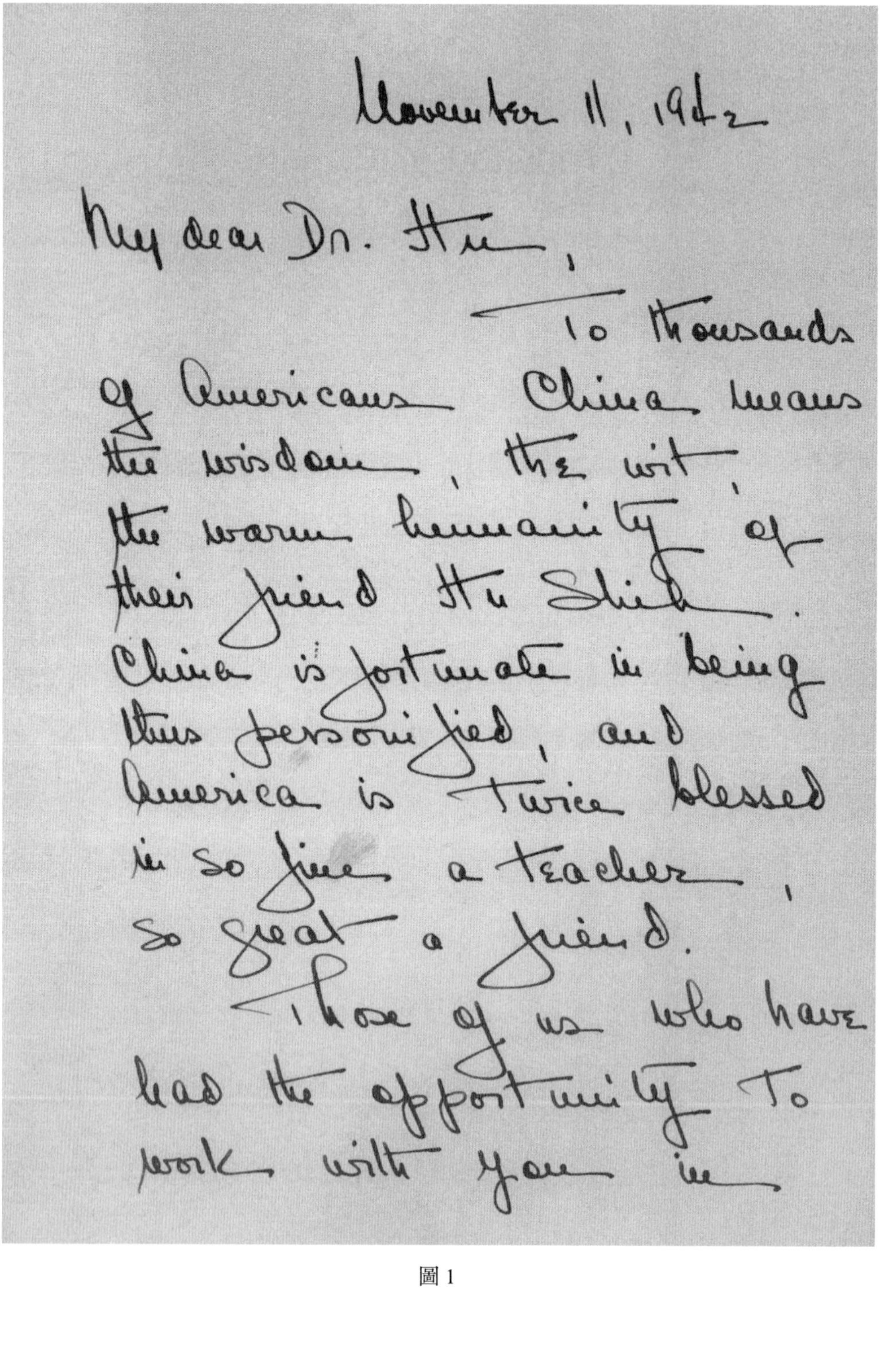

November 11, 1942

My dear Dr. Hu,

To thousands of Americans, China means the wisdom, the wit, the warm humanity of their friend Hu Shih. China is fortunate in being thus personified, and America is twice blessed in so fine a teacher, so great a friend.

Those of us who have had the opportunity to work with you in

圖 1

November 11, 1942

My dear Dr. Hu,

To thousands of Americans China means the wisdom, the wit, the warm humanity of their friend Hu Shih. China is fortunate in being thus personified, and America is twice blessed in so fine a teacher, so great a friend.

Those of us who have had the opportunity to work with you in

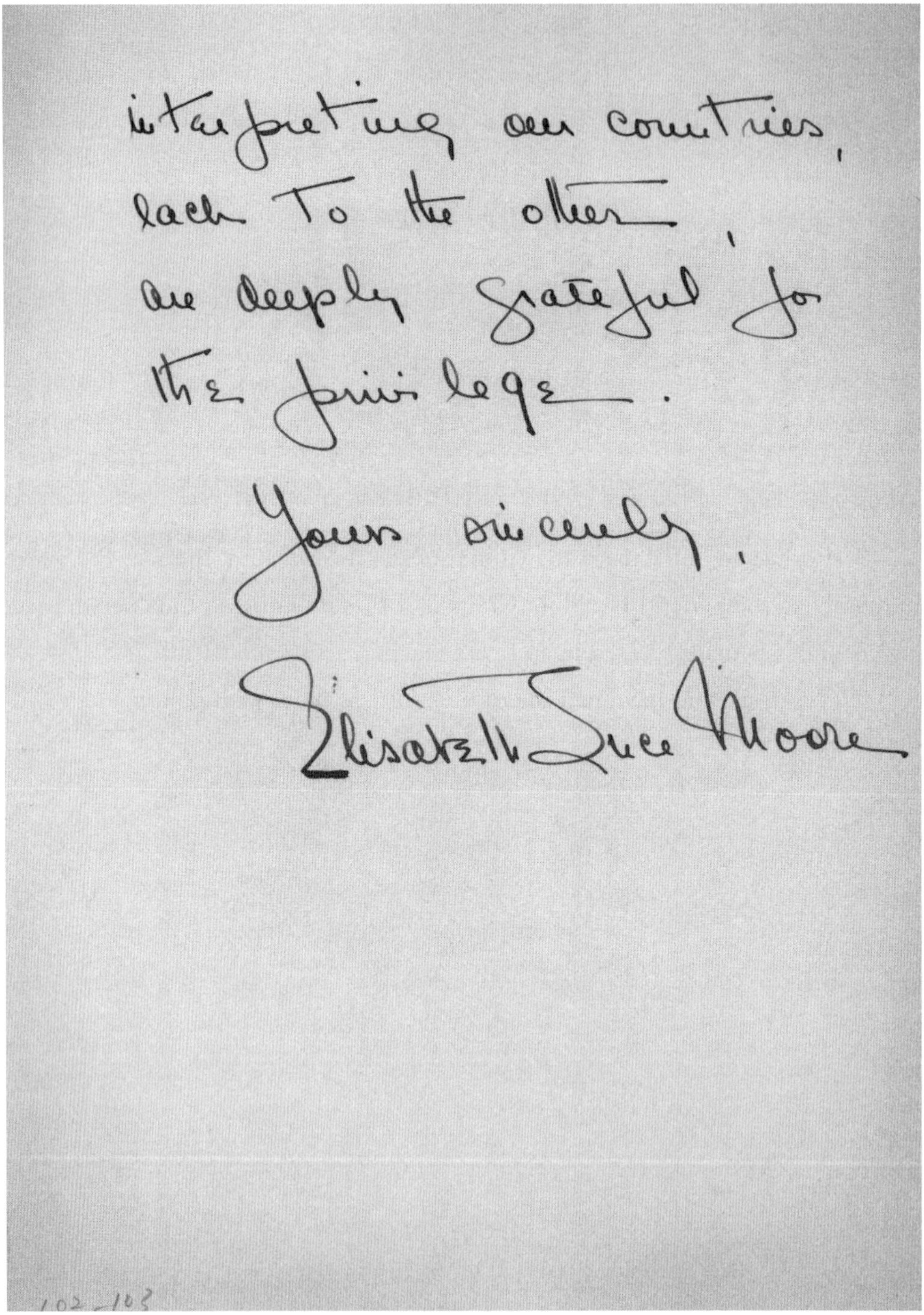

interpreting our countries,
each to the other,
are deeply grateful for
the privilege.

Yours sincerely,

Elisabeth Luce Moore

圖 2

interpreting our countries, each to the other, are deeply grateful for the privilege.

Yours sincerely,
Elizabeth Luce Moore

Eric M. North

作者生平不詳。

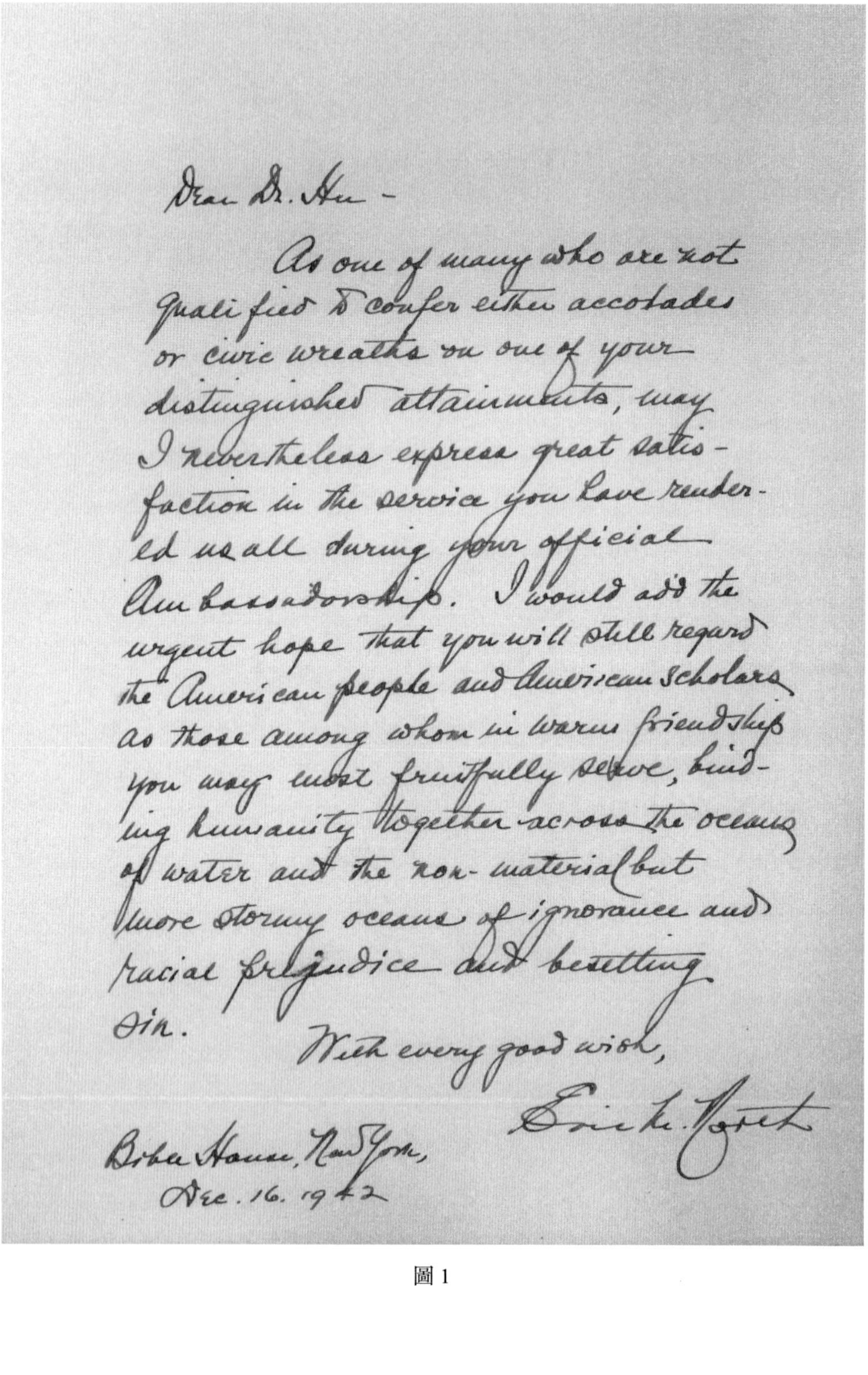

Dear Dr. Hu —

As one of many who are not qualified to confer either accolades or civic wreaths on one of your distinguished attainments, may I nevertheless express great satisfaction in the service you have rendered us all during your official Ambassadorship. I would add the urgent hope that you will still regard the American people and American scholars as those among whom in warm friendship you may most fruitfully serve, binding humanity together across the oceans of water and the non-material but more stormy oceans of ignorance and racial prejudice and besetting sin.

With every good wish,

Erich M. North

China House, New York,
Dec. 16, 1942

圖 1

Dear Dr. Hu—

As one of many who are not qualified to confer either accolades or civic wreaths on one of your distinguished attainments, may I nevertheless express great satisfaction in the service you have rendered us all during your official Ambassadorship. I would add the urgent hope that you will still regard the American people and American scholars as those among whom in warm friendship you may most fruitfully serve, binding humanity together across the oceans of water and the non-material but more stormy oceans of ignorance and racial prejudice and besetting sin.

With every good wish,
Eric M. North

Bible House, New York
Dec. 16, 1942

Eugene E. Barnett

　　Eugene E. Barnett（1888—1970），鮑乃德，美國傳教士。1910 年來華，任杭州基督教青年會總幹事。1925—1935 年任上海中華基督教青年會全國協會城市部幹事兼中華基督教男青年會首席幹事，後任副總幹事和總幹事。著有《我在中國的生活，1910—1936》(*My Life in China, 1910—1936*)。北京檔收藏有 Barnett 致胡適書信兩封，分別爲 1942 年 9 月 2 日和 1944 年 3 月 17 日，第一封信主要内容爲聽説胡適卸任駐美大使後，對胡適在任期間的貢獻表示敬意。

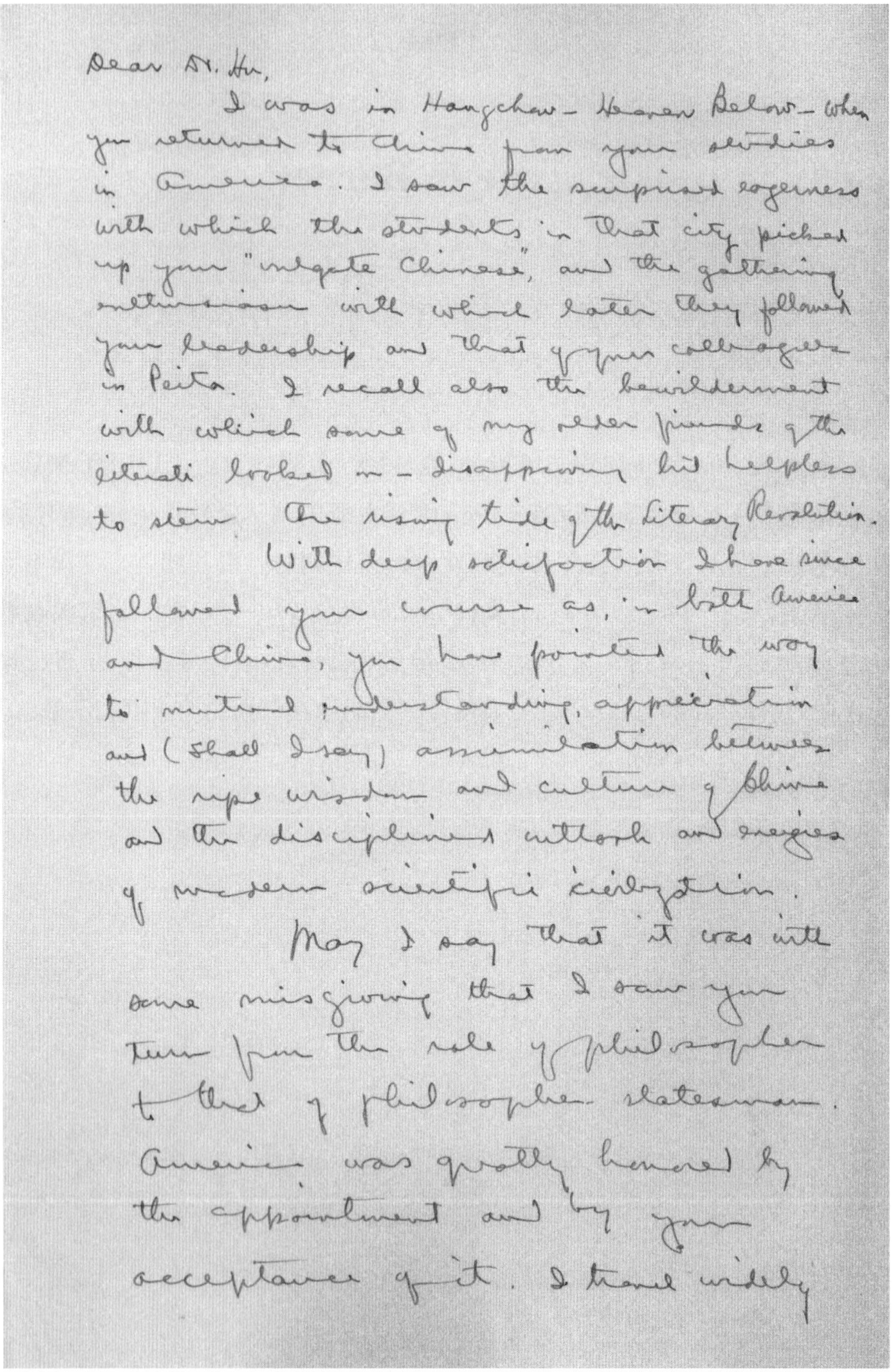

Dear Dr. Hu,

    I was in Hangchow — Heaven Below — when you returned to China from your studies in America. I saw the surprised eagerness with which the students in that city picked up your "inelegant Chinese", and the gathering enthusiasm with which later they followed your leadership and that of your colleagues in Peita. I recall also the bewilderment with which some of my older friends of the literati looked on — disapproving but helpless to stem the rising tide of the Literary Revolution.

    With deep satisfaction I have since followed your course as, in both America and China, you have pointed the way to mutual understanding, appreciation and (shall I say) assimilation between the ripe wisdom and culture of China and the disciplined outlook and energies of modern scientific civilization.

    May I say that it was with some misgiving that I saw you turn from the role of philosopher to that of philosopher-statesman. America was greatly honored by the appointment and by your acceptance of it. I travel widely

圖 1

Dear Dr. Hu,

I was in Hangchow—Heaven Below—when you returned to China from your studies in America. I saw the surprised eagerness with which the students in that city picked up your "vulgate Chinese" and the gathering enthusiasm with which later they followed your leadership and that of your colleagues in Peita. I recall also the bewilderment with which some of my older friends of the literati looked on— disapproving but helpless to stem the rising tide of the Literary Revolution.

With deep satisfaction I have since followed your course as, in both America and China, you have pointed the way to mutual understanding, appreciation and (shall I say) assimilation between the ripe wisdom and culture of China and the disciplined outlook and energies of modern scientific civilization.

May I say that it was with some misgiving that I saw you turn from the role of philosopher to that of philosopher-statesman. American was greatly honored by the appointment and by your acceptance of it. I travel widely and almost continually back and forth across America, and I have seen the "reservoir" of respect, admiration, and good will for your people overflowing among the people of America during your Ambassadorship. You will say that the credit for this belongs to your people and to qualities they have demonstrated during this period, but you yourself must accept large credit because of the distinguished manner in which you have represented them.

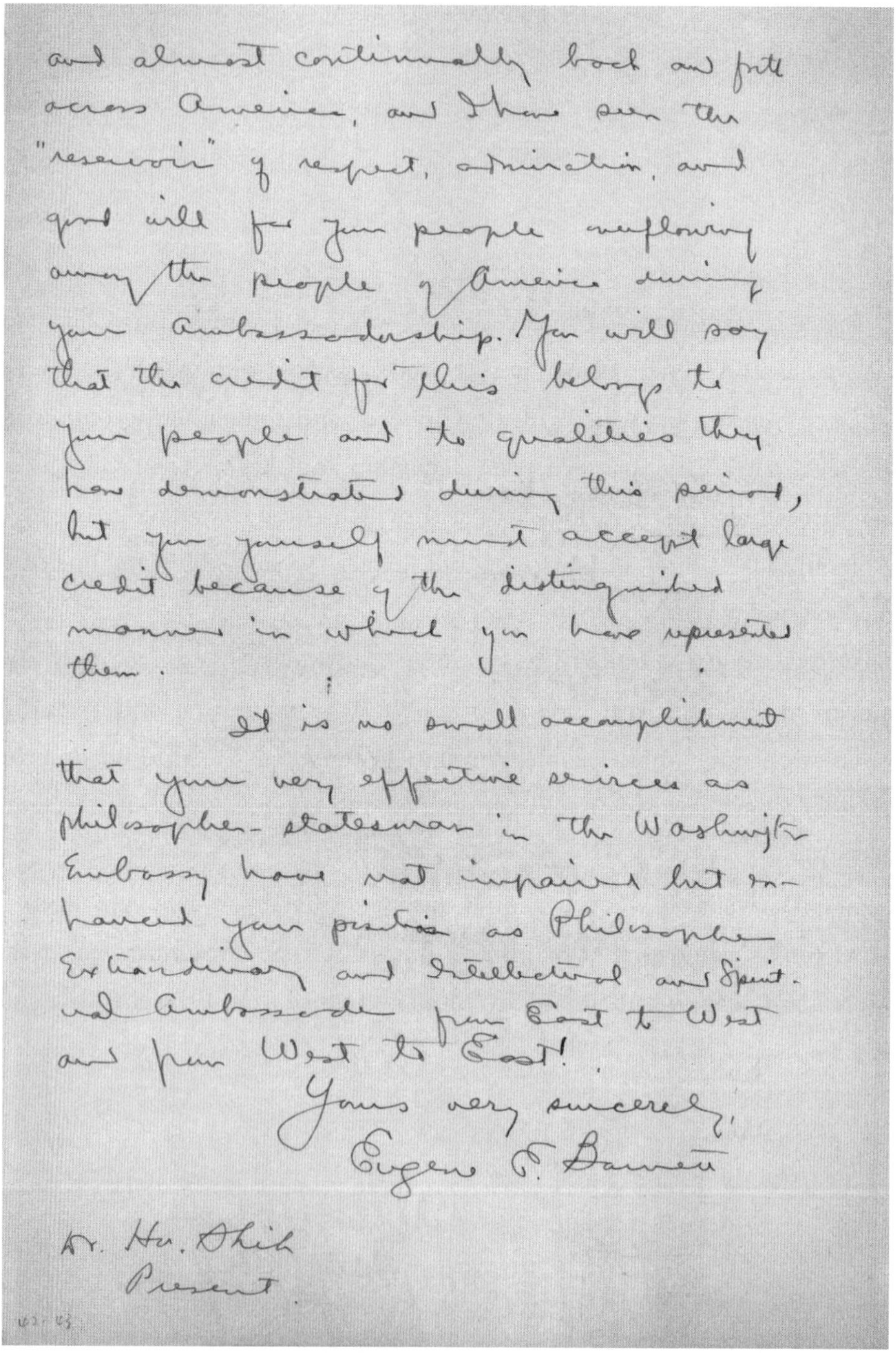

It is no small accomplishment that your very effective services as philosopher-statesman in the Washington Embassy have not impaired but enhanced your position as Philosopher Extraordinary and Intellectual and Spiritual Ambassador from East to West and from West to East!

Yours very sincerely,
Eugene E. Barnett

Dr. Hu Shih
Present

圖2

and almost continually back and forth across America, and I have seen the "reservoir" of respect, admiration, and good will for your people overflowing among the people of America during your Ambassadorship. You will say that the credit for this belongs to your people and to qualities they have demonstrated during this period, but you yourself must accept large credit because of the distinguished manner in which you have represented them.

It is no small accomplishment that your very effective services as philosopher-statesman in the Washington Embassy have not impaired but enhanced your position as Philosopher Extraordinary and Intellectual and Spiritual Ambassador from East to West and from West to East!

Yours very sincerely,
Eugene E. Barnett

Dr. HU Shih
Present

Felix Frankfurter

　　Felix Frankfurter（1882—1965），生於奥地利維也納，12 歲時移民美國。美國著名律師、法學家，時任美國最高法院大法官。1902 年畢業於紐約城市大學，後獲哈佛大學法學院法學士學位。一戰期間任美國軍法署署長，後任哈佛大學法學院教授。1939—1962 年任美國最高法院大法官。胡適任駐美大使前後與其有交往。胡適在 1939 年 3 月 11 日的日記中説："與最高法院新推事 Felix Frankfurter 夫婦吃飯。"北京檔有 Frankfurter 致胡適書信四封，其中三封日期不詳，另一封爲 1937 年 12 月 17 日。

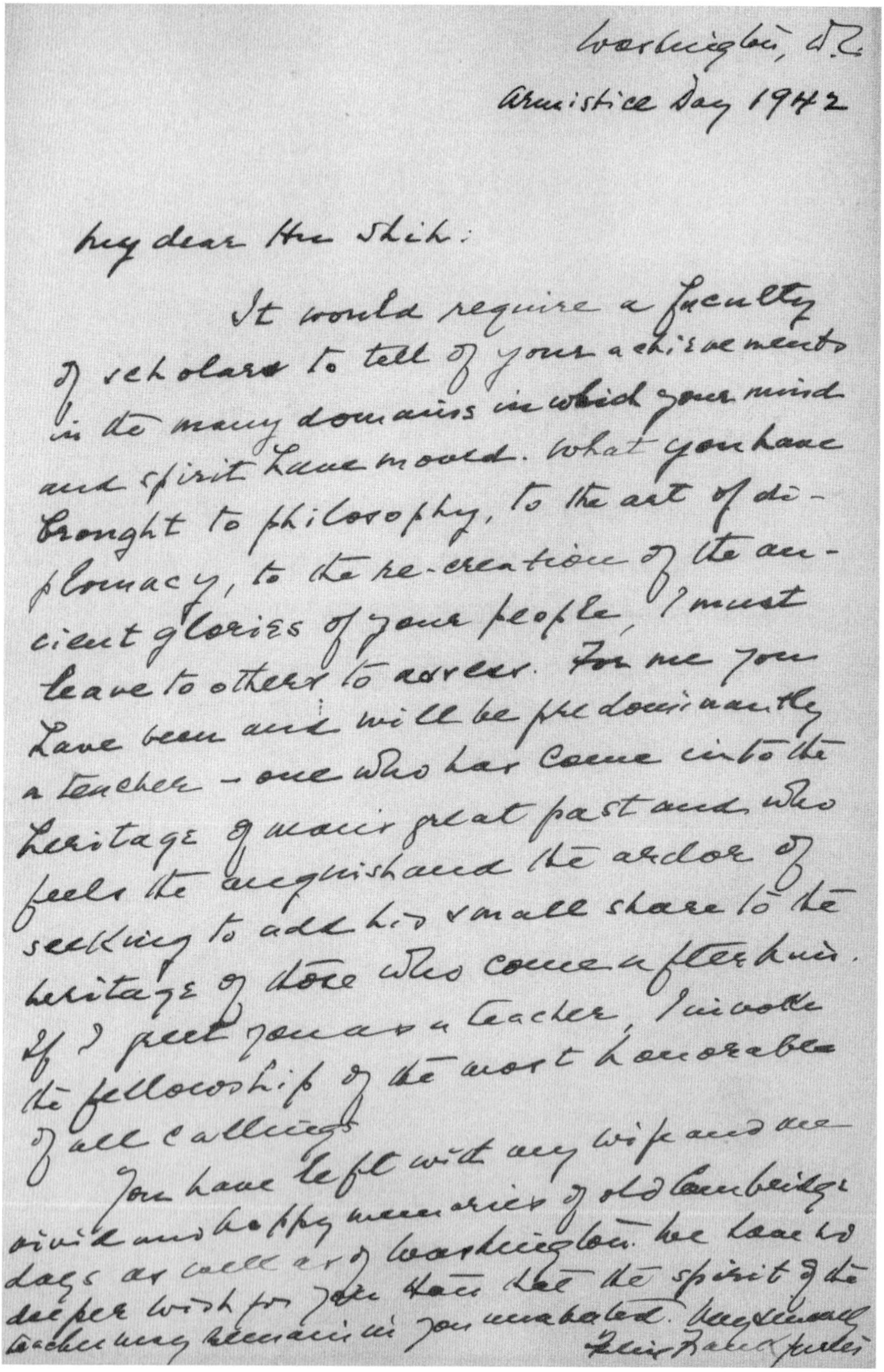

Washington, D.C.
Armistice Day 1942

My dear Hu Shih:

It would require a faculty of scholars to tell of your achievements in the many domains in which your mind and spirit have moved. What you have brought to philosophy, to the art of diplomacy, to the re-creation of the ancient glories of your people, I must leave to others to assess. For me you have been and will be predominantly a teacher — one who has come into the heritage of man's great past and who feels the anguish and the ardor of seeking to add his small share to the heritage of those who come after him. If I greet you as a teacher, I invoke the fellowship of the most honorable of all callings.

You have left with my wife and me vivid and happy memories of old Cambridge days as well as of Washington. We have no deeper wish for you than that the spirit of the teacher may remain in you unabated. Very sincerely

Felix Frankfurter

圖1

Washington, D.C.
Armistice Day 1942

My dear Hu Shih:

It would require a faculty of scholars to tell of your achievements in the many domains in which your mind and spirit have moved. What you have brought to philosophy, to the art of diplomacy, to the re-creation of the ancient glories of your people, I must leave to others to assess. For me you have been and will be predominantly a teacher—one who has come into the heritage of man's great past and who feels the anguish and the ardor of seeking to add his small share to the heritage of those who come after him. If I greet you as a teacher, I invoke the fellowship of the most honorable of all callings.

You have left with my wife and me vivid and happy memories of old Cambridge days as well as of Washington. We have no deeper wish for you than that the spirit of the teacher may remain in you unabated.

Very sincerely
Felix Frankfurter

Fiorello H. LaGuardia

　　Fiorello H. LaGuardia（1882—1947），意大利裔美國人，生於紐約市，時任紐約市長。先後畢業於紐約大學和紐約大學法學院。1916年當選爲美國衆議院議員，一戰時加入美國空軍。1923—1933年任美國衆議院議員。1934—1945年任紐約市長。1946年任聯合國善後救濟總署總幹事。

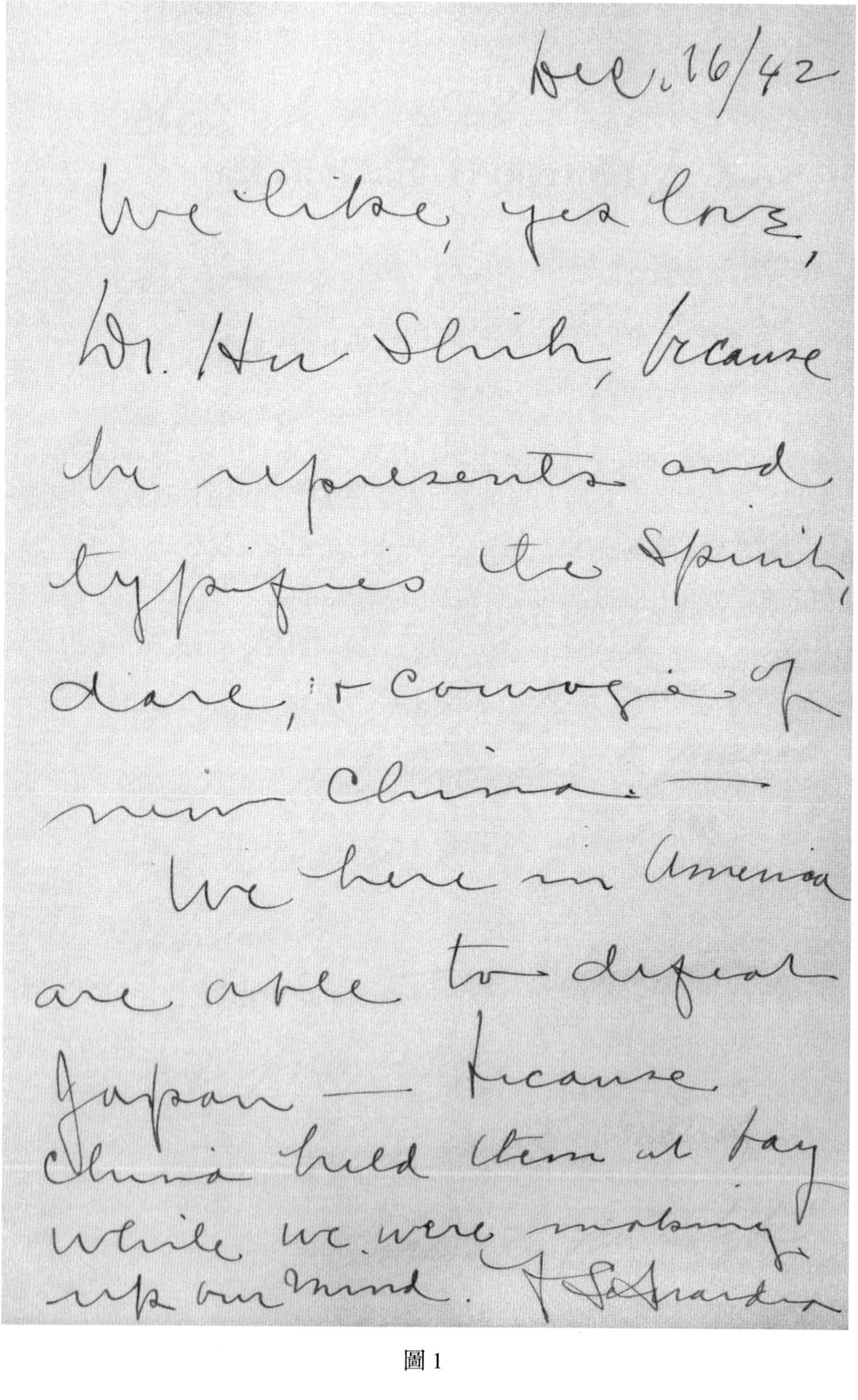

Dec. 16/42

We like, yea love, Dr. Hu Shih, because he represents and typifies the spirit, dare, & courage of new China. —

We here in America are able to defeat Japan — because China held them at bay while we were making up our mind. J. S. Strauder

圖 1

Dec. 16/42

We like, yes love, Dr. Hu Shih, because he represents and typifies the spirit, dare, & courage of new China.

We here in America are able to defeat Japan—because China held them at bay while we were making up our mind.

F. LaGuardia

Francis S. Hutchins（何欽思）

　　Francis S. Hutchins，中文名何欽思，生卒年不詳。1928—1938 年任美國雅禮會駐華代表。曾任美國肯塔基州伯里亞學院院長。胡適任駐美大使期間與此人有交往，北京檔藏有胡適與其往來書信五封，時間從 1940 年 5 月到 1942 年 9 月。

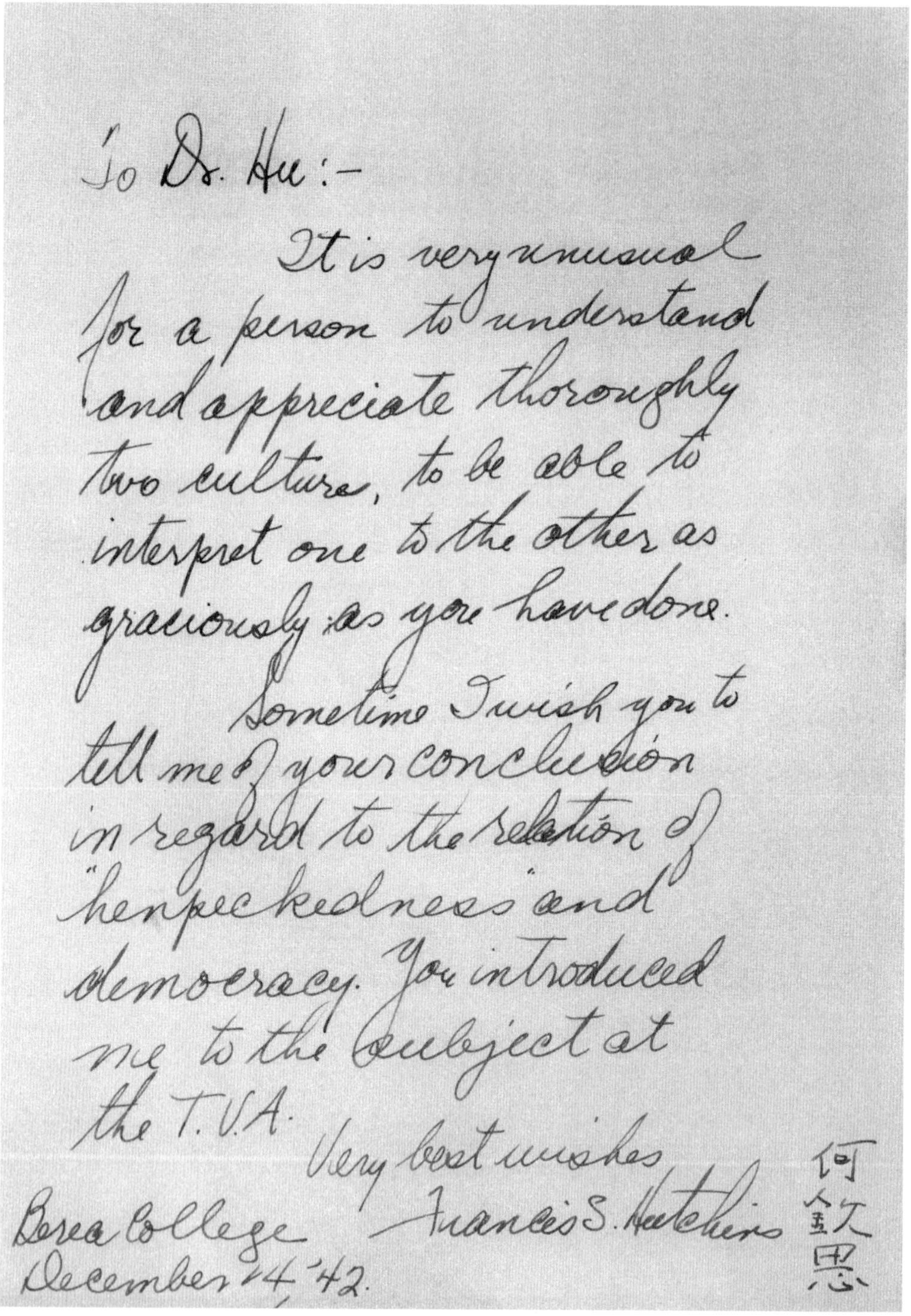

To Dr. Hu:—

It is very unusual for a person to understand and appreciate thoroughly two cultures, to be able to interpret one to the other as graciously as you have done.

Sometime I wish you to tell me of your conclusion in regard to the relation of "henpeckedness" and democracy. You introduced me to the subject at the T.V.A.

Very best wishes
Francis S. Hutchins

Berea College
December 14, '42.

何欽思

圖1

To Dr. Hu:—

It is very unusual for a person to understand and appreciate thoroughly two cultures, to be able to interpret one to the other as graciously as you have done.

Sometime I wish you to tell me of your conclusion in regard to the relation of "henpeckedness" and democracy. You introduced me to the subject at the T.V.A.

Very best wishes
Francis S. Hutchins 何欽思

Berea College
December 14, '42

Francis Biddle

　　Francis Biddle（1886—1968），生於法國巴黎，美國律師、政治家，時任美國司法部長。1909 年獲哈佛大學文學士學位，1911 年獲哈佛大學法學士學位。後在費城從事律師職業 27 年。1930 年被任命爲美國全國勞資關係委員會主席。1939 年被任命爲美國聯邦第三巡迴上訴法院法官。次年任美國檢察長。1941—1945 年任美國司法部長。後任紐倫堡審判美國法官。1950 年任美國民主行動協會主席。

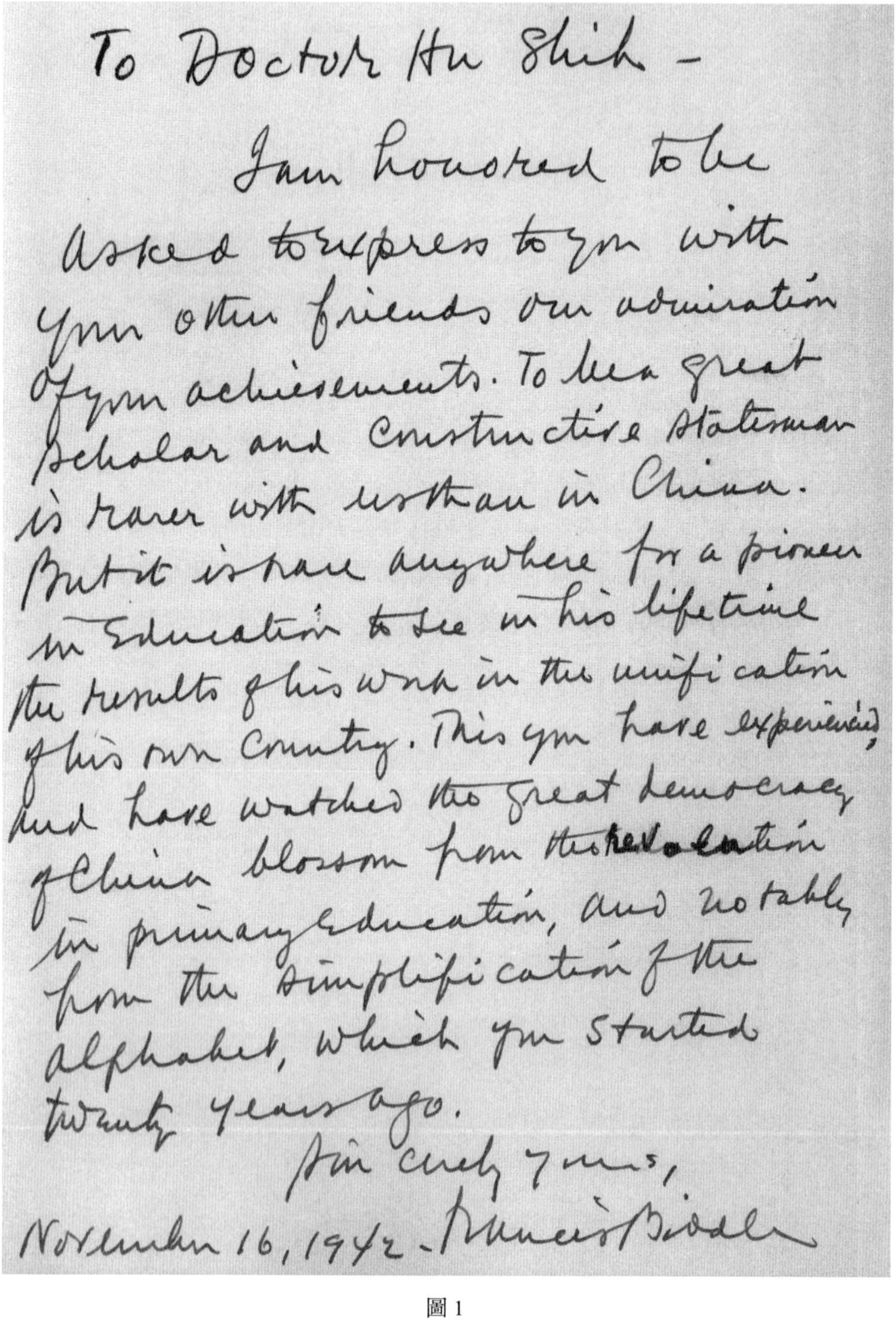

To Doctor Hu Shih —

I am honored to be asked to express to you with your other friends our admiration of your achievements. To be a great scholar and constructive statesman is rarer with us than in China. But it is rare anywhere for a pioneer in Education to see in his lifetime the results of his work in the unification of his own country. This you have experienced, and have watched the great democracy of China blossom from the revolution in primary education, and notably from the simplification of the alphabet, which you started twenty years ago.

Sincerely yours,
Francis Biddle

November 16, 1942.

圖 1

To Doctor Hu Shih—

I am honored to be asked to express to you with your other friends our admiration of your achievements. To me a great scholar and constructive statesman is rarer with us than in China. But it is rare anywhere for a pioneer in education to see in his lifetime the results of his work in the unification of his own country. This you have experienced, and have watched the great democracy of China blossom from the revolution in primary education, and notably from the simplification of the alphabet, which you started twenty years ago.

Sincerely yours,
Francis Biddle

November 16, 1942

Frank Co Tui

　　Frank Co Tui（1897—1983），許肇堆，生於廈門，五歲到菲律賓，1914年入菲律賓大學，後獲醫學博士學位。長期在美國從事醫學、藥學和心理學的教學與科研。曾任美國紐約大學醫學院醫藥學教授和實驗外科手術系教授、紐約科學學會研究員、美國科學促進會會員和美國藥理學會會員，美國原子能委員會醫學專家。曾應聘任菲律賓總統府科技顧問、菲律賓科學發展署顧問、美菲科學基金會副會長。1937年11月在紐約與他人發起創建"美國醫藥援華會"。1942年，在其技術支持下，中國成爲世界上第七個能生産盤尼西林的國家。1942年、1946年分别獲得中國政府頒發的碧玉勳章和勝利勳章。晚年回菲律賓，1983年在馬尼拉去世。胡適任駐美大使期間與此人有交往，北京檔有胡適致許肇堆和Donald D. Van Slyke一封信，時間爲1942年1月5日。

Hu Shih and Benjamin Franklin had strikingly parallel careers. Philosophers and scholars, they were both beloved by the nations to which they were Envoys. Franklin was in France when France was crucial to American Independence; Hu Shih was Ambassador to America when America was crucial to China's survival. Both forged strong ties of sympathy between their peoples and the peoples to which they were Envoys.

Having achieved the golden age of Chinese diplomacy, Hu Shih has now become China's spiritual and cultural ambassador. He symbolizes to America the acme of Chinese culture, to China the best in American education, and to both countries the friendship that links them.

CoTui

圖1

Hu Shih and Benjamin Franklin had strikingly parallel careers. Philosophers and scholars, they were both beloved by the nations to which they were Envoys. Franklin was in France when France was crucial to American independence; Hu Shih was Ambassador to America when America was crucial to China's survival. Both forged strong ties of sympathy between their peoples and the peoples to which they were Envoys.

Having achieved the golden age of Chinese diplomacy, Hu Shih has now become China's spiritual and cultural Ambassador. He symbolizes to America the acme of Chinese culture, to China the best in American education; and to both countries the friendship that links them.

Co Tui

Frank T. Cartwright

Frank T. Cartwright（1884—? ），葛惠良，美國美以美會傳教士。1917年來華，在福州傳教。曾任衛理公會（Division of Foreign Missions of the Board of Missions and Church Extension）副秘書長。著有《從福州到內地》（*From Foochow to the Interior*）。

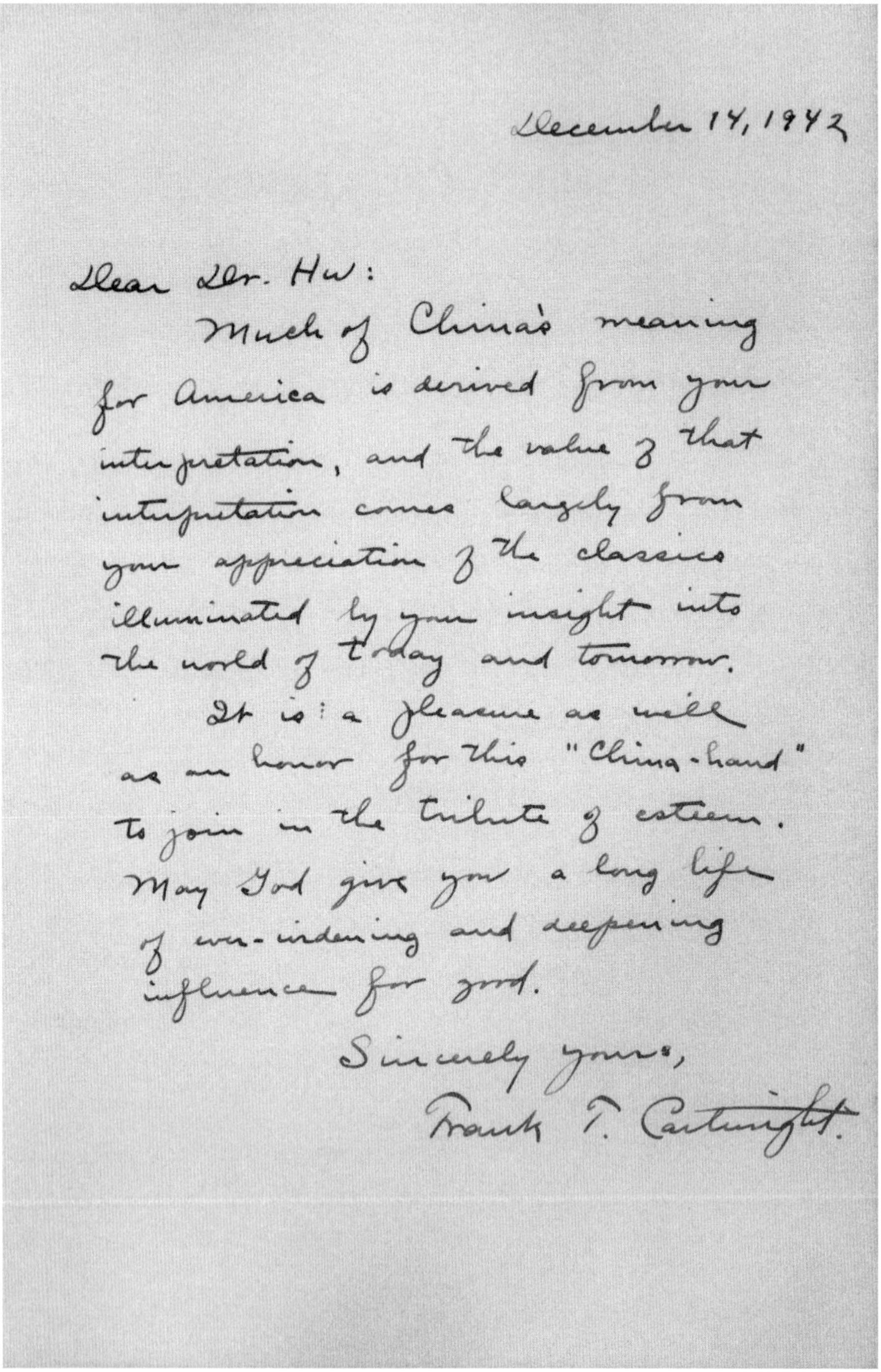

December 14, 1942

Dear Dr. Hu:

Much of China's meaning for America is derived from your interpretation, and the value of that interpretation comes largely from your appreciation of the classics illuminated by your insight into the world of today and tomorrow.

It is a pleasure as well as an honor for this "China-hand" to join in the tribute of esteem. May God give you a long life of ever-widening and deepening influence for good.

Sincerely yours,
Frank T. Cartwright

圖1

December 14, 1942

Dear Dr. Hu:

Much of China's meaning for America is derived from your interpretation, and the value of that interpretation comes largely from your appreciation of the classics illuminated by your insight into the world of today and tomorrow.

It is a pleasure as well as an honor for this "China-hand" to join in the tribute of esteem. May God give you a long life of ever-widening and deepening influence for good.

Sincerely yours,
Frank T. Cartwright

Frank Knox

Frank Knox（1874—1944），生於美國波士頓，美國政治家、報紙編輯和出版人，時任美國海軍部長。早年獲阿爾瑪學院文學士學位。曾參加美西戰爭，戰後在密歇根州大急流城任報紙編輯。一戰期間到法國參戰，任炮兵官員。1940年任美國海軍部長，直至1944年去世。

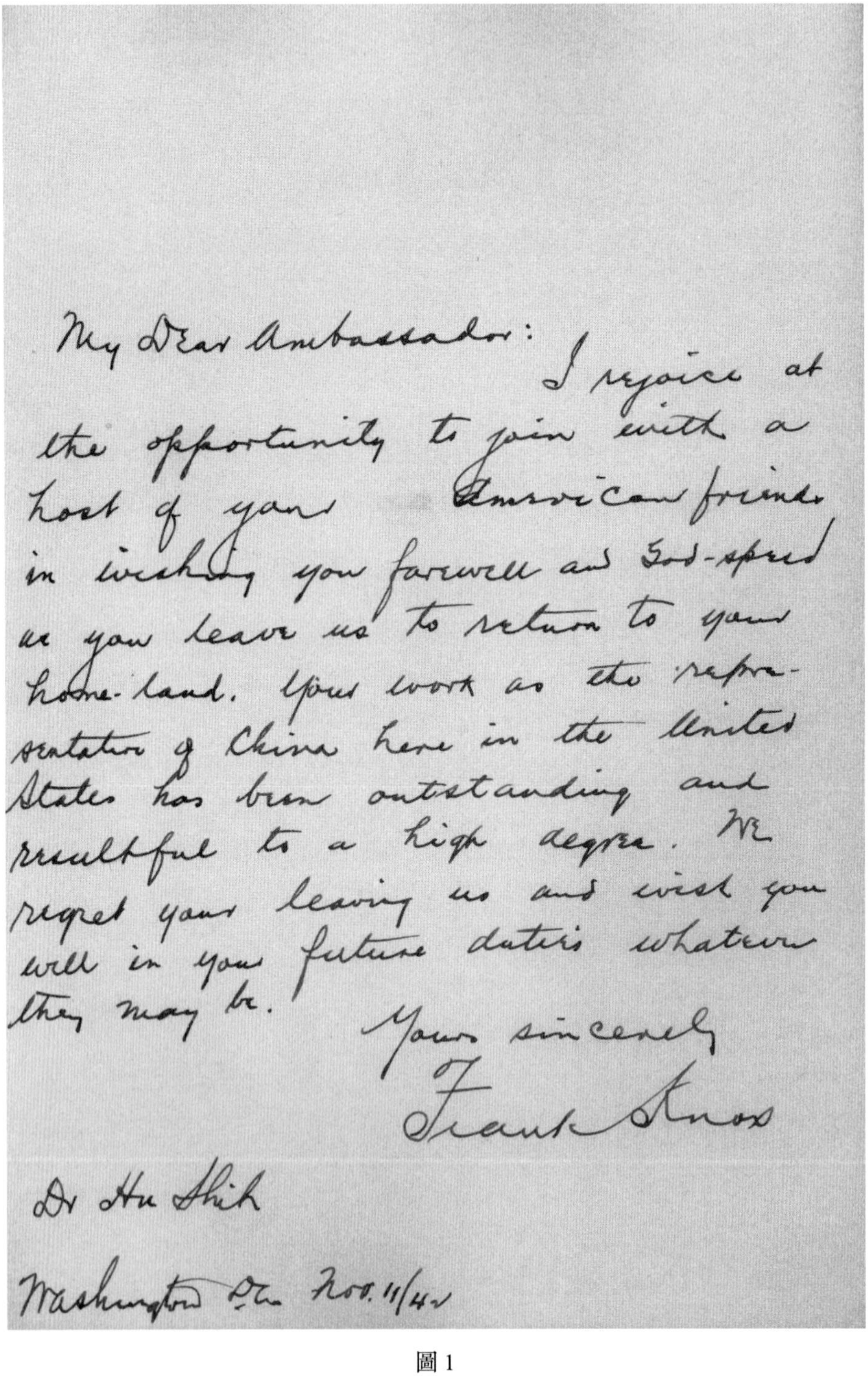

My Dear Ambassador:

I rejoice at the opportunity to join with a host of your American friends in wishing you farewell and God-speed as you leave us to return to your home-land. Your work as the representative of China here in the United States has been outstanding and resultful to a high degree. We regret your leaving us and wish you well in your future duties whatever they may be.

Yours sincerely

Frank Knox

Dr Hu Shih

Washington D.C. Nov. 11/42

圖1

My dear Ambassador:

I rejoice at the opportunity to join with a host of your American friends in wishing you farewell and God-speed as you leave us to return to your homeland. Your work as the representation of China here in the United States has been outstanding and resultful to a high degree. We regret your leaving us and wish you well in your future duties whatever they may be.

Yours Sincerely
Frank Knox

Dr. Hu Shih
Washington, D.C. Nov. 11/42

Frank Meleney

　　Frank Meleney（1889—1963），1916 年畢業於哥倫比亞大學，畢業後參加一戰。後到北京四年，任洛克菲勒基金會外科醫生。1925 年重回哥倫比亞大學。北京檔藏有其致胡適書信四封，時間從 1942 年 11 月到 1945 年 4 月。

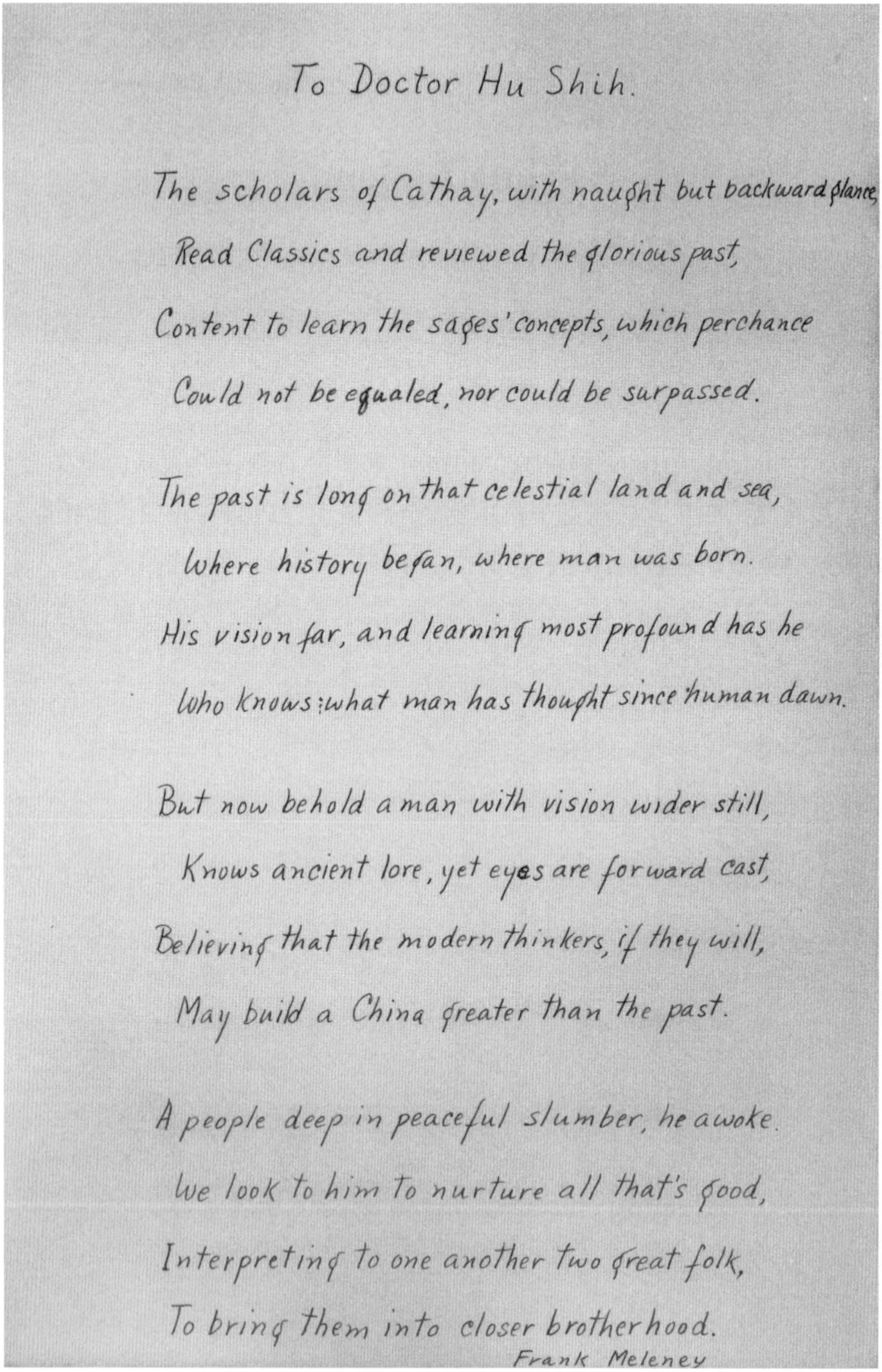

To Doctor Hu Shih.

The scholars of Cathay, with naught but backward glance,
   Read Classics and reviewed the glorious past,
Content to learn the sages' concepts, which perchance
   Could not be equaled, nor could be surpassed.

The past is long on that celestial land and sea,
   Where history began, where man was born.
His vision far, and learning most profound has he
   Who knows what man has thought since human dawn.

But now behold a man with vision wider still,
   Knows ancient lore, yet eyes are forward cast,
Believing that the modern thinkers, if they will,
   May build a China greater than the past.

A people deep in peaceful slumber, he awoke.
   We look to him to nurture all that's good,
Interpreting to one another two great folk,
   To bring them into closer brotherhood.

                Frank Meleney

圖 1

To Doctor Hu Shih.

The scholars of Cathay, with naught but backward glance,
Read Classics and reviewed the glorious past,
Content to learn the sages' concepts, which perchance
Could not be equaled, nor could be surpassed.

The past is long on that celestial land and sea,
Where history began, where man was born.
His vision far, and learning most profound has he
Who knows what man has thought since human dawn.

But now behold a man with vision wider still,
Knows ancient lore, yet eyes are forward cast,
Believing that the modern thinkers, if the will,
May build a China greater than the past.

A people deep in peaceful slumber, he awoke.
We look to him to nurture all that's good,
Interpreting to one another two great folk,
To bring them into closer brotherhood.

Frank Meleney

Franklin D. Roosevelt

Franklin D. Roosevelt（1882—1945），羅斯福，1933—1945 年任美國總統。

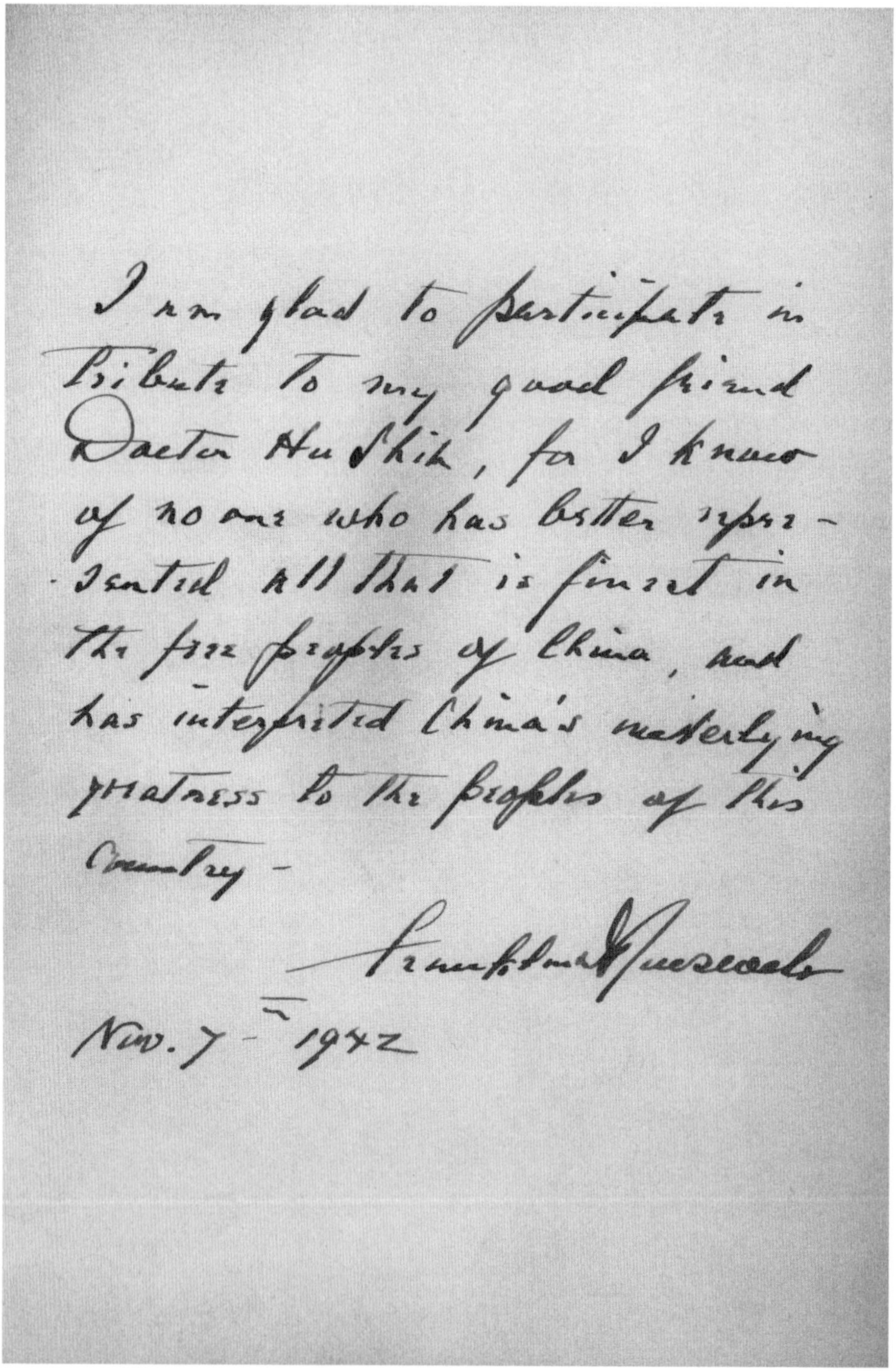

I am glad to participate in tribute to my good friend Doctor Hu Shih, for I know of no one who has better represented all that is finest in the free peoples of China, and has interpreted China's underlying greatness to the peoples of this country —

Franklin D Roosevelt

Nov. 7 - 1942

圖1

I am glad to participate in tribute to my good friend Doctor Hu Shih, for I know of no one who has better represented all that is finest in the free peoples of China, and has interpreted China's underlying greatness to the peoples of this country.

Franklin D. Roosevelt

Nov. 7, 1942

Frederick H. Wood

Frederick H. Wood,生平不詳,北京檔藏有其致胡適書信一封,日期爲 1942 年 11 月 6 日。

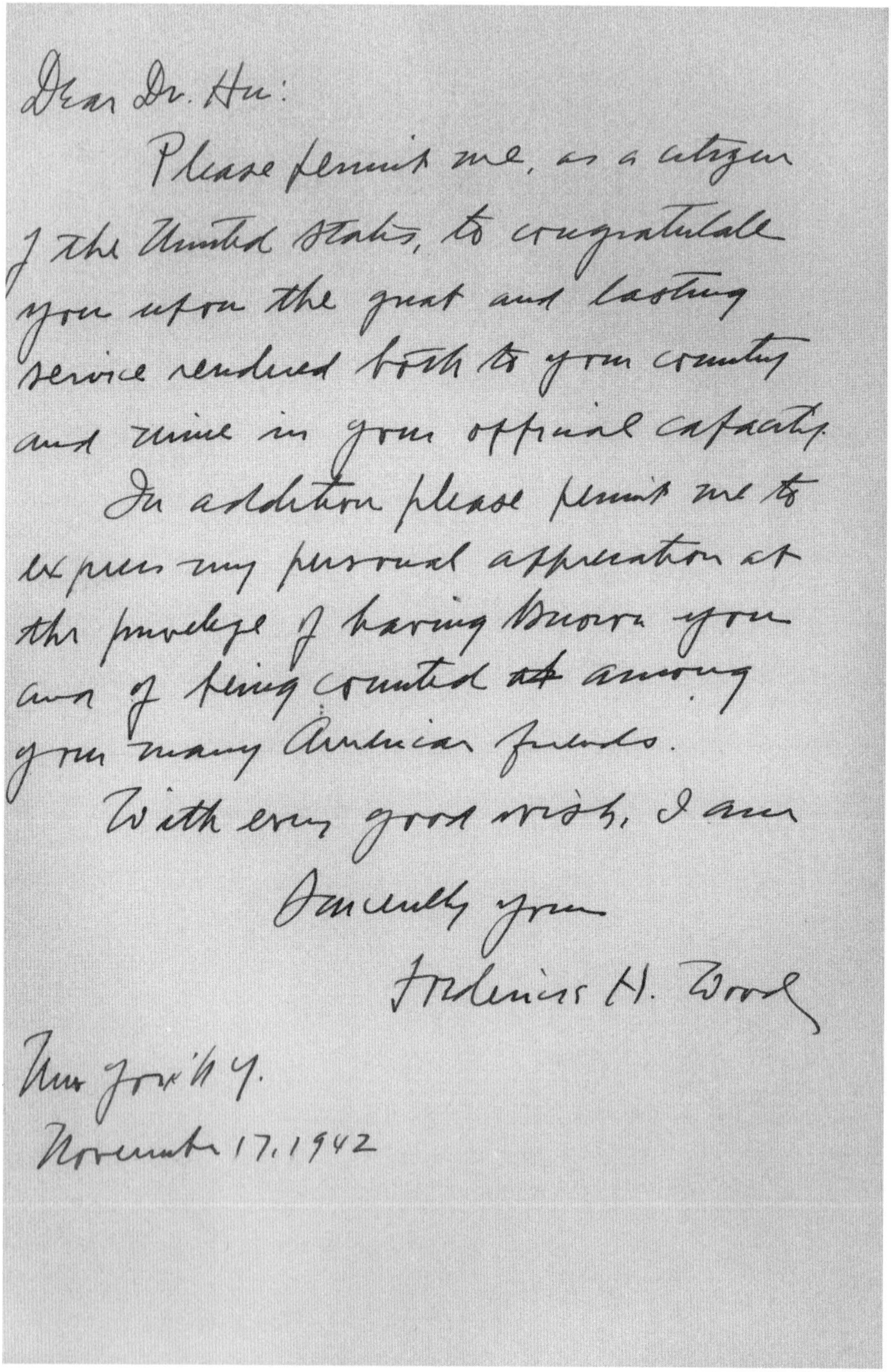

Dear Dr. Hu:

Please permit me, as a citizen of the United States, to congratulate you upon the great and lasting service rendered both to your country and mine in your official capacity.

In addition please permit me to express my personal appreciation at the privilege of having known you and of being counted at among your many American friends.

With every good wish, I am

Sincerely yours

Frederick H. Wood

New York N.Y.
November 17, 1942

圖 1

Dear Dr. Hu:

Please permit me, as a citizen of the United States, to congratulate you upon the great and lasting service rendered both to your country and mine in your official capacity.

In addition please permit me to express my personal appreciation at the privilege of having known you and of being counted among your many American friends.

With very good wish, I am
Sincerely yours,
Frederick H. Wood

New York, N. Y.
November 17, 1942

G. Harold Welch

G. Harold Welch（1896—1992），紐黑文銀行家和房地產開發商。

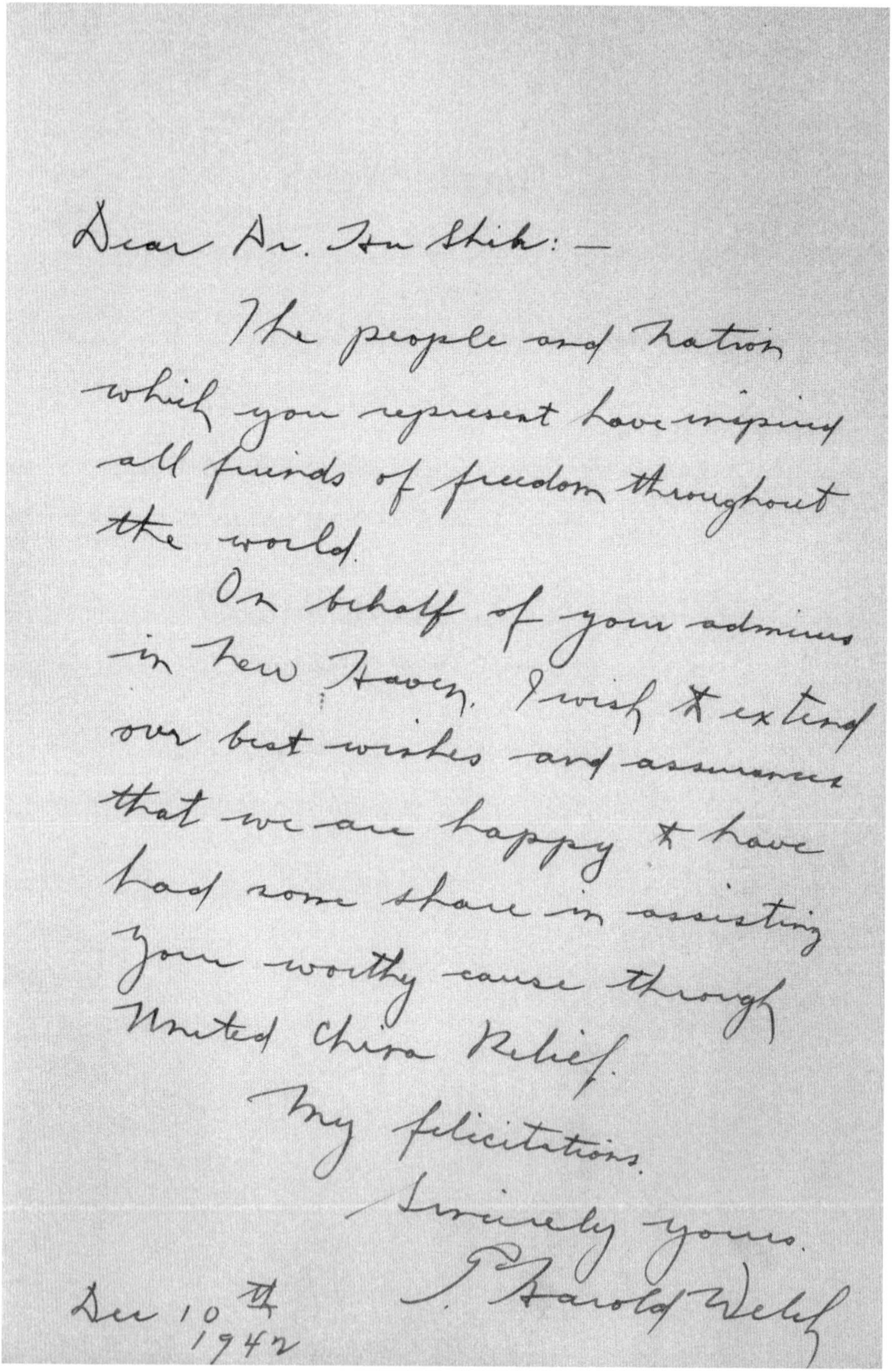

Dear Mr. Hu Shih: —

The people and nation which you represent have inspired all friends of freedom throughout the world.

On behalf of your admirers in New Haven, I wish to extend our best wishes and assurances that we are happy to have had some share in assisting your worthy cause through United China Relief.

My felicitations.

Sincerely yours,

T. Harold Welch

Dec 10th 1942

圖 1

Dear Dr. Hu Shih:—

The people and nation which you represent have inspired all friends of freedom throughout the world.

On behalf of your admirers in New Haven, I wish to extend our best wishes and assurances that we are happy to have had some share in assisting your worthy cause through United China Relief.

My felicitations.
Sincerely yours,
G. Harold Welch

Dec. 10th, 1942

Galen M. Fisher

　　Galen M. Fisher（1873—1955），1897年到日本傳教，1898—1919年任日本基督教青年會會長。1919年回美國，後獲加州大學碩士學位。1921—1934年任職於洛克菲勒基金資助的社會和宗教研究學院。後任加州大學伯克利分校政治學副研究員，太平洋關係學會顧問。

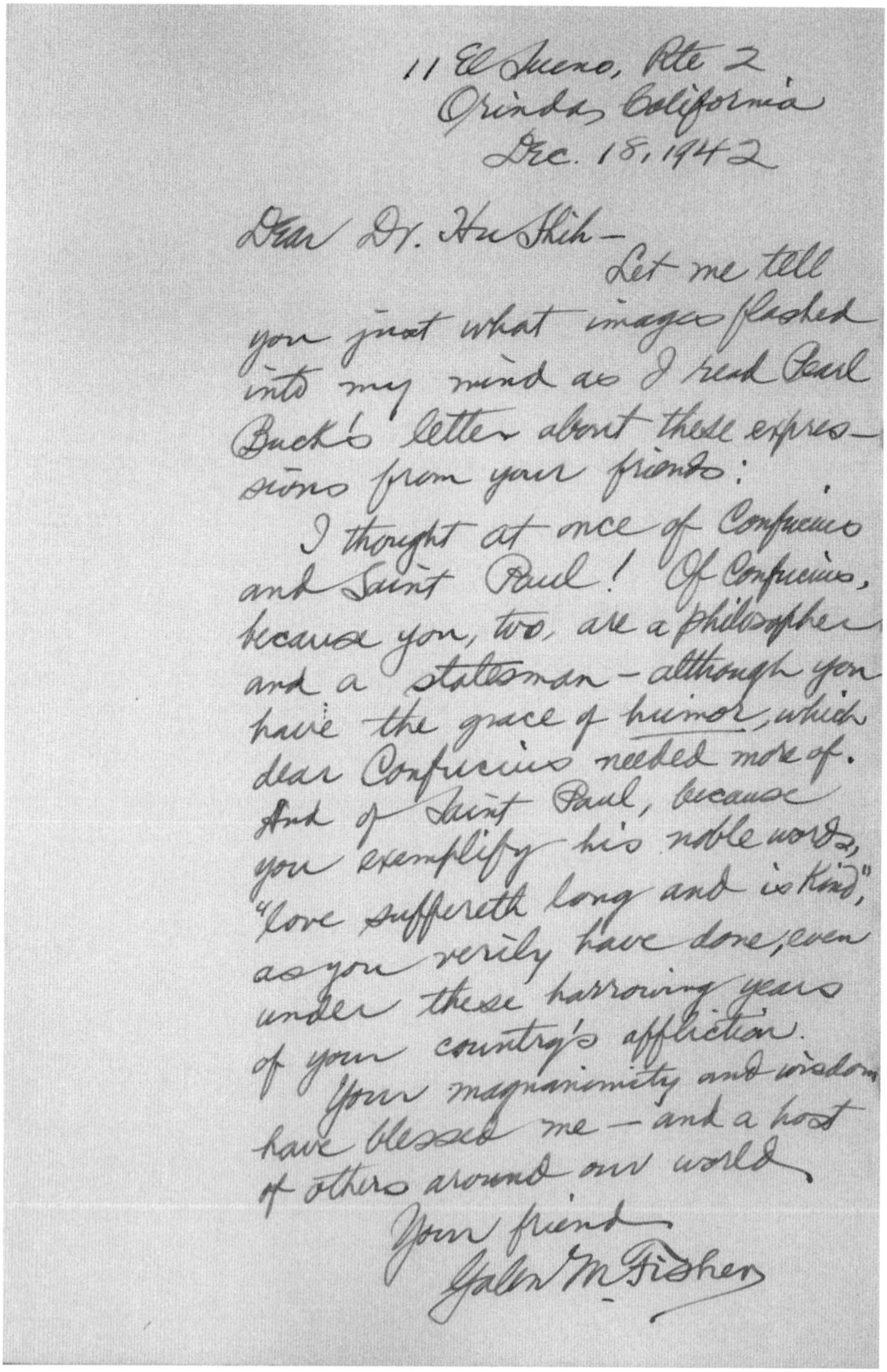

11 El Sueno, Rte 2,
Orinda, California
Dec. 18, 1942

Dear Dr. Hu Shih —

Let me tell you just what images flashed into my mind as I read Pearl Buck's letter about these expressions from your friends:

I thought at once of Confucius and Saint Paul! Of Confucius, because you, too, are a philosopher and a statesman — although you have the grace of humor, which dear Confucius needed more of. And of Saint Paul, because you exemplify his noble words, "Love suffereth long and is kind", as you verily have done, even under these harrowing years of your country's affliction.

Your magnanimity and wisdom have blessed me — and a host of others around our world.

Your friend
Galen M. Fisher

圖 1

11 El Jueno, Rte 2
Orinda, California
Dec. 18, 1942

Dear Dr. Hu Shih—

Let me tell you just what images flashed into my mind as I read Pearl Buck's letter about these expressions from your friends:

I thought at once of Confucius and Saint Paul! Of Confucius, because you, too, are a philosopher and a statesman—although you have the grace of humor, which dear Confucius needed more of. And of Saint Paul, because you exemplify his noble words, "love suffereth long and is kind," as you verily have done, even under these harrowing years of your country's affliction.

Your magnanimity and wisdom have blessed me—and a host of others around our world.

Your Friend
Galen M. Fisher

George T. Marchmont

作者生平不詳。

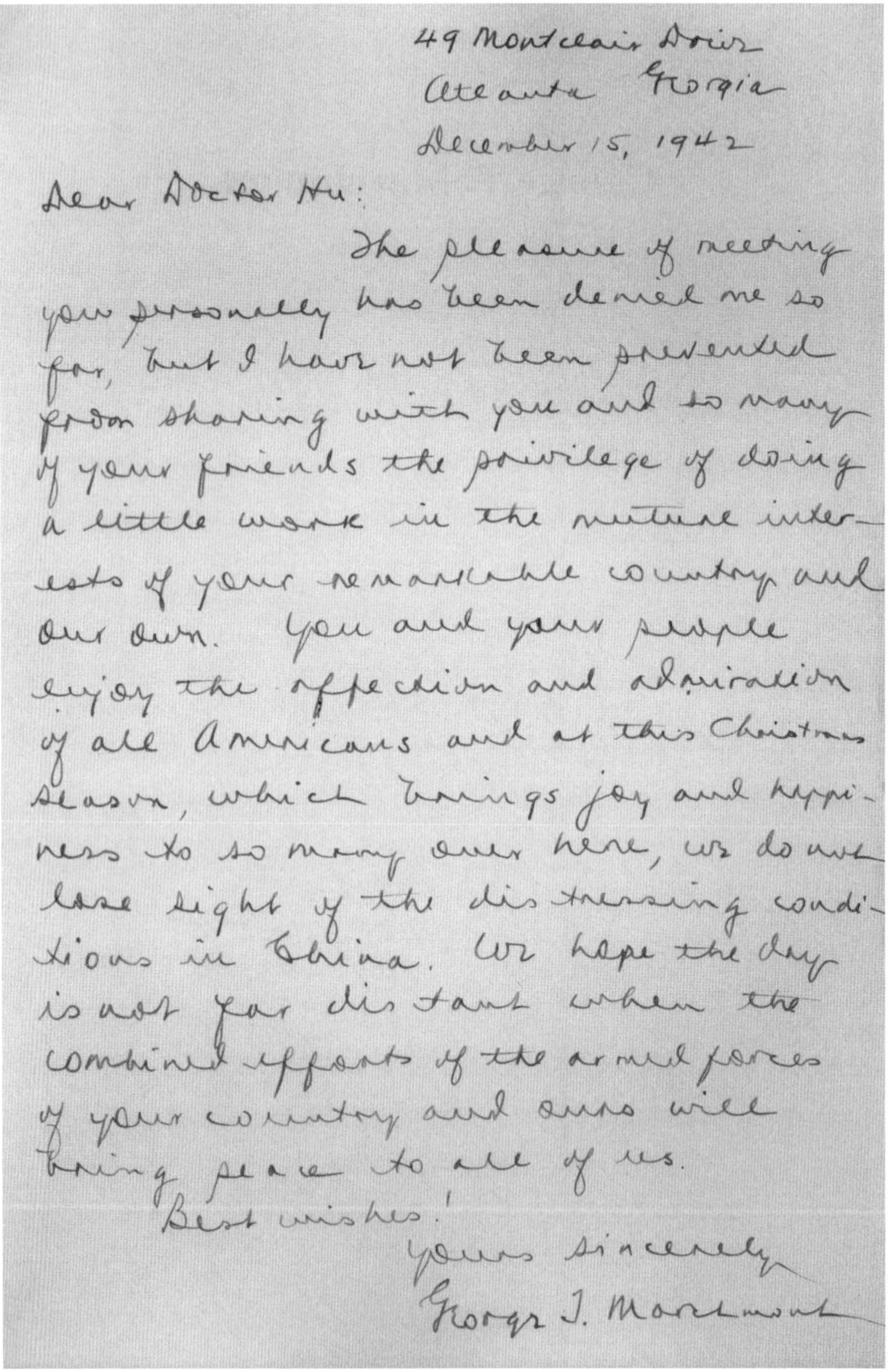

49 Montclair Drive
Atlanta Georgia
December 15, 1942

Dear Doctor Hu:

The pleasure of meeting you personally has been denied me so far, but I have not been prevented from sharing with you and so many of your friends the privilege of doing a little work in the mutual interests of your remarkable country and our own. You and your people enjoy the affection and admiration of all Americans and at this Christmas season, which brings joy and happiness to so many over here, we do not lose sight of the distressing conditions in China. We hope the day is not far distant when the combined efforts of the armed forces of your country and ours will bring peace to all of us.

Best wishes!

Yours sincerely
George J. Montmount

圖 1

49 Montclair Drive
Atlanta, Georgia
December 15, 1942

Dear Doctor Hu:

The pleasure of meeting you personally has been denied me so far, but I have not been prevented from sharing with you and so many of your friends the privilege of doing a little work in the mutual interests of your remarkable country and our own. You and your people enjoy the affection and admiration of all Americans and at this Christmas season, which brings joy and happiness to so many over here, we do not lose sight of the distressing conditions in China. We hope the day is not far distant when the combined efforts of the armed forces of your country and ours will bring peace to all of us.

Best wishes!

Yours sincerely
George T. Marchmont

H. E. Yarnell

　　H. E. Yarnell（1875—1959），生於美國愛荷華州。1893 年入美國海軍學院，畢業後在美國海軍服役，曾參加美西戰爭和第一、二次世界大戰，曾任美國海軍上將。胡適任駐美大使期間與其有交往，在 1939 年 9 月 5 日的日記中有拜訪 Yarnell 的記載。另北京檔藏有 Yarnell 1941 年 12 月 26 日致胡適書信一封。

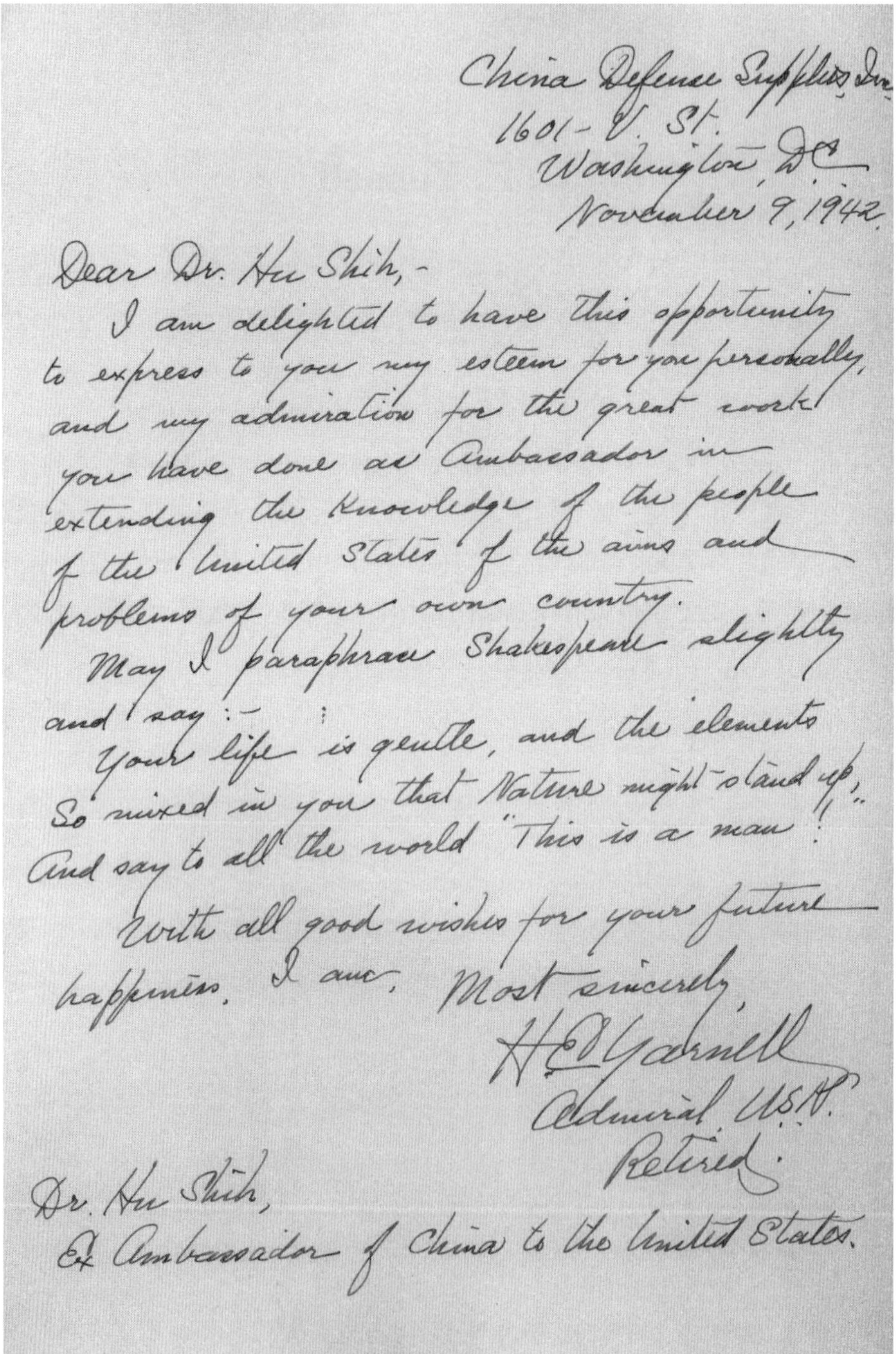

China Defense Supplies, Inc.
1601 V. St.
Washington, D.C.
November 9, 1942.

Dear Dr. Hu Shih,-

I am delighted to have this opportunity to express to you my esteem for you personally, and my admiration for the great work you have done as Ambassador in extending the knowledge of the people of the United States of the aims and problems of your own country.

May I paraphrase Shakespeare slightly and say:-

Your life is gentle, and the elements so mixed in you that Nature might stand up, And say to all the world "This is a man".

With all good wishes for your future happiness, I am,

Most sincerely,
H. E. Yarnell
Admiral, U.S.N.
Retired.

Dr. Hu Shih,
Ex Ambassador of China to the United States.

圖1

China Defense Supplies, Inc.
1601-V. St.
Washington D.C.
November 9, 1942

Dear Dr. Hu Shih, —

I am delighted to have this opportunity to express to you my esteem for you personally, and my admiration for the great work you have done as Ambassador in extending the knowledge of the people of the United States of the aims and problems of your own country.

May I paraphrase Shakespeare slightly and say: —

Your life is gentle, and the elements so mixed in you that Nature might stand up, and say to all the world: "This is a man!"

With all good wished for your future happiness, I am

Most sincerely,
H. E. Yarnell
Admiral, U.S.N.
Retired

Dr. Hu Shih,
Ex Ambassador of China to the United States.

H. R. Ekins

　　H. R. Ekins（？—1963），新聞記者，編輯。二十世紀二十年代曾任合衆社（United Press）駐火魯奴奴、馬尼拉分社負責人，三十年代初曾任合衆社駐上海分社負責人，後任北平分社負責人，1938年回國。1939年任合衆社羅馬分社負責人。

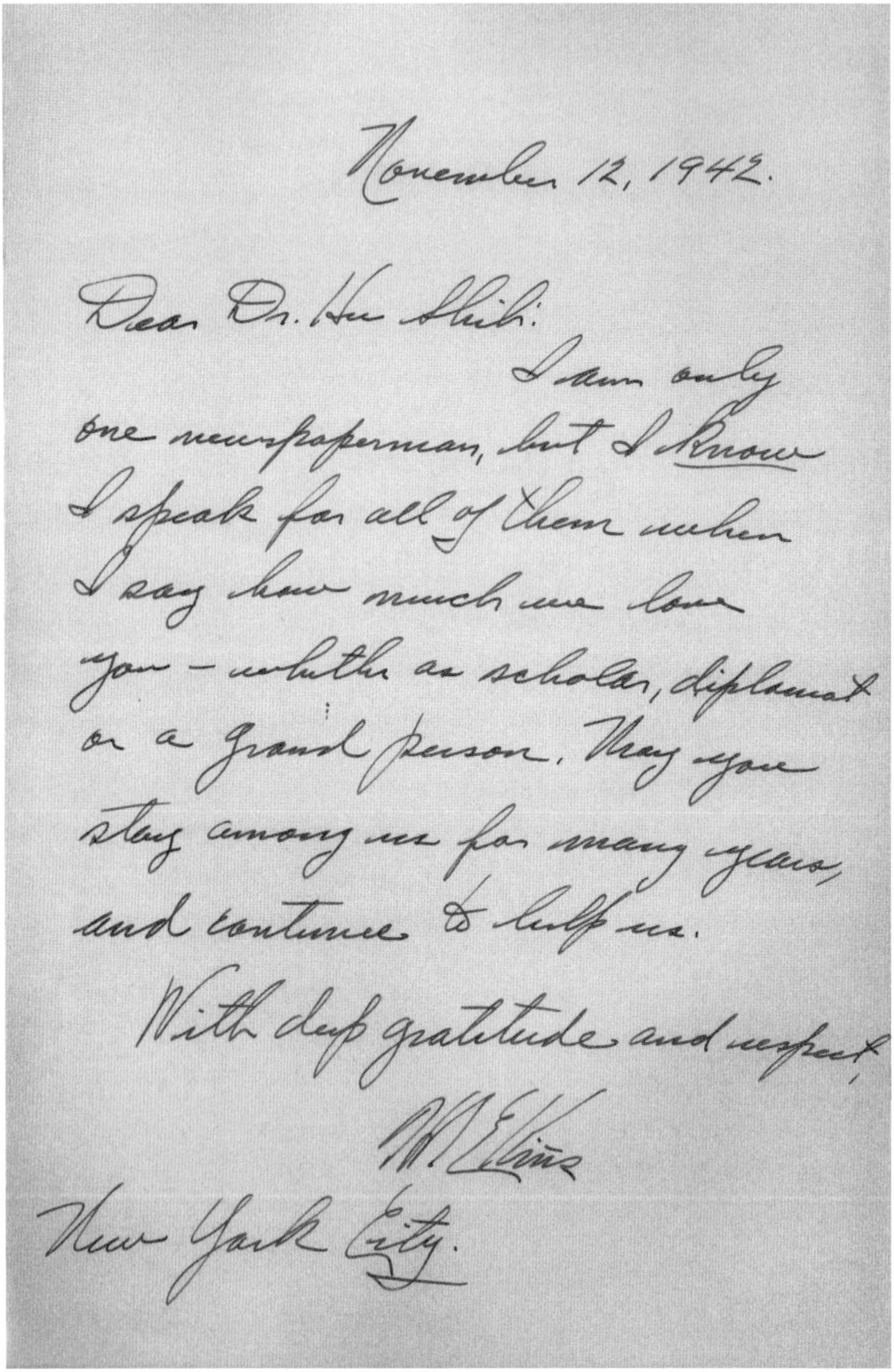

November 12, 1942.

Dear Dr. Hu Shih:

I am only one newspaperman, but I know I speak for all of them when I say how much we love you — whether as scholar, diplomat or a grand person. May you stay among us for many years, and continue to help us.

With deep gratitude and respect,

W. Elins

New York City.

圖 1

November 12, 1942

Dear Dr. Hu Shih:

I am only one newspaperman, but I <u>know</u> I speak for all of them when I say how much we love you—whether as scholar, diplomat or a grand person. May you stay among us for many years, and continue to help us.

With deep gratitude and respect,
H. R. Ekins

New York City

Harlan Fiske Stone

　　Harlan Fiske Stone（1872—1946），生於美國新罕布什爾州切斯特菲爾德。律師、政治家，時任美國最高法院首席大法官。1894 年畢業於艾姆赫斯特學院，曾任美國司法部長、最高法院大法官等職。胡適任駐美大使前後與其有交往，北京檔藏有 Stone 致胡適書信兩封，時間爲 1940 年 5 月 30 日和 1943 年 10 月 18 日。

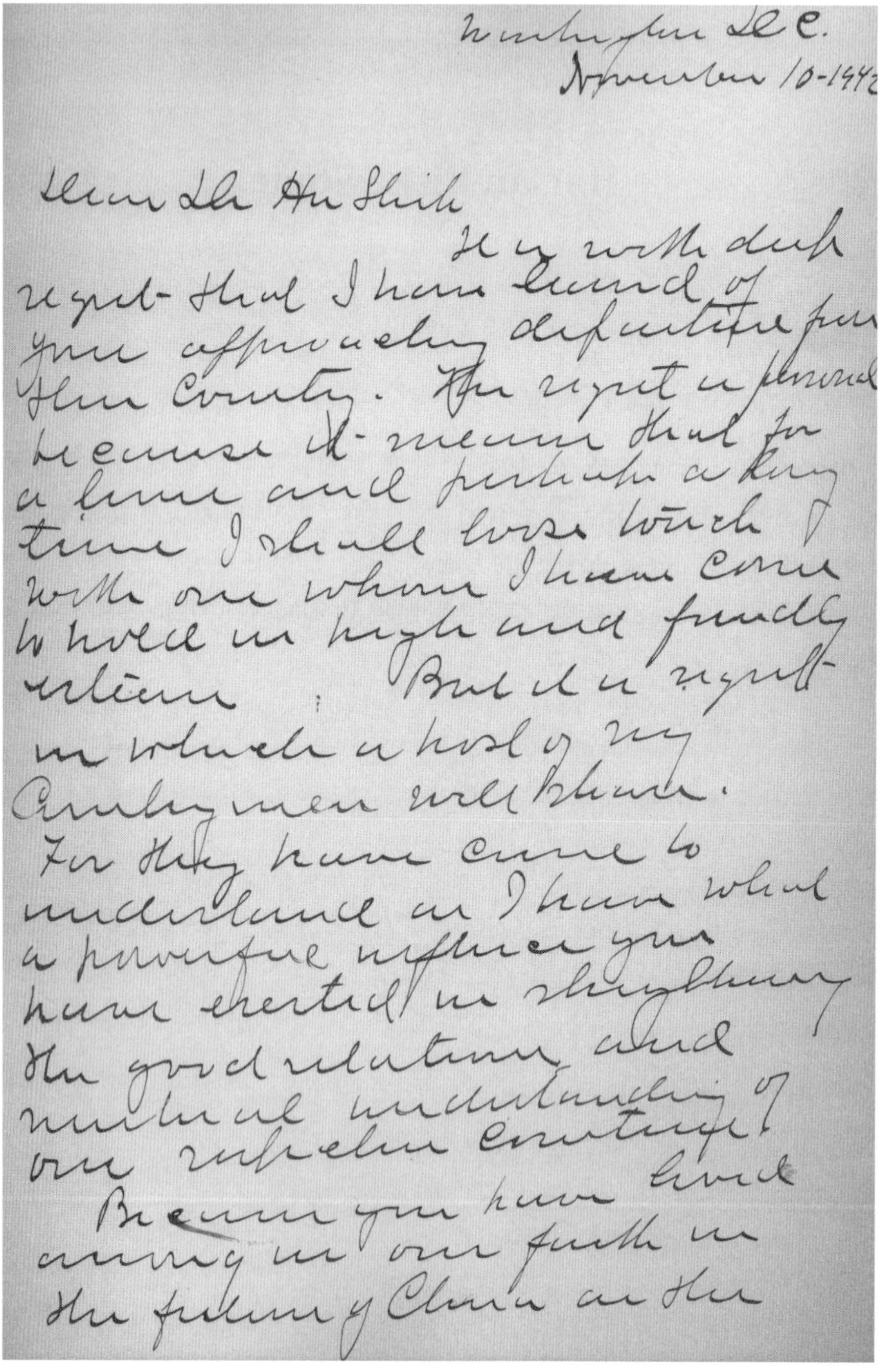

Washington D.C.
November 10-1942

Dear Dr. Hu Shih

It is with deep regret that I have learned of your approaching departure from this country. The regret is personal because it means that for a time and perhaps a long time I shall lose touch with one whom I have come to hold in high and friendly esteem. But it is regret in which a host of my countrymen will share. For they have come to understand as I have what a powerful influence you have exerted in strengthening the good relations and mutual understanding of our respective countries.

Because you have lived among us our faith in the future of China is the

圖1

Washington D.C.
November 10 - 1942

Dear Dr. Hu Shih

It is with deep regret that I have learned of your approaching departure from this country. The regret is personal because it means that for a time and perhaps a long time I shall lose touch with one whom I have come to hold in high and friendly esteem. But it is regret in which a host of my countrymen will share. For they have come to understand as I have what a powerful influence you have erected in strengthening the good relation and mutual understanding of our respective countries.

Because you have lived among us our faith in the future of China as the great force for peace and the civilized life in the end — and our determination to give her the helping hand have been revived and strengthened.

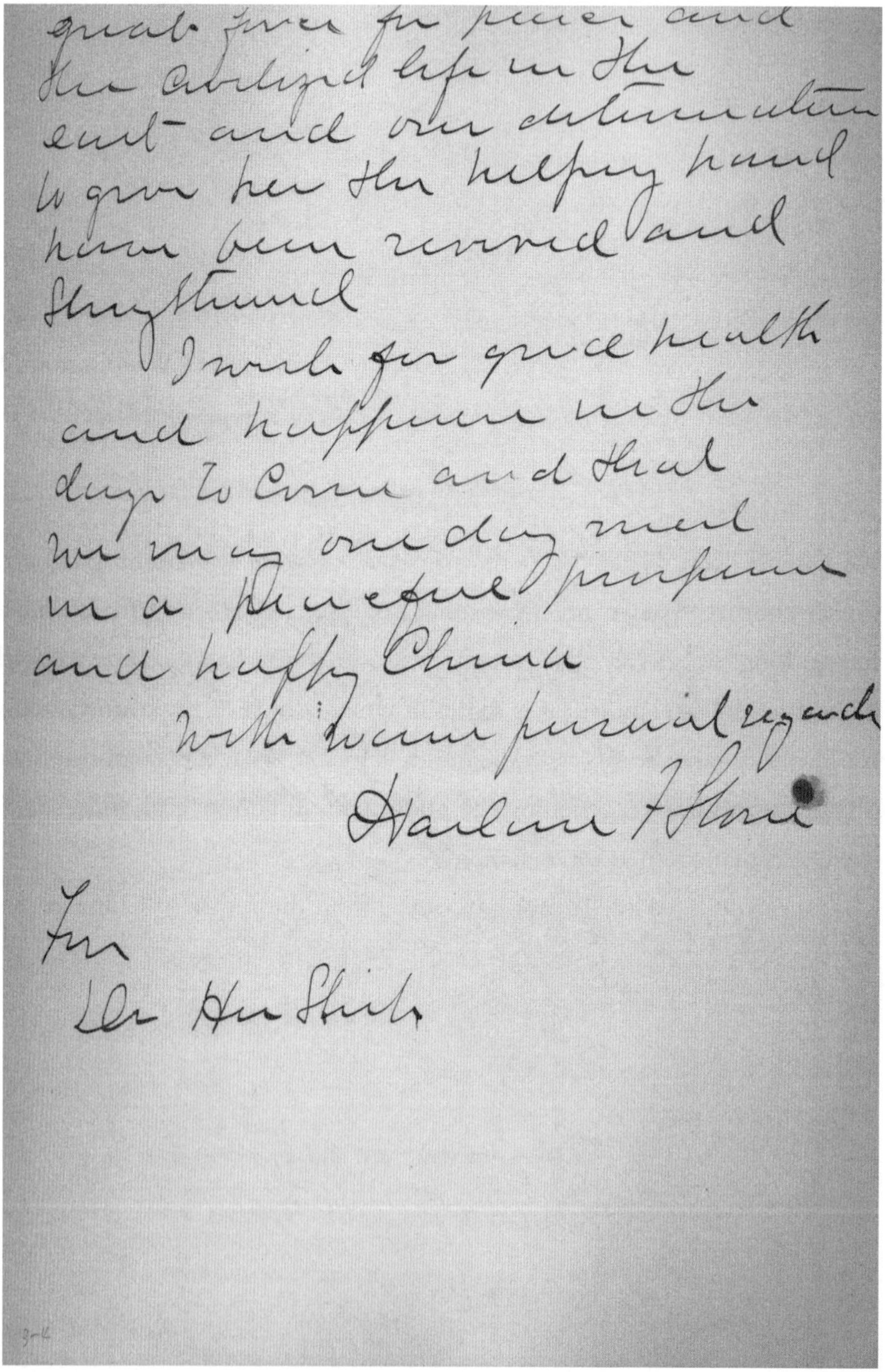

I wish for good health and happiness in the days to come and that we may one day meet in a peaceful, prosperous and happy China.

With warm personal regards

Harlan F Stone

For
Dr Hu Shih

圖 2

great force for peace and the civilized life in the east and our determination to give her the helping hand have been revived and strengthened.

I wish for good health and happiness in the days to come and that we may one day meet in a peaceful prosperous and happy China.

With warm personal regards
Harlan F. Stone

For Dr. Hu Shih

Harold E. Stassen

Harold E. Stassen（1907—2001），生於美國明尼蘇達州，時任該州州長。1927年獲明尼蘇達大學文學士學位，1929年獲該校法學士學位。1939—1943年任明尼蘇達州州長。1941—1942年任全美州長協會主席。1948—1953年任賓州大學校長。1953年任共同安全署署長。1953—1955年任援外事務管理署署長。

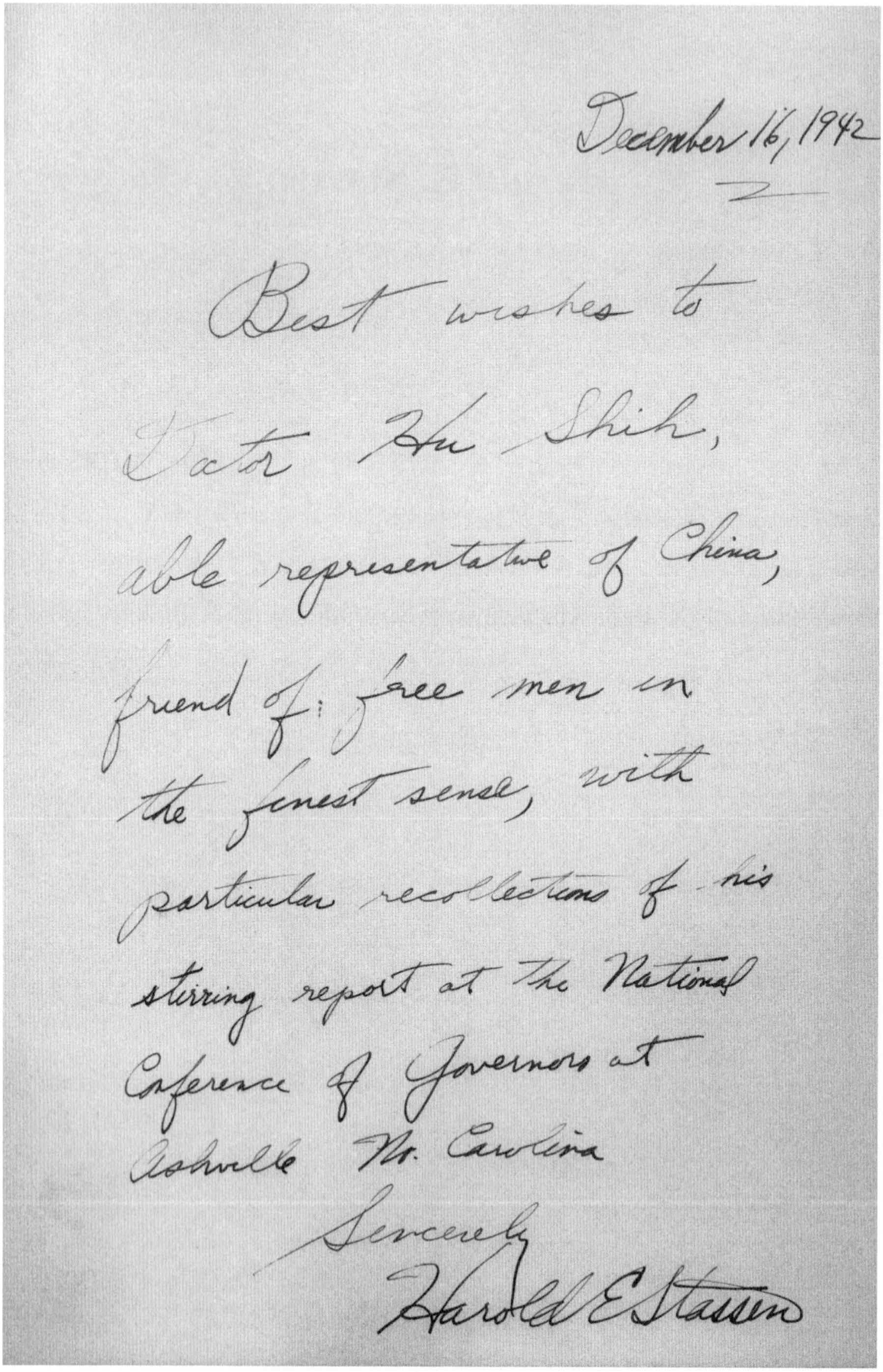

December 16, 1942

Best wishes to Dato Hu Shih, able representative of China, friend of free men in the finest sense, with particular recollections of his stirring report at the National Conference of Governors at Asheville N. Carolina

Sincerely
Harold E Stassen

圖 1

December 16, 1942

Best wishes to Doctor Hu Shih, able representative of China, friend of free men in the finest sense, with particular recollections of his stirring report at the National Conference of Governors at Asheville No. Carolina.

Sincerely

Harold E. Stassen

Harold L. Ickes

　　Harold L. Ickes（1874—1952），生於美國賓夕法尼亞州，時任美國內政部長。1897 年獲芝加哥大學文學士學位，1907 年獲芝加哥大學法學院法學士學位。1933—1946 年任美國內政部長。胡適任駐美大使期間與其有交往，曾於 1939 年 9 月 22 日致信 Ickes，寄贈紀念郵票。

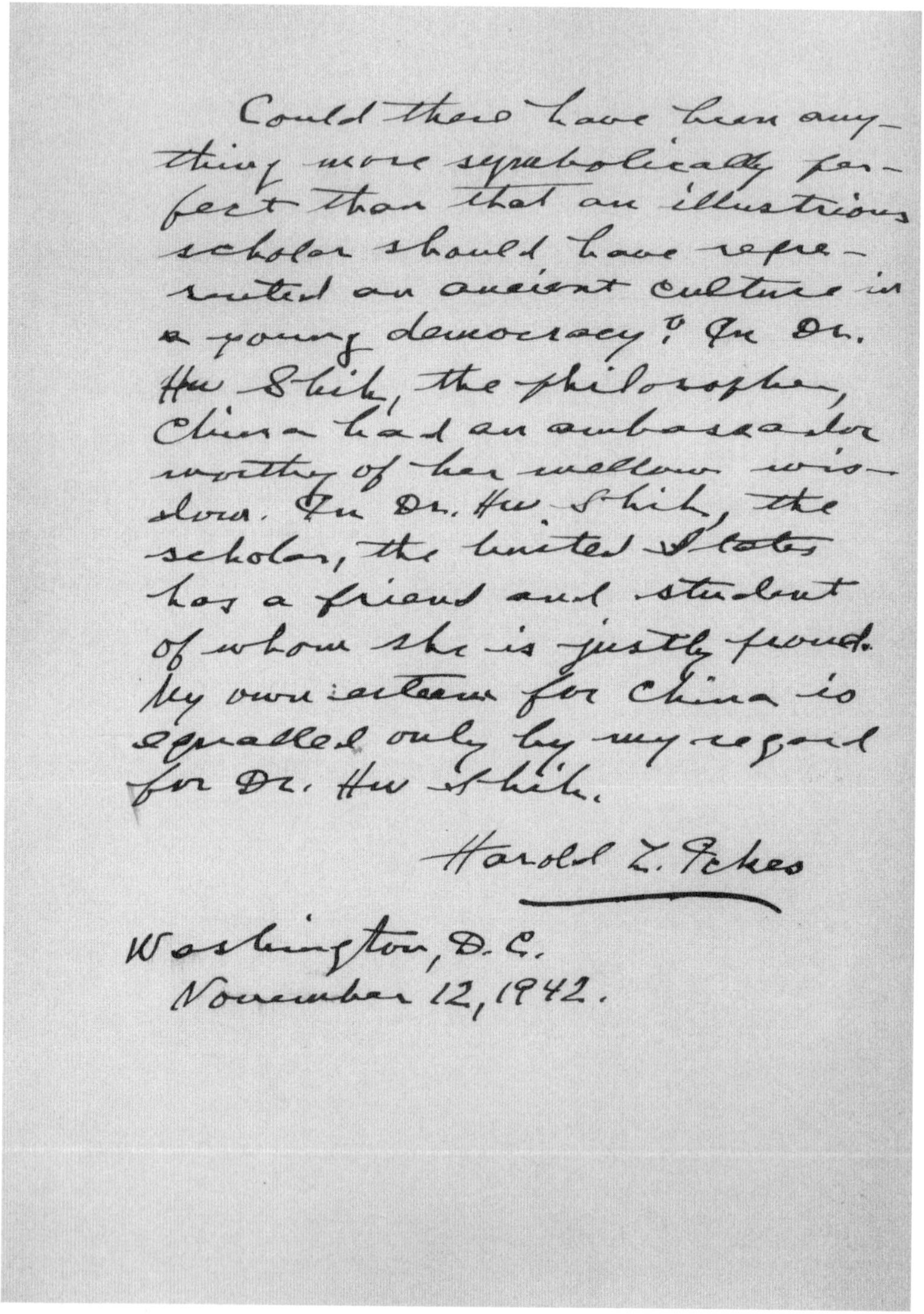

Could there have been anything more symbolically perfect than that an illustrious scholar should have represented an ancient culture in a young democracy? In Dr. Hu Shih, the philosopher, China had an ambassador worthy of her mellow wisdom. In Dr. Hu Shih, the scholar, the United States has a friend and student of whom she is justly proud. My own esteem for China is equalled only by my regard for Dr. Hu Shih.

Harold L. Ickes

Washington, D. C.
November 12, 1942.

圖1

Could there have been anything more symbolically perfect than that an illustrious scholar should have represented an ancient culture in a young democracy? In Dr. Hu Shih, the philosopher, China had an ambassador worthy of her mellow wisdom. In Dr. Hu Shih, the scholar, the United States has a friend and student of whom she is justly proud. My own esteem for China is equalled only by my regard for Dr. Hu Shih.

Harold L. Ickes

Washington, D.C.
November 12, 1942

Harper Sibley, Georgiana Sibley

　　Georgiana Sibley（1887—1980），生於美國紐約州米爾布魯克。美國基督教普世運動領導者。1945年任婦女教會聯合會官方觀察員，1946—1948年任該聯合會主席。美國廢除種族歧視、控制核武器運動領導者。

　　Harper Sibley，生平不詳。

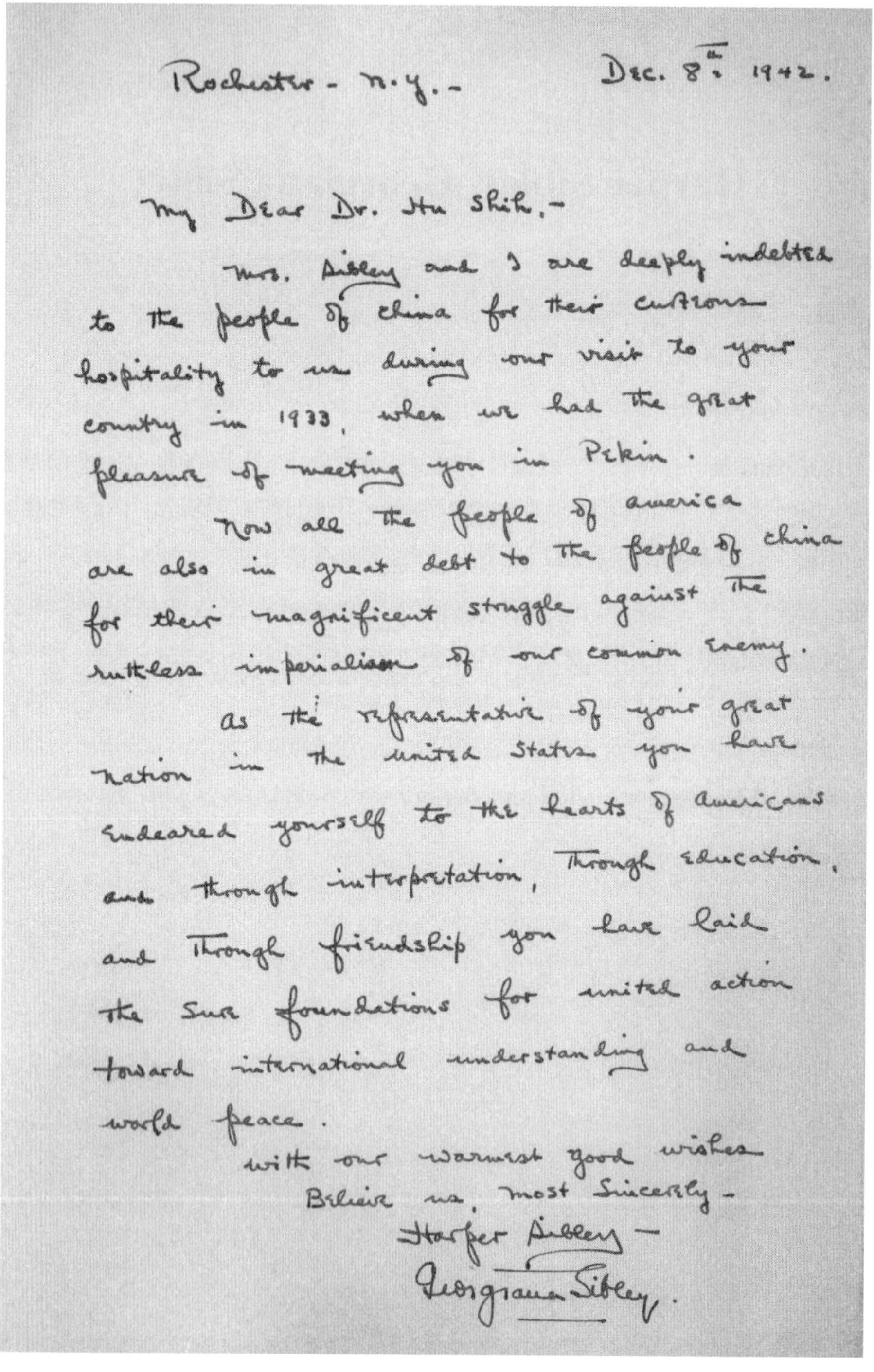

Rochester - N.Y. -   Dec. 8th. 1942.

My Dear Dr. Hu Shih, -

Mrs. Sibley and I are deeply indebted to the people of China for their courteous hospitality to us during our visit to your country in 1933, when we had the great pleasure of meeting you in Pekin.

Now all the people of America are also in great debt to the people of China for their magnificent struggle against the ruthless imperialism of our common enemy.

As the representative of your great nation in the United States you have endeared yourself to the hearts of Americans and through interpretation, through education, and through friendship you have laid the sure foundations for united action toward international understanding and world peace.

With our warmest good wishes
Believe us, most sincerely -
Harper Sibley -
Georgiana Sibley.

圖 1

Rochester—N.Y.— Dec. 8th, 1942

My Dear Dr. Hu Shih,—

Mrs. Sibley and I are deeply indebted to the people of China for their courteous hospitality to us during our visit to your country in 1933, when we had the great pleasure of meeting you in Pekin.

Now all the people of America are also in great debt to the people of China for their magnificent struggle against the ruthless imperialism of our common enemy.

As the representative of your great nation in the United States you have endeared yourself to the hearts of Americans and through interpretation, though education, and through friendship you have laid the sure foundations for united action toward international understanding and world peace.

With our warmest good wishes

Believe us, most sincerely—

Harper Sibley

Georgiana Sibley

Harry B. Price

　　Harry B. Price，生平不詳，抗戰期間曾任職於全美助華聯合總會（United China Relief）。北京檔中收有胡適1941年6月14日致Price書信一封。另有Price 1941年9月26日致胡適書信一封。

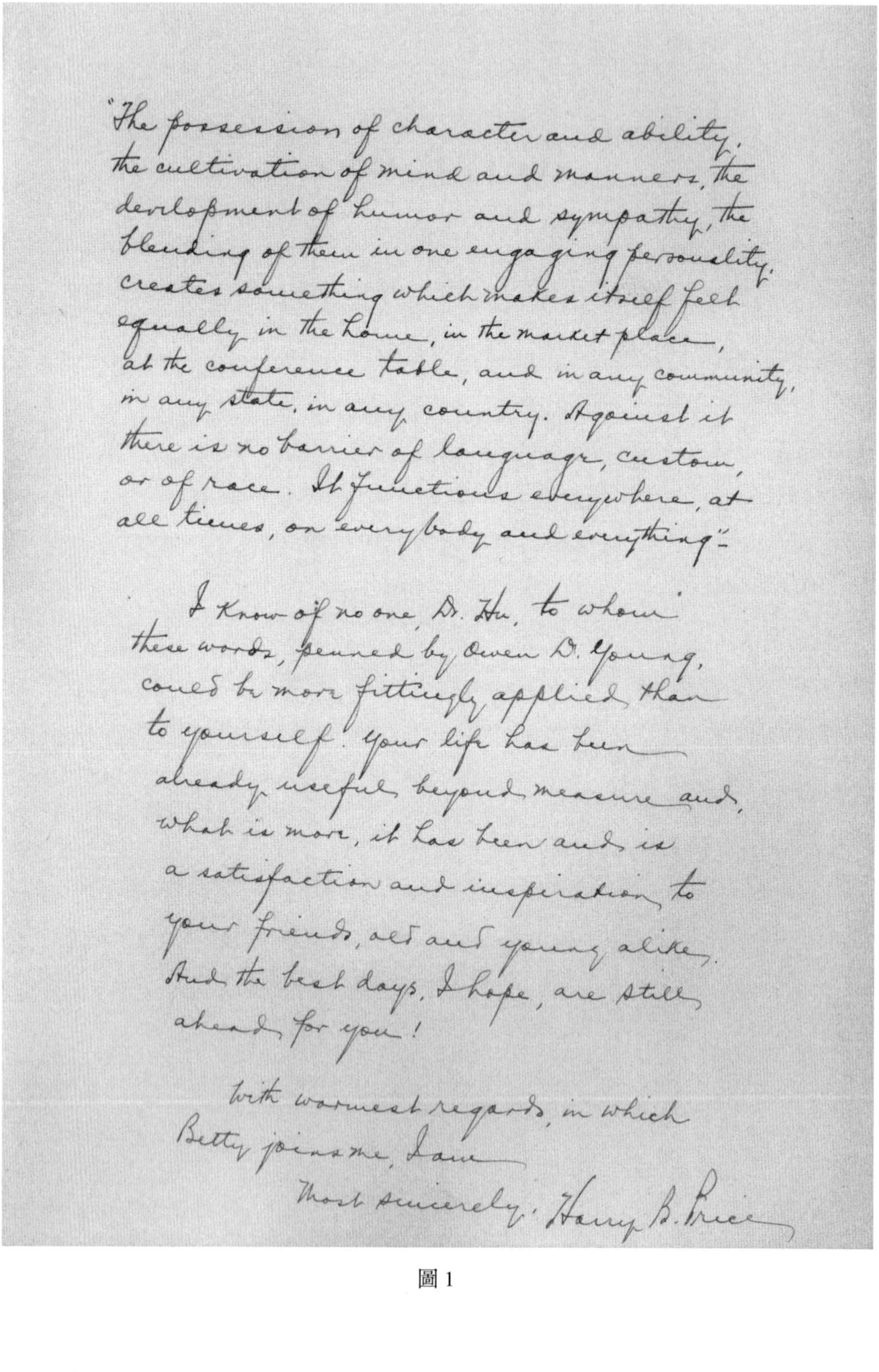

"The possession of character and ability, the cultivation of mind and manners, the development of humor and sympathy, the blending of them in one engaging personality, creates something which makes itself felt equally in the home, in the market place, at the conference table, and in any community, in any state, in any country. Against it there is no barrier of language, custom, or of race. It functions everywhere, at all times, on everybody and everything"—

I know of no one, Dr. Hu, to whom these words, penned by Owen D. Young, could be more fittingly applied than to yourself. Your life has been already useful beyond measure and, what is more, it has been and is a satisfaction and inspiration to your friends, old and young alike. And the best days, I hope, are still ahead, for you!

With warmest regards, in which Betty joins me, I am

Most sincerely, Harry B. Price

圖 1

"The possession of character and ability, the cultivation of mind and manners, the development of humor and sympathy, the blending of them in one engaging personality, creates something which makes itself feel equally in the home, in the market place, at the conference table, and in any community, in any state, in any country. Against it there is no barrier of language, custom, or of race. It functions everywhere, at all times, on everybody and everything."

I know of no one, Dr. Hu, to whom these words, penned by Owen D. Young, could be more fittingly applied than to yourself. Your life has been already useful beyond measure and, what is more, it has been and is a satisfaction and inspiration to your friends, old and young alike. And the best days, I hope, are still ahead for you!

With warmest regards, in which Betty joins me, I am

Most sincerely, Harry B. Price

Harvey S. Firestone, Jr

　　Harvey S. Firestone, Jr.（1898—1973），早年就讀於美國北卡羅來納州的阿什維爾學校。一戰期間爲海軍飛行員。1920年畢業於普林斯頓大學。畢業後在家族企業凡士通輪胎與橡膠公司工作，1941年出任該公司董事會主席。爲國際音樂聯誼會Delta Omicron的主要贊助人。

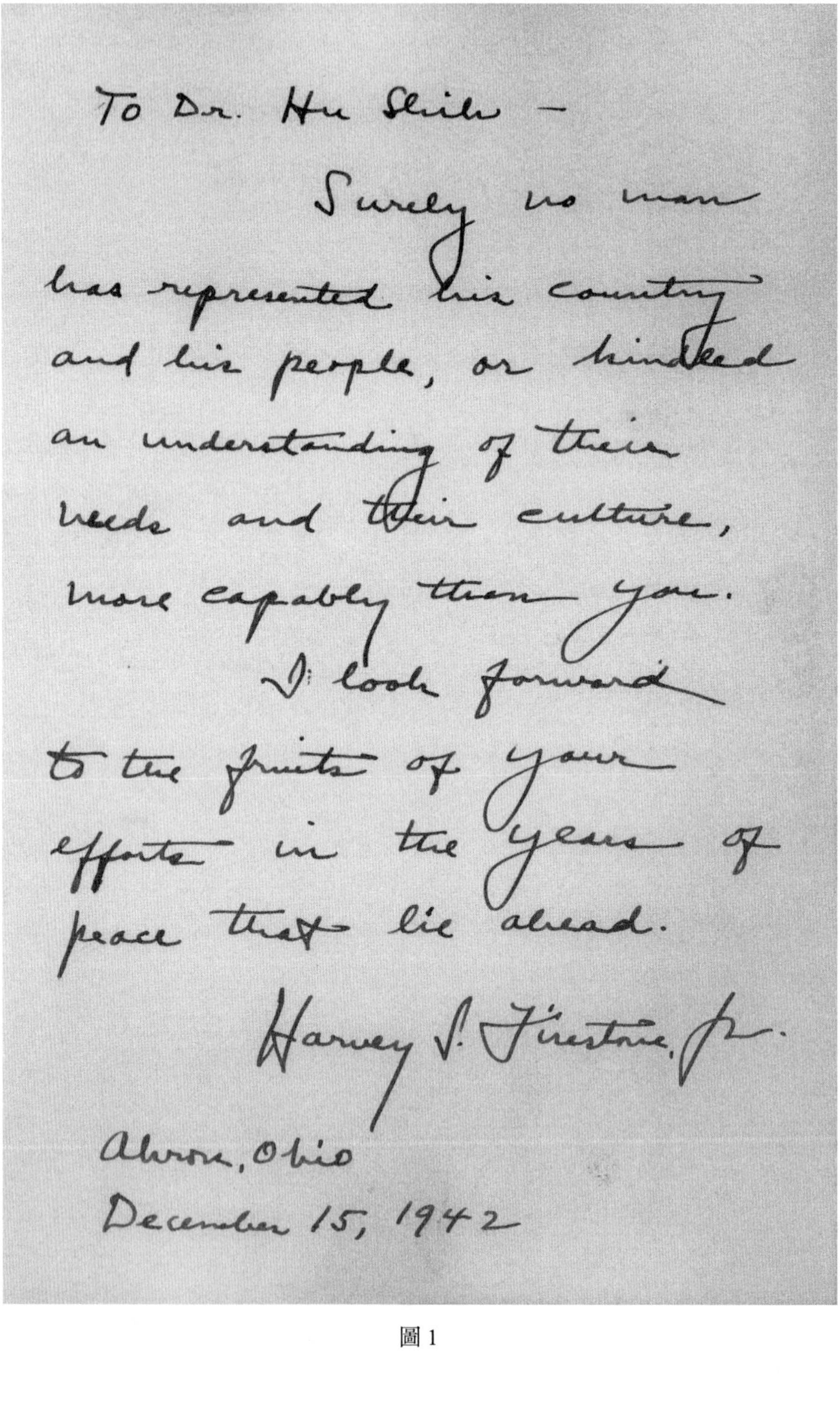

To Dr. Hu Shih —

Surely no man has represented his country and his people, or kindled an understanding of their needs and their culture, more capably than you.

I look forward to the fruits of your efforts in the years of peace that lie ahead.

Harvey S. Firestone, Jr.

Akron, Ohio
December 15, 1942

圖1

To Dr. Hu Shih—

Surely no man has represented his country and his people, or kindled an understanding of their needs and their culture, more capably than you.

I look forward to the fruits of your efforts in the years of peace that lie ahead.

Harvey S. Firestone, Jr.

Akron, Ohio
December 15, 1942

Helen Rogers Reid

Helen Rogers Reid（1882—1970），生於美國威斯康辛州阿普爾頓。1903年畢業於巴納德學院。畢業後曾擔任美國駐英國和法國大使夫人秘書。1918年任職於《紐約先驅報》，後將該報與《紐約論壇報》合併。1950年當選美國人文與科學院院士。曾任紐約大都會藝術博物館董事，雷德基金會主席。胡適任駐美大使前後與其有交往，北京檔收錄有其致胡適電報一通。

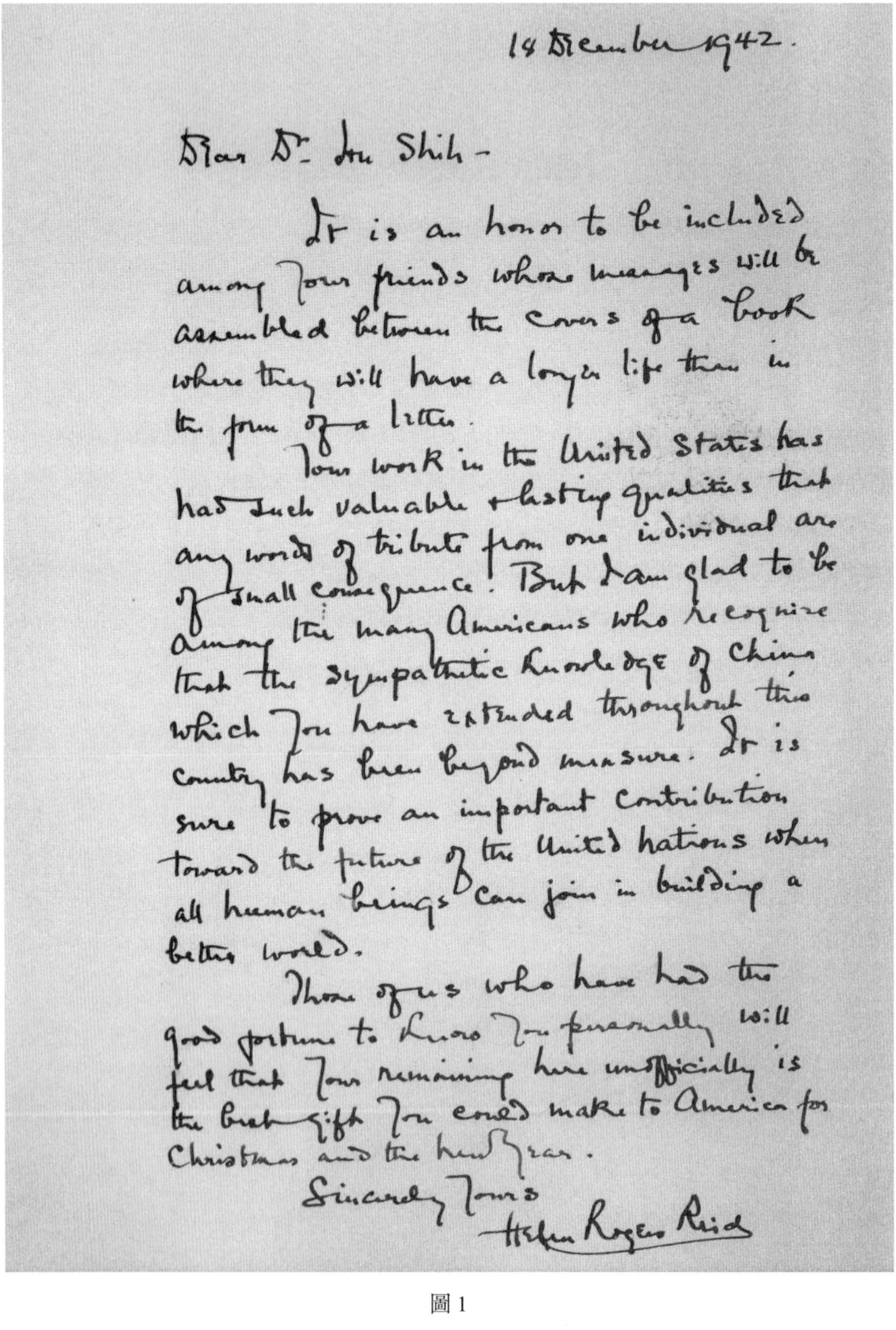

18 December 1942.

Dear Dr. Hu Shih —

It is an honor to be included among your friends whose messages will be assembled between the covers of a book where they will have a longer life than in the form of a letter.

Your work in the United States has had such valuable & lasting qualities that any words of tribute from one individual are of small consequence. But I am glad to be among the many Americans who recognize that the sympathetic knowledge of China which you have extended throughout this country has been beyond measure. It is sure to prove an important contribution toward the future of the United Nations when all human beings can join in building a better world.

Those of us who have had the good fortune to know you personally will feel that your remaining here unofficially is the best gift you could make to America for Christmas and the New Year.

Sincerely yours
Helen Rogers Reid

圖1

18 December 1942

Dear Dr. Hu Shih—

It is an honor to be included among your friends whose messages will be assembled between the covers of a book where they will have a longer life than in the form of a letter.

Your work in the United States has had such valuable & lasting qualities that any words of tribute from one individual are of small consequence. But I am glad to be among the many Americans who recognize that the sympathetic knowledge of China which you have extended throughout this country has been beyond measure. It is sure to prove an important contribution toward the future of the United Nations when all human beings can join in building a better world.

Those of us who have had the good fortune to know you personally will feel that your remaining here unofficially is the best gift you could make to America for Christmas and the New Year.

Sincerely yours
Helen Rogers Reid

Henry R. Luce

　　Henry R. Luce（1898—1967），生於山東登州（今煙臺市蓬萊區），曾就讀於芝罘學校。15 歲回美國，就讀於康涅狄格州霍奇科斯學校，並編輯《霍奇科斯文學月刊》。後入耶魯大學，並任《耶魯日報》主編，1920 年畢業。後到牛津大學學習歷史一年。1921 年到《巴爾的摩新聞報》工作。1922 年與布里頓·哈登成立時代公司，次年發行《時代》雜誌。1930 年創辦《財富》雜誌，1936 年收購《生活》雜誌並改爲週刊。此後又創辦多種有影響的雜誌。被譽爲"他的時代最具影響力的美國公民"。胡適任駐美大使前後與魯斯有交往，北京檔收錄有胡適與魯斯往來函電十通，時間從 1941 年 2 月到 1943 年 11 月。

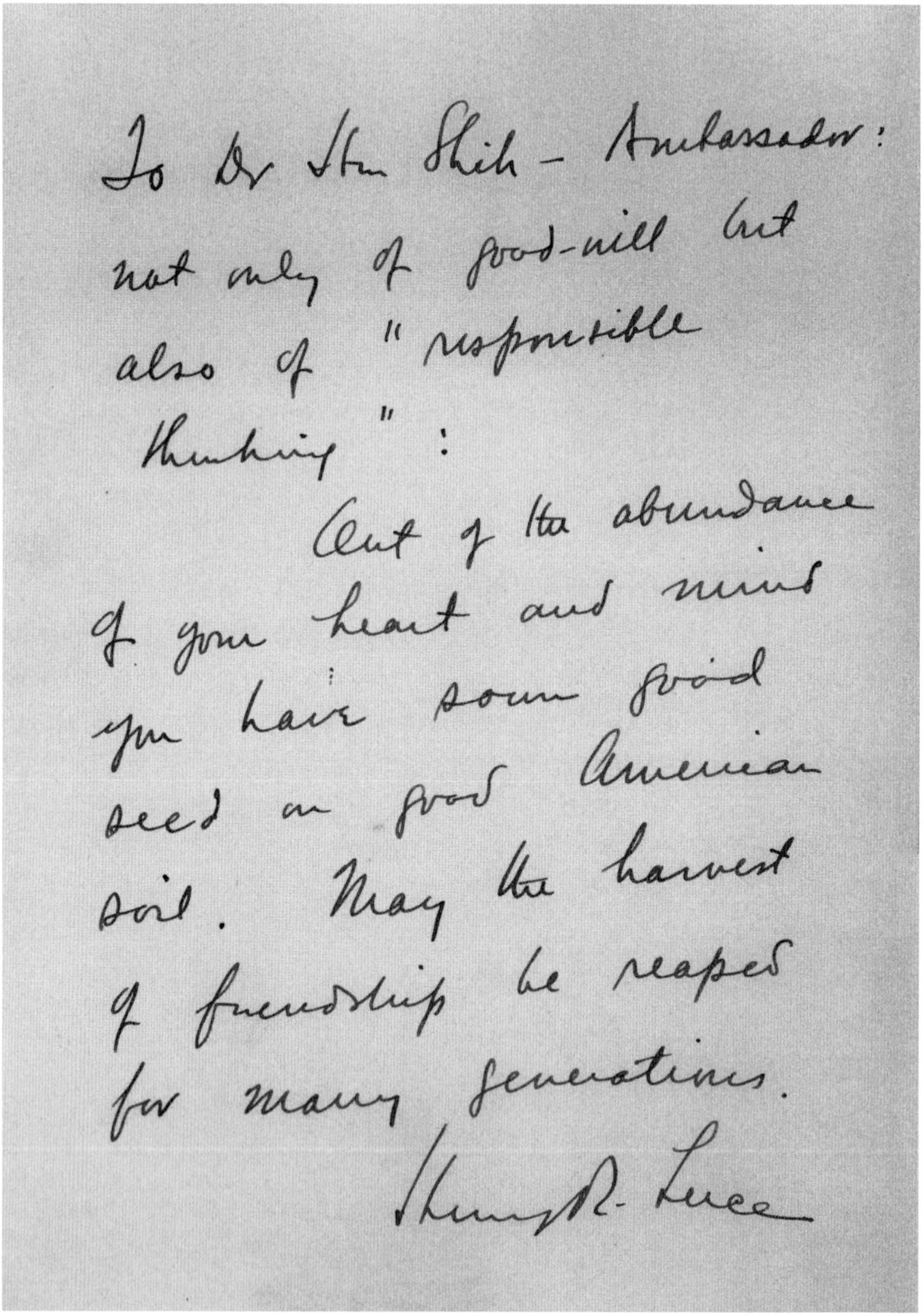

To Dr Hu Shih — Ambassador:

not only of good-will but also of "responsible thinking":

Out of the abundance of your heart and mind you have sown good seed on good American soil. May the harvest of friendship be reaped for many generations.

Henry R. Luce

圖1

To Dr. Hu Shih—Ambassador:

    not only of good-will but also of "responsible thanking":

    Out of the abundance of your heart and mind you have some good seed on good American soil. May the harvest of friendship be reaped for many generations.

Henry R. Luce

Henry St. George Tucker

　　H. St. George Tucker（1874—1959），生於美國弗吉尼亞州。1895 年畢業於弗吉尼亞大學，獲碩士學位。後獲弗吉尼亞聖公會神學院神學學士學位。1899 年到日本傳教，前後達 24 年，曾任東京聖保羅學院校長。1923 年回美國。1927 年任弗吉尼亞大主教。後任美國聖公會第 19 任大主教。

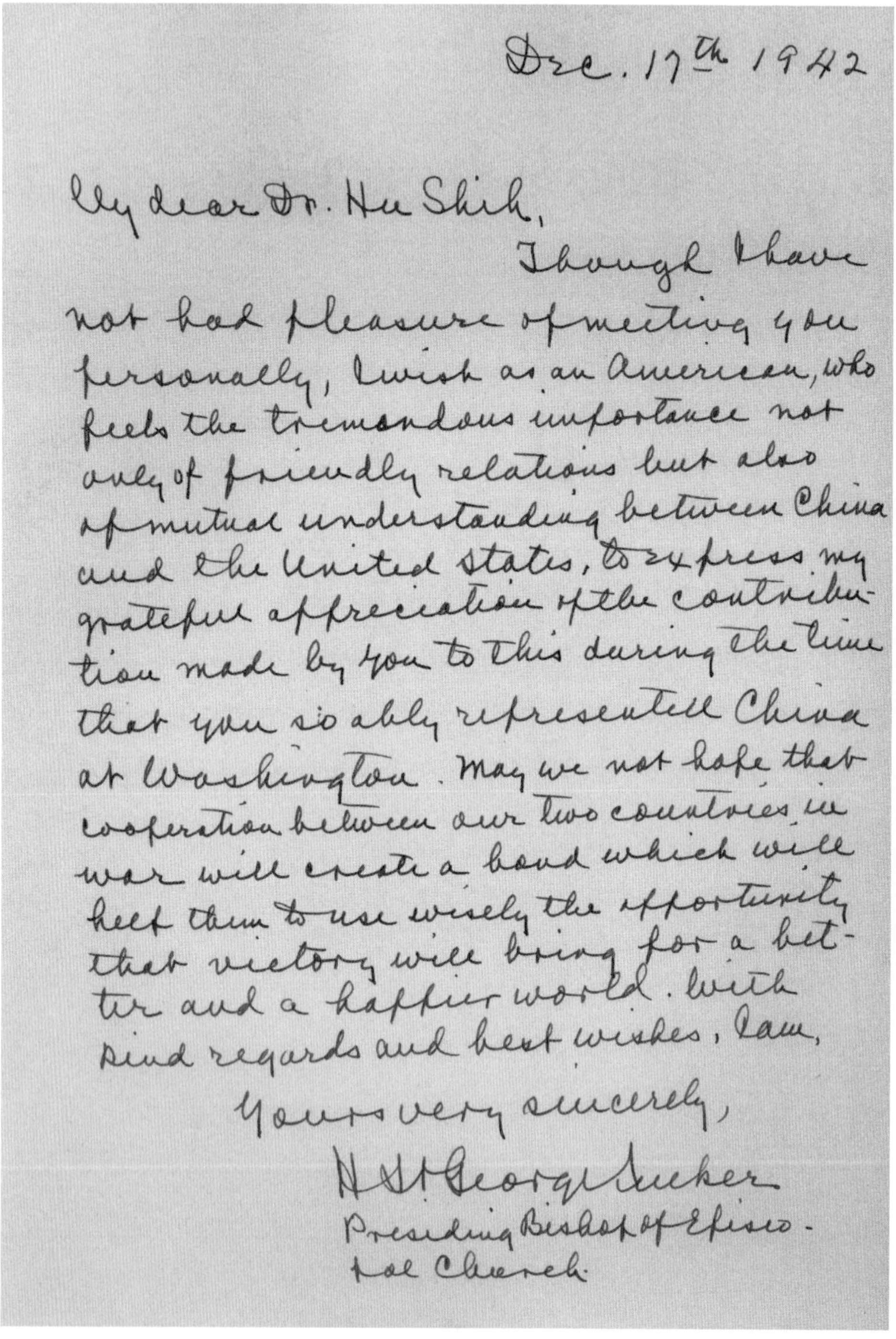

Dec. 17th 1942

My dear Dr. Hu Shih,

Though I have not had pleasure of meeting you personally, I wish as an American, who feels the tremendous importance not only of friendly relations but also of mutual understanding between China and the United States, to express my grateful appreciation of the contribution made by you to this during the time that you so ably represented China at Washington. May we not hope that cooperation between our two countries in war will create a bond which will help them to use wisely the opportunity that victory will bring for a better and a happier world. With kind regards and best wishes, I am,

Yours very sincerely,
H St George Tucker
Presiding Bishop of Episcopal Church.

圖 1

Dec. 17th, 1042

My dear Dr. Hu Shih,

Though I have not had pleasure of meeting you personally, I wish as an American, who feels the tremendous importance not only of friendly relations but also of mutual understanding between China and the United States, to express my grateful appreciation of the contribution made by you to this during the time that you so ably represented China at Washington. May we not hope that cooperation between our two countries, in war will create a bond which will help them to use wisely the opportunity that victory will bring for a better and a happier world. With kind regards and best wishes, I am,

Yours very sincerely

H. St. George Tucker

Presiding Bishop of Episcopal Church

Henry W. Hobson

　　Henry W. Hobson（1891—1983），1914 年畢業於耶魯大學，一戰期間任步兵軍官。1920 年畢業於麻省劍橋聖公會神學院。1930 年到辛辛那提，任南俄亥俄聖公會教區主教，直至去世。

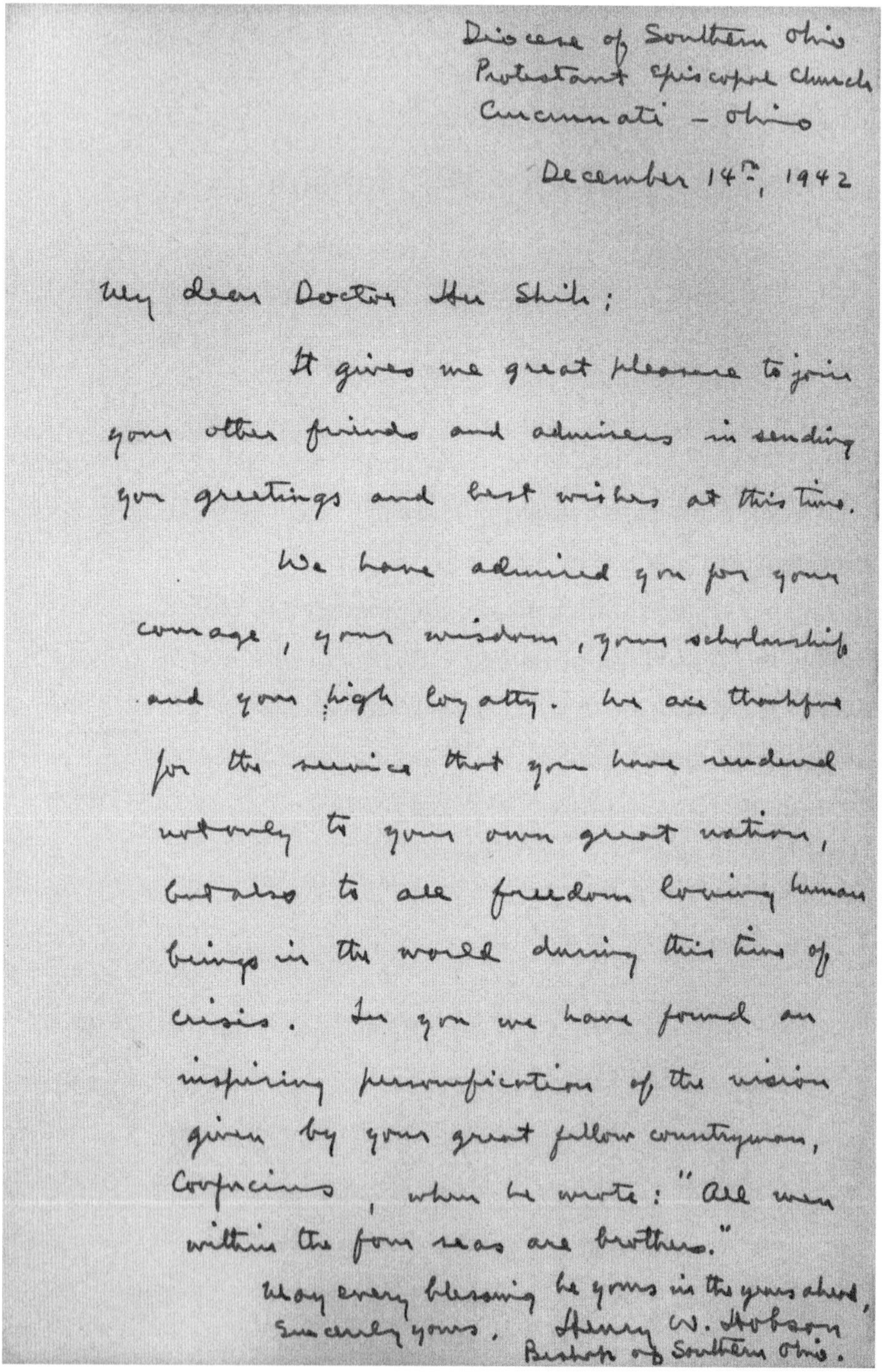

Diocese of Southern Ohio
Protestant Episcopal Church
Cincinnati — Ohio

December 14th, 1942

My dear Doctor Hu Shih:

It gives me great pleasure to join your other friends and admirers in sending you greetings and best wishes at this time.

We have admired you for your courage, your wisdom, your scholarship and your high loyalty. We are thankful for the service that you have rendered not only to your own great nation, but also to all freedom loving human beings in the world during this time of crisis. In you we have found an inspiring personification of the vision given by your great fellow countryman, Confucius, when he wrote: "All men within the four seas are brothers."

May every blessing be yours in the years ahead.
Sincerely yours, Henry W. Hobson
Bishop of Southern Ohio.

圖1

Diocese of Southern Ohio
Protestant Episcopal Church
Cincinnati-Ohio
December 14th, 1942

My dear Doctor Hu Shih:

It gives me great pleasure to join your other friends and admirers in sending you greetings and best wishes at this time.

We have admired you for your courage, your wisdom, your scholarship and your high loyalty. We are thankful for the service that you have rendered not only to your own great nation, but also to all freedom loving human beings in the world during this time of crisis. In you we have found an inspiring personification of the vision given by your great fellow countryman, Confucius, when he wrote: "All men within the four seas are brothers."

May every blessing be yours in the years ahead,

Sincerely yours,

Henry W. Hobson

Bishop of Southern Ohio

Henry Morgenthau, Jr

　　Henry Morgenthau, Jr.（1891—1967），生於紐約，時任美國財政部長。早年畢業於康奈爾大學。1929 年任美國紐約州農業顧問委員會主席。1934—1945 年任美國財政部長。胡適任駐美大使前後與其有交往，1939 年、1940 年日記中有多處訪問 Morgenthau 或請其吃飯的記錄。

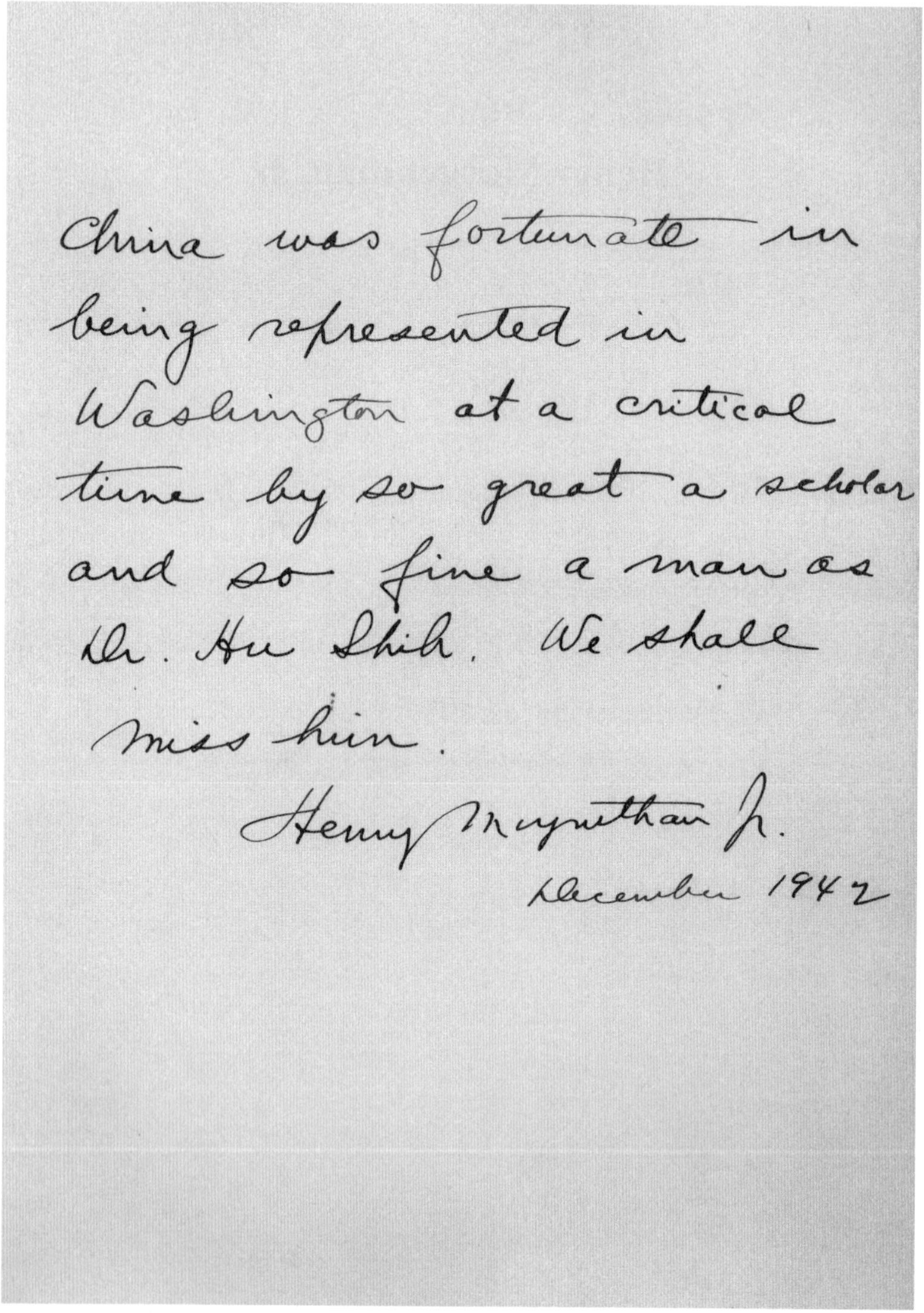

China was fortunate in being represented in Washington at a critical time by so great a scholar and so fine a man as Dr. Hu Shih. We shall miss him.

Henry Moynihan Jr.

December 1942

圖 1

China was fortunate in being represented in Washington at a critical time by so great a scholar and so fine a man as Dr. Hu Shih. We shall miss him.

Henry Morgenthau, Jr.
November 1942

Herbert H. Lehman

　　Herbert H. Lehman（1878—1963），生於美國紐約，時任紐約州州長。1899年畢業於威廉姆斯學院，獲文學士學位。畢業後從事紡織業和金融投資。一戰期間任美軍中校。1929—1932年任紐約州副州長。1933—1942年任紐約州州長。1943—1946年任聯合國善後救濟總署總署長。1949—1957年任美國參議員。胡適任駐美大使前後與其有交往，北京檔藏有胡適與其往來書信五封，時間從1942年9月到11月，其中1942年9月4日Lehman致胡適書信，對胡適卸任駐美大使表示遺憾，稱讚胡適任大使期間的貢獻。

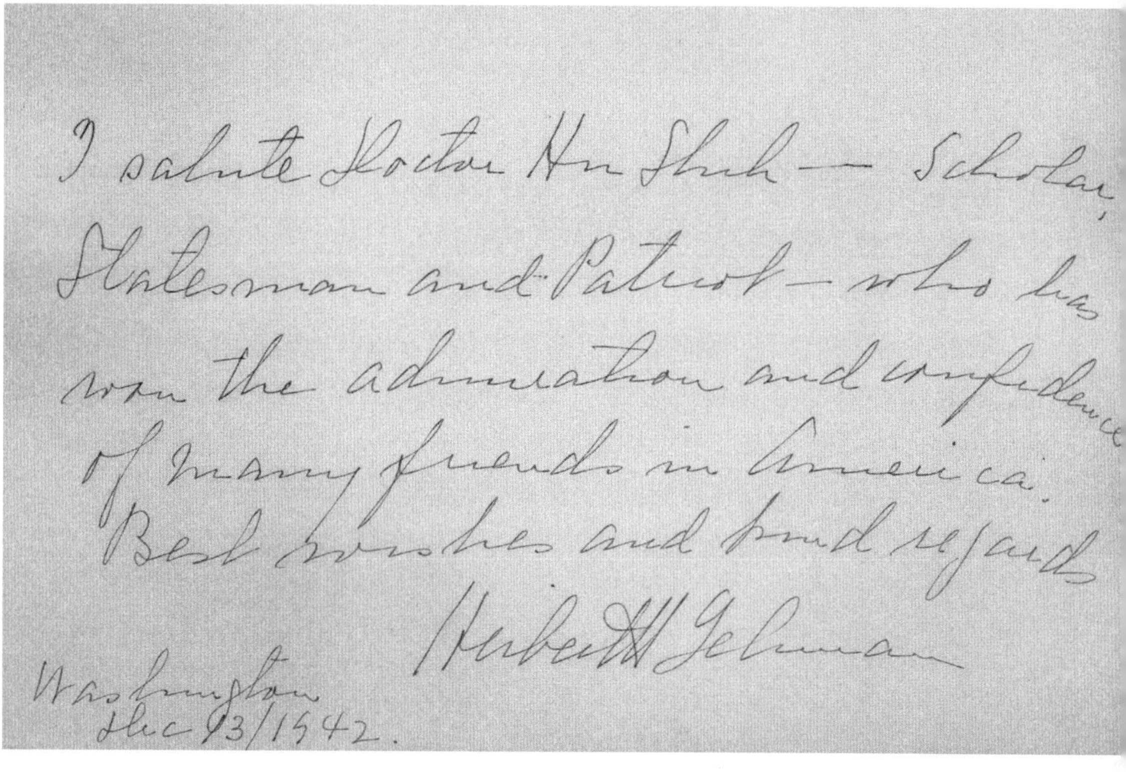

I salute Doctor Hu Shih — Scholar, Statesman and Patriot — who has won the admiration and confidence of many friends in America. Best wishes and kind regards

Herbert H. Lehman

Washington
Dec 13/1942.

圖 1

I salute Doctor Hu Shih—Scholar, Statesman and Patriot—who has won the admiration and confidence of many friends in America.

Best wishes and kind regards

Herbert H. Lehman

Washington
Dec. 13/1942

Herbert Welch

Herbert Welch（1862—1969），生於美國紐約。1887年獲衛斯理安大學（Wesleyan University）文學士學位。1905—1916年任衛斯理安大學校長。曾任美以美會、衛理公會、聯合衛理公會大主教。

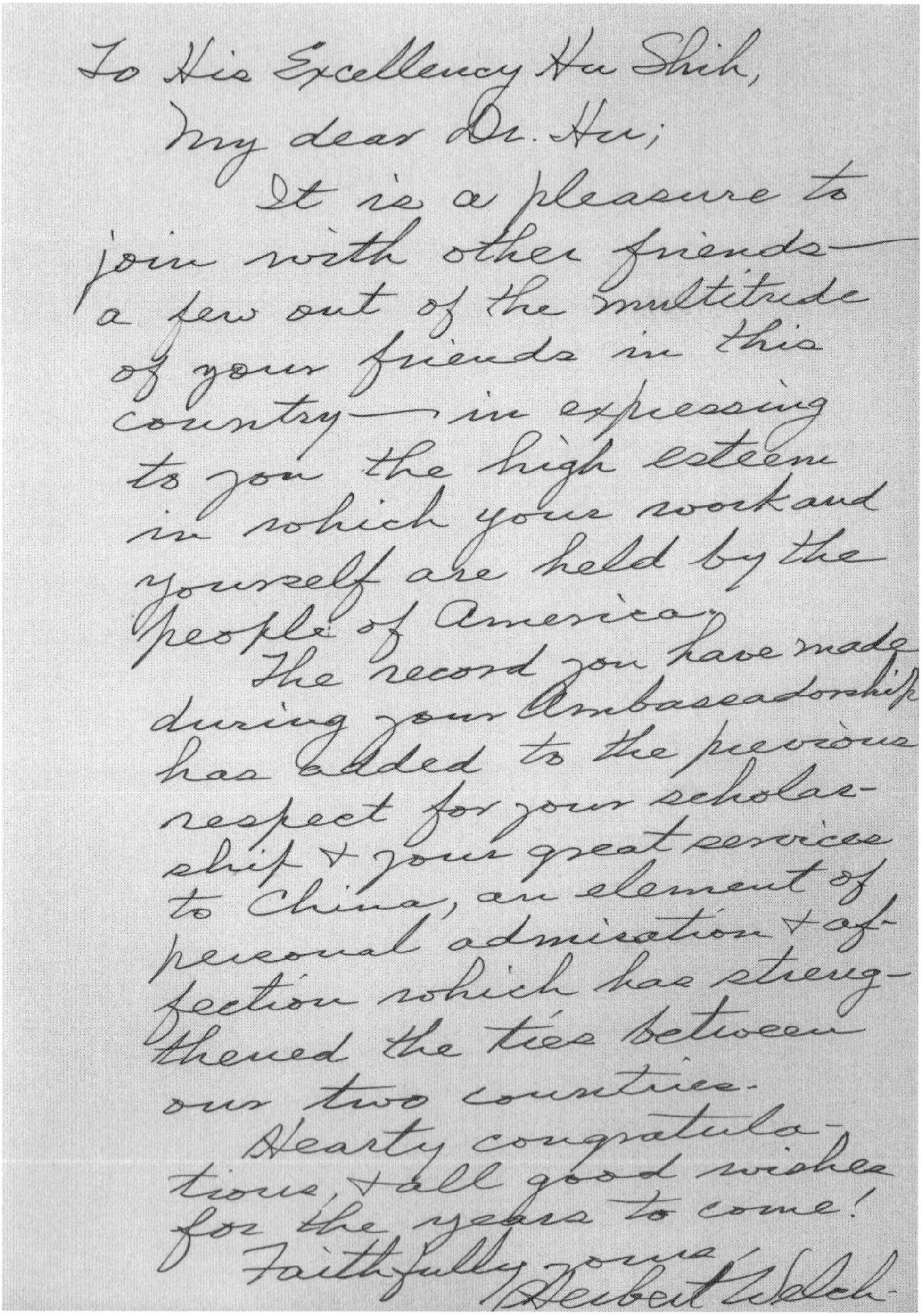

To His Excellency Hu Shih,
My dear Dr. Hu;

It is a pleasure to join with other friends — a few out of the multitude of your friends in this country — in expressing to you the high esteem in which your work and yourself are held by the people of America.

The record you have made during your Ambassadorship has added to the previous respect for your scholarship & your great services to China, an element of personal admiration & affection which has strengthened the ties between our two countries.

Hearty congratulations, & all good wishes for the years to come!

Faithfully yours,
Herbert Welch

圖 1

To His Excellency Hu Shih,

My dear Dr. Hu;

It is a pleasure to join with other friends—a few out of the multitude of your friends in this country—in expressing to you the high esteem in which your work and yourself are held by the people of America.

The record you have made during your Ambassadorship has added to the precious respect for your scholarship & your great services to China, an element of personal admiration & affection which has strengthened the ties between our two countries.

Hearty congratulations & all good wishes for the years to come!

Faithfully yours,
Herbert Welch

Hugo L. Black

　　Hugo L. Black（1886—1971），生於美國阿拉巴馬州阿什蘭，美國政治家及法學家，時任美國最高法院大法官。1906年畢業於阿拉巴馬大學法學院，1927年至1937年任民主黨阿拉巴馬州參議員，1937年至1971年任美國最高法院大法官。

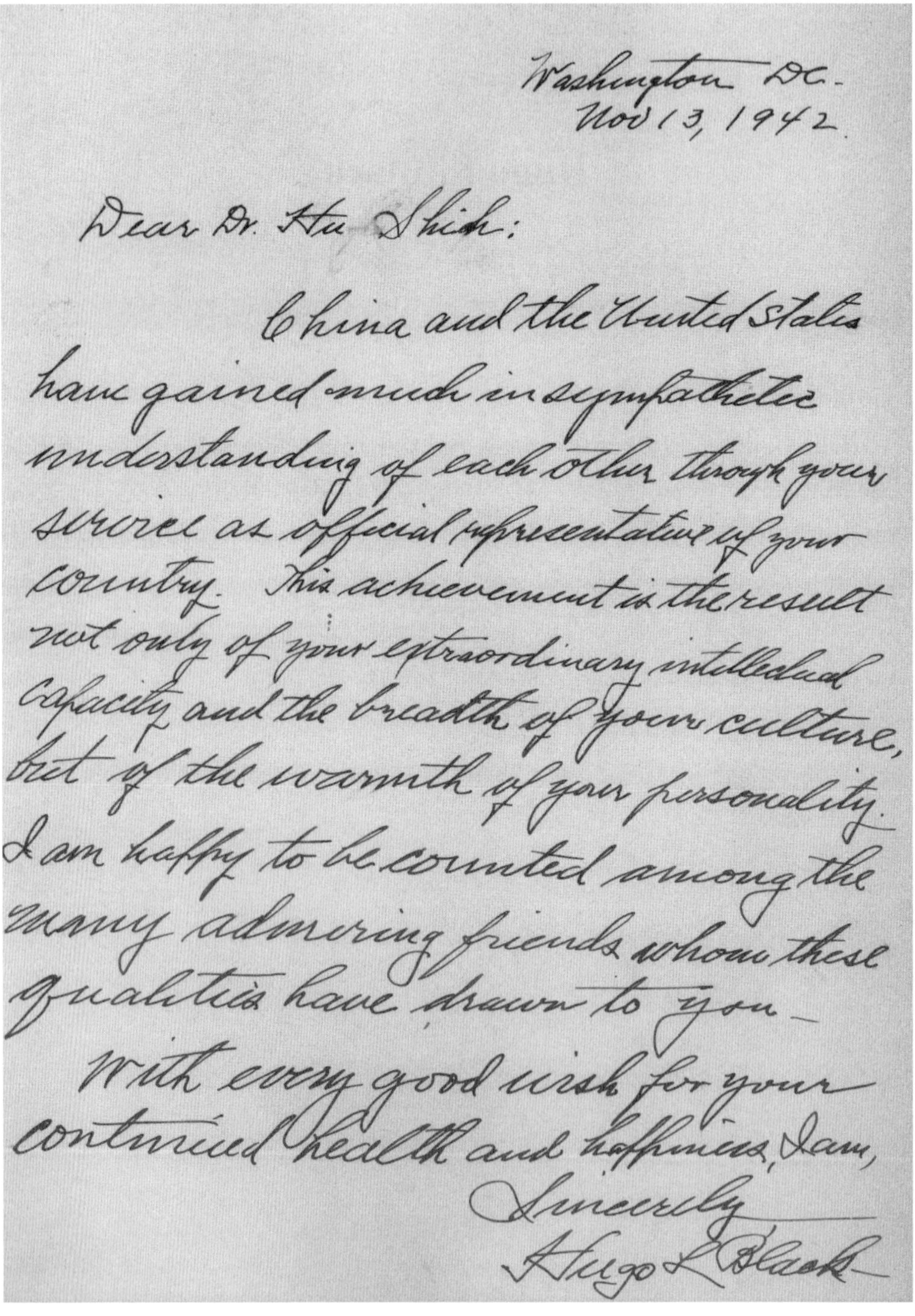

Washington D.C.
Nov 13, 1942.

Dear Dr. Hu Shih:

China and the United States have gained much in sympathetic understanding of each other through your service as official representative of your country. This achievement is the result not only of your extraordinary intellectual capacity and the breadth of your culture, but of the warmth of your personality. I am happy to be counted among the many admiring friends whom these qualities have drawn to you.

With every good wish for your continued health and happiness, I am,

Sincerely
Hugo L Black

圖1

Washington DC.
Nov. 13, 1942

Dear Dr. Hu Shih:

China and the United States have gained much in sympathetic understanding of each other through your service as official representative of your country. This achievement is the result not only of your extraordinary intellectual capacity and the breadth of your culture, but of the warmth of your personality. I am happy to be counted among the many admiring friends whom these qualities have drawn to you.

With every good wish for your continued health and happiness, I am,

Sincerely,
Hugo L. Black

J. W. Decker

J. W. Decker，生平不詳。北京檔收藏有 Decker 致胡適書信兩封，時間分別爲 1944 年 3 月 16 日和 4 月 18 日。

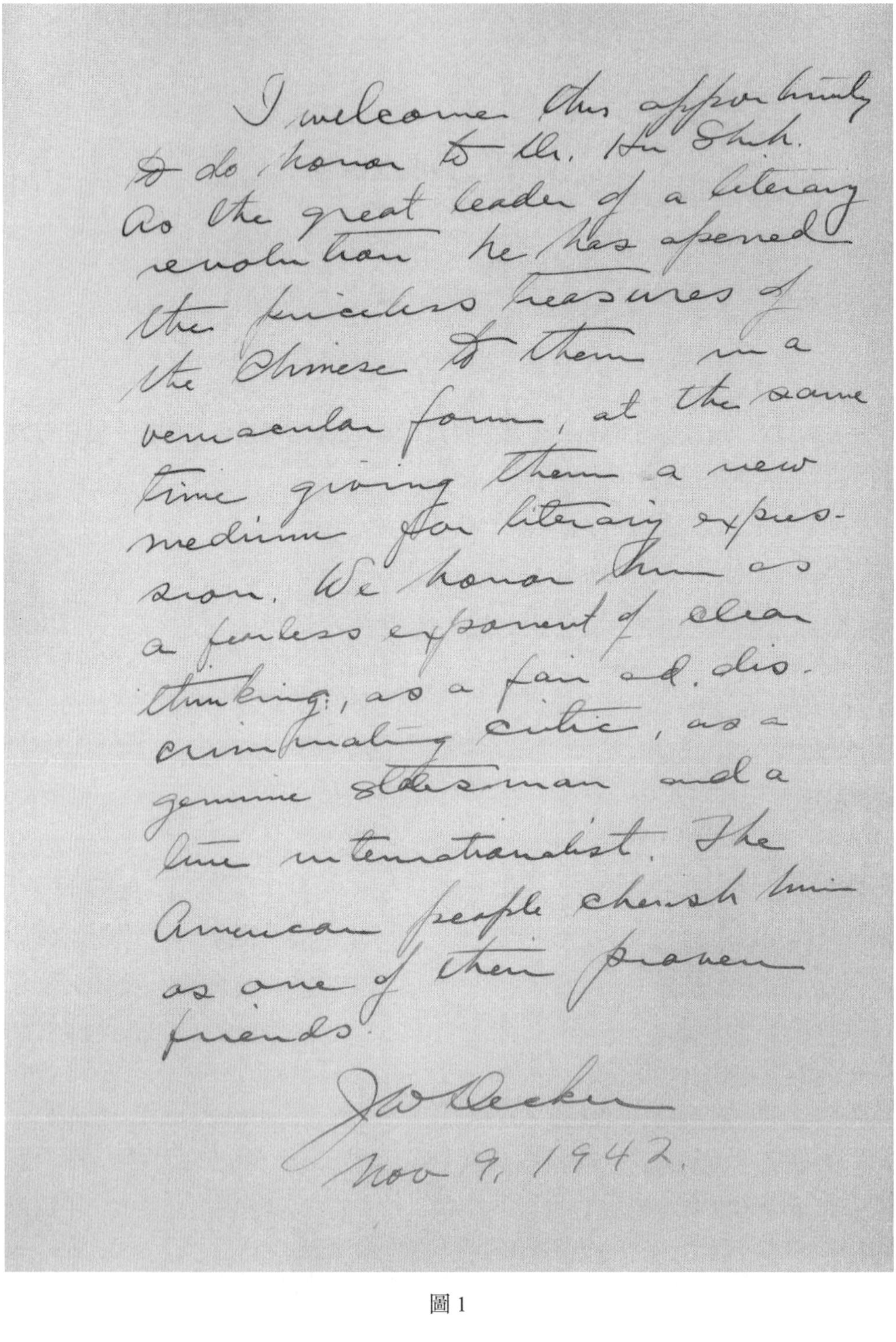

I welcome this opportunity to do honor to Dr. Hu Shih. As the great leader of a literary revolution he has opened the priceless treasures of the Chinese to them in a vernacular form, at the same time giving them a new medium for literary expression. We honor him as a fearless exponent of clear thinking, as a fair and discriminating critic, as a genuine statesman and a true internationalist. The American people cherish him as one of their proven friends.

J W Decker
Nov 9, 1942.

圖1

I welcome this opportunity to do honor to Dr. Hu Shih. As the great leader of a literary revolution he has opened the priceless treasures of the Chinese to them in a vernacular form, at the same time, giving them a new medium for literary expression. We honor him as a fearless exponent of clear thinking, as a fair and discriminating critic, as a genuine statesman and a true internationalist. The American people cherish him as one of their proven friends.

J. W. Decker
Nov. 9, 1942

James G. Blaine

James G. Blaine，1941 年任 The United China Appeal 主席，餘不詳。胡適任駐美大使期間與其有交往，北京檔收藏有胡適與其往來函電十通。

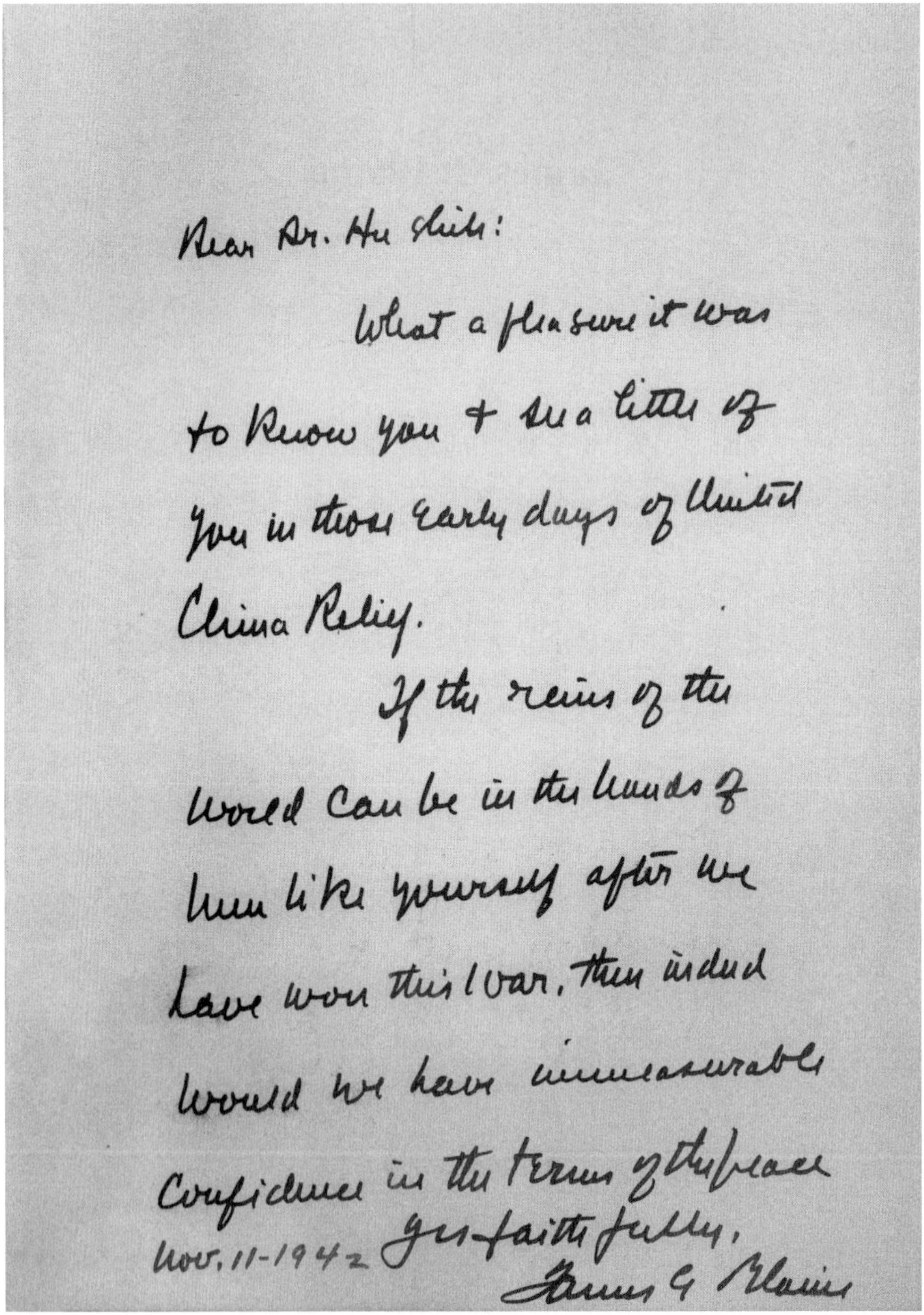

Dear Dr. Hu Shih:

What a pleasure it was to know you & see a little of you in those early days of United China Relief.

If the reins of the world can be in the hands of men like yourself after we have won this war, then indeed would we have immeasurable confidence in the terms of the peace

Nov. 11-1942

Yrs faithfully,
James G Blaine

圖1

Dear Dr. Hu Shih:

What a pleasure it was to know you & see a little of you in those early days of United China Relief.

If the reins of the world can be in the hands of men like yourself after we have won this war, then indeed would we have immeasurable confidence in the terms of the peace.

Yours faithfully,
James G. Blaine

Nov. 11-1942

James L. McConaughy

　　James L. McConaughy（1887—1948），生於美國紐約，1909年畢業於耶魯大學，1911年獲布朗大學碩士學位。1913年獲哥倫比亞大學博士學位。1915年獲達特茅斯學院碩士學位。1909—1915年在鮑登學院講授英語和教育學。1918—1925年任達特茅斯學院教育學教授。1925—1943年先後任諾克斯學院、衛斯理安大學校長。1929—1941年任康涅狄格州副州長。1942年任美國援華聯合會主席。1947—1948年任康涅狄格州州長。胡適任駐美大使期間與其有交往，北京檔藏有胡適與其往來書信十七封，時間從1939年2月到1942年12月。

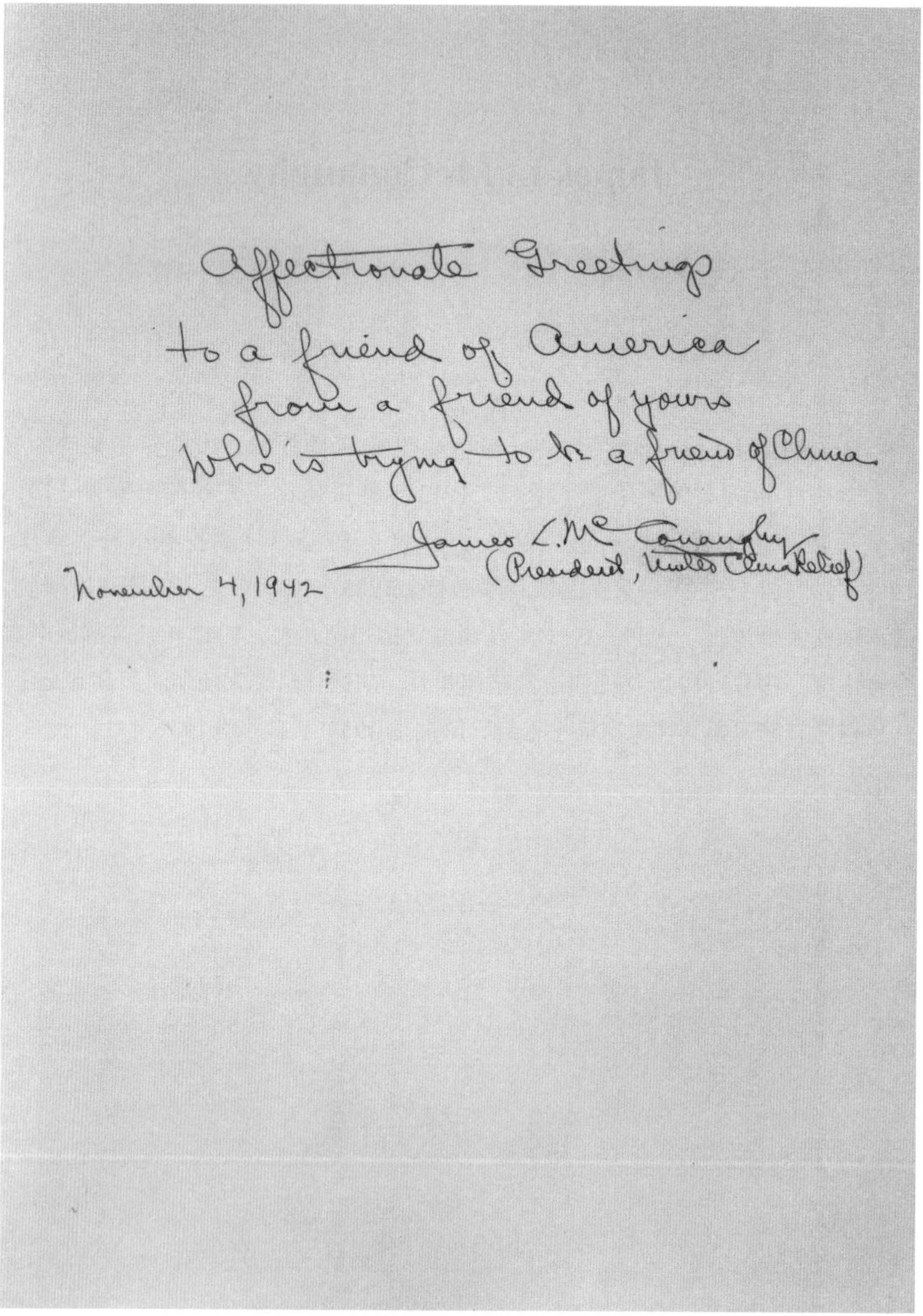

Affectionate Greetings
to a friend of America
from a friend of yours
who is trying to be a friend of China

James L. McConaughy
(President, United China Relief)

November 4, 1942

圖 1

Affectionate Greetings

to a friend of America from a friend of yours who is trying to be a friend of China.

James L. McConaughy
(President, United China Relief)

November 4, 1942

James R. Angell

　　James R. Angell（1869—1949），美國心理學家，教育學家。生於美國佛蒙特州。1890年獲密歇根大學學士學位，次年獲碩士學位。1892年獲哈佛大學心理學碩士學位。1895年任教於芝加哥大學。1905年任芝加哥大學心理系主任。1918年任芝加哥大學代理校長。1919年任美國國家科學研究委員會主席。1921—1937年任耶魯大學校長。1932年當選美國文理科學院院士。胡適任駐美大使期間與其有交往，北京檔藏有Angell1942年9月6日致胡適書信一封，對胡適卸任駐美大使深表遺憾。

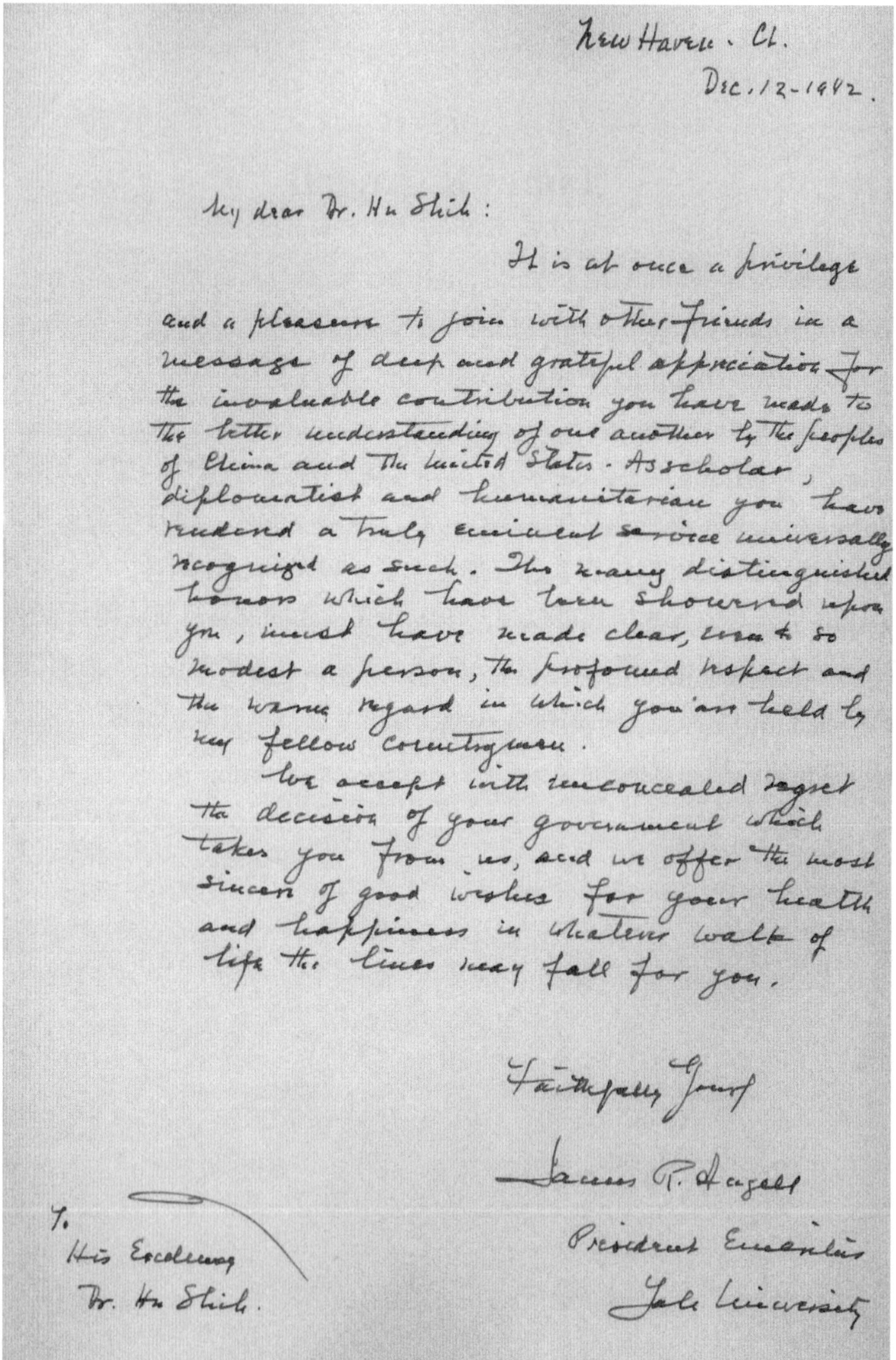

New Haven, Ct.
Dec. 12-1942.

My dear Dr. Hu Shih:

It is at once a privilege and a pleasure to join with other friends in a message of deep and grateful appreciation for the invaluable contribution you have made to the better understanding of one another by the peoples of China and the United States. As scholar, diplomatist and humanitarian you have rendered a truly eminent service universally recognized as such. The many distinguished honors which have been showered upon you, must have made clear, even to so modest a person, the profound respect and the warm regard in which you are held by my fellow countrymen.

We accept with unconcealed regret the decision of your government which takes you from us, and we offer the most sincere of good wishes for your health and happiness in whatever walk of life the lines may fall for you.

Faithfully Yours

James R. Angell
President Emeritus
Yale University

To:
His Excellency
Dr. Hu Shih.

圖 1

New Haven, Ct.
Dec. 12-1942

My dear Dr. Hu Shih:

It is at once a privilege and a pleasure to join with other friends in a message of deep and grateful appreciation for the invaluable contribution you have made to the better understanding of one another by the peoples of China and the United States. As scholar, diplomatist and humanitarian you have rendered a truly excellent service universally recognized as such. The many distinguished honors which have been showered upon you, must have made clear, even to so modest a person, the profound respect and the warm regard in which you are held by my fellow countrymen.

We accept with unconcealed regret the decision of your government which takes you from us, and we offer the most sincere of good wishes for your health and happiness in whatever walk of life this lines may fall for you.

Faithfully Yours
James R. Angell
President Emeritus
Yale University

To
His Excellency
Dr. Hu Shih

James V. Forrestal

　　James Forrestal（1892—1949），生於美國紐約州，時任美國海軍部副部長。1911年入達特茅斯學院，後轉學普林斯頓大學，獲文學士學位。一戰期間參加海軍，成爲海軍航空兵。一戰後到華爾街從事金融業。1940年被羅斯福總統任命爲海軍部副部長，1944—1947年任美國最後一任内閣級海軍部長。1947—1949年任美國首任國防部長。

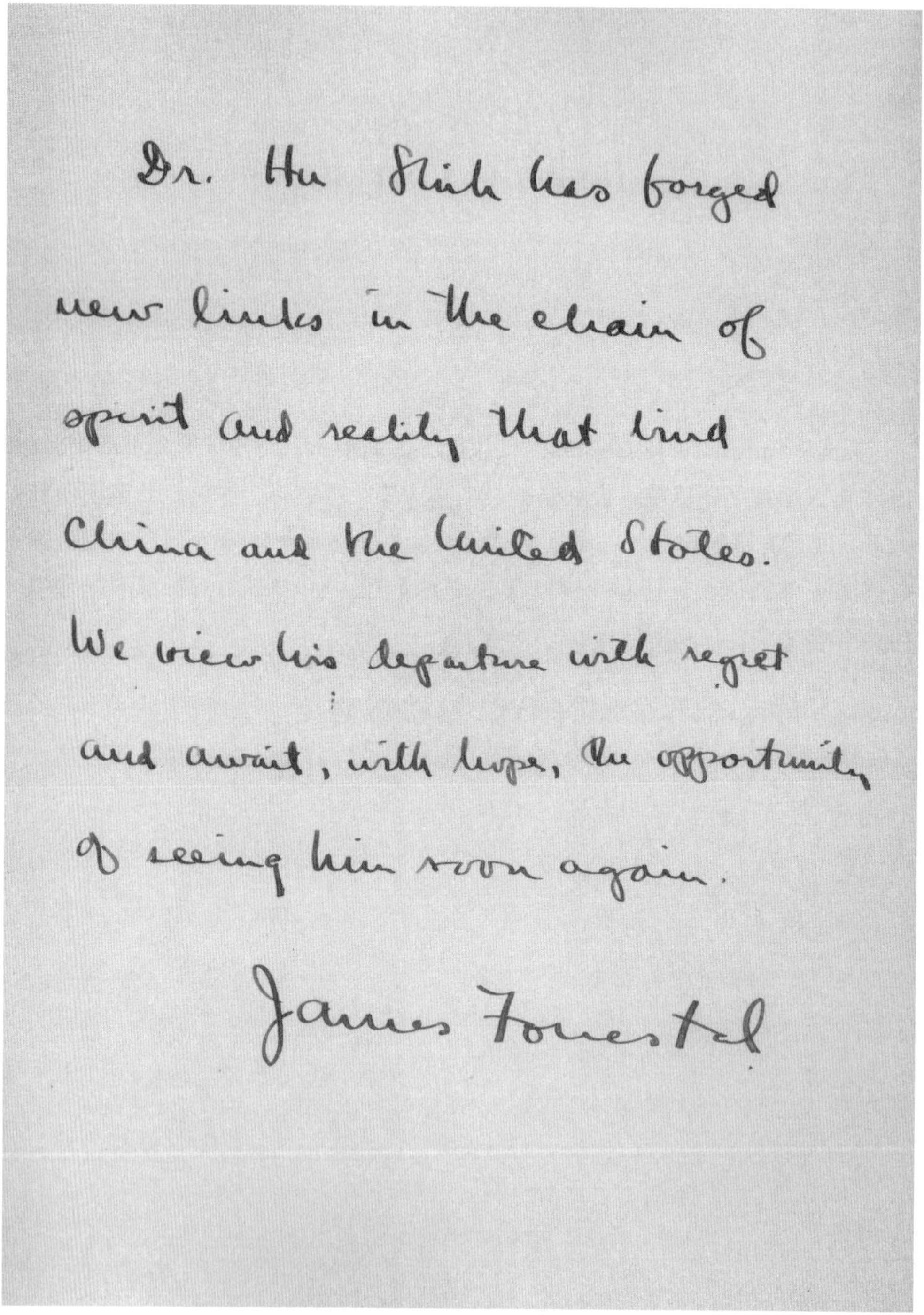

Dr. Hu Shih has forged new links in the chain of spirit and reality that bind China and the United States. We view his departure with regret and await, with hope, the opportunity of seeing him soon again.

James Forrestal

圖1

Dr. Hu Shih has forged new links in the chain of spirit and reality that bind China and the United States. We view his departure with regret and await, with hope, the opportunity of seeing him soon again.

James Forrestal

Jesse D. Gard

　　Jesse D. Gard，時任美國國家銀行（United States National Bank）副總裁，餘不詳。

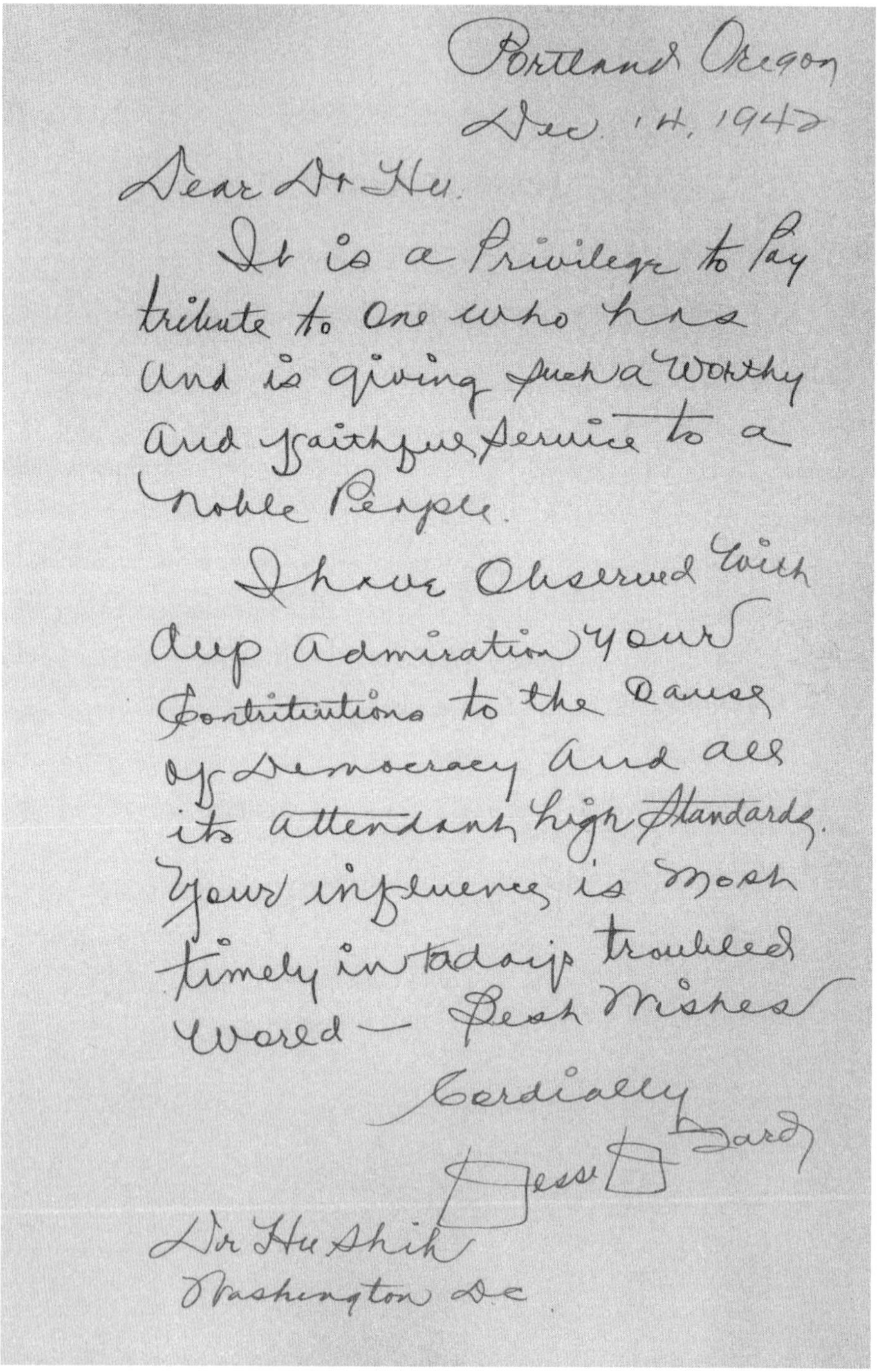

Portland Oregon
Dec. 14, 1942

Dear Dr Hu.

It is a privilege to pay tribute to one who has and is giving such a worthy and faithful service to a noble people.

I have observed with deep admiration your contributions to the cause of democracy and all its attendant high standards. Your influence is most timely in today's troubled world — Best wishes

Cordially
Jess Sard

Dr Hu Shih
Washington DC

圖1

Portland Oregon
Dec. 14, 1942

Dear Dr. Hu:

It is a privilege to pay tribute to one who has and is giving such a worthy and faithful service to a noble people.

I have observed with deep admiration your contributions to the cause of Democracy and all its attendant high standards. Your influences is most timely in today's troubled world—Best wishes

Cordially
Jesse D. Gard

Dr. Hu Shih
Washington D.C.

Jesse H. Jones

Jesse H. Jones（1874—1956），美國民主黨政治家，時任美國商務部長。生於美國田納西州，14歲經營烟草工廠，後到休斯頓經營伐木場，逐漸發展到房地產、商業建築和銀行業。

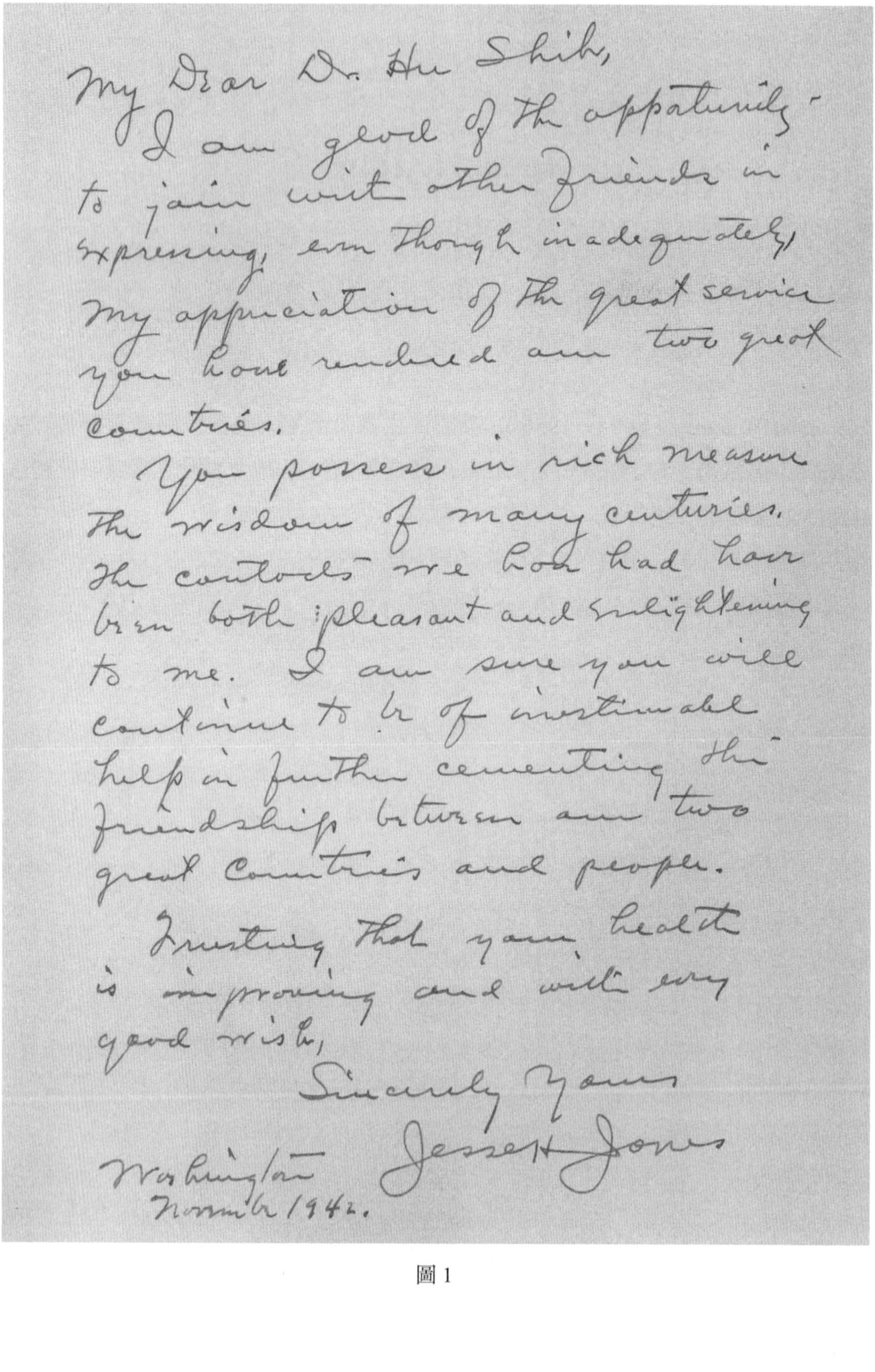

My Dear Dr. Hu Shih,

I am glad of the opportunity to join with other friends in expressing, even though inadequately, my appreciation of the great service you have rendered our two great countries.

You possess in rich measure the wisdom of many centuries. The contacts we have had have been both pleasant and enlightening to me. I am sure you will continue to be of inestimable help in further cementing the friendship between our two great countries and people.

Trusting that your health is improving and with every good wish,

Sincerely yours
Jesse H Jones

Washington
November 1942.

圖 1

My Dear Dr. Hu Shih,

I am glad of the opportunity to join with other friends in expressing even though inadequately, my appreciation of the great service you have rendered our two great countries.

You possess in rich measure the wisdom of many centuries, the contacts we have had have been both pleasant and enlightening to me. I am sure you will continue to be of inestimable help in further cementing this friendship between our two great countries and people.

Trusting that your health is improving and with every good wish,

Sincerely yours
Jesse H. Jones

Washington
November 1942

John D. Rockefeller, 3rd

John D. Rockefeller, 3rd（1906—1978），美國洛克菲勒家族第三代長子。1929年獲普林斯頓大學科學學士學位。主要從事慈善事業和國際關係，推動建立多個慈善基金組織和公共組織，曾是外交學會和太平洋關係學會委員。1952年創辦人口理事會，1956年創辦亞洲學會。

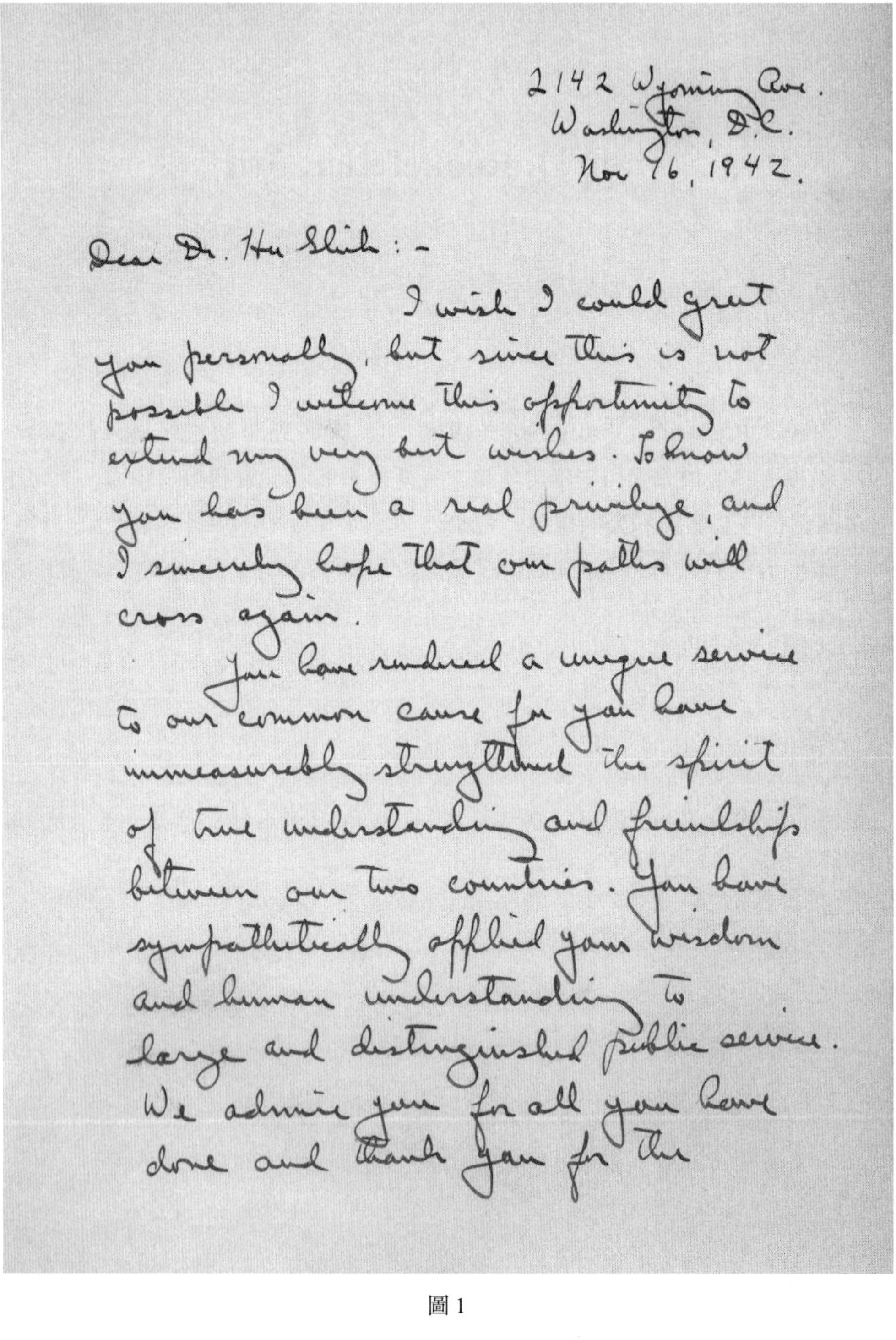

2142 Wyoming Ave.
Washington, D.C.
Nov 26, 1942.

Dear Dr. Hu Shih:-

I wish I could greet you personally, but since this is not possible I welcome this opportunity to extend my very best wishes. To know you has been a real privilege, and I sincerely hope that our paths will cross again.

You have rendered a unique service to our common cause for you have immeasurably strengthened the spirit of true understanding and friendship between our two countries. You have sympathetically applied your wisdom and human understanding to large and distinguished public service. We admire you for all you have done and thank you for the

圖1

2142 Wyoming Ave.
Washington, D. C.
Nov. 16, 1942

Dear Dr. Hu Shih:—

I wish I could greet you personally, but since this is not possible I welcome this opportunity to extend my very best wishes. To know you has been a real privilege, and I sincerely hope that our paths will cross again.

You have rendered a unique service to our common cause for you have immeasurably strengthened the spirit of true understanding and friendship between our two countries. You have sympathetically applied your wisdom and human understanding to large and distinguished public service. We admire you for all you have done and thank you for the

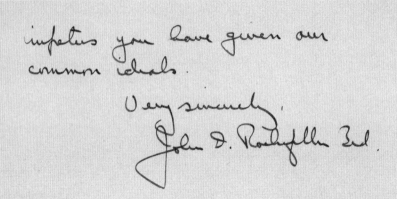

圖 2

impetus you have given our common ideals.

Very sincerely,

John D. Rockefeller 3rd

John E. Miles

John E. Miles（1884—1971），生於美國田納西州，時任美國新墨西哥州州長。1939—1943年任美國新墨西哥州州長，1949—1951年任美國眾議院議員。

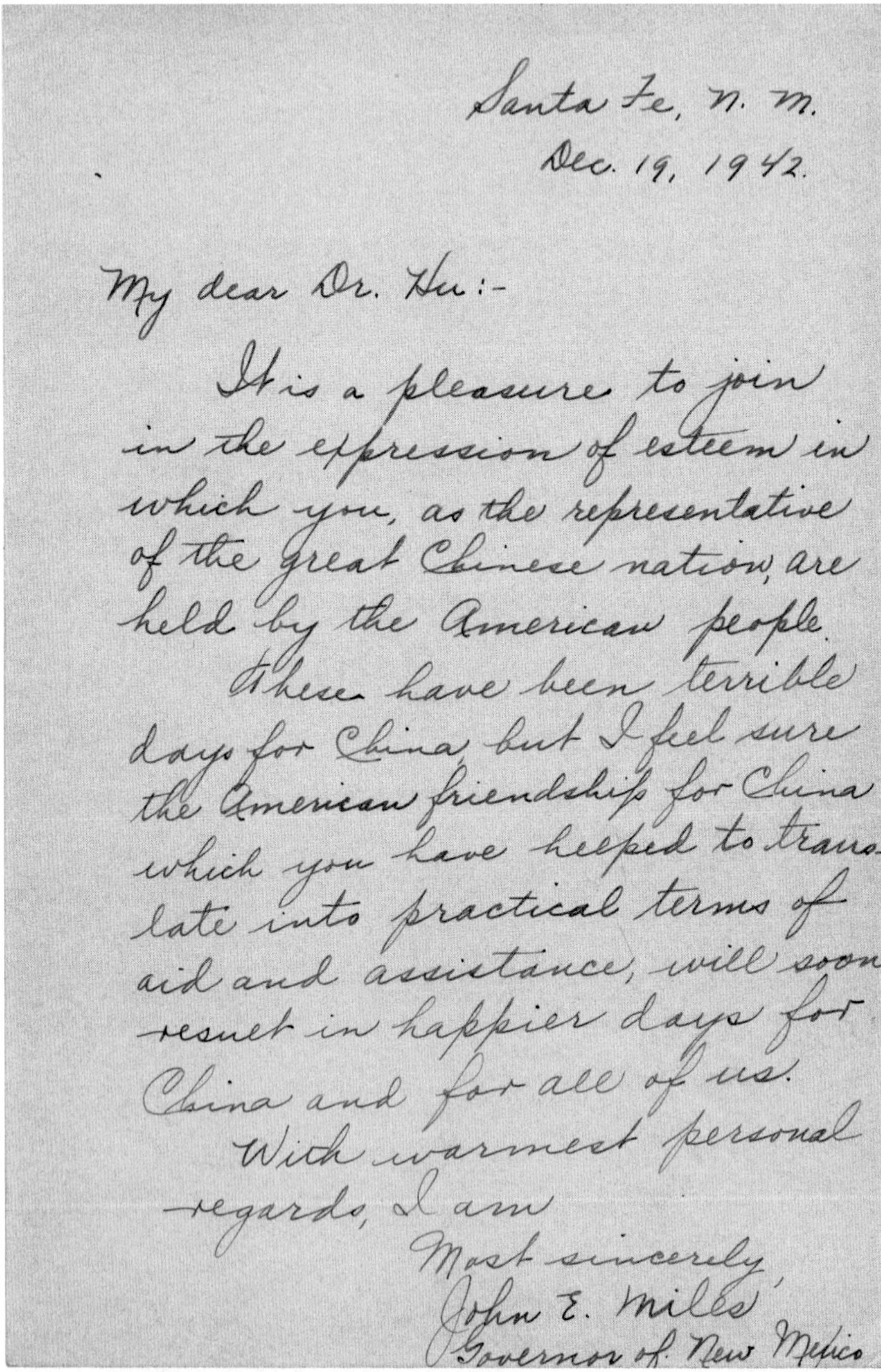

Santa Fe, N. M.
Dec. 19, 1942.

My dear Dr. Hu:-

It is a pleasure to join in the expression of esteem in which you, as the representative of the great Chinese nation, are held by the American people.

These have been terrible days for China, but I feel sure the American friendship for China which you have helped to translate into practical terms of aid and assistance, will soon result in happier days for China and for all of us.

With warmest personal regards, I am

Most sincerely,
John E. Miles
Governor of New Mexico

圖 1

Senate Fe, N.M.
Dec. 19, 1942

My dear Dr. Hu: —

It is a pleasure to join in the expression of esteem in which you, as the representative of the great Chinese nation, are held by the American people.

These have been terrible days for China but I feel sure the American friendship for China which you have helped to translate into practical terms of aid and assistance, will soon result in happier days for China and for all of us.

With warmest personal regards, I am

Most sincerely,
John E. Miles
Governor of New Mexico

John R. Mott

　　John R. Mott（1865—1955），生於美國紐約州沙利文縣。1888年獲康奈爾大學學士學位。曾擔任1910年世界宣教會議主席。後到歐洲和亞洲推動普世教會合一運動。1920—1928年任世界基督教學生聯盟主席。1946年獲諾貝爾世界和平獎。

15-6 Fifth Ave., New York
December 14", '42

Dear Doctor Hu Shih,

It is a great privilege to associate myself with your many friends, near and far, in an expression of high regard for you. My own friendship for you has been an ever-deepening one from student days in China, and later at our common University, Cornell, and has been fostered by our many contacts across the years in Orient and Occident. I have a profound appreciation of your distinguished services in your own great land and in my own country, as well as of your notable contribution in the realm of sound international relations. Never were you more needed than you will be in the coming fateful years, and, to this end, I wish you a most hearty godspeed. Anything I can do to strengthen your hands in the constructive undertakings which await you I will ever esteem it an honor to do.

Faithfully yours,
John R. Mott

圖 1

156 Fifth Ave., New York
December 14, '42

Dear Doctor Hu Shih,

It is a great privilege to associate myself with your many friends, near and far, in an expression of high regard for you. My own friendship for you has been an ever-deepening one from student days in China, and later at our common University, Cornell, and has been fostered by our many contacts across the years in Orient and Occident. I have a profound appreciation of your distinguished services in your own great land and in my own country, as well as of your notable contribution in the realm of sound international relations. Never were you made needed than you will be in the coming fateful years, and, to this end, I wish you a most hearty Godspeed. Anything I can do to strengthen your hands in the constructive understandings which await you I will ever esteem it an honor to do.

Faithfully yours
John R. Mott

John Gunther

　　John Gunther（1901—1970），生於美國芝加哥。美國新聞工作者、作家。1922年畢業於芝加哥大學。曾任職於《芝加哥每日新聞報》，長期擔任該報駐英國分部記者。臺北胡適紀念館藏有 John Gunther 寫的胡適傳記（*Biography of Dr. Hu Shih, Former Chinese Ambassador to the U. S.*）。大約寫於二十世紀四十年代。

For Dr. Hu Shih

In warmest admiration

John Gunther

New York City
Xmas 1942

For Dr. Hu Shih
    In warmest admiration

                                                    John Gunther

New York City
Xmas 1942

Julean Arnold

Julean Arnold（1876—1946），安立德，生於美國加州。1902 年獲加州商學院理學學士學位。1904 年任美國駐上海領事館副領事，1914 年任駐漢口總領事。1914—1917 年，任駐日、華兩國商務參贊。1920—1941 年任駐華商務參贊。著有《中國商務指南》(*A Commercial Handbook of China*)、《中美關係之蠡測》(*China Through the American Window*) 等。胡適日記中記錄的與 Arnold 最早的交往是在 1928 年 3 月 30 日，"爲 Julean Arnold *Some Bigger Issues in China's Problems* 作序"。北京檔藏有胡適與其往來書信四封，時間自 1943 年 10 月到 1945 年 5 月，以及胡適 Foreword to Julean Arnold, *Some Bigger Issues in China's Problems* 打印稿兩頁。

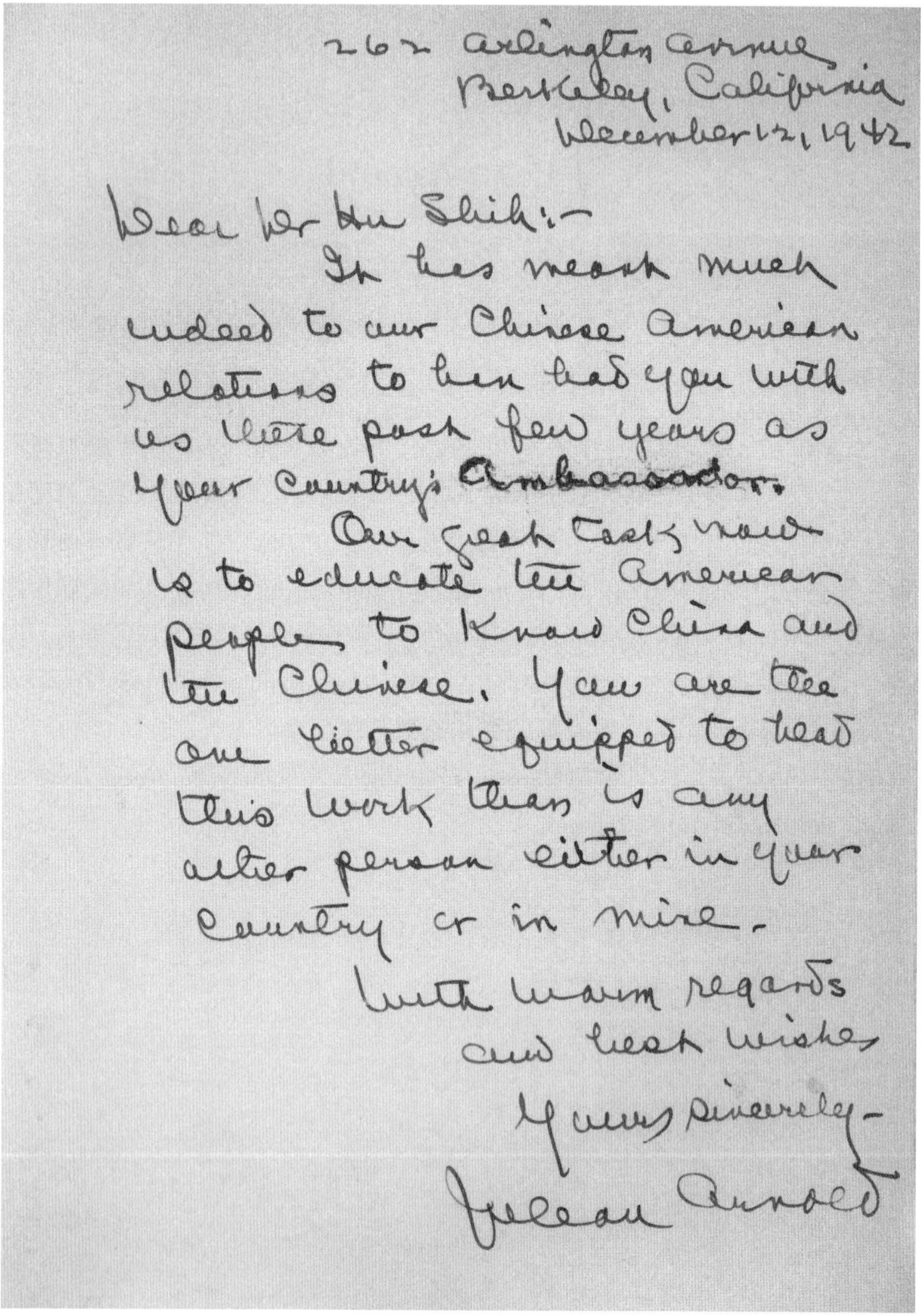

262 Arlington Avenue
Berkeley, California
December 12, 1942

Dear Dr Hu Shih:-

It has meant much indeed to our Chinese American relations to have had you with us these past few years as your country's Ambassador.

Our great task now is to educate the American people to know China and the Chinese. You are the one better equipped to head this work than is any other person either in your country or in mine.

With warm regards and best wishes

Yours sincerely-

Julean Arnold

圖1

262 Arlington Avenue
Berkeley, California
December 12, 1942

Dear Dr. Hu Shih:—

It has meant much indeed to our Chinese American relations to have had you with us these past few years as your country's ambassador.

Our great task lead us to educate the American people to know China and the Chinese. You are the one better equipped to head this work than is any other person either in your country or in mine.

With warm regards
And best wishes
Yours sincerely—
Julean Arnold

Julius Klein

　　Julius Klein（1901—1984），生於美國芝加哥。二十世紀二十年代任 The State Herald 記者，並在美國創辦首家德語廣播。創辦《星條旗報》南太平洋版。1933 年加入伊利諾伊國民衛隊，1941 年任中校。1947 年任美國猶太退伍老兵聯合會全國領導人。胡適任大使期間曾於 1940 年 7 月 22 日致電 Julius Klein，邀請其參加 7 月 25 日在大使館舉行的晚宴。

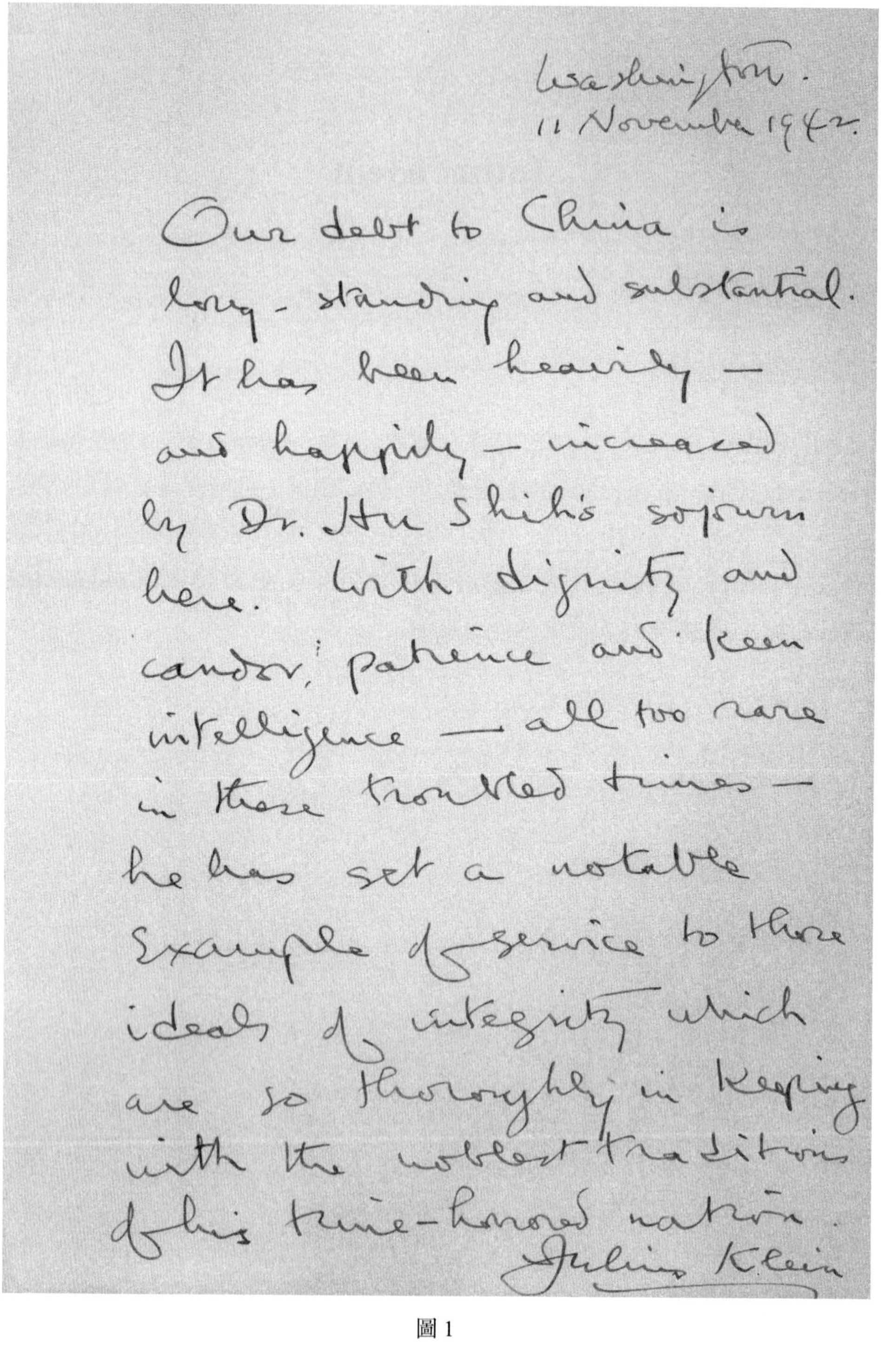

Washington.
11 November 1942.

Our debt to China is long-standing and substantial. It has been heavily — and happily — increased by Dr. Hu Shih's sojourn here. With dignity and candor, patience and keen intelligence — all too rare in these troubled times — he has set a notable example of service to those ideals of integrity which are so thoroughly in keeping with the noblest traditions of his time-honored nation.

Julius Klein

圖1

Washington

11 November 1942

Our debt to China is long-standing and substantial. It has been heavily—and happily—increased by Dr. Hu Shih's sojourn here. With dignity and candor, patience and keen intelligence—all too rare in these troubled times—he has set a notable example of service to those ideals of integrity which are so thoroughly in keeping with the noblest traditions of his time-honored nation.

Julius Klein

Karl T. Compton

　　Karl T. Compton（1887—1954），生於美國俄亥俄州，美國著名物理學家。1908 年畢業於伍斯特大學，獲哲學學士學位，次年獲碩士學位。1909—1910 年任伍斯特大學化學系講師。1912 年獲普林斯頓大學哲學博士學位。1913 年改任里德學院物理學講師。1915 年回普林斯頓，任物理學副教授，1919 年升任全職教授。1927 年任普林斯頓帕爾默實驗室主任，1929 年任物理系主任。1923 年當選美國哲學學會會員，1924 年當選美國國家科學院會員，1927—1930 年任該會物理分會主席。1927 年任美國物理學會主席。1930—1948 年任麻省理工學院校長。

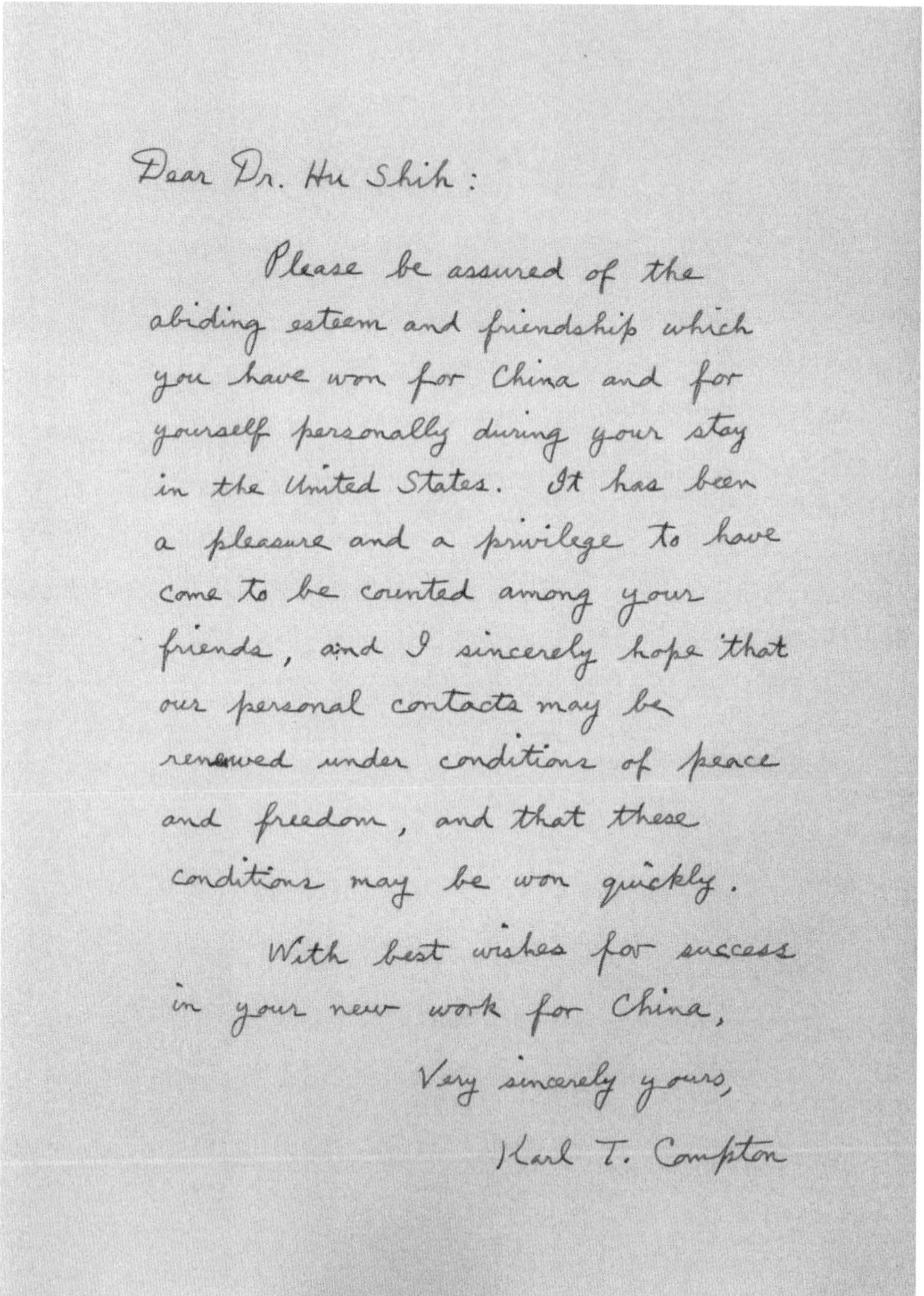

Dear Dr. Hu Shih:

  Please be assured of the abiding esteem and friendship which you have won for China and for yourself personally during your stay in the United States. It has been a pleasure and a privilege to have come to be counted among your friends, and I sincerely hope that our personal contacts may be renewed under conditions of peace and freedom, and that these conditions may be won quickly.

  With best wishes for success in your new work for China,

    Very sincerely yours,
    Karl T. Compton

圖 1

Dear Dr. Hu Shih:—

Please be assured of the abiding esteem and friendship which you have won for China and for yourself personally during your stay in the United States. It has been a pleasure and a privilege to have come to be counted among your friends, and I sincerely hope that our personal contacts may be renewed under conditions of peace and freedom, and that these conditions may be won quickly.

With best wishes for success in your new work for China.

Very sincerely yours,
Karl T. Compton

L. A. Weigle

　　L. A. Weigle，即 Luther Allan Weigle（1880—1976），生於美國賓夕法尼亞州。1900 年畢業於蓋茨堡學院（Gettysburg）。1935 年曾來華六個月，訪問教會學校。其間曾與胡適見面。1905 年獲耶魯大學博士學位。1905—1916 年主要任明尼蘇達州卡爾頓學院哲學教授，其中 1909—1914 年任該學院教務長。1914—1915 年任耶魯大學神學院訪問教授。1916 年任耶魯大學神學院教授，1928—1949 年任神學院院長。1949 年自耶魯大學退休，1952 年完成《聖經》標準修訂版的編輯工作。

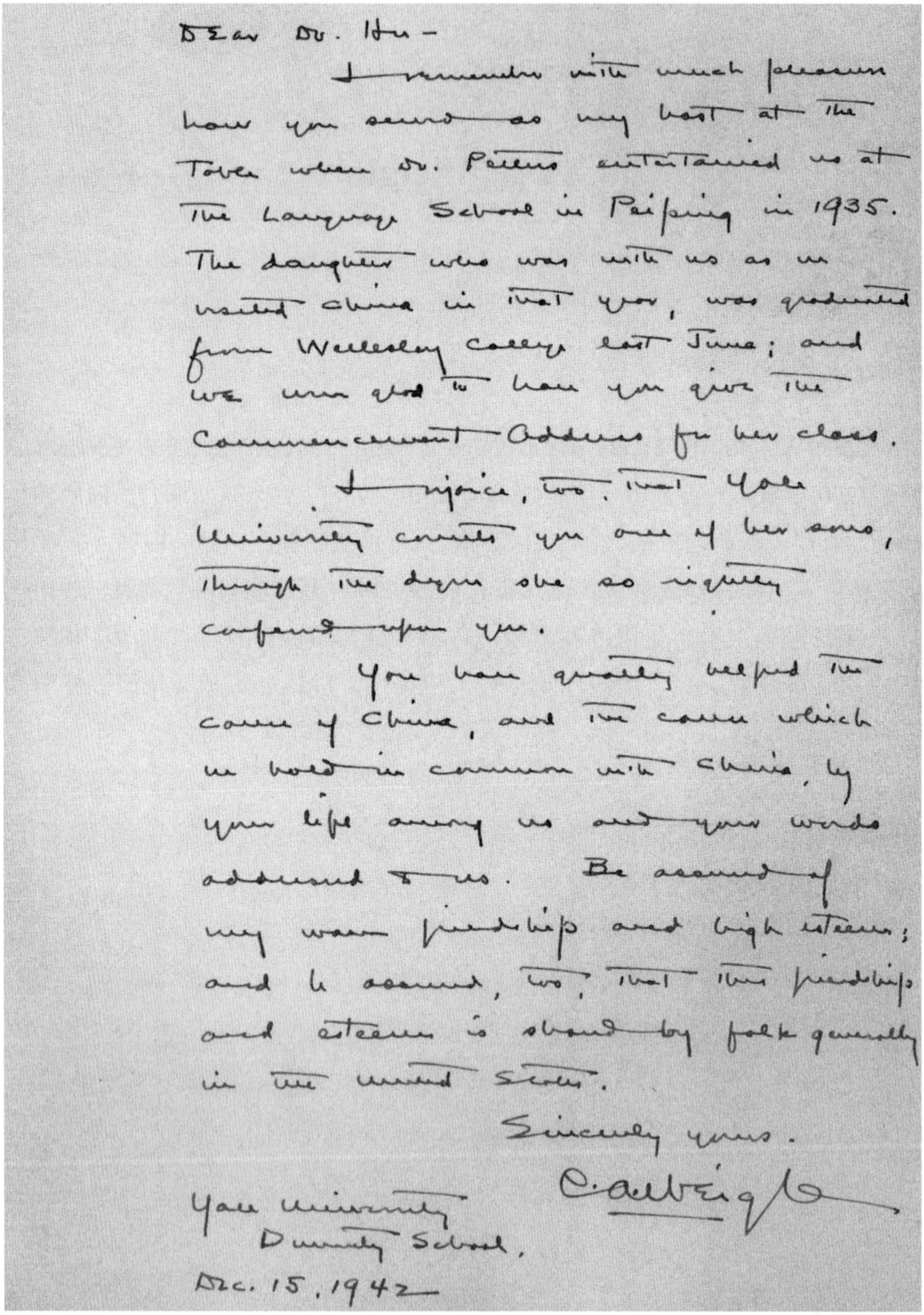

Dear Dr. Hu —

I remember with much pleasure how you served as my host at the Tower when Dr. Peters entertained us at the Language School in Peiping in 1935. The daughter who was with us as we visited China in that year, was graduated from Wellesley College last June; and we were glad to have you give the Commencement Address for her class.

I rejoice, too, that Yale University counts you one of her sons, through the degree she so justly conferred upon you.

You have greatly helped the cause of China, and the cause which we hold in common with China, by your life among us and your words addressed to us. Be assured of my warm friendship and high esteem; and be assured, too, that this friendship and esteem is shared by folk generally in the United States.

Sincerely yours,

C. A. Wright

Yale University
Divinity School,
Dec. 15, 1942

圖1

Dear Dr. Hu —

I remember with much pleasure how you served as my host at the table when Dr. Pettus entertained us at the Language School in Peiping in 1935. The daughter who was with us as we visited China in that year, was graduated from Wellesley College last June; and we were glad to have you give the Commencement Address for her class.

I rejoice, too, that Yale University counts you one of her sons, through the degree she so rightly conferred upon you.

You have greatly helped the cause of China, and the cause which we hold in common with China, by your life among us and your words addressed to us. Be assured of my warm friendship and high esteem; and be assured, too, that this friendship and esteem is shared by folk generally in the United States.

Sincerely yours,
L. A. Weigle

Yale University
Divinity School,
Dec. 15, 1942

Lauchlin Currie

　　Lauchlin Currie（1902—1993），生於加拿大，時任美國總統羅斯福秘書。早年就讀於倫敦經濟學院，1931 年獲哈佛大學博士學位，畢業後任哈佛大學講師至 1934 年。1939 年被提名爲羅斯福總統白宮經濟學家。1941 年、1942 年兩度被派往中國。1943—1944 年任美國外國經濟管理局副局長。胡適任駐美大使期間與其有交往，北京檔藏有 Currie 1943 年 1 月 12 日致胡適書信一通。

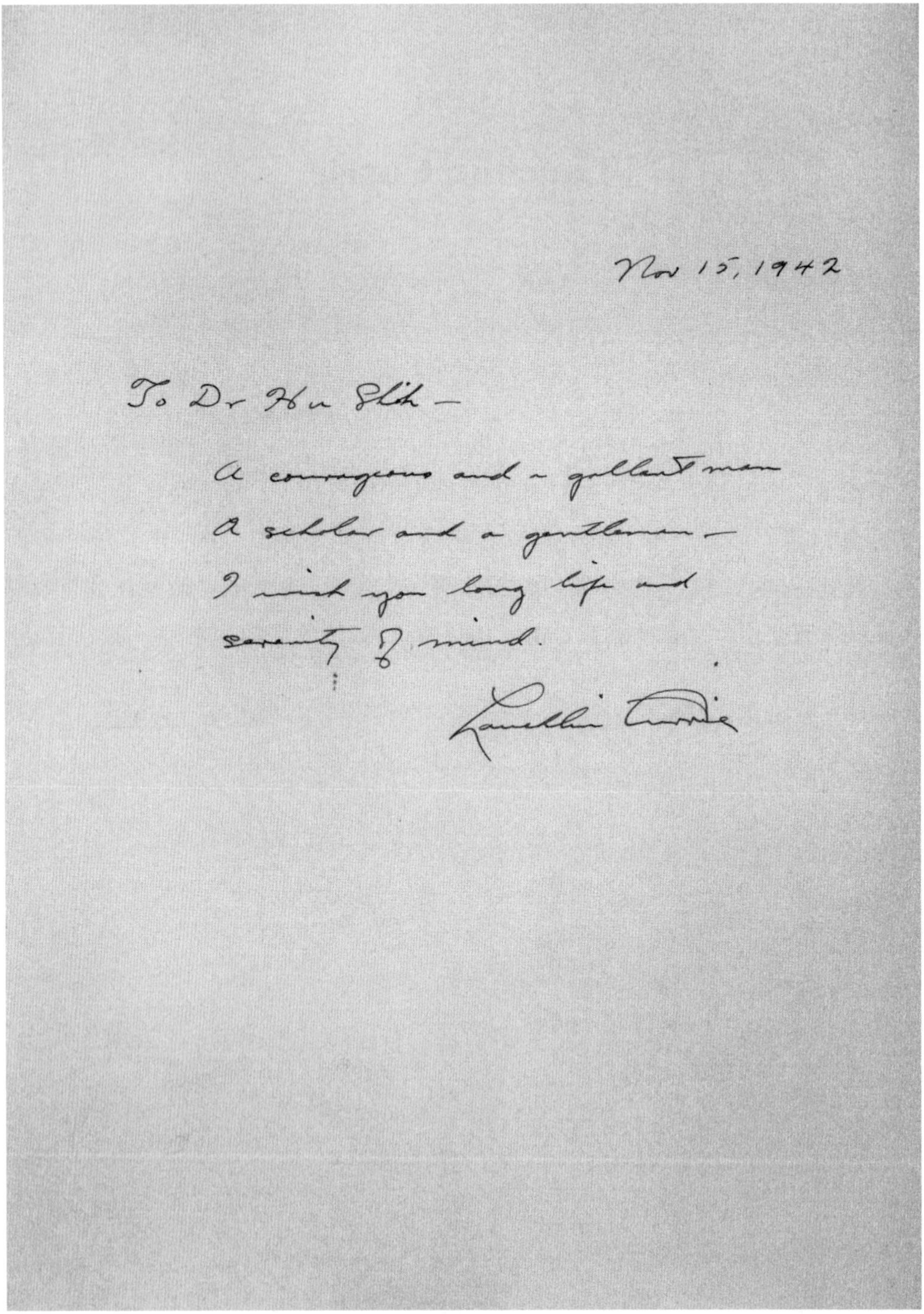

Nov 15, 1942

To Dr Hu Shih —

A courageous and a gallant man
A scholar and a gentleman —
I wish you long life and
serenity of mind.

Lauchlin Currie

圖1

Nov. 15, 1942

To Dr. Hu Shih—

    A courageous and a gallant man

    A scholar and a gentleman,

    I wish you long life and serenity of mind.

                                            Lauchlin Currie

Lenning Sweet

Lenning Sweet，生平不詳，北京檔藏有 Sweet 致胡適書信三封，第一封時間爲 1938 年 10 月 13 日，內容爲祝賀胡適擔任駐美大使，第三封日期爲 1942 年 9 月 1 日，內容爲對胡適卸任駐美大使表示遺憾，感謝他任職期間對中美友誼的貢獻。

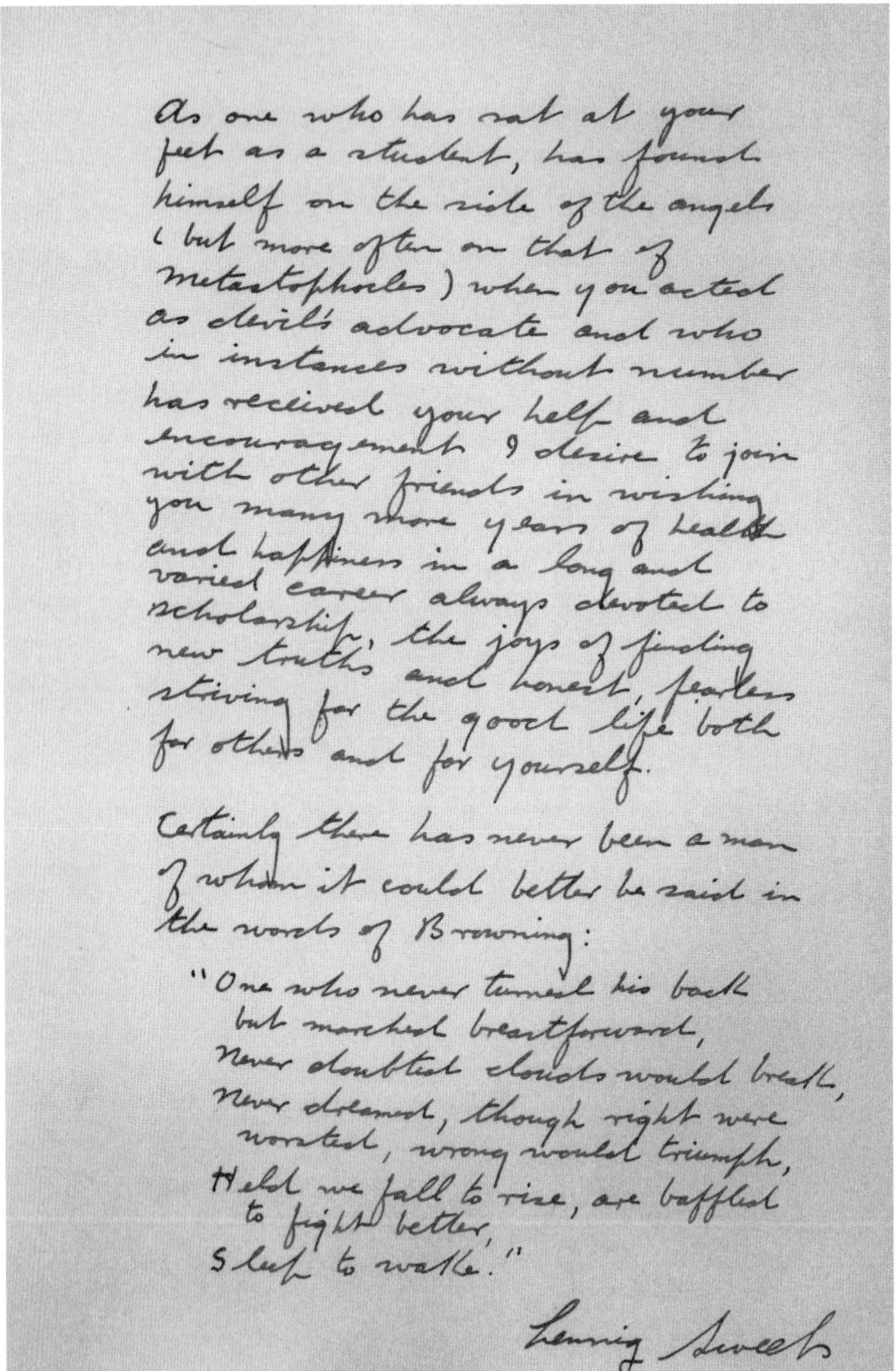

As one who has sat at your feet as a student, has found himself on the side of the angels (but more often on that of Mestastophocles) when you acted as devil's advocate and who in instances without number has recieved your help and encouragement I desire to join with other friends in wishing you many more years of health and happiness in a long and varied career always devoted to scholarship, the joys of finding new truths and honest, fearless striving for the good life both for others and for yourself.

Certainly there has never been a man of whom it could better be said in the words of Browning:

"One who never turned his back
but marched breastforward,
Never doubted clouds would break,
Never dreamed, though right were worsted, wrong would triumph,
Held we fall to rise, are baffled
to fight better,
Sleep to wake'."

Henning Sweet

圖 1

As one who has sat at your feet as a student, has found himself on the side of the angels (but more often on that of metastophocles [似爲 mephistopheles 之誤]) when you acted as devil's advocate and who in instances without number has received your help and encouragement I desire to join with other friends in wishing you many more years of health and happiness in a long and varied career always devoted to scholarship, the joys of finding new truths and honest, fearless striving for the good life both for others and for yourself.

　　Certainly there has never been a man of whom it could better be said in the words of Browning:

"One who never turned his back but marched breast forward,
Never doubted clouds would break,
Never dreamed, though right were worsted, wrong would triumph,
Held we fall to rise, are baffled to fight better,
Sleep to wake."

Lenning Sweet

Marion Fitch Exter

Marion Fitch Exter（1911—2009），美國來華北長老會傳教士、上海中華基督教青年會幹事費吳生（George Ashmore Fitch, 1883—1979）之女，生於上海。畢業於美國伍斯特學院（The College of Wooster）。

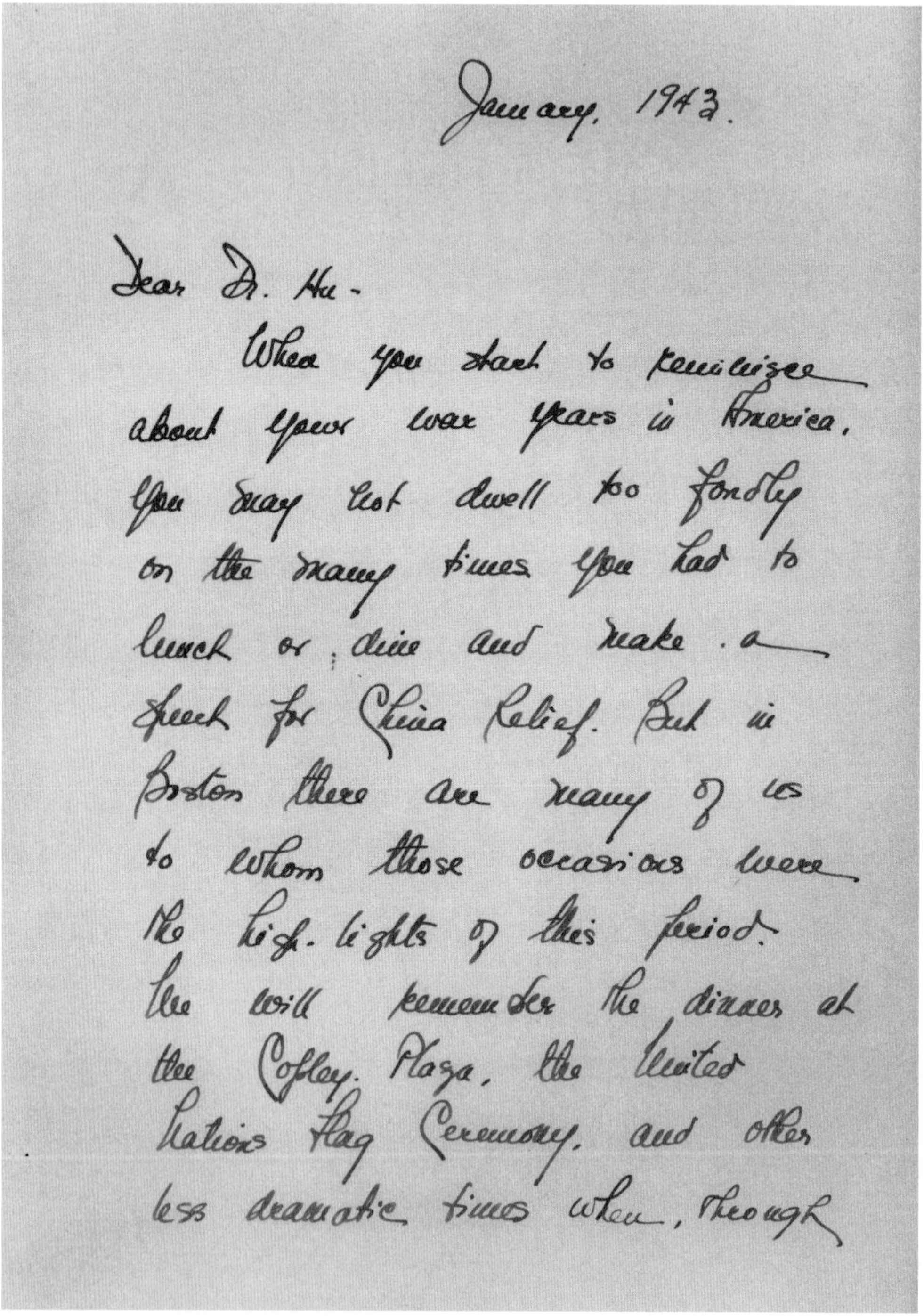

January, 1943.

Dear Dr. Hu -

When you start to reminisce about your war years in America, you may not dwell too fondly on the many times you had to lunch or dine and make a speech for China Relief. But in Boston there are many of us to whom those occasions were the highlights of this period. We will remember the dinners at the Copley Plaza, the United Nations Flag Ceremony, and other less dramatic times when, though

圖1

January, 1943

Dear Dr. Hu,

When you start to reminisce about your war years in America, you may not dwell too fondly on the many times you had to lunch or dine and make a speech for China Relief. But in Boston there are many of us to whom those occasions were the high lights of this period. We will remember the dinner at the Copley Plaza, the United Nations Flag ceremony, and other less dramatic times when, through you, we came closer to the people of your country.

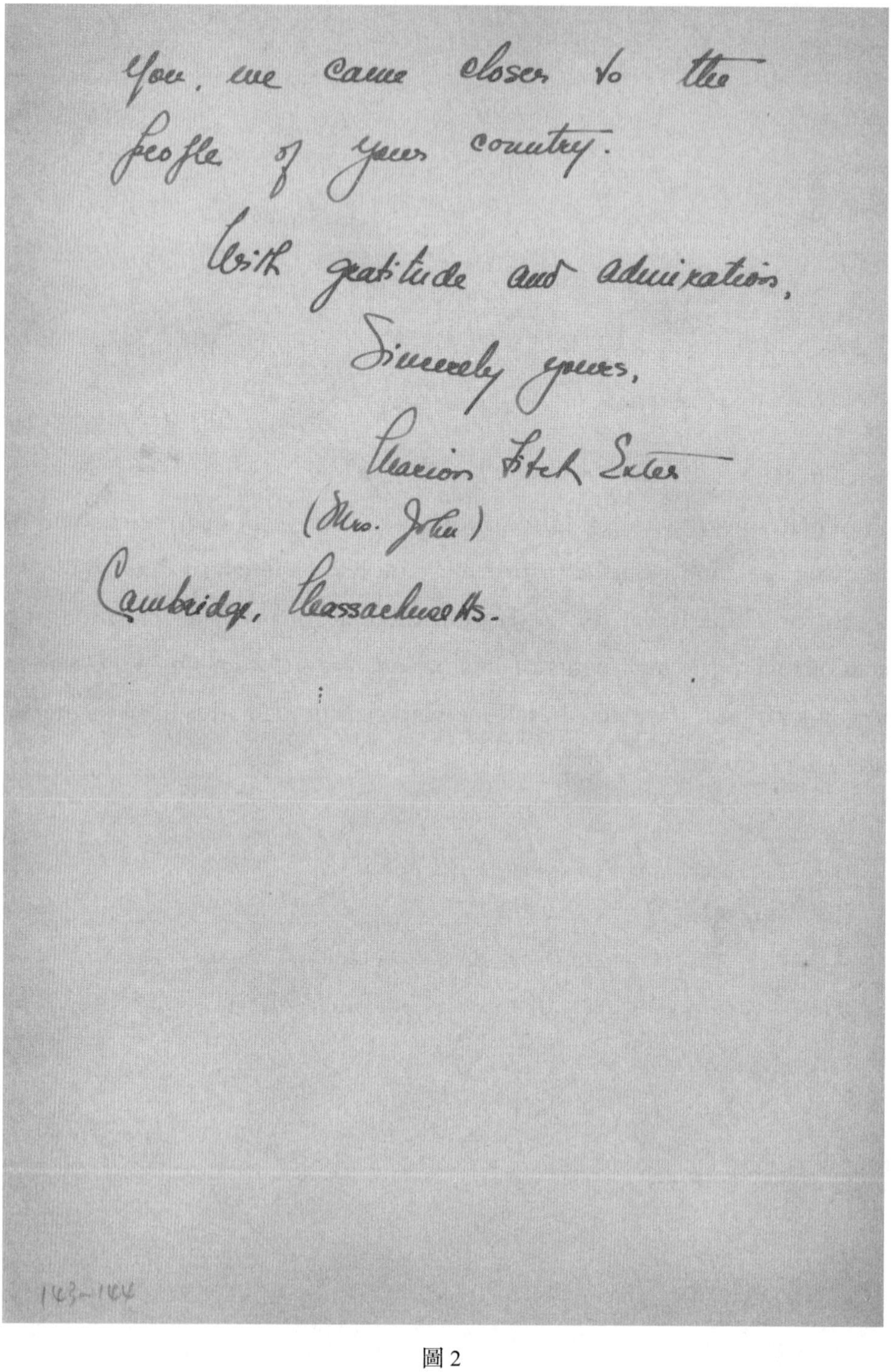

With gratitude and admiration,

Sincerely yours,

Marion Fitch Exter
(Mrs. John)

Cambridge, Massachusetts.

圖 2

you, we came closer to the people of your country.

With gratitude and admiration,

Sincerely yours,

Marion Fitch Exter

(Mrs. John)

Cambridge, Massachusetts

Martha Finley (Mrs. John H.)

Martha Finley (Mrs. John H.)（？—1956），其夫 John H. Finley 曾任《紐約時報》編輯，據信中內容，曾到過中國。餘不詳。

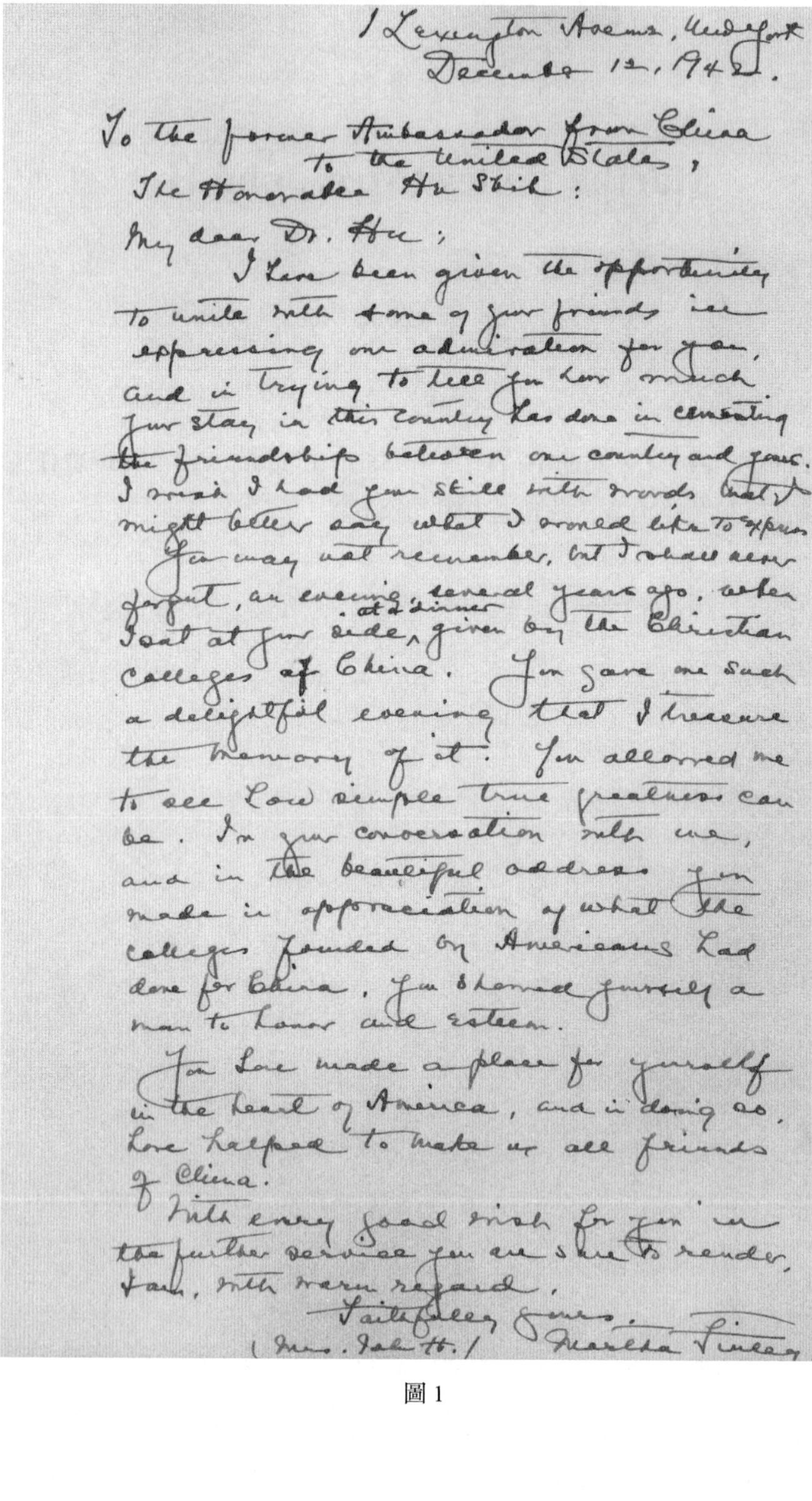

1 Lexington Avenue, Medefort.
December 12, 1942.

To the former Ambassador from China
to the United States,
The Honorable Hu Shih:
My dear Dr. Hu:

I have been given the opportunity to unite with some of your friends in expressing our admiration for you, and in trying to tell you how much your stay in this country has done in cementing the friendship between our country and yours. I wish I had your skill with words that I might better say what I would like to express.

You may not remember, but I shall never forget, an evening several years ago, at a dinner when I sat at your side, given by the Christian Colleges of China. You gave me such a delightful evening that I treasure the memory of it. You allowed me to see how simple true greatness can be. In your conversation with me, and in the beautiful address you made in appreciation of what the colleges founded by Americans had done for China, you showed yourself a man to honor and esteem.

You have made a place for yourself in the heart of America, and in doing so, have helped to make us all friends of China.

With every good wish for you in the further service you are sure to render, I am, with warm regards,

Faithfully yours,
(Mrs. Job H.) Martha Finley.

圖1

1 Lexington Avenue, New York

December 12, 1942

To the former Ambassador from China to the United States,

The Honorable Hu Shih:

My dear Dr. Hu:

I have been given the opportunity to unite with some of your friends in expressing our admiration for you, and in trying to tell you how much your stay in this country has done in cementing the friendship between our country and yours. I wish I had your skill with words that I might better say what I would like to express.

You may not remember, but I shall never forget, an evening several years ago, when I sat at your side at a dinner given by the Christian Colleges of China. You gave me such a delightful evening that I treasure the memory of it. You allowed me to see how simple true greatness can be. In your conversation with me, and in the beautiful address you made in appreciation of what the colleges founded by Americans had done for China, you showed yourself a man to honor and esteem.

You have made a place for yourself in the heart of America, and in doing so, have helped to make us all friends of China.

With every good wish for you in the further service you are sure to render, I am, with warm regard,

Faithfully yours,

(Mrs. John H.) Martha Finley

Maurice William

　　Maurice William（？—1973），美國作家，餘不詳。胡適任駐美大使前後與其有交往，日記中有1940年、1943年與其交談、共餐的記錄。北京檔藏有胡適與其往來函電九通，時間從1939年7月到1940年7月。

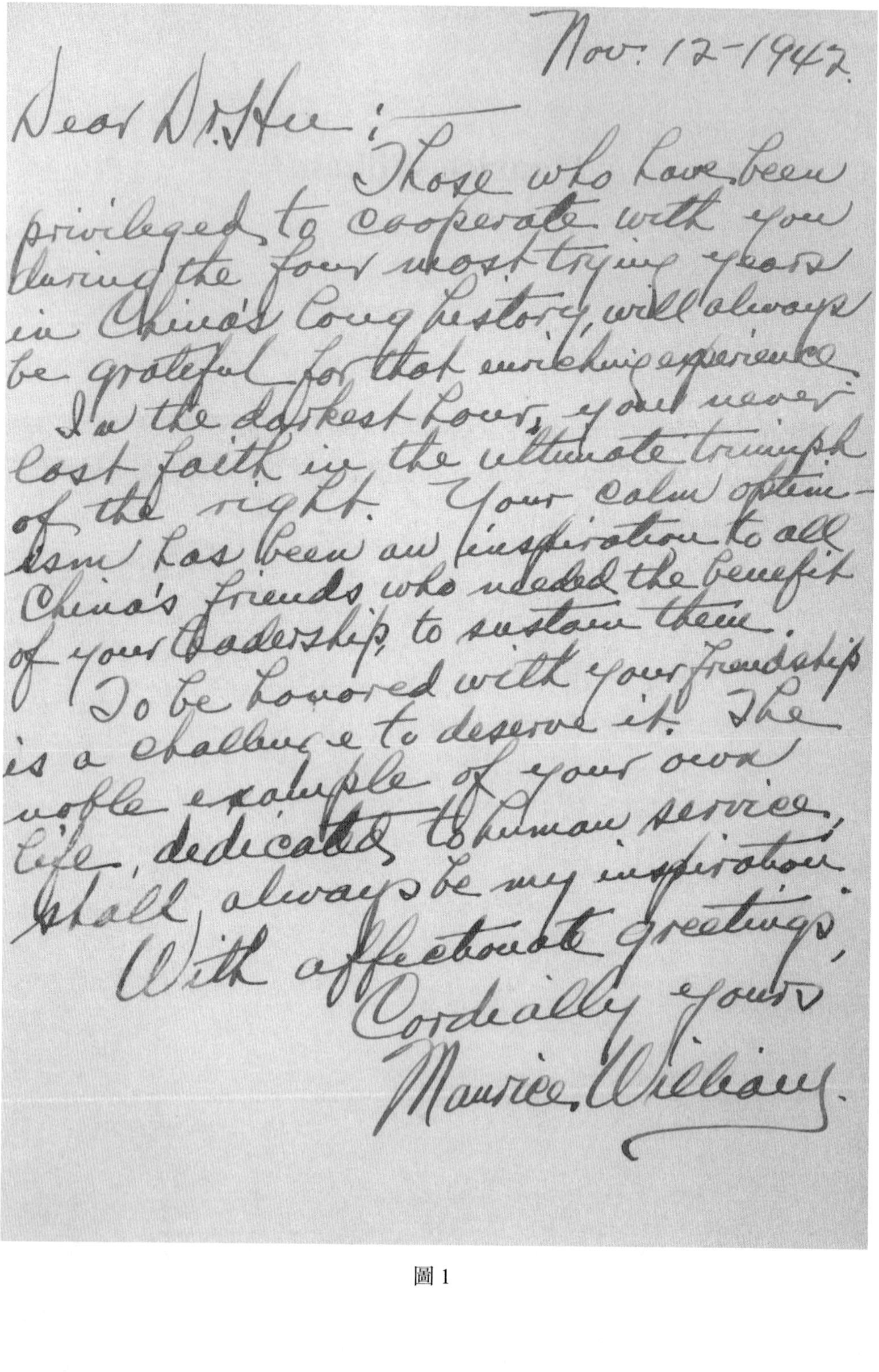

Nov. 12-1942.

Dear Dr. Hu:—

Those who have been privileged to cooperate with you during the four most trying years in China's long history, will always be grateful for that enriching experience.

In the darkest hour, you never lost faith in the ultimate triumph of the right. Your calm optimism has been an inspiration to all China's friends who needed the benefit of your leadership to sustain them.

To be honored with your friendship is a challenge to deserve it. The noble example of your own life, dedicated to human service, shall always be my inspiration.

With affectionate greetings,

Cordially yours,
Maurice William

圖 1

Nov. 12-1942

Dear Dr. Hu:—

Those who have been privileged to cooperate with you during the four most trying years in China's long history, will always be grateful for that enriching experience.

In the darkest hour, you never lost faith in the ultimate triumph of the right. Your calm optimism has been an inspiration to all China's friends who needed the benefit of your leadership, to sustain them.

To be honored with your friendship is a challenge to deserve it. The noble example of your own life, dedicated to human service shall always be my inspiration.

With affectionate greetings,
Cordially yours
Maurice William

Mildred H. McAfee

　　Mildred H. McAfee（1900—1994），生於美國密蘇里州帕克維爾。先後獲瓦薩學院學士學位、芝加哥大學碩士學位。先後任美國中央學院和歐柏林學院女生訓導長。1936年任韋爾斯利學院院長。二戰期間擔任美國婦女海軍志願服役負責人。1945年成爲美國第一位接受海軍優秀服務獎章的女性。後在美國基督教會聯合會和世界基督教會聯合會擔任領導工作。胡適任駐美大使前後與其有交往，北京檔藏有胡適與其往來函電十三通，時間從1941年7月到1942年6月。

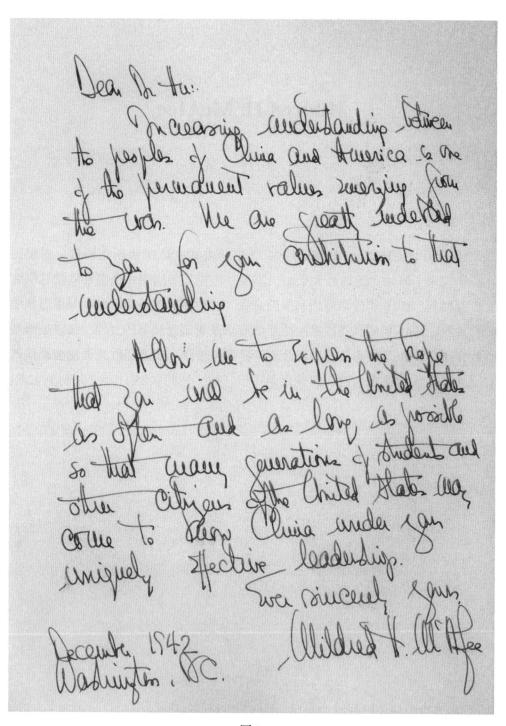

圖 1

Dear Dr. Hu:

Increasing understanding—between the people of China and America—is one of the permanent values emerging from the war. We are greatly indebted to you for your contribution to that understanding.

Allow me to express the hope that you will be in the United States as often and as long as possible so that many generations of students and other citizens of the United States may come to New China under your uniquely effective leadership.

Ever sincerely yours,
Mildred H. McAfee

December 1942
Washington, D. C.

Mildred Hughes (Mrs. James E.)

　　Mildred Hughes，曾任 Far East-American Council of Commerce and Industry, Inc. 行政副主席。

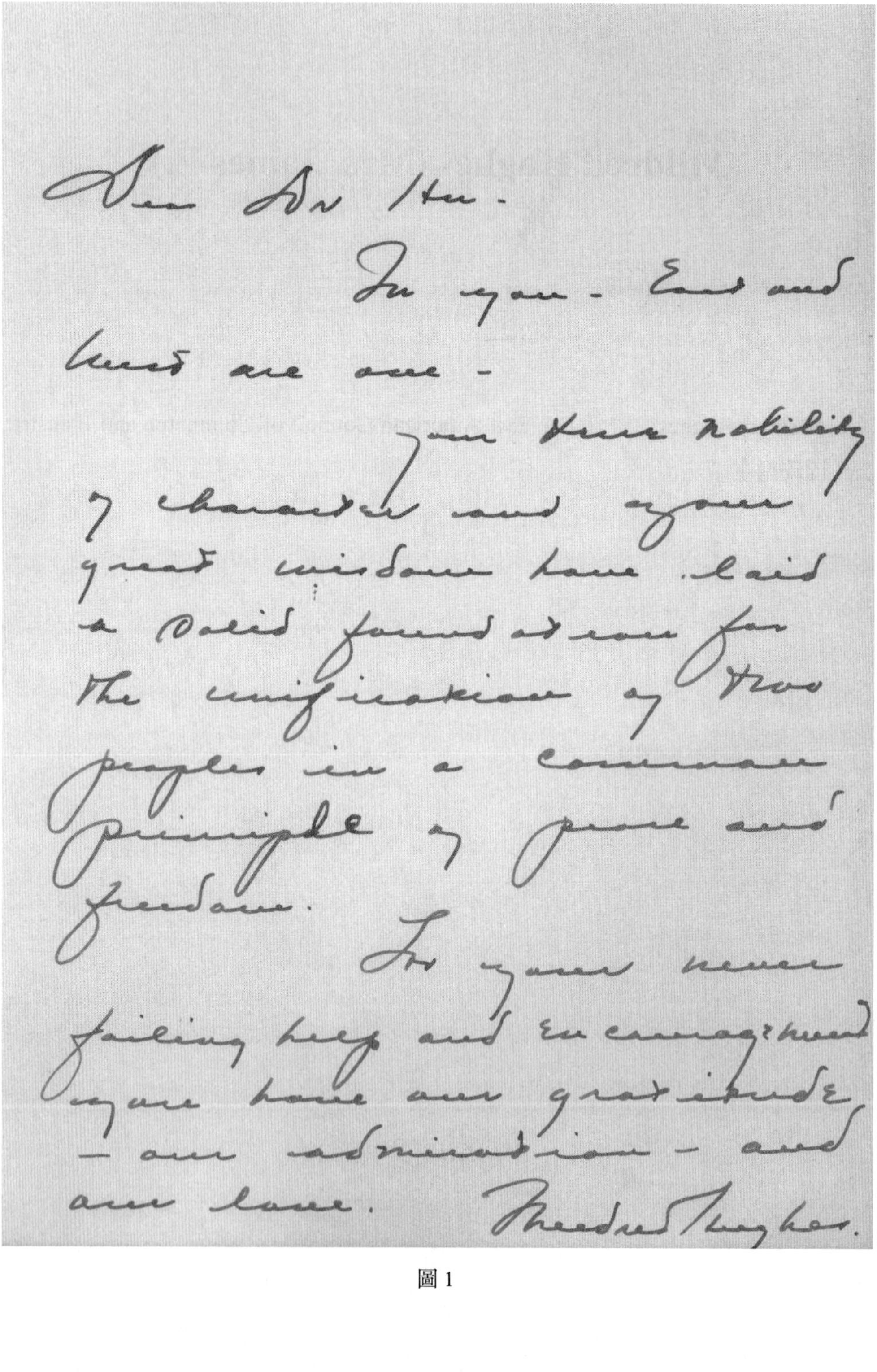

Dear Dr Hu,

In you — East and West are one —

Your sheer nobility of character and your great wisdom have laid a solid foundation for the unification of two peoples in a common principle of peace and freedom.

For your never failing help and encouragement you have our gratitude — our admiration — and our love. Theodore Hughes.

圖 1

Dear Dr. Hu,

In you, East and West are one.

Your true nobility of character and your great wisdom have laid a solid foundation for the unification of two peoples in a common principle of peace and freedom.

In your never failing help and encouragement you have our gratitude, our admiration, and our love.

Mildred Hughes

Myron C. Taylor

　　Myron C. Taylor，即 Myron Charles Taylor（1874—1959），生於美國紐約州萊昂斯。1894 年畢業於康奈爾大學法學院。1900 年到紐約華爾街從事公司法律事務，後從事紡織和商業郵遞。1925 年當選立法院財政委員會委員，1929 年擔任主席。1932—1938 年任美國鋼鐵公司董事會主席兼總裁。

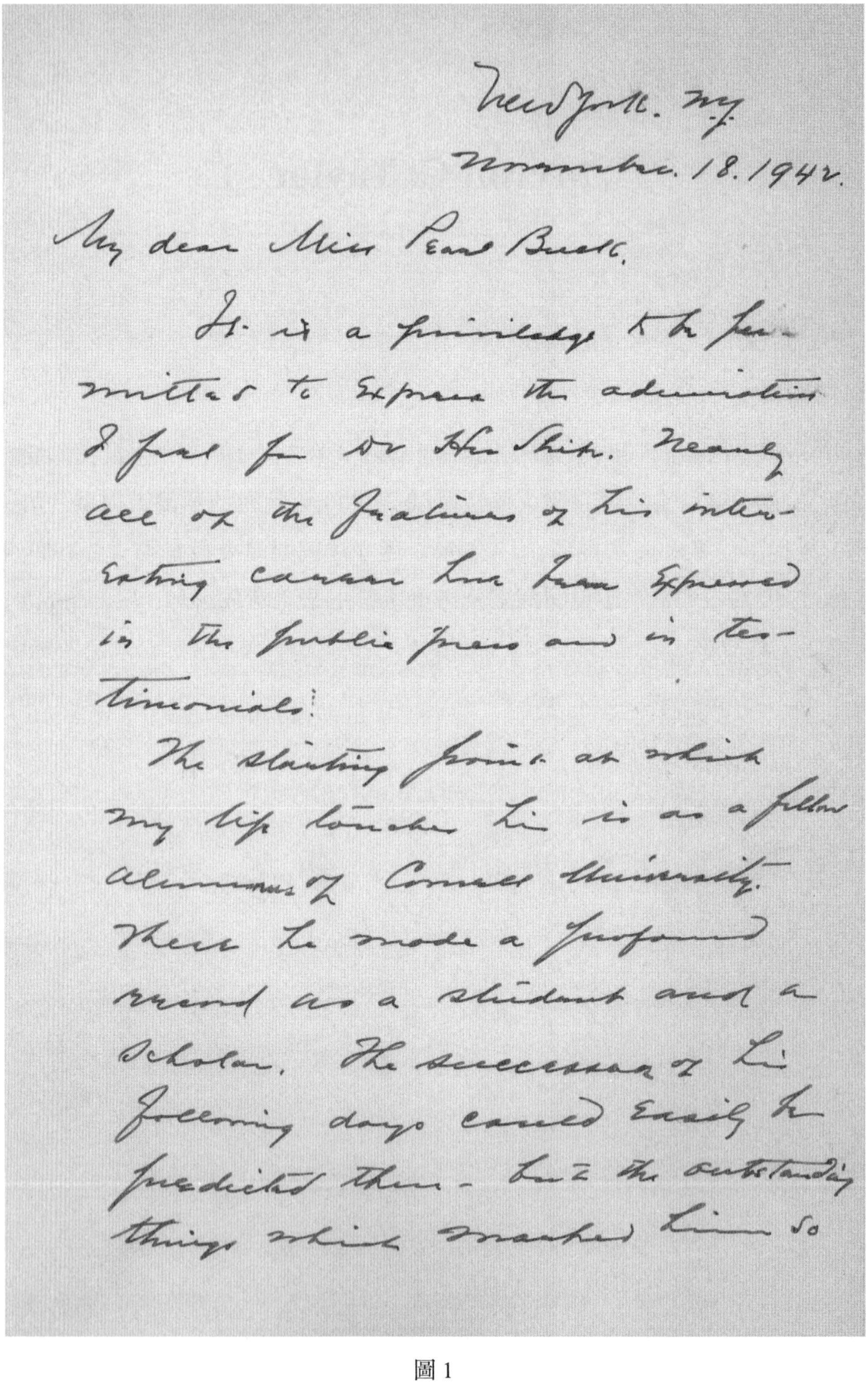

New York, N.Y.
November. 18. 1942.

My dear Miss Pearl Buck,

It is a privilege to be permitted to express the admiration I feel for Dr. Hu Shih. Nearly all of the features of his interesting career have been expressed in the public press and in testimonials.

The starting point at which my life touches his is as a fellow alumnus of Cornell University. There he made a profound record as a student and a scholar. The successes of his following days could easily be predicted then — but the outstanding things which marked him so

圖 1

New York, N. Y.
November 18, 1942

My dear Miss Pearl Buck,

It is a privilege to be permitted to express the admiration I feel for Dr. Hu Shih. Nearly all of the features of his interesting career have been expressed in the public press and in testimonials.

The starting point at which my life touches his is as a fellow alumnus of Cornell University, where he made a profound record as a student and a scholar. The successes of his following days could easily be predicted then—but the outstanding things which marked him so distinctly were his great modesty, his calm under trial and his unfailing courtesy. These distinctive qualities reflect traditional backgrounds of those great seers, philosophers, and poets of the days far back in the long history of his Chinese motherland. In the field of diplomacy these many attributes combined in a single individual furnish a befitting equipment for dealing with the tremendous questions of an ever changing world. He has possessed them. He has used them well. May the distressed world of our day long have the continued benefit of his wisdom and his art.

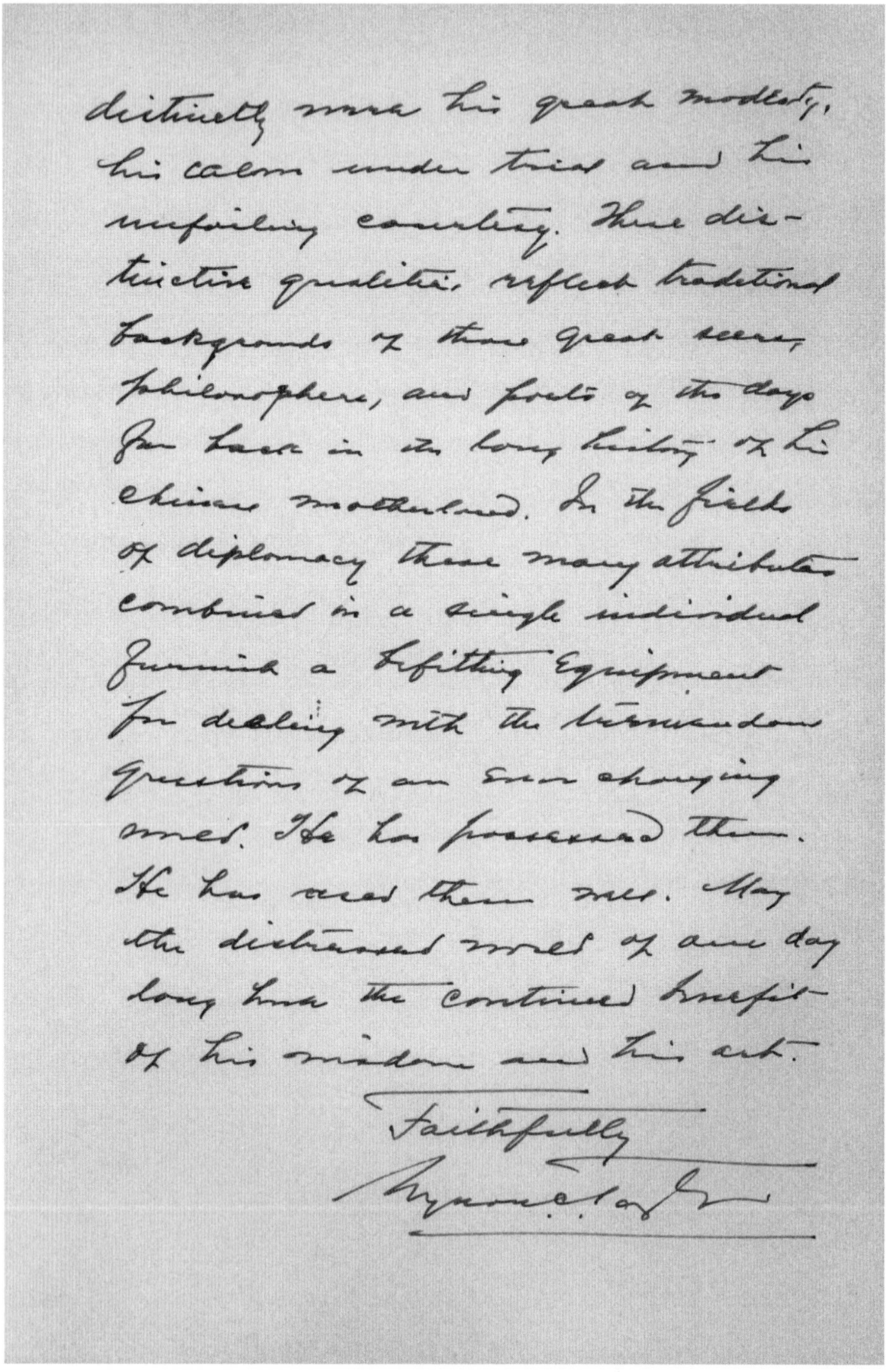

Faithfully
[signature]

圖 2

distinctly were his great modesty, his calm under trial and his unfailing courtesy. These distinctive qualities reflect traditional backgrounds of those great seers, philosophers, and poets of the days far back in the long history of his Chinese motherland. In the fields of diplomacy these many attributes combined in a single individual furnish a befitting equipment for dealing with the tremendous questions of our ever changing world. He has possessed them. He has used them well. May the distressed world of our day long have the continued benefit of his wisdom and his art.

Faithfully
Myron C. Taylor

Otis Peabody Swift

　　Otis Peabody Swift（1895—1971），美國新聞人、作家。早年就讀於哥倫比亞新聞學院，一戰曾參加美國海軍。二十世紀二十年代早期在歐洲任海外記者。1923年回美國後主要在紐約和芝加哥從事新聞工作。二十世紀三十年代成爲作家和公關人員。抗戰期間曾任全美助華聯合總會主席。胡適在任駐美大使期間與其有交往。北京檔藏有Swift致胡適函電三通，及胡適私人秘書代復Swift函電兩通，時間從1941年3月到9月。

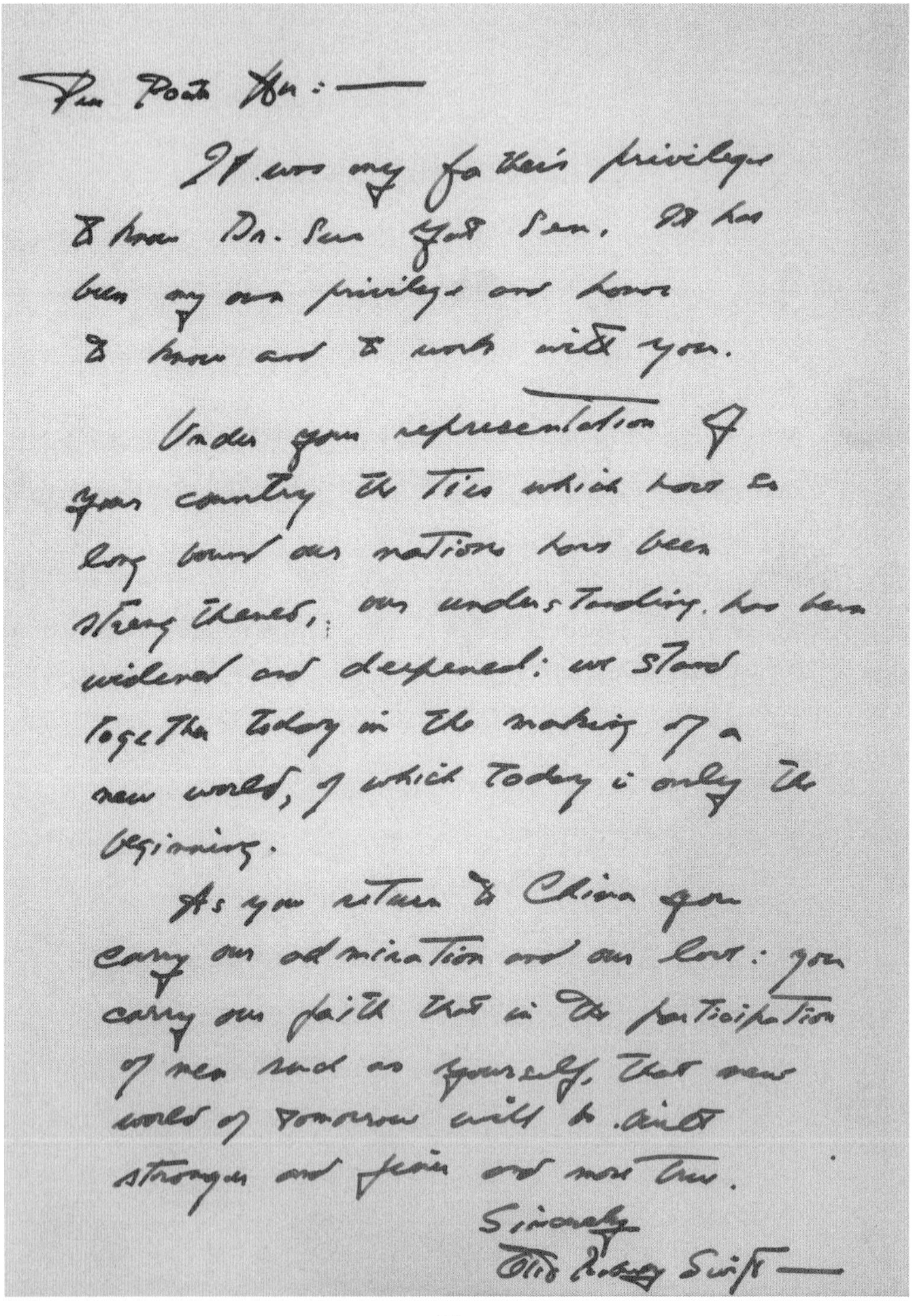

Dear Doctor Hu:—

It was my father's privilege to know Dr. Sun Yat Sen. It has been my own privilege and honor to know and to work with you.

Under your representation of your country the Ties which have so long bound our nations have been strengthened; our understanding has been widened and deepened: we stand together today in the making of a new world, of which today is only the beginning.

As you return to China you carry our admiration and our love: you carry our faith that in the participation of men such as yourself, that new world of tomorrow will be built stronger and fairer and more true.

Sincerely
Otis Robert Swift—

圖 1

Dear Doctor Hu: —

It was my father's privilege to hear Dr. Sun Yat Sen. It has been my own privilege and honor to hear and to work with you.

Under your representation of your country the ties which have so long bound our nations have been strengthened, our understanding have been widened and deepened: we stand together today in the making of a new world, of which today is only the beginning.

As you return to China you carry our admiration and our love: you carry our faith that in the participation of men such as yourself, that new world of tomorrow will be □ stronger and firmer and more true.

Sincerely
Otis Peabody Swift

Paul G. Hoffman

　　Paul G. Hoffman（1891—1974），生於美國伊利諾伊州。18歲從芝加哥大學退學，推銷斯圖貝克汽車，34歲即成爲百萬富翁，1935—1948年任斯圖貝克總裁。1950—1953年任福特基金會主席。1966—1972年任聯合國發展計劃負責人。1974年被尼克松總統授予總統自由勳章。胡適任駐美大使前後與其有交往，北京檔藏有胡適與其往來函電十通，時間從1941年9月到1943年6月。

Dear Dr Hu Shih:-

You are a great scholar - your many honorary degrees from great universities attest that.

You are China's greatest educator - that is a matter of record.

You also were a great ambassador. Since the beginning of time yours is the greatest of all contributions to the growth of understanding and friendship between your people and ours. That puts the world much in your debt because its future peace and progress depend in no small way upon accord between the east and the west.

But it is not the great scholar, educator + statesman for whom I feel such a deep and overwhelming affection. Rather it is for the human being Hu Shih, a gentleman out of the top drawer who is filled to overflowing with sweetness and light.

Sincerely yours,

Paul G Hoffman

Mar. 5. 1942

圖1

Dear Dr. Hu Shih:

You are a great scholar—your many honorary degrees from great universities attest that.

You are China's greatest educator—that is a matter of record.

You also were a great ambassador & since the beginning of time yours is the greatest of all contributions to the growth of understanding and friendship between your people and ours. That puts the world much in your debt, because its future peace and progress depend in no small way upon accord between the east and the west.

But it is not the great scholar, educator & statesman for whom I feel such a deep and overwhelming affection. Rather it is for the human being Hu Shih, a gentleman out of the type drawn who is filled to overflowing with sweetness and light.

Sincerely yours
Paul G. Hoffman

Dec. 5, 1942

Paul Monroe

　　Paul Monroe（1869—1947），孟禄，生於美國印第安納州，1890年畢業於印第安納州富蘭克林學院，1897年獲芝加哥大學博士學位。1899年任哥倫比亞大學教授，曾任該校教育學院院長。曾任教於耶魯大學和加州大學。1913年獲北京大學榮譽博士學位。二十世紀二三十年代曾多次來華，爲中美教育交流做出了貢獻。曾任《教育學年鑒》主編，華美協進社董事會主席。胡適日記中與其最早的見面記錄是1921年9月5日。胡適任大使期間與其書信往來頗多，北京檔藏有二人1938年至1944往來函電十六通。

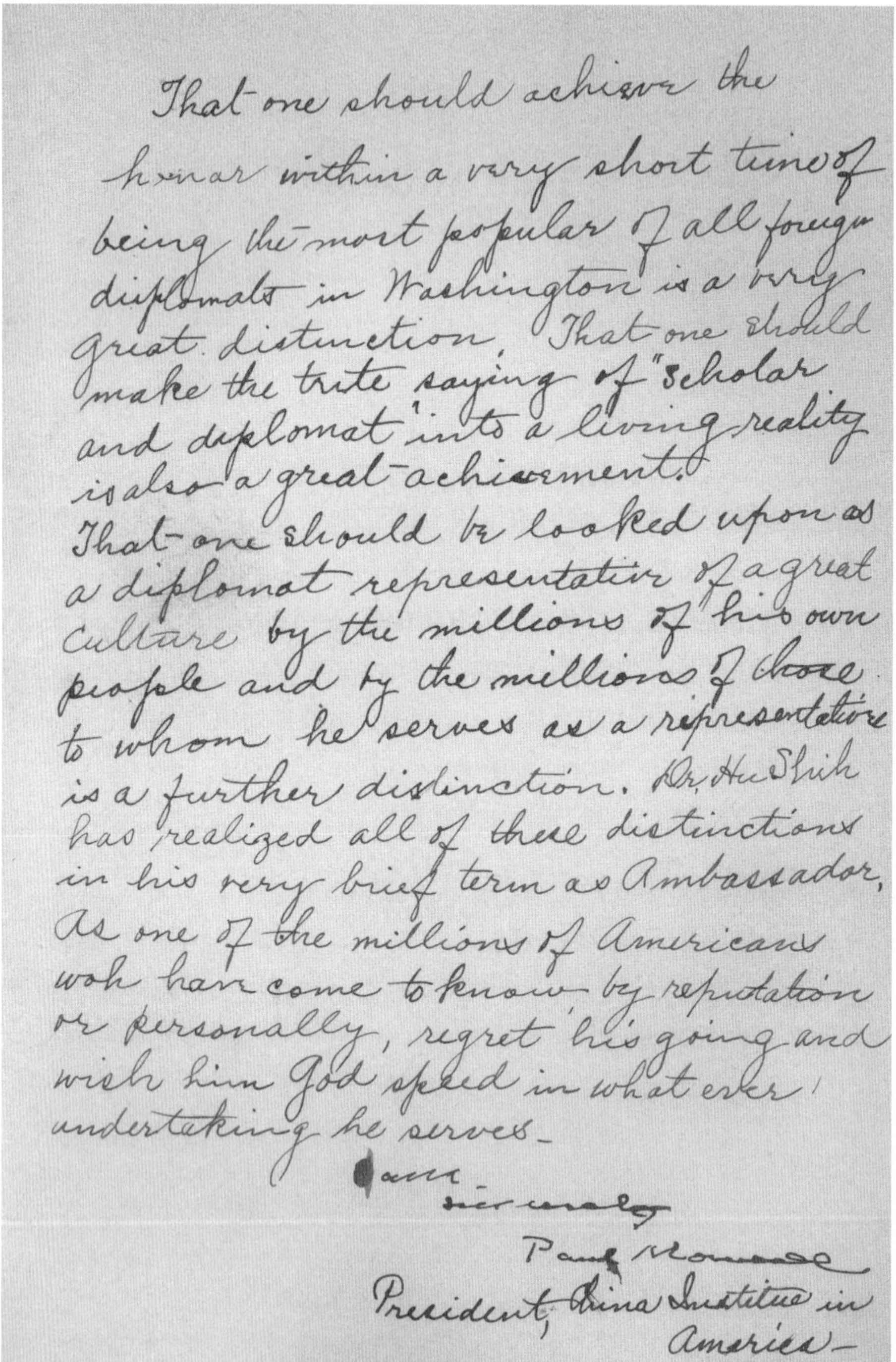

That one should achieve the honor within a very short time of being the most popular of all foreign diplomats in Washington is a very great distinction. That one should make the trite saying of "scholar and diplomat" into a living reality is also a great achievement. That one should be looked upon as a diplomat representative of a great culture by the millions of his own people and by the millions of those to whom he serves as a representative is a further distinction. Dr. Hu Shih has realized all of these distinctions in his very brief term as Ambassador. As one of the millions of Americans woh have come to know by reputation or personally, regret his going and wish him God speed in what ever undertaking he serves.

I am ~~sincerely~~

Paul Monroe

President, China Institute in America.

圖1

That one should achieve the honor within a very short time of being the most popular of all foreign diplomats in Washington is a very great distinction. That one should make the trite saying of "scholar and diplomat" into a living reality is also a great achievement.

That one should be looked upon as a diplomat representative of a great culture by the millions of his own people and by the millions of those to whom he serves as a representative is a further distinction. Dr. Hu Shih has realized all of these distinctions in his very brief term as Ambassador. As one of the millions of Americans who have come to know by reputation or personally, regret his going and wish him God speed in whatever undertaking he serves.

I am
Sincerely
Paul Monroe
President, China Institute in America

Pearl S. Buck

　　Pearl S. Buck（1892—1973），賽珍珠，美國女作家。生於美國西弗吉尼亞州，父親爲在華長老會傳教士，五個月時隨家庭到中國。1911年回美國，就讀於倫道夫・梅康女子學院，1914年畢業，同年返回中國。1921—1931年任金陵大學英國文學教授。1935年返回美國。以小説《大地》（*The Good Earth*）成名，1938年獲諾貝爾文學獎。北京檔藏有胡適任駐美大使前後賽珍珠致胡適函電五通，其中1942年9月6日的書信裏，賽珍珠對胡適卸任駐美大使表示遺憾，並對胡適的貢獻給予了高度評價。

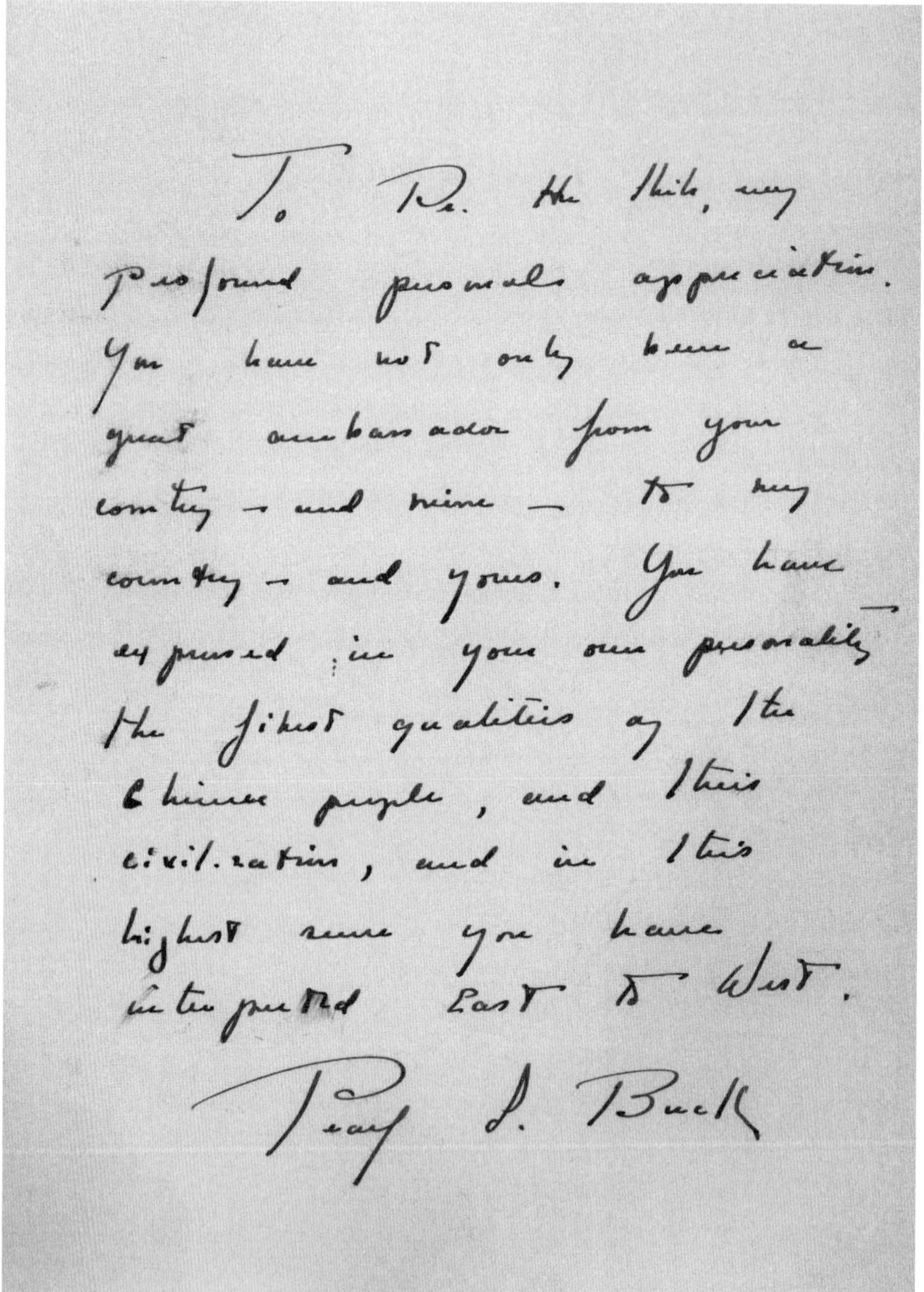

To Dr. Hu Shih, my profound personal appreciation. You have not only been a great ambassador from your country — and mine — to my country — and yours. You have expressed in your own personality the finest qualities of the Chinese people, and their civilization, and in this highest sense you have interpreted East to West.

Pearl S. Buck

圖 1

To Dr. Hu Shih, my profound personal appreciation. You have not only been a great ambassador from your country—and mine—to my country—and yours. You have expressed in your own personality the finest qualities of the Chinese people, and this civilization, and in this highest sense you have interpreted East to West.

Pearl S. Buck

Ralph A. Bard

　　Ralph A. Bard（1884—1975），生於美國俄亥俄州克利夫蘭，時任美國海軍部助理部長。1906年畢業於耶魯大學。1941—1944年任海軍部助理部長，1944—1945年任海軍部副部長。

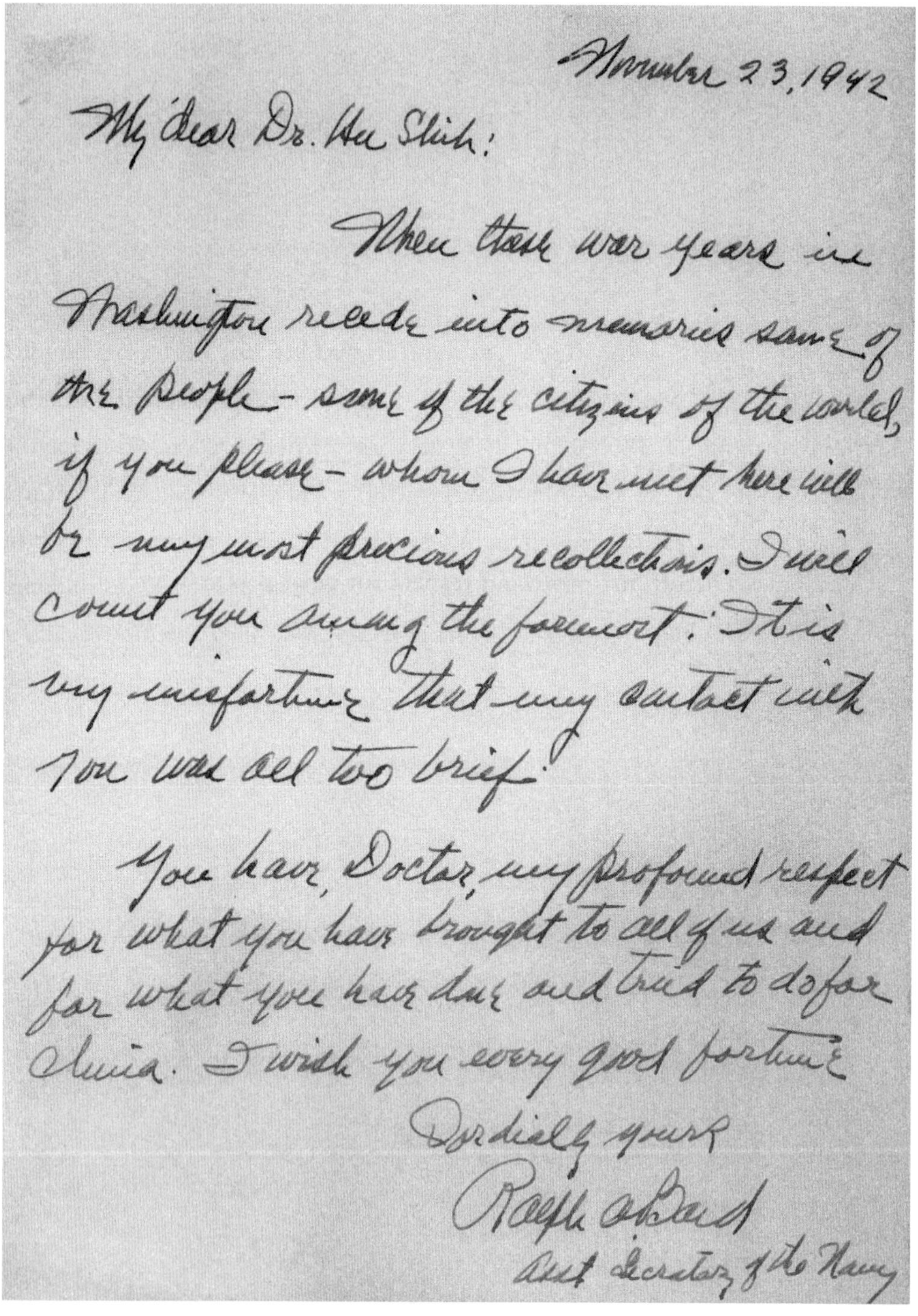

November 23, 1942

My dear Dr. Hu Shih:

When these war years in Washington recede into memories some of the people — some of the citizens of the world, if you please — whom I have met here will be my most precious recollections. I will count you among the foremost. It is my misfortune that my contact with you was all too brief.

You have, Doctor, my profound respect for what you have brought to all of us and for what you have done and tried to do for China. I wish you every good fortune.

Cordially yours,

Ralph A Bard
Asst Secretary of the Navy

圖1

November 23, 1942

My dear Dr. Hu Shih:

When these war years in Washington recede into memories some of the people—some of the citizens of the world, if you please—whom I have met here will be my most precious recollections. I will count you among the foremost. It is my misfortune that my contact with you was all too brief.

You have, Doctor, my profound respect for what you have brought to all of us and for what you have done and tried to do for China. I wish you every good fortune.

Cordially yours
Ralph A. Bard
Asst. Secretary of the Navy

Ralph E. Diffendorfer

　　Ralph E. Diffendorfer（1879—1951），生於美國俄亥俄州，牧師。早年畢業於俄亥俄州衛斯理大學。1904—1906 年任傳教士教育運動（Missionary Education Movement）秘書。1916—1917 年任 Board of Home Missions and Church Extension 和 Board of Foreign Missions of the Methodist Episcopal Church 秘書。1919—1920 年任 Home Missions Survey of the Inter-church world movement 會長。1920 年被聘爲 Committee on Conservation and Advance of the Methodist Episcopal Church 教育部秘書。曾任美國衛理會海外傳教會秘書。胡適在 1939 年 11 月 30 日致 Earl H. Cressy 的信中通知，中國決定授予包括 Ralph E. Diffendorfer 在内四位美國人"雙十"國慶榮譽勛章。

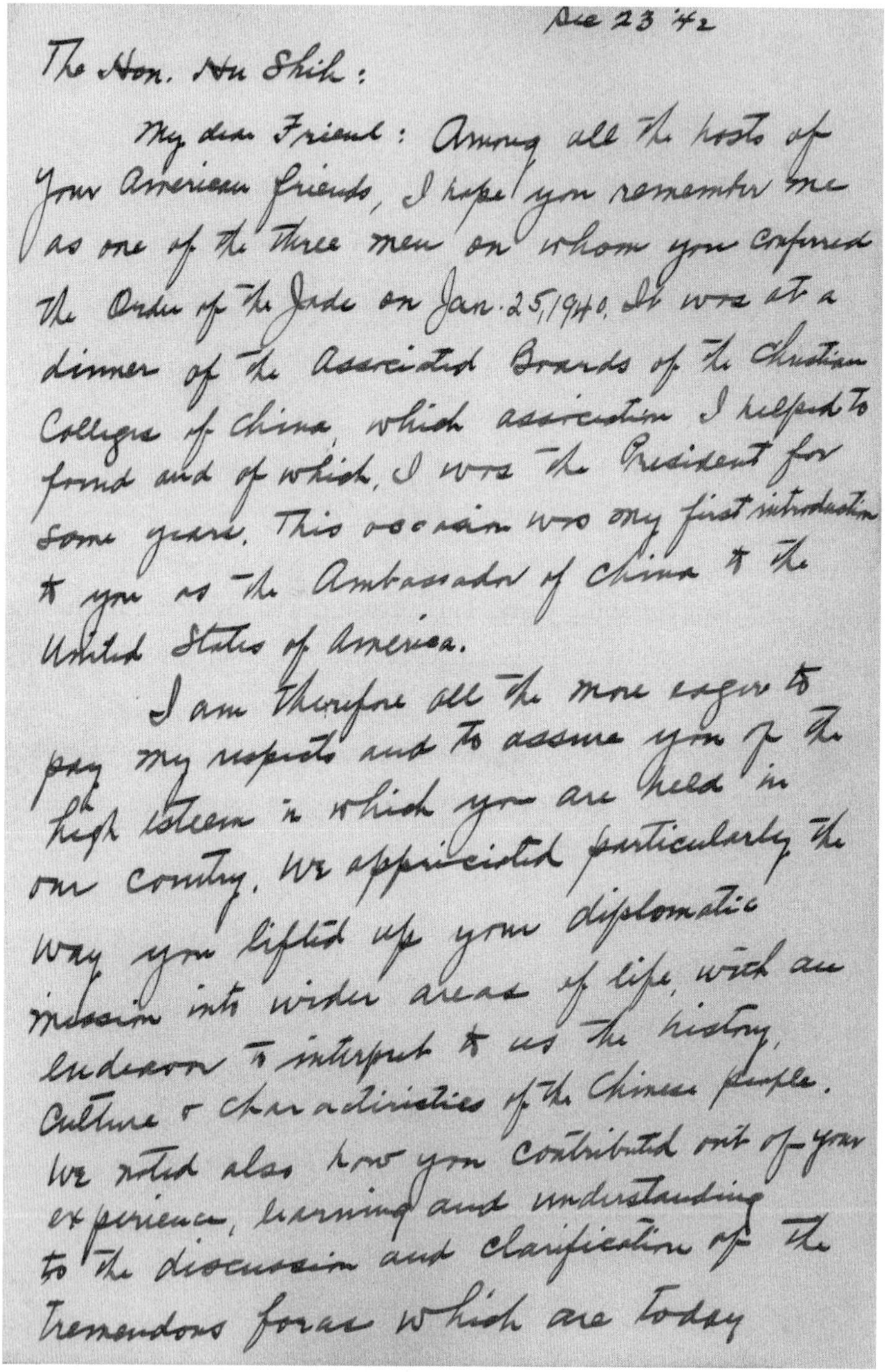

Dec 23 '42

The Hon. Hu Shih:

My dear Friend: Among all the hosts of your American friends, I hope you remember me as one of the three men on whom you conferred the Order of the Jade on Jan. 25, 1940. It was at a dinner of the Associated Boards of the Christian Colleges of China, which association I helped to found and of which I was the President for some years. This occasion was my first introduction to you as the Ambassador of China to the United States of America.

I am therefore all the more eager to pay my respects and to assure you of the high esteem in which you are held in our country. We appreciated particularly the way you lifted up your diplomatic mission into wider areas of life, with an endeavor to interpret to us the history, culture & characteristics of the Chinese people. We noted also how you contributed out of your experience, learning and understanding to the discussion and clarification of the tremendous forces which are today

圖1

Dec. 23, '42

The Hon. Hu Shih:

My dear Friend: Among all the hosts of your American friends, I hope you remember me as one of the three men on whom you conferred the Order of the Jade on Jan. 25, 1940. It was at a dinner of the Associated Boards of the Christian College of China, which association I helped to found and of which, I was the President for some years. This occasion was my first introduction to you as the Ambassador of China to the United States of America.

I am therefore all the more eager to pay my respects and to assure you of the high esteem in which you are held in our country. We appreciated particularly the way you lifted up your diplomatic mission with wider areas of life, with an endeavor to interpret to us the history, culture & characteristics of the Chinese people. We noted also how you contributed out of your experience, learning and understanding to the discussion and clarification of the tremendous forces which are today sweeping over the modern world.

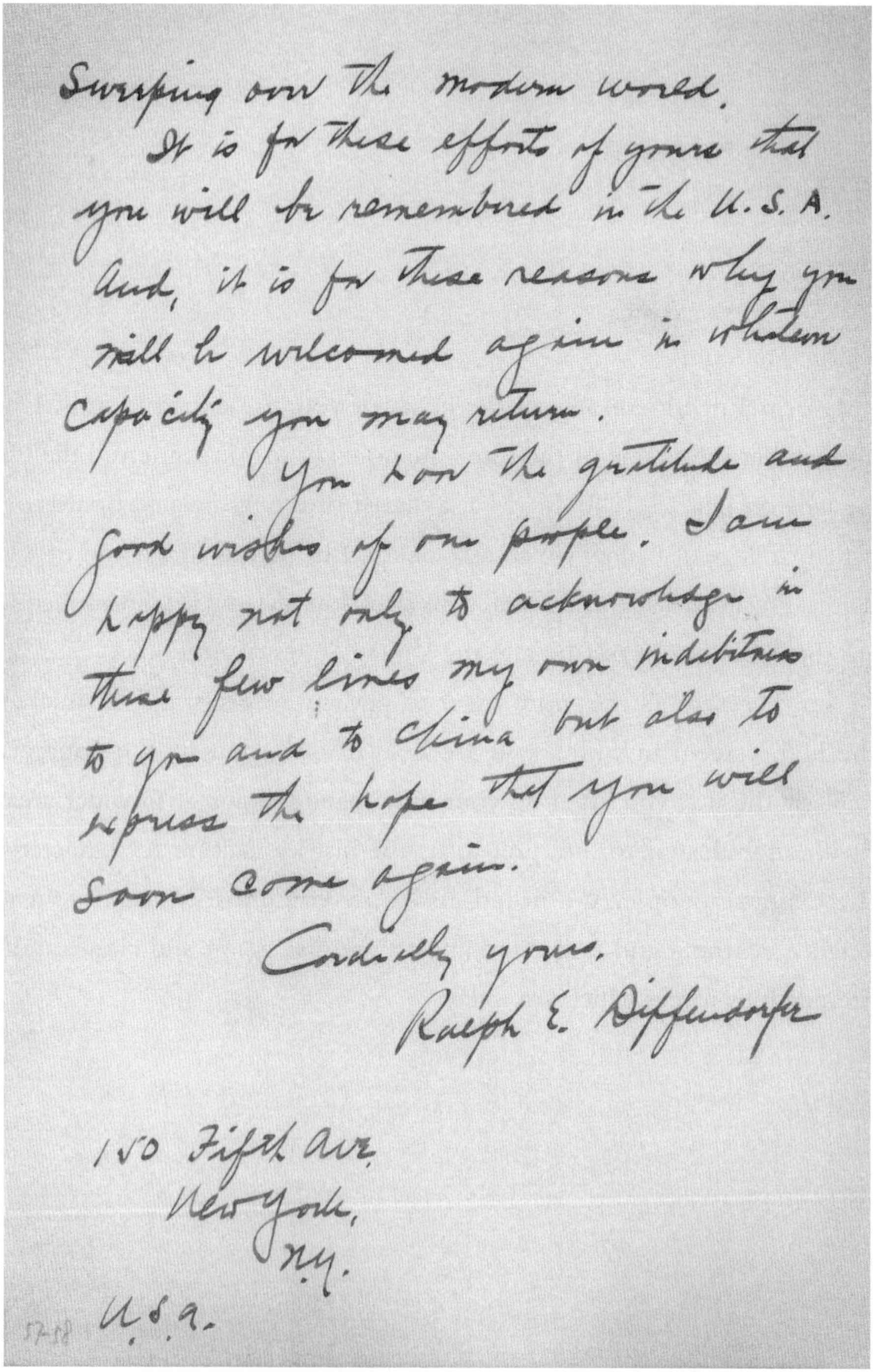

It is for these efforts of yours that you will be remembered in the U.S.A. And, it is for these reasons why you will be welcomed again in whatever capacity you may return.

You have the gratitude and good wishes of our people. I am happy not only to acknowledge in these few lines my own indebtness to you and to China but also to express the hope that you will soon come again.

Cordially yours,
Ralph E. Diffendorfer

150 Fifth Ave,
New York,
N.Y.
U.S.A.

圖 2

sweeping over the modern world.

It is for these efforts of yours that you will be remembered in the U.S.A. And, it is for these reasons why you will be welcomed again in whatever capacity you may return.

You have the gratitude and good wishes of our people. I am happy not only to acknowledge in these few lines my own indebtedness to you and to China but also to express the hope that you will soon come again.

Cordially yours,
Ralph E. Diffendorfer

150 Fifth Ave.
New York
N.Y.
U.S.A

Ralph L. Carr

　　Ralph L. Carr（1887—1950），生於美國科羅拉多州，時任該州州長。1912年獲科羅拉多大學法學士學位。1939—1943年任科羅拉多州州長。北京檔中藏有 Ralph L. Carr 於 1942 年 6 月 29 日致胡適書信一封，大意爲很高興見到胡適並聽胡適的演講。

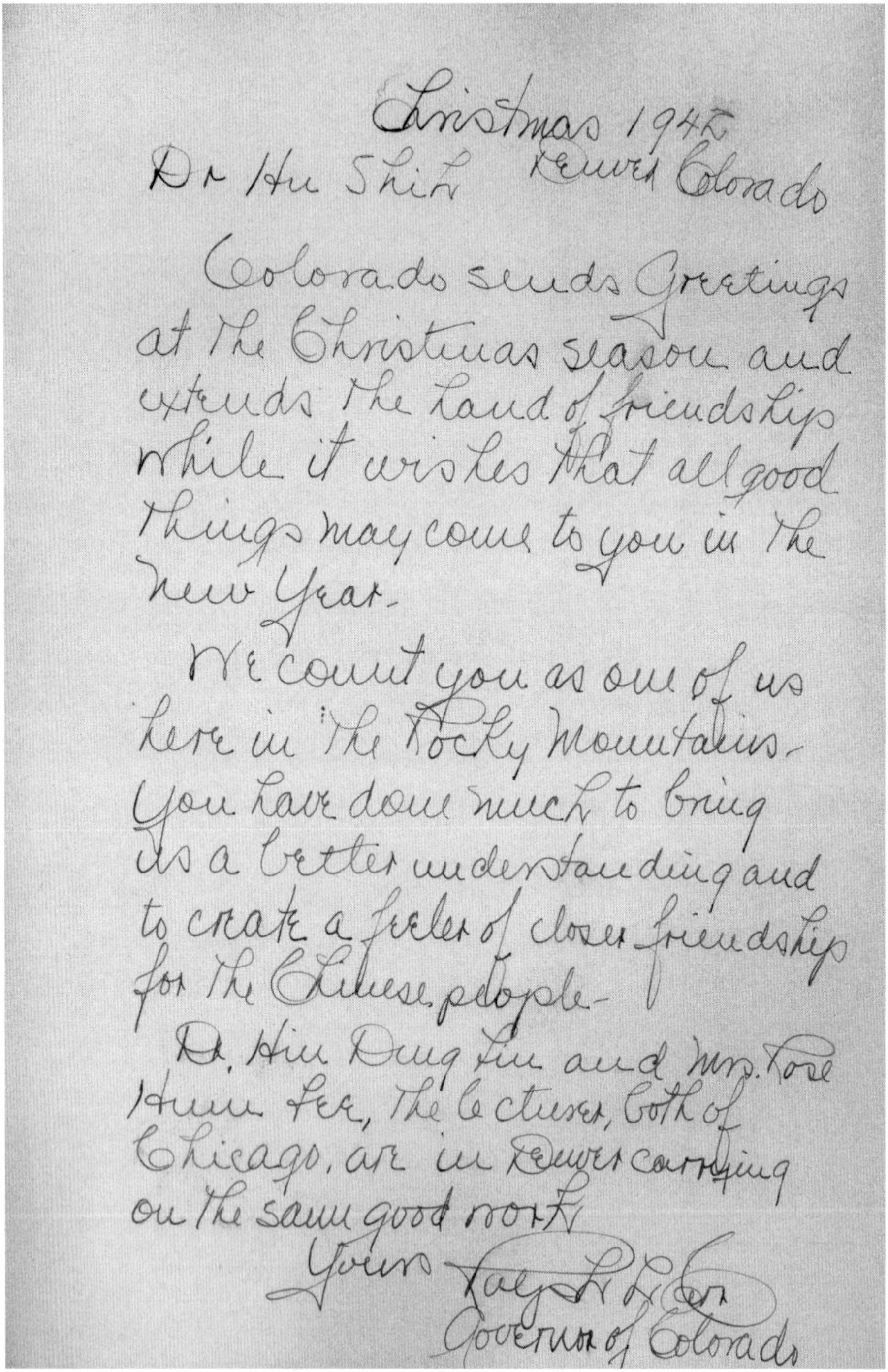

Christmas 1945
Denver Colorado

Dr Hu Shih

Colorado sends Greetings at the Christmas season and extends the hand of friendship while it wishes that all good things may come to you in the New Year.

We count you as one of us here in the Rocky Mountains. You have done much to bring us a better understanding and to create a feeler of closer friendship for the Chinese people.

Dr. Hin Ding Fu and Mrs. Rose Hum Lee, the lecturer, both of Chicago, are in Denver carrying on the same good work.

Yours
Ralph L. Carr
Governor of Colorado

圖1

Christmas 1942
Denver Colorado

Dr. Hu Shih

Colorado sends greetings at the Christmas season and extends the hand of friendship while it wishes that all good things may come to you in the New Year.

We count you as one of us here in the Rocky Mountains, you have done much to bring us a better understanding and to create a feeler of closer friendship for the Chinese people.

Dr. Hie Ding Lin and Mrs. Rose Hum Lee, the lecturer, both of Chicago, are in Denver carrying on the same good work.

Yours
Ralph L. Carr
Governor of Colorado

Ray Lyman Wilbur

　　Ray Lyman Wilbur（1875—1949），生於美國愛荷華州。1896 年獲加州大學文學士學位。1899 年獲舊金山庫珀醫學院博士學位。1896 年任教於斯坦福大學，1911—1916 年任斯坦福大學醫學院院長。1916—1943 年任斯坦福大學校長。北京檔藏有 Wilbur 1940 年 11 月 28 日在 America's Town Meeting of the Air 發表的演說 What Kind of World Order Do We Want? 的記錄稿。

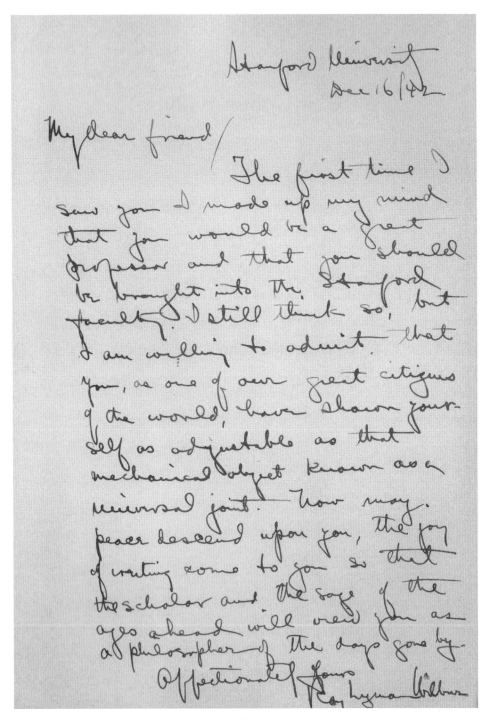

圖 1

Stanford University
Dec. 16/42

My dear friend

The first time I saw you I made up my mind that you would be a great professor and that you should be brought into the Stanford faculty. I still think so, but I am willing to admit that you, as one of our great citizens of the world, have shown yourself as adjustable as that mechanical object known as a universal joint. Now may peace descend upon you, the joy of writing come to you so that the scholar and the sage of the ages ahead will view you as a philosopher of the days gone by.

Affectionately yours
Ray Lyman Wilbur

Raymond Clapper

　　Raymond Clapper，美國廣播和報紙評論員和新聞分析員，生於美國堪薩斯州。早年畢業於堪薩斯大學。1916 年開始爲合衆國際社工作，次年升任該社西北分社經理。1923 年到華盛頓報道政治新聞，六年後任合衆國際社華盛頓經理。1934 年受聘《華盛頓郵報》。二十世紀三四十年代曾任美國互動廣播公司新聞主播。胡適 1941 年 2 月 21 日曾記錄與 Clapper 船上同行並交談。

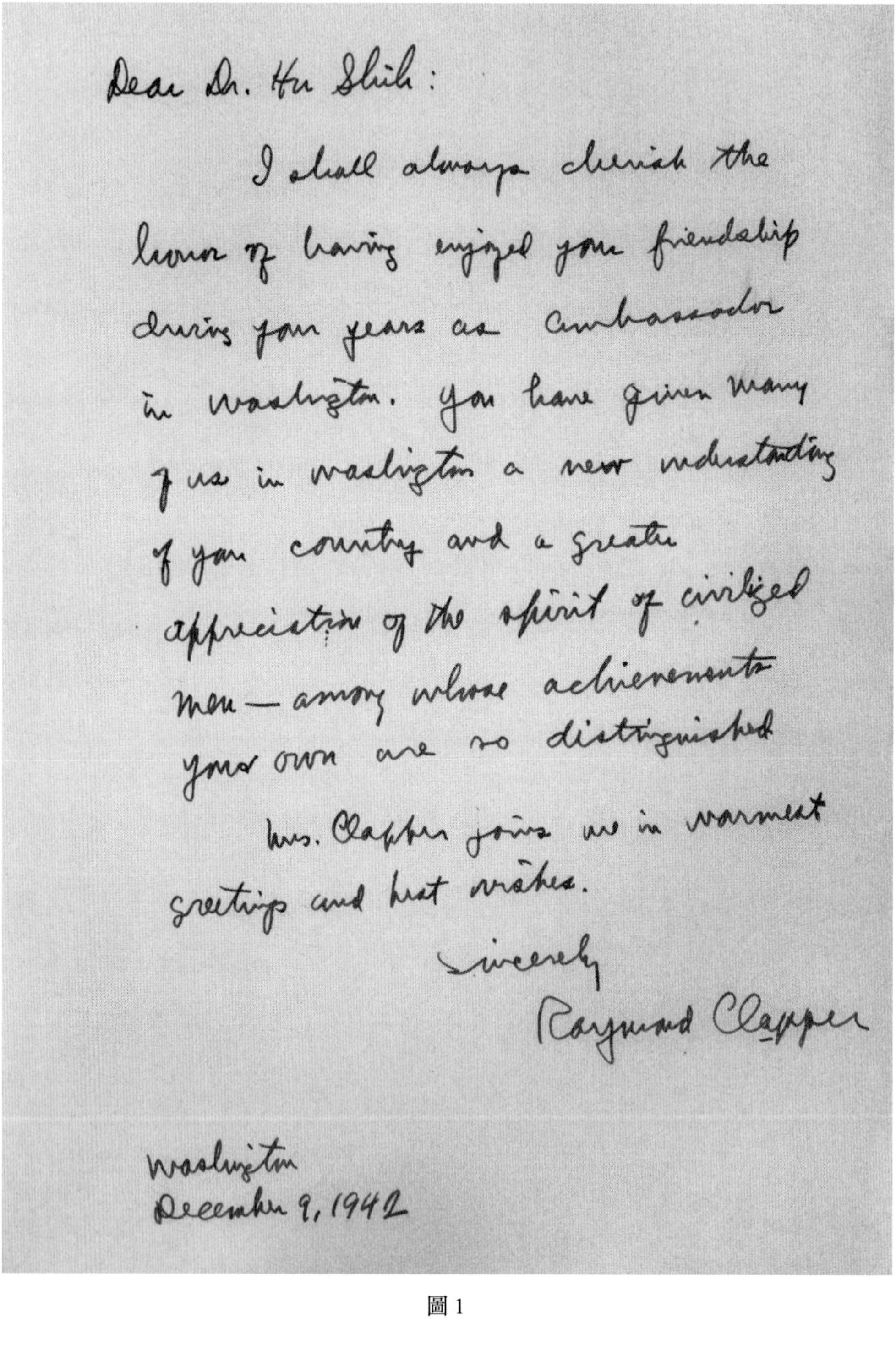

Dear Dr. Hu Shih:

I shall always cherish the honor of having enjoyed your friendship during your years as Ambassador in Washington. You have given many of us in Washington a new understanding of your country and a greater appreciation of the spirit of civilized men — among whose achievements your own are so distinguished.

Mrs. Clapper joins me in warmest greetings and best wishes.

Sincerely
Raymond Clapper

Washington
December 9, 1942

圖1

Dear Dr. Hu Shih:

I shall always cherish the honor of having enjoyed your friendship during your years as Ambassador in Washington. You have given many of us in Washington a new understanding of your country and a greater appreciation of the spirit of civilized men—among whose achievements your own are so distinguished.

Mrs. Clapper joins me in warmest greetings and best wishes.

Sincerely
Raymond Clapper

Washington
December 9, 1942

Richard J. Walsh

　　Richard J. Walsh（1886—1960），賽珍珠丈夫，出版家，擁有John Day Company 出版公司，曾任《亞洲》雜志編輯。北京檔藏有胡適任駐美大使前後與其往來函電二十一封，時間從 1940 年 9 月至 1943 年 7 月。

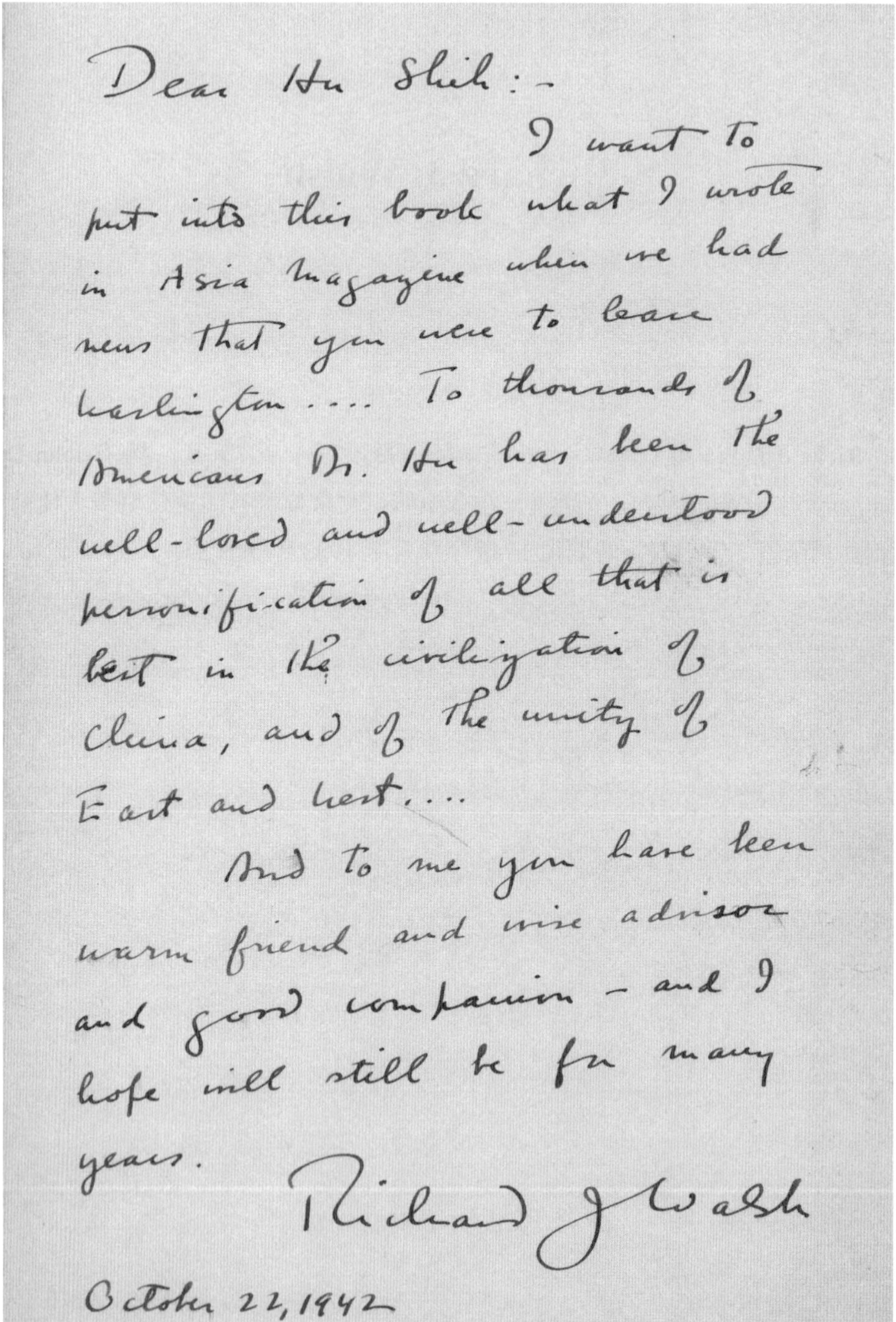

Dear Hu Shih:-

I want to put into this book what I wrote in Asia magazine when we had news that you were to leave Washington.... To thousands of Americans Dr. Hu has been the well-loved and well-understood personification of all that is best in the civilization of China, and of the unity of East and West....

And to me you have been warm friend and wise advisor and good companion — and I hope will still be for many years.

Richard J Walsh

October 22, 1942

圖 1

Dear Hu Shih:—

I want to put into this book what I wrote in Asia magazine when we had news that you were to leave Washington... To thousands of Americans Dr. Hu has been the well-loved and well-understood personification of all that is best in the civilization of China, and of the unity of East and West...

And to me you have been warm friend and wise advisor and good companion—and I hope will still be for many years.

Richard J. Walsh

October 22, 1942

Robert A. Millikan

　　Robert A. Millikan（1868—1953），美國實驗物理學家。1891年畢業於歐柏林學院，1895年獲哥倫比亞大學博士學位。1896年任教於芝加哥大學，1910年任教授。1923年獲諾貝爾物理學獎。

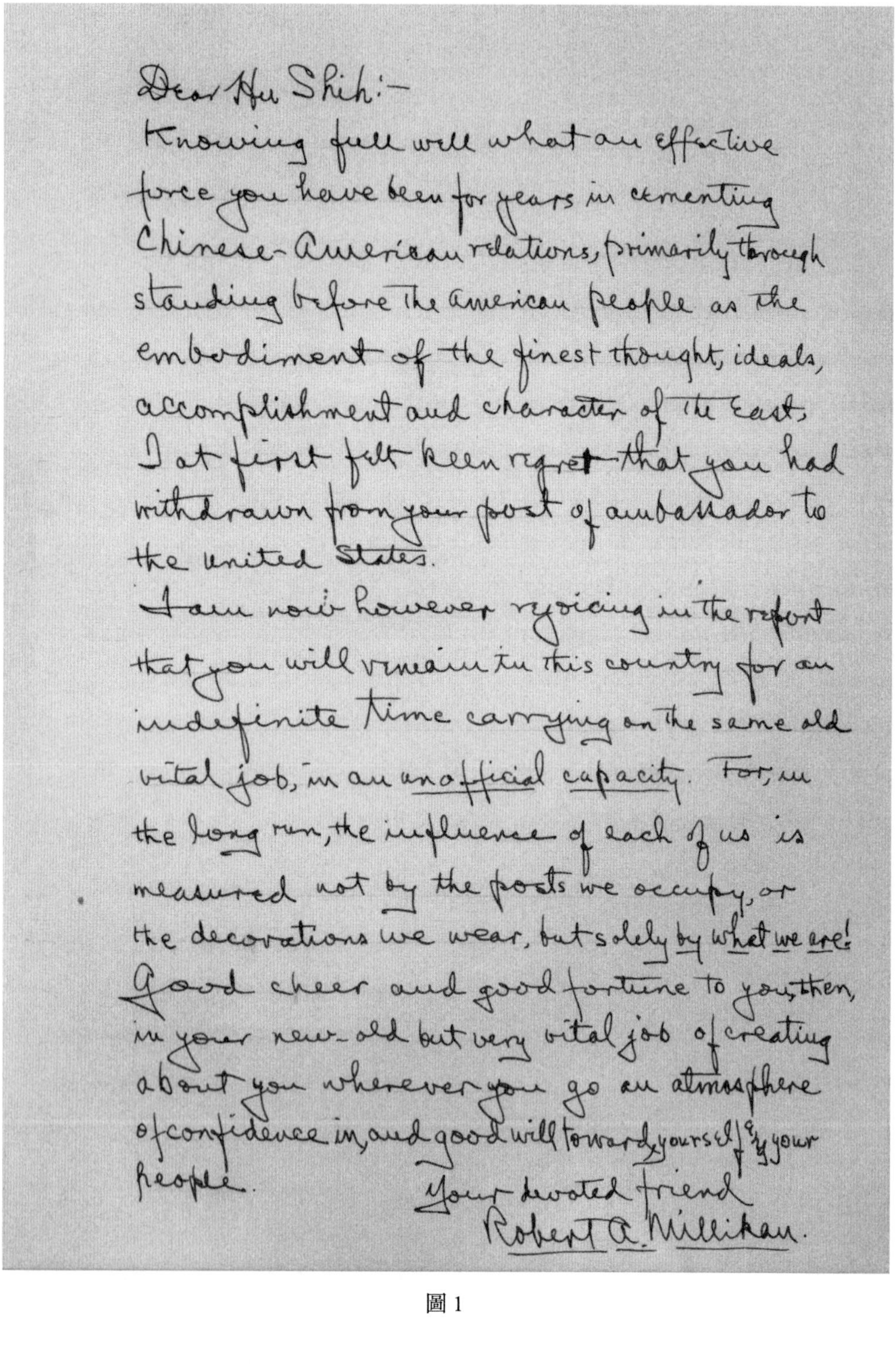

Dear Hu Shih:—

Knowing full well what an effective force you have been for years in cementing Chinese-American relations, primarily through standing before the American people as the embodiment of the finest thought, ideals, accomplishment and character of the East, I at first felt keen regret that you had withdrawn from your post of ambassador to the United States.

I am now however rejoicing in the report that you will remain in this country for an indefinite time carrying on the same old vital job, in an unofficial capacity. For, in the long run, the influence of each of us is measured not by the posts we occupy, or the decorations we wear, but solely by what we are! Good cheer and good fortune to you, then, in your new-old but very vital job of creating about you wherever you go an atmosphere of confidence in, and good will toward yourself & your people.

Your devoted friend
Robert A. Millikan.

圖 1

Dear Hu Shih:—

Knowing full well what an effective force you have been for years in cementing Chinese-American relations, primarily through standing before the American people as the embodiment of the finest thought, ideals, accomplishment and character of the East, I at first felt keen regret that you had withdrawn from your post of ambassador to the United States.

I am now however rejoicing in the report that you will remain in this country for an indefinite time carrying on the same old vital job, in an unofficial capacity. For, in the long run, the influence of each of us is measured not by the posts we occupy, or the decorations we wear, but solely by what we are! Good cheer and good fortune to you then, in your new-old but very vital job of creating about you wherever you go an atmosphere of confidence in, and good will towards yourself and your people.

Your devoted friend
Robert A. Millikan

Robert Gordon Sproul

　　Robert Gordon Sproul（1891—1975），生於加州舊金山。1913年畢業於加州大學伯克利分校。1914年開始在加州大學從事財政與商業事務。1930—1952年任加州大學伯克利分校校長。1952—1958年任加州大學總校長。

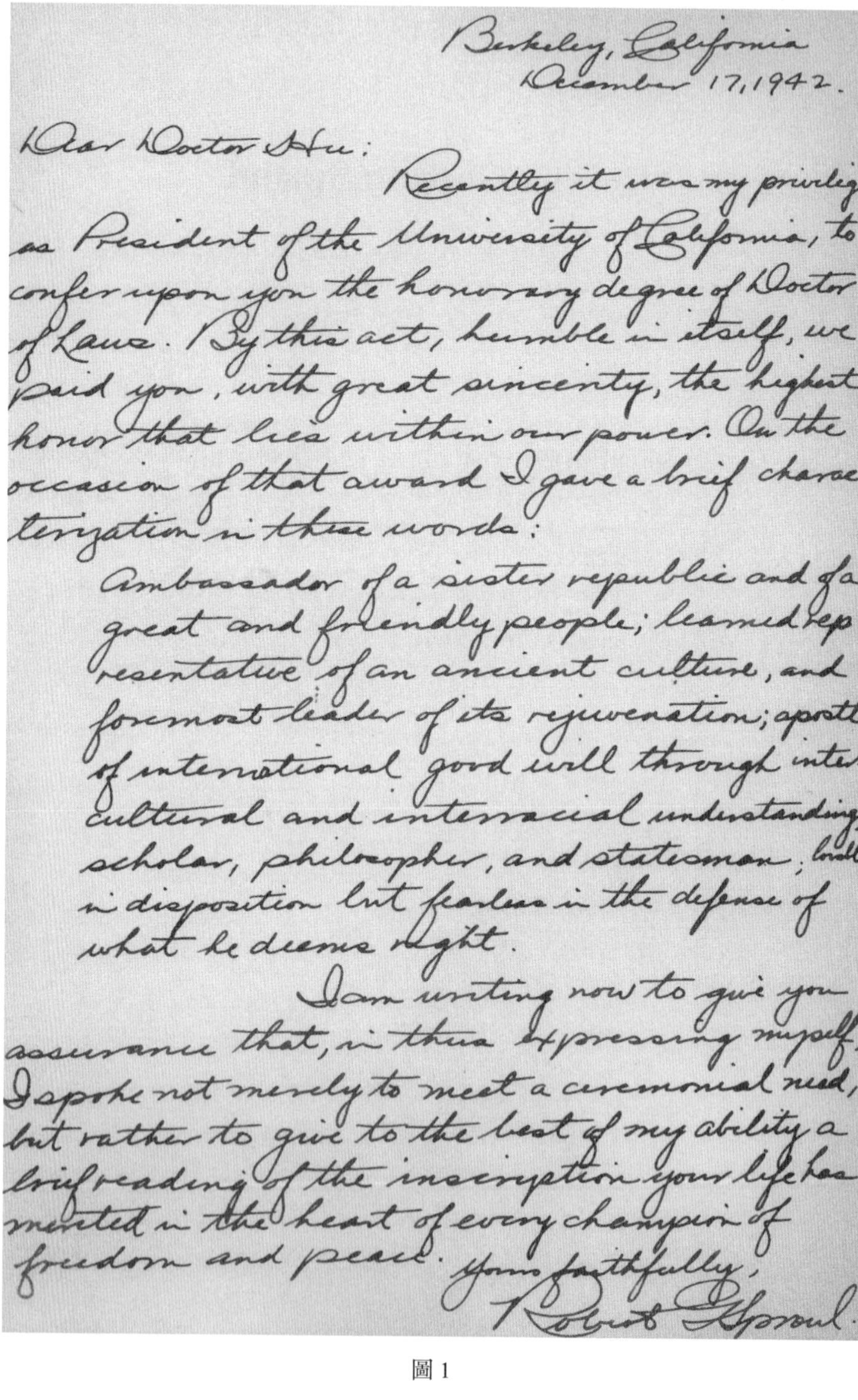

Berkeley, California
December 17, 1942.

Dear Doctor Hu:

Recently it was my privilege, as President of the University of California, to confer upon you the honorary degree of Doctor of Laws. By this act, humble in itself, we paid you, with great sincerity, the highest honor that lies within our power. On the occasion of that award I gave a brief characterization in these words:

> Ambassador of a sister republic and of a great and friendly people; learned representative of an ancient culture, and foremost leader of its rejuvenation; apostle of international good will through intercultural and interracial understanding; scholar, philosopher, and statesman; bridle in disposition but fearless in the defense of what he deems right.

I am writing now to give you assurance that, in thus expressing myself, I spoke not merely to meet a ceremonial need, but rather to give to the best of my ability a brief reading of the inscription your life has merited in the heart of every champion of freedom and peace. Yours faithfully,

Robert Gordon Sproul.

圖1

Berkeley, California
December 17, 1942

Dear Doctor Hu:

Recently it was my privilege, as President of the University of California, to confer upon you the honorary degree of Doctor of Laws. By this act, humble in itself, we paid you, with great sincerity, the highest honor that lies within our power. On the occasion of that award I gave a brief characterization in these words:

Ambassador of a sister republic and of a great and friendly people; learned representative of an ancient culture, and foremost leader of its rejuvenation; apostle of international good will through intercultural and interracial understanding; scholar, philosopher, and statesman; lovable in disposition but fearless in the defense of what he deems right.

I am writing now to give you assurance that, in thus expressing myself, I spoke not merely to meet a ceremonial need, but rather to give to the best of my ability a brief reading of the inscription your life has minted in the heart of every champion of freedom and peace.

Yours faithfully,
Robert G. Sproul

Robert H. Jackson

　　Robert H. Jackson（1892—1954），生於美國賓州，美國政治家、法學家，時任美國最高法院大法官。1912年獲美國聯合大學阿爾伯尼法學院法學士學位。1940年至1941年任司法部長，1941年至1954年任美國最高法院大法官。曾在紐倫堡審判中擔任美國的總檢察官。胡適曾於1939年4月21日參加美國新聞編輯協會年度晚宴，其間曾聽到四人演說，其中就包括Jackson。

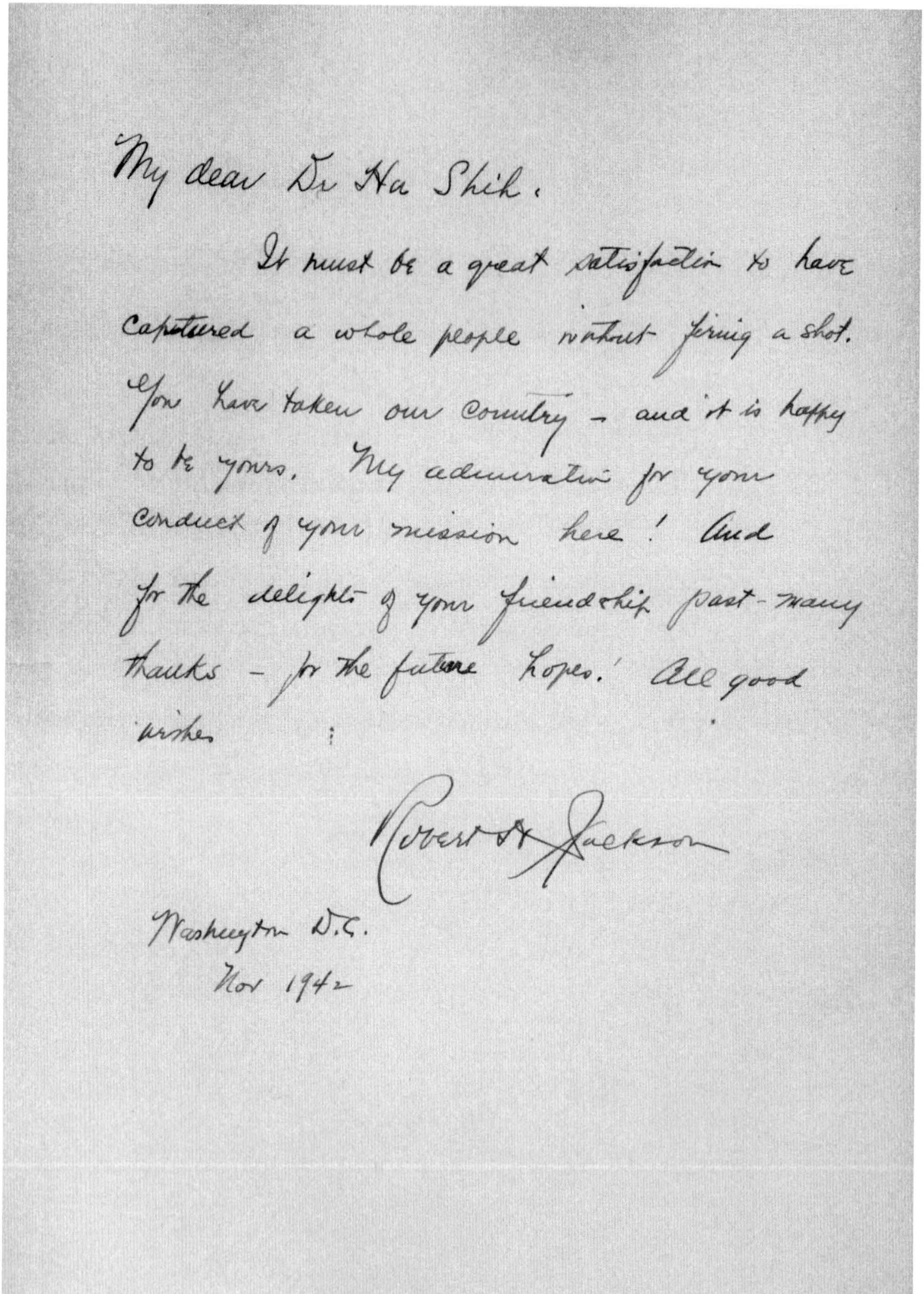

My dear Dr Hu Shih.

It must be a great satisfaction to have captured a whole people without firing a shot. You have taken our country — and it is happy to be yours. My admiration for your conduct of your mission here! And for the delight of your friendship past — many thanks — for the future hopes! All good wishes

Robert H Jackson

Washington D.C.
Nov 1942

圖1

My dear Dr. Hu Shih:

It must be a great satisfaction to have captured a whole people without firing a shot. You have taken our country—and it is happy to be yours. My admiration for your conduct of your mission here! And for the delight of your friendship past—many thanks—for the future hopes! All good wishes.

Robert H. Jackson

Washington D. C.
Nov. 1942

Robert L. Smith

　　Robert L. Smith，曾任全美助華聯合總會（United China Relief）南加州委員會代表，1942 年 2 月 25 日曾與胡適一起在全美助華聯合總會南加州委員會與 The Kiwanis Club in the Biltmore 聯合舉辦的演講會上作演講。

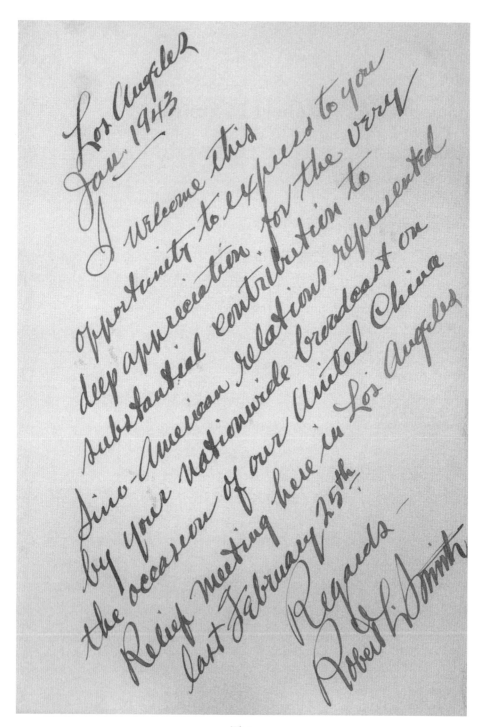

圖 1

Los Angeles
Jan. 1943

I welcome this opportunity to express to you deep appreciation for the very substantial contribution to Sino-American relations represented by your nationwide broadcast on the occasion of our United China Relief meeting here in Los Angeles last February 25th.

Regards,
Robert L. Smith

Robert P. Patterson

　　Robert P. Patterson（1891—1952），生於美國紐約州，時任美國戰争部副部長。早年先後畢業於美國聯合大學聯合學院、哈佛大學法學院。一戰時從軍。1930年任美國南區地方法院法官。1940年任美國戰争部副部長，1945年任部長，1947年離任。胡適任駐美大使期間，於1940年9月26日舉行Book of Hope贈送儀式招待會，Patterson曾經參加。

November 10/42

Dear Dr. Hu:

To us in America you have been a symbol of the perseverance and resolution of the people of China. You have ably interpreted their will to win and in doing so have inspired our people with the same will to win.

I wish you every success in your new assignment.

Sincerely,

Robert P Patterson
Under Secretary
of War.

圖 1

November 10/42

Dear Dr. Hu:

To us in America you have been a symbol of the perseverance and resolution of the people of China. You have ably interpreted their will to win and in doing so have inspired our people with the same will to win.

I wish you every success in your new assignment.

Sincerely,
Robert P. Patterson
Under Secretary
of War

Roy W. Howard

　　Roy W. Howard（1883—1964），美國著名辦報人。曾先後任《印第安納波利斯星報》、史克利普斯-麥克雷報系記者。一戰期間到歐洲擔任戰地記者。1920 年到史克利普斯報業，1922 年成爲 E. W. 史克利普斯公司總裁，長達四十年。曾於 1933 年到中國東北采訪，1936 年曾采訪斯大林。胡適 1933 年 6 月 25 日的日記中曾記與 Howard 閑談，稱 Howard 爲美國出版聯合會的主席。北京檔藏有 Howard 1942 年 9 月 3 日致胡適書信一封，內容爲很遺憾胡適卸任駐美大使。

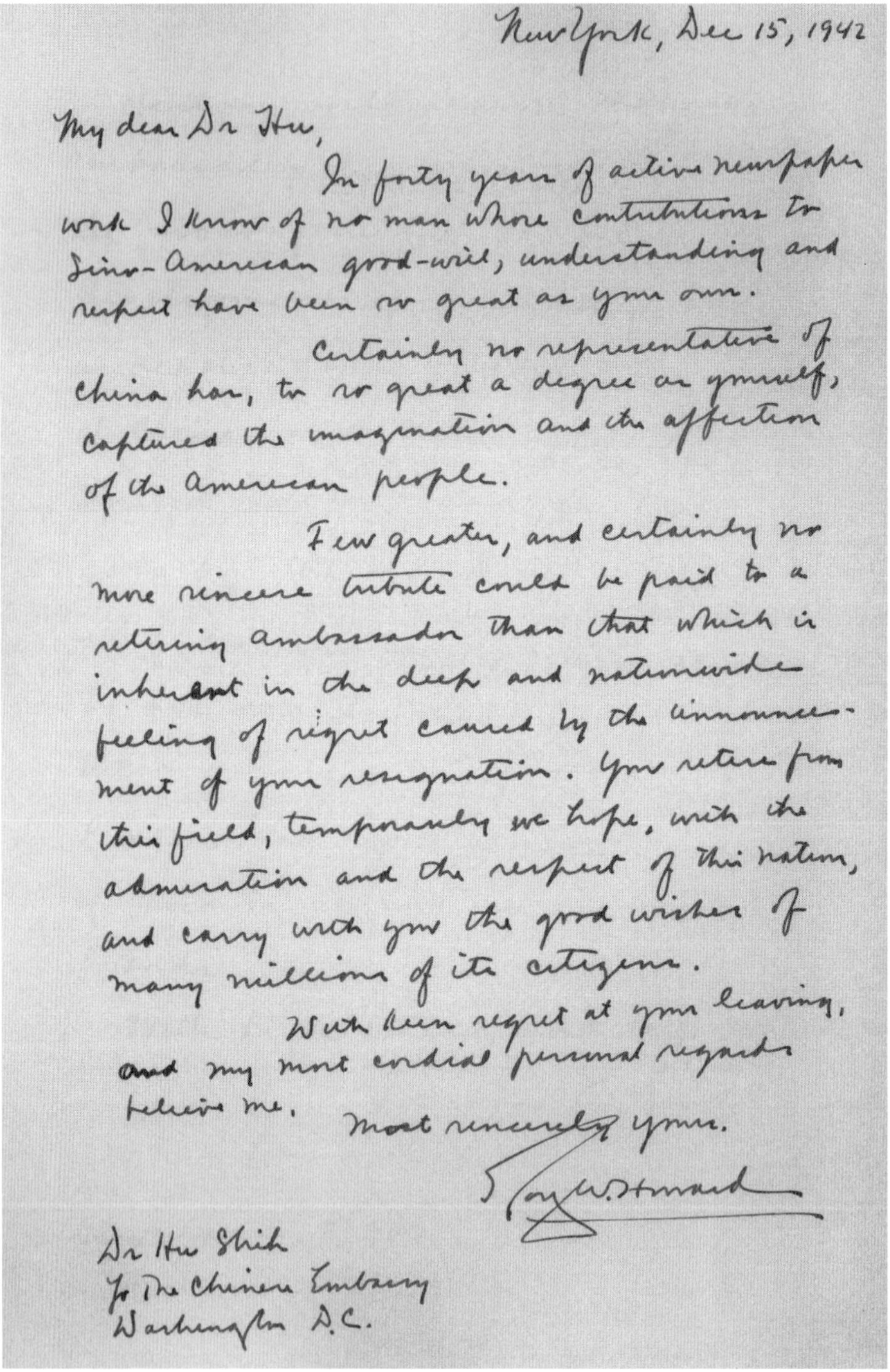

New York, Dec 15, 1942

My dear Dr Hu,

In forty years of active newspaper work I know of no man whose contributions to Sino-American good-will, understanding and respect have been so great as your own.

Certainly no representative of China has, to so great a degree as yourself, captured the imagination and the affection of the American people.

Few greater, and certainly no more sincere tribute could be paid to a retiring ambassador than that which is inherent in the deep and nationwide feeling of regret caused by the announcement of your resignation. You retire from this field, temporarily we hope, with the admiration and the respect of this nation, and carry with you the good wishes of many millions of its citizens.

With keen regret at your leaving, and my most cordial personal regards believe me.

Most sincerely yours,

Roy W. Howard

Dr Hu Shih
% The Chinese Embassy
Washington D.C.

圖 1

New York, Dec. 15, 1942

My dear Dr. Hu,

In forty years of active newspaper work I know of no man whose contributions to Sino-American good-will, understanding and respect have been so great as your own.

Certainly no representative of China has, to so great a degree as yourself, captured the imagination and the affection of the American people.

Few greater, and certainly no more sincere tribute could be paid to a retiring Ambassador than that which is inherent in the deep and nationwide feeling of regret caused by the announcement of your resignation. You retire from this field, temporarily we hope, with the admiration and the respect of this nation, and carry with you the good wishes of many millions of its citizens.

With keen regret at your leaving, and my most cordial personal regards

Believe me,

Most sincerely yours,
Roy W. Howard

Dr. Hu Shih
c/o The Chinese Embassy
Washington D. C.

Rufus M. Jones

　　Rufus M. Jones（1863—1948），美國宗教領袖、作家、雜志編輯、大學教授，20世紀最具影響力的貴格會成員。生於中國南部，1885年畢業於美國賓州哈弗福德學院，1886年獲碩士學位。1893—1934年任教於哈弗福德學院。1893—1912年任Friends' Review雜志編輯。1901年獲哈佛大學文學碩士學位。曾任美國教友會會長。北京檔藏有美國教友會助理秘書John F. Rich1942年9月2日致胡適書信一封，內容爲很遺憾得知胡適卸任駐美大使，美國教友會會長Jones希望能在胡適離開美國之前拜訪他。北京檔另藏有Jones與James B. Blaine等人於1941年12月11日聯名發給胡適的電報，內容爲：全美助華聯合總會國家委員會(National Committee)擬舉行募款活動以吸引資金提供醫療照顧、食物與必需品給受難的中國人，邀請胡適參與。

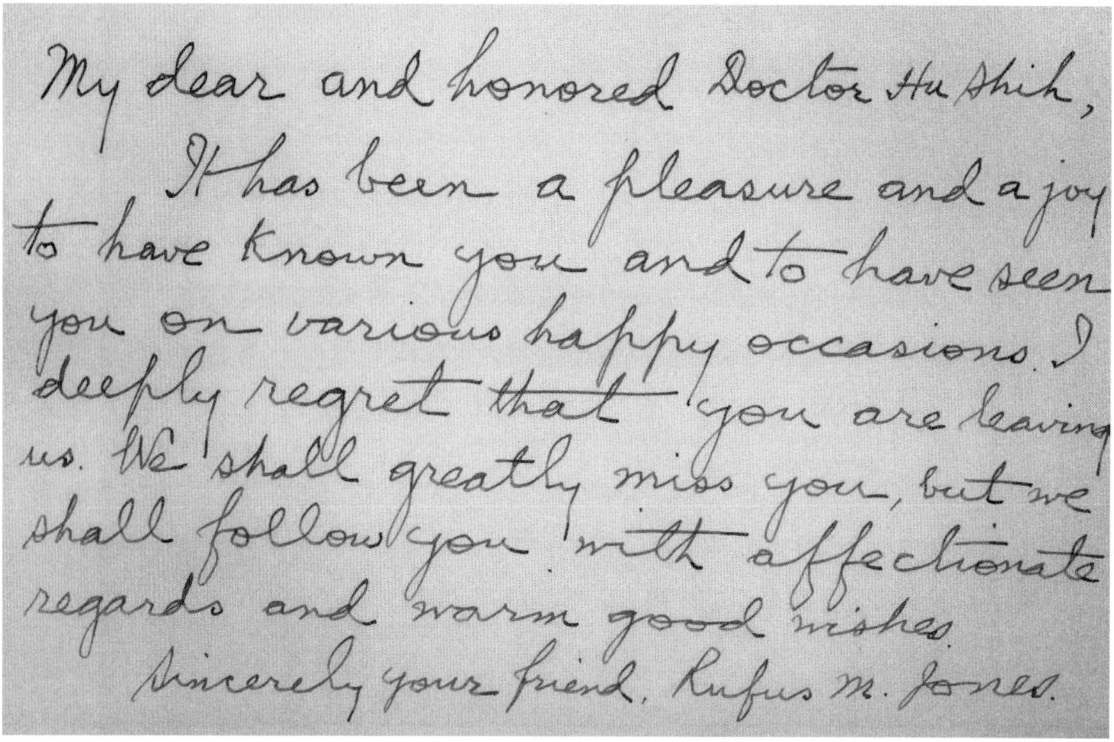

My dear and honored Doctor Hu Shih,

It has been a pleasure and a joy to have known you and to have seen you on various happy occasions. I deeply regret that you are leaving us. We shall greatly miss you, but we shall follow you with affectionate regards and warm good wishes.

Sincerely your friend, Rufus M. Jones.

圖 1

My dear and honored Doctor Hu Shih,

It has been a pleasure and a joy to have known you and to have seen you on various happy occasions. I deeply regret that you are leaving us. We shall greatly miss you, but we shall follow you with affectionate regards and warm good wishes.

Sincerely your friend
Rufus M. Jones

Sidney D. Gamble

Sidney D. Gamble（1890—1968），甘博，生於美國俄亥俄州辛辛那提。1912 年畢業於普林斯頓大學。曾於 1908 年、1917—1919 年、1924—1927 年、1931—1932 年四次來華，1918 年任北京中華基督教青年會幹事，不久改任燕京大學社會學教授。以做社會調查和拍攝關於北京和華北的照片聞名。回國後任普林斯頓大學教授，曾任基督教青年會全國委員會委員、普林斯頓在亞洲負責人和名譽主席。著有《北京社會調查》《1900—1924 年北京的物價、工資和生活標準》《定縣：一個華北農村社區》《華北鄉村：1933 年以前的社會、政治及經濟活動》等。

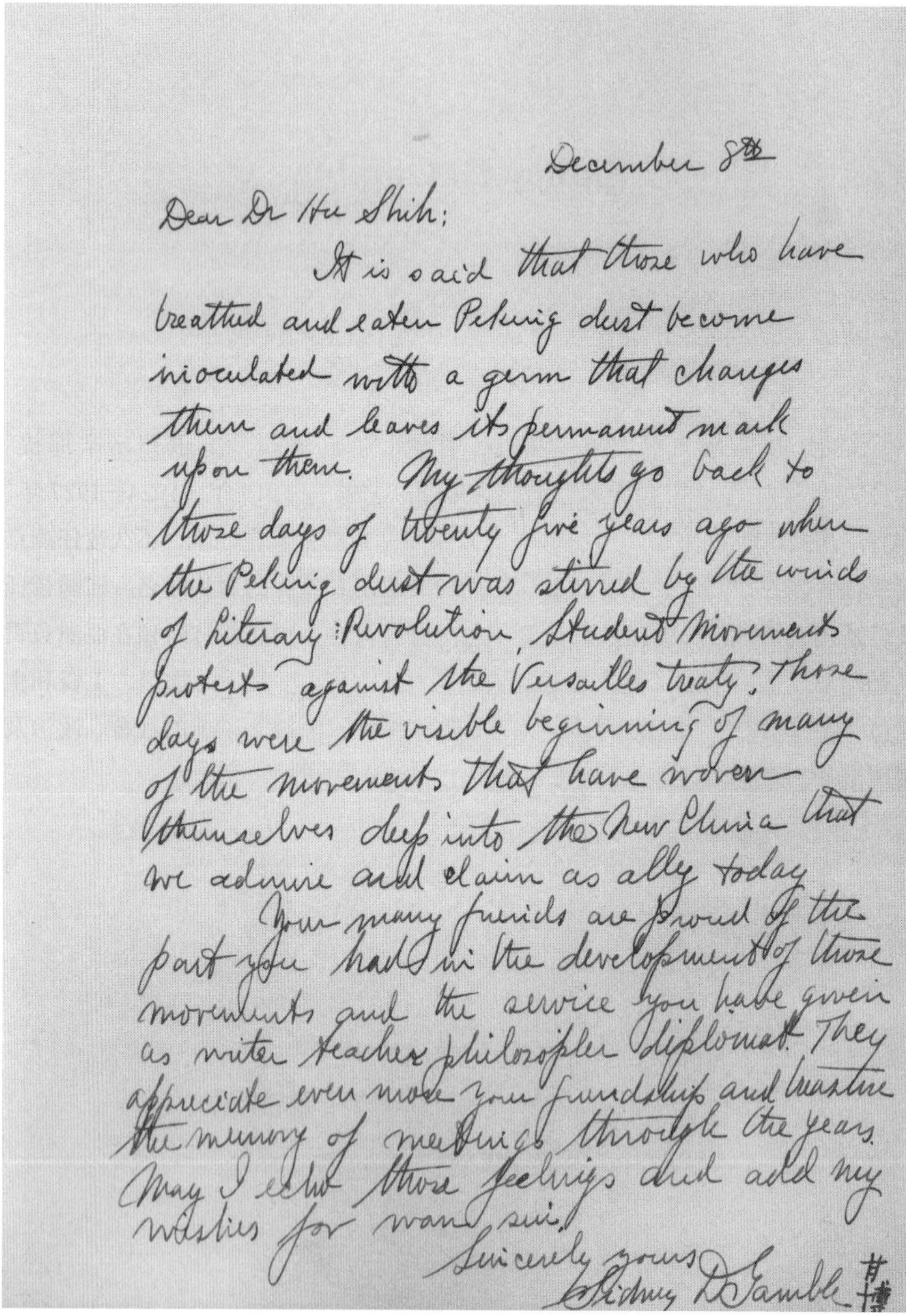

December 8th

Dear Dr Hu Shih;

It is said that those who have breathed and eaten Peking dust become inoculated with a germ that changes them and leaves its permanent mark upon them. My thoughts go back to those days of twenty five years ago when the Peking dust was stirred by the winds of Literary Revolution, Student Movements, protests against the Versailles treaty. Those days were the visible beginning of many of the movements that have woven themselves deep into the New China that we admire and claim as ally today.

Your many friends are proud of the part you had in the development of those movements and the service you have given as writer teacher philosopher diplomat. They appreciate even more your friendship and treasure the memory of meetings through the years. May I echo those feelings and add my wishes for many, sir,

Sincerely yours
Sidney D Gamble

圖 1

December 8th

Dear Dr. Hu Shih:

It is said that those who have breathed and eaten Peking dust become inoculated with a germ that changes them and leaves its permanent mark upon them. My thoughts go back to those days of twenty five years ago when the Peking dust was stirred by the winds of literary Revolution, Student movements protest against the Versailles Treaty, those days were the visible beginning of many of the movements that have woven themselves deep into the new China that we admire and claim as ally today.

Your many friends are proud of the part you had in the development of those movements and the service you have given as writer teacher philosopher diplomat. They appreciate even more your friendship and treasure the memory of meetings through the years. May I echo those feelings and add my wishes for wan sui.

Sincerely yours

Sidney D. Gamble 甘博

Sidney P. Osborn

Sidney P. Osborn（1884—1948），生於美國亞利桑那州，時任該州州長。早年曾任報紙記者、編輯。1912—1919 年任亞利桑那州第一秘書。1941—1948 年任亞利桑那州州長。

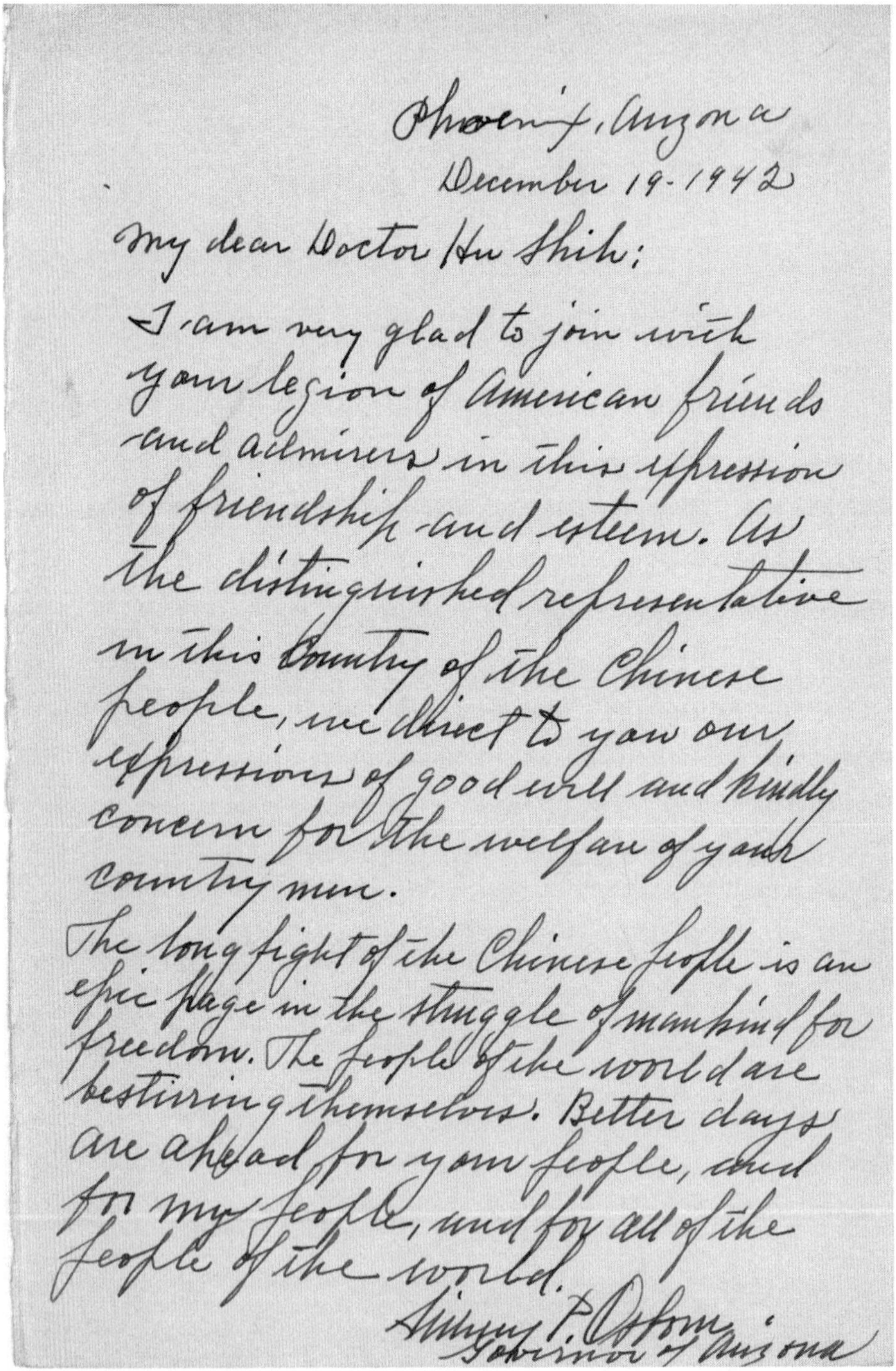

Phoenix, Arizona
December 19, 1942

My dear Doctor Hu Shih:

I am very glad to join with your legion of American friends and admirers in this expression of friendship and esteem. As the distinguished representative in this country of the Chinese people, we direct to you our expressions of good will and kindly concern for the welfare of your countrymen.

The long fight of the Chinese people is an epic page in the struggle of mankind for freedom. The people of the world are bestirring themselves. Better days are ahead for your people, and for my people, and for all of the people of the world.

Sidney P. Osborn,
Governor of Arizona

圖1

Phoenix, Arizona
December 19-1942

My dear Doctor Hu Shih:

I am very glad to join with your legion of American friends and admirers in this expression of friendship—and esteem. As the distinguished representative in this country of the Chinese people, we direct to you our expressions of good will and kindly concern for the welfare of your country men.

The long fight of the Chinese people is an epic page in the struggle of mankind for freedom. The people of the world are bestirring themselves. Better days are ahead for your people, and for my people, and for all of the people of the world.

Sidney P. Osborn
Governor of Arizona

Silas H. Strawn

　　Silas H. Strawn（1866—1946），生於美國伊利諾伊州渥太華。高中畢業後在渥太華律師所學習法律。1889 年開始從事律師工作，後成爲芝加哥著名律師。1913 年當選芝加哥律師事務所聯合會主席。1921—1922 年擔任伊利諾伊州律師事務所聯合會主席。1927 年擔任全美律師事務所聯合會主席。

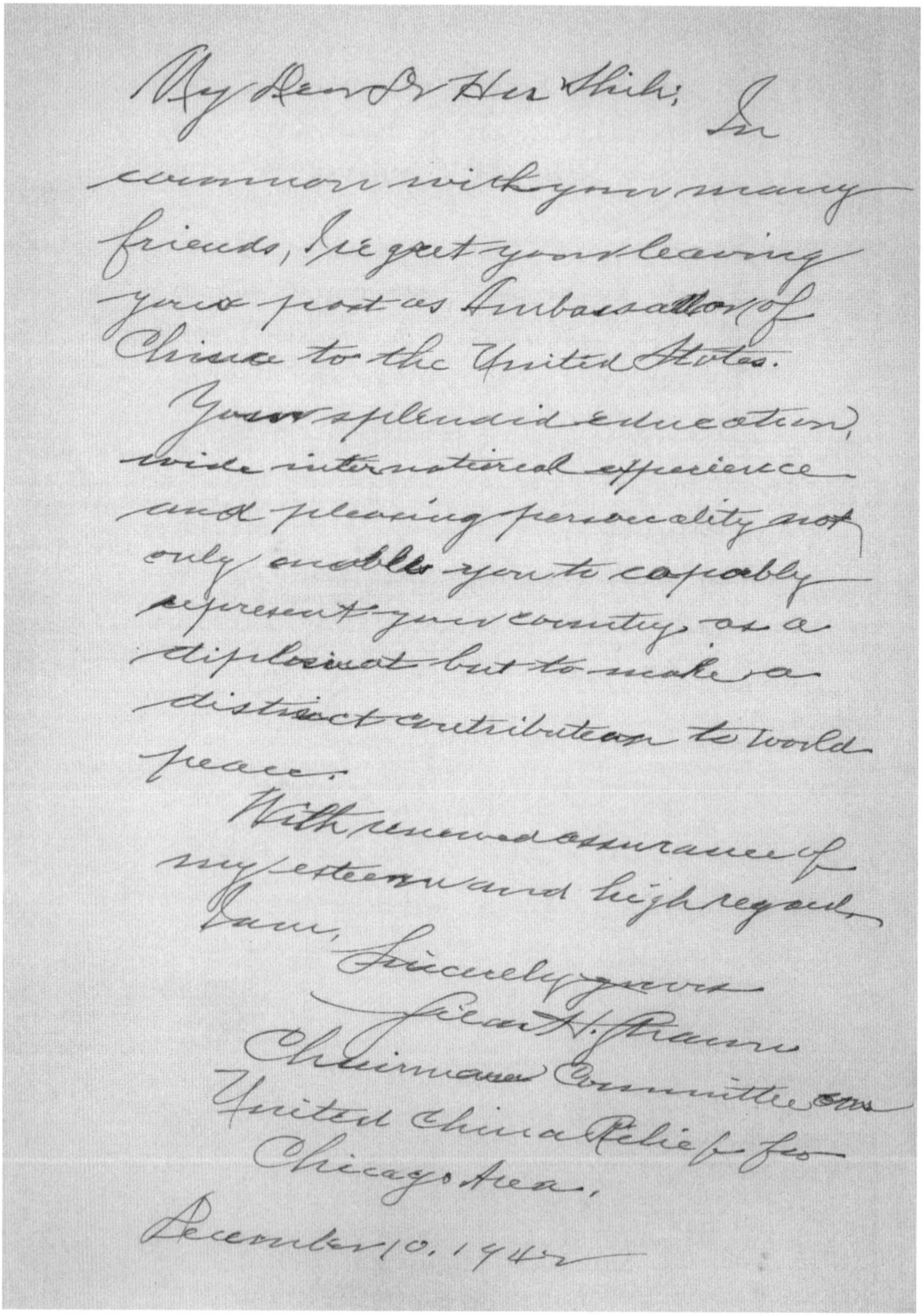

My Dear Dr Hu Shih:

In common with your many friends, I regret your leaving your post as Ambassador of China to the United States. Your splendid education, wide international experience and pleasing personality not only enables you to capably represent your country as a diplomat but to make a distinct contribution to world peace.

With renewed assurance of my esteem and high regard,

I am,
Sincerely yours
Silas H. Strawn
Chairman Committee on
United China Relief for
Chicago Area.

December 10, 1942

圖 1

My dear Dr. Hu Shih:

In common with your many friends, I regret your leaving your post as Ambassador of Chinese to the United States.

Your splendid education, wide international experience and pleasing personality not only enable you to capably represent your country as a diplomat but to make a distinct contribution to world peace.

With sincered assurance of my esteem and high regards,

I am,

Sincerely yours

Silas H. Strawn

Chairman Committee

United China Relief for

Chicago Area,

December 10, 1942

Stanley Reed

Stanley Reed（1884—1980），生於美國肯塔基州梅森縣，時任美國最高法院大法官。1902 年、1906 年先後獲肯塔基衛斯理安學院、耶魯大學學士學位，後又在弗吉尼亞大學、哥倫比亞大學學習法律。1935 年任美國聯邦總律師（Solicitor General）。1938—1957 年任美國最高法院大法官。

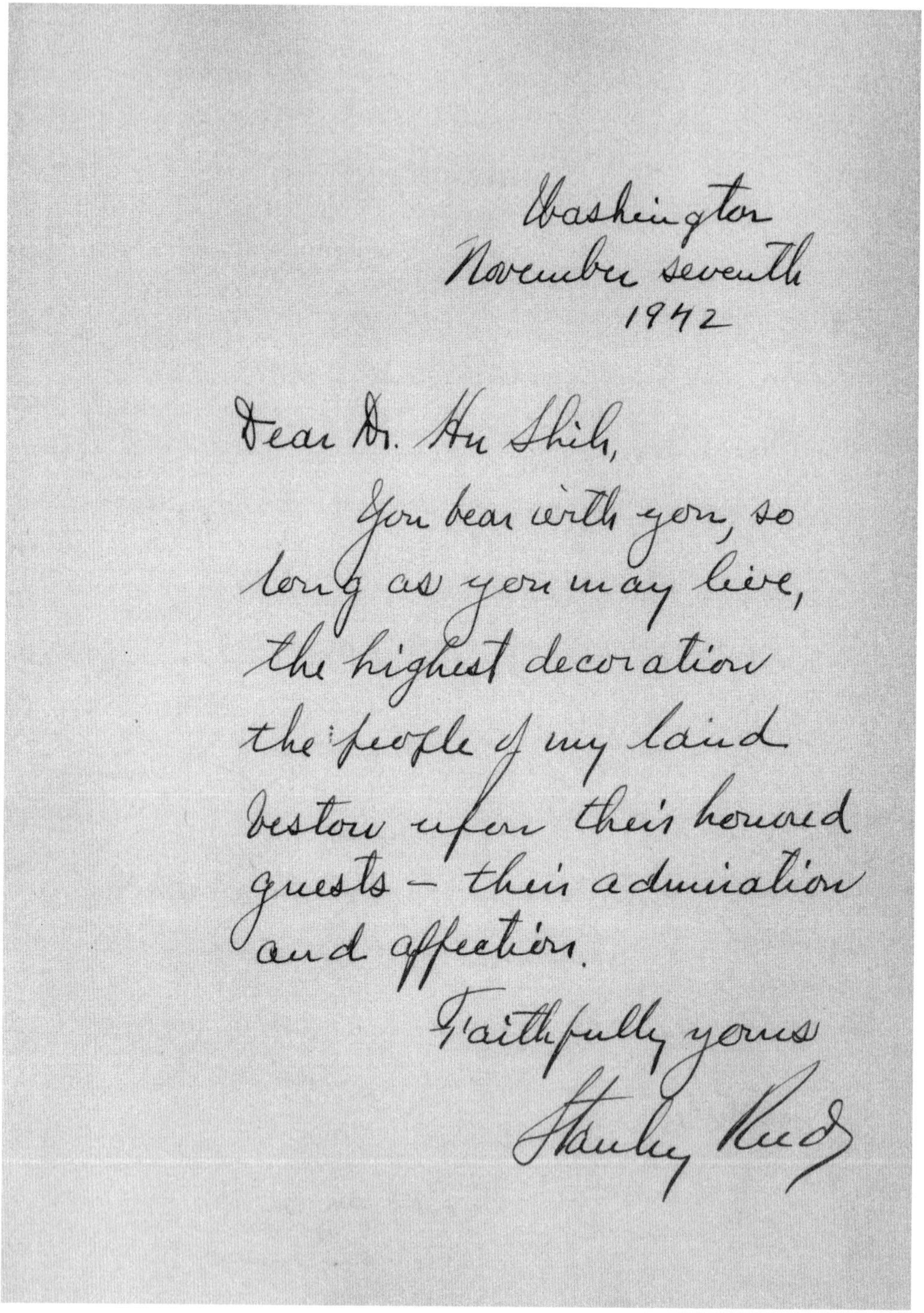

Washington
November seventh
1942

Dear Dr. Hu Shih,

You bear with you, so long as you may live, the highest decoration the people of my land bestow upon their honored guests — their admiration and affection.

Faithfully yours

Stanley Reed

圖1

Washington
November Seventh
1942

Dear Dr. Hu Shih,

You bear with you, so long as you may live, the highest decoration the people of my land bestow upon their honored guests—their admiration and affection.

Faithfully yours
Stanley Reed

Sumner Welles

　　Sumner Welles（1892—1961），生於紐約，時任美國副國務卿。1914年畢業於哈佛大學。早年從事拉美外交工作，1933年任拉美事務助理國務卿。1937—1943年任美國副國務卿。胡適任駐美大使前後與Welles有交往，他在1938年10月7日的日記中説："下午去見代外長Sumner Welles。"這是胡適初任駐美大使時拜見Welles。

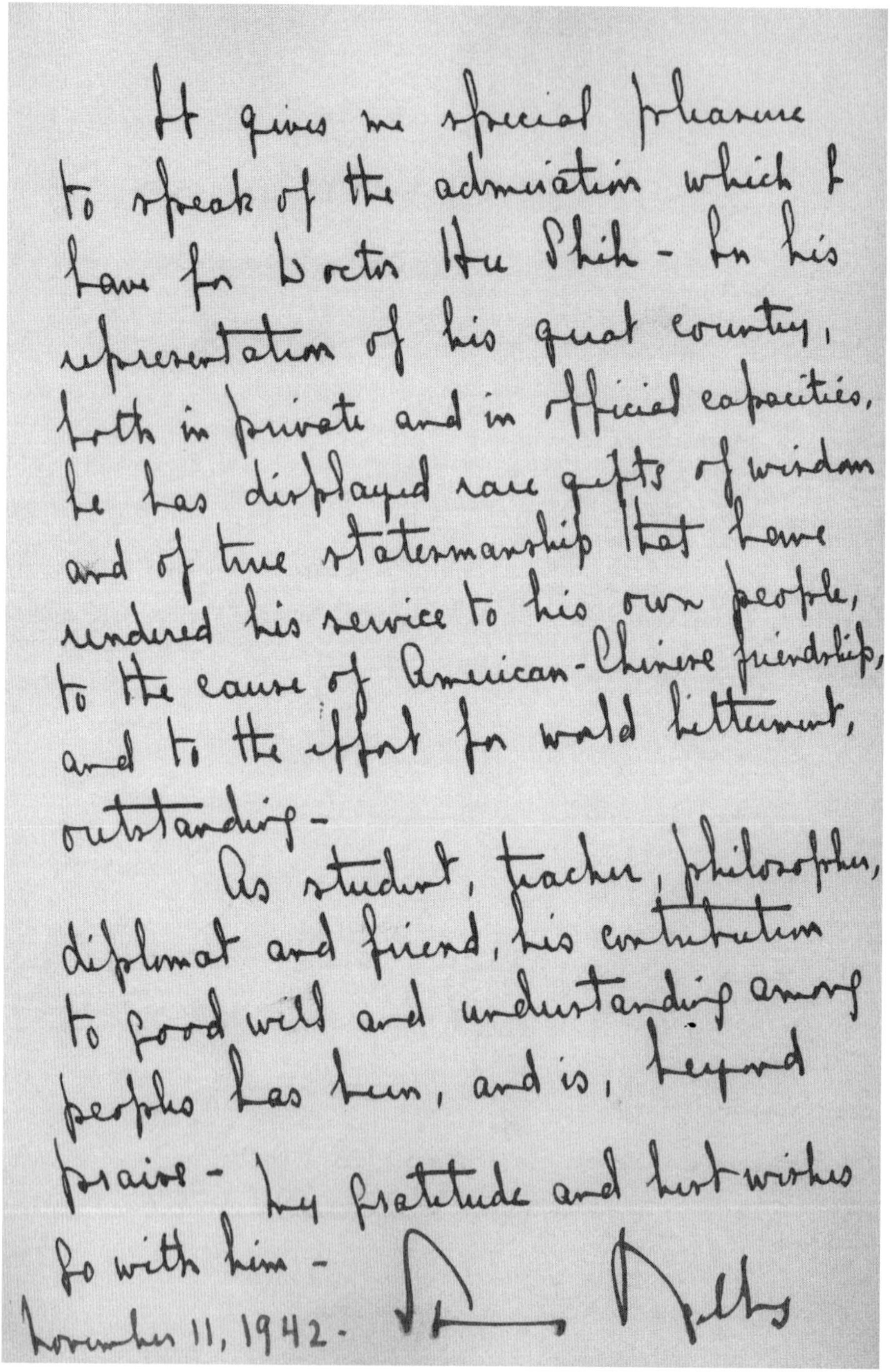

It gives me special pleasure to speak of the admiration which I have for Doctor Hu Shih — In his representation of his great country, both in private and in official capacities, he has displayed rare gifts of wisdom and of true statesmanship that have rendered his service to his own people, to the cause of American-Chinese friendship, and to the effort for world betterment, outstanding —

As student, teacher, philosopher, diplomat and friend, his contribution to good will and understanding among peoples has been, and is, beyond praise — My gratitude and best wishes go with him —

November 11, 1942.

圖 1

It gives me special pleasure to speak of the admiration which I have for Doctor Hu Shih. In his representation of his great country, both in private and in official capacities, he has displayed rare gifts of wisdom and of true statesmanship that have rendered his service to his own people, to the cause of American-Chinese friendship, and to the effort for world betterment, outstanding.

As student, teacher, philosopher, diplomat and friend, his contribution to good will and understanding among peoples has been, and is, beyond praise.

My gratitude and best wishes go with him.

Sumner Welles

November 11, 1942.

Thomas J. Watson

　　Thomas J. Watson（1874—1956），生於美國紐約州。早年曾學習會計和商業，曾任郵局會計、推銷員，後加入 NCR 公司。1914 年受聘爲 IBM 公司的前身 CTR 公司總經理，不久出任該公司總裁。1924 年將 CTR 公司更名爲 IBM，並擔任總裁和董事會主席，直至 1956 年。胡適任駐美大使期間與 Watson 有交往，1940 年 9 月 26 日在雙橡園駐美大使館舉行 Book of Hope 贈送儀式及晚宴，Watson 夫婦受邀參加。

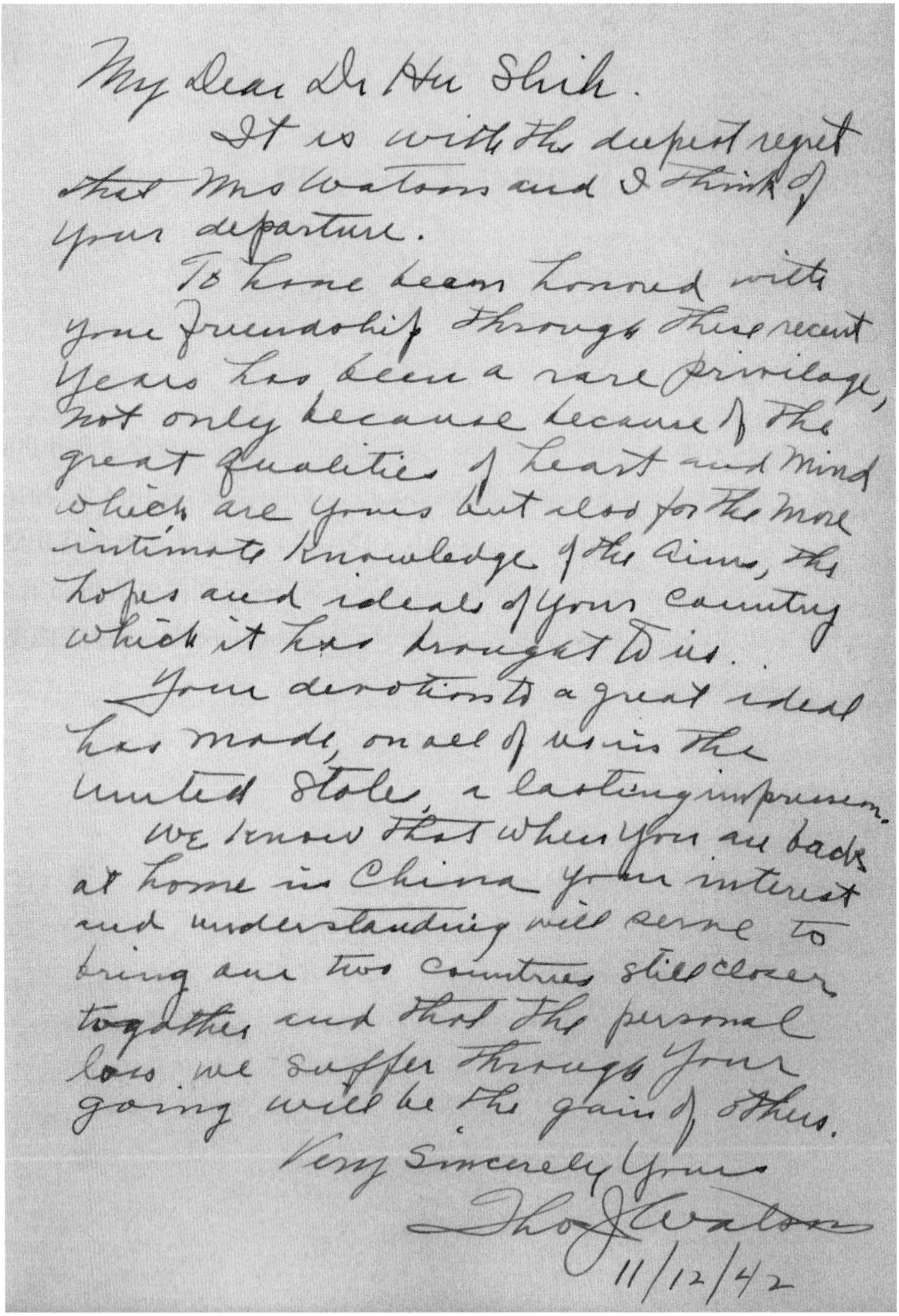

My dear Dr Hu Shih.

It is with the deepest regret that Mrs Watson and I think of your departure.

To have been honored with your friendship through these recent years has been a rare privilege, not only because because of the great qualities of heart and mind which are yours but also for the more intimate knowledge of the aims, the hopes and ideals of your country which it has brought to us.

Your devotion to a great ideal has made, on all of us in the United State, a lasting impression.

We know that when you are back at home in China your interest and understanding will serve to bring our two countries still closer together and that the personal loss we suffer through your going will be the gain of others.

Very Sincerely Yours
Thos J Watson
11/12/42

圖 1

My Dear D. Hu Shih

It is with the deepest regret that Mrs. Watson and I think of your departure.

To have been honored with your friendship through these recent years has been a rare privilege, not only because [because] of the great qualities of heart and mind which are yours but also for the more intimate knowledge of the aims, the hopes and ideals of your country which it has brought to us.

Your devotion to a great ideal has made, on all of us in the United States, a lasting impression.

We know that when you are back at home in China your interest and understanding will serve to bring our two countries still closer together and that the personal loss we suffer through your going will be the gain of others.

Very sincerely yours
Thomas J. Watson
11/12/42

Thomas L. Sidlo

　　Thomas L. Sidlo（1888—1955），生於美國克利夫蘭。1909年畢業於西儲大學（Western Reserve University）。1910年獲該校文學碩士學位，1912年獲該校法學學士學位。畢業後在克利夫蘭市任職。1924—1936年，任斯克里普斯—霍華德報系、美聯社、報業協會財務主管、財務總監、法律總顧問。退休後曾任北俄亥俄歌劇協會主席、音樂藝術聯合會主席、克利夫蘭自然史博物館館長等職。

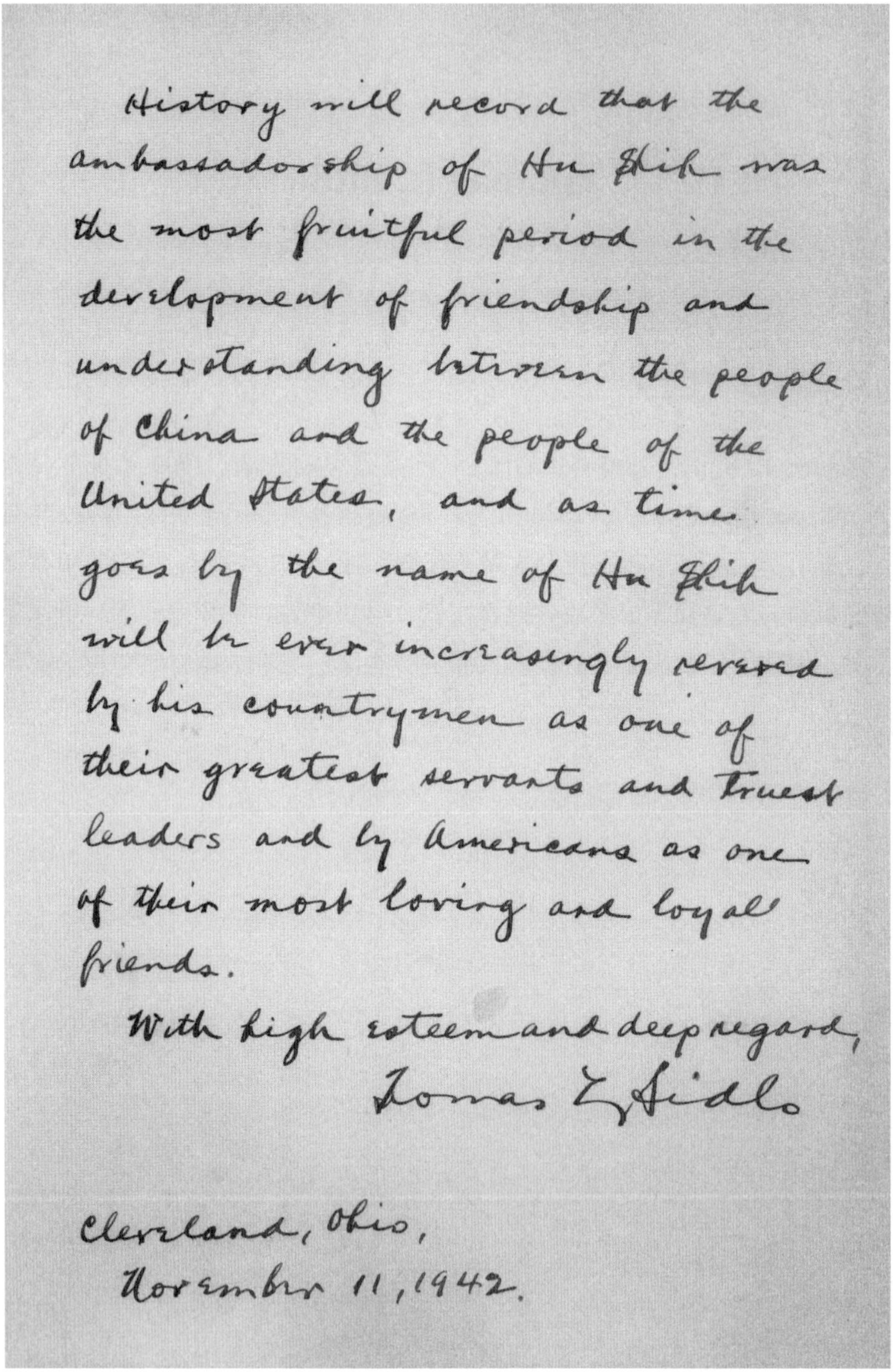

History will record that the ambassadorship of Hu Shih was the most fruitful period in the development of friendship and understanding between the people of China and the people of the United States, and as time goes by the name of Hu Shih will be ever increasingly revered by his countrymen as one of their greatest servants and truest leaders and by Americans as one of their most loving and loyal friends.

With high esteem and deep regard,

Tomas T. Sidlo

Cleveland, Ohio,
November 11, 1942.

圖 1

History will record that the ambassadorship of Hu Shih was the most fruitful period in the development of friendship and understanding between the people of China and the people of the United States, and as time goes by the name of Hu Shih will be ever increasingly revered by his countrymen as one of their greatest servants and truest leaders and by Americans as one of their most loving and loyal friends.

With high esteem and deep regard,

Thomas L. Sidlo

Cleveland, Ohio,
November 11, 1942

Thomas W. Lamont

　　Thomas W. Lamont（1870—1948），美國銀行家。生於美國紐約州卡拉夫拉克。1892年畢業於哈佛大學。同年任職於《紐約論壇報》。後從商，並加入銀行家托拉斯，後擔任第一國家銀行副總裁。胡適任駐美大使前後與其有交往，北京檔藏有胡適1941年4月19日致Lamont書信一封。另全美助華聯合總會James B. Blaine等人聯合簽名請胡適參加全美助華聯合總會國家委員會擬舉行的募款活動，Lamont也爲簽名者之一。

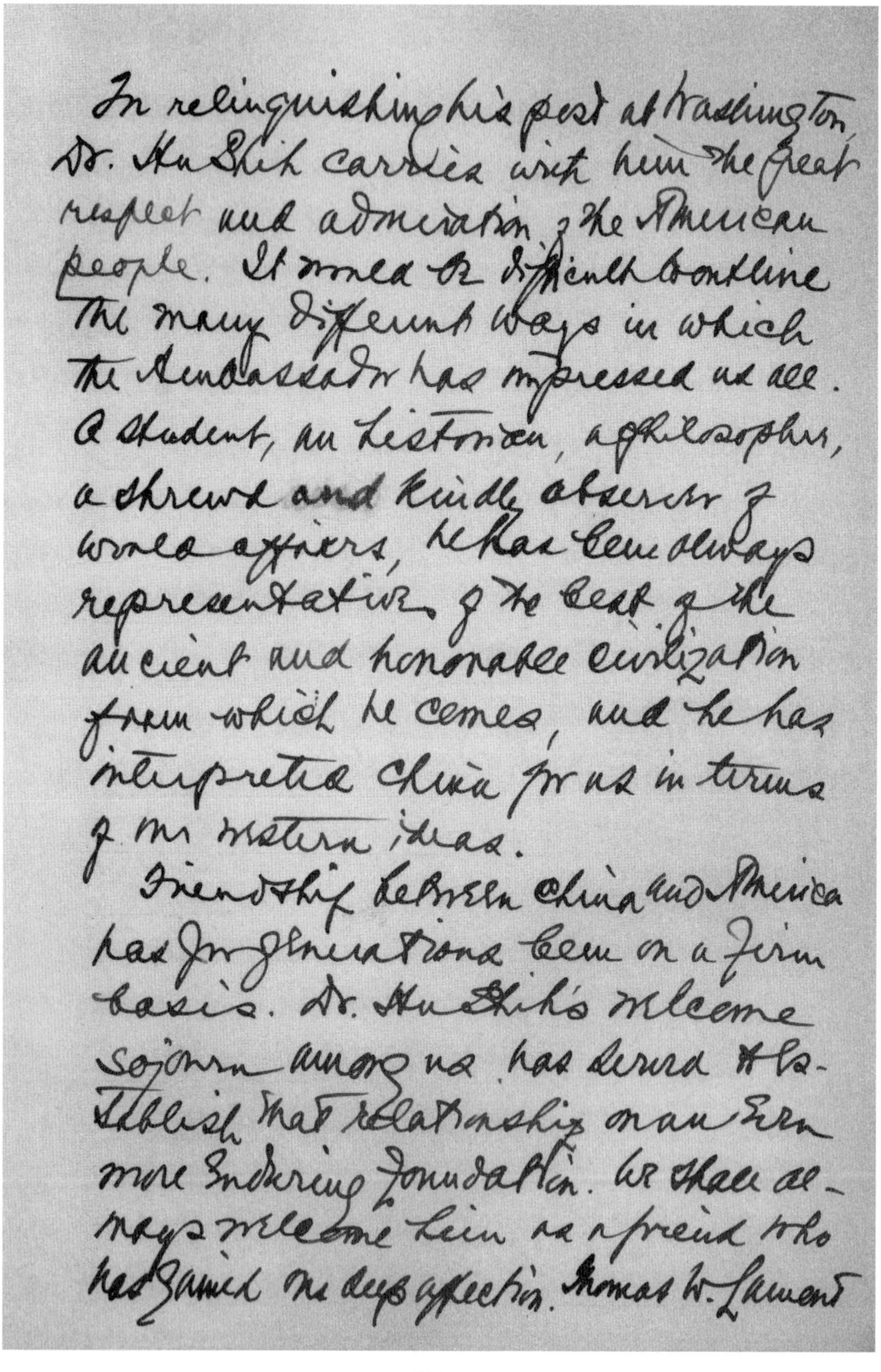

In relinquishing his post at Washington, Dr. Hu Shih carries with him the great respect and admiration of the American people. It would be difficult to outline the many different ways in which the Ambassador has impressed us all. A student, an historian, a philosopher, a shrewd and kindly observer of world affairs, he has been always representative of the best of the ancient and honorable civilization from which he comes, and he has interpreted China for us in terms of our western ideas.

Friendship between China and America has for generations been on a firm basis. Dr. Hu Shih's welcome sojourn among us has served to establish that relationship on an even more enduring foundation. We shall always welcome him as a friend who has gained our deep affection. Thomas W. Lamont

圖 1

In relinquishing his post at Washington, Dr. Hu Shih carries with him the great respect and admiration of the American people. It would be difficult to outline the many different ways in which the Ambassador has impressed us all. A student, a[n] historian, a philosopher, a shrewd and kindly observer of world affairs, he has been always representative of the best of the ancient and honorable civilization from which he comes, and he has interpreted China for us in terms of our western ideas.

Friendship between China and America has in generations been on a firm basis. Dr. Hu Shih's welcome sojourn among us has served & establish that relationship on an even more enduring foundation. We shall always welcome him as a friend who has gained our deep affection.

Thomas W. Lamont

W. R. Herod

　　W. R. Herod，曾任美國通用電氣公司總裁，美國援華聯合會主席。胡適任駐美大使前後與其有交往，北京檔藏有二人往來函電八通，時間基本爲1942年，胡適卸任駐美大使之前。

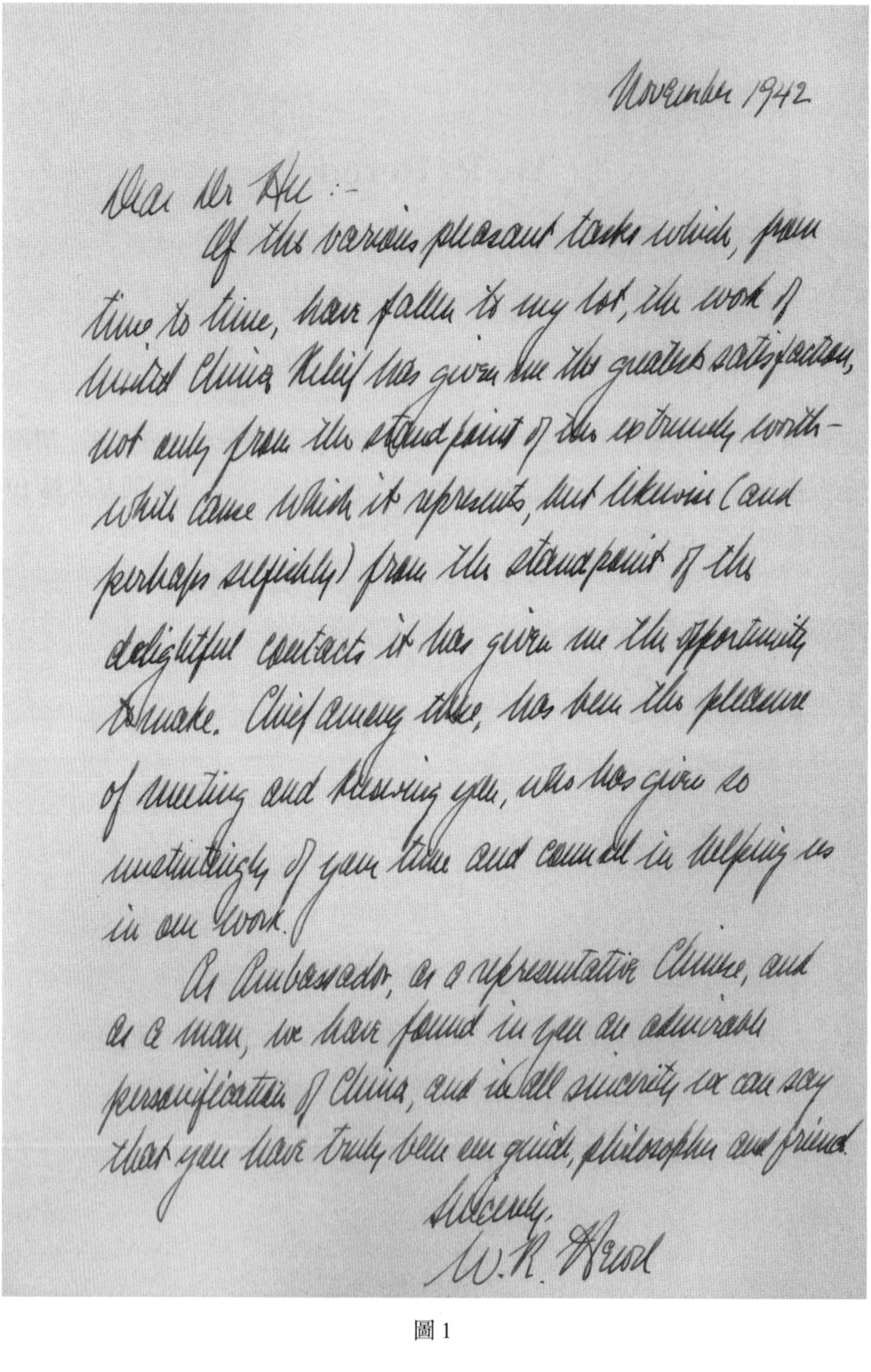

November 1942

Dear Dr Hu:—

Of the various pleasant tasks which, from time to time, have fallen to my lot, the work of United China Relief has given me the greatest satisfaction, not only from the standpoint of the extremely worth-while cause which it represents, but likewise (and perhaps selfishly) from the standpoint of the delightful contacts it has given me the opportunity to make. Chief among these, has been the pleasure of meeting and knowing you, who has given so unstintingly of your time and counsel in helping us in our work.

As Ambassador, as a representative Chinese, and as a man, we have found in you an admirable personification of China, and in all sincerity we can say that you have truly been our guide, philosopher and friend.

Sincerely,
W. R. Herod

圖 1

November 1942

Dear Dr. Hu:—

Of the various pleasant tasks which, from time to time, have fallen to my lot, the work of United China Relief has given me the greatest satisfaction, not only from the standpoint of the extremely worthwhile cause which it represents, but likewise (and perhaps selfishly) from the standpoint of the delightful contacts it has given me the opportunity to make. Chief among these, has been the pleasure of meeting and knowing you, who has given so unstintingly of your time and counsel in helping us in our work.

As Ambassador, as a representative Chinese, and as a man, we have found in you an admirable personification of China, and in all sincerity we can say that you have truly been our guide, philosopher and friend.

Sincerely,
W. R. Herod

Walter B. Cannon

　　Walter B. Cannon（1871—1945），生於美國威斯康辛州，生理學家。1896年獲哈佛大學學士學位，1900年獲哈佛大學醫學博士學位。畢業後任哈佛大學生理系講師。1906年任哈佛醫學院生理系主任、教授，直至1942年。1914—1916年任美國生理學會會長。胡適任駐美大使期間，Cannon曾於1940年1月5日覆信胡適，答謝聖誕新年賀卡。胡適任駐美大使前後與其有交往，北京檔藏有Cannon致胡適書信兩封，其中一封日期爲1940年1月5日。

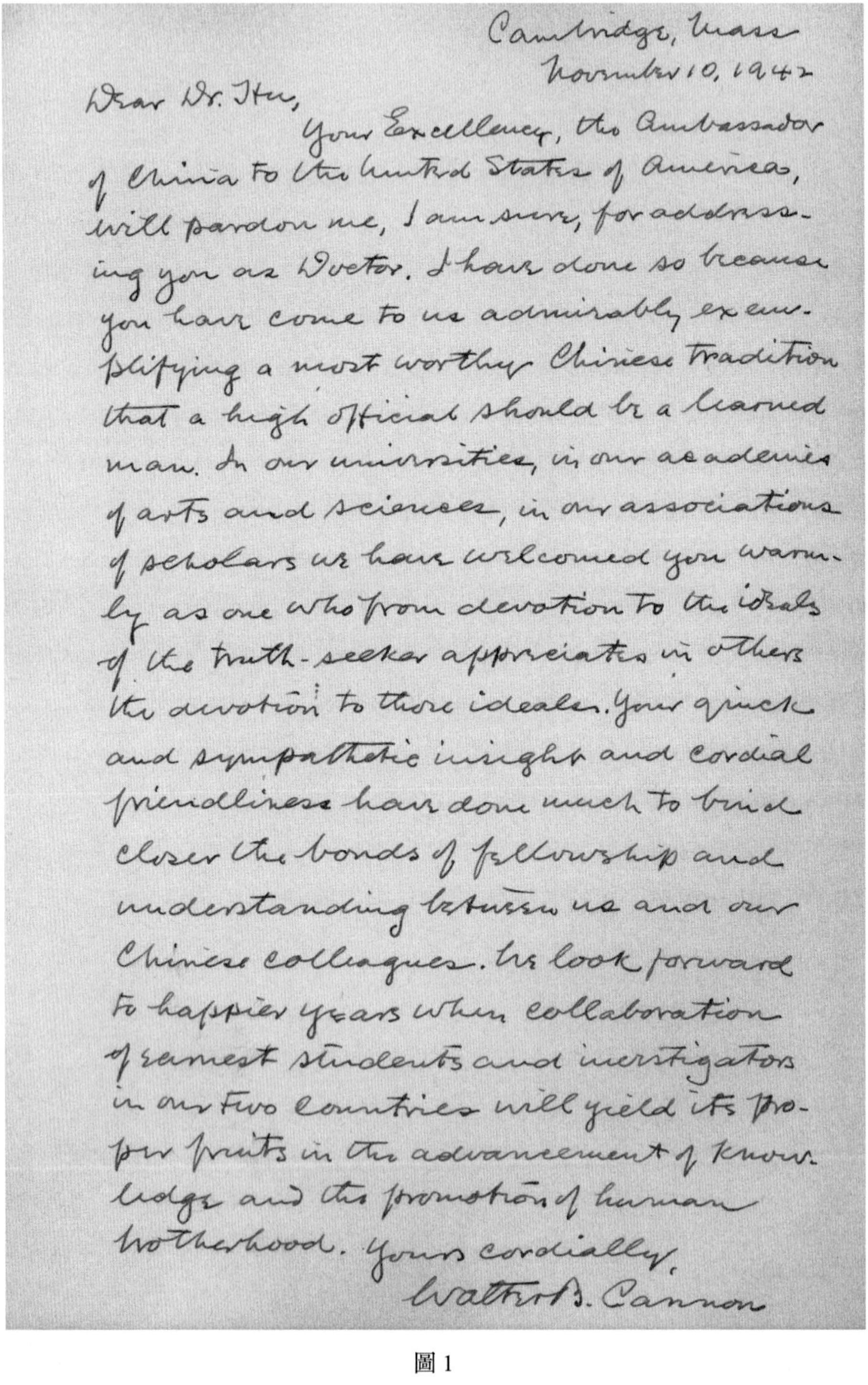

Cambridge, Mass
November 10, 1942

Dear Dr. Hu,

Your Excellency, the Ambassador of China to the United States of America, will pardon me, I am sure, for addressing you as Doctor. I have done so because you have come to us admirably exemplifying a most worthy Chinese tradition that a high official should be a learned man. In our universities, in our academies of arts and sciences, in our associations of scholars we have welcomed you warmly as one who from devotion to the ideals of the truth-seeker appreciates in others the devotion to those ideals. Your quick and sympathetic insight and cordial friendliness have done much to bind closer the bonds of fellowship and understanding between us and our Chinese colleagues. We look forward to happier years when collaboration of earnest students and investigators in our two countries will yield its proper fruits in the advancement of knowledge and the promotion of human brotherhood. Yours cordially,

Walter B. Cannon

圖1

Cambridge, Mass.
November 10, 1942

Dear Dr. Hu,

Your Excellency, the Ambassador of China to the United States of America, will pardon me, I am sure, for addressing you as Doctor. I have done so because you have come to us admirably exemplifying a most worthy Chinese tradition that a high official should be a learned man. In our universities, in our academies of arts and sciences, in our associations of scholars we have welcomed you warmly as one who from devotion to the ideals of the truth-seeker appreciates in others the devotion to those ideals. Your quick and sympathetic insight and cordial friendliness have done much to bind closer the bonds of fellowship and understanding between us and our Chinese colleagues. We look forward to happier years when collaboration of earnest students and investigators in our two countries will yield its proper fruits in the advancement of knowledge and the promotion of human brotherhood.

Yours cordially,
Walter B. Cannon

Walter G. Hiltner

Walter G. Hiltner,美國長老會傳教士,曾在上海中國哈佛醫學院任解剖學教授,後在南京外國醫院行醫。

It is an unusual man that rises above the level of the leaders of his generation. Less often does such fame come to one who is not in politics or in the affairs of war. A few times in history men have stood above their peers because of intellectual gifts that were expressed in philosophical, social or scientific achievements. But rare indeed is one, who still in the bloom of youth has attained such honor, not only in his own nation; but in the lands across the seas.

To you Dr Hu, there is even more. There is not only the admiration of our people for you; but for your people as well. One can sense a mutual growing esteem and respect of our nationals toward your Chinese nationals and much of this you have helped to develop.

You have already given much. But may I wish for you, that your most fruitful years shall lie ahead. Through your great gifts of mind and heart, may you join with others, or stand alone, in trying to bring understanding and respect — confidence and love, into this saddened and disillusioned world. Walter G. Hiltner

圖 1

It is an unusual man that rises above the level of the leaders of his generation. Less often does such fame come to one who is not in politics or in the affairs of war. A few times in history men have stood above their peers because of intellectual gifts that were expressed in philosophical, social or scientific achievements. But rare indeed is one, who still in the bloom of youth has attained such honor, not only in his own nation; but in the lands across the seas.

In you Dr. Hu, there is even more. There is not only the admiration of our people for you; but for your people as well, one can sense a mutual growing esteem and respect of our nationals toward your Chinese nationals and much of this you have helped to develop.

You have already given much. But may I wish for you, that your most fruitful years shall lie ahead. Through your great gifts of mind and heart, may you join with others, or stand alone, in trying to bring understanding and respect—confidence and love, into this saddened and disillusioned world.

Walter G. Hiltner

Walter Parker

　　Walter Parker，生平不詳，據北京檔有關資料，似曾參加全美助華聯合總會工作。C. Scott Fletcher 1942 年 5 月 15 日致胡適函中說，已請 Walter Parker、James A. Note 轉交全美助華聯合總會的電報和信函給胡適，關於募集捐助資金之事。

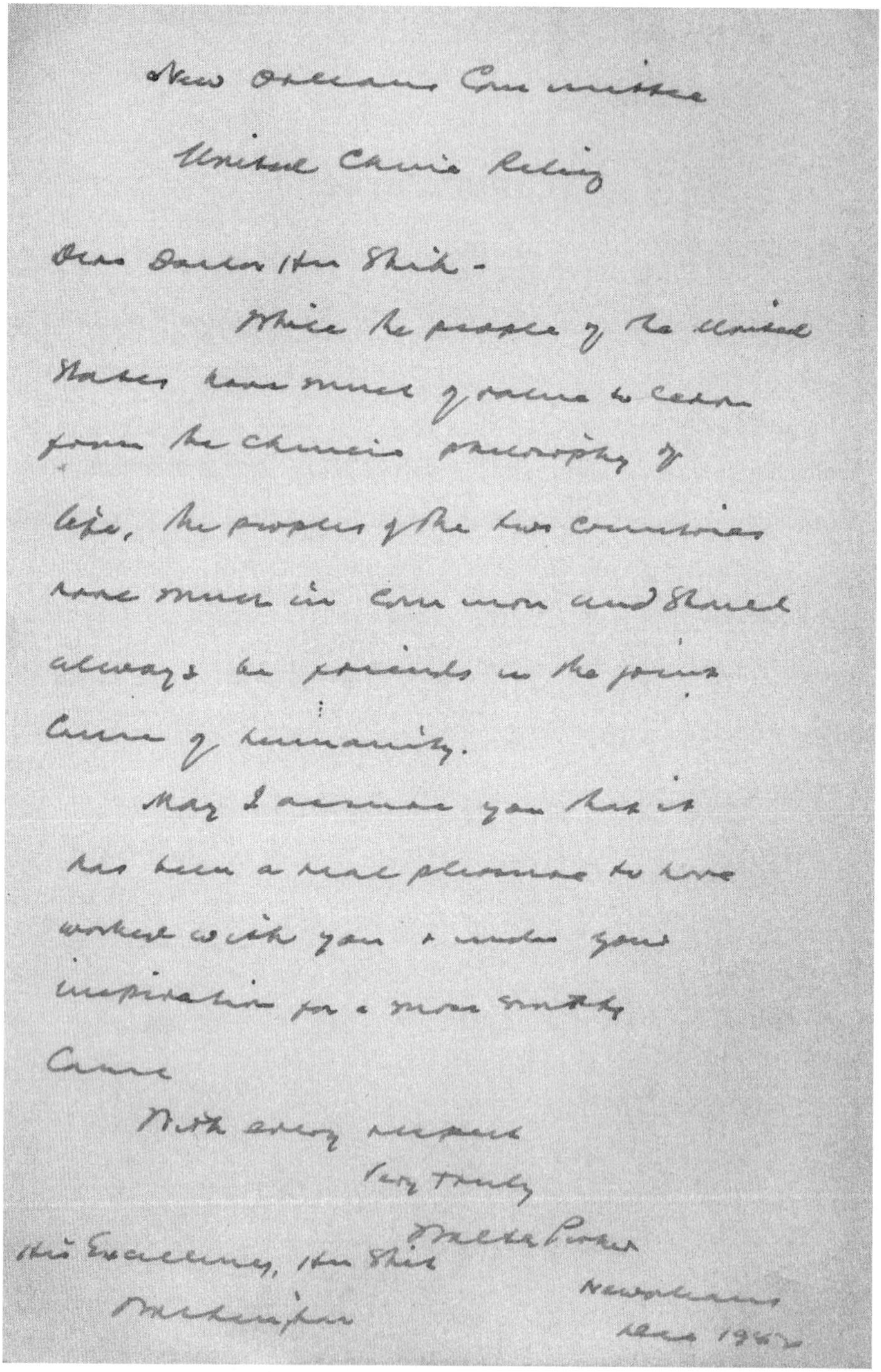

> New Orleans Committee
>   United China Relief
>
> Dear Doctor Hu Shih —
>
> While the people of the United States have much of value to learn from the Chinese philosophy of life, the peoples of the two countries have much in common and should always be friends in the joint cause of humanity.
>
> May I assure you that it has been a real pleasure to have worked with you & under your inspiration for a more worthy cause.
>
> With every respect
>   Very truly
>   Walter Parker
>
> His Excellency, Hu Shih
>   Washington
>   New Orleans
>   June 1942

圖1

New Orleans Committee
United China Relief

Dear Doctor Hu Shih—

While the people of the United States have much of value to learn from the Chinese philosophy of life, the peoples of the two countries have much in common and should always be friends in the joint cause of humanity.

May I assure you that it has been a real pleasure to have worked with you & under your inspiration for a more justly cause.

With every respect
Very truly
Walter Parker
New Orleans
Dec. 1942

His Excellency, Hu Shih
Washington

Wayne Chatfield Taylor

　　Wayne Chatfield Taylor（1893—1967），生於美國芝加哥，時任美國商務部副部長。1945—1946年任華盛頓進出口銀行行長。曾任羅斯福總統任內商務部副部長、財政部助理部長。

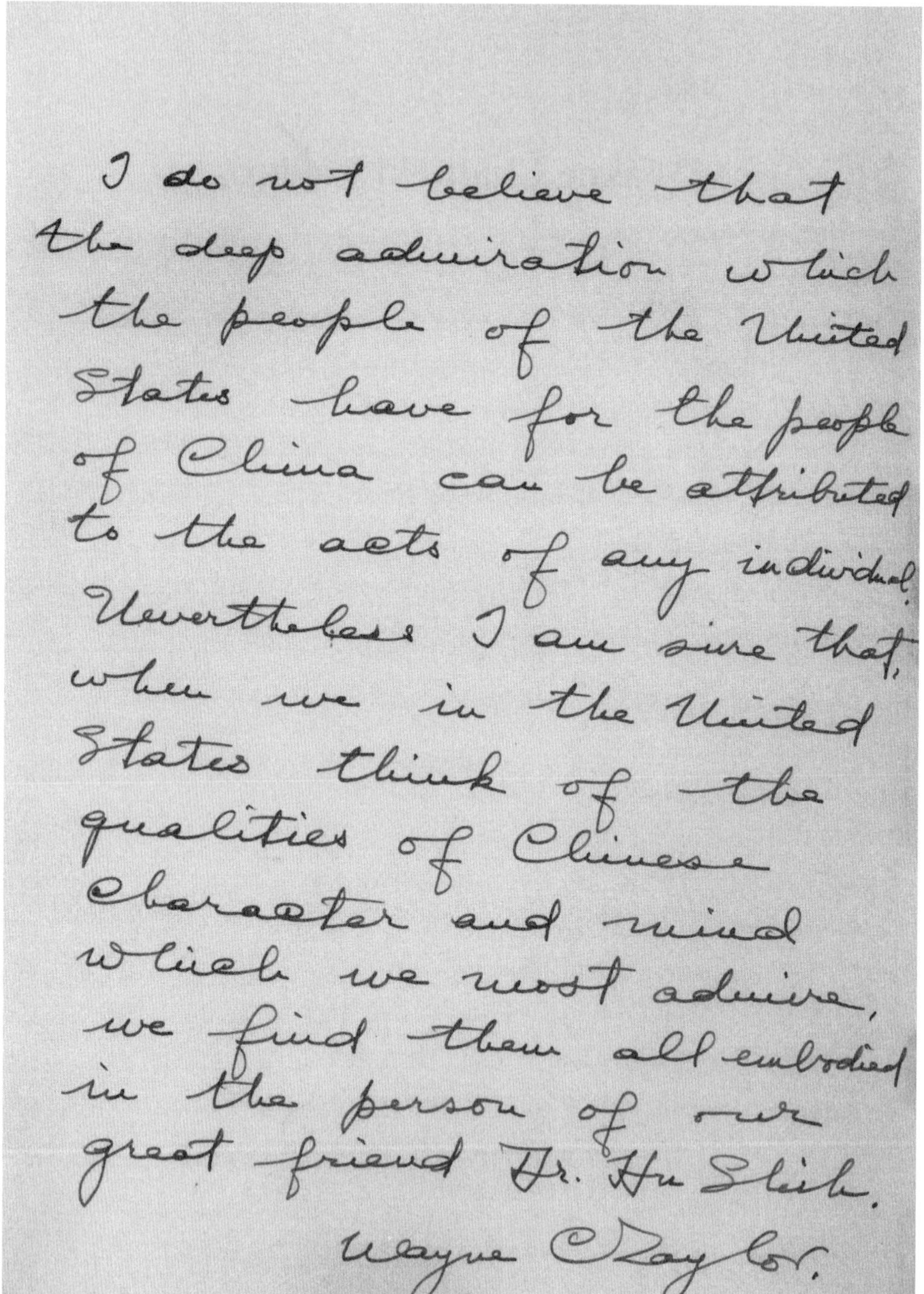

I do not believe that the deep admiration which the people of the United States have for the people of China can be attributed to the acts of any individual. Nevertheless I am sure that when we in the United States think of the qualities of Chinese character and mind which we most admire, we find them all embodied in the person of our great friend Dr. Hu Shih.

Wayne Taylor.

圖1

I do not believe that the deep admiration which the people of the United States have for the people of China can be attributed to the acts of any individual. Nevertheless I am sure that, when we in the United States think of the qualities of Chinese character and mind which we most admire, we find them all embodied in the person of our great friend Dr. Hu Shih.

Wayne C. Taylor

Wendell L. Willkie

　　Wendell L. Willkie，即 Wendell Lewis Willkie（1892—1944），生於美國印第安納州。1913 年畢業於印第安納大學。1916 年畢業於印第安納大學法學院。畢業後從事律師職業，一戰期間參軍，曾爲參戰士兵辯護。1919 年任凡世通輪胎橡膠公司法律辦公室主任，後轉入其他律師公司。1929 年任聯邦與南方公司律師。1933 年任該公司總裁。胡適任駐美大使期間與 Willkie 有交往，北京檔藏有胡適與其往來書信兩封，另有胡適秘書劉鍇代致 Willkie 電文一通，時間均在 1941 年。

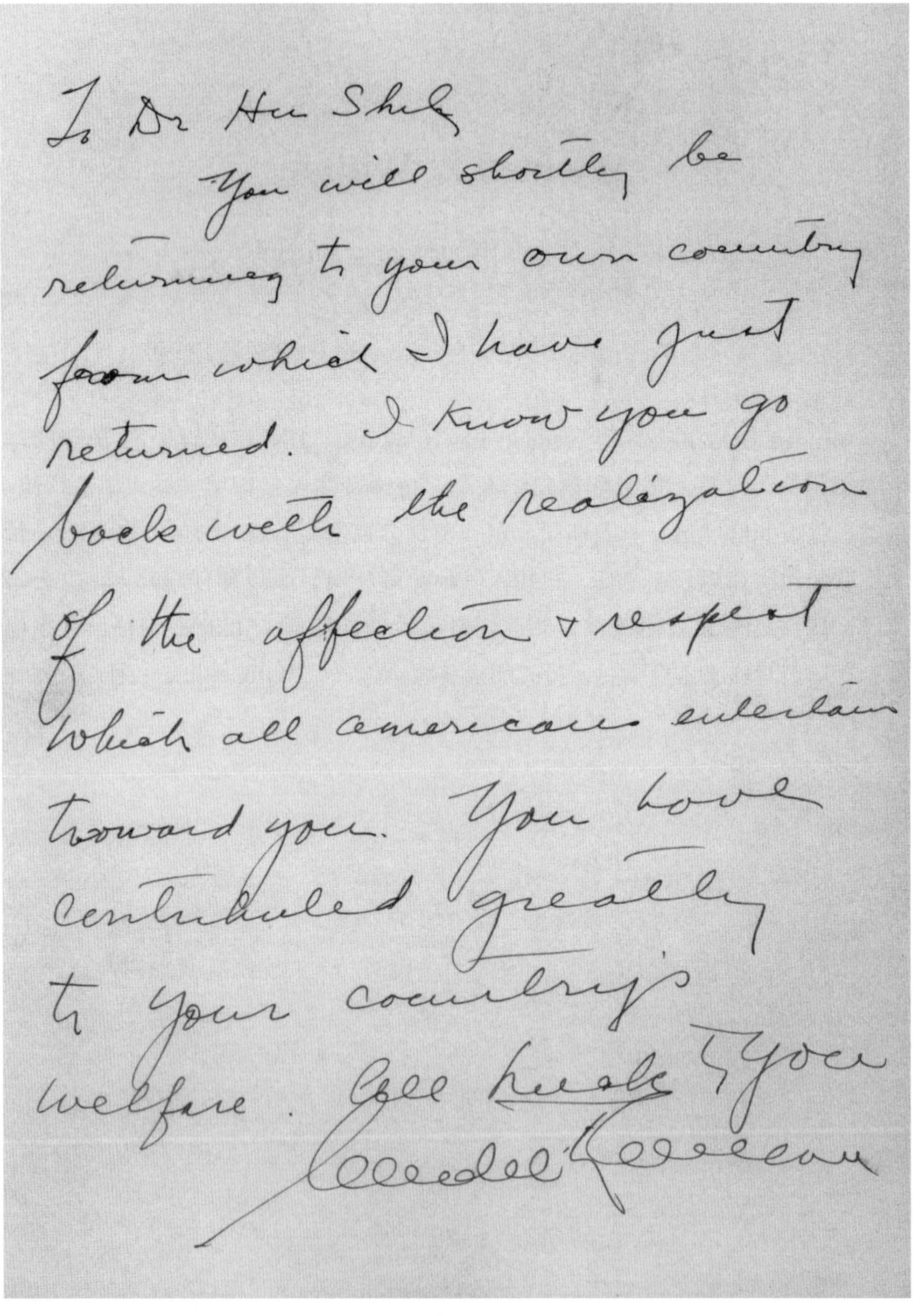

To Dr Hu Shih,

You will shortly be returning to your own country from which I have just returned. I know you go back with the realization of the affection & respect which all americans entertain toward you. You have contributed greatly to your country's welfare. All husks to you

[signature]

圖 1

To Dr. Hu Shih

You will shortly be returning to your own country from which I have just returned. I know you go back with the realization of the affection & respect which all American entertain toward you. You have contributed greatly to your country's welfare.

All luck to you

Wendell L. Willkie

William D. Leahy

William D. Leahy（1875—1959），生於美國愛荷華州漢普頓市。美國海軍五星上將，1897年畢業於美國海軍學院，時任美軍總司令參謀長。此外曾任美國海軍作戰部長、波多黎各總督、美國駐法國大使等職。胡適曾分別於1939年3月30日、5月11日的日記中提及與其交往，或共進晚餐，或交談。北京檔收藏的胡適書信中有胡適1939年5月18日致Leahy書信一封，以及Leahy同年5月22日的回信，主要內容爲對Leahy出任波多黎各總督的祝賀以及Leahy的答謝。

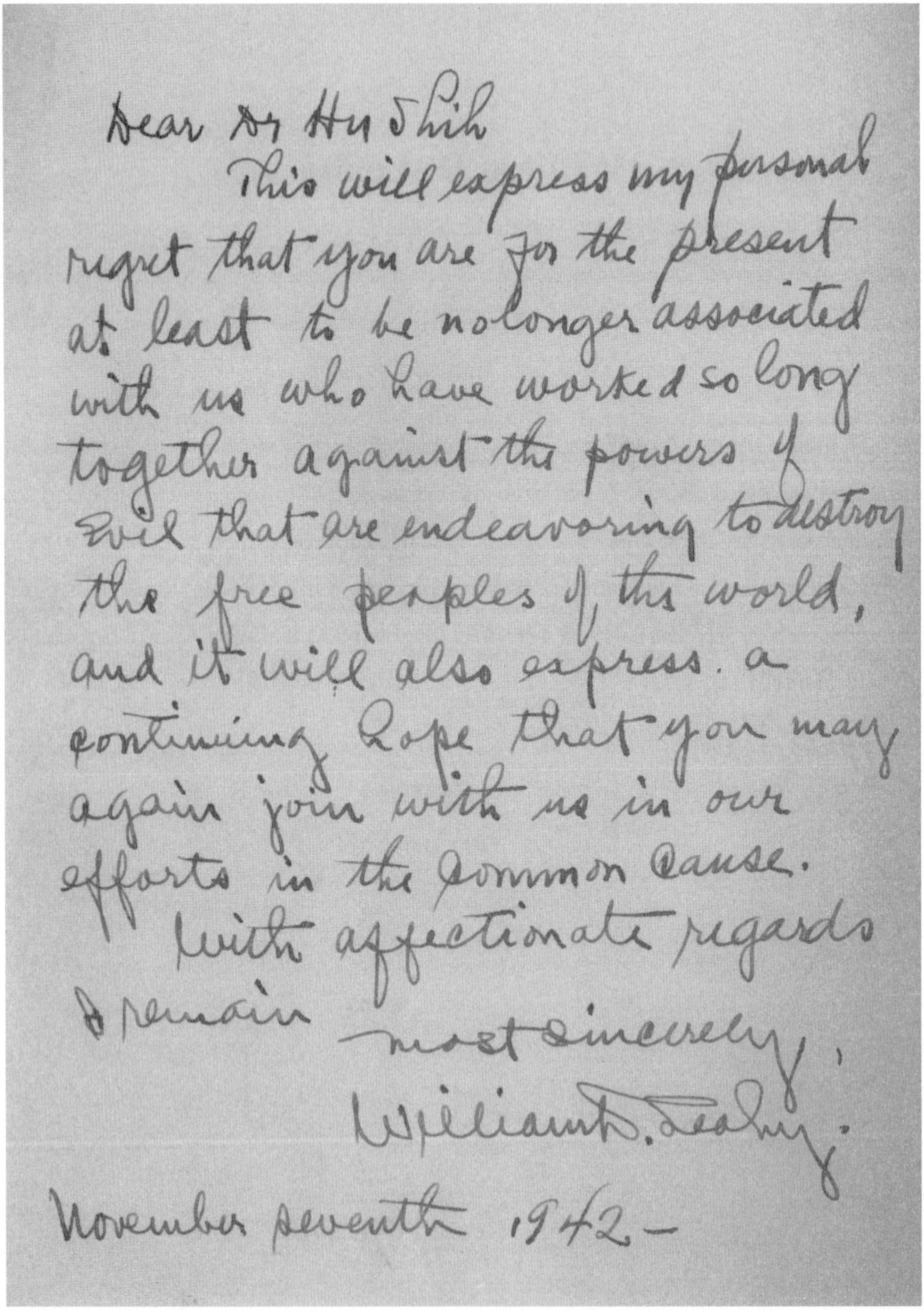

Dear Dr Hu Shih

This will express my personal regret that you are for the present at least to be no longer associated with us who have worked so long together against the powers of evil that are endeavoring to destroy the free peoples of the world, and it will also express a continuing hope that you may again join with us in our efforts in the common cause.

With affectionate regards I remain most sincerely,

William D. Leahy

November seventh 1942.—

图 1

Dear Dr. Hu Shih:

This will express my personal regret that you are for the present at least to be no longer associated with us who have worked so long together against the powers of evil that are endeavoring to destroy the free peoples of the world, and it will also express a continuing hope that you may again join with us in our efforts in the Common Cause.

With affectionate regards I remain

most sincerely,
William D. Leahy

November Seventh 1942

William O. Douglas

William O. Douglas（1898—1980），生於美國明尼蘇達州，時任美國最高法院大法官。1920年畢業於惠特曼學院。1925年畢業於哥倫比亞大學法學院。先後任教於哥倫比亞大學法學院、耶魯大學法學院。1939—1975年任美國最高法院大法官。

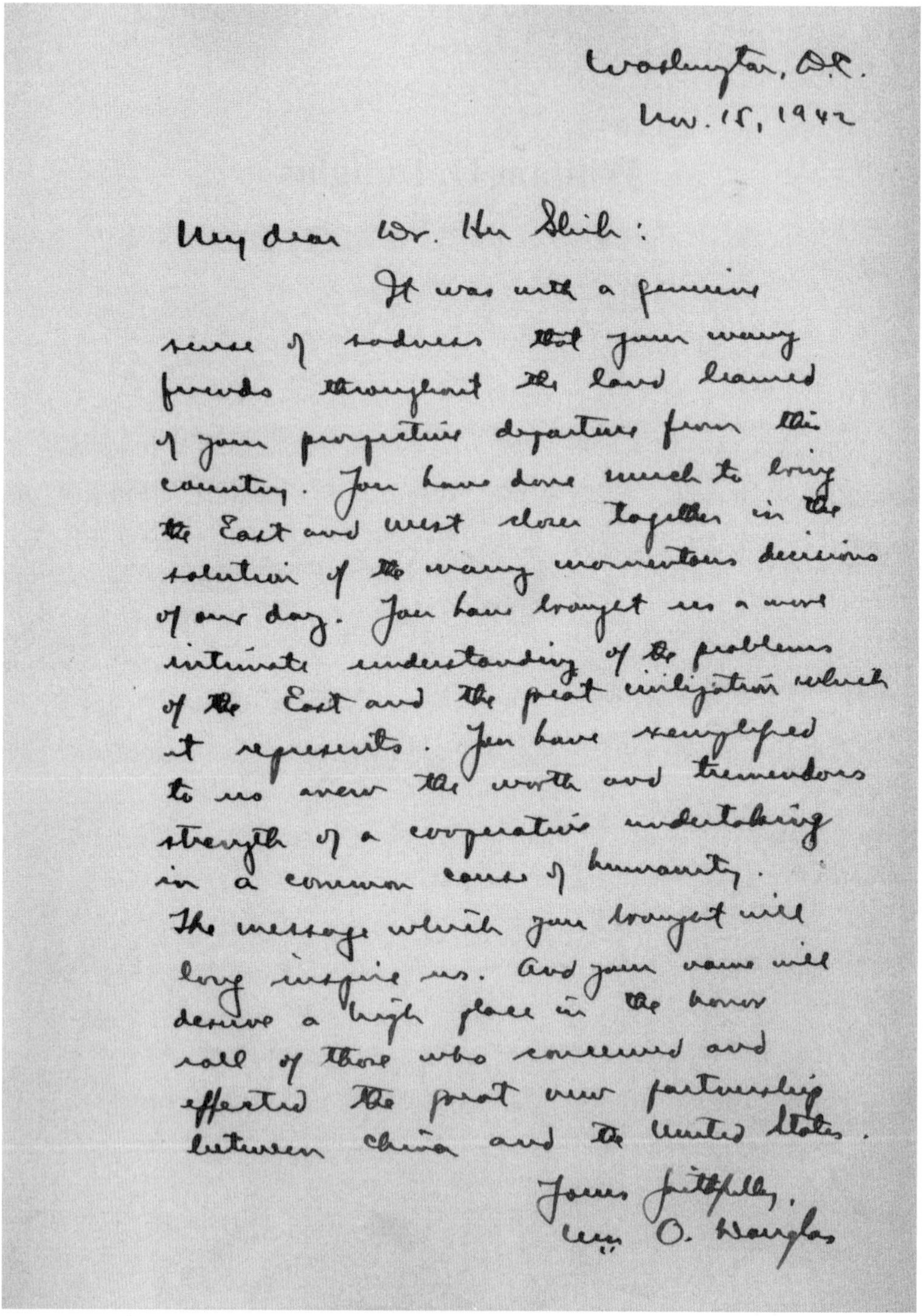

Washington, D.C.
Nov. 15, 1942

My dear Mr. Hu Shih:

It was with a genuine sense of sadness that your many friends throughout the land learned of your prospective departure from this country. You have done much to bring the East and West closer together in the solution of the many momentous decisions of our day. You have brought us a more intimate understanding of the problems of the East and the great civilization which it represents. You have reemphasized to us anew the worth and tremendous strength of a cooperative undertaking in a common cause of humanity. The message which you brought will long inspire us. And your name will derive a high place in the honor roll of those who conceived and effected the great new partnership between China and the United States.

Yours faithfully,
Wm. O. Douglas

圖 1

Washington, D.C.
Nov. 15, 1942

My dear Dr. Hu Shih:

It was with a genuine sense of sadness that your many friends throughout the land learned of your prospective departure from this country. You have done much to bring the East and West closer together in the solution of the many momentous decisions of our day. You have brought us a most intimate understanding of the problems of the East and the great civilization which it represents. You have exemplified to us anew the worth and tremendous strength of a cooperative undertaking in a common cause of humanity.

The message which you brought will long inspire us. And your name will deserve a high place in the honor roll of those who convened and effected the great new partnership between China and the United States.

Yours faithfully,
Wm. O. Douglas

William Philip Simms

William Philip Simms，時任美國海軍上將，餘不詳。

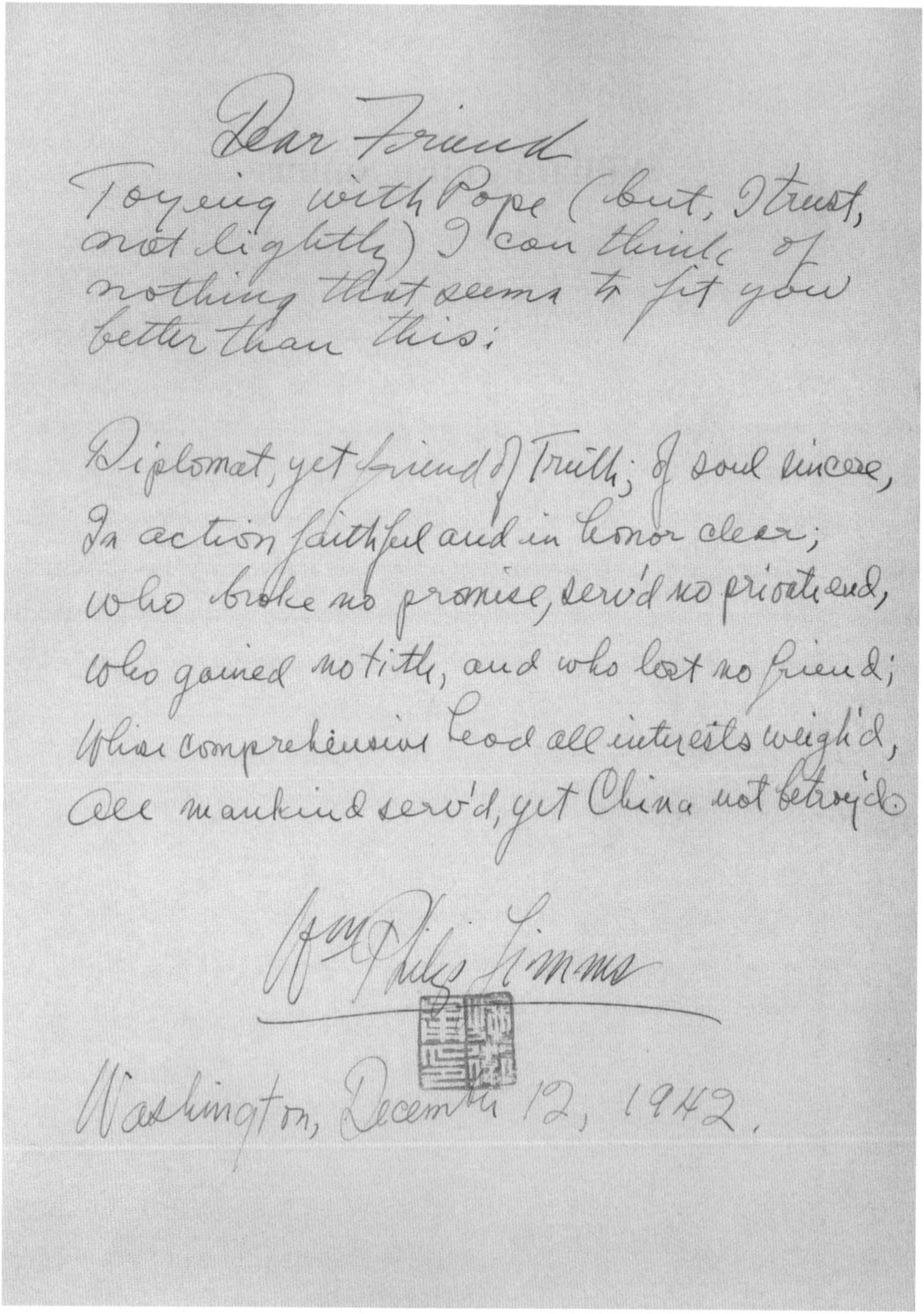

Dear Friend

Toying with Pope (but, I trust, not lightly) I can think of nothing that seems to fit you better than this:

Diplomat, yet friend of Truth; of soul sincere,
In action faithful and in honor clear;
Who broke no promise, serv'd no private end,
Who gained no title, and who lost no friend;
Whose comprehensive head all interests weigh'd,
All mankind serv'd, yet China not betray'd

William Philip Simms

Washington, December 12, 1942.

圖 1

Dear Friend

Toying with Pope (but, I trust, not lightly) I can think of nothing that seems to fit you better than this:

Diplomat, yet friend of Truth; of soul sincere, in action faithful and in honor clear; who broke no promise, serv'd no private end, who gained no title, and who lost no friend; whose comprehensive head all interests weighed, all mankind serv'd, yet China not betrayed.

Wm. Philip Simms

Washington, December 12, 1942

William Green

William Green（1873—1952），生於美國俄亥俄州，美國工會領導者，年輕時即從事工會活動，1910年當選俄亥俄州議員。1924—1952年任美國勞工聯合會主席。

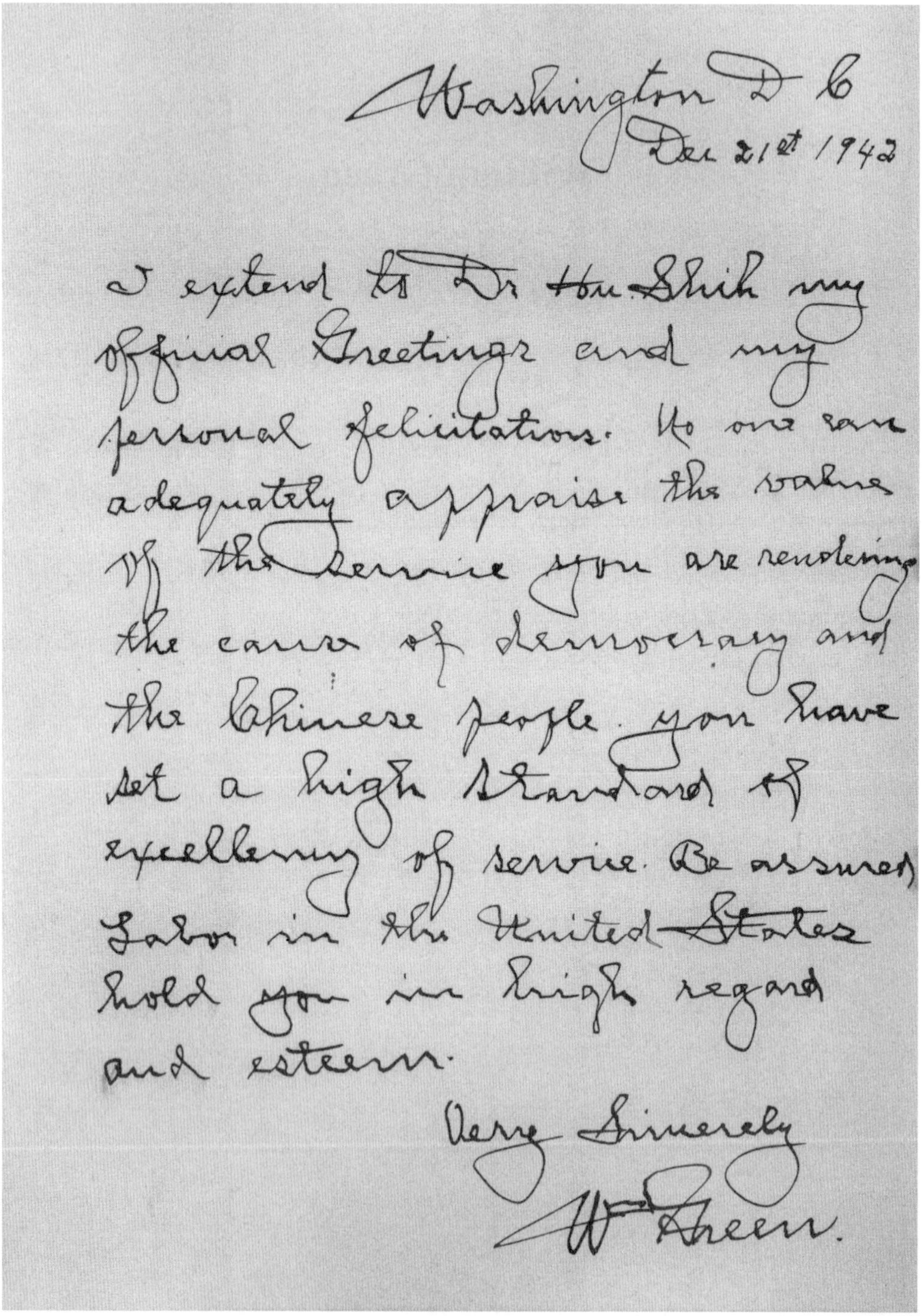

Washington D C
Dec 21st 1942

I extend to Dr. Hu Shih my official Greetings and my personal felicitations. No one can adequately appraise the value of the service you are rendering the cause of democracy and the Chinese people. You have set a high standard of excellency of service. Be assured Labor in the United States hold you in high regard and esteem.

Very Sincerely
Wm Green.

圖 1

Washington D.C.
Dec. 21st 1942

I extend to Dr. Hu Shih my official Greetings and my personal felicitations. No one can adequately appraise the value of the service you are rendering the cause of democracy and the Chinese people. You have set a high standard of excellency of service. Be assured Labor in the United States hold you in high regard and esteem.

Very Sincerely
W. Green

Wilson Compton

Wilson Compton（1890—1967），生於美國俄亥俄州。1915年畢業於普林斯頓大學，獲哲學博士學位。在達特茅斯學院任職一年，後到聯邦貿易委員會工作。1918—1944年任聯邦木業製造委員會秘書長。1944年任華盛頓州立學院首任院長。

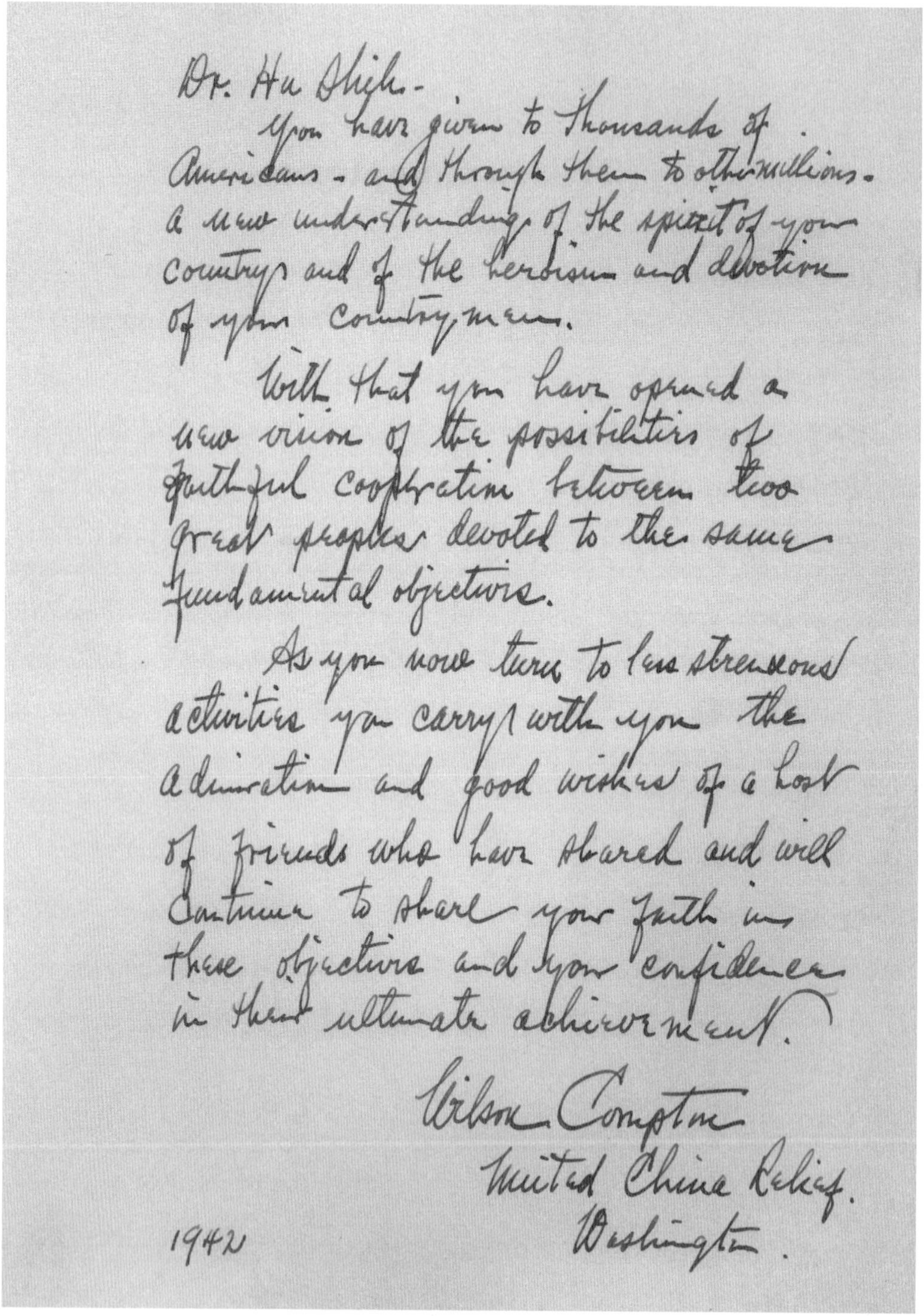

Dr. Hu Shih —

You have given to thousands of Americans — and through them to other millions — a new understanding of the spirit of your country and of the heroism and devotion of your countrymen.

With that you have opened a new vision of the possibilities of faithful cooperation between two great peoples devoted to the same fundamental objectives.

As you now turn to less strenuous activities you carry with you the admiration and good wishes of a host of friends who have shared and will continue to share your faith in these objectives and your confidence in their ultimate achievement.

Wilson Compton
United China Relief.
Washington.

1942

圖 1

Dr. Hu Shih—

You have given to thousands of Americans—and through them to other millions—a new understanding of the spirit of your country and of the heroism and devotion of your countrymen.

With that you have opened a new vision of the possibilities of faithful cooperation between two great peoples devoted to the same fundamental objectives.

As you now turn to less strenuous activities you carry with you the admiration and good wishes of a host of friends who have shared and will continue to share your faith in these objectives and your confidence in their ultimate achievement.

Wilson Compton
United China Relief
Washington

1942

Wynn C. Fairfield

Wynn C. Fairfield，曾任美國公理會差會秘書，餘不詳。

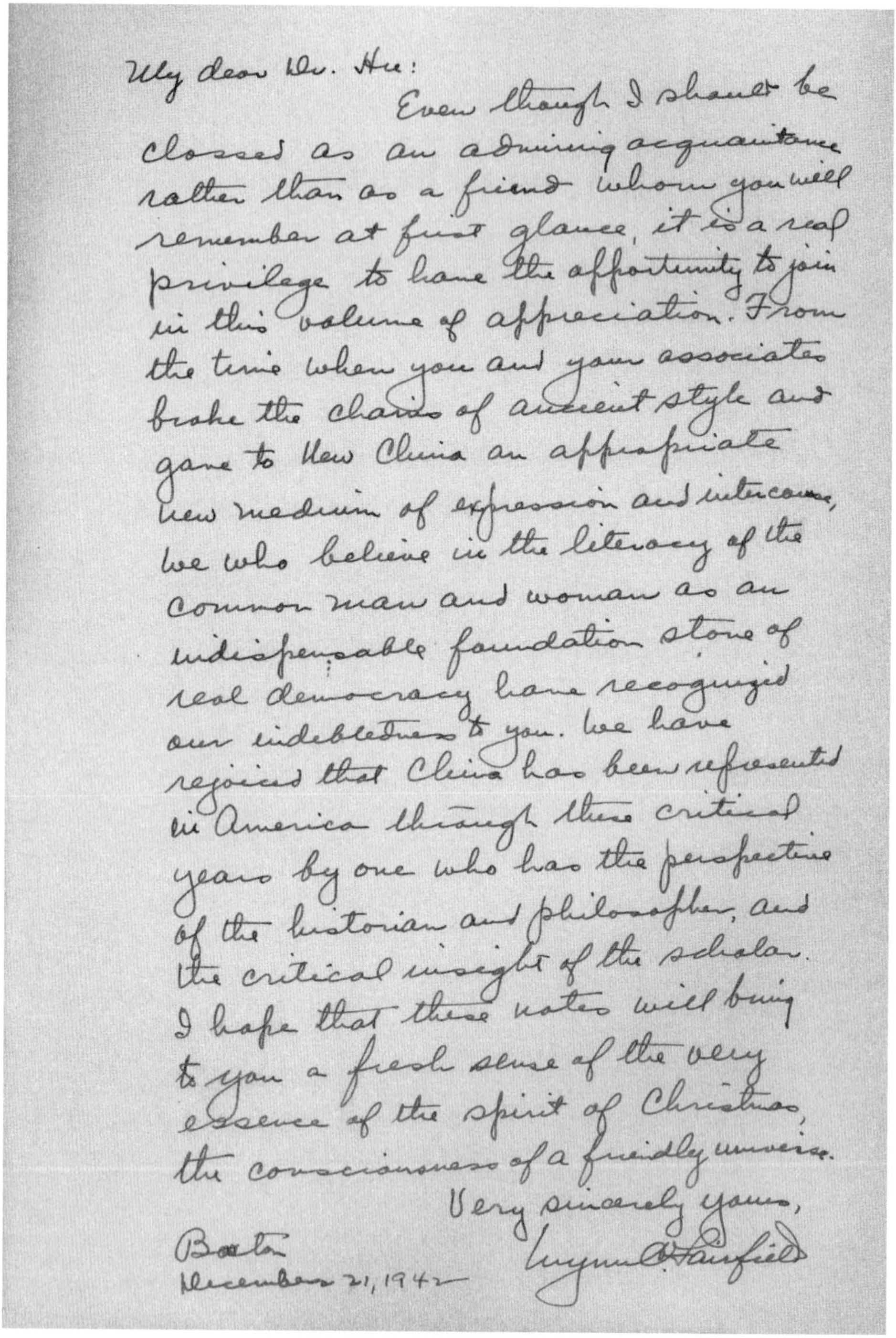

My dear Dr. Hu:

Even though I should be classed as an admiring acquaintance rather than as a friend whom you will remember at first glance, it is a real privilege to have the opportunity to join in this volume of appreciation. From the time when you and your associates broke the chains of ancient style and gave to New China an appropriate new medium of expression and intercourse, we who believe in the literacy of the common man and woman as an indispensable foundation stone of real democracy have recognized our indebtedness to you. We have rejoiced that China has been represented in America through these critical years by one who has the perspective of the historian and philosopher, and the critical insight of the scholar. I hope that these notes will bring to you a fresh sense of the very essence of the spirit of Christmas, the consciousness of a friendly universe.

Very sincerely yours,

Wynne Fairfield

Boston
December 21, 1942

圖1

My dear Dr. Hu:

Even though I should be classed as an admiring acquaintance rather than as a friend whom you will remember at first glance, it is a real privilege to have the opportunity to join in this volume of appreciation. From the time when you and your associates broke the chains of ancient style and gave to New China an appropriate new medium of expression and intercourse, we who believe in the literacy of the common man and woman as an indispensable foundation stone of real democracy have recognized our indebtedness to you. We have rejoiced that China has been represented in America through these critical years by one who has the perspective of the historian and philosopher, and the critical insight of the scholar. I hope that these notes will bring to you a fresh sense of the very essence of the spirit of Christmas, the consciousness of afriendly universe.

Very sincerely yours,
Wynn C. Fairfield

Boston
December 21, 1942